BATTLES
THAT CHANGED HISTORY

BATTLES
THAT CHANGED HISTORY

KEY BATTLES THAT DECIDED
THE FATE OF NATIONS

© 2010 Amber Books Ltd

This 2010 edition published by 3C Publishing Ltd
by arrangement with Amber Books Ltd.

3C Publishing Ltd
Sky House
Raans Road
Amersham
Bucks, HP6 6JQ

Editorial and design by:
Amber Books Ltd
Bradley's Close
74–77 White Lion St
London N1 9PF
United Kingdom
www.amberbooks.co.uk

Project editor: Michael Spilling
Editorial assistance: Kieron Connolly
Design: Hawes Design
Picture research: Terry Forshaw

ISBN: 978-1-906842-12-3

Printed and bound in China

1 3 5 7 9 10 8 6 4 2

Parts of this book have been previously published in the following titles:
Battles of the Ancient World, Battles of the Bible, Battles of the
Medieval World, Battles of the Crusades, Battles of the American
Civil War and Battles That Changed Warfare.

PICTURE CREDITS

All maps and black-and-white line artworks produced by JB Illustrations (© Amber Books).

AKG-Images: 42 (Peter Connolly), 45, 50, 52 & 59 (Peter Connolly), 65 & 70 (Peter Connolly), 81 (Peter Connolly), 88/89 (Peter Connolly), 94, 100/101tc (Peter Connolly), 115 (British Library), 122 (Erich Lessing), 137, 166, 171br, 192, 318/319bl, 329, 356 (Ullstein Bild)
Amber Books: 23, 31, 287br, 292tl, 293, 297
Ancient Art & Architecture Collection: 49 (Prisma), 72/73 (Ronald Sheridan), 82 (Mike Andrews), 91 (Prisma), 92 & 104 (Ronald Sheridan)
Art Archive: 90 (Gianni Dagli Orti/Musée Municipal Sémur en Auxois), 143 (Gianni Dagli Orti/National Museum of Damascus)
Art-Tech/Aerospace: 327b, 349, 358, 360, 361 (both), 365, 369tl, 372b, 384, 385, 395t, 409, 423t, 437
Art-Tech/John Batchelor: 215
Art-Tech/De Agostini: 204, 327t, 351, 357br, 359, 377, 393, 401, 403, 423br, 424tl, 433br
Art-Tech/MARS: 112, 114, 118/119, 173, 191br, 193, 221, 259, 261, 269, 270, 275, 282, 313, 323, 324 tl, 376, 390, 402, 406, 410, 411, 414, 415, 417, 418
Bridgeman Art Library: 7 (Look & Learn), 8tr, 151 (Ken Welsh), 156 (K. Savitsky Art Museum, Penza), 164 (Agra Art, Warsaw), 170/171tl (Museum Naradowe), 174, 218 (Royal Library, Stockholm), 226 (Bonhams, London), 227 (National Army Museum, London), 255 (State Central Military Museum, Moscow), 262 (State Central Artillery Museum, St. Petersburg), 274 (Haynes Fine Art, Bindery Galleries, Broadway)
Cody Images: 8b, 9, 146, 178, 180, 306, 336, 342, 344, 367, 369bl, 372tl, 375tr, 378, 386, 387, 407, 432, 433tl, 435
Corbis: 10 (Gianni Dagli Orti), 12 (Hulton-Deutsch Collection), 17 (Gianni Dagli Orti), 18 (Richard T. Nowitz), 19 (Archivo Iconografico, S.A.), 20 (Jose Fuste Raga), 22 (Charles & Josette Lenars), 26 (Stapleton Collection), 29 (Carl & Ann Purcell), 54 (Johansen Krause), 60t (Alfredo Dagli Orti), 68 (Bettmann), 85 (Vanni Archive), 97 (Bettmann), 110 (Werner Forman Archive), 111 (Vanni Archive), 124 (Richard T. Nowitz), 126 (Gianni Dagli Orti), 130 & 132 (Bettmann), 140 (Bettmann), 141 (Hanan Isachar), 147, 161 & 167 (Bettmann), 179 (Bettmann), 191t (Chris Hellier), 194 (Dave Bartruff), 196 (Charles & Josette Lenars), 201 (Asian Art & Archaeology, Inc.), 202tr (Ric Ergenbright), 202bl (Werner Forman Archive), 203 (Asian Art & Archaeology, Inc.), 220 (Arte & Immagini Srl), 230 & 234 (Bettmann), 236 & 239tr (Bettmann), 260 (Alexander Burkatovski), 284 (Bettmann), 353, 366 (Bettmann), 368, 400 & 408 (Bettmann), 416 (Christian Simonpietri/Sygma), 422 (Geneviève Chauvel/Sygma), 424br & 425 (David Rubinger)
De Agostini Picture Library: 60bl (G. Cozzi), 61 (G. Dagli Orti)
Getty Images: 62 & 69 (Hulton Archive), 76 (Hulton Archive), 77 (Time & Life Pictures), 103 (Hulton Archive), 131 (Time & Life Pictures), 154 (Hulton Archive), 163 (Time & Life Pictures), 181 & 341 (Hulton Archive), 350 & 419 (Hulton Archive), 439
Heritage Images: 38 (Spectrum Colour Library), 127 (Art Media), 160 (Ann Ronan Picture Library), 184 (British Library), 319tr (Ann Ronan Picture Library)
Library of Congress: 235, 239bl, 279, 286, 287tl, 292br, 294, 296, 300, 301, 302, 303, 304, 307, 315tl, 326, 379
Mary Evans Picture Library: 13 (Hubertus Kanus), 27, 28, 30, 36 (Edwin Wallace), 37, 39, 40, 41, 44 (Edwin Wallace), 51, 79, 80/81tl, 106, 120bl, 120/121tr, 123, 133, 134, 152, 153, 172, 175, 182, 183, 197, 283, 328, 333, 340, 352, 357tl
Military & Historical Image Bank: 290/291 (Don Troiani), 314 (Don Troiani)
Oliver Missing: 382, 395b
Bertl Olofsson/Krigsarkivet: 345
Photos 12: 93 & 187 (ARJ), 190 & 207 (ARJ), 231 (Oronoz), 266 & 267 (Fondation Napoléon), 316 (Ullstein Bild), 324/325br (Ullstein Bild)
Photos.com: 206, 211, 214, 222, 238 (both), 243, 254, 278, 337
Photoshot: 246 (UPPA), 250 & 251bl (World Illustrated), 442 & 443 (WpN)
Peter H. Proctor: 332
Public Domain: 32, 219, 228, 276
TopFoto: 100bl (Charles Walker)
Ukrainian State Archive: 383, 392, 394, 398, 399
U.S. Department of Defense: 309, 315br, 348, 364, 373, 374, 375br, 391 (both), 426, 427, 428, 429, 434 (both), 436, 438

CONTENTS

INTRODUCTION

THROUGHOUT HISTORY, THERE HAVE BEEN NUMEROUS CLIMACTIC BATTLES THAT HAVE RESHAPED HISTORY. THIS WORK EXAMINES A SELECTION OF THESE SEMINAL ENCOUNTERS, BRINGING ALIVE THE REALITY OF THE PARTICIPANTS' EXPERIENCES WHILE EXPLORING THE PROFOUND IMPACT THESE BATTLES EXERTED UPON SUBSEQUENT EVENTS.

The 47 decisive encounters presented here span the centuries from the first properly recorded battle (Meggido, 1457 BC), through Agincourt (1415) to the American-led invasion of Iraq (2003). These momentous actions also span the globe: they range across Europe from north-western Russia (Peipus, 1242) down to the waters off Greece (Salamis, 480 BC); they also range across the Middle East (Kadesh, 1285 BC; Jerusalem, 1099), into Asia (Nagashino, 1576), and onto the Americas (Siege of Quebec 1759; Second Manasses, 1862). These influential clashes also occurred in various environments; from the waters off Japan (Tsushima, 1905), through the forests of Germania (Teutoberger Wald, AD 9) and Israel's arid mountains (Hattin, 1187), and on to the world's great cities (Tyre, 332 BC; Constantinople, 1453). Drawing upon expert knowledge, this volume presents the reader with fresh insights into an unprecedented array of climactic battles that have changed history.

These battles have decisively impacted on subsequent history, helping either to reshape to prevent the reshaping of the domestic, regional or international political, military, economic, social, and cultural landscapes. These individual battles, moreover, have exerted such decisive impacts in four principal ways. First, there have been encounters that have brought to an end a monumental conflict (Alesia, 52 BC; Siege of Jerusalem, 1099; Berlin, 1945), thus influencing the ensuing political environment. Second, there have been battles that have been the turning point in a given climactic conflict; while the war itself

This British grenadier from the 1770s is armed with the trusty Brown Bess musket. The grenadiers constituted the elite element of British infantry units. In North America, the unorthodox tactics of American colonial militias and the wilderness environment often undermined conventional infantry tactics.

continued, these actions proved to be the 'end of the beginning' or 'the beginning of the end' of their respective conflict (Guagamela, 331 BC; Yorktown, 1781; Gettysburg, 1863; Normandy Landings, 1944.) Third, there have been battles that have seen the introduction of new technology, new tactics, or some combination of the two (Meggido, 1457 BC; Cambrai, 1917; the Sinai, 1973; the Gulf War, 1991), which has profoundly influenced how warfare has been subsequently waged. Finally, there are encounters (Agincourt, 1415; the Charge of the Light Brigade, 1854; the Somme, 1916) that still exert a profound impact on modern public consciousness.

DECISIVE ENCOUNTERS

Some of the battles examined here have brought to an end some of history's most monumental military struggles. At Alesia (52 BC), Julius Caesar's Roman Legions took the surrender of the Gallic armies that over the preceding years had fiercely resisted the Republic's attempts to subjugate them. This defeat ended Gallic resistance to Rome's expansion and propelled Caesar's career upwards until he became 'Dictator' – in all but name the first of 83 subsequent Roman Emperors that ruled Europe's predominant political entity for over five centuries.

Similarly, the 1945 Soviet capture of Berlin – which triggered the suicide of the Nazi German *Führer*, Adolf Hitler – precipitated the end of World War II in Europe. This was a victory of staggering historic significance: it destroyed the evil of Nazism, freed the peoples of Europe from ruthless German occupation, and rescued Europe's surviving Jewish and Roma populations from genocidal Nazi mass-murder. This triumph over militant European Fascism, moreover, created two new global super-powers: the communist Soviet Union and the capitalist United States. The ensuing Cold War – the 45-year-long bi-polar division of Europe and the wider international system into two opposed blocs – horrifyingly brought the world on several occasions to the brink of global thermo-nuclear war.

TURNING POINTS

Secondly, there have been battles that have been decisive by being the turning point in a given climactic conflict. At Gettysburg (1863), the Confederate Army of North Virginia failed to defeat the Union Army of the Potomac. With this failure, the Confederates lost their last realistic chance of progression towards strategic victory, and subsequently the Union's superior mobilization capacity ground the

This modern painting of the battle of Salamis (480 BC) shows a Greek vessel ramming a taller Persian ship. Sails were not normally carried in battle, ideally being left behind on shore.

In this painting by Robert Hillingford, the Duke of Wellington salutes his Guardsman at the end of the battle of Waterloo, 18 June 1815. The victory at Waterloo brought an end to any return to power by Napoleon Bonaparte.

Confederacy down into final defeat during 1865. The Union victory ensured that slavery would be eradicated across the North American continent.

In similar vein, on 6 June 1944 the Western Allies successfully secured an irreversible beachhead along the Normandy coast of German-occupied France in the D-Day Landings. This achievement now locked the German armed forces into an unrelenting three-front attritional struggle that they could not win. Just 11 months later, the Allies finally won the World War II in Europe – an achievement that, as we have seen above, exerted a fundamental impact not just on Europe but on the entire world.

NEW TECHNOLOGY

Third, some of the battles explored here have been momentous because they witnessed the introduction of new technology and/or tactics that have

impacted significantly on the way in warfare has subsequently been conducted. At Nagashino (1576), the Oda-Tokugawa army defeated their Takeda opponents, thanks to the disciplined massed volley-fire of the foot soldiers armed with matchlock arquebus; the traditional Japanese way of warfare with Samurai-led cavalry charges, even when augmented by archers and 'modern' firearm-equipped soldiers, could no longer effectively resist such disciplined delivery of massed firepower.

Similarly, at Cambrai (1917), the British Army employed tanks en masse to support the infantry's assault of the German trench system; motorized armoured fighting vehicles (AFVs) have played a crucial role in most battles waged subsequently. In similar vein, during the 1991 Gulf War, the American forces employed cutting-edge intelligence-gathering assets, novel 'stealth' aircraft undetectable by enemy radar, precision-guided missiles, and high-tempo

US infantry wade ashore at Omaha Beach, Normandy, 6 June 1944. The German defenders were heavily dug in to the steep shelf of land rising behind the beach, and US forces suffered up to 3000 casualties in what was the bloodiest of the D-Day landings.

advances by the latest generation of AFVs to defeat the enemy forces defending Iraqi-occupied Kuwait.

BATTLES THAT ENDURE

Finally, there have been crucial encounters that today still profoundly shape the popular consciousness. On 25 October 1854, during the Battle of Balaklava in the Crimean War, a series of command misunderstandings meant that the 670 cavalrymen of the British Light Brigade mounted a mass charge along the 'Valley of Death' against well-prepared Russian positions. Despite encountering withering Russian fire, the British cavalry nevertheless reached the end of the valley and drove back the defenders before themselves being forced to withdraw, again in the face of fierce Russian fire; the result was the devastation of the force, with around 300 casualties and the survivors scattered. One French observer observed, *'C'est magnifique, mais ce n'est pas la guerre'* ('It's magnificent, but it's not war.') Immortalized in Tennyson's poetry, the charge has subsequently become etched into the British consciousness as a potent symbol of the incredible valour and the horrifying tragedy that often accompanies war. Similarly, the Battle of the Somme (1916) has become engrained in the modern British psyche as the epitome of futile industrial-scale warfare. During the second half of 1916,

Anglo-French forces conducted a 142-day offensive designed to break through the German trench system in the Somme valley of north-eastern France. All that the Allies managed to achieve was a 13km (8 mile) advance, well short of the intended decisive breakthrough. Some historians view the battle as a success in that it was the harsh crucible in which the Allies developed improved tactics that led ultimately to Germany's 1918 defeat. Whatever the success achieved, this was bought only at an appalling human cost – 632,000 Allied and 230,000 German casualties. The aspect most deeply scored into the British consciousness is the offensive's first day. Tragically, as Allied troops assaulted the German trenches they were cut down by withering enemy fire: 57,470 British soldiers became casualties that day, including 19,240 killed, in the most egregious blood-letting the British Army has ever experienced.

Whether it is the shocking slaughter of the Great War trenches, the tumult of the titanic 1973 Israeli-Egyptian armoured onslaught in the Sinai, or the fearsome clash of the Persian and Greek fleets at Salamis (480 BC), *Battles That Changed History* has a wealth of exciting accounts that not only illustrate how and why such seminal battles were fought, but crucially how and why these actions changed subsequent history.

June 1954: Viet Minh soldiers march triumphantly through a Vietnamese city, celebrating their victory over French forces at Dien Bien Phu. The surrender at Dien Bien Phu marked the beginning of the end of the French presence in Indochina.

MEGIDDO
1457 BC

MEGIDDO IS THE FIRST BATTLE TO HAVE BEEN RECORDED IN A METHODICAL MANNER. IT IS NOTEWORTHY FOR THE EXTREME RISKS TAKEN BY THE EGYPTIAN COMMANDER IN MAKING HIS APPROACH MARCH. THE GAMBLE PAID OFF AND RESULTED IN A COMPLETE VICTORY FOR THE EGYPTIAN ARMY AND ITS DISCIPLINED CHARIOT FORCE.

WHY DID IT HAPPEN?

WHO An Egyptian army under the command of Pharaoh Thutmose III (d. 1425 BC) versus a Canaanite army under Durusha, king of Kadesh.

WHAT The Egyptians took a risky and unexpected route to the battlefield and achieved surprise.

WHERE Near the ancient city of Megiddo, Canaan; now in Israel.

WHEN 1457 BC (some sources suggest other dates).

WHY The Canaanites had rebelled against their Egyptian overlords.

OUTCOME After being defeated in the field, the rebels fled into the city and were besieged.

Thutmose III was a child when his father, Thutmose II, died, in 1479 BC. His stepmother Hatshepsut (d. 1457 BC), who was also his aunt, became regent over all the dominions of Egypt until such time as Thutmose was old enough to assume the throne. However, Egyptian politics were complex, and within a couple of years Hatshepsut was declared 'king' despite being a woman.

Although Thutmose was not deposed, the young pharaoh was sidelined. In theory, he and his stepmother ruled as co-regents and shared power. In practice, his position was nebulous and he was kept out of the way while Hatshepsut ruled. Thutmose was married to Hatshepsut's daughter, further consolidating his claim to the throne, yet for the first 22 years of his reign he did not rule. As Hatshepsut consolidated her hold on power in Egypt, there was a period of growth and security, which the nation needed. Trade routes were re-established and the economy grew vastly. This was the beginning of the wealth for which ancient Egypt is now famed.

Meanwhile, Thutmose studied and became widely respected for his learning. He also gained renown as commander of the army, and made a name for himself as a good general who was also wise in victory.

Finally, Hatshepsut died and Thutmose emerged from the shadows. He indulged himself in a certain amount of spite aimed at his stepmother, ordering her image to be removed from temples and her statues to be destroyed. However, he had urgent matters to occupy his attention.

News had arrived in Egypt that trouble was brewing in Canaan. The region

Although depicted as Pharaoh in this relief sculpture, Thutmose III had little power in the early years of his reign. After the death of Hatshepsut, his stepmother, ...came a strong and effective leader.

EGYPTIAN CHARIOT

Chariots were invented in Canaan, and were still experimental at the time of Thutmose III's Megiddo campaign. It is possible to date some Egyptian sculptures quite accurately by their depiction of chariot wheels. Although Thutmose' chariots still used rather fragile four-spoked wheels, they were effective in action. At Megiddo, the Egyptians used their chariots as the advanced shock troops to disorientate and harass the Canaanites before they were fully formed for battle.

The driver did not fight but concerned himself with handling the vehicle while the warrior shot his bow at the enemy. At closer quarters, the warrior had a javelin to throw and could then fight with sword or mace. He protected himself and his driver with a shield when necessary. The light frame of the chariot was little protection from arrows or javelins, but rapid movement provided a good defence by making the vehicle a hard target.

contained many small kingdoms and states, most of which were Egyptian vassals. The area had been strongly controlled in the past, but in recent times Egyptian influence had begun to be replaced with that of foreign princes. Now word came that a confederation of princes were in open revolt, under the leadership of Durusha, king of Kadesh.

The revolt was probably triggered by the death of Hatshepsut. The death of a ruler often resulted in a period of reorganization or even political infighting. In such circumstances, mounting an effective response was not always possible, so for the Canaanite princes seeking their independence this was the best opportunity they were likely to have.

However, Thutmose had two advantages. First, there was no real period of dislocation. As co-regent, power fell to him in a manner that felt natural to the Egyptians – after all, he had been pharaoh for the past two decades! In addition, Thutmose was commander-in-chief of the army, and had been for many years. Thus he was ideally placed to meet this challenge to his rule.

Within a very short period, Thutmose mobilized his army and set out across the Sinai Desert in the direction of Canaan with about 20,000 men. His army was well provisioned, and the route was scouted to

ensure that water and other supplies could be located along the way. The army marched along a well-established road through the desert, which had been improved recently when Thutmose himself campaigned in the region.

CHARIOT ARMY

The main strength of Thutmose' army was its chariots. The horses of the time were too weak for cavalry work, though scouts and messengers sometimes rode. The invention of the stirrup, which would allow cavalry to become a truly effective battle-winning weapon, was some centuries off. The prestige and capabilities later associated with cavalry rested with the chariot corps.

The chariot was invented in Canaan, the land into which Thutmose now marched. Drawn by two small horses, the war chariot of the time was a fairly small vehicle composed of a wooden frame and basketwork sides. Experimentation was still in progress regarding the best position for the axle. Wheels had four spokes, which was later found to be inadequate. Eight- and finally six-spoked wheels were eventually used, but in the time of Thutmose III the chariot had relatively fragile wheels. The pharaoh's army contained a mobile chariot workshop – the ancient equivalent of an armoured formation's armoured recovery vehicles and field workshops.

LOCATION

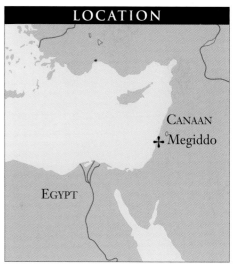

The city of Megiddo has been the site of three major battles, two of them in biblical times. Tradition also has it that it will be the site of the battle of Armageddon at the end of the world.

11

Each chariot had a crew of two men. The charioteer drove the vehicle, freeing his companion to fight from the small deck. The warrior was equipped with a mace or short sword plus a shield, a bow and a javelin.

The army also contained infantry and archers, and was organized into combined-arms divisions of 5000 men. These contained standard-bearers and support elements as well as fighting units. This level of organization enabled the army to cover ground quickly and efficiently, resulting in a much more rapid response to the situation than Thutmose' enemies were expecting.

The army marched from the frontier fortress of Tjel in Egypt to Gaza, a distance of 241km (150 miles), in 10 days. From there, it took 11 days to cover the 129km (80 miles) to Yehem. This slower pace was probably due to a combination of greater caution and a need to forage for supplies in the rich surrounding lands.

Although the king of Kadesh and his rebel allies were surprised and alarmed at the speed of the Egyptian response, they announced that they would await Thutmose' host in the vicinity of Megiddo. This was commonplace for the time; there were rules and formalities associated with the conduct of a campaign, and these were – at least sometimes – followed.

Thutmose now had a difficult choice to make. North of him stood the Carmel Ridge. At 600m (1969ft) high in places, it presented a major obstacle to his army. Beyond it was the plain of Esdraelon, where the city of Megiddo stood and battle awaited. There were three passes through the ridge, of which two – the northerly and southerly passes – offered a slow but relatively safe approach to the plain.

The central route, the Aruna Pass, was an altogether different prospect. Much more direct, it offered the chance for a rapid approach but placed the army in jeopardy. The pass was so narrow that, in places, men would have to go in single file and chariots would need to be manhandled over obstacles. An ambush in the pass would be devastating, and even if one did not materialize, the army would be strung out. It would take time to assemble into fighting formation. If the lead elements were attacked while re-forming, they might be defeated before reinforcements could clear the pass.

COUNCIL OF WAR

Thutmose held a council of war, as was not uncommon at the time. This was a curious business in that as pharaoh, Thutmose was the absolute authority and could not be spoken to directly by his subordinates, who were nevertheless charged with giving their opinions without fear. The result was a situation in which Thutmose' officers each 'spoke in his presence' but not directly to him.

The pharaoh's officers were opposed to the central route, arguing that it was far too dangerous, and wanted to choose one of the

The land of Canaan as it is today. The hills of Galilee are to the north, across a barren plain. The observer is at Samaria, which was for a time the capital of the Israelites who came to dominate the region.

The Egyptians were highly organized in both peace and war. They built great monuments such as the Temple of Amun at Luxor, and fought in well-disciplined formations.

THE OPPOSED FORCES

EGYPTIANS (estimated)

Total: **20,000**

CANAANITES (estimated)

Total: **20,000**

other passes. Ultimate authority on earth he might be, but a wise pharaoh did not ignore the counsel of his officers, especially when their advice was unanimous. Leaving aside the possibility that they might be right, disregarding their advice was politically (and upon occasion, personally) dangerous.

Yet Thutmose did so. He was resolved to take the central pass. However, instead of ordering his commanders to follow him, he simply stated that he was going to take the Aruna road, alone if necessary. The officers could do nothing but immediately declare that they were going to do likewise.

EGYPTIAN ADVANCE

At first light the following day, the Egyptian army moved into the pass of Aruna, and in the next 12 hours the whole army moved through it

successfully. Meanwhile, Durusha of Kadesh had deployed his army. He predicted that Thutmose would take the southerly route, and was waiting in prepared positions near Taanach.

Durusha's position was good. If the Egyptians came via the southerly pass, they would have to fight in

Massed ranks of Egyptian infantry. Uniformity of equipment and regularity of formations are hallmarks of a well-organized and disciplined military force.

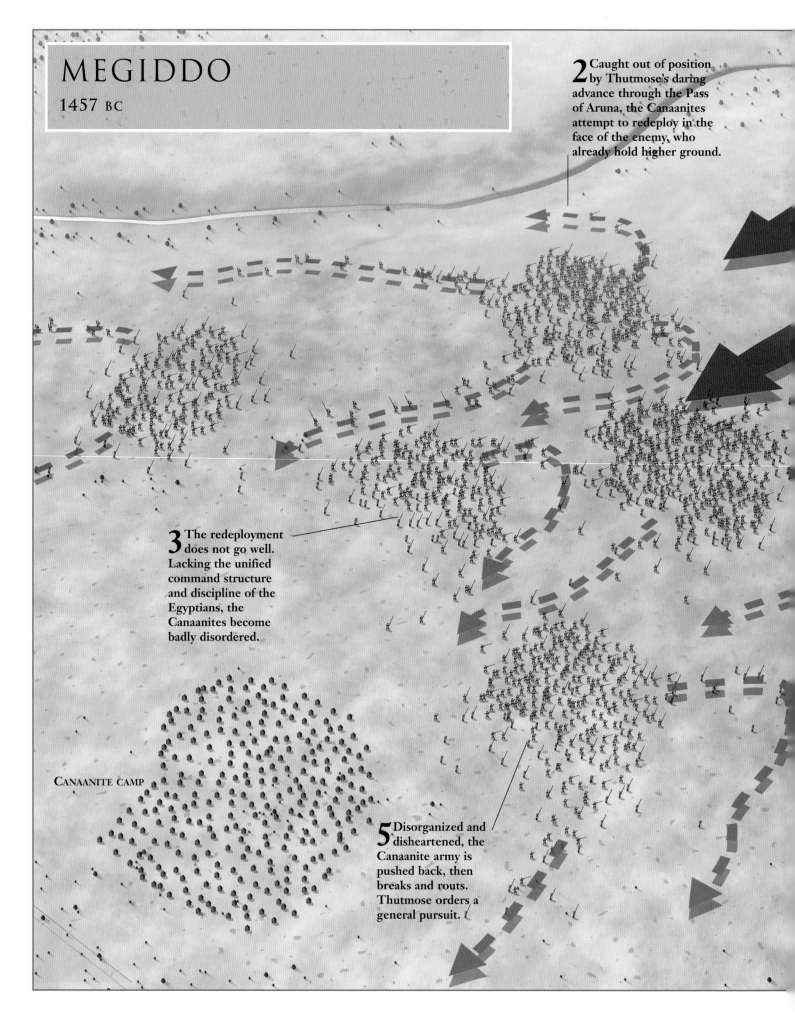

MEGIDDO
1457 BC

2 Caught out of position by Thutmose's daring advance through the Pass of Aruna, the Canaanites attempt to redeploy in the face of the enemy, who already hold higher ground.

3 The redeployment does not go well. Lacking the unified command structure and discipline of the Egyptians, the Canaanites become badly disordered.

CANAANITE CAMP

5 Disorganized and disheartened, the Canaanite army is pushed back, then breaks and routs. Thutmose orders a general pursuit.

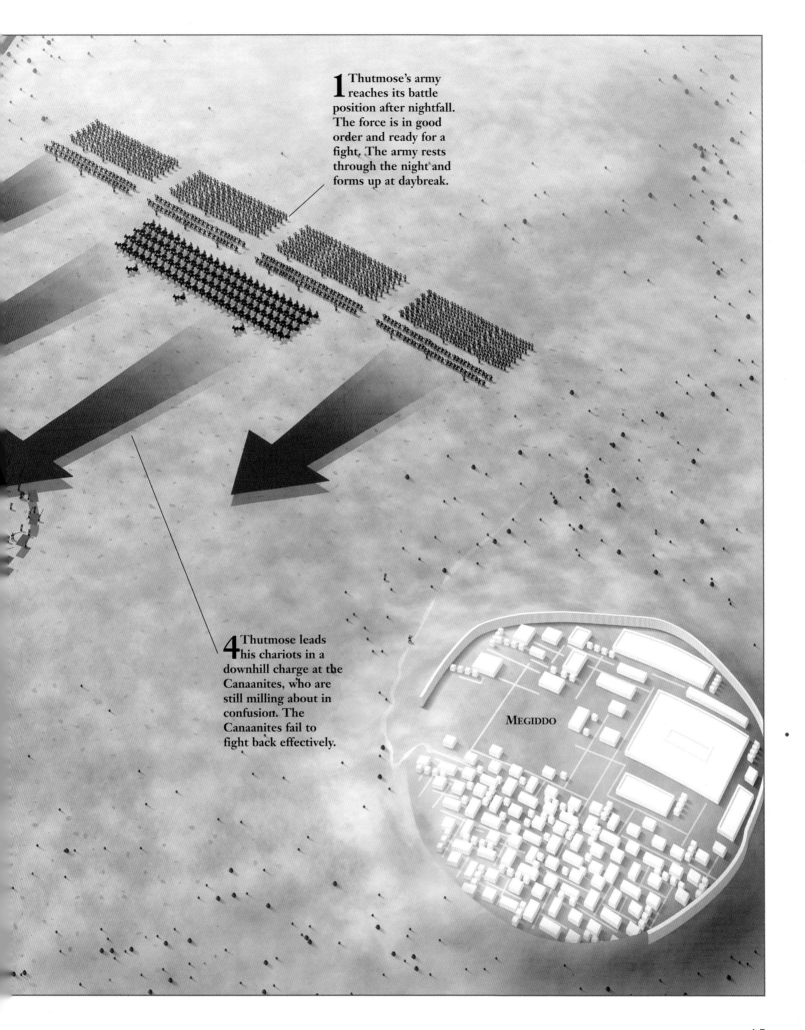

1 Thutmose's army reaches its battle position after nightfall. The force is in good order and ready for a fight. The army rests through the night and forms up at daybreak.

4 Thutmose leads his chariots in a downhill charge at the Canaanites, who are still milling about in confusion. The Canaanites fail to fight back effectively.

MEGIDDO

its mouth against a prepared enemy on ground of the latter's choosing. If they went north, there would be plenty of time for scouts to bring word, as this entailed a long detour. Durusha's army would be able to redeploy to meet them without being compromised.

Instead, the Egyptians emerged from the Aruna Pass and deployed on the plain of

This diagram shows the process by which early, solid chariot wheels were made from the trunk of a tree. A plank is cut from the centre of log. The plank is then halved: one half forms the middle plank of the wheel. The other half is further divided to form the two remaining sections.

Esdraelon, appearing on Durusha's flank and causing alarm in the enemy camp. The Canaanite princes under Durusha's command were not a unified army in the way that the Egyptians were, and their response was uncoordinated and panicky. No scouts had been posted to watch the central pass and now the seriousness of that mistake was becoming apparent.

The two armies reached their battle positions in the dark, with only a little light from the new moon to see by. This was seen as a good omen by the Egyptians, as Thutmose' family were favoured by the moon goddess. Thutmose himself made sacrifices to Amon and to Montu, god of battle, before retiring to his tent.

Canaanite chariots were more advanced than those of the Egyptians. Notably, they had better wheels that broke less often. They were used in much the same way as those of the Egyptians.

THE BATTLE

The Egyptian account of the Battle of Megiddo suggests that the forces under Durusha's hand were huge, containing several million infantrymen, hundreds of thousands of chariots and the oddly precise figure of 330 kings. In all likelihood, the Canaanite force was no larger than that of the Egyptians. It was composed of the individual contributions of a large number of nobles and princes, and it is unlikely to have possessed good enough logistics to support a very large number of troops.

Durusha's forces, however big they may have been, were still redeploying as the

Opposite: The Egyptian god Amun had many aspects at different times. Amun was credited with the victories of Pharoahs, who raised great temples to him in the hope of continued success.

Egyptians prepared to attack. Never very well organized, the Canaanites were thrown into chaos by the conflicting orders of the various princes and were further confused by arguments among the many contributors to the host about who was senior to whom, and about who was to blame for the whole debacle anyway.

The Egyptian army was much better organized and was drawn up on higher ground than its enemies. Its left flank was close to the city of Megiddo; its right was anchored on a hill by the Kina Stream. Thutmose himself commanded the centre, where he had concentrated his chariots for the decisive blow.

The pharaoh wore a blue leather crown rather than a battle helm. He stood in his command chariot, which was decorated in gold and shone in the dawn sunlight, and gave the signal for his chariots to advance. The chariot was at that time mainly used as a mobile firing platform, and it was as mobile archers that the Egyptian charioteers made their first attack. Advancing rapidly downhill, they closed to short bow range before opening fire. Behind them, the infantry crashed their weapons against their shields, and trumpets added to the din.

CHARIOT ATTACK

Thutmose' chariot force advanced confidently and began pouring arrows into the disorganized Canaanites. The Egyptians' rapid approach was alarming, and no coherent response could be made to their shooting. In the Canaanite force, disorder turned to demoralization and then quickly to rout.

Seeing the Canaanite army breaking up and men fleeing, Thutmose' chariots followed as closely as they could, and the pharaoh ordered his infantry to make a general pursuit. However, many of the infantry paused to loot the enemy camp, and so a large segment of Durusha's army

The ruins of Megiddo. The city stood in a strong, high place and was protected by good fortifications. These almost proved the undoing of the defeated Canaanites, who could not get into the city.

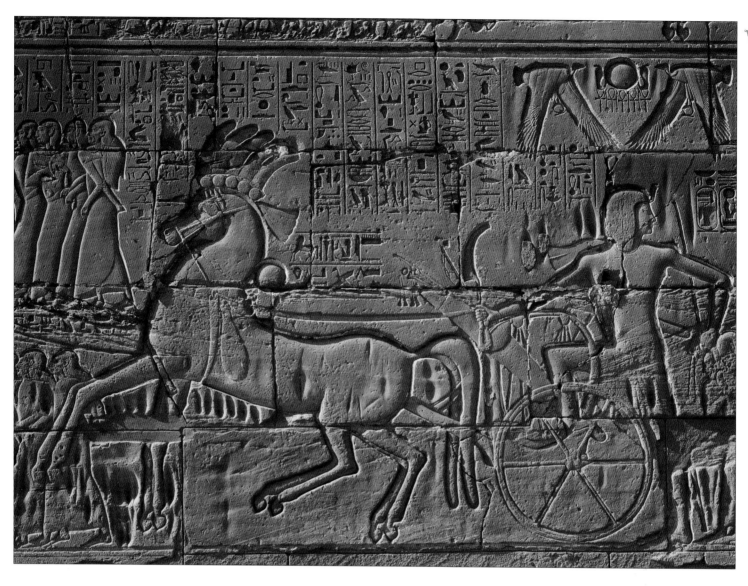

was able to reach the city of Megiddo. However, the gates were closed when Durusha arrived, and there was the possibility that his army would be pinned against the city and utterly smashed. Many of the Canaanite troops did manage to get inside while the Egyptians were rifling their belongings in the camp. The lord of Megiddo as well as the king of Kadesh himself were hauled up the wall on ropes made of clothing.

THE SIEGE OF MEGIDDO

The Egyptians laid siege to Megiddo, throwing up fortifications consisting of a moat and wall right around the city to ensure that no one escaped. With his enemies bottled up, Thutmose campaigned across the region for seven months, leaving a segment of his force to watch Megiddo. After a number of successes, including the capture of Damascus, Thutmose returned

to Megiddo and took its surrender. It was commonplace at the time to put the defenders of a city to the sword when it fell, but Thutmose spared Megiddo. His mercy was rewarded with oaths of loyalty from the former rebels, though some of the leaders were taken to Egypt as hostages.

Durusha of Kadesh was able to escape somehow, but it mattered little to the outcome. The revolt had been put down and governors installed in the region. With the challenge to his authority dealt with, Thutmose returned to Egypt and took up the reins of power in earnest. It was almost a year since he had set out on this, his first campaign as sole ruler. Throughout the campaign, Thutmose referred to it as his first. It seems that even in those early days he expected to lead many more. He had commanded two military campaigns while co-regent and would eventually lead no less than 17 as pharaoh.

This sunk-relief depiction of a charioteer at the Temple of Amun dates from later than Thutmose's campaign. The chariot uses six-spoked wheels, which supplanted other designs.

KADESH
1285 BC

ARMOURED VEHICLES, DECAPITATION STRIKES, HIDDEN FORCES AND AN ADVANCED CHAIN OF COMMAND PLAYED DECISIVE ROLES IN A CONFLICT OF CULTURES IN THE MIDDLE EAST. DISINFORMATION AND PERSONAL LEADERSHIP DROVE THOUSANDS INTO AN EPIC BATTLE LOST IN THE MISTS OF TIME.

WHY DID IT HAPPEN?

WHO The rich and powerful kingdom of Egypt under Pharaoh Ramses II (d. 1213 BC) clashed in northern Syria with the militarily innovative Hittite Empire under their king Muwatallis.

WHAT Egyptian chariots and light-armed infantry played a sanguinary game of hide-and-seek around the walls of a fortified city until finally an all-out clash resulted.

WHERE Kadesh was a rich and powerful fortified city that offered an excellent outpost to defend an empire, or to expand one from.

WHEN 1285 BC.

WHY Kadesh was a Hittite obstacle to Ramses' efforts to make Egypt's claims of world supremacy more than empty boasting.

OUTCOME Hittite cunning and technology were almost too much for Egyptian numbers and organization. A tactical victory for the Egyptians, a strategic one for the Hittites, and in the end – a draw.

When empires expand, there is resistance – from native peoples, established smaller states; and in the case of another expanding empire, resistance takes its strongest form. Ramses II's great battle of 1285 BC was the product of a young king's desire to surpass the achievements of an illustrious ancestor – and the success of the Hittite Empire's ongoing expansion southwards from Asia Minor. The two competing imperial tides clashed around the walls of a fortified city in one of the most fought-over regions on earth.

For a long time Ramses' own account of the battle of Kadesh – carved with loving care onto temple after temple – provided the only account of the action. Predictably, the Pharaoh portrayed the struggle as his personal victory over treachery in the face of overwhelming odds. Recently, however, cuneiform tablets unearthed at Boghazköy, Turkey, provide some of the other side's perspective, and the results of the battle do not quite match up with the account the ruler of Egypt left for posterity.

BACKGROUND

By the New Kingdom epoch (1539–1075 BC), Egypt had an established, and better documented, history of military activity in lands far distant from the Nile. Egypt was a rich strip of land on either side of the desert, but there were wider vistas to the north. There was a long and wide vein of racial supremacy in the character of Egyptian foreign policy – their art depicted foreign nations as helpless captives, bound to await the will of Pharaoh.

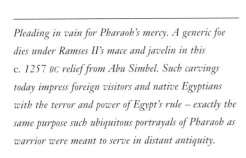

Pleading in vain for Pharaoh's mercy. A generic foe dies under Ramses II's mace and javelin in this c. 1257 BC relief from Abu Simbel. Such carvings today impress foreign visitors and native Egyptians with the terror and power of Egypt's rule – exactly the same purpose such ubiquitous portrayals of Pharaoh as warrior were meant to serve in distant antiquity.

SUMERIAN CHARIOT

Combined traditions at Kadesh led to the development of this later Sumerian chariot that combined the best traits of the two differing varieties of fighting vehicles hurled into the fray by Egyptian and Hittite builders. This later chariot is four-wheeled, like the more heavily armoured and stable vehicles of the Hittite warriors. The extra horse power of two extra asses gave the heavier vehicle greater speed, in an effort to equal the velocity of the lighter horse-drawn Egyptian chariots at Kadesh.

Imperialism came as naturally to Egypt's rulers as did their belief in themselves as the children of the Sun-God on earth. That military impulse endured and often prompted the rulers of Egypt to aggressive war. After thousands of years of experience, the pharaohs had come to be in possession of proven ways of projecting force abroad. Centuries of experimentation was a large part of Egyptian military prowess, that which the ages had taught being left for future generations to learn in texts, sculpture and monuments.

On the walls of his ancestors' temples, Ramses himself could read and benefit from the experiences of Egypt's former warrior pharaohs, including the inscription modern scholars study today detailing Thutmose III's great battle at Megiddo in 1458 BC, two centuries before. So epic were the achievements of that warrior pharaoh that even the Christian Bible's prophecy of

Armageddon, 'the hill at Megiddo', may be an echo of Thutmose's titanic struggle with the King of Kadesh and his allies the Mitanni, forerunners of the Hittites. Ramses would win his own glory – or try to – from the same source.

Some things had changed in 200 years, however. The Hittites were Egypt's most formidable opponents yet. Starting in the central regions of what is now Turkey, the smaller city-states and kingdoms of the northern Middle East had come under the centralized dominion of the Hittite Empire. With the resources of the north behind them, they were a far more formidable foe than the Mitanni – but they had taken Kadesh from Egypt, and Ramses wanted both it back and the glory of recapturing the site of Thutmose's triumph.

The Hittite king Muwatallis had no inclination to yield to the dictates of Ramses' perceived destiny, and, possessing

LOCATION

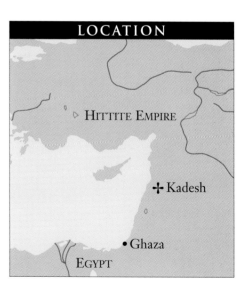

HITTITE EMPIRE

✝ Kadesh

● Ghaza

EGYPT

Ramses' campaign was an attempt to win back territory that had been Egypt's a few centuries before. Although he failed to regain all of the lost lands, he nonetheless secured a lasting peace.

the advantages of the defender, made his own preparations to exploit them.

RAMSES' ARMY

The understanding in Egypt that peasants had to be levied, trained and fed for great undertakings went back to the Old Kingdom's massive construction projects, some of which still survive in the pyramids looming over Cairo. Ramses would once more employ the vast human resources of Ancient Egypt.

While the Nile flooded and the crops grew, the wealth of Egypt could take idle fellahin and mobilize them into armies, as well as the construction gangs that had left the glories of the past. The richness of Egyptian agriculture could equip these levies for war, but training and controlling them in battle would prove a very difficult task. War was more complicated an affair than dragging one more stone up onto the sides of a pyramid. With king fighting king on the chessboard of battle, both sides enjoyed a unified supreme command

Terror on the battlefield – and hopefully in international relations – was the objective behind the gruesome images portrayed in this relief from the vast temple of Ramses II at Thebes. For the education of his subjects and the intimidation of his enemies, Pharaoh's exploits needed and received the florid magnification of skilled artists to leave a lasting impression.

structure, but the simple limitations on the abilities of a single man to control an army nonetheless required compensatory measures.

The Egyptian solution, which is the one Ramses recorded on his own inscription describing the battle, was a fairly effective one. Ramses divided his army of approximately 20,000 men into four divisions of equal size under trusted subordinates, men with positions and possessions back in Egypt and hence a stake in victory. Ramses hit upon a useful combination of divine patronage and unit identity by naming each of his divisions

THE OPPOSED FORCES

EGYPTIANS (estimated)

Chariots:	2000
Infantry:	18,000
Total:	**20,000**

HITTITES (estimated)

Chariots:	3000
Infantry:	20,000
Total:	**23,000**

*The prototypical armoured fighting vehicle. Chariots
such as these offered a degree of stability and protection
to the Hittite archers stationed within them.
The sturdy wild asses pulling them offered endurance,
as their top speed was no more than the primitive
construction of the chariots could endure.*

*The wealthier Egyptians favoured a faster, lighter –
and less stable – horse-drawn version of the chariot.*

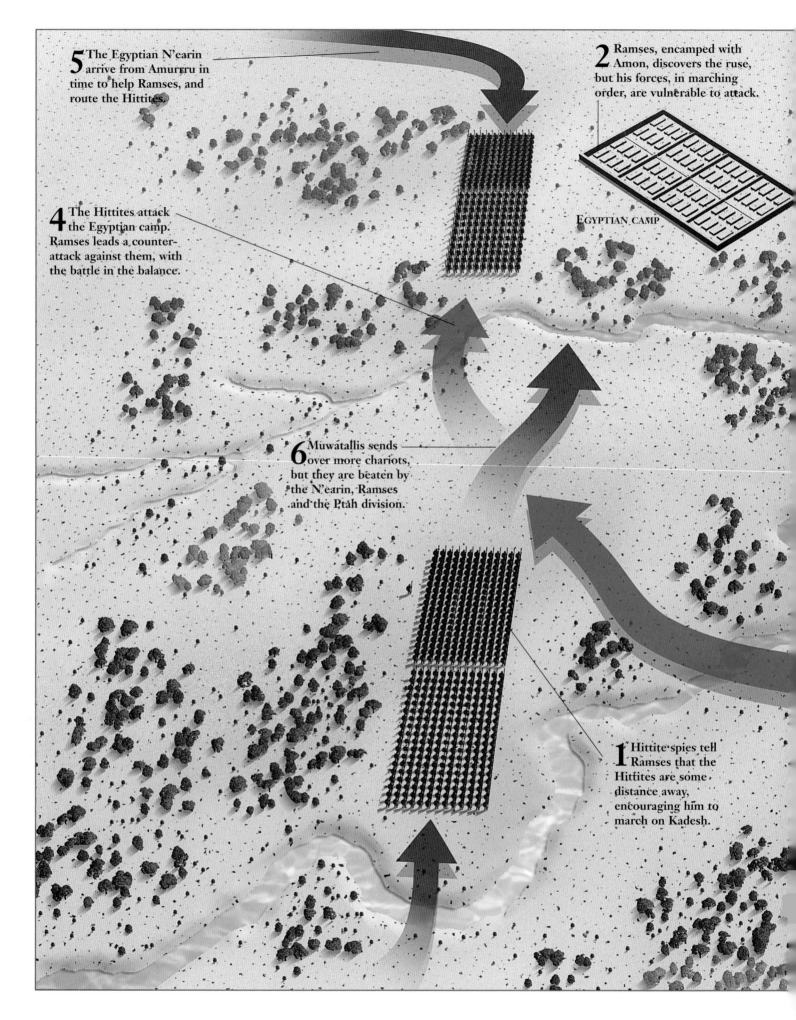

5 The Egyptian N'earin arrive from Amurrru in time to help Ramses, and route the Hittites.

2 Ramses, encamped with Amon, discovers the ruse, but his forces, in marching order, are vulnerable to attack.

EGYPTIAN CAMP

4 The Hittites attack the Egyptian camp. Ramses leads a counter-attack against them, with the battle in the balance.

6 Muwatallis sends over more chariots, but they are beaten by the N'earin, Ramses and the Ptah division.

1 Hittite spies tell Ramses that the Hitfites are some distance away, encouraging him to march on Kadesh.

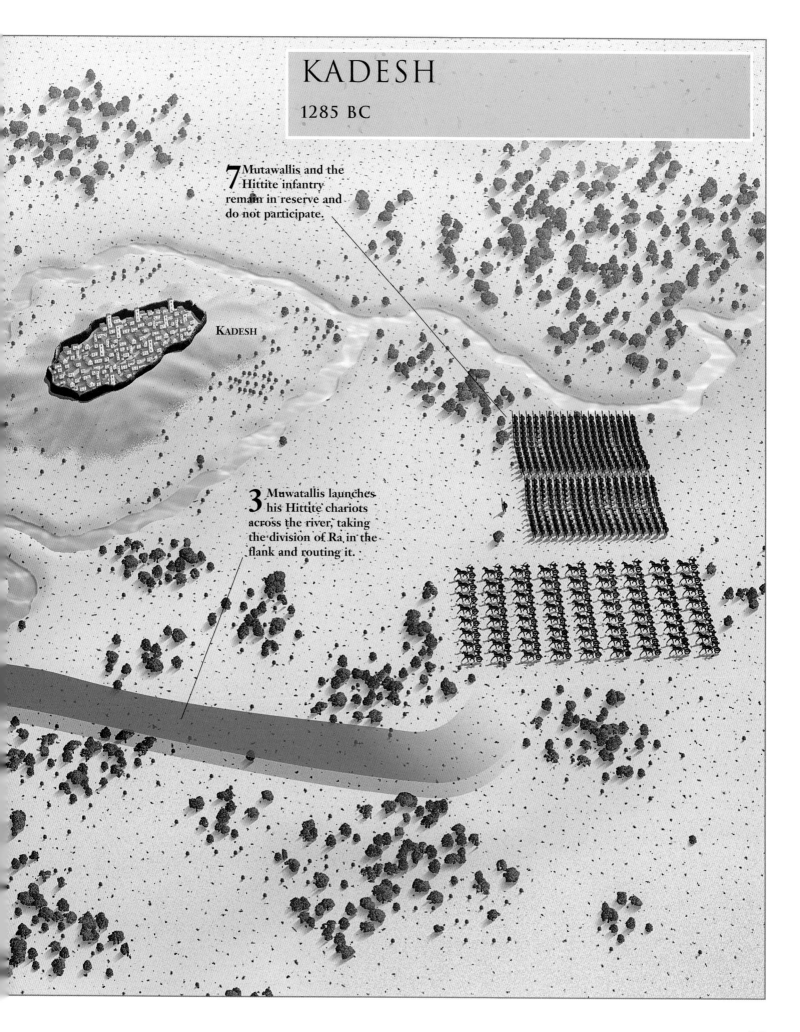

KADESH

1285 BC

7 Mutawallis and the Hittite infantry remain in reserve and do not participate.

KADESH

3 Muwatallis launches his Hittite chariots across the river, taking the division of Ra in the flank and routing it.

In this mural depicting Ramses II's carefully propagandized exploits at Kadesh, the exaggerated sizes of Pharaoh and the targeted city emphasize the respective importance of each in the mental picture the image is intended to create. The terror of the defenders and the absolute order of the Egyptian ranks were more the products of wishful thinking by Ramses than historical reality.

after a divine patron, those being Amon, Ra, Ptah and Sutekh, while at the same time keeping his own person, bodyguard and immediate subordinates outside of that structure in a separate, mobile unit. The Egyptian officer corps' task would be to get the most out of their mostly raw troops by localized supervision.

THE CAMPAIGN

During Ramses' march toward Kadesh, these four divisions moved at some distance apart, a tactical trade-off between access to such roads as there were and the need for time to let assorted water sources and reservoirs be refilled or replenished, and the considerable, and in this case realized, risk of the army's component parts encountering the enemy while still separated and being destroyed in detail. Still, the Egyptians were successfully moving huge numbers of men a great distance, the very essence of aggressive war. The Hittites were facing no minor threat.

Some details in text do survive of exactly what an Egyptian called up for the wars could expect, in addition to 'no clothes, no sandals … a march uphill through the mountains … water every third day … body ravaged by illness'. Pharaoh's wealth provided the infantry with orders, a short linen skirt, a leather helmet and a cowhide shield with the pelt turned outwards. But at least there were a lot of their fellows about them to share the burden of war, if they could be fed, if they could be given water.

Organization and wealth allowed Ramses both to employ mercenaries to support his native levies and to make a very rapid march from Egypt to the north of Syria where the battle took place. The speed of the Egyptian march risked causing problems in supply and sudden attack, but the advantage was very great in terms of surprise and preparation. The expertise of the mercenaries was a definite asset to the Egyptians, and drained the pool of talent available to the Hittites.

The wealth of Egypt found expression in the copper and bronze heads of the knife, mace, sword and spear shown here. As much a soldier's tool as a weapon, the knife would have been of greatest value at close quarters or at mealtimes. The mace was at its best against the skull of an unhelmeted enemy, being the first weapon specifically designed to slaughter humankind, while as a lance, pike or throwing weapon, the humble spear made up the classic mainstay of any ancient soldier's fighting gear.

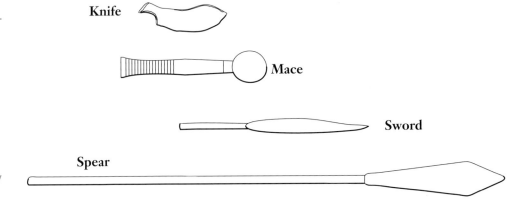

Knife

Mace

Sword

Spear

Fear of the enemy (or his own pets) seems to exhibit itself in this nineteenth-century visualization of Ramses II at the climax at Kadesh. The Egyptians did train large cats such as cheetahs for hunting, but their legendary accounts of the Pharaoh using pet lions in war call for scepticism. The Pharaoh and, more importantly, the horses drawing his chariot might well have had their doubts about the behaviour of a large carnivore in the midst of carnage such as depicted here.

Muwatallis, however, was no supine foe. The Hittite king managed, at what the Egyptian account notes as considerable expense and disruption, to produce a matching army of his own by the time the Egyptian forces approached the walled city of Kadesh.

THE BATTLE

Always involved in any exercise of command and control is the flow of information to and from the commander. Muwatallis cannily fed some 'disinformation' into Ramses' control apparatus by planting two spies in the path of Ramses' army. The captured pair informed Ramses that the Hittite army was still some distance off, prompting Ramses to make another tactical gamble and take his foremost division, that of Ra, and his own command and bodyguard to Kadesh with the hope of seizing the city before the Hittites arrived. Ramses and his bodyguard encamped to the north of the city while the division of Amon rendezvoused with them the following morning.

The Hittite army, probably smaller than the Egyptian army, accordingly had two great advantages besides the simple, greatest one of more battle experience. Ramses was unaware of their actual position, and they themselves were unified, in a position to annihilate the division of Ra and win perhaps the war by capturing or killing Ramses himself.

For all the advantage having the king as commander gave ancient armies, like the chess game that reflects them, struggles in which the king was the cause could be lost with the neutralization of one man.

With visual reconnaissance being the only sort Ramses apparently saw need to employ, the Hittite army's simple strategy of using Kadesh itself as cover worked quite well against the Egyptians. As the Amon and Ra divisions approached from the south and west of the city, the Hittites moved to the east, poised to move across the Egyptian line of march.

Muwatallis' decision to hold his army outside of the city was a very sound one. The difficulties of controlling an army in an urban environment are very serious even today, and in those days, using his complete force for a tactical offensive within the city would have been impossible for Muwatallis as walls and streets would have blocked audible and visual signals and disrupted his unit formations.

The Hittites struck the second of Ramses' divisions – Ra – as it approached their new positions and hit it in the flank. The Egyptians, surprised, panicked and fled for safety to the division of Amon and threw that formation into disorder and confusion as well, just as the victorious Hittites

'Shield high, stay in ranks,' were basic commands that could be taught and under ideal conditions adhered to by fellahin levied into the Egyptian infantry by Ramses' officers. In equipment, bare, in training, poor, such chariot-fodder as these lacked everything but numbers and a desire for loot and glory. In those Egypt was wealthy enough to pose a sizeable threat to even so sophisticated and skilled an opponent as the expanding Hittite Empire.

attacked again from the south directly across the Egyptians' escape route. Disaster loomed.

At that point of the battle Ramses and Muwatallis each faced differing problems in controlling their armies. The panic and disorder of fully half of his forces left Ramses physically unable to transmit countering orders to his own troops, and no message could be sent that would dramatically hasten the impending arrival of the divisions of Ptah and Sutekh to the battlefield where they were desperately needed. Muwatallis, for that matter, found his own ability to command his forces disintegrating as his men stopped to plunder the Egyptians' camp, including the tents of the Pharaoh, as the disorganized Egyptian forces gave ground.

Moreover, Muwatallis himself apparently made a lapse of reconnaissance and intelligence-gathering and remained unaware that the other half of the Egyptian army was marching directly into his rear, while a formation of mercenaries hired by Ramses was moving in from the Mediterranean coast and about to take him squarely in his eastern flank with more trained ferocity than the raw Egyptians could achieve.

Ramses and his army would live or die upon his ability to regain control of his forces, and the Pharaoh took the only, therefore the best, means of doing it, by very visibly leading his own bodyguard into a headlong counter-attack against the advancing Hittites. Instantly, every Egyptian on the field knew where his commander was and where his own duty lay, and a general movement against the Hittites allowed the division of Ptah to strike the

Hittites in the rear just as the mercenaries pitched into them from the flank.

Muwatallis withdrew in some confusion. It is worth noting that in even the most autocratic of armies retreat is a decision democratically arrived upon, when the majority of soldiers 'vote with their feet', and force even the officer corps to retire with them. Moving into Kadesh, the Hittites were sheltered against any further Egyptian surprises but did forfeit the substantial psychological advantage of holding the battlefield.

AFTERMATH

Ramses' reverses prompted him to withdraw his remaining forces from the vicinity of Kadesh, while the Hittites had seen enough of Egypt's military resources to agree to a lasting peace after the battle. Both sides had shown good and bad exercises of central command, both sides had had their failures of communication, and the result was a tactical win for the Egyptians, a strategic victory for the Hittites, and, in the light of the treaty, an international 'draw'.

At Kadesh, Ramses did inflict a great deal of damage on the Hittite army, at a considerable, and inadvertent, risk of losing his crown and life due to his own belief in the information planted by the two captured spies. At considerable cost in time, treasure and the blood of both armies, Ramses did secure a peace treaty and security on his northern frontier, not to mention a stele of his own to rival the enduring military glory of Thutmose III and the other warrior pharaohs. In his own view – and no one else's mattered – the battle was a success, whatever else shows up under the glaring spotlight of modern analysis.

Opposite: The massive statue of Ramses II fronting the temple of Ramses II at Abu Simbel, near Lake Nasser in modern Egypt, was built to mark the ancient kingdom's southern border and is testament to the Pharaoh's power.

MARATHON
490 BC

THE MARATHON IS THE ONLY OLYMPIC EVENT NAMED AFTER A BATTLE, A RACE OF 26 MILES TO RETRACE THE DISTANCE THE GREEK RUNNER PHILIPPIDES RAN FROM MARATHON TO ATHENS, ANNOUNCING THAT GREEK ARMIES FROM THERE AND THEIR ALLIED CITY PLATAEA HAD DEFEATED A LARGE PERSIAN INVASION FORCE. WITH THIS VICTORY THE THREAT TO THE CITY HAD SUBSTANTIALLY DECREASED.

WHY DID IT HAPPEN?

WHO An Athenian army under Miltiades attacked a Persian invasion force commanded by King Darius' general Datis.

WHAT The Greek hoplites charged the Persian line, broke the light infantry on the flanks and turned in on the heavy infantry in the centre. The Persians were pursued to their ships and great numbers were killed.

WHERE Marathon, 42km (26 miles) from Athens, in Greece.

WHEN 490 BC

WHY Darius invaded Greece to punish Athens for its support of a rebellion of the Ionian Greek cities in Asia Minor.

OUTCOME The Persian army was all but wiped out, and the Greek peninsula was saved from Persian conquest.

If one visited the site of the battle only a year before the modern Olympics returned to Athens in 2004, one was greeted with a broken monumental plinth, graffiti spray-painted on all man-made surfaces, and a museum that was rarely visited. The battlefield, on which perhaps the greatest battle in Ancient Greece's history had been fought, was not only neglected, it was abused – all except the two grave mounds. In one are the cremated remains of the 192 Athenians who fell on that day, in the other the remains of the unnumbered Plataeans. These mounds are said to have been erected on opposite ends of where the Greek soldiers were lined up before they had burst

The famous Immortals armed with spear, bow and arrows, in the service of Darius for the Persian king's invasion of Greece in 490 BC. The illustration is taken from enamelled tiles in Susa, modern-day Iran.

into their surprising, well-nigh insane charge and gained victory. These mounds stand now as they stood nearly 2400 years ago, a remembrance of the brave men who had saved their cities and land from Persian conquest.

PERSIAN EXPANSIONISM

As the calendar turned to what would later be reckoned as the first year of the fifth century BC, the Persian Empire was the largest state in the Eastern Mediterranean region. Only 41 years before, in 559 BC, Cyrus I 'the Great' had become king of Persia and had started immediately to add to his realm. By the time of his death 30 years later he had extended his borders to include Media, Central Asia, Babylon and almost all of Asia Minor, including Lydia and the Greek colonies of Ionia. No force had successfully stood in his way. Cyrus' army so outnumbered its enemies that it simply crushed any opposition with its size and power, and his navy was so numerous that it simply swept any other fleet away. There was really no intelligence to tactics such as these.

However, Cyrus was a strategic genius. He knew how to campaign, moving armies and supplies with the greatest of ease. And after his death, in 529 BC, his son, Cambyses, continued his father's practices, adding Egypt to the kingdom before accidentally wounding himself in the thigh with his own sword and dying of gangrene during a civil war with his brother, Bardiya, in 522 BC.

Up to this time, military encounters with the Greeks had been few. Ionia was hardly populated enough to put up much of a defence against the Persians, and so had fallen with very little opposition. Nor had mainland Greece been threatened, as the thrust of Persian conquest during most of Cyrus' and all of Cambyses' reigns had been toward Babylon and Egypt. But after the new emperor, Darius – at best only a distant relation of the Cyrus family – seized the throne in 521 BC, the danger of Graeco-Persian conflict grew. In 513 BC, having secured his throne, Darius entered Scythia. In two more years he conquered Thrace. However, then and now without historical

rationale, his further progress into the region stopped. Darius pulled out of open conquest of Greece and left Artaphernes as governor of the region. A tenuous peace between the Greek cities and Persia followed for a few years. In 507 BC

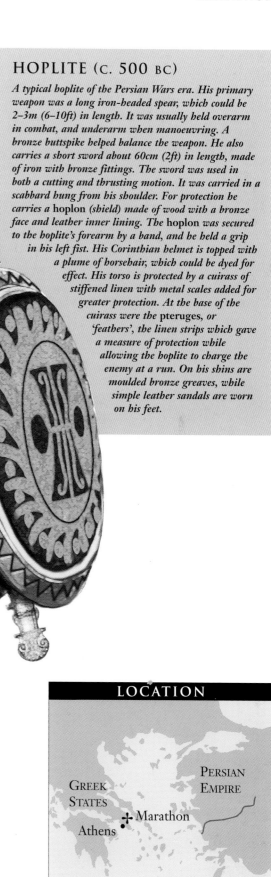

HOPLITE (C. 500 BC)

A typical hoplite of the Persian Wars era. His primary weapon was a long iron-headed spear, which could be 2–3m (6–10ft) in length. It was usually held overarm in combat, and underarm when manoeuvring. A bronze buttspike helped balance the weapon. He also carries a short sword about 60cm (2ft) in length, made of iron with bronze fittings. The sword was used in both a cutting and thrusting motion. It was carried in a scabbard hung from his shoulder. For protection he carries a hoplon (shield) made of wood with a bronze face and leather inner lining. The hoplon was secured to the hoplite's forearm by a band, and he held a grip in his left fist. His Corinthian helmet is topped with a plume of horsehair, which could be dyed for effect. His torso is protected by a cuirass of stiffened linen with metal scales added for greater protection. At the base of the cuirass were the pteruges, or 'feathers', the linen strips which gave a measure of protection while allowing the hoplite to charge the enemy at a run. On his shins are moulded bronze greaves, while simple leather sandals are worn on his feet.

LOCATION

GREEK STATES

Athens

✝ Marathon

PERSIAN EMPIRE

Myth has it that Philippides ran the 42km (26 miles) back to Athens to proclaim the victory before dying of exhaustion. In the nineteenth century, the 'Marathon' road race was instituted in his honour.

MARATHON

Bronze hoplite helmet. It was made of a solid piece of bronze shaped and cut to fit the head. The skull and neck were well protected by the helmet, while the long nose guard and cheek pieces covered the face.

THE OPPOSED FORCES

GREEKS

Athenian hoplites:	9600
Plataean hoplites:	400
Total:	**10,000**

PERSIANS

Cavalry:	1000
Infantry:	19,000
Total:	**20,000**

have questioned how dissatisfied the Ionians could have been, as the Persians had allowed them almost complete political and economic autonomy. There may have been some urging by other Greek cities – most notably Athens and Eretria – as these immediately assisted their cross-Aegean neighbours. However, as the rebels' immediate target was Sardis, the Lydian capital of Persian western Asian Minor – which was burned – perhaps there was more dissatisfaction with outside governance than previously thought.

Herodotus reports that Darius replied with a huge army and navy. Within five years the revolt had been crushed, resulting in an almost complete loss of autonomy for the Ionian Greeks. By that time, Athenian and Eretrian support for the Ionians had diminished, but it seems that Darius would not forgive those who had previously given him 'earth and water', having a slave whisper 'Remember Athens!' to him while serving his evening meals.

THE PERSIAN INVASION

In 491 BC Darius began his campaign against mainland Greece. First, he sent ambassadors to each Greek *polis* (city-state) demanding its submission. Athens, Sparta, Eretria, and many others refused. But the Saronic island state of Aegina, certainly frightened by Persia and not very friendly towards Athens, agreed. Aegina under the control of Persia meant that the sea lanes to and from the Greek peninsula would be blocked, disrupting trade and threatening security. Athens, together with Sparta, which also felt threatened by this alliance, demanded that the Aeginetans withdraw their submission to Persia. This was just the provocation Darius needed, and he began to put his plans for an invasion of the mainland into action.

In recounting the history that followed, including the battle of Marathon, the historian is constrained by the existence of only a single source, the Greek historian Herodotus. Although justifiably called the 'father of history' and judged by many modern historians to be a reliable source, Herodotus is nevertheless naturally biased, especially in his reporting of events that turned out to be so successful for the

the Athenians even presented Artaphernes with 'earth and water', their friendship and allegiance, although later historians have wondered how serious an obeisance this was.

THE IONIAN REVOLT

In 499 BC this peace was broken, when Ionia revolted. Why the still underpopulated Ionia chose to rebel at this time cannot be determined from the meagre historical sources that remain. It seems to have been an internal plot, although some historians

Various drill positions used by hoplites around 500 BC. From left to right: the hoplite standing at ease; at attention awaiting orders; the position adopted when advancing into battle; and when thrusting his spear overarm.

Greeks. For example, his description of the Persian invading force as 'a huge army' transported to Marathon on 600 triremes almost no one accepts as credible. Much more believable is Herodotus' chronology. Datis, the Persian commander, first moved against Eretria, which he captured in short order – after two of the city's leaders opened the gates for him – afterwards destroying it and enslaving the population. Then he rowed his fleet to Marathon.

THE OPPOSING ARMIES

The Athenians had been aware of Persian movements even before Eretria was attacked. They immediately mustered their army and at the same time sent their swiftest messenger, the legendary Philippides (sometimes called Pheidippides), to Sparta for military assistance. The Athenian army has recently been described as a citizen-army, because it was reputed to have been drawn from its general population. Although not requiring all of its citizens to serve in the army as Sparta did, Athens relied on them to provide almost all of its soldiers. Each infantry soldier was to be outfitted with greaves, a helmet, and a

hoplon, the large and heavy round metal-faced shield, from which the term for these soldiers – hoplite – was derived. Most also wore a cuirass (torso armour), either styled to emphasize or exaggerate the musculature – hence the modern name 'muscle cuirass' – or in the form of a composite corslet, leather armour to which metal scales were added. Leather flanges descending from the waist on both sides added protection for the groin. Each also carried a strong spear, tipped with a sharp iron spearhead, and most also had a sword for close-quarters fighting or if they lost or broke their spear.

Despite being recruited from the citizenry, Athenian infantry were disciplined and well trained. They could manoeuvre as units, called phalanxes, both offensively and defensively. Athenian cavalry carried javelins and swords and always wore a cuirass – as they could not carry the *hoplon* – and sometimes arm guards. They were trained primarily to operate as missile troops throwing javelins or to clash with their spears against opposing cavalry. Archers and slingers were largely hired from elsewhere as mercenaries. At Marathon the Athenians, supported by a

MARATHON
490 BC

5 Philippides allegedly runs the 42km (26 miles) to Athens to proclaim the news of the Greek victory before dying of fatigue.

2 In the centre the Persian line counter-charges, and successfully breaks through the Athenian phalanx.

1 The Greek phalanx advances at a run towards the Persians, whose flanks quickly give way under pressure.

3 At the crucial moment, the Greek wings abandon their pursuit and attack the flanks of the Persian centre.

4 The Persian centre routs and flees back to their fleet. Approximately one-third of the Persian army is killed.

unit of 400 Plataean hoplites, numbered around 10,000 infantry.

Less is known about Persian troops of the early fifth century BC. Like the Greeks, a Persian army was principally an infantry force, but unlike its opponent, both heavy and light infantry were used. Once thought to have worn only cloth tunics or robes and hats, because that is all that can be seen in most artistic portrayals, it is now believed that heavy infantry were outfitted in armour and helmets underneath this outer apparel. They also carried spears, swords, kidney-bean-shaped shields and sometimes bows. Light infantry wore similar tunics, robes and hats and may have been unarmoured except for the large oblong wooden shields each carried. They threw javelins, shot

bows, and – in close combat – wielded spears. Most of the Persian infantry were professional, paid soldiers, although many of the light infantry could also be recruited from subject peoples.

A select group of heavy infantry, numbered at no less than 10,000, were known as the Immortals, a band whose bravery, experience and fraternity made them feared throughout the Ancient World. Persian cavalry were similarly equipped to their infantry, and – as at Marathon – were usually more numerous than Greek cavalry. Historians judge the size of the Persian army at Marathon to be 19,000 infantry and 1000 cavalry.

The leadership of the two armies differed considerably. Persian leaders were appointed most often because of the skills that they had shown in previous campaigns and engagements, but sometimes also because of their political proximity to the throne or court. Datis, the Persian general at Marathon, was a combination of the two: he was a favourite of Darius, but this favour

The so-called Darius Vase (painted in the fourth century BC and currently in the Naples Museum) shows Persian king Darius I holding a council of war before launching his invasion of Greece in 491 BC. His land campaign ended with the battle of Marathon.

Opposite: At the battle of Marathon, Miltiades, with 9600 Athenian and 400 Plataean hoplites, defeated a Persian force of double the size, including 10,000 Immortals, demonstrating the value of the phalanx infantry formation.

Relief of the Persian Immortals from the Apadana, Persepolis, Iran. The Immortals were an elite infantry force of the Persian army. Only ethnic Persians or Medeans could be members of a unit which, according to Herodotus, always numbered 10,000.

had resulted from the military leadership he had previously shown. The Athenians were led by a corps of ten elected generals. These made decisions as a council, with no single general carrying more weight than another. Overall command of the army was rotated daily among these ten. Of these leaders, the most prominent – although primarily because of his leadership at Marathon – was the vengeful Miltiades, whose previous political leadership of the Chersonese peninsula in northern Asia Minor had been ended by Persian conquest.

THE DECISION TO FIGHT

Philippides' mission to Sparta essentially failed. The Spartans were prepared to come to the aid of the Athenians, but not until their religious celebrations tied to the appearance of the full moon were completed. A militaristic society, the Spartans were nevertheless a highly religious people who, as Thermopylae would later confirm, let nothing – even war – interrupt their festivities and rituals. Philippides returned to the Athenian army with the news. It is not known whether the

Greeks had reached Marathon before or after receiving Philippides' report.

According to Herodotus, Marathon was selected by the Persians based on the advice of an exiled Athenian, Hippias, who had seen the battlefield in a vision. While not doubting Hippias' role, modern historians have surmised that it was selected because the flatness of the plain rising up from the beach provided good ground for Datis to make effective use of his cavalry. If this was the case, however, it must be wondered why the Persian cavalry was not arrayed in a very good tactical position, especially as there were several days between the army's landing and the battle. It is far more probable that Datis selected this disembarkation point because of its broad unguarded beaches and its proximity to Athens. It was the Athenians who chose to meet the Persians there rather than to try and shelter behind their city walls as the Eretrians had attempted to do.

But when the Athenians saw the immense size of the Persian force at Marathon they wavered in their decision to fight them there. A dispute arose in the war

council between those who favoured withdrawal, at least until the arrival of the Spartans, and those who desired to do battle with the Persians then and there. Herodotus claims that the vote between these two proposals was a tie. This left the decision to the War Archon, Callimachus, whose position of leadership on the right wing of the army gave him decision-making authority when just such a situation occurred. But before he could cast the deciding vote, Miltiades approached him. In the words of Herodotus, Miltiades promoted the idea of fighting: 'If we do not fight, I look to see a great disturbance at Athens which will shake men's resolutions, and then I fear they will submit themselves, but if we fight the battle before any

unsoundness show itself among our citizens, let the gods but give us fair play, and we are able to overcome the enemy. On you therefore we depend in this matter, which lies wholly in your own power. You have only to add your vote to my side and your country will be free, and not free only, but the first state in Greece. Or, if you prefer to give your vote to them who would decline the combat, then the reverse will follow.' Callimachus voted to fight.

Miltiades was clearly the influential force in the choice of this course of action, and the other leaders responded by giving him overall command of the Greek forces. Because of the ultimate success of the endeavour, historians have always honoured him. And, yet, was his role not more

The battle of Marathon ended dramatically with the collapse of the Persian line and a flight to the beached Persian ships. All but seven of the Persian vessels escaped capture. Greek historian Herodotus numbered the Persian dead at 6400.

Following the Greek victory at Marathon, the Athenian runner Philippides delivered the news to the worried Athenians 42km (26 miles) away. He is said to have dropped dead from exhaustion after passing on his message, although this is disputed. The modern marathon race celebrates his feat.

incautious and vengeful, rather than tactically astute? Surely he must have known of the impending approach of the Spartans, whose numbers at the very least would have made his forces more even in strength to the Persians, not to mention adding the inestimable advantage of their legendary bellicosity.

But Miltiades not only ignored this, he waited until he could lead the Greeks on his own day of command, which turned out to be only a single day prior to the Spartan arrival. Had the battle ended in failure, no doubt the blame for this would have rested on this decision.

THE BATTLE

On a day in August or September 490 BC as yet undetermined by modern historians, Miltiades formed his Athenian and Plataean troops into their battle formation. With the force stretched thinly in the middle – 'only a few ranks deep', according to Herodotus – to approximate the length of the deeper Persian line that faced them, the two wings were actually stronger than the centre. As War Archon, Callimachus placed his troops on the right wing, while the Plataeans, no doubt to reward their allegiance, were placed on the left wing.

Was this a planned or accidental formation? Most historians believe that Miltiades made his centre thinner accidentally, in order to approximate the length of the Persian line. But other ancient commanders, most notably Hannibal at the battle of Cannae, used such a formation as a tactic, to lure their opponents into a weakened centre in order to collapse the stronger two wings onto them.

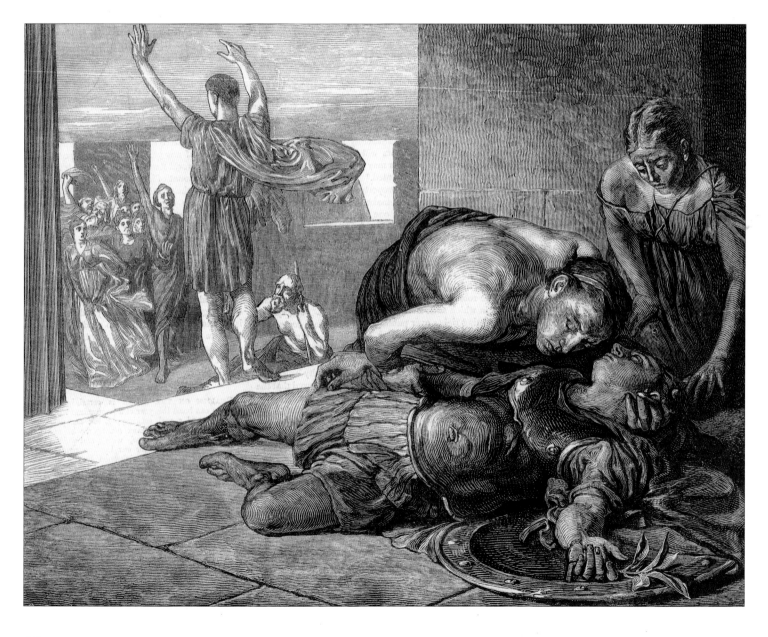

One thing that might suggest that this was not a planned formation is what happened next. Herodotus writes: 'When their [the Greeks'] battle lines were drawn up and the omens from the sacrifices were favourable, the Athenians were released, and charged the invaders at a run. The distance between the two armies was no less than eight stades. When the Persians saw the Athenians running towards them … they thought the Athenians must be mad – mad enough to bring about their utter destruction – because they could see how few of them there were, and that they were unsupported by cavalry or archers.'

Eight stades equals roughly 1.6km (1 mile), which some historians regard as too far for the Greeks to carry out the 'mad' charge that Herodotus claims, but it does fit the battlefield. If the Greeks were deployed between the later grave mounds at the beginning of their charge, then the Persian army, as it is reported to have been lined up in front of the marshlands near the beach, was roughly 1.6km (1 mile) away.

Still, an army charging 1.6km (1 mile) does surprise us. Herodotus reports that it also surprised the Persians at the battle of Marathon. The clash of the two forces must have been loud and violent. Quickly the two wings of the Persian army began to fail, but the centre held and soon began to gain the upper hand against the Greeks who faced them. However, by this time, it seems, the soldiers on the Persian wings had begun to flee to the beach. Instead of pursuing them, though, the Greek wings folded in on the Persian centre; 'the two wings combined into a single fighting unit', writes Herodotus. Whatever early advantage these troops, among whom were the Immortals, had gained on their opponents soon dissolved, as they began to be attacked on all sides. They too eventually fled towards the beached Persian ships.

The Greeks had won the battle, but the threat to Athens clearly remained if a significant number of soldiers were able to escape. So, despite the fatigue that had obviously begun to overtake the hoplites, they pursued their enemy to the beaches, continuing the fight the entire way. There the Persians had regrouped to establish a defensive wall, and they defended their

ships there with a ferocity previously unseen in the battle. The desire for survival is, of course, a very strong one, and the Persians knew they had been defeated. They wanted some of their number to stay alive. It was a valiant effort, paying off in the end when all but seven ships were able to escape, although Herodotus numbers the Persian dead at 6400.

AFTERMATH

Philippides made his run to Athens; the Athenians were elated at the news; the Spartans arrived the next day on the battlefield and congratulated their fellow Greeks on the victory; and the fallen soldiers of the victorious side were cremated and their remains interred in the mounds that still remain today. They and the other Athenians and Plataeans who fought that day at Marathon were heroes. They had kept their peninsula free from Persian conquest and it would remain so for the next ten years.

One veteran of the battle of Marathon, Aristides, later served in several Athenian governmental positions. His advice helped determine further Greek victories at the battles of Salamis and Plataea, leading to the ultimate defeat of the Persians.

SALAMIS
480 BC

THE BATTLE OF SALAMIS WAS ANCIENT GREECE'S GREATEST VICTORY IN ITS LIFE-AND-DEATH STRUGGLE AGAINST THE PERSIAN EMPIRE. IT EFFECTIVELY ENDED XERXES' PLAN TO CONQUER ALL OF GREECE, AND ESTABLISHED ATHENS AS THE GREATEST SEA POWER OF THE MEDITERRANEAN.

WHY DID IT HAPPEN?

WHO A Persian fleet of at least 700 triremes, under the immediate command of the Phoenician admiral Ariabignes, but with King Xerxes (d. 465 BC) in command of the nearby land army, was opposed by a fleet of about 310 ships contributed by member states of the Greek League, under the official command of the Spartan general Eurybiades, although the credit for victory by rights belongs to the admiral of the Athenian squadron, Themistocles.

WHAT The battle took place between the Greek and Persian fleets, with marine exchanges of arrows and javelins succeeded by ramming and boarding of enemy vessels.

WHERE In the Salamis Strait, between the island of Salamis and the mainland of Attica in Greece.

WHEN 20 September 480 BC.

WHY The Persian king Xerxes had launched a massive invasion to conquer Greece, in revenge for Greek interference in a Persian rebellion and the Athenian victory over a Persian force at Marathon in 490 BC. The Persians had already occupied northern and central Greece, but had to defeat the allied fleet before they could move on, by both land and sea, to invade the Peloponnese.

OUTCOME Thanks especially to a cunning strategy plotted by Themistocles of Athens, the Greeks won a resounding victory over the Persians. The Persians lost over 200 ships sunk and many more captured and disabled. Their fleet no longer viable, the Persians had to withdraw from Greece.

King Xerxes came to the throne of the Persian Empire in 486 BC eager to restore Persian honour after the defeat of his father's invasion by the Athenians at the battle of Marathon in 490 BC. As soon as his throne was secured, Xerxes began plans for a massive invasion of Greece by both land and sea. The first target was the city of Athens, but Xerxes also intended to conquer the entire Greek peninsula and make it a province of the empire. Both an enormous land army and a massive fleet (numbering over 1200 triremes) were mustered, the warships especially intended to protect the supply ships that were needed to provision the army.

The states of Greece knew for years that this invasion was coming. In desperation, the governments in particular of central and southern Greece (the Peloponnese) united in a military league, trying to set aside centuries of mutual suspicion and hatred for the common good. Of all the states of the league, the one that did the most to prepare to resist was the one most threatened by Persian vengeance – Athens. Already a maritime power, it was at this time that Athens became a naval giant. The brilliant

A Greek pentecontor dating from around 600 BC, with its sail hoisted. This early vessel has a keel but no ram. It is unclear exactly when rams were first introduced onto naval vessels in the Mediterranean, but their first documented use was in 535 BC by the Phocaeans against a larger Carthaginian fleet.

statesman Themistocles argued for years that Athens needed to increase the size of its fleet, against strong resistance from more conservative citizens.

Unlike infantry fighting, it required major government expenditure to build a fleet of triremes, the long, narrow fighting ships that dominated Mediterranean naval warfare during this period. These ships were themselves weapons, each fitted with a bronze ram designed to pierce enemy ships below the waterline as its primary weapon. But each trireme required 170 oarsmen, tightly packed into the ship in three tiers, to give it the speed and power for effective ramming. These rowers, men who could not afford the equipment to fight as hoplites, had to be paid, raising the expense of a fleet still further. When a major silver vein was discovered in the state silver mine in 484–483 BC, Themistocles convinced the Athenian assembly to invest the money in new triremes, and, working at top speed, the dockyards produced 200 new vessels by the time the Persians arrived.

THE INVASION
When Xerxes marched with his army into Greece, the first significant obstacle he encountered was in central Greece in mid-August, where an infantry force tried to stop the Persians at Thermopylae, while the united Greek fleet met the enormous Persian fleet at nearby Artemisium. Thanks to two storms that wreaked havoc among the Persian fleet, the Greeks held their own at Artemisium, but were forced to pull back when the Persian land force defeated the Spartans at Thermopylae. This withdrawal left Attica, the territory of Athens, open to the Persians.

The united Greek fleet drew back to the strait of Salamis, an island off the coast of Attica. The ships were needed to protect and speed the complete evacuation of Attica, including Athens, since it could not be defended against the far superior Persian force. The Athenians in desperation put all their trust in their fleet, sending many of the city's infantrymen to fight as marines (each Greek ship had a complement of ten marines and three or four archers), inspired or at least encouraged by the Delphic oracle, which had proclaimed that the

PERSIAN MARINE (C. 480 BC)
At the battle of Salamis, Xerxes relied heavily on marines, placing at least 30 on each vessel. At the heart of this decision was probably Persian distrust of sea power and failure to recognize the effectiveness of the ship itself as the primary weapon. Xerxes may also have distrusted his Egyptian, Phoenician, and Ionian Greek subjects, who manned the ships, and sought to assure their loyalty with a strong Persian marine presence. Impressive as they appeared, the marines probably did Xerxes' cause more harm than good. They were so tightly packed on the ships that they could not fight effectively and their lack of body armour and light weapons were no match for the Greeks. Many drowned in the battle, since few Persians could swim.

'wooden wall only shall not fail, but help you and your children' – interpreted by Themistocles to mean the wooden hulls of the Athenian ships.

HOLDING SALAMIS
The combined Greek fleet assembled in three harbours on the island of Salamis on 27 August. More cities had joined the league since the battle of Artemisium, so more Greek ships were present at Salamis than at that battle, although some Greek squadrons fled as soon as the Persian fleet appeared on 29 August. The total number of Greek ships engaged at the battle of Salamis was about 310, according to the best estimates. The Greeks who fled when they saw the Persians arrive had good cause: the lowest estimate of Persian triremes at

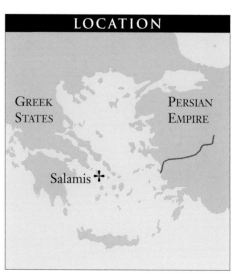

LOCATION
GREEK STATES

PERSIAN EMPIRE

Salamis

The Persian Empire had been expanding westwards for some time, and the Greek states were an obvious, rich target. If they had lost at Salamis, the Greek states would surely have been overrun.

SALAMIS

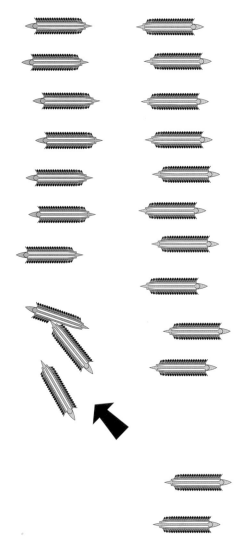

the battle is at least 700. There is no reason to suppose that the Persian ships were in any way inferior to those of the Greeks. In fact, many of them had been built and were manned by Ionian Greek subjects of Persia. Egypt and other Persian provinces that bordered the Mediterranean such as Halicarnassus also provided squadrons of ships, including a large Phoenician contingent. These ships were for the most part more seaworthy than those of the allied navy, since they had been beached, dried out and recaulked in northern Greece at the beginning of the invasion. Each ship also carried more than double the number of marines found on a Greek vessel – 30 instead of the 13 or 14 typical on a mainland Greek trireme.

According to the Greek historian Herodotus, the admirals of the various state squadrons debated vigorously whether to stay and fight the Persians at Salamis or to withdraw to the Isthmus, where the Greek land army was frantically digging into a defensive position. At Salamis the fleet was in a position to protect the Athenian refugees on the island, at least for a time. Most of the city-states that had provided ships for the fleet were from the Peloponnese, though, and most wanted to withdraw to protect their own territory. Themistocles, speaking for Athens, had to threaten to withdraw its fleet completely – about two-thirds of the total number of ships – before his fellow commanders agreed to remain where they were to fight.

The following morning, the allied Greeks signalled their resolve by sending for the sacred images of the hero Aeacus and his sons, the legendary protectors of Salamis.

In fact, the Salamis Strait was an ideally chosen location in which to engage the Persian fleet, as well as to protect the Athenian refugees on the island. The passage between the isle of Salamis and the mainland is approximately 1.6km (1 mile) wide, and a little over 4.8km (3 miles) long. A fight in the strait would neutralize the Persian fleet's overwhelming numerical superiority, whereas on the open sea Xerxes' navy would have been able to surround the Greeks and destroy them utterly.

Xerxes, no military fool, was perfectly aware that he would throw away his advantage if he committed his fleet to battle in the strait. Yet he had a two-fold problem: how to reach Salamis to attack the Athenian refugees there while the Greek fleet was still in position, and how to march on to the Peloponnese if the Greek fleet was still intact to harry his supply lines. Xerxes'

efforts to deal with these difficulties demonstrate both his ingenuity and his understanding of the distrust and arguments among the Greek allies. His first step was to attempt to attack the fleet from the rear, by taking Salamis and depriving the ships of their base. Relying on his immense reserves of manpower, he ordered a causeway built across the Salamis channel, so he could attack the island by land. The initial stages of this work progressed well, but as the causeway neared the island the Greeks set Cretan archers to harass the labourers. They caused so many casualties that Xerxes had to abandon his plan.

Xerxes also tried to force at least the Peloponnesian squadrons of the fleet to abandon their strong position at Salamis. He sent a large force of troops toward the Isthmus, expecting the Peloponnesians of the fleet to break away to defend their homeland. It is clear that he had detailed reports of the disagreements within the Greek high command, and fully expected the alliance to break apart in acrimony.

The Sea Battle of Salamis – a romantic depiction of the battle by German artist Wilhelm von Kaulbach (1804–1874).

THE OPPOSED FORCES

GREEKS (estimated)

Triremes:	310
Oarsmen:	52,700
Marines:	4300
Total:	**57,000**

PERSIANS (estimated)

Triremes:	700
Oarsmen:	119,000
Marines:	21,000
Total:	**140,000**

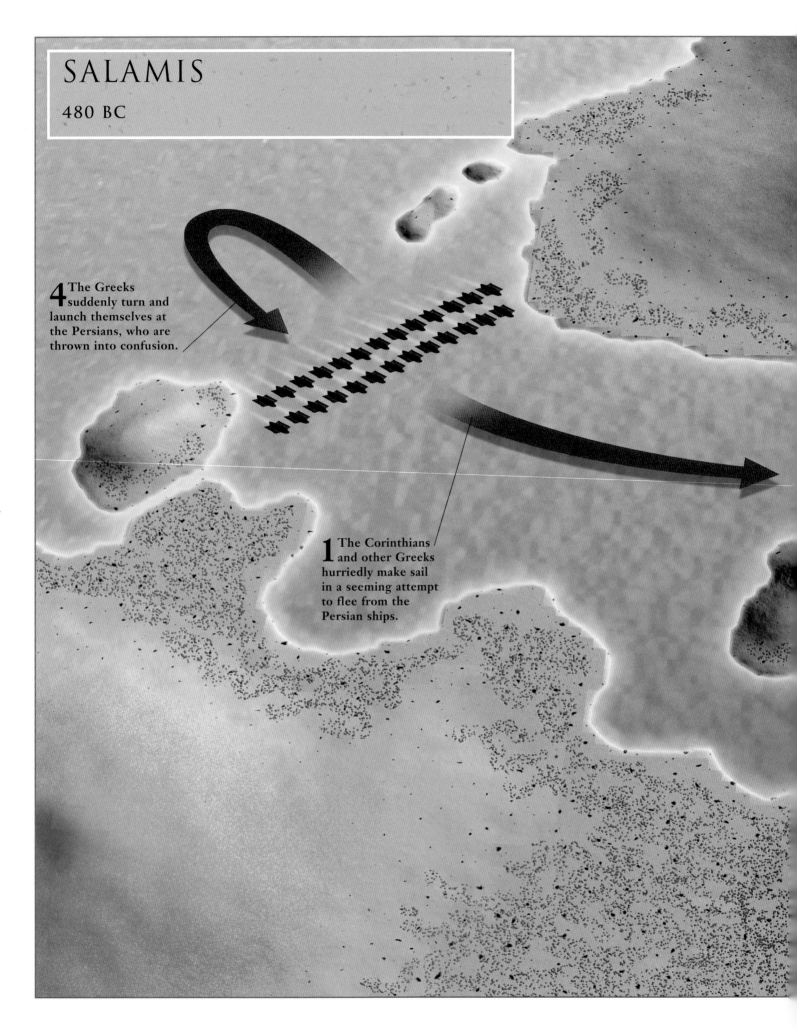

SALAMIS

480 BC

4 The Greeks suddenly turn and launch themselves at the Persians, who are thrown into confusion.

1 The Corinthians and other Greeks hurriedly make sail in a seeming attempt to flee from the Persian ships.

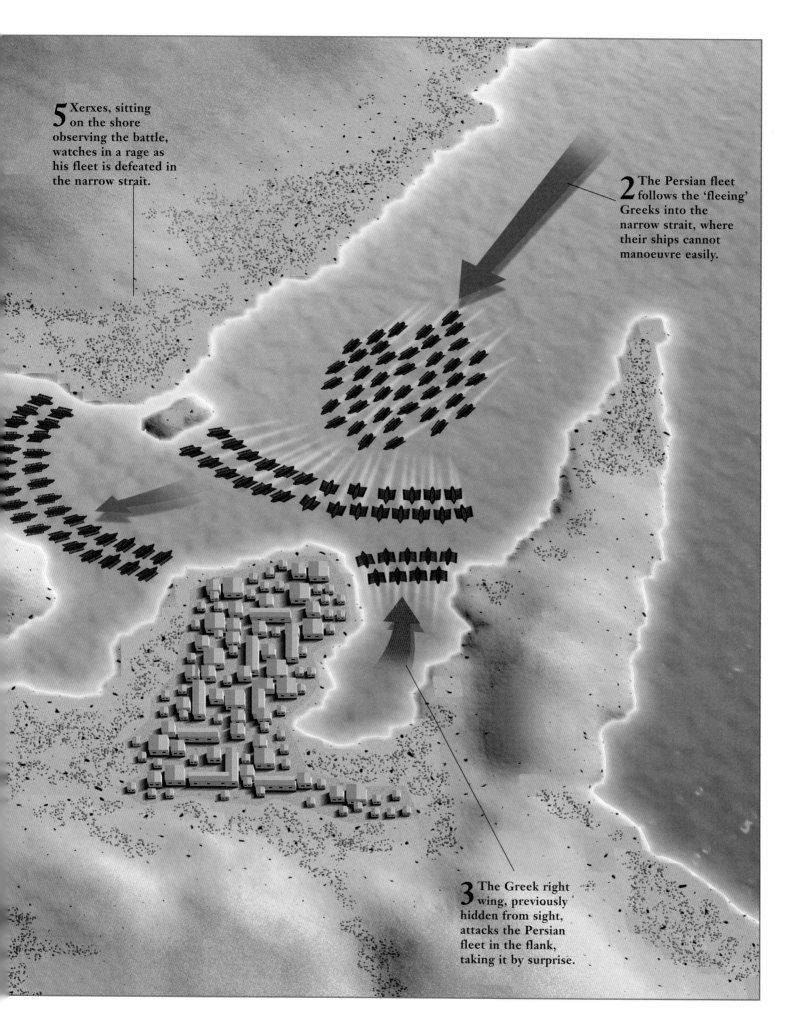

5 Xerxes, sitting on the shore observing the battle, watches in a rage as his fleet is defeated in the narrow strait.

2 The Persian fleet follows the 'fleeing' Greeks into the narrow strait, where their ships cannot manoeuvre easily.

3 The Greek right wing, previously hidden from sight, attacks the Persian fleet in the flank, taking it by surprise.

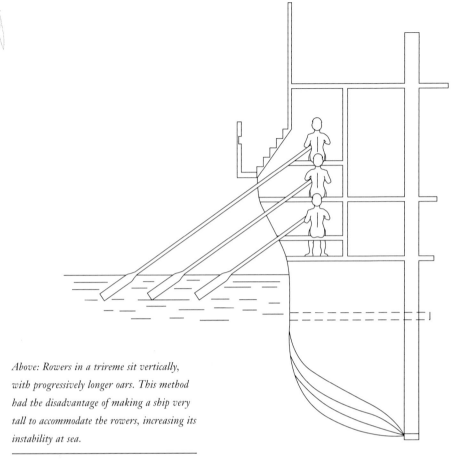

Above: Rowers in a trireme sit vertically, with progressively longer oars. This method had the disadvantage of making a ship very tall to accommodate the rowers, increasing its instability at sea.

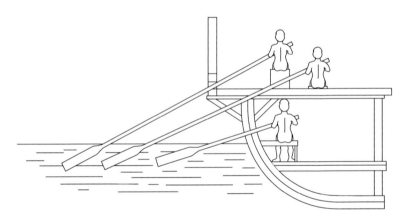

Alternative seating arrangements. Staggering the rowers resulted in a much lower, wider and therefore more stable ship. In the upper example, the lowest rower is partially below the waterline.

Thus it is unlikely that Xerxes was at all surprised when he received evidence that his plan was succeeding, evidence that was in fact a carefully laid trick by the Greek high command.

Themistocles' ruse at Salamis is the most debated detail of the battle, and some scholars have argued that it never happened. It is first recorded in Aeschylus' play *The Persians*. This was performed only eight years after the battle, so Themistocles' action is likely to have really occurred. Doubtless with the agreement of the other Greek commanders, Themistocles sent a message to Xerxes, in which he presented himself as a wronged man who was disgusted with his reluctant allies, professed himself ready to defect to the Persian side, and warned that the Greek fleet planned to escape during the night. Xerxes and his commanders believed this report, because it was inherently plausible.

THE BATTLE

Xerxes therefore set up an ambush to catch the Greek triremes as they left the strait. He sent a squadron of Egyptian triremes to block the Megara channel at the western end of the strait, while two other squadrons blocked the channels around the small island of Psyttáleia at the eastern opening of the channel and another squadron patrolled the south coast of the island. The Persian ships held their position all night, waiting for the anticipated escape attempt.

Although no ships sailed during the night, on the morning of 20 September Themistocles' report that the Greeks intended flight still seemed to be true. Xerxes had set up the Persian headquarters on the slope of Mount Aegaleus, a well-chosen site from which he and his officers could see the whole channel and coordinate the fleet's movements.

In the early morning, he was able to see the Corinthian squadron of 50 ships hurry northwest up the channel, to all appearances panicked by the sight of the Persian

Opposite: This nineteenth-century painting of the battle of Salamis gives a good sense of the chaos of an ancient naval battle, although the use of sails during combat is anachronistic.

squadrons guarding Psyttáleia. The ships had their sails up, while the usual custom for trireme combat was to leave both sails and mast on shore, so it seemed clear that they were in fact running rather than intending to fight. Soon the Athenian and Peloponnesian squadrons followed the Corinthian lead. It appeared that the Persian ambush had been set up perfectly: the Greek triremes would encounter the Egyptian ships stationed at the mouth of the western channel, and if Xerxes committed the eastern parts of his fleet to chase them, the Greeks would be caught, with an overwhelming force both before and behind them. Therefore, Xerxes ordered squadron after squadron into the narrow channel to give chase.

There was indeed a trap, but it caught the Persians rather than the Greeks. The flight had been a ruse and once the Persian fleet had entered the channel, the 'fleeing' ships turned to face them, redeploying into three lines abreast. The Persians had rushed into the strait in disorder due to overconfidence, and as squadrons were added they found their ships too tightly bunched together to manoeuvre. Disarray and disorientation must have followed rapidly, as the Greek squadrons from Aegina and Megara, hidden in a side channel, burst out and hit the exposed Persian left flank, the position held by Xerxes' Ionian Greek subjects.

Matters rapidly grew worse for the Persians. The Salamis Strait had indeed been well chosen for a Greek stand, as the Athenians, who would have known the local waters, were well aware. Sailors could depend on a rising swell in the morning, and it duly appeared at about 9.00 a.m. The weather conditions gave a decided advantage to triremes of mainland Greek design over those constructed by Persia's subject allies, whether Phoenicians, Egyptians or Ionian Greeks.

The triremes used by the Greek League were heavier than their counterparts, with a centre of gravity much closer to the waterline. They were not even completely decked, and the small complements of marines were trained to sit or even lie down while throwing javelins. The Persian triremes, by contrast, were constructed to give a much larger role to marines. They had full decks, high prows and sterns, and each had at least twice as many marines as a Greek ship. All this weight above the waterline made the Persian ships top-heavy in bad weather. As the swell increased, the Persian ships pitched, disrupting the rowers' stroke and even slewing the vessels around so they presented their sides to the Greek rams.

The Persian ships were largely unable to manoeuvre, and even those with open water around them had no clear idea what to do; the Phoenician admiral Ariabignes was killed very early in the action, there was no recognized second-in-command, and Xerxes from his distant observation point could not convey orders rapidly enough in

A woodcut of Xerxes watching the battle from the hill called Xerxes' Throne. Depicted here as a leisurely spectator, in reality Xerxes needed a full view of the strait to give effective commands.

an age before modern communications systems. The Phoenician squadron, which formed the Persian right wing, was the first to break and flee. Their flight left a gap for the Athenians to exploit: they advanced and hit yet another Persian squadron. Some of the Phoenician triremes ran aground on the mainland, only to have their commanders beheaded on the orders of a furious Xerxes.

The last of the Persian forces to continue to fight in the strait were the Ionian Greeks, who held their own for some time. But the Athenians stopped their pursuit and came back to hit the Ionians from the flank and rear until they, too, broke and ran. The Greeks then harried the retreating Persians relentlessly until night fell. Among those retreating was Queen Artemisia of Halicarnassus, one of Persia's subject allies. Hotly pursued by a Greek ship, she rammed a ship of her own side to make the Greek pursuer think that she was in fact an ally rather than an enemy. Her trick worked and she escaped to safety. Xerxes saw her dashing action and thought she had brought down a Greek ship; he is reported to have said, seeing it: 'My men have turned into women, my women into men.'

AFTERMATH

Persian losses were very heavy. At least 200 ships of the Persian fleet were sunk, and many more were captured, while the Greeks lost 40 ships. Casualties were also disproportionately high for the Persians, since many Greek oarsmen and marines swam safely to Salamis, while few of the Persian marines could swim. Many more of Xerxes' ships were damaged and had suffered serious losses during the day's fight. In a final action of the day, Greek marines landed on the isle of Psyttáleia, where 400 Persian infantrymen had been posted, and massacred them.

The Greeks spent 21 September frantically labouring to make their ships seaworthy, clearly expecting another attack and not realizing how much damage they had done. After Salamis, though, the Persian fleet was no longer capable of fighting. Many of the surviving ships were disabled and morale was extremely low. The number of battleworthy ships the king had at his command was now no longer even equal to that of the Greeks. Xerxes accepted the inevitable. He removed the marines from his surviving ships, placing them among the army. Then on the night of 21/22 September, the Persian fleet set out for the Hellespont, its mission to guard the Persian army's retreat. For without the fleet, the army had to withdraw. It could not be supplied, and it could not hope to carry the war on to the Peloponnese successfully. Although a sizeable Persian land army remained in Attica, to be defeated at Plataea the following year, Salamis marks the true end of the Persian dream to dominate the Greek world.

An engraving of an ancient marble bust of the Athenian statesman and admiral Themistocles (525–460 BC). The bust is an idealized image, meant to emphasize Themistocles' military valour.

SIEGE OF TYRE
332 BC

THE PHOENICIAN CITY OF TYRE WAS ONE OF THE BEST-FORTIFIED CITIES OF ALL TIME, YET SUBDUING IT WAS VITAL TO ALEXANDER THE GREAT'S PLANS FOR CONQUEST OF THE PERSIAN EMPIRE. THE MOST CHALLENGING OF MORE THAN 20 SIEGES CONDUCTED BY ALEXANDER, THE SEVEN-MONTH SIEGE AND FINAL CONQUEST OF TYRE DISPLAY MACEDONIAN MILITARY SKILLS AT THEIR VERY BEST.

WHY DID IT HAPPEN?

WHO Alexander the Great's (356–323 BC) Macedonian and Greek army of about 30,000 men, aided by an allied fleet provided by several Phoenician cities and Cyprus, versus Tyre, a major Phoenician city subject to Persia, with a population of about 50,000.

WHAT Macedonian siege of Tyre, which resisted Alexander in his effort to control the eastern seaboard of the Mediterranean.

WHERE Tyre (modern Sur, southern Lebanon), at that time an island about 4.4km (2.75 miles) in circumference, approximately 0.8km (0.5 miles) off the Phoenician coast.

WHEN January to August 332 BC.

WHY Alexander's conquest of Persia was impossible without control of the sea. He did not have a sufficient naval force to meet the Persian fleet, so he set out to eliminate the threat by taking the Persian-held seaports of the eastern Mediterranean coast, including Tyre.

OUTCOME After seven months of increasingly desperate resistance, Alexander took Tyre, killing most of the male population and enslaving the women and children.

In 334 BC, the Macedonian king, Alexander the Great, launched his invasion of the mighty Persian Empire, which in this period controlled Phoenicia and Palestine. In his first encounter with the Persians, he defeated a Persian field army at Granicus. Instead of proceeding immediately inland to attack the Persian imperial heartland, though, Alexander next began a bold strategy to assure his supply lines before undertaking the march into the Asian hinterland.

Alexander did not have sufficient sea power to challenge the Persian-controlled Phoenician fleet; and although some of his Greek allies, such as Athens, were naval powers, Alexander did not trust their loyalty. His only option, therefore, to win the eastern Mediterranean from the hostile Persians was a plan to capture the Phoenician naval bases

Alexander and his Companion Cavalry cross the Granicus River. Although more famous for his field battles, some historians regard Alexander's sieges as the true mark of his military brilliance.

along the Mediterranean coast, making it impossible for their ships to work against Macedonian interests.

Thus, after Granicus, Alexander soon set out southwards along the Mediterranean coast of Anatolia and then Phoenicia. Most of the Phoenician cities, never very happy as Persian subjects, opened their gates to the Macedonian conqueror. Tyre, however, was at bitter enmity with its fellow Phoenician city Sidon, so when Sidon went over to Alexander, the Tyrians decided to resist.

THE PERFECT FORTIFICATION

The Tyrians had every right to be confident in their ability to withstand Alexander. Expectation was high that the Persian King Darius III would arrive soon with a much larger force than had been mustered at Granicus, an army that would wipe out the presumptuous barbarians. (In fact, Darius never appeared; his failure to respond in a timely fashion to Alexander's threat remains a mystery.)

Even without Darius, the townsmen felt they would have little to fear. Tyre was situated on an island 0.8km (0.5 miles) off the coast of the mainland. While strongly fortified all around, Tyre's walls on the landward side were a staggering 46m (150ft) in height, rising from the edge of the sea so that no attacker could gain a foothold from which to stage an assault. Catapults were mounted all around the walls. Even slow starvation of the defenders seemed unlikely, since two good harbours, on the north and south sides of the island, made supplying the city by sea an easy matter. A strong Tyrian fleet of about 80 ships, mostly triremes, was sufficient to keep the waterways open.

The Tyrians would also have known that their city had withstood sieges by the greatest military powers of earlier ages. The Assyrians had tried and failed to take Tyre in the seventh century BC. The Babylonians, successors to Assyrian power in the Levant, had also besieged the island fortress – for a staggering 13 years – but eventually gave up the attempt. It seemed very likely that Tyre would prove to be the rock upon which Alexander would break his army. Indeed, Darius might have counted on Tyre's ability

to hold the Macedonians as he slowly assembled his army.

OPENING MOVES

Alexander's siege began in January 332 BC. The most compelling military need was to find a way to approach the island city's walls. Therefore, Alexander almost immediately began construction of a mole, a causeway from the mainland that gradually inched towards the island city. The chief planners were probably Alexander's two greatest siege engineers, Charias and Diades, who had benefited from major advances in Greek siege warfare during the reign of Alexander's father, King Philip II (382– 336 BC). Construction of the mole posed several challenges.

Although not technically demanding, the magnitude of the task called for major manpower resources. The manual labour was unpopular with Alexander's soldiers, but

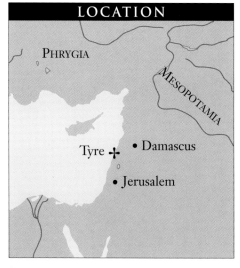

LOCATION

PHRYGIA

MESOPOTAMIA

Tyre ✝ • Damascus

• Jerusalem

Tyre's position in the middle of the eastern Mediterranean coastline allowed it to dominate sea travel in the region, making its conquest essential to Alexander's success in Persia.

SIEGE DEFENCES

In ancient sieges, the advantage lay on the defenders' side. Artillery that could break walls had not yet been invented, and gravity-propelled missiles helped the defenders drive away enemies who tried to bring a ram up to the wall. The defenders were, however, vulnerable to enemy missiles shot from bows or early catapults, whether from the ground or from siege towers. Against these large shields or screens were mounted defensively on the wall.

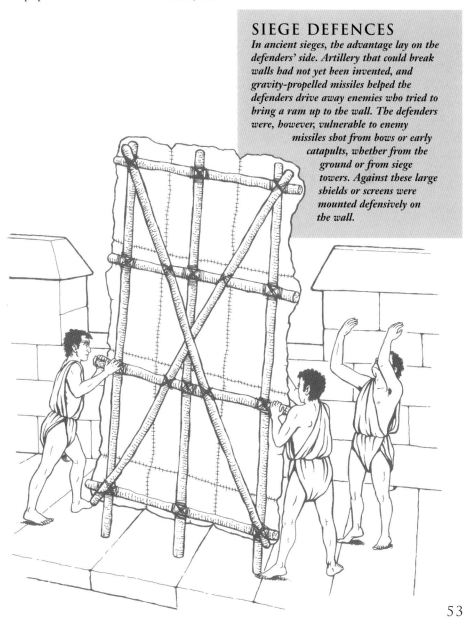

SIEGE OF TYRE

Alexander's father, King Philip II of Macedon (359–336 BC), was the creator of the Macedonian army that Alexander used to such magnificent effect. This gold coin from Tarsus is a symbol of Philip's wide reach.

THE OPPOSED FORCES

MACEDONIANS (estimated)
Macedonian and Greek infantry:
30,000
Phoenician and Cypriot triremes:
200
Marines and rowers: 40,000
Total: **70,000**

TYRIANS (estimated)
Men of military age: 15,000
Other civilians: 15,000
Tyrian triremes crews: 20,000
Total city population: **70,000**

Alexander dealt with the matter personally by impressing large numbers of locals into labour gangs to work alongside the soldiers. He also directed the men himself, and gave large gifts to encourage his soldiers. Stone was readily available, from the ruins of Old Tyre on the coast, and the nearby forests of Lebanon provided trees. At first, work proceeded rapidly, since the water was shallow near the mainland, although closer to Tyre it deepened to 5m (18ft).

As the mole inched towards Tyre, Tyrian soldiers attacked the workers, employing torsion catapults mounted on the city walls while also drawing close to the mole with their ships to pelt the workers with arrows and missiles from small shipboard catapults. Alexander responded to the threat of ship harassment by erecting a palisade to shelter his work gangs. He also constructed two siege towers at the end of the mole. They stood 46m (150ft) high, perhaps the tallest siege towers ever built, a necessary measure if the arrow-shooting catapults placed in them were to be able to strike the catapults and their operators on Tyre's high walls.

The siege towers, draped with fresh hides, were impervious to ordinary measures to burn them down. So the ingenious Tyrians hatched a more comprehensive plan to destroy them. They modified a cavalry transport ship, filling it with combustibles, including sulphur and pitch; cauldrons containing more flammable materials were slung on the ship's yardarms. The crew weighted the ship's stern so that the bow would be able to run further up onto land. Tyrian triremes then towed the fire ship towards the end of the mole, casting off at the last possible moment; the transport's crew started fires, then swam for their lives.

The ship succeeded in igniting both Macedonian towers. As the towers burned, Tyrian soldiers in small boats tore down the palisade that Alexander had erected to help protect the workers and set much of Alexander's smaller siege machinery alight.

Soon afterwards, high seas submerged most of the mole. Clearly, the Tyrians had won the first round.

SIEGE FROM THE SEA

The assault on the mole exposed the key weakness of Alexander's position – he needed ships, without which the Tyrian fleet could harass his men at will, and Tyre could be resupplied by sea. Fortunately for the Macedonian king at this point, the surrender of the other Phoenician naval bases to the Macedonians paid off. A fleet of 80 Phoenician triremes arrived at Sidon, discovered that the city now supported Alexander and followed its lead in accepting Alexander's overlordship.

The Cypriot fleet soon also appeared to add itself to Alexander's command. Between them, the two fleets provided the Macedonian king with more than 200 triremes, more than enough to put a stop to

Tyrian fleet activities. Alexander's new fleet promptly defeated the Tyrians in a naval battle, then proceeded to blockade both Tyrian harbours.

The Tyrian ships confined to the northern harbour (the Harbour of Sidon) made a spirited attempt to break the naval blockade. They screened their plans by hanging sails over the mouth of the harbour, and tried to break out with three quinqueremes, three quadriremes and seven triremes. Their surprise attack caught the Cyprian seamen off guard, sinking several ships and driving others onto the shore. Damage was limited, though, because Alexander quickly led the Phoenician squadron around from the south harbour and defeated the Tyrians.

Meanwhile, Alexander and his engineers began construction of a new mole, following a line rather further to the north and widening the causeway to about

Alexander's mole, an artificial causeway, was gradually built out to Tyre, allowing the Macedonians to bring two great siege towers against the island city's walls.

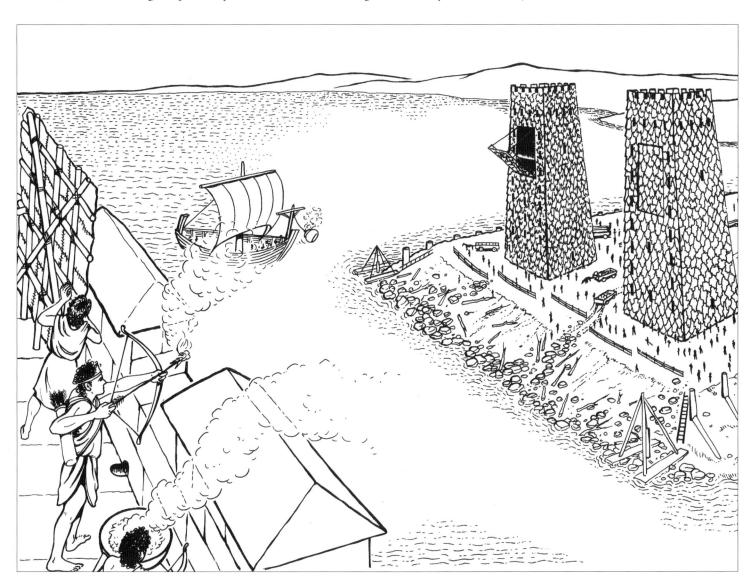

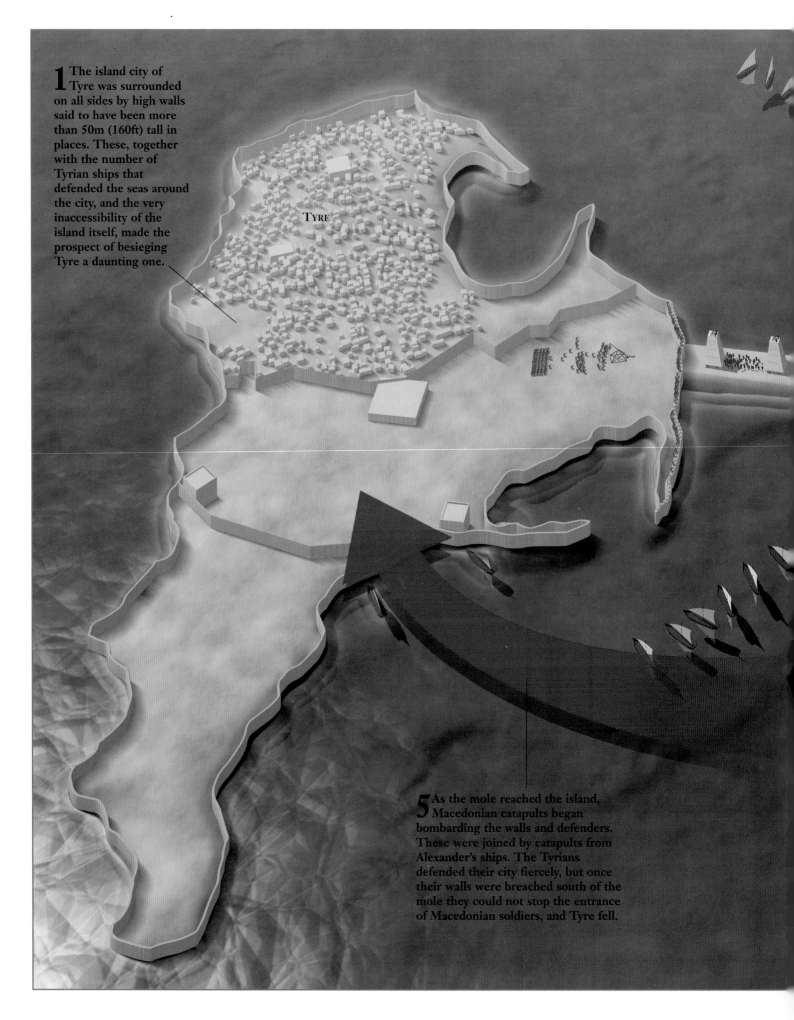

1 The island city of Tyre was surrounded on all sides by high walls said to have been more than 50m (160ft) tall in places. These, together with the number of Tyrian ships that defended the seas around the city, and the very inaccessibility of the island itself, made the prospect of besieging Tyre a daunting one.

Tyre

5 As the mole reached the island, Macedonian catapults began bombarding the walls and defenders. These were joined by catapults from Alexander's ships. The Tyrians defended their city fiercely, but once their walls were breached south of the mole they could not stop the entrance of Macedonian soldiers, and Tyre fell.

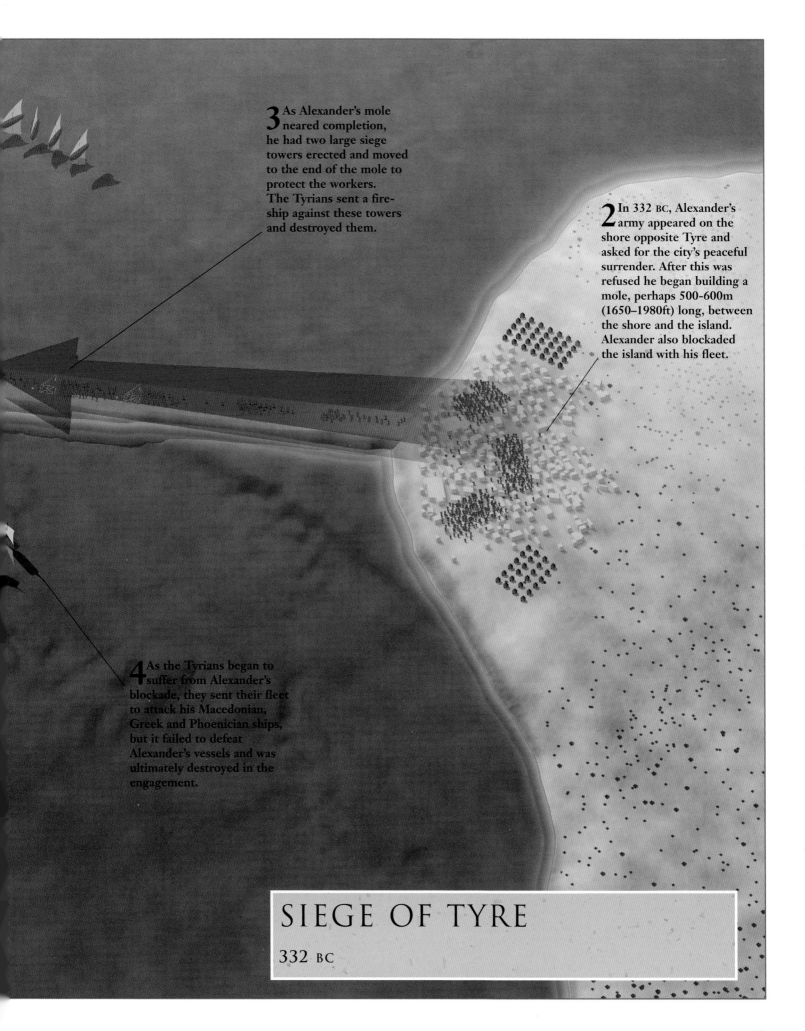

3 As Alexander's mole neared completion, he had two large siege towers erected and moved to the end of the mole to protect the workers. The Tyrians sent a fire-ship against these towers and destroyed them.

2 In 332 BC, Alexander's army appeared on the shore opposite Tyre and asked for the city's peaceful surrender. After this was refused he began building a mole, perhaps 500-600m (1650–1980ft) long, between the shore and the island. Alexander also blockaded the island with his fleet.

4 As the Tyrians began to suffer from Alexander's blockade, they sent their fleet to attack his Macedonian, Greek and Phoenician ships, but it failed to defeat Alexander's vessels and was ultimately destroyed in the engagement.

SIEGE OF TYRE

332 BC

61m (200ft) for greater stability against storms. The remains of this second mole can still be seen, forming the basis of the isthmus that now links Sur, Lebanon, permanently to the mainland.

New siege towers protected the work, and this time the patrolling ships of Macedon's new allies made another naval attack impossible. Alexander also began to probe Tyre's sea walls with floating battering rams: he had ships tied together so that they could provide stable platforms for rams, the ship platforms moored close against a segment of wall with anchors all around.

Tyrian divers succeeded in cutting the ships' anchor cables, causing several to run aground. Then, however, Alexander switched to mooring chains, and the onslaught continued. Alexander's new fleet also proved its usefulness by clearing away the large boulders the Tyrians had placed in the sea before their walls to keep ships away.

THE ASSAULT

As the summer progressed, the siege rapidly grew in intensity, the Tyrians fighting for their city with ever-increasing desperation. The Tyrians captured some of Alexander's men and paraded them on the walls before executing them and throwing their bodies into the sea. They also killed some Macedonian heralds, which might explain the violence of Alexander's revenge against the city.

The Tyrians also put up a highly innovative defence as the Macedonians approached their walls. The historian Diodorus Siculus tells that Alexander, contrary to normal ancient practice, used stone-throwing torsion catapults so large that they were able to damage walls – and that the Tyrians responded by padding their walls. Less likely is his story that the Tyrians mounted rapidly spinning mechanical wheels on the walls to deflect Macedonian catapult bolts.

Although Alexander's fleet mostly consisted of triremes, he also used lighter and more manoeuvrable biremes, propelled by two banks of oars, as in this illustration.

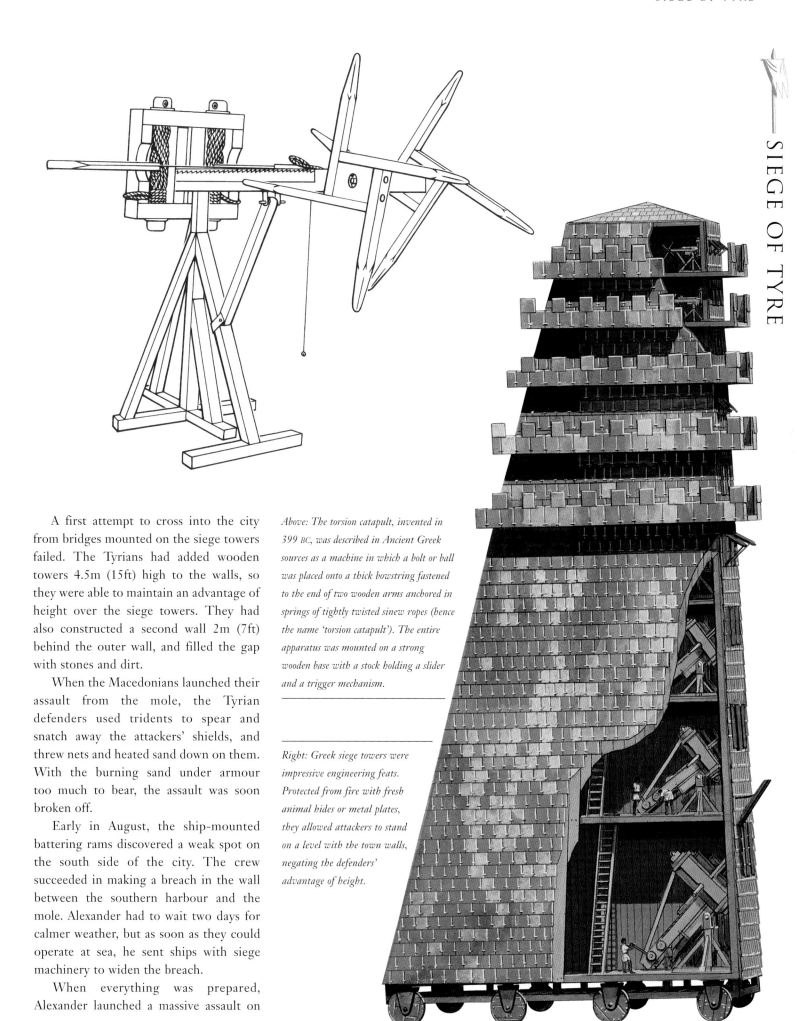

A first attempt to cross into the city from bridges mounted on the siege towers failed. The Tyrians had added wooden towers 4.5m (15ft) high to the walls, so they were able to maintain an advantage of height over the siege towers. They had also constructed a second wall 2m (7ft) behind the outer wall, and filled the gap with stones and dirt.

When the Macedonians launched their assault from the mole, the Tyrian defenders used tridents to spear and snatch away the attackers' shields, and threw nets and heated sand down on them. With the burning sand under armour too much to bear, the assault was soon broken off.

Early in August, the ship-mounted battering rams discovered a weak spot on the south side of the city. The crew succeeded in making a breach in the wall between the southern harbour and the mole. Alexander had to wait two days for calmer weather, but as soon as they could operate at sea, he sent ships with siege machinery to widen the breach.

When everything was prepared, Alexander launched a massive assault on

Above: The torsion catapult, invented in 399 BC, was described in Ancient Greek sources as a machine in which a bolt or ball was placed onto a thick bowstring fastened to the end of two wooden arms anchored in springs of tightly twisted sinew ropes (hence the name 'torsion catapult'). The entire apparatus was mounted on a strong wooden base with a stock holding a slider and a trigger mechanism.

Right: Greek siege towers were impressive engineering feats. Protected from fire with fresh animal hides or metal plates, they allowed attackers to stand on a level with the town walls, negating the defenders' advantage of height.

Above: This Roman floor mosaic, dating from the second century BC, gives a good impression of a trireme's grace in the water.

Left: The ruins of Tyre. After Alexander's conquest of the city, it was soon rebuilt and maintained its importance as a seaport in Roman times.

all fronts. He himself led the attack on the breach, using, for the purpose, two transport ships loaded with his best infantry. The attack was co-ordinated with ship attacks all around Tyre, major fleet assaults on both harbours and a fresh attempt at escalade from the mole. The Tyrians did not have enough defenders to fight off so many challenges at once. Alexander's force beat its way through the breach, the fleets broke into both harbours and started fighting street to street, and the main Macedonian force was then able to enter the city along the mole.

AFTERMATH

Although Alexander was noted for his mercy to defeated enemies, he made an example of Tyre. In part, this was typical ancient fighting practice: if a city refused to surrender and had to be taken by force, the triumphant army had a widely recognized right to slaughter, rape and pillage indiscriminately.

It was not uncommon for all male defenders to be killed, especially if the defenders were members of another race. Alexander might have been more generous, but the Tyrians themselves had not 'played fair'. In particular, they had killed not just Macedonian prisoners but also heralds.

So Tyre was burned, and the assault is known to have cost the lives of about 8000 Tyrians. There were about 2000 adult male survivors, and Alexander now ordered their crucifixion. Still, he showed himself surprisingly kind by the standards of the age by saving everyone who had taken refuge in the temple of Melkart, whom Alexander identified with the Greek god Heracles.

Those who survived included the king of Tyre, who was treated honourably. However, the Tyrians had decided partway through the siege to send their women and children to their colony of Carthage in North Africa – a decision made too late. Alexander took control of the sea before it could be carried out, and those non-combatants who had survived the assault were now sold into slavery.

The Macedonians had lost a valuable seven months besieging Tyre, but the Persian king's lethargy prevented this delay from being catastrophic for Alexander. Morevoer, he lost only about 400 troops, a sign of how careful he was to protect his men whenever possible.

In return, the young Macedonian king won control of the eastern Mediterranean, thereby gaining a foothold in Phoenicia and Palestine (which would remain in Greek hands for nearly two centuries). He was perhaps the greatest siege commander of all time.

Alexander on horseback, from the 'Alexander Sarcophagus' (c. 310 BC). Note the ram's horns, a sign of Alexander's divinity as son of the Egyptian god Ammon.

GAUGAMELA
331 BC

ELITE FORCES FACED RESURRECTED AND EXOTIC TACTICS AND WEAPONRY IN THE BATTLE THAT DECIDED THE FATE OF THE KNOWN WORLD IN THE NEAR EAST. COULD THE MILITARY GENIUS OF ALEXANDER THE GREAT OVERCOME THE COLLECTED RESOURCES OF THE WORLD'S LARGEST EMPIRE?

WHY DID IT HAPPEN?

WHO Alexander the Great (356–323 BC) and his battered Macedonian army faced the final stand of the Persian Great King Darius (reigned 336–330 BC), who was well-prepared and on ground of his own choosing.

WHAT War elephants from India stood ready to smash the legendary Macedonian phalanx – while scythed chariots and picked bodies of special troops awaited their own part in the final struggle for control of the Persian Empire.

WHERE Gaugamela near the city of Arbela, in modern northern Iraq.

WHEN 1 October 331 BC

WHY To Alexander and the Greeks before him, the Persian Empire stood as the very definition of world power. That taken, Alexander and his army would neither face nor fear a rival.

OUTCOME In a staggering display of tactical adaptability and superb military training, Alexander's army resisted and destroyed every Persian weapon and tactic. One subordinate's error resulted in a crisis, however, of Macedonian command.

Gaugamela, as the greatest victory of the Ancient World's undisputedly greatest military genius, deserves study from all angles as the tactical masterpiece it was. Under careful review, the battle takes on the appearance of having such intricate and careful construction that the very difficulties Alexander faced in controlling and preserving his own army in the face of the Persians ended up augmenting Alexander's plan, instead of hindering it.

Arrian's excellent *Anabasis* of Alexander's battles is the preferred source here.

DARIUS' ARMY

Alexander had been blessed in his principal opponent, Darius III, during his campaigns from 336 to 331 BC. For five years the boy-king of Macedon had laboured brilliantly to complete his father's dream of conquering the Persian Empire and territories in the East. The Persian Great King Darius was a

In this nineteenth-century magazine illustration, Alexander is shown as a young man listening to his tutor, the philosopher Aristotle (384–322 BC), while they sit in a palace in ancient Pella, Greece, c. 342 BC.

good leader but a below-par general, whose ability to bring huge numbers of Persia's military assets into the field did not live up to his skill in using them. Moreover, as it had been since Kadesh, the king was still the cause – if Darius could be captured, Persian organized resistance to the invasion could, and in the end did, collapse.

As a result, in every battle with Alexander, the circumstances of his position prompted Darius to make ever greater demands upon his empire's reserves of manpower as they became available. Alexander would not find many Persians of military age able or willing to resist him away from the battlefields where Darius' poor skills got many of them slaughtered or put to humiliating flight. As the centre of Persian command, Darius necessarily fled the battlefield as soon as Alexander's own advance posed a credible threat to his person. Such pusillanimity had not been the case when the Persians themselves had tried a 'decapitation strike' on Alexander at the battle of the Granicus in 334 BC. Alexander's bodyguard had prevented the Persian cavalry's effort to despatch him, while Alexander kept control of his anxieties and his army and won battle after battle.

At the core of Darius' forces were the celebrated, and dreaded, Immortals, the elite division of the Persian army. The unit's name came from the Persian practice of replacing each casualty in that 10,000-man unit with another picked soldier, whose spear would bear the golden pomegranate of the elite. The goal had been to raise the lighter Persian infantry to a level where they could face heavier Greek hoplites and prevail. At times they had come close, such as during the Persian Wars in Greece at Thermopylae and Plataea. Darius' ranks also included the assembled nobility of the Persian Empire, sons of all the empire's powerful families serving in the cavalry divisions under Bessus and Mazaeus.

In addition to these elite forces, Darius employed a sizeable force of Greek mercenary hoplites, hardened professionals who continued in Persian service despite the gruesome example Alexander had made of the Greeks in Persian service who had

penetrated the Macedonian Phalanx at Issus, two years before. Many of the Greeks came from lands already subjugated by the Macedonians, eager to strike a blow – even for the hated Persians – against Alexander and the Macedonian conquerors. Darius' assurance in facing Alexander received additional support from the Persian king's confidence in two secret weapons he had procured in the time for preparation granted him by Alexander's two-year campaign south to Egypt.

From his Indian subjects, Darius had secured a number of war elephants, transported at great expense in time and fodder from the easternmost frontiers of Persian suzerainty. Untrained horses could endure neither the sight nor appearance of the strange monsters, who bore archers and javelin throwers upon their backs, and whose strength, Darius thought, might crack the Macedonian phalanx.

Alexander's entire army was aimed directly at him. Darius intended to be more than ready. Besides the elephants, Darius also had in his arsenal 200 of the most terrifying weapons from the traditions of

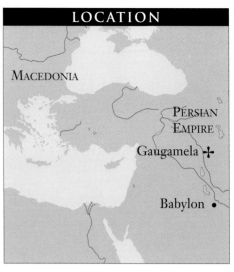

LOCATION

MACEDONIA

PERSIAN EMPIRE

Gaugamela

Babylon

Gaugamela was the last stand of the Persian Empire. Darius escaped the staggering defeat Alexander inflicted upon his army, only to be executed by a subordinate disgusted by his cowardice and failures.

COMPANION CAVALRY

Companion Cavalry were literally that, the sons of the Macedonian nobility, raised along with Alexander under Philip's supervision and trained in the tactics Philip had learned from the Theban Epaminondas. Many of them were personal friends to whom he owed his life.

Companion Cavalry carried the shorter cavalry sarissa *and lighter armour, and always fought under Alexander's personal command. To the cavalry was given the decisive role in Alexander's battles. When the lumbering phalanx created a gap in the enemy's line, the cavalry would charge through and disrupt and destroy the enemy ranks by carrying out flanking attacks.*

GAUGAMELA

63

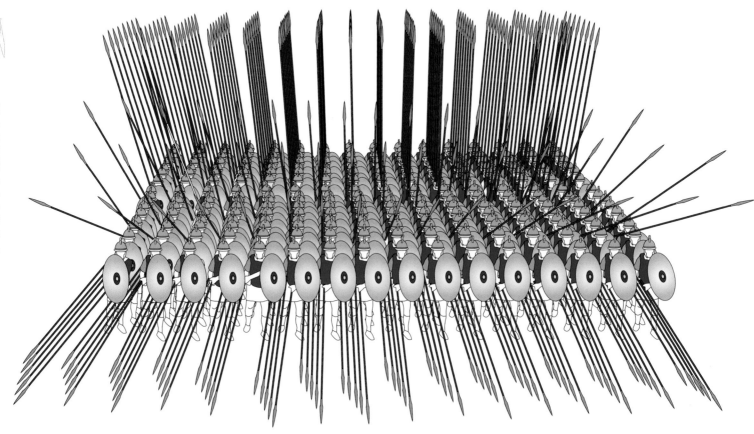

A forest of spears. A frontal view of a Macedonian speira, the unit making up the larger infantry phalanx. The ranks behind the front five would hold their counter-weighted pikes aloft until required to fill a gap, and in the hope of deflecting incoming missiles.

THE OPPOSED FORCES

MACEDONIANS (estimated)
Cavalry:	7000
Infantry:	40,000
Total:	**47,000**

PERSIANS (estimated)
Cavalry:	30,000
Infantry:	56,000
Chariots:	200
War elephants:	15
Total:	**86,000**

Eastern warfare: chariots equipped with scythe blades upon their wheels and traces, weapons designed to inflict dire casualties upon Alexander's infantry.

DISPOSITIONS

Darius took advantage of his ability to control Alexander's movements by being himself the objective of Alexander's campaign. He chose a wide and level battlefield near the city of Arbela, going so far as to have the terrain levelled to assist the operation of his chariots. For his own part, however, Alexander had taken the precaution of scouting the battlefield thoroughly. Darius' preparations provided his enemy with a very good idea about his plans. By giving Darius time enough to collect so great an agglomeration of resources and men, Alexander had either gambled heavily or allowed ample time for the final collection of resistance to be drawn together at a place where it could be found and destroyed. The outcome would determine which was the case.

Alexander, with the pragmatism of a genius, camped 6.4km (4 miles) from Darius' army, just far enough to prevent a

surprise attack, and had one last interview with his sub-commanders. The leader's very confidence became a command asset in itself, for Alexander chose to leave his troops comfortably encamped, rather, than as their Persian counterparts, in arms and watchful throughout the course of a long and cold desert night. The commanding general himself managed such a good night's sleep that he had to be roused for action the following day.

With some justification, Alexander had come to feel that his subordinates were not quite worthy adjuncts to his genius. Alexander's father's adjutant and most competent general Parmenio approached him with his own plan for the battle, that being the very night attack the Persians were dreading. Contrary to Parmenio's usual reputation in the sources for prudence, such a suggestion was, in fact, bold and consequently risky. Controlling an army in broad daylight was hard enough, doing so in darkness legendarily difficult. Alexander's dismissive rejection, that he would not 'steal a victory', was the final word against such action, but Parmenio's very anxiety about the battle became yet another liability-turned-asset in Alexander's master plan.

It was a tendency of soldiers to move to the right in the course of an advance, as each sought to cover the exposed portion of his body with the shield of his comrade next in the line. The great Theban military genius Epaminondas had learned to exploit that tendency with an obliquely directed and focused attack on an advancing enemy line as it stretched and thinned in response. Philip himself had spent time in Thebes, and the tactic became an integral and vital part of Macedonian success in the decades following. Alexander's plan made full use of it when he formed his lines on the morning of the battle. Both Alexander's elite cavalry and the awe-inspiring Macedonian phalanx would move at the oblique angle into the much longer Persian line, impact, as usual, being set directly for Darius' visible position in the centre of his line. Layer after layer of the dreaded Macedonian pike, the *sarissa*, would menace the Persians and hold their attention. The Macedonian line would move at an angle as it advanced, and create a gap in the ranks of the apprehensive enemy.

While his attack was being launched, Alexander knew that Darius' cavalry, chariots and elephants would attempt to flank him and get behind his forces. His counter were his own selected special forces. These consisted of a unit new in Western warfare, crack light infantry, called 'hypaspists'. Experienced veterans, these men could move rapidly to oppose an attack with support from Alexander's allied Thessalian cavalry positioned at either end of his line. Both the hypaspists and the Thessalians fought in small units capable of dispersing in the face of a threat, then re-forming at need. In the course of the battle, these sub-formations would move aside in the face of elephants and chariots, showering javelins on those and the cavalry as they would inevitably be driven back by the Persian thrusts at Alexander's flanks.

Such was the genius of the Macedonian commander that the retreat of these smaller units became an asset to Alexander's grand plan. Behind his front line, under the worried Parmenio, Alexander placed a reserve phalanx, another rectangle of bristling pikes as difficult to attack as the

In this illustration, Alexander leads his Companion Cavalry across the Granicus, seizing the initiative from the Persians. Like most successful military commanders, Alexander was no stranger to luck.

GAUGAMELA

331 BC

3 The Persian left tries to outflank the Macedonians, but they cannot get past the light troops and cavalry.

1 The Macedonian phalanx marches obliquely towards the Persian line. The Persian chariots are repulsed by javelins.

4 Alexander and the Companions break through a weak spot in the Persian line and swing leftwards.

2 Darius' secret weapons, his Indian war elephants and scythe-armed chariots, prove to be a disappointment.

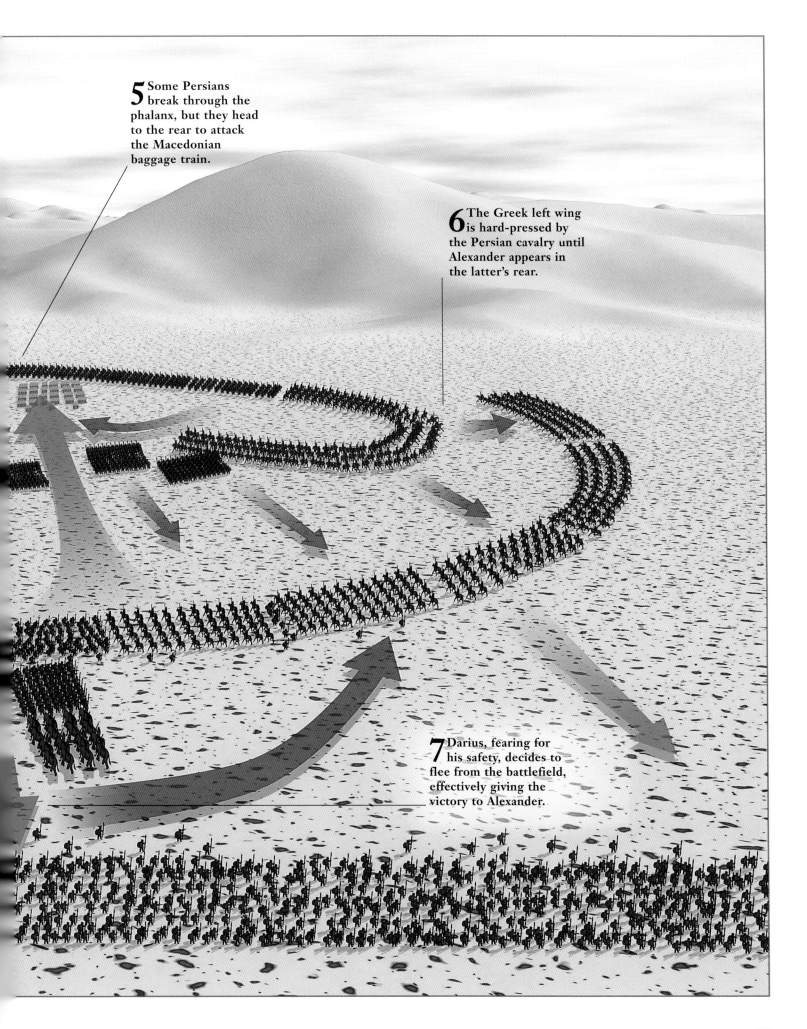

5 Some Persians break through the phalanx, but they head to the rear to attack the Macedonian baggage train.

6 The Greek left wing is hard-pressed by the Persian cavalry until Alexander appears in the latter's rear.

7 Darius, fearing for his safety, decides to flee from the battlefield, effectively giving the victory to Alexander.

Darius breathes his last in this nineteenth-century depiction of the Persian ruler's death. Alexander's propagandists claimed that Darius had survived long enough to will his empire to Alexander with his dying gasp. Alexander found it more expedient after the battle to pose as Darius' successor, rather than rule as a foreign conqueror.

front line. The Thessalians and hypaspists would fall back into contact with the second line. In effect, as his smaller army waded into the massed Persian forces, Alexander's formation would become a forerunner of the British 'square' of the nineteenth century, a formation that became the stronger as it was driven into itself.

THE BATTLE

For the most part, the plan worked. Alexander's archers and javelin throwers killed the charioteers of the scythed chariots. In employing these, Darius had made another of his disastrous errors. The legendary ferocity of the chariots had come from their use by earlier empires to increase the slaughter of a disorganized and retreating en___ as ___ scythes took a fearful toll on fr__ __ed and defenceless men. In the face of Alexander's disciplined veterans, they failed miserably. Darius' second secret weapon proved no more successful. As often happened with elephants in warfare, the great beasts felt no

stake in the battle sufficient to wade into the bristling spears and arrows of the enemy, and proved useless and uncontrollable. Meanwhile Alexander's pike-equipped cavalry and infantry bore inexorably down, at the oblique angle, upon Darius' standard.

Meanwhile, Darius had nothing to stop the slow advance of the Macedonian infantry and cavalry toward a point near where he and his entourage clustered in mounting anxiety. Alexander was making an enduring demonstration of the utility of sending the strength of an army's forces against a single chosen spot in the enemy's front. Two British officers, Colonels Basil Liddell-Hart and J.F.C. Fuller, would cite Gaugamela as their inspiration when after the battle of Cambrai in 1917 they developed a new plan of battle. What those two officers outlined featured the concentration of force at a weak spot in an enemy line, penetration by an army's most mobile units to attack from the rear and spread havoc in the enemy's rear areas, culminating in the remaining frontal resistance of the enemy being crushed by infantry. The plan's adoption and successful use by the German army would give it its name: *Blitzkrieg*.

The moment of danger for Alexander and his army came when the onrushing Persian cavalry got past the Thessalians and hypaspists on the flank and drove for the Macedonian rear. Parmenio had not been able to keep the reserve in good order, the result of that failure coming as the Persians drove through his reserve line and moved miles to the rear to plunder the Macedonian camp. Only those Persians would have any taste of victory. Distance and Alexander's pressure upon him cost Darius the control of the most dangerous part of his army at that moment. Darius had no way of either summoning his victorious cavalry to his rescue or ordering it to take Alexander's line in the rear as a desire to win, as opposed to a desire to loot, should have prompted.

The Macedonian advance ground onwards, and as previously Darius' nerve failed. This final retreat was his most ignominious, as the Persian king abandoned his army and camp in wild flight. For a while longer at Gaugamela, however, the armies fought on. Alexander's plan had not survived contact with the enemy. Parmenio himself, under pressure and out of contact with Alexander's line, had abandoned the original idea of a box and sent frantically to the front to Alexander for assistance. Alexander returned to find that his Thessalian cavalry had counter-attacked, Parmenio had reversed the direction of the reserve advance and destroyed the Persians to the rear, and that Darius had, yet again, escaped him.

There would be a reckoning with Parmenio for his premature panic and disagreement with Alexander's plans and tactics, but, although it was not clear at the time, Alexander was for the rest of his life the virtual master of the entire Greek and Persian worlds.

AFTERMATH

Darius only bought a few more weeks of life by his flight. His disgusted subordinate Bessus executed his own monarch and attempted in vain to lead further resistance himself. Alexander wanted it all, and had the genius and the means to get it. He asked no more of his army than he himself was willing to give, but his army eventually lost its own willingness to march ever onward for more conquests, and Alexander's empire left him when a body wracked by wounds and disease could no longer support the powerful mind that had prevailed so brilliantly at Gaugamela. He died in the legendary city of Babylon in 323 BC.

Winning hearts and minds was Alexander's purpose behind his kindly treatment of Darius' surrendered family, depicted here in a 1566 painting by Paolo Veronese. Alexander went so far as to marry one of Darius' daughters, but his plan for a fusion of Persians and Macedonians under his rule did not long survive him.

CANNAE
216 BC

AFTER THE BATTLES OF TREBIA (218 BC) AND TRASIMENE (217 BC), AT CANNAE HANNIBAL WON HIS THIRD AND GREATEST VICTORY OVER THE ARMIES OF ROME IN ITALY. A TACTICAL MASTERPIECE, THIS BATTLE HAS PROVIDED A MODEL FOR GENERALS FOR OVER 2000 YEARS. YET ROME SURVIVED THIS CATASTROPHE TO DEFEAT THE CARTHAGINIANS.

WHY DID IT HAPPEN?

WHO A Roman army under the consul Varro moved to attack the Carthaginians under Hannibal Barca (247–183 or 182 BC).

WHAT The Roman cavalry were driven from the field by the Carthaginian cavalry. The Roman and allied infantry, in a very deep formation, pushed the enemy back until their own flanks were exposed to the longer Carthaginian line which squeezed their formation even more. The returning Carthaginian cavalry attacked the rear of the Roman infantry, severely restricting the ability of individuals to respond.

WHERE Apulia, Italy.

WHEN 216 BC.

WHY Hannibal was attempting to wrest Rome's recently acquired Italian allies from her and so weaken her ability to continue the war.

OUTCOME More than half the Roman force was cut down. But Rome raised another army and continued the war to ultimate victory.

In its early manifestation Rome was a city-state, just like all the others in Greece and Italy. However, Rome first defeated and then formed alliances with the other city-states in Italy. Rome was also aware of the older city of Carthage, which had great influence amongst the numerous independent cities on the island of Sicily. This became the centre of the first Punic War (264–241 BC) and ended with the defeat of Carthage. Thirty years later another area of dispute arose in Spain. In this, the second war between Carthage and Rome, half of the latter's power base comprised fairly recently acquired Italian allies. By taking the war to Italy the Carthaginian general Hannibal Barca hoped to break at least some of those alliances and reduce Rome's power in the field, while other Carthaginian leaders continued the struggle in Spain, where much of the second Punic War (218–202 BC) was fought.

THE CAMPAIGN

Roman strategy had been, initially, to immediately confront the invader in the field. This proved disastrous as Hannibal out-thought his amateur opponents on every occasion and slaughtered Roman soldiers in their tens of thousands. There was then a change of tack, and a policy of attrition was introduced by the consul Fabius Maximus: Hannibal was to be denied a victory in the field and his army was to be allowed to wither in the open countryside. Unfortunately, a lot of the countryside belonged to powerful politicians who didn't

Hannibal entering a northern Italian town in triumph. Elephants had helped Hannibal in his crossing of the Alps, but once the Roman troops and cavalry became inured to these strange beasts, they were relatively ineffective on the battlefield.

appreciate their farms and incomes being destroyed in this way.

To avoid the possibility of a popular army commander taking over the state and declaring himself king, the army of the Roman Republic was commanded by a pair of annually elected politicians, called consuls, each in charge on alternate days. In the year 216 BC the consuls Paullus and Varro were elected to command. They could not have been more different. Paullus was cautious, thoughtful and valued the lives of the men he had been entrusted with, while Varro was brash and full of unfounded confidence. Neither had held high command before. The consuls, bringing reinforcements which increased the field force by half, joined the army near Samnium, close to Hannibal's base camp. The Roman force was billeted in two camps, one smaller than the other.

FORAGING

Hannibal had his own problems. The army had eaten out the surrounding countryside and had only ten days' food left. Also, the lack of battle and thus plunder was making his largely mercenary troops discontented almost to the point of desertion. Inevitably, with two hostile armies so close, there was a lot of skirmishing between scouting and foraging parties. Within days of the consuls arriving, the Romans had the best of a large skirmish which left 1700 enemy soldiers dead for the loss of about 100 Romans. Paullus, in charge that day, called off any pursuit, suspecting a trap.

This is exactly what Hannibal planned for the following night. His army stole out of camp fully armed and ready for battle but leaving behind some of their tents, food and treasure. The baggage train also set off in plain view along a rising valley making it look as though he was fleeing in some haste. But the army was hidden either side of this valley, infantry one side, cavalry the other. Would the Romans take the bait and follow the baggage?

It was Varro's turn to command and he was nearly taken in, being on the point of ordering a precipitate advance. Luckily, Paullus sent word that the omens from a sacrifice of chickens were bad, foretelling disaster (how right they were!) and two

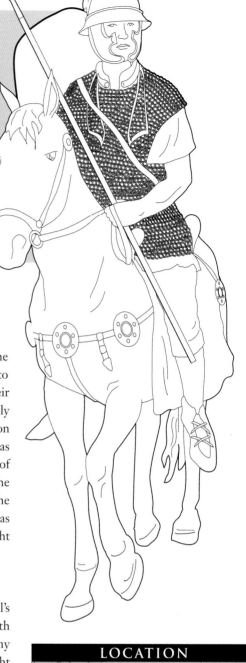

Roman captives who had escaped from the Carthaginian host returned just in time to expose the ruse. Both sides returned to their respective camps. To alleviate his supply problems, Hannibal decided to move on into Apulia. He set out leaving the camp as he had before at night and with all sorts of paraphernalia lying around. By the time the Romans had cautiously scouted the area he was well ahead of them. However, he was tracked and soon the Roman army caught up with him near the village of Cannae.

DISPOSITIONS

This was no whim or accident. Hannibal's position at Cannae provided him with several advantages. Firstly, his army deployed on hills giving them a height advantage. Secondly, they had their backs to the prevailing wind, which was prone to kick up dust squalls and impair the vision of anyone advancing into it. Thirdly, but perhaps most importantly of all, the frontage was restricted. He knew the Roman army outnumbered him almost two to one. The ground he chose forced them to deploy with a river on their right and steep hills to their left. This restricted their frontage, the gap being only 3.2km (2 miles) wide, and forced their infantry into a much denser formation than normal.

However many men they had, only the front rank could fight. The Athenians had used the same ploy in their first battle with the Syracusan army 200 years earlier and it

LOCATION

ROMAN REPUBLIC

Rome

Cannae ✛

Cannae was perhaps Rome's greatest defeat, but typically the Republic soon recovered, and Hannibal, neglecting to march on the capital, was effectively isolated in the south of Italy.

CANNAE

THE OPPOSED FORCES

CARTHAGINIANS

Heavy infantry:	32,000
Light auxiliaries:	8000
Cavalry:	10,000
Total:	**50,000**

ROMANS

Legionaries:	58,000
Light auxiliaries:	16,000
Cavalry:	6000
Total:	**80,000**

would be used again by the English at Agincourt some 1600 years later. This negated the principal Roman advantage at a stroke. Hannibal's genius would turn that negated advantage into a crushing millstone around the neck of the Roman army.

When the Romans arrived they again fortified two separate camps on either side of the small river Aufidus. Again, skirmishing took place with the Numidian cavalry in the pay of the Carthaginians, causing havoc amongst the Romans as they went to fetch water from the river. Meanwhile, the consuls argued bitterly as to the right course of action. On Varro's day, without consulting his fellow commander, he led the army out and deployed for battle in the traditional style, with infantry in the

centre and cavalry on each wing. This time the Roman cavalry was on the right wing next to the river, next to them the Roman infantry, then the allied infantry and finally the allied cavalry. Along the front of the infantry were the skirmishers, armed with a throwing javelin, bows or slings. Many of these had been loaned by Syracuse, at that time allied with Rome.

Hannibal had a plan. Like the Romans, he placed unarmoured infantry skirmishers, including slingers from the Balearic Islands, along his front. On his left, facing the Roman cavalry, he deployed his own Gallic and Spanish cavalry. Gallic and Spanish mercenaries made up the main infantry centre. If they died he would not have to pay them. The line was deliberately bellied

out towards the Romans. This line, right and left, was tipped by his African infantry, now sporting the Roman armour captured in previous victories. On his right flank were his famous Numidian cavalry.

THE ROMAN ARMY

The Roman army was relatively homogeneous. It always included priests and purified beasts for sacrifice to try and placate the gods. It is likely the Carthaginians did the same. The infantry was organized in legions of about 5000 men. These deployed in a standard way. The front line consisted of light infantry skirmishers, *velites*, armed with javelins and carrying a round shield. The second and third lines were of *hastati* and *principes*

armed with the heavy throwing javelin, for which the Romans were famous, known as the *pilum*, and carrying a large, flat, oval shield. The richer members of this class would wear a mail shirt, otherwise a simple square of bronze worn on the chest had to suffice for protection. The last line was formed of *triarii*. They were equipped with a long thrusting spear and, being the older members of the community, were more able to afford mail armour. The second, third and fourth lines normally deployed in companies of around 80 men, maniples, arranged in a chequerboard formation. This allowed mutual support and maximum flexibility as well as breaking up the rigid battle lines of many of their opponents. The restricted frontage at Cannae must have

The site of the battle at Cannae today. Stand on the ridge above the river as Hannibal must have done and let your imagination conjure up the enthusiastic Romans rushing into your trap. Then go down by the river and dwell upon the despair and frustration of the men who were so hemmed in by their fellows they could not strike back as they were cut down.

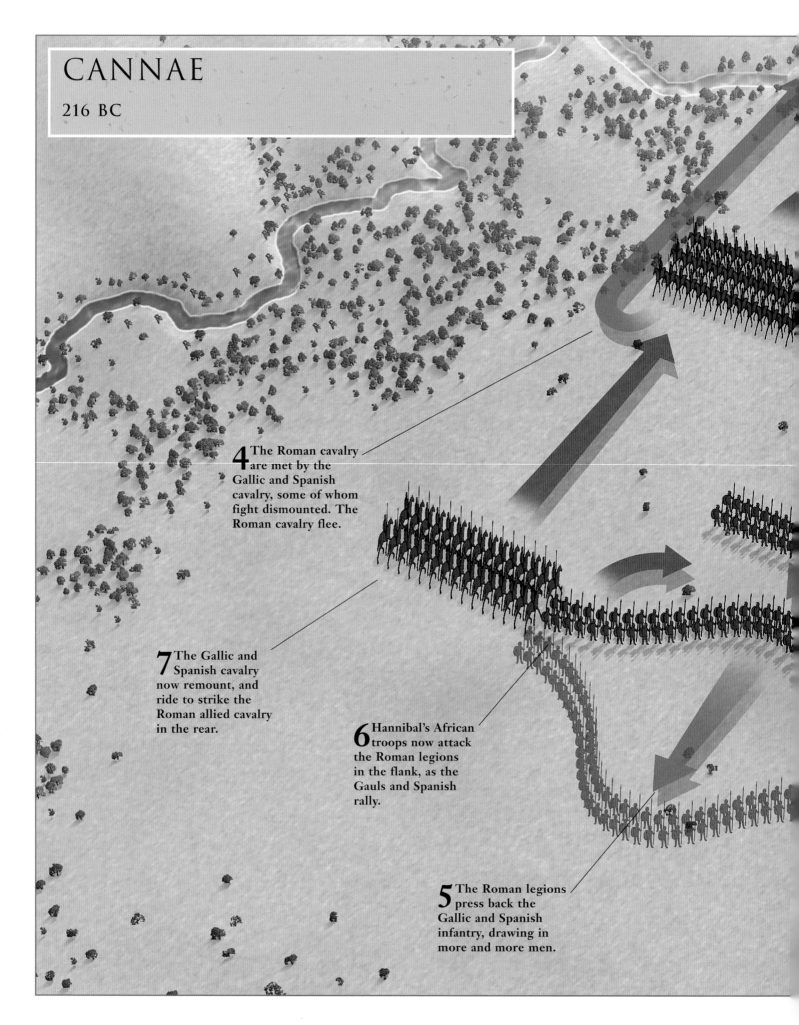

CANNAE
216 BC

4 The Roman cavalry are met by the Gallic and Spanish cavalry, some of whom fight dismounted. The Roman cavalry flee.

7 The Gallic and Spanish cavalry now remount, and ride to strike the Roman allied cavalry in the rear.

6 Hannibal's African troops now attack the Roman legions in the flank, as the Gauls and Spanish rally.

5 The Roman legions press back the Gallic and Spanish infantry, drawing in more and more men.

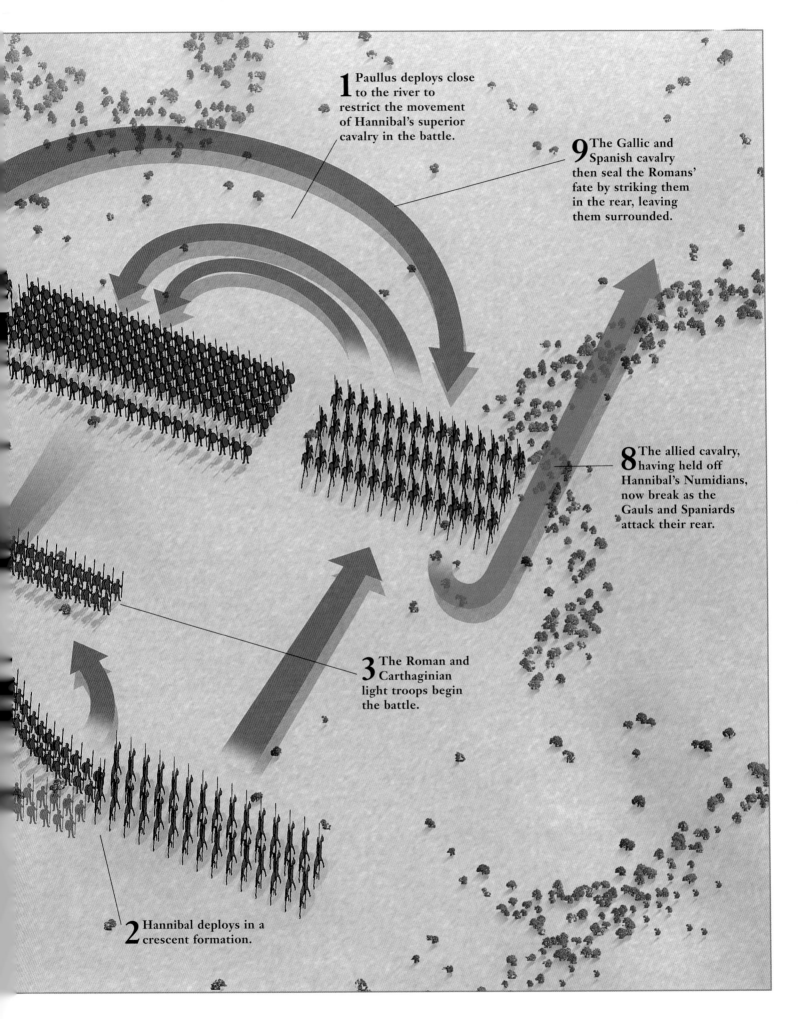

1 Paullus deploys close to the river to restrict the movement of Hannibal's superior cavalry in the battle.

9 The Gallic and Spanish cavalry then seal the Romans' fate by striking them in the rear, leaving them surrounded.

8 The allied cavalry, having held off Hannibal's Numidians, now break as the Gauls and Spaniards attack their rear.

3 The Roman and Carthaginian light troops begin the battle.

2 Hannibal deploys in a crescent formation.

Roman cavalry shields. From left to right: a round, spined design from 200 BC; a first century BC Celtic style; a typical first century AD oval design; an AD 300 design, with a rounder, more dished shape.

cancelled the chequerboard formation and the resulting departure from their training contributed to their defeat.

Have sympathy for the poor Roman cavalryman. His was a much under-developed branch of the army. There were no stirrups, so he had to maintain his own balance, grip with his knees and control his reins with his left hand which also held his shield. At the same time he had to wield his spear in his right hand, listen for orders and

try to spear the man facing him before he was speared himself. Although he wore a muscled cuirass in thin bronze, his shield was made of buffalo hide which tended to go soft in damp conditions. His principal weapon, a light javelin, was not really up to the job either. It was too thin, making it wobble and difficult to aim at the vital moment. When it broke, there was no butt spike and he was left wielding a broken stick! Even though he carried a sword, vital

seconds would be lost in drawing it just when the opponent was upon him, and by then it might well be too late.

The principal weakness of the Roman army at this period was a collective belief in their own invincibility. This often led to rash command decisions, as we shall see, and to the soldiers clamouring to get at the enemy, not to mention unauthorized advances. A large part of the army would have been trained but inexperienced. Rome had already lost 30,000 men in the previous two years in battles against Hannibal. Yet tactics and equipment remained unchanged. Although about half the army was provided by Rome's allies, they were similarly armed and organized. In this battle Varro commanded the allies on the left wing while Paullus commanded the Roman right.

HANNIBAL'S ARMY

The Carthaginian army was a very different beast. Hannibal had brought some troops with him from Africa and collected many more mercenaries on his long march from Spain where they had already won many victories. The core of the army was African spearmen from both Carthage and Libya. They wore a tunic to below the knee, an iron helmet and carried a large oval shield. The principal weapon was a spear about 1.8m (6ft) long, quite short for the period. By the time of Cannae many of these spearmen were wearing armour looted from the Roman dead at previous battles.

Cavalry from the city carried a round shield and wore muscled bronze breastplates. These horsemen were supplemented by numerous Numidian cavalry from the pre-desertified hinterland. A simple sleeveless tunic to the thigh, a shield and a few javelins were their equipment. They were nevertheless fearsome in their charge and formidable horsemen. They had mastered the art of

Opposite: The death of the Roman general Paullus at the battle of Cannae. This Eighteenth-century illustration shows legionaries wearing a form of armour introduced nearly 300 years after the battle and a breed of horse popular in the Eighteenth century. But it does confirm Cannae's place in world history as the defeat of overconfidence by intelligent planning.

controlling their horses with only their knees and body weight and did not encumber their shield arms with reins. This gave them a tremendous advantage in a melee. Although Hannibal had also brought elephants from Africa they had all died, mainly from the cold, two years before.

In Spain he recruited large numbers of native Celtiberians. These warriors sported black helmets made from sinew, a large oval shield and their typical dress was a white tunic with a purple border. They used a

Romans and Carthaginians contest the battle of Lake Trasimene (217 BC) during the second Punic War.

A Numidian light cavalryman from around 200 BC. He is armed with a javelin and small shield. These horsemen were such good riders that they had no need of a bridle to control their mount.

completely iron javelin, the *angon*, not unlike the Roman pila in effect. They also provided a contingent of cavalry. The Spanish cavalry carried a small shield of boiled leather and a pair of robust javelins so they could be hurled in a close-quarters mounted scrum without disarming the rider. Hannibal's only significant missile force was a number of slingers from the Balearic Islands.

In Gaul he added more tribal infantry and cavalry, again with big oval shields, javelins and long, slashing swords. They were the only ones in either army to wear trousers! The Gallic mounted warriors carried the wooden shield like their infantry and a stout spear. These separate groups spoke different languages and fought in different styles. The Gauls preferred a huge, wild, headlong charge whereas the Celtiberians threw their javelins and charged like the Romans.

Hannibal also had greater control in the field. For this battle his right wing, opposite the allied cavalry, was commanded by Marhabal. The Gallic and Spanish cavalry facing the Roman horse were under the command of his brother Hasdrubal. Hannibal personally led the centre with his brother Mago. He had four experienced battle commanders facing just two novices. It is an oft-omitted tribute to Hannibal's abilities that he managed to weld this disparate group into an army that regularly beat the Romans and kept it in the field in Italy for about 16 years.

THE BATTLE

The Roman cavalry were the first to give way. They were hemmed in by the river on one side and the massed infantry on the other. Frankly, the Romans should have placed all the cavalry in reserve ready to plug gaps or exploit success as required and held the riverside with infantry. Outclassed by the veteran Gallic and Spanish cavalry, the Romans first gave ground and then turned tail and fled.

The skirmishers exchanged missiles and withdrew through the ranks of the main infantry as they closed. When they met it was with a tremendous clamour. Buoyed up by the war horns and shouts of their own side they would have appeared to hesitate about 30m (32 yards) apart, while the *hastati* and *principes* on the Roman side and the Gauls and Spanish on the other hurled their javelins at each other.

To the war cries and clash of weapons would be added the screams of the injured. Then the lines would quickly collide in melee, raising the noise to painful levels as shield clashed against shield and swords began their deadly work, seeking out unguarded limbs and bodies. More screams and a bass undertone of grunting, shoving men in a mortal scrum added to the din. Slowly but surely the Roman and allied infantry pushed back the centre of the Gallic/Spanish line.

But this was Hannibal's trap. As the Romans pushed forward the line flattened then went concave. As it did so the already

Opposite: Despondency in Rome after defeat at Cannae. Hannibal still did not feel strong enough to besiege the city. So a stalemate ensued in Italy and the seat of the war moved to Spain. It ended with the Roman invasion of Africa and the battle of Zama in 202 BC.

This nineteenth-century illustration shows Hannibal and his army stripping the defeated Romans of arms and armour after their victory at Cannae.

cramped Roman and allied infantry became increasingly crowded, restricting the space they needed to wield their weapons. The Gauls and Spaniards started to run in feigned rout. This also left the two tips of African troops on the wings of the infantry. These fresh troops now launched themselves at the flanks of the tiring Roman infantry. The Romans had observed that a man can fight with maximum vigour for

about eight minutes. To fight and beat one enemy takes a lot of energy. To be then faced by a new, fresh foe is a blow to the spirit as well as a physical challenge. Added to that, the encircling movement they could perceive to their rear would have further sapped the Romans' will. However, they were not yet ready to throw in the towel. They desperately turned to face the new foe but they were already bloodied and

reported to have said: 'They might as well be delivered up to me in chains.'

On the Roman left about 500 of the Numidian cavalry had pretended to desert and were escorted through the allied cavalry lines. When the cavalry battle on this flank became general they showed their true colours and attacked the allied cavalry in the rear with weapons they had hidden earlier. Outnumbered and attacked front and rear, it was just a question of time before the allied cavalry too fled the field.

As casualties mounted and men started to leave the field Hasdrubal, Hannibal's brother, who commanded a reserve of Numidian cavalry, launched them in a bloody slaughter of the fugitives, for it is when an army breaks and is pursued that most casualties are inflicted.

In the early stages of this pursuit they cut down the consul Paullus who was still trying to make a fight of it. The Gauls and Spaniards were now recalled to the fight for the Africans were tiring of the butchery. The instinct to fight or flee is a strong one. When fighting becomes suicide, flight takes over and so it was at Cannae that day. The Roman army lost cohesion under this onslaught and fugitives ran in all directions: 10,000 made it to the larger camp, 7000 to the smaller and 2000 to the unfortified village of Cannae. Varro escaped with 70 cavalry to Venusia. The dead numbered 48,000. The Carthaginians captured 4500.

AFTERMATH

Although it was another great victory and he had now killed nearly 80,000 Roman soldiers in three years, Hannibal still did not feel strong enough to attempt to storm Rome. Meanwhile, Roman general Publius Scipio was subjugating Spain. A decade later, he went on to invade Africa and beat Hannibal at the battle of Zama, so ending the second Punic War in 202 BC.

Hannibal escaped and went to serve the Seleucid king Antiochus, who in turn became one of Rome's bitterest opponents. In the final war between these great powers the Romans besieged and captured the city of Carthage in 146 BC, slaughtering all the inhabitants and salting the surrounding countryside in the hope that Carthage would never rise again.

Dating from the third century BC, this Roman cavalry helmet – without its cheek guards – was recovered from excavations in Italy.

disorganized. They didn't stand a chance.

As the African steamroller hit, the confused Romans were thrown closer and closer together, unable to fight back. The sources speak of butchery rather than fighting. A slingshot had injured Paullus, commanding the right wing of the army. Unable to stay mounted he ordered his bodyguard to dismount to continue the fight. When he learned this Hannibal is

ALESIA
52 BC

THE FALL OF ALESIA WAS THE DEATH KNELL FOR GALLIC INDEPENDENCE. DEFEATED BY THE ROMAN ARMIES UNDER GAIUS JULIUS CAESAR, THE GAULS FELL UNDER THE SWAY OF THE EXPANDING REPUBLICAN EMPIRE. OPERATIONS CONTINUED INTO THE FOLLOWING YEAR BUT IT WAS AT ALESIA THAT THE GAULS WERE BROKEN.

WHY DID IT HAPPEN?

WHO Roughly 70,000 Roman troops under Gaius Julius Caesar (100–44 BC), versus around 80,000 infantry and 15,000 cavalry under the Gallic chieftain Vercingetorix (d. 46 BC) besieged inside the fortress. Perhaps as many as 250,000 more Gauls formed the relief army.

WHAT The Roman forces built extensive field fortifications to pen the Gauls within their fortress and to prevent relief. Gallic reinforcements and relief efforts were beaten off and the siege was maintained.

WHERE Mount Auxois, near what is now Dijon in France.

WHEN 52 BC.

WHY Julius Caesar embarked on a campaign to pacify Gaul and bring the Gallic tribes within the empire. The Gauls resisted fiercely.

OUTCOME Break-out and relief attempts were contained, and finally the starving Gauls were forced to surrender.

It has been said many times that history is written by the victors. In the case of *The Gallic War*, this is literally true – Julius Caesar himself wrote the definitive account of the campaign and his role in it. He uses a third-person perspective throughout, giving the illusion of objectivity, but the fact is that Caesar wrote the history of his own campaign. How much of his account is self-publicity and how much is truthful journalism is open to conjecture. Additional books were written by others after the mopping-up operations in 51 BC and generally agree with Caesar's account of events during the campaign.

Gaius Julius Caesar rose to military prominence fairly late in life, in his forties. He did have a solid background as a solider

of Rome, however, having won a *corona civica* whilst on campaign in Asia in 80–78 BC. He was taken hostage by pirates on his voyage home, and after being ransomed took his revenge. On his own initiative, Caesar raised local forces and smashed the pirates. He probably served as a military tribune in 72 BC and may have fought in the campaign against Spartacus' revolt, which began the previous year.

Like all Roman field commanders he was a political figure as well as a military one. He had held office as praetor and *Pontifex Maximus*, and governorship of three provinces had been conferred on him. He was thus responsible for both military and political command (the two were inextricably entwined) within a large region

A reconstructed fort at modern-day Alesia. The double ditch and abatis (sharp poles projecting from the wall) were not intended to stop intruders so much as to slow them down so that missile fire from within the fort could kill more of them. After a struggle through the ditch under fire, the wall with its brushwood palisade and frequent towers was a formidable obstacle.

of the empire, which included Transalpine Gaul and Cisalpine Gaul.

Later Caesar would use 'his' army to make him master of Rome but at the outset of the campaign in 58 BC, Caesar was no more than an officer of the Republic tasked with the subjugation of Gaul and given the resources to tackle this difficult task. He was an important and powerful man when he led his army into Gaul, but it was during the Gallic campaigns that he went beyond being a servant of Rome and became potentially her master.

THE CAMPAIGN OPENS

Caesar's Gallic campaign was triggered by the migration of the Helvetii people in search of more fertile land to support their growing population. This move would take them into Transalpine Gaul, and Caesar was determined to prevent any incursions into Roman territory. He rushed to the frontier to take stock of the situation.

Although the Helvetii requested permission to move through Roman territory and gave guarantees of their good conduct whilst doing so, Caesar refused, though not immediately. After stalling the Helvetii for nearly three weeks, he gave notice that their request would be rejected. In the intervening time, Caesar's legions had built field fortifications. These were defended against all incursions and the Helvetii eventually chose to take a different route into Gaul.

Caesar, who was out to make a reputation for himself and seeking plunder, was determined to fight the Helvetii. At the head of a force consisting of five legions plus supporting troops, he advanced against the Helvetii, citing complaints from Roman-allied tribes that they had been raided. The Helvetii, hit hard, tried to negotiate a settlement whereby the Romans would give them a place to settle in return for peace, but Caesar wanted none of it. After a period of manoeuvre and skirmish, Caesar's force brought the Helvetii to battle and soundly defeated them. Most of the survivors were returned to their old home, though some were allowed to settle with local tribes allied to Rome.

THE CONFLICT BROADENS

Whilst still in Gaul, Caesar received requests for aid from allied tribes. A Germanic army numbering some 120,000 had invaded Gaul. Despite some trepidation in the ranks, Caesar led his legions against this new foe and, after a fierce fight, defeated them.

Having beaten two major enemies in a single year, Caesar had won great fame and glory, but he was not yet satisfied. He had under his hand a powerful and well-honed tool in the form of his army, and he was determined to use it to best effect. Thus in the following year he marched against the Belgae and, despite some reverses, defeated them. He then divided his command to undertake several minor campaigns all over Gaul in 56 BC.

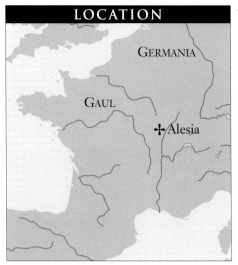

GERMANIA

GAUL

✛ Alesia

The town of Alesia is now called Alise-Ste.-Reine, on Mount Auxois, near the source of the Seine river. It was in Central Gaul, a province that Caesar himself had added to Rome's empire.

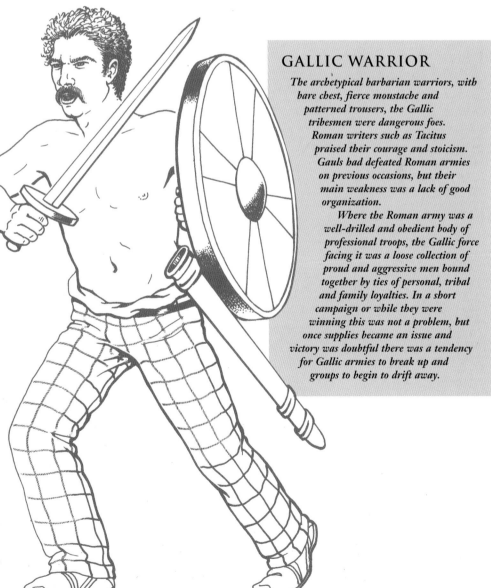

GALLIC WARRIOR

The archetypical barbarian warriors, with bare chest, fierce moustache and patterned trousers, the Gallic tribesmen were dangerous foes. Roman writers such as Tacitus praised their courage and stoicism. Gauls had defeated Roman armies on previous occasions, but their main weakness was a lack of good organization.

Where the Roman army was a well-drilled and obedient body of professional troops, the Gallic force facing it was a loose collection of proud and aggressive men bound together by ties of personal, tribal and family loyalties. In a short campaign or while they were winning this was not a problem, but once supplies became an issue and victory was doubtful there was a tendency for Gallic armies to break up and groups to begin to drift away.

ALESIA

ALESIA

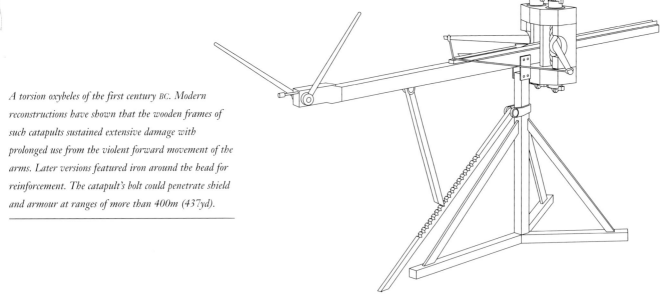

A torsion oxybeles of the first century BC. Modern reconstructions have shown that the wooden frames of such catapults sustained extensive damage with prolonged use from the violent forward movement of the arms. Later versions featured iron around the head for reinforcement. The catapult's bolt could penetrate shield and armour at ranges of more than 400m (437yd).

The ballista. In the third century BC, the Romans began adopting Greek siege warfare technology. The ballista was a new version of the stone-throwing lithobolos. The frame and base were now sturdier, the holes through which the rope was inserted and the washers by which it was secured went from being square in earlier models to an oval shape. This allowed more rope to be used in the springs and these were also twisted tighter. The springs were now exclusively made of sinew, much stronger than the old horsehair versions. All of this gave the machine much greater range and accuracy.

Caesar's campaigns took him across the Rhine in 55 BC, and even to Britain in the same year and in 54 BC, and it seemed that he was unstoppable. All the while his stock was rising in Roman politics, and much of what he did was planned to increase his wealth and standing. Inevitably, however, the Gauls were provoked into a more serious response, and in the winter of 54–53 BC, Caesar discovered that he had a fight on his hands.

The Belgae rose up against Rome and inflicted some defeats on Caesar's army.

The relatively green XIV Legion, with some additional troops attached, was caught by surprise in winter quarters. After some fighting its commander negotiated a withdrawal. However, in an ambush that foreshadowed events in the Teutoberger Wald half a century later, the legion was set upon in forest where it could not form up properly and was massacred.

A similar attack on another legion was fended off long enough for Caesar to march to its relief, and early in the new year Caesar launched a series of punitive expeditions to put down what was becoming a widespread revolt. This quietened things for a while, but the following winter (53–52 BC), the Gauls rose up again. This time they were acting together, though it could not be said that they were entirely in concert. Many important figures led the war against Rome, but Vercingetorix, a chieftain of the Arverni, emerged as the overall leader.

THE OPPOSED FORCES

ROMANS (estimated)
12 Roman legions, with auxiliaries
Total: 60,000

GAULS (estimated)
Besieged warriors: 80,000
Relief forces: 150–200,000
Total: 230–280,000

VERCINGETORIX MAKES WAR

The Gauls were fierce fighters, with a military system based upon duty to tribal leaders. The Gauls were mainly organized in warbands around their nobles, who tended to be ferocious warriors and courageous leaders. The bulk of Gallic soldiery were armed with spear and shield, though well-made swords were prized possessions as well as deadly weapons. The Gauls were nothing like as well organized as the Roman invaders, who had well-established practices for logistics and line of supply. However, Vercingetorix and his followers did seek to establish adequate supplies for their army and were consequently able to take the field with more men than the Gauls had previously been able to manage, and keep them concentrated.

At first the Gauls were successful. Raids were launched against Roman and pro-Roman Gallic settlements. Traders were massacred and troops in winter quarters came under attack. Caesar was at this time in Cisalpine Gaul, attending to his duties as governor, and had to make a choice between calling his legions to him, which might look like a withdrawal as well as leaving them open to attack and defeat in detail, or establishing local defence with minor forces and going to the legions himself.

Caesar chose the latter course, and even managed to lead an attack into Arvernian lands which caused dismay among the rebel chieftains. As Vercingetorix marched to meet this threat, which was actually fairly minor but reported as a major Roman army by panicked local leaders, Caesar rejoined his legions and concentrated them for a decisive battle.

His supply situation was not good as it was very early in the year, but with Vercingetorix on the march he had to act.

Modern-day Alesia in the Burgundy region of France.
The site of the battle is seen here from Caesar's position.
The hill offered Vercingetorix obvious defensive
advantages, but once surrounded it became a deathtrap.

Delay would make matters worse as the Gauls won minor successes which might persuade more chiefs to join their cause. Caesar had to act, and quickly.

The usual Roman response to an uprising was aggressive, and Caesar followed this course. Demanding grain from allied tribes to supply his army, he advanced towards where Vercingetorix was besieging Gorgobina, seizing supplies on the march and destroying targets of opportunity such as minor rebel strongholds along the way. Caesar's approach caused Vercingetorix to break off his siege and go to meet the Romans. After a cavalry action around Noviodunum,

ALESIA
52 BC

5 A large relief army of about 250,000 men arrives, and makes three serious attempts to lift the siege of the town.

4 The women and children are forced out of Alesia to save food, and have to camp between the two forces.

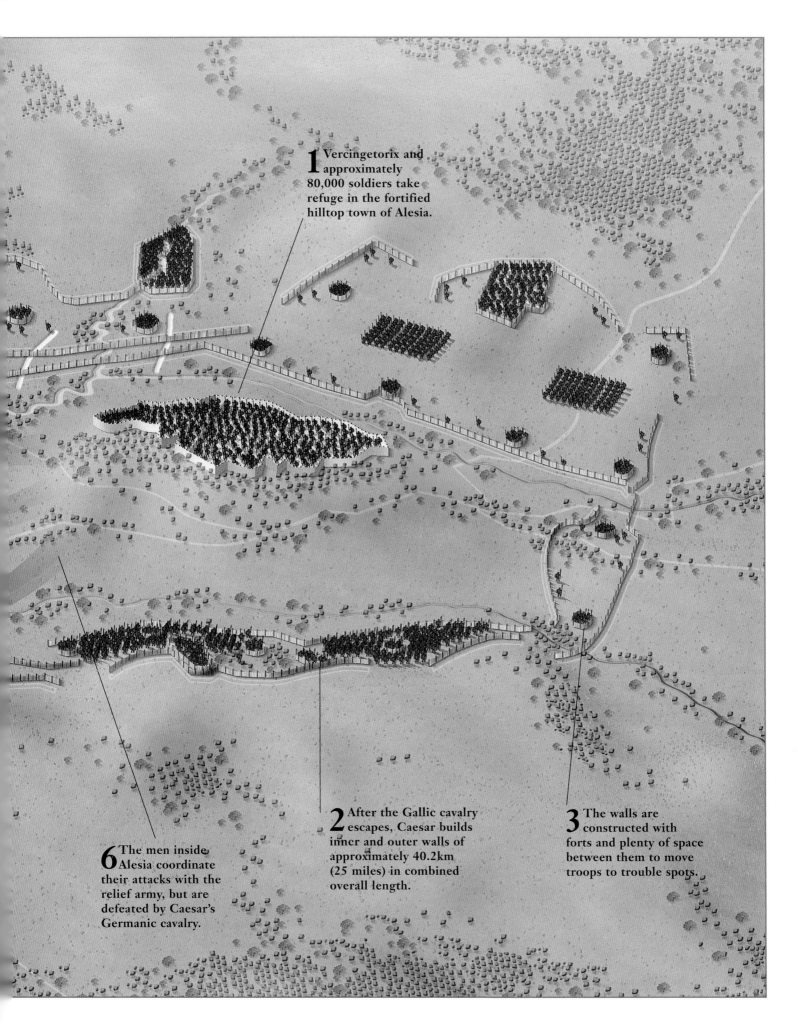

1 Vercingetorix and approximately 80,000 soldiers take refuge in the fortified hilltop town of Alesia.

2 After the Gallic cavalry escapes, Caesar builds inner and outer walls of approximately 40.2km (25 miles) in combined overall length.

3 The walls are constructed with forts and plenty of space between them to move troops to trouble spots.

6 The men inside Alesia coordinate their attacks with the relief army, but are defeated by Caesar's Germanic cavalry.

A L E S I A

which went in the Romans' favour, Caesar advanced on Avaricum.

Instead of allowing himself to be drawn into a decisive battle, Vercingetorix settled down to play a long game, choking the Roman army by cutting off its supplies whilst wearing down its strength by ambushes and small actions. The struggle went on like this for some time, with Caesar's forces besieging Avaricum whilst the Gallic army effectively tried to besiege the Roman field army. Supplies were getting short in both armies, and Caesar was having trouble obtaining more. Some allies had nothing more to send, and others were reconsidering their position. However, the Gauls were also running short of supplies and in general lacked the patience for such a protracted action.

CAESAR'S INITIATIVE

With the Romans steadily reducing Avaricum and his commanders becoming restless, Vercingetorix allowed himself to be talked into taking more direct action. Moving up closer to the town, he offered battle from a strong position but Caesar refused to sanction what would have been a costly assault. The siege continued, with the Romans gradually gaining the upper hand. The warriors Vercingetorix had sent into the town now attempted to fight their way out, but were contained. Shortly afterwards the legions stormed the town and put the defenders to the sword, capturing large stocks of grain into the bargain.

Caesar now went on the offensive, launching attacks against other rebel towns in rapid succession. His legions and auxiliaries were being worn down by the constant fighting and rapid marching, but there was no time to be lost.

In the meantime, the fall of Avaricum had actually strengthened Vercingetorix's political position as he had argued against defending it in the first place. More tribes came to join him, and rebellion broke out even among tribes previously staunch allies

Legionaries construct defensive works around the perimeter of Alesia. The Roman army were unparalleled in the Ancient world as builders of small fortresses for siege warfare.

ALESIA

In this illustration by artist Henri Paul (1846–1922), Roman soldiers are depicted operating an onager at the siege of Alesia. The weapon and its crew are protected from counter-fire by simple but effective fortifications.

Fearing that he had lost the initiative and that more Gauls would be encouraged to join the rising, Caesar launched a counter-offensive and called in his detached forces. He also raised more auxiliaries and hired mercenaries from the German tribes. Vercingetorix had also been reinforced, and a fierce running battle developed, mainly between the cavalry of both armies, along the line of march.

After a long and hard fight, Caesar's army drove off the Gauls and pursued them for the remainder of that day. The Gallic army rallied and re-formed on a hill outside the town of Alesia and the Romans, who now had more than sufficient supplies, decided to besiege it.

THE SIEGE BEGINS

The Romans were not great originators of siege technology. Indeed, much of what was available to them was copied from foreign powers, mainly the Greeks. What the Romans were very good at was what might today be called combat engineering. Experts at erecting field fortifications, the Romans were able to quickly throw up an entire ring of defences – a line of circumvallation – around the Gallic camp, making it difficult for Vercingetorix to sally out and for supplies to get in.

However, the Roman army was deep within hostile territory, and it faced attack from outside the town, so a second line of defences – a line of contravallation – facing outwards was also built. The inner line, containing the defenders, was 17.7km (11 miles) long. The outer line, protecting the besiegers, was 22.5km (14 miles) long.

The defences were formidable. Initially a makeshift set-up with a ditch and a wall no more than 1.8m (6ft) in height, the fortifications were rapidly developed into a very impressive set of works. A 6m (20ft) wide ditch ran right around the Gallic position to slow down any advance by Vercingetorix and buy time for reserves to assemble to meet an assault. The main belt consisted of a 3.6m (12ft) earth-and-timber wall fronted by two 4.6m (15ft) wide ditches to break up an attack.

In some places these ditches were flooded and in others they were reinforced with sharp stakes and small pits. Wooden

of Rome. Caesar brought the situation under control and inflicted defeats on the Gauls, but matters remained serious.

THE DECISIVE PHASE

After a surprise attack on a Gallic force near Gergovia, the aggression of the legions got out of control. This led to a disorganized and chaotic attempt to storm the city. Despite early successes, the assault was broken and the Romans suffered heavy casualties, including no less than 46 centurions. Caesar withdrew from the town to deal with other problems including further uprisings and the massacre of Roman garrisons along his supply route.

frameworks from which iron spikes projected were buried in some areas as well. Alone, these obstacles would not contain the Gauls, but this was not their purpose. They were intended to inflict some casualties but above all impose delay on a force assaulting the Roman besiegers. Every moment longer taken to reach the defenders meant another hail of missiles from the wall, another maniple of reserves rushed up to the endangered section, and an ever smaller chance of success. The outward-facing line of contravallation was equally formidable, and both lines were strengthened by the inclusion of towers every 24m (80ft) along the line as well as independent strongpoints.

According to Caesar's own account of events, around 80,000 Gauls were trapped within the fortifications. This figure is suspect, since the besiegers can only have numbered around 40,000–70,000, but whatever the exact figure, what is certain is that Vercingetorix commanded a very substantial force within the camp. He also enjoyed massive support all across Gaul. It has been estimated that as many as 250,000 Gallic warriors were available to come to the assistance of the besieged army. However, supplying such a huge force was beyond the means of the tribes; there was no chance of a quarter of a million warriors all turning up at once.

RELIEF ARRIVES

The Gauls were not idle during the construction of the siegeworks, but despite launching many raids and spoiling attacks were not able to prevent the ring from closing on them. Cut off from additional supplies, Vercingetorix had to hope that relief would reach him, and to extend the time he could hold out, he expelled all non-combatants from the town. Already Vercingetorix's cavalry (numbering some 15,000 according to Caesar) had been sent out to join the relief force. It forced its way through the defences at the second attempt, though with heavy losses. Now women, children and anyone else who could not fight were sent out of the town and the Gallic camp, but Caesar would not allow them through his lines. Thus these innocents were left to starve between the

two armies. The campaign had entered its final, desperate phase.

The Gallic relief army reached Alesia soon after the expulsion of non-combatants. While Caesar's figure of 250,000 infantry and 8000 cavalry seems excessive, nonetheless this force was probably very large. Caesar was now forced to defend his positions from attack from outside, while Vercingetorix was leading an attack from within. As the besieged Gauls worked to fill in parts of the ditch, a cavalry melee developed on the plains outside. This was eventually won by the Roman heavy horse, who routed the Gallic cavalry and massacred their supporting light infantry.

The following day was quiet, but at midnight that night, the relief army launched its attack and Vercingetorix responded by attacking from within the circle of fortifications. A confused and bloody battle erupted with Roman troops

A statue of Julius Caesar in Vienna. Caesar literally changed the world, converting Rome from a republic to an empire, and casts a long shadow over world history. Some later words for 'emperor' (Kaiser, Tsar) are derived from his name.

Vercingetorix led the Gauls rather than commanded them, which limited his options. He was successful in fighting a guerrilla war and wearing down the Romans, but when forced into open battle his forces were outmatched by better tactics and superior equipment.

defending their positions using javelins and light siege engines called scorpions, and hurling stones that had been readied for just such an occasion. A hail of missile fire – arrows, javelins and slingstones – was sent against the Roman positions as Gallic infantry tried to gain a foothold on the fortifications. Matters were in doubt for some time, but Roman reinforcements led by Mark Antony and another of Caesar's legates were able to stabilize the situation and drive the assaults back.

CRISIS POINT

At midday the next day, a force some 60,000 strong (according to Caesar) made an assault on one of the Roman forts while other forces made diversionary attacks at various points along the line. There was no way to inform Vercingetorix of what was planned, but when he heard the noise of battle he again led his forces out to assault the Roman positions.

The Romans were hard-pressed, but they were tough, tenacious and highly disciplined. They stood and fought stubbornly wherever they were attacked, and this bought time for Caesar to make use of the Romans' other great advantage, the ability to manoeuvre quickly. Time and again Caesar called up reserves from elsewhere in the line and fed them into a crisis point. He also sent the legate Labienus with five cohorts to reinforce the beleaguered fort. Labienus had complete latitude to do as he had to. He could deploy his cohorts and the two legions already in the fort as he saw fit, and had permission to abandon the position and fight his way out if need be.

THE LAST HURRAH

Knowing that this was the best and perhaps the last chance he would be offered, Vercingetorix launched an all-out assault on the Roman positions. A massive hail of missiles swept the defenders from the wall, and under its cover the Gauls made their final assault.

The attack was a success. Gallic warriors began destroying the defences and some gained the ramparts. Caesar ordered Decimus Brutus to throw them back, and Brutus led several cohorts into a counter-attack. The fighting was still desperate, so

Caesar ordered the legate Gaius Fabius to Brutus' aid with virtually all the available troops. Between them they were able to retake the defences. Vercingetorix's assault faltered and with it any hope of linking up with the relief army was gone.

Meanwhile, Caesar himself gathered a final reserve from lightly engaged sectors and led it to the assistance of Labienus, whose troops had been forced off the ramparts but were holding out inside the fort. Supported by a force of cavalry, Caesar's troops threw back the Gauls, who broke and were vigorously pursued by the cavalry. This disheartened the relief force, which gradually melted away leaving the siege unbroken.

AFTERMATH

The following day, the starving defenders of Alesia agreed to Caesar's demand for their unconditional surrender. Vercingetorix, dressed in his most impressive armour and riding a fine horse, laid down his weapons before Caesar and was taken away as a prisoner.

The surrender of Vercingetorix was not quite the end of the rebellion. A smaller uprising took place in 51 BC but was quickly put down. Treatment of the vanquished varied. Some tribes were treated leniently in the hope of winning them back over to Roman allegiance. Some were punished very harshly as an example to others. Vercingetorix himself was kept captive in Rome for six years before being publicly executed by strangulation.

So many prisoners were taken in the campaign that every man in Caesar's army was given one to sell as a slave. Caesar himself became fabulously wealthy from the campaign, even after paying off the huge debts he had started out with.

Caesar's reputation was made in the Gallic campaign – in Rome, but more importantly with the Roman army. It was this army that was at his back when he crossed the Rubicon and entered Italy, and this army that defeated Pompey in the civil war that followed. In Rome, political and military power were inextricably mixed. Caesar knew this, and exploited it to the full.

Entitled 'Vercingetorix Throwing His Weapon's at the Feet Of Caesar', Lionel-Noël Royer's (1852–1926) depiction of Vercingetorix offers a romanticized view of the Gallic leader's surrender. Caesar is portrayed dressed as a political figure rather than a soldier. To Rome, the two were often the same thing.

TEUTOBERGER WALD
AD 9

TEUTOBERGER WALD WAS A SHOCKING DEFEAT FOR THE ROMAN EMPIRE, AND ONE THAT ENSURED THAT THE GERMANIC FRONTIER WAS NEVER FULLY PACIFIED. THE BATTLE HAD CONSEQUENCES THAT CHANGED THE COURSE OF EUROPEAN HISTORY.

WHY DID IT HAPPEN?

WHO Three Roman legions under Publius Quinctilius Varus (d. AD 9), with supporting cavalry, versus Germanic troops of the Cherusci tribe under their chief Arminius (?18 BC– AD 19), who was supposedly a Roman ally.

WHAT The Roman forces were betrayed, ambushed and massacred by the Cherusci in the forests of the Teutoberger Wald.

WHERE Along the line of march towards winter quarters in the deep forest, near Osnabrück in northwest Germany. There were many actions and the exact locations are hard to place.

WHEN September–October AD 9

WHY Tiring of Roman policies, the Cherusci turned on their allies and used guerrilla tactics to destroy them in the forests where standard legionary formations were ineffective.

OUTCOME Three Roman legions and supporting troops were annihilated. The Roman Empire never regained control of the Germanic frontier.

In AD 6, when Publius Quinctilius Varus was appointed governor of the province of Germania, the Roman army was apparently an unstoppable war machine. Formed around a professional core of long-service regulars backed up by auxiliary troops where necessary, the Roman army was years ahead of its time in terms of organization and fighting power.

The Romans enjoyed many advantages over their enemies. Individual soldiers were well equipped, thoroughly trained and physically tough. Fighting with their short stabbing swords (*gladii*) while protected by shields and good armour, individual Roman soldiers were deadly combatants. Yet for all this the main strength of the empire was not its individual soldiers. Many barbarian tribes and foreign nations produced fighting men every bit as physically powerful as the Roman solider. Often bigger, stronger and every bit as motivated and aggressive, these warriors fell before the swords of the legions and were assimilated into the empire. The reason was not individual skill or courage, but organization.

In battle, the Roman soldier did not fight in closely packed ranks but had sufficient space to manoeuvre as he needed to. However, he did fight as part of a unit. Part of his training involved being aware of the men on each side of him. A legionary who got into trouble could expect prompt assistance from his companions in the front

The Roman general Publius Quinctilius Varus prepares to commit suicide as his legions are slaughtered around him in the Teutoberger forest. Varus imposed harsh financial penalties on colonized peoples which lost him much local support.

rank, or replacement by a fresh man from the rear. Roman policy was that no man could fight effectively for more than 15 minutes at a time, and troops were rotated out of the front line as they tired. This was trained for and well practised; where a barbarian warrior would battle on until he dropped, a Roman soldier would fight for a period, then retire to catch his breath before returning to the fray. This took place on a larger scale too. Manoeuvre and drill were an important part of the Roman army's training, so gaps in the line could be quickly plugged, maniples wheeled to face a new threat on the flanks, and tiring units replaced in the front line – all without confusion or loss of cohesion.

Thus the Roman legion was composed of formidable fighters but was more than the sum of its parts. Advancing confidently to contact with the enemy, releasing a hail of *pila* (heavy javelins) just before impact, then entering hand-to-hand combat as a coherent and mutually supporting whole, it was impressive. But what made the Roman army really stand head and shoulders above its foes was the fact that it could maintain its cohesion and combat capability through a long engagement. As its foes tired, the legion simply kept on going.

This was the war machine that Varus had at his disposal when he took over from Augustus' stepson (and future successor) Tiberius in AD 6, and its capabilities were enhanced by allied and auxiliary troops which provided specialist functions (skirmishers, scouts, and so forth) and raw numbers to cover ground.

FAILURES OF POLICY

Despite the fact that Varus had over 15,000 Roman troops at his disposal, this was not sufficient to pacify such a large region if the inhabitants rose up together against Rome. A conquered or occupied region only stays that way if the inhabitants consent to remain pacified. So long as the local tribes were divided, the frontier was safe. And so it was in AD 6. Some tribes were allied to Rome; some were hostile but cowed by the threat of force or by the example that had been made of others that opposed Rome; some were neutral so long as Roman interference was minimal.

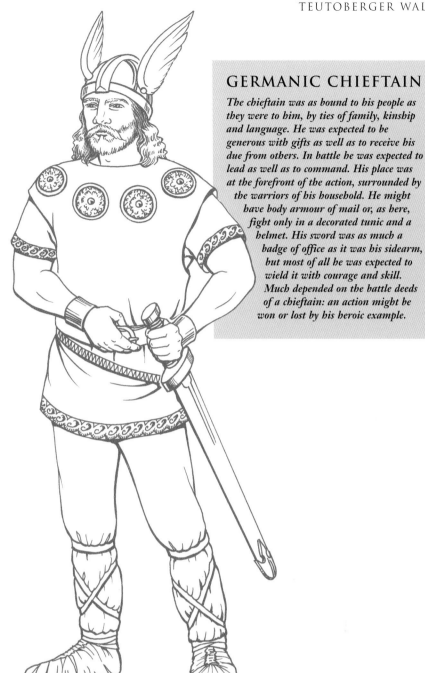

Varus' mission was to continue the work of Tiberius in making the Germanic frontier safe and secure. The key to this was cooperation of the local tribes such as the Cherusci, which could field large numbers of highly capable fighting men. While revolts and local opposition could be put down easily enough, it was important that Varus built long-term relationships with the tribal leaders, playing them off against one another and gradually creating a 'natural order' of things on the frontier whereby Rome was the master but the tribes were respected allies and 'Friends of Rome'.

But Varus instead undertook policies that alienated the tribal leaders and their people. Heavy taxation and lack of respect for Germanic culture, coupled with

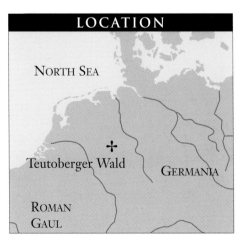

LOCATION

NORTH SEA

Teutoberger Wald

GERMANIA

ROMAN GAUL

Germania was the frontier of Roman-controlled territory. But for the events of AD 9, Germania might have eventually been absorbed into the empire. After Teutoberger Wald there was little chance that would ever happen.

arrogance on the part of Varus and his fellows, drove the neutral tribes to rebellion and even the allied ones to reconsider their position.

By the summer of AD 9, Varus and his remaining allies were engaged in putting down rebellions along the frontier. While the summer campaign was successful, Varus' arrogance and overconfidence led him to disaster at the end of the campaign season.

WINTER QUARTERS

During the summer, Varus had taken the field with an impressive force – three entire legions, six independent cohorts and three squadrons of cavalry, totalling around 18,000 Roman infantry and 1800 cavalry, plus a large force of troops supplied by the allied chief Arminius of the Cherusci tribe. About 10,000 camp-followers accompanied the Roman army on its campaign.

Arminius had by this time had quite enough of Varus and of Rome, and had decided to remove the Roman presence from the frontier. His growing disaffection had been noticed but Varus disregarded warnings that the Cherusci might rise up against him and continued to treat the tribe as close allies. He depended on guides and scouts from the Cherusci and made no attempt to guard himself against any change of allegiance. At this point, having defeated rebel and hostile tribes during the summer, Varus probably thought he was winning.

As the campaign season drew to a close, Varus retired towards his winter quarters.

The Cherusci were in close contact. The route chosen by Varus was through the densely forested Teutoberger Wald. The thick forest was tough going, made worse by appalling weather conditions that included very heavy rainfall. As the Roman army slogged through the forest, dragging its baggage and shepherding its many camp-followers along, the well-drilled formations that were the great strength of the Roman army became disorganized and fragmented. Troops became lost and straggled off into the forests and contact was lost with the Germanic allies. Shortly after that, the attacks began.

ASYMMETRIC WARFARE

There is asymmetry in all conflict, of course. One side always has better weapons, tactics, technology, training or other factors that give advantages that may lead to victory. However, asymmetric warfare is a somewhat different concept. Essentially it means engaging a superior or more advanced force in a manner that negates some of its advantages. Asymmetric warfare is rarely the first choice of a state or group;

Roman standards from the first century AD. From left to right are two manipular standards with bravery awards attached, and a vexillarum. Standards did more than show troops where to rally and where their officers could be found: they inspired the legion by reminding its members of their unit's past glory and challenging them to live up to its reputation.

THE OPPOSED FORCES

GERMANIC TRIBES (estimated)

Warriors: 32,000

ROMANS (estimated)
3 Legions and 6 auxiliary cohorts
Total: 21,000

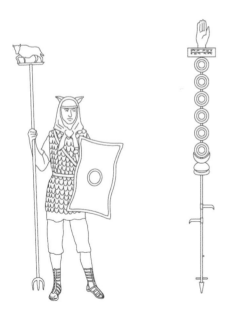
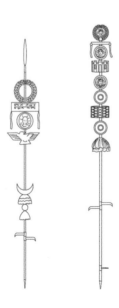
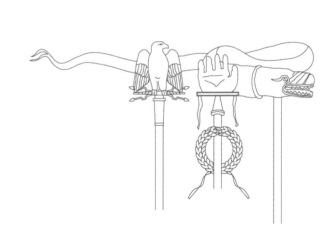

where it is possible to engage in conventional warfare with a reasonable chance of victory, this is the usual course. The raids, ambushes and general nuisance-causing tactics of asymmetric warfare are generally the preserve of the underdog. For example, a major naval power will usually build ships to win decisive battles; a weaker power plans to cause damage to commerce instead because it cannot take on the greater fleet in open battle. The Romans faced several opponents who used asymmetric warfare against them. Resistance groups in occupied areas made life difficult for the conquerors, but rarely did these tactics meet with any real success. The Parthians, who countered the deadly but ponderous legions with fast-moving horse archers, were a notable exception. And as events on those terrible days in AD 9 were to show, the Germanic tribes were another.

Dispersed throughout the forest, in many cases lost, tired and dispirited, the legions were at their most vulnerable. Their formations were ineffective, their command and control had broken down completely. They could not see the enemy, who moved quickly through the forests to strike wherever he would. The annihilation of the legions began with hit-and-run attacks by Germanic tribesmen at various points on the fragmented column. The slow-moving baggage and camp-followers meant that the legionaries could only plod on through the forest between attacks. It was not hard to pick one of the groups, mass a suitable force, and fall upon it from ambush at an advantageous moment.

The Romans fought back hard, their long training and excellent combat skills giving small groups of legionaries a fighting chance even against enemies who sprang out from ambush with no warning. Where possible, junior officers and experienced soldiers led aggressive counter-attacks that roughly handled some of the ambushes. Sometimes it was possible to dash to the rescue of a nearby group that was under attack – and equally, sometimes the reinforcements were themselves ambushed, or their unguarded charges wiped out in their ambush.

Gradually the Roman force was worn down despite the best efforts of the

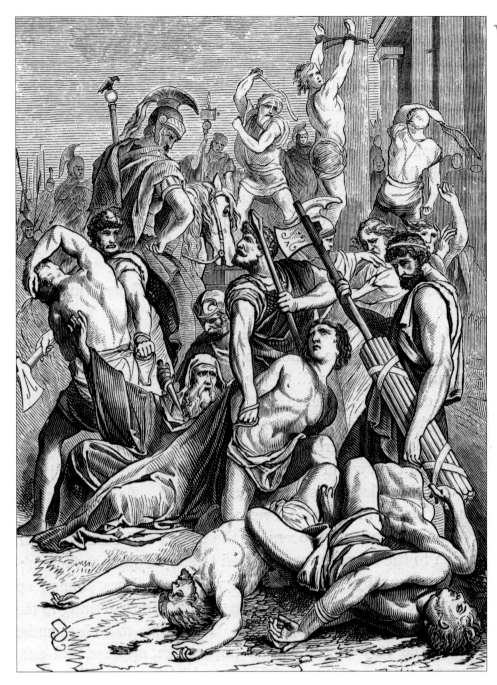

legionaries. Unable to abandon or even go far from their baggage and camp-followers, the Romans had lost the initiative to the attackers. They could only meet each onslaught as it came and drive it back if possible, resuming the long hard slog when it was over.

SURVIVAL MEASURES

No doubt the Roman commanders and Varus himself knew by this time that they were under severe threat. Contact between different groups was all but impossible in the forest, where a messenger would be quickly ambushed and killed. Perhaps the local commanders formed roving 'reaction

A depiction of Varus punishing the tribes under his jurisdiction. Varus did immeasurable damage to Roman relations with the Germanic people, and paid the price.

TEUTOBERGER WALD

AD 9

2 Germanic warriors launch hit-and-run attacks, isolating parts of the column and destroying them, then melting into the forest when reinforcements arrive.

1 Struggling onward through the forests en route for winter quarters, the vanguard of the column is left largely unmolested at first.

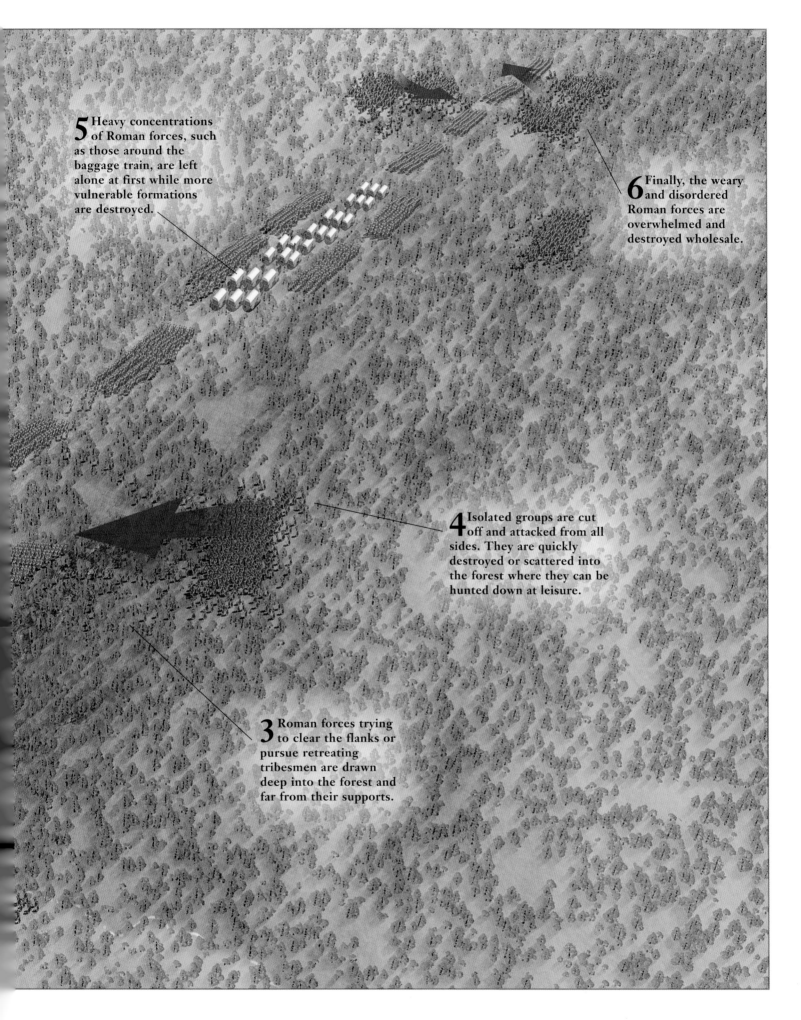

5 Heavy concentrations of Roman forces, such as those around the baggage train, are left alone at first while more vulnerable formations are destroyed.

6 Finally, the weary and disordered Roman forces are overwhelmed and destroyed wholesale.

4 Isolated groups are cut off and attacked from all sides. They are quickly destroyed or scattered into the forest where they can be hunted down at leisure.

3 Roman forces trying to clear the flanks or pursue retreating tribesmen are drawn deep into the forest and far from their supports.

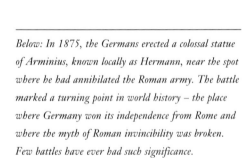

Below: In 1875, the Germans erected a colossal statue of Arminius, known locally as Hermann, near the spot where he had annihilated the Roman army. The battle marked a turning point in world history – the place where Germany won its independence from Rome and where the myth of Roman invincibility was broken. Few battles have ever had such significance.

forces' to move up and down their section of the column and deal with problems as they occurred. Perhaps some groups struck off into the forest to try to fight their way clear, or became lost and wandered away to meet their fate far from any possible help.

What is known is that the situation was very confused and increasingly desperate, but the Romans battled on towards their winter quarters. If they could reach suitable ground they might be able to re-form and defeat their foe in a traditional set-piece action – the sort of battle that the Roman army was designed for and had a long history of winning. But it was not to be.

Perhaps at first the Romans hoped that their Germanic allies would return to their aid, but as the nightmare march continued, it became apparent that those very 'allies' were among the dimly seen figures attacking out of the depths of the forest. With each weary hour, with each new assault or group of friends and comrades found slaughtered on the path ahead, hope faded until it became obvious that to press on was certain death.

The power of the legions was based very much on being able to work as a unit and bring concentrated force to bear on the enemy, such as throwing pila. In the forest of the Teutoberger Wald, however, Roman organization was undermined as the legionaries were separated and picked off in smaller groups.

Now the fight was a lot more equal, for within the camp the excellent organization of the Roman army reasserted itself. Junior leaders commanded sections of the defences, knowing that reserves were available to assist them from unengaged sections of the perimeter or the inner reserve in the camp. Few they might be, but now they were fighting on their own terms and making the enemy pay. If they could just hold on a little longer, surely the tribesmen would tire of being slaughtered on the defences and melt away. They might yet fight free of the forest deathtrap.

The camp held out for several days, during which additional groups straggled in. All were sadly depleted. They described a rain-soaked nightmare of ambush and sudden death; the forest filled with vast numbers of tribesmen; sudden and bloody death waiting behind every tree. Out in the forest, the tribesmen picked off the stragglers and the groups that had failed to find the camp or become detached. Gradually the Roman force was whittled down until only those holding out in their fort were left alive. Now the field fortification had become a prison around which the tribesmen gathered their strength. When they were ready, the final attack went in.

THE ROMANS DIG IN

Varus ordered his section of the column to halt and to prepare a fortified camp. This was the other thing that the Roman army did very well indeed. It hit hard and overthrew its opponents with shock action, and it could prepare excellent field fortifications. Each legionary knew how to build a fortified camp and had had plenty of practice – on the march, the legion dug in every night.

Despite the attentions of Germanic warriors, Varus' legionaries fortified themselves with earthworks and cut logs, creating formidable defences. The baggage and camp-followers were placed within, defended by legionaries who were fighting for their very lives.

Undoubtedly, morale rose within the camp. No longer subject to sudden ambushes from the forest, now the troops' backs were protected by their comrades. The enemy were without the camp and had to attack across defended obstacles where they could be made to pay dearly for their audacity.

THE END COMES SWIFTLY

After bottling the last coherent Roman force up in their fort while they destroyed all the easy targets still blundering around in the forest, the barbarians gathered their strength for a massive assault. The Roman infantry on the walls of the camp put up a good fight. They were weary beyond measure but they were desperate. They knew they could expect no mercy if the camp fell, and behind them sheltered the helpless camp-followers, who included families of some legionaries. The Cherusci

A legion shown in full. It was divided into ten cohorts. The first cohort had five centuries of about 160 men each, the remainder had six centuries of about 80 men. Each legion had an attachment of about 120 horsemen to act as scouts and despatch riders. The legion was commanded by a legate, a senator appointed by the emperor.

tribesmen paid a price to cross the ditch and scale the earthworks, their charge met with *pilum* and *gladius* as the Romans fought for their lives.

For a while it seemed that superior equipment and discipline, coupled with sheer desperation, might prevail over the raw courage of the tribal warriors, but there were simply too many of them. More and more barbarians poured into the camp, overwhelming what reserves there were and forcing the defenders away from their fortifications, back into the camp. It was all over but for the massacre.

The Roman cavalry, which had numbered about 1800 at the beginning of the action, made an attempt to break out and escape. Charging out of the fortifications, it met momentary success but was dragged to a halt and cut down by the horde of attackers. Now no distractions remained and the full fury of the attackers hammered into the last hold-outs among the legionaries.

Seeing that all was lost, Publius Quinctilius Varus committed suicide in the traditional manner, by falling upon his own sword and thereby avoiding capture. Many tribunes and centurions also evaded the disgrace of capture by suicide or, more often, by being cut down as they fought to the bitter end. Few Romans survived the catastrophe. Some stragglers did manage to escape and eventually make their way back to Roman territory. For most, things were far more grim. Most were killed in battle or the massacre that followed, some being tortured to death. Most of the camp-followers met the same fate as their soldiers, though some were captured and enslaved.

The head of Publius Quinctilius Varus was sent to the Emperor Augustus in Rome as a token of the utter defeat his force had suffered. Those tribunes and centurions who survived long enough to be captured were used as human sacrifices to the Germanic gods.

AFTERMATH

Although punitive expeditions were launched across the Germanic frontier and Rome won several victories, the region was never fully pacified. A campaign to recover the standards of the three legions involved – the XVII, XVIII and XIX – could not change the fact that three entire legions had been destroyed. The image of Rome as the invincible conqueror had been shattered at Teutoberger Wald. Now the tribes of the frontier knew that they could defeat the legions if they came again. Peace and stability of a sort was restored to the region eventually, and a frontier along the Rhine was established. This was not the original goal; all of Germania was to have been incorporated into the empire, but after Teutoberger Wald this was not possible.

Rome never pacified the Germanic frontier, and the German people retained their culture intact rather than being heavily influenced by Mediterranean civilization. This had some very important ramifications for the future of Europe. Indeed, many historians believe that the Saxon tribes would never have migrated to England, which would have profoundly altered the history of Britain. More importantly, it also ensured that the Germanic tribes thrived and grew outside of Roman influence. It was these same tribes that came to destroy Rome many centuries later.

Whatever the consequences for the rest of Europe, the catastrophe that befell the Roman army at Teutoberger Wald ensured the independence of Germany and limited the expansion of the Roman Empire. It also shook the myth of Roman invincibility to its core and may have inspired other groups to take on the might of Rome. Who can say whether the failure of Rome to bring the German tribes to heel was due to its impossibility or simply the fear that such a disaster might strike again? Perhaps if the defeat had been less total, the campaign to avenge it might have been carried out with more confidence and determination.

The disaster certainly affected the confidence of Rome and shocked the Emperor Augustus, who is said to have exclaimed upon hearing the news, 'Give me back my legions!' What is certain is that the massacre in the Teutoberger Wald was one of the worst defeats suffered by the Roman Empire. It is a strong candidate for one of the worst military disasters of all time.

In this classically styled painting, Roman general Germanicus defeats Arminius of the Cherusci at the battle of the Weser river (AD 16), in revenge for the defeat at the Teutoberger Wald seven years earlier.

ADRIANOPLE
AD 378

THE BATTLE OF ADRIANOPLE WAS THE ONLY GREAT VICTORY IN A PITCHED BATTLE OF THE GERMANS WHO OVERRAN THE WESTERN EMPIRE. THE GOTHIC VICTORY DEMONSTRATED ROMAN WEAKNESSES AND EXPOSED THE EMPIRE TO FURTHER ATTACK, BEGINNING A DOMINO EFFECT THAT ENDED IMPERIAL RULE IN THE WEST.

WHY DID IT HAPPEN?

WHO The field army of the Eastern Roman Empire, commanded by the Emperor Flavius Valens (AD 328–378), met a mixed Gothic army, with a core consisting of the Tervingi tribe under Fritigern, supported by Greuthungi led by Alatheus and Saphrax, as well as other tribes.

WHAT The battle took place between the rebellious Goths and a Roman army that had been called together to suppress the rebellion.

WHERE About 13km (8 miles) from Adrianople, modern Edirne in European Turkey.

WHEN 9 August AD 378.

WHY Having made a treaty with the Romans in AD 376 that allowed them to settle within the empire, the Goths rebelled against the ill-treatment they received. Valens intended to end this Gothic threat but attacked based on a mistaken report of Gothic strength, without waiting for the Western Roman army under Emperor Gratian (AD 359–383) to arrive.

OUTCOME The Roman army was completely defeated. Two-thirds of the Roman forces, perhaps 10,000 men, were killed, including Valens.

The Goths were not a distinct group, but rather shifting alliances of eastern Germanic tribes, with little sense of ethnic identity. Nineteenth-century historians oversimplified them, dividing them into 'Visigoths' and 'Ostrogoths'. The reality was more complex. Both major Gothic divisions, the Tervingi and the Greuthungi, fought at Adrianople. In the year AD 376 the Tervingi received permission to settle in Roman territory to escape attacks by the Huns. They crossed the Danube, only to suffer systematic abuse from the Roman authorities placed over them. The Romans had promised provisions and land for settlement, in return for which the Goths would fight for the Romans. But Roman policy-makers were increasingly alarmed by the presence of a Germanic tribe within the empire, and local officials made matters much worse by making outrageous demands on the refugees. The contemporary Roman author Ammianus Marcellinus tells that they demanded Gothic children as slaves, in return providing dead dogs for food. Faced with starvation, the Goths attempted to force the Romans to honour their treaty by applying increasing pressure. They broke into full rebellion after the local Roman commander attempted to assassinate their leaders, Fritigern and Alavivus. Fritigern survived the attempt and led his followers to raid Roman territory.

The Goths travelled from place to place with their families, slaves, and all their goods in wagons, hoping to receive or take a place they could settle. They defeated a regional Roman army at Marcianople in AD 376 and fought another, indecisive, battle with the Romans at Ad Salices in AD 377. Thanks to these two engagements, the Goths at Adrianople would mostly have been using Roman arms and armour. Their position, however, remained desperate.

THE CAMPAIGN

By AD 378, continuing Gothic rampages were proving to be a major embarrassment to the Eastern Roman emperor, Valens. He was an unpopular ruler, especially because of his religious policy, which favoured Arian Christians over both Catholics and non-Christians. Valens was, however, an experienced and successful commander, who had spent much of his reign in the field. About 50 years old at the time of the battle of Adrianople, he had won several noteworthy battles against Goths in the 360s. Valens was cautious, though. He arranged for the Western emperor, his

A gold coin of Roman emperor Valens (reigned AD 364–378), later converted into a necklace. Valens was one of the last Roman emperors to appear on coins in civilian garb.

nephew Gratian, to join forces with the Eastern field army in a joint attack against the Goths. It is clear from this level of preparation that the Roman emperors regarded the Goths as a major threat.

Valens assembled the Eastern field army outside Constantinople, in a temporary camp, and joined them there on 12 June. And then he waited for the Western army, while Gratian was delayed by a campaign in the West. By the time Valens and his army had sat doing nothing for two months, morale had plummeted. Moreover, Valens had received word that his co-emperor was bringing only a small force, not the major field army anticipated. According to Ammianus Marcellinus, Valens was also jealous of his nephew's military successes, and wanted all the glory of victory for himself.

Valens' opportunity appeared to have arrived when scouts reported that the Gothic force that was approaching contained only about 10,000 fighting men. In response to this news, Valens moved his force the short distance to Adrianople, close to which the Goths had been sighted. He then decided to wait no longer for his co-emperor, Gratian, both because he believed his Eastern army outnumbered that of the Goths and because the Gothic force was trying to manoeuvre between Valens and Constantinople in a bid to cut the Roman supply lines. Thus Valens decided to join battle on 9 August.

THE SIZE OF THE ARMIES

Valens' decision to fight brings to the forefront the question of how many Gothic and Roman warriors fought at Adrianople. Historians have credited the Goths with up to an impossible 200,000 fighting men, but recent scholarship has reconsidered the issue. The key to number estimates is the report given to Valens shortly before the battle that only about 10,000 Goths were in the opposing force.

It is interesting to note that Valens did not immediately decide to attack when he heard this but rather had his military council debate the next step to take, which suggests that the Roman army was not a great deal larger than the 10,000 reported

Goths. The number now most commonly accepted for the Roman army is about 15,000. While the entire Roman military in AD 378 consisted of about 500,000 men, the vast majority of these were permanently stationed on Rome's enormous frontier, while others were committed to ongoing wars against the Persians in the East and the Alamanni in the West.

The truth of the matter is that the Goths had more than 10,000 men; the remainder, perhaps as many as another 10,000, joined the battle at a key moment. So instead of the numerical superiority Valens had expected, the Romans were outnumbered, but not by a great deal. The Gothic leader Fritigern's eagerness to negotiate a peace with Valens bears out this argument in favour of roughly equal forces. On the night before the battle,

ALAN HEAVY CAVALRYMAN

It is likely that the Roman and Gothic forces at Adrianople both contained at least some heavy cavalry, sometimes known as cataphracts. Mounted on heavy horses that could bear the weight of their own body armour (27–36kg/60–80lb) as well as the weight of their armoured riders (an additional c. 18kg/40lb of metal), such horsemen could break up an enemy line by their sheer weight on impact. Since their armoured horses were less susceptible to crippling injuries, such troops were also more willing to close with the enemy, where their weapon of choice – the thrusting spear – could be devastatingly effective.

LOCATION

GOTHS

Adrianople ✝

• Constantinople

ASIA MINOR

Adrianople guarded the European land approach to Constantinople, one of the Roman Empire's great metropolitan centres. Valens met the Goths there to prevent their move into more heavily populated lands.

ADRIANOPLE

Emperor Valens concludes a treaty with the leader of the Goths in AD 376, just two years before the massacre at Adrianople.

THE OPPOSED FORCES

GOTHS (estimated)
Cavalry:	10,000
Infantry:	10,000
Total:	**20,000**

ROMANS (estimated)
Cavalry:	5000
Infantry:	10,000
Total:	**15,000**

Fritigern sent a priest to try to make peace. Just before the battle, as the Romans deployed, he sent two more sets of envoys. It has been suggested that Fritigern was just stalling, waiting for the other Gothic group, the Greuthungi, to join him. Since his envoys declared that Fritigern himself was willing to go to the Roman positions to speak directly to the emperor (in return for hostages), though, it appears much more likely that he was not willing to commit his troops to a near equal battle, even if he knew how close his reinforcements were. Similarly, Valens did in fact listen to the final envoys and began to arrange an exchange of hostages, a step that would have been highly unlikely if his numerical superiority had been so great that he felt completely confident of victory.

THE BATTLE

On the morning of 9 August AD 378 the Roman army marched about 13km (8 miles) from its camp outside Adrianople to where the Gothic army had been sighted north of the city. They reached the site at about 2.00 p.m. to discover that the Goths had assumed a defensive position. They had created a wagon circle, within which their women, children, elderly, slaves and goods were placed for safety. While some warriors would have been posted to defend the wagons, most of Fritigern's force was lined up along a ridge, from which they could charge the Roman army at full speed. Most of these Gothic fighters were probably infantry; it became clear at a decisive point in the battle that the cavalry had been off foraging in the neighbourhood.

When the Romans arrived, they began to deploy in a traditional formation: two lines of heavy infantry formed the centre with a screen of skirmishers thrown out before them, and cavalry on both flanks. Ammianus describes the Roman army as 'mixed', which probably means that it included many veterans and that the units were more diversified than usual. It is almost certain that the cavalry included both regular heavy cavalry and horse archers. Most of the heavy infantry would have been equipped with chain mail, round or oval shields, and the longer swords favoured by the late Roman military, and there were also archers. The Roman army then waited, without food or water in the August sun, while their emperor proceeded to negotiate with the Goths. Probably at this point, the Goths lit grassfires upwind of the Romans, so the Roman troops also had to cope with added smoke and heat.

At this stage, everything was shaping up for a classic late Roman battle, one that would rely mostly on infantry. The only essential difference from an earlier imperial army was that the number of cavalry had grown in the course of the fourth century, and formed perhaps one quarter of the Roman force at Adrianople. While the parley was still in progress, though, things started going wrong.

The fault appears to have lain with the badly disciplined Roman cavalry, which had never been fully integrated into Roman warfare and had for decades been unpredictable on the battlefield. The Roman right-wing cavalry advanced while the negotiations continued, probably to probe for weak points in the Gothic line. Without orders, two cavalry units, probably a mix of elite cavalry and horse archers, proceeded to attack the Goths. It seems likely that the ill-disciplined troopers had seriously underestimated the 'barbarians' and regarded them with a very risky contempt. The Roman cavalry attack, unplanned and unsupported, was soon driven back.

The engagement became general. The Romans were still not fully deployed from their march; the cavalry of the left wing in particular had been at the rear of the column and were not fully formed up.

Gothic cavalry charging. Unlike the nomadic peoples of the steppe, who relied on mounted archers, Gothic cavalry fought in Greco-Roman style, with short thrusting spears and swords.

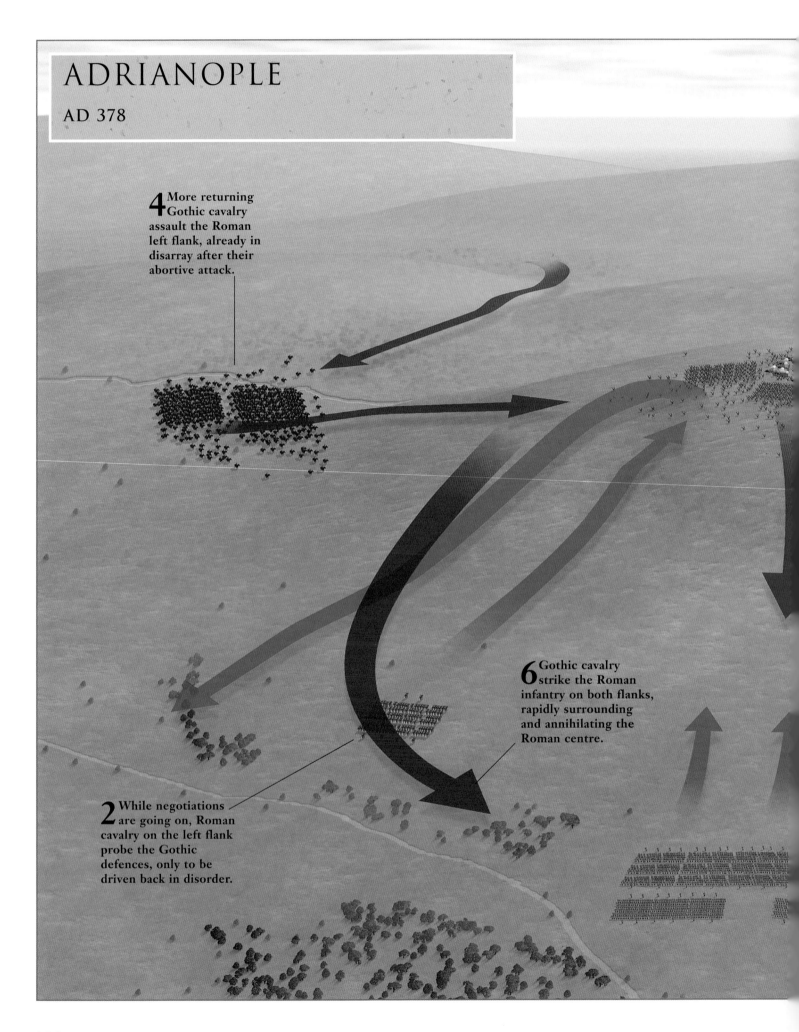

ADRIANOPLE

AD 378

4 More returning Gothic cavalry assault the Roman left flank, already in disarray after their abortive attack.

6 Gothic cavalry strike the Roman infantry on both flanks, rapidly surrounding and annihilating the Roman centre.

2 While negotiations are going on, Roman cavalry on the left flank probe the Gothic defences, only to be driven back in disorder.

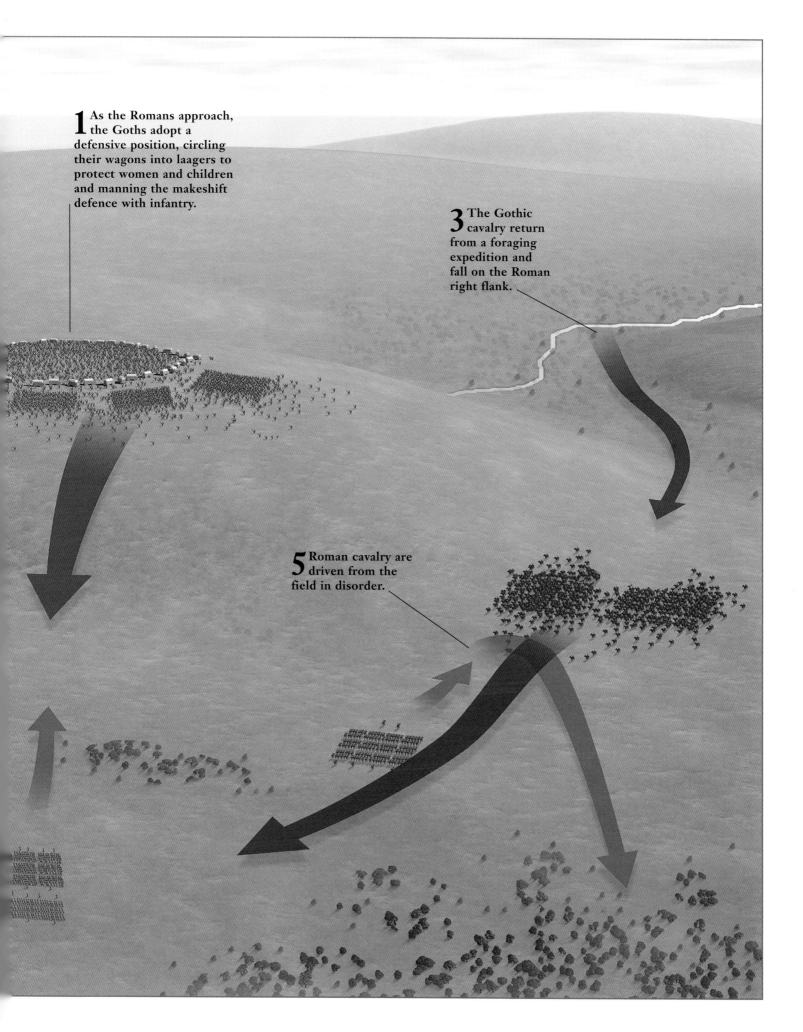

1 As the Romans approach, the Goths adopt a defensive position, circling their wagons into laagers to protect women and children and manning the makeshift defence with infantry.

3 The Gothic cavalry return from a foraging expedition and fall on the Roman right flank.

5 Roman cavalry are driven from the field in disorder.

Detail from the huge Ludovisi Sarcophagus (c. AD 250–260), showing Roman troops in battle against Germans. The sarcophagus is housed in the National Museum of Rome.

At this point, catastrophe struck the Romans. While the emperor's scouts had probably been accurate in reporting about 10,000 Goths in their camp, they had completely overlooked another large Gothic force, which had been foraging in the neighbourhood. This second group, Greuthungi under the command of Alatheus and Saphrax, also included Huns and Alans, and appears to have been mostly mounted. They appeared on the battlefield just as the Roman left wing's attack stalled and was certainly in need of reinforcement from their still unprepared comrades. The newly arrived Greuthungi achieved a complete tactical surprise. They fell on this Roman force and shattered it while the rest of the Roman left wing was still forming up to come to their support. The surviving Romans of the left wing fled for their lives, completely abandoning the battlefield.

While the Roman left wing was being routed, the Tervingi, who until then had held their position on the ridge, deployed all along the Roman infantry line. This action alone would not have caused serious worry – after all, Roman infantry had frequently defeated much larger Germanic armies in the recent past, relying on discipline and teamwork. But in this case, the Roman infantrymen were close to exhaustion from heat, hunger, and thirst before they began fighting. Much worse, the flight of the Roman cavalry had left the infantry flank fully exposed.

By the later fourth century, Roman infantry typically fought in very close order. When the Greuthungi cavalry, having driven their Roman counterparts from the field, returned and smashed into the open Roman left flank, few of the hapless infantrymen could even turn to respond effectively. Under heavy attack from both the front and the flank, the Romans were rapidly compressed still further, until they could not manoeuvre or even draw their swords to defend themselves. They soon found themselves mostly surrounded, Gothic archers adding to the confusion and panic by shooting deep into the Roman ranks.

Nonetheless, a part of the wing was sent in to attack, perhaps to draw the Goths' attention from inflicting further damage on the Roman right wing. At first this second cavalry group made good progress. They pushed the Goths back to their wagon circle, and nearly took the wagon laager itself in a spirited assault.

Most of the Roman soldiers soon broke and fled, to be cut down by Gothic cavalrymen as they tried to escape. Only two elite legions, maybe 1500 men (a fourth-century legion was only 1000 men at full strength), held firm in a desperate last stand. Emperor Valens was apparently with them. One account tells that he ordered two commanders to bring up the Roman reserves – only to find that the reserves had been among the first to flee, at the same time that the cavalry left the field. It is unlikely that any of these men survived; the emperor himself certainly did not. There are two alternative stories of Valens' death. According to one, he was killed by an arrow, and his body was never found in the carnage. A more detailed report tells that Valens was wounded, then taken to a nearby farmhouse by a few members of his bodyguard. A group of Goths attacked and, meeting resistance, burned the place down without realizing that such a valuable potential captive was inside. In all, Ammianus Marcellinus tells that two-thirds of the Roman army was left dead on the battlefield, probably amounting to some 10,000 men.

WHAT WENT WRONG?

Historians used to credit the Gothic victory to their supposed use of the stirrup, an invention that did not in fact reach Europe for several more centuries. In reality, the Roman and Gothic armies, both cavalry and infantry, would have had quite similar equipment. Nor did a vast horde of barbarians simply overwhelm a much smaller Roman force; if the Goths enjoyed numerical superiority, it was not too great. Instead, one must look to failures in the Roman army at Adrianople when seeking reasons for this military disaster. Three problems in particular stand out: 1) Low morale. The Roman army that fought at Adrianople was tired, hungry and thirsty. Moreover, their ranks were torn by religious controversy between Arian Christians, Catholic Christians and non-Christians. Many soldiers must have seen the defeat, as contemporary Catholic churchmen did, as a divine judgment against Emperor Valens for supporting the Arians. 2) Poor scouting. A traditional Roman weakness, in this case the misinformation provided by inadequate or untrained scouts was catastrophic. 3) Poorly trained and disciplined cavalry. While the Roman army employed increasing numbers of cavalry in the fourth century, during this period of transition to the largely cavalry forces of the Byzantine Empire this branch of the army appears to have been badly officered and was several times an embarrassment on the battlefield.

AFTERMATH

On 10 August, the day after the battle, the Gothic army tried to take Adrianople by assault, aiming in particular for the imperial treasury that had been left there. They failed, having no experience of attacking walled cities, and probably suffered greater losses there than they had in the main battle. So they went on to loot Thrace.

Emperor Theodosius I (*c.* AD 346–395) replaced the dead Valens, and both he and the Western emperor Gratian devoted their energies to defeating the Goths. They could not do so, nor could the Goths achieve another significant victory over the new Roman armies that came against them. Finally, after four years of warfare, in AD 382 the two sides made another treaty. The terms were essentially the same as the treaty of AD 376: the Goths were to receive land for settlement and autonomous status within the Roman Empire, in return for which they would provide warriors for Rome's armies.

Things appeared to be back where they had started, as if the battle of Adrianople were only a bad dream. In reality, though, much had changed. The Romans who fell at Adrianople included a high proportion of veterans, who would have been an inestimable help in ongoing battles against the Goths and Rome's other enemies. More importantly, the Roman authorities were forced to accept, once and for all, the presence of Germanic tribes on Roman soil. The Goths had proven to themselves and to the world that they could meet and defeat a Roman emperor in the field, which emboldened them in their demands. If it had not been for Adrianople, the Goths would surely never have dreamed of the course that led them, in AD 410, to sack the city of Rome itself.

Emperor Theodosius I (reigned AD 379–395). A successful general before being named Eastern emperor, Theodosius later reigned as sole ruler of a reunited empire, the last emperor to do so.

HASTINGS
1066

MEDIEVAL WARFARE HAD VERY FEW DECISIVE MILITARY ENGAGEMENTS, BUT ONE CERTAINLY WAS THE BATTLE OF HASTINGS, FOUGHT BETWEEN DUKE WILLIAM THE CONQUEROR'S INVADING NORMAN TROOPS AND KING HAROLD II GODWINSON'S ANGLO-SAXON ARMY. THE BATTLE WOULD LEAD TO A NEW ERA IN ENGLISH HISTORY.

WHY DID IT HAPPEN?

WHO A Norman army under William the Conqueror (1028–87) invaded England and fought a battle against an Anglo-Saxon force led by King Harold II Godwinson (c.1022–66).

WHAT The battle was fought largely between Norman cavalry who charged several times up a hill into a shield wall formed by Anglo-Saxon infantry.

WHERE At Senlac Hill, 11.2km (7 miles) north of Hastings, now called Battle.

WHEN 14 October 1066.

WHY William the Conqueror fought the battle in an effort to press his claim to the throne of England.

OUTCOME In a lengthy battle, after numerous Norman cavalry charges up Senlac Hill against the Anglo-Saxon shield wall, and two feigned retreats, many of the Anglo-Saxon infantry broke from their formation and ran down the hill into defeat.

It would still take Duke William time to complete his conquest of the rest of England; however, his victory gave him almost decisive control over the country, especially as not only Harold Godwinson, but also his two brothers, Gyrth and Leofwine, were slain. Duke William of Normandy's conquest of England in 1066 was instigated by the political chaos of the kingdom of the previous 50 years. After fending off more than two centuries of Viking invasions, in 1013 England finally fell to the Danish king, Svein Forkbeard, who defeated and slew King Ethelred II. Ethelred's reign had never been secure, and in order to preserve power in his kingdom, in 1002 he married Emma, daughter of Duke Richard I of Normandy. This move

A romantic portrayal of William the Conqueror from a nineteenth-century illustration. Born an illegitimate son of Duke Robert of Normandy, he became one of the greatest military leaders in history, not only fighting off rebels in his own duchy, but also conquering Maine, parts of Brittany, and England.

had not worked, as Svein Forkbeard's conquest proved. Yet, Emma's marriage to Ethelred, and then to Svein's successor, Cnut, introduced Normandy in a significant way into the political future of England.

Cnut ruled England until 1035, but once he died a succession crisis beset the kingdom. Two of Cnut's sons claimed the English throne: one, Harold I Harefoot, although an illegitimate son by Cnut's mistress, Ælfgifu, was in England at the time of the death of his father and thus became king. The other claimant, Harthacnut, was Cnut's legitimate son, by Emma, but he was ruling Denmark. However, in 1039 or 1040, Harold died, and Harthacnut returned to England and ascended the throne. However, his reign also was short, and he died in 1042.

EDWARD THE CONFESSOR

Neither of these kings had children, and with Cnut's line ended, the throne passed to Ethelred's remaining son, Edward the Confessor, who had been living in exile in Normandy. Edward's succession was welcomed. He further shored up his rule by marrying Edith, the only daughter of Godwin, the most powerful earl in England, and appointing two of her brothers to earldoms. The second of these, Harold, would succeed his father as Earl of Wessex in 1053, serving for the remaining years of Edward's reign as the chief counsellor to the king. This was when William the Conqueror appeared on the scene. He had become Duke of Normandy in 1035, but he was the illegitimate son of Duke Robert of Normandy, who had died on pilgrimage to the Holy Land. He was also young and was met immediately by rebellions among his nobles, but these were put down rather quickly, at first by barons loyal to William and later by the duke himself. William the Conqueror began to gain military experience and to develop expertise in generalship, especially when it came to waging cavalry warfare. By 1066, he had won not only Normandy, but also the county of Maine and parts of the counties of Brittany and Ponthieu.

Before 1052, William had little interaction with England. During that year, while Earl Godwin and his family were in

exile, he visited the island. It is this visit that most historians link to the promise of his inheritance of the throne, although when the Godwin family returned shortly thereafter – and despite Godwin's death the following year – it was Harold, not the Duke of Normandy, who became the obvious heir to Edward the Confessor's throne. But sometime in 1063–64 Harold is purported to have visited Normandy, either being driven off course while at sea or for a diplomatic meeting with William. Most importantly, Norman sources claim that while in Normandy Harold swore his allegiance to the Norman duke and his willingness to aid him in acquiring the English throne after Edward died.

CONTESTED SUCCESSION

However, even if this made William the rightful heir to the throne of England, on his deathbed, on 5 January 1066, Edward the Confessor recognized Harold Godwinson as the new King of England.

However, three claimants to the English crown disputed Harold's coronation. Svein

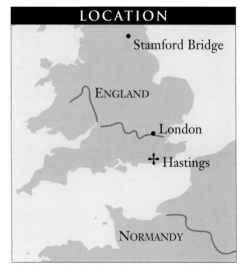

Landing on England's southern coast near Hastings, William quickly built five motte-and-bailey castles, establishing a foothold. Harold's march to counter this incursion met the invader at Senlac Hill.

William the Conqueror's campaign to gain the English throne is depicted here in the Bayeux Tapestry. In the top sequence, after being shipwrecked in France, the chief English earl, Harold Godwinson, is rescued from a Breton lord by William and his Norman cavalry. In the second panel, a grateful Harold promises to support William's claim by making an oath on two relics. He then returns by Norman ship to England. And in the third panel an ailing King Edward the Confessor dies. He is carried for burial to Westminster Abbey, whereupon Harold Godwinson, breaking his oath to the Duke of Normandy, takes the English throne and thereby provokes William's conquest.

Estrithson, King of Denmark, whose claim was based on his kinship to Cnut, decided not to do anything about it. The other two, King Harald Hardrada of Norway and Duke William of Normandy, planned to immediately invade England. Harald Hardrada's claim to the English throne was weak and distant; mostly he believed that England had been weakened by the succession of Harold Godwinson, a belief seemingly confirmed by Harold's estranged brother, Tostig Godwinson, who had fled to Norway after being outlawed in 1065. Tostig was also willing to accompany Harald's Norwegian army on their invasion of England.

THE CAMPAIGN

Harald Hardrada and William the Conqueror were ready to launch their invasions by the summer of 1066. Harold

Godwinson certainly knew that the latter was planning an attack on his kingdom; he may also have thought that William was the greater of the two threats, or he may not have known of Harald Hardrada's plans, or even of Tostig's flight to him. Whatever the reason, his army remained waiting for William's invasion along the southern coast of England until 8 September.

However, because of poor weather in the English Channel, William had been unable to launch his invasion. Harald Hardrada was able to set sail, however, and in September 1066 he went first to the Orkney Islands and then to Scotland, where a few allied troops – although not many – joined his army. Finally, the Norwegians sailed along the northeastern coast of England to the Humber River. On 20 September, Harald landed his fleet in the Humber at Ricall and marched towards

York. In the way of his march, at Fulford Gate outside York, were the armies of two English earls, the brothers Morkere of Northumbria and Edwin of Mercia. Yet they proved no match for the much more numerous and skilled Norwegians, who quickly won the battle.

Harald Hardrada proceeded to York, where the town's leaders surrendered to him, and then he marched to Stamford Bridge, where he waited for the payment of promised tribute. His soldiers could relax in the knowledge that there was no one else in northern England to oppose him.

Or so they thought. It is not known when Harold learned of the Norwegian invasion nor when he began his army's march north to counter the threat. It is certain, however, that what he accomplished was an impressive feat – a swift march of his army to Tadcaster and then on to York, 306km (190 miles) north of London. It was achieved at an incredible pace of 32–40km (20–25 miles) per day.

Four days after Harald Hardrada landed at Ricall and no more than two days after he had arrived at Stamford Bridge, on 24 September, the English forces also arrived at the Humber River, in Tadcaster, and the next day they marched through York to Stamford Bridge. Their early morning approach completely surprised the Norwegians, some of whom were caught across the Derwent River away from their camp and their armour. The Battle of

The Norman conquest of England remained of interest throughout the Middle Ages as evidenced in this illumination from a manuscript of miscellaneous chronicles painted between 1280 and 1300 and housed today in the British Library. Accuracy was clearly not an issue, as it shows both sides on horseback and William personally killing Harold.

Stamford Bridge was over quickly, with the Norwegians decidedly defeated, although how this was accomplished cannot be determined from contemporary sources. Both Harald Hardrada and Tostig Godwinson were slain.

Two days after Stamford Bridge, while Harold Godwinson and his men enjoyed

---

English shield wall, mid-eleventh century. The troops are mainly spearmen, although some hold axes and swords. The formation depended upon the mutual support of the men within it for its strength.

THE OPPOSED FORCES

NORMANS (estimated)

Cavalry:	1–2000
Infantry:	5–6000
Total:	**6–8000**

ANGLO-SAXONS (estimated)

Huscarls:	1000
Infantry:	5–6000
Total:	**6–7000**

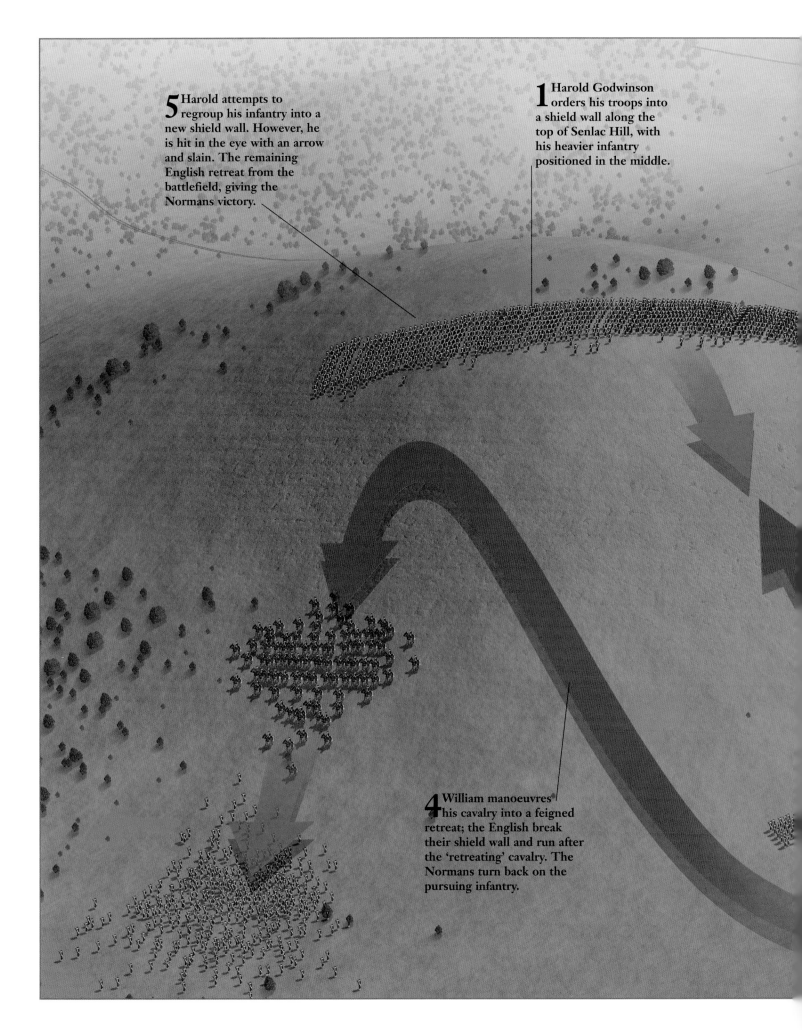

5 Harold attempts to regroup his infantry into a new shield wall. However, he is hit in the eye with an arrow and slain. The remaining English retreat from the battlefield, giving the Normans victory.

1 Harold Godwinson orders his troops into a shield wall along the top of Senlac Hill, with his heavier infantry positioned in the middle.

4 William manoeuvres his cavalry into a feigned retreat; the English break their shield wall and run after the 'retreating' cavalry. The Normans turn back on the pursuing infantry.

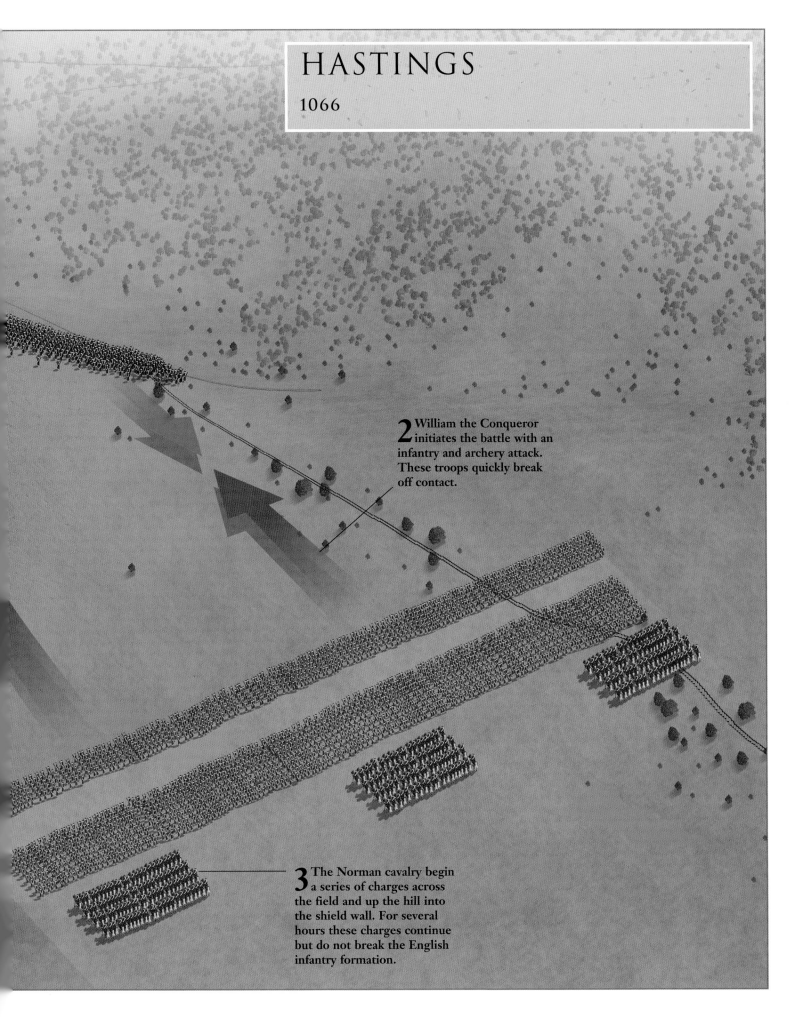

HASTINGS
1066

2 William the Conqueror initiates the battle with an infantry and archery attack. These troops quickly break off contact.

3 The Norman cavalry begin a series of charges across the field and up the hill into the shield wall. For several hours these charges continue but do not break the English infantry formation.

HASTINGS

The Bayeux Tapestry, perhaps the most famous artistic depiction of medieval warfare, shows William the Conqueror's campaign to gain the English throne. This scene portrays the attack of Norman cavalry against the Anglo-Saxon infantry shield wall at the Battle of Hastings. Note that while one or two cavalry lances are shown to be couched, most are thrust down on the infantry, indicating that at this time there was no single preferred position.

their victory celebrations in York, William the Conqueror got his favourable weather and crossed the English Channel. His army landed without opposition at Pevensey on the south coast of England. They immediately erected an earth-and-wood motte-and-bailey castle, the first of five such constructions that William built in England before the Battle of Hastings. The castles were intended to provide the Normans with permanent bases from which they could operate and reinforce, in the

event that the conquest of England turned into a lengthy campaign. William's permanent positions would also have the effect of drawing Harold towards him and precipitating battle.

DISPOSITIONS

King Harold Godwinson learned of the Norman landing only a few days later, probably on or around 1 October. The king retraced his route. Repeating the speed of his earlier march, he passed through London and continued for another 80–96km (50–60 miles) to Senlac Hill. Here, some 600–800m (656–731 yards) along the crest, or slightly below it, facing south, he found terrain that he believed was favourable for a stand against the invading Normans. He estimated, correctly, that William wanted to fight a battle, and that this would keep the Duke of Normandy from avoiding his army, even if they occupied the better position.

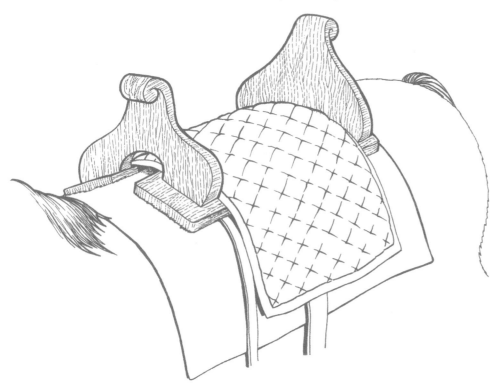

Technological improvements to the saddle, most notably the high cantle and pommel invented in the early twelfth century, increased the stability of a cavalry soldier. A high cantle, sitting against the rider's back, prevented him being thrown over the horse's rump. An equally high pommel protected the rider's genitals and lower stomach as well as preventing him being thrown over his horse's head.

Harold lined up his troops using a well-known tactic, the shield wall. His infantry and dismounted cavalry stood in a tightly packed formation, their shields overlapping one another in what was in effect a field fortification. If they could hold their position, it was almost impossible to break through this formation. The Anglo-Saxons were experienced warriors, many of whom had served with Harold in his victorious attacks on the Welsh in 1063 and all of whom had fought at the Battle of Stamford Bridge. In the centre of the shield wall fought the royal huscarls, Harold's most trusted and skilled troops, armoured in lengthy mail coats and able to fight with all weapons, but especially feared for their use of the two-handed battle-axe. On the wings of the shield wall were the fyrd, a well-trained and skilled militia, adept with the spear and sword. They, too, were well armed and well armoured. A few archers also fought with the English forces, although their numbers were likely small.

While his army was not entirely composed of cavalry, they were certainly

NORMAN CAVALRY

During the eleventh century, Norman horsemen dominated five military theatres: England, northern France, southern Italy, Sicily and the Holy Land. Their body armour, called a hauberk by this time, was mail, made in one piece. Most hauberks reached to the knees and were divided down the front and back by slits that allowed greater freedom of movement and comfort to a horseman. Some leaders and other more wealthy soldiers were also outfitted in mail leggings, or chausses. Other defensive equipment included the kite shield and helmet. A long lance was the chief weapon of the Norman horseman, while a sword could be used for close-combat situations.

King Harold II Godwinson was the son of the powerful Earl Godwin. Before ascending to the throne of England, Harold had served King Edward the Confessor as earl, first of East Anglia and then of Wessex, since 1044–45. His inheritance of the crown in January 1066 from the childless Edward was contested by the Kings of Denmark and Norway and the Duke of Normandy.

HAROLD.

Second Son of Godwin Earl of Kent, in 1065. seized the Crown Sep.3.1066. Will.™ Duke of Normandy made a descent upon the Coast of Sussex, with a great Army, to claim the Crown of England; came to an Engagement with Harold, 14. Oct. who was killed on the Spot, and his Army entirely defeated. He was bur.⁴ at Waltham Abbey in Essex.

This Portrait is taken from one of his Coins. NB. the Drapery is added.

the primary arm of William the Conqueror's force at Hastings. These horsemen were also very experienced warriors, with many having served the duke in his military adventures for many years. Most were from Normandy, but others had been recruited from the counties of Boulogne and Flanders. These, too, were quite experienced men. This was undoubtedly the most superb cavalry force in Europe since the time of Charlemagne.

William's tactics at the Battle of Hastings were simple, but also quite risky: his cavalry were to charge up the hill against the Anglo-Saxon shield wall. If stopped, they were to retreat, regroup, and charge again and again. It was hoped that this charge would break the line and send his opponents in rout from the field. William reasoned that under these continuous charges the English shield wall would eventually weaken, giving the Normans victory. There were also Norman archers and footsoldiers at the Battle of Hastings, but their roles, like their counterparts', seem to have been limited.

THE BATTLE BEGINS

William the Conqueror began the battle early in the morning by dividing his cavalry into three divisions, with most historians believing that these were then ordered across a single front. The Norman cavalry, led by William himself, were in the centre; on his left were Breton cavalry; and on his right were a mixture of other mounted soldiers, called 'French' by most Norman chroniclers, but probably Flemish and Boulognese cavalry. In front of the cavalry lines were the Norman archers and infantry.

These dismounted Norman troops began the battle by attacking the English infantry, but this turned out to be rather unimportant to the outcome. This may have been William's decision. He may have curtailed his infantry's attacks, as it was not honourable to his more noble cavalry to keep them out of the battle for too long. The cavalry charges soon began; 'those who were last became first', wrote the eyewitness William of Poitiers, referring to the reversal in the Norman formation.

Contemporary sources claim that the Norman cavalry was not as numerous as their Anglo-Saxon infantry opponents. They delivered their initial charge with a heroism equalled by few other warriors in history, 'brave to the extreme', according to William of Malmesbury. But this charge was halted by the shield wall. So, too, was the next charge, and the next, and the next. No one, contemporary or modern, can agree on just how many cavalry charges were made by the Normans at the Battle of Hastings. But all were stopped by the extremely

disciplined English footsoldiers, who could not be moved from their strong defensive position. William of Poitiers describes the scene thus: 'this was a strange kind of battle, one side with all the mobility and initiative, and the other just resisting as though rooted to the soil.'

It was also quite a long battle. Most medieval battles were decided in a very short time, no more than an hour or even less. But not the Battle of Hastings. The

Norman cavalry delivered charge after charge. None broke the English infantry shield wall. Few were killed or wounded on either side, with the horses stopping their assaults on the infantry before actually clashing with them. However, at one time, well into the battle, a rumour passed through the Norman ranks that William the Conqueror had fallen. In an era before heraldry, such a mistake was excusable, as all Norman horsemen looked alike, as

The death of King Harold as recorded in the Bayeux Tapestry. In this panel he is shot in the eye with an arrow. In the following panel he is shown cut down by a sword. Other contemporary sources confirm these methods of death. They also indicate that his body was so mutilated following the battle that it could only be identified by his mistress, Edith Swan's Neck.

Since the time of the Battle of Hastings, the battlefield has been secured. On the crest of Senlac Hill, near the site of the Anglo-Saxon shield wall (and from where this photo was taken), William the Conqueror built an abbey, in part as penance for his participation in the battle.

confirmed by the contemporary Bayeux Tapestry. William is also shown in the tapestry to quash this rumour by lifting his helmet and showing his face. His cavalry immediately regrouped for another charge.

FEIGNED RETREAT

That William was still fighting with them seemed to re-energize the Norman cavalry, enough at least to pull off one of the most widely used but difficult cavalry tactics: the feigned retreat. Recorded in Vegetius' *De re militari* – the military manual read most frequently in the Middle Ages – the feigned

retreat demanded skill and discipline, for those 'retreating' had to look as though they were genuinely fleeing the battlefield, only to wheel and charge again in formation and unity. Such a tactic could not be performed too early in the battle, and rarely more than once – although at Hastings, the Normans attempted two feigned retreats, according to eyewitness testimony. Should a feigned retreat work, however, usually by drawing the opposing line into a celebratory pursuit, the battle would be over quickly. On the other hand, should it not work, military history had shown that, demoralized by

their failure, those who had attempted the tactic might actually flee the field in earnest.

At Hastings, the second feigned retreat worked well. Some Anglo-Saxon troops were able to remain in their lines, but many others broke and pursued the 'retreating' Normans, only to realize too late that the cavalry had turned around and returned to the attack. Very few of the English troops who had run down the hill after the Normans could escape the re-charging horsemen and they were ridden down and slain. Among these were Harold's two brothers, Gyrth and Leofwine, who had served as his lieutenants that day.

The battle had changed so quickly that Harold Godwinson could do little more than try to regroup those soldiers who had not fallen for the Normans' tactical trick. He attempted to form them again into a shield wall; however, this group proved to be too

fatigued and disorganized to resist the Normans for long. They remained with their king until he was killed, the Bayeux Tapestry and William of Poitiers recording that this was by an arrow that struck him in the eye.

AFTERMATH

The last Anglo-Saxon/Anglo-Scandinavian army had been defeated, and it was a defeat from which the remaining military and governmental powers in England could not recover. William still had to face some opposition in the kingdom, primarily in the north from Earls Edwin and Morkere, who had been defeated at Fulford Gate and had not followed Harold Godwinson to Hastings. But they were defeated quite easily. William the Bastard, Duke of Normandy and Count of Maine, had become William the Conqueror, King of England, as well.

The Norman army as displayed in the Bayeux Tapestry consists of cavalry and archers. Other contemporary sources indicate that the cavalry greatly outnumbered the archers, but the latter's role in the death of King Harold Godwinson no doubt accounts for their exaggerated presence.

The most fearsome military tactic of the Middle Ages was perhaps the cavalry charge, as demonstrated here by Norman horse. At a time when success in battle often depended more on forcing one's enemies to flee the battlefield than on actually killing them, resisting such a charge depended on the discipline of much lower-class infantry troops and the leadership of their officers.

JERUSALEM
1099

ON 15 JULY 1099, THE FIRST CRUSADE REACHED ITS ULTIMATE GOAL – THE CHURCH OF THE HOLY SEPULCHRE – BUT ONLY AFTER A BLOODY ASSAULT THAT SHOWED YET AGAIN THE VERSATILITY, MILITARY SKILL, AND PERSEVERANCE OF THE CRUSADER FORCES.

WHY DID IT HAPPEN?

WHO The remnants of the Christian armies of the First Crusade fought the Fatimid Egyptian garrison of Jerusalem, under the command of the governor Iftikhar-ad-Daulah.

WHAT In an extended and hard-fought assault, the Crusaders broke into Jerusalem and claimed it as Christian territory.

WHERE Jerusalem.

WHEN 13–15 July 1099.

WHY By 1099 the whole focus of the First Crusade had been the conquest of the city of Jerusalem, to regain the city of Christ's death and resurrection as the natural and God-given possession of Christendom.

OUTCOME The Crusaders took the city and established a Christian state with Jerusalem as its capital, electing Duke Godfrey of Lorraine as 'advocate' of the Holy Sepulchre.

It took a very long time for the Christian forces of the First Crusade to reach Jerusalem, their ultimate goal. While the Crusaders were still at Antioch, far to the north, another army had conquered Jerusalem – that of the Egyptian Fatimid Caliphate, a Shi'ite state that had long fought the Turks for control of Palestine. The Fatimid vizier of Egypt almost immediately opened negotiations with the leaders of the Christian army, apparently believing that the Crusaders were mostly concerned with halting Turkish aggression and territorial gain. Some of the Crusade leaders were indeed content to secure territories such as Antioch and Edessa, and lent the Fatimids a willing ear. It took a near revolt by the Crusader rank and file to force

the army back onto the road towards Jerusalem. The renewal of the march apparently took the Fatimids by surprise. Their recently gained territory was unprepared for war, with small garrisons that could not hope to keep out the Crusaders.

Thus the Crusaders' march south was largely peaceful. Some Fatimid cities on the coast negotiated free passage for the Crusaders; others, resenting Fatimid encroachment, even promised to accept Crusader overlordship – if the Crusaders succeeded in conquering Egypt. The major port of Jaffa was completely abandoned before the Crusaders got there, its walls slighted so the Crusaders could not use them for defence.

The Citadel of Jerusalem that can be seen today was built in the sixteenth century. A citadel has stood on this site, however, since the period of the ancient Israelite monarchy.

Jerusalem itself was only moderately ready to withstand a siege. The Fatimids had apparently repaired the walls after their seizure of the city in August 1098. The garrison, however, does not appear to have been large, although extant sources give us little clue of its size. We know it was a mixed force; Crusader accounts mention especially the presence of Ethiopian troops. At the last minute, the Fatimid vizier sent 400 elite cavalry to reinforce the defenders. It is unlikely that the garrison numbered more than 2000–3000. The Fatimid governor, Iftikhar-ad-Daulah, made no effort to weaken the Crusader army with sallies before the assault. After the assault, he retreated to the citadel but surrendered almost immediately, suggesting that at least by that point in the battle he did not have sufficient manpower to put up an effective fight. The fear of internal treachery also led the governor to expel most of the Christian population from the city, lest one of them open the city to their co-religionists, as had happened at Antioch.

PREPARING TO ATTACK

The Crusader army reached Jerusalem on 7 June 1099, walking barefoot as penitents and overcome with joy at the sight of the holy city. Almost immediately, the council of Crusade leaders planned an assault. They had good reason to hurry. Not only were the Crusaders eager to reach the city, which most of them had spent three years of their lives to gain, but once again the Crusaders were in a desperate situation. They were far from any Christian assistance. Food supplies were adequate, but the only reliable water source was over 2km (1.3 miles) away from the Crusader camps.

Worst of all, the Crusaders intercepted messengers who revealed (under torture) that a large Egyptian relief force was on its way to Jerusalem. A siege was simply not an option. The Crusaders did not have time for such a measure, and could not even fully invest the city for fear of sudden surprise assaults from the defenders if they split up their forces into small groups. Instead, the Christians concentrated their forces near Jerusalem's western walls, the northern French forces to the north and Raymond of Toulouse's Provencals further south.

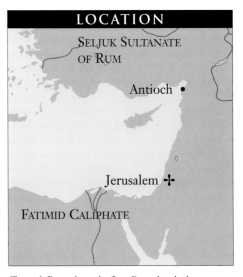

Raymond soon decided that the section of defences he faced was too strong to penetrate, and moved to the southwest corner of the city, despite the objections of many of his own men.

The Crusaders attempted an escalade on 13 June. Apparently, the Crusade leaders, who had quarrelled seriously ever since Antioch, disagreed on this approach, and Count Raymond of Toulouse and his Provencal army did not take part in the assault at all. The attack was pitiful. The Crusader assault was spirited but, unable to find much wood for siege equipment, they had only a single scaling ladder. Despite their best efforts, the attacking Christians were soon driven off.

Clearly, the city would not fall without proper siege equipment, but finding the heavy timber and necessary expertise was a serious problem – until a fleet of six Italian

LOCATION

SELJUK SULTANATE OF RUM

Antioch •

Jerusalem ✝

FATIMID CALIPHATE

To reach Jerusalem, the first Crusaders had to pass through the Sultanate of Rum in Asia Minor, then march down the coastal road via Antioch. Jerusalem itself is well inland.

JERUSALEM

The crusaders used siege engines like this traction trebuchet in their attack on Jerusalem. A team of men would heave the ropes together on command, making the bowl with its ammunition shoot upwards.

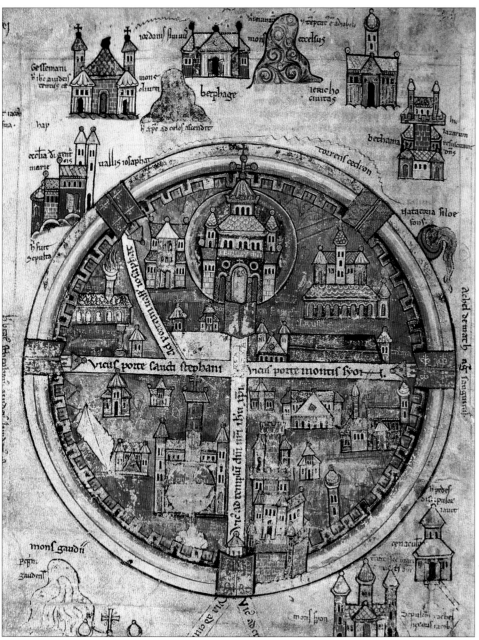

ships arrived at Jaffa on 17 June, carrying supplies and the vital timber. The Crusaders sent a large force to protect the sailors in the devastated port, only to be ambushed while on their way to the coast. The fleet itself was trapped in the harbour by an Egyptian fleet. So the sailors burned five of their ships (one escaped to the open sea), then marched to the Crusader camp outside Jerusalem with their large supply train.

The sailors included expert woodworkers; Count Raymond hired a Genoese craftsman to build him a siege tower. With wood and workers now available, the Crusaders began to prepare for a fresh assault. They built two siege towers, one in the northern French camp to the north of the city, and one in the Provencal camp to the south; the northern French also constructed a very large ram, suspended in a framework that was moved on rollers or wheels. The Crusaders also constructed many more assault ladders and a number of mangonels and other stone- and bolt-throwing devices. They also made smaller siege equipment such as mantlets to protect the men dragging the towers and ram up to the walls. To complete their preparations, on 8 July the Crusaders

In this medieval map of Jerusalem, from Robert the Monk's chronicle of the First Crusade, Jerusalem is a microcosm of the world as medieval geographers perceived it.

conducted a penitential procession around the walls of Jerusalem, culminating in sermons on the Mount of Olives. Their leaders managed at least a superficial reconciliation on this occasion.

THE BATTLE

The Crusaders made two largely independent assaults on Jerusalem, one by the northern French army (commanded by Duke Godfrey of Lorraine, Tancred, Duke Robert of Normandy and Hugh of Vermandois) and one by the Provencals under Count Raymond. While this may have been a purposeful tactic to weaken the garrison by forcing them to fight at two widely separated points, Crusade chronicles suggest that the immediate reason was Count Raymond's ongoing quarrel with the northern French leaders.

The first stages of the assault began on 9 July with the long, dangerous process of levelling ground and filling in the ditch before the walls so that the siege equipment could be moved in close enough. The process was straightforward for the southern army, but in the north, however,

the Crusade leaders made a move that caught the defenders by surprise. On the night of 9–10 July they partially disassembled the siege tower that had been built in Duke Godfrey's camp, and moved it about 1km (0.6 miles) further north, positioning it to assault the wall about 100m (300 feet) from Herod's Gate. The defenders had been strengthening the defences closest to the site where the siege tower was being built, but had no time to do the same at the new position. After moving the tower, the northern Crusaders proceeded to fill in the ditch and level the ground, then set up their siege tower, ram and three mangonels.

The assault proper commenced on Wednesday 13 July at the north of the city. Jerusalem's defences here consisted of a forewall and a wider, higher inner wall; the battle on 13 and 14 July was for control of the forewall. The French Crusaders brought their ram up to the wall, with the defenders trying to stop them with a barrage of missiles. By aiming their mangonels at the troops on the walls, the Crusaders were also able to inflict serious

THE OPPOSED FORCES

FATIMID GARRISON
  Infantry: No good estimate exists.
  Force certainly included Arabs and
  Ethiopians as well as Egyptians.
  Cavalry:
    Elite Egyptian horsemen   400
  Total: **10,000**

CRUSADER ARMY
  Knights: 1200–1300
  Infantry: c. 12,000
  Total: **c. 13,200**

This fourteenth-century illustration shows Godfrey of Lorraine, after he has become ruler of Jerusalem, commanding a siege. In reality, bowmen at ground level would have been at a serious disadvantage against a city's defenders.

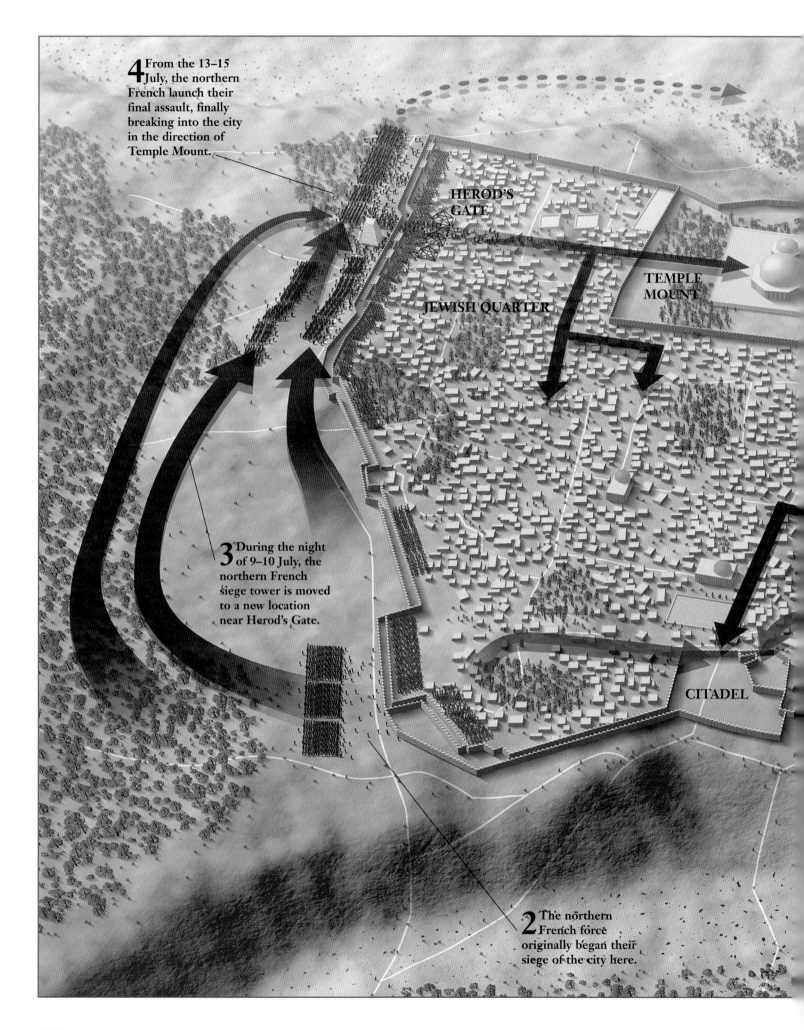

4 From the 13–15 July, the northern French launch their final assault, finally breaking into the city in the direction of Temple Mount.

HEROD'S GATE

TEMPLE MOUNT

JEWISH QUARTER

3 During the night of 9–10 July, the northern French siege tower is moved to a new location near Herod's Gate.

CITADEL

2 The northern French force originally began their siege of the city here.

JERUSALEM

1099

1 Route of crusader penitential procession on 8 July, ending at the Mount of Olives.

6 As word spreads that the crusaders have broken into the city, the Fatimid garrison flees to the citadel, where they are trapped and eventually slaughtered.

SIEGE ARTILLERY

ZION GATE

5 A second assault comes from the other side of the city from the Provençal troops, led by Count Raymond of Toulouse.

JERUSALEM

damage on the Muslims. As the Crusaders positioned the ram at the foot of the wall, the enemy worked desperately to burn it, with flaming arrows, fire pots and even Greek fire, while the Crusaders expended much of their precious water to protect it. Despite the defenders' efforts, the men operating the ram succeeded in bringing down a portion of the outer wall.

The inner wall was apparently too strong for the ram, and the space was very narrow, causing the ram itself to block the progress of the siege tower. So the Christians now set the ram alight themselves, while the defenders desperately tried to put out the flames. When the ram was finally destroyed, the Crusaders were able to move their siege tower close to the inner wall. The tower was a massive structure, standing about 15–17m (49–56ft)

high and looming above the wall. As was usual in such situations, the tower's purpose was to act as a platform for firing down on the wall's defenders, thus making it possible for other attackers to raise siege ladders and climb the walls in relative safety. The Muslim soldiers were well aware of their danger and aimed a large number of mangonels against the tower, but the Crusaders had covered the structure with woven osiers to buffer it from the shock of stones striking; they had also covered it with wet hides so that the defenders could not set it alight. As the tower reached the wall, the defenders even tried to tip it over, swinging a heavy beam against it that they had suspended with ropes between two of the wall's towers; the Crusaders, however, succeeded in cutting the ropes that supported the beam, using blades attached to long poles for the purpose.

Duke Godfrey and his brother Eustace commanded from the top of the siege tower, showing how much the Crusader plan depended on it. In its shadow, forces still on the ground were able to bring up a number of ladders. More unusually, some men in the siege tower also got onto the wall, climbing over on a tree trunk. Once on the walls, the Crusaders spread out, some of them opening the Josaphat Gate some distance to the east to admit their compatriots.

THE SOUTHERN ASSAULT

While the northern assault had the advantage of surprise over enemies who did not have time to reinforce the walls there, the southern assault, led by Raymond of Toulouse, had been forced to prepare in full sight of the enemy. While the northerners fought for the forewall on their side of the city, the Provencals continued to fill in the ditch before the southern wall, a necessary step before moving their siege tower forward. Their main defence against missiles from the walls would have been large shields made of woven branches. The defenders fought with fire, to very good effect. When, on the morning of 15 July, the Christians brought their petrariae (large stone-slinging engines) forward, the enemy made fireballs of fat, hair and other combustibles, and launched them against the Crusader machines, succeeding in

Joseph-François Michaud's 1875 History of the Crusades *idolized Duke Godfrey of Lorraine. In this illustration from Michaud's history, by Gustav Doré, Godfrey is shown leading his troops into the city.*

This illustration by M Meredith Williams (1910) shows the men from Duke Godfrey's siege tower battling their way onto the wall of Jerusalem, as their comrades mount scaling ladders.

Below: This simple mangonel was operated by torsion: the arm was pulled against the resistance of tightly coiled rope, which launched the missile when the arm was released.

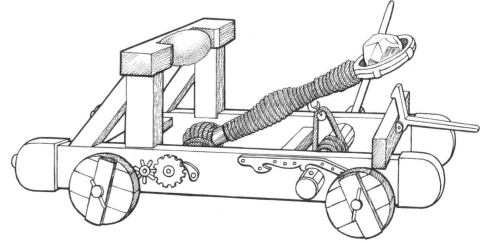

causing major fires in Raymond's camp. Unlike the defenders to the north of the city, they also succeeded in damaging Raymond's siege tower so badly that it could not be brought up to the wall.

The Provencal assault was flagging badly when word arrived that the northern attack was succeeding. The Provencals then launched a mad scramble for the wall with ladders and ropes, and they too succeeded in winning their way into the city. The surviving members of the garrison retreated before the Crusaders into the citadel, but

surrendered almost immediately when Raymond promised to protect them.

THE AFTERMATH

The battle was effectively over at that point. The Crusaders swept into the town and began an orgy of killing and looting. That in itself was typical when an army took a city by assault. Much of the native population in fact survived the initial Crusader onslaught – but three days later, the Crusader leaders ordered the massacre of all prisoners. The reason was simple: an Egyptian army was on its way, and the council of leaders determined to meet the enemy outside of the city. They simply could not leave a large number of enemies and potential enemies behind them in the newly conquered city. This logic, however, does not explain the slaughter of women and children as well as adult men. Before leaving the city for Ascalon, where the Crusaders fought their last battle, the leaders had make an important decision: now that the holiest of cities was in Christian hands, who would rule and protect it? The churchmen argued that the first step should be the choice of a Latin patriarch.

The secular leaders, however, overrode them, deciding that one of their own should be the effective ruler: Godfrey of Bouillon, Duke of Lorraine. Godfrey refused to be crowned king of the place where Christ was crowned with thorns, but accepted the title 'advocate' of the Holy Sepulchre. Thus was established the Latin kingdom of Jerusalem (Godfrey's successor did not feel the same qualms about being named king), the focal point of Muslim–Christian struggle for the next two centuries.

*Opposite: This Gustav Doré illustration (1875) is an
imaginative re-creation of the siege engines employed
at Jerusalem. Although inaccurate in details, it gives
a good impression of the scale of the enterprise.*

HATTIN
1187

THIS BATTLE MARKED THE TURNING POINT IN THE CRUSADES. THE MORE INTELLIGENT STRATEGY AND FLEXIBLE TACTICS OF THE ISLAMIC ARMY DELIVERED A CATASTROPHIC DEFEAT TO THE ARMY OF JERUSALEM. THE CHRISTIANS WOULD NEVER AGAIN HOLD AS MUCH TERRITORY AS THEY HAD PREVIOUSLY.

WHY DID IT HAPPEN?

WHO A Crusader army of 32,000 men under King Guy of Jerusalem (reigned 1186–92), opposed by 50,000 Seljuk Turks under Saladin (1138–93).

WHAT Thirsty, tired and dispirited Crusaders en route to relieve a castle could not catch the more nimble Turks until they were too exhausted to fight. Only then did the Turks surround and attack the remaining Crusaders.

WHERE The Horns of Hattin, near Tiberias on the Sea of Galilee in modern Israel.

WHEN June 1187.

WHY The Turks were responding to the Crusaders who had breached a truce by raiding a Turkish caravan.

OUTCOME Most of the Crusaders were killed or captured. The Turks went on to recapture Jerusalem.

The Crusades were an extraordinary phenomenon. Recruited by the clergy of a peace-professing religion, waves of invaders and their reinforcements were raised in Europe to conquer and convert both non-believers and heretics in Spain, the Pyrenees, Central Europe and the Baltic. For more than 1000 years the Romans and their successor state the Byzantines struggled to maintain their rule over Palestine and the holy sites of three great religions. Following the crushing defeat of the Byzantines by the Seljuk Turks at Manzikert in 1071 Pope Urban II

A thirteenth-century portrait of Salah ad-Din Yusuf Ibn Ayyub, known to us as 'Saladin', from a manuscript by an unknown Persian artist. This is a rare contemporary image of Saladin, who was Sultan of Egypt and Syria.

(c.1042–1099) called for a Crusade to occupy and hold the Christian sites in Turkish Syria. The Crusaders carried with them the social structures, attitudes and ambitions of the society they left, and met, when they arrived in Saracen lands, a completely different set of customs and outlooks and a different way of waging war. These strange Saracen lands were in fact the Seljuk Turkish Sultanates of Rum and Syria. They stretched from southern Turkey to the Persian Gulf and east to Afghanistan.

The Sultan Nur ad-Din incorporated Egypt into his empire and set Saladin to be its governor and thence sultan. The relatively tiny Crusader territories on the western edge of this vast empire ebbed and flowed like the tide as they struggled against their more numerous foes. This strange enemy did not seem to pin all on headlong rushes into combat but was content to shoot arrows from horseback, particularly at the horses which were too valuable in the West to be so targeted, and retire until he perceived it advantageous to close for hand-to-hand combat. By this time of course, if the Saracens had judged their moment right, the knights and footsoldiers of the Crusading armies were tired, desperately thirsty and disorganized.

Successive newly arrived and headstrong Crusader leaders did not always listen to the experiences of their predecessors and learnt the hard way, paying for their lessons with the lives of their own men. Their independent attitude also led to many feuds and disputes with their fellow Crusaders over land, precedence and women, but above all over power. They had no clear, accepted head of state to direct affairs and enforce unity. In such a long-drawn-out war, truces and periods of relative peace were inevitable, as were their breaches.

In the autumn of 1186 Reynald de Chatillon (c.1125–1187), Lord of Kerak and one of history's most brutal rulers, raided a Muslim caravan, breaking a long-standing truce. Both Saladin and King Guy of Jerusalem demanded the prisoners and stolen goods be returned but Reynald refused. Saladin declared war and summoned his own host from just a portion of his empire: northern Syria, Aleppo, Damascus and Egypt.

His first move in May 1187 was to send four of his *amirs* (troop commanders) and about 6500 men on a reconnaissance. Coincidentally the Grand Masters of the Knights of the Hospital and Temple were in the area to resolve a dispute between Count Raymond of Tripoli, who had negotiated the original truce, and King Guy of Jerusalem. The Grand Masters had little more than their immediate bodyguards.

They set off with just 140 knights and 350 infantry to intercept the Muslims. These they found watering their horses at the Spring of Cresson (also known as Kishon). The knights charged immediately, leaving their infantry behind. Not surprisingly they were almost all massacred – the odds were over 40:1. Only the Grand Master of the Temple, Gerard de Ridefort, and two of his brethren escaped. The Muslims' reconnaissance mission went on, via Tiberias on the Sea of Galilee, to massacre the Christian forces in Nazareth.

Through the deaths of their knights the Grand Masters had succeeded in their objective as Count Raymond and King Guy set aside their differences to deal with the new threat. By then King Guy had a mere 700 knights and men-at-arms left in his small kingdom.

THE CAMPAIGN

The city of Acre on the coast was chosen as the rendezvous of the Crusader host. It had a huge harbour and infrastructure to support the assembling troops before they set out. Here 2200 knights assembled. The feudal obligations of the component parts of the kingdom are recorded by various chroniclers at between 636 and 749 knights. The Temple had already lost two-thirds of its strength so could only provide about 40 true Templar knights.

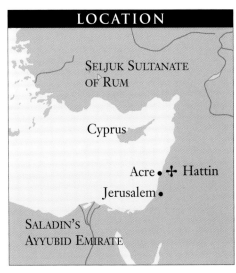

LOCATION

SELJUK SULTANATE OF RUM

Cyprus

Acre • ✝ Hattin

Jerusalem •

SALADIN'S AYYUBID EMIRATE

King Guy of Jerusalem set out to relieve the castle at Tiberias, but was cut off from his water supply by Saladin's larger Muslim army. The battle took place around two rocky outcrops – the Horns of Hattin.

HOSPITALLER KNIGHT (C.1190)

The Order of the Hospital of St John was originally founded to care for pilgrims around 1070. They became a militant order around 1148 when a brother knight is first recorded. They were governed by a Constable, Marshal and Master. Their members (brothers) were recruited from Christian soldiers, Turcopoles and converted Arabs. They fought as knights, sergeants, crossbowmen and Turcopole light cavalry. Knights were accompanied by two esquires, sergeants by one. The rank of standard bearer also commanded the force in the absence of the Marshal, in which case the standard would be carried by an esquire.

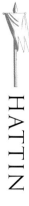

Turcopole archers – whether on foot or mounted – were employed in large numbers by Crusader armies in the Kingdom of Jerusalem, since they added a valuable skirmishing element to match the enemy light cavalry. Most were recent converts to Christianity.

THE OPPOSED FORCES

MUSLIMS (estimated)

Askari:	12,000
Turcomans & other cavalry:	26,000
Infantry:	12,000
Total:	**50,000**

CRUSADERS (estimated)

Knights of the Holy Orders:	120
Feudal knights:	700
Mercenary men-at-arms:	1380
Turcopoles:	4000
Infantry:	32,000
Total:	**38,200**

The Hospitaller strength is generally estimated to be about the same; deducting their losses at Cresson gives around 80 true Hospitallers. This means that more than half the knights were secular and mercenary. Although they would fight well, they were less motivated by their pay than the Templar and Hospitaller knights were by their religious fervour. More lightly armoured and armed with sword, light lance and bow were 4000 Turcopole skirmishing cavalry. Local mercenaries who had converted to Christianity, they provided a vital skirmishing and scouting capability the Crusader armies otherwise lacked. The mass of the army was made up of 32,000 infantry – a motley crew, some veterans of earlier campaigns, some newly arrived pilgrims. Weapons would include spear and crossbow and many would have worn mail and a helmet for protection. Spearmen also carried a shield.

Saladin's host of perhaps 50,000 was reviewed and is recorded as including 12,000 regular Egyptian and Syrian cavalry (*Askari*) – five times the number of Crusader knights. These received regular pay and were fully equipped, mail-coated (some with plate reinforcement sewn on) cavalry, armed with bow as well as lance and shield. They were as well equipped as their Christian counterparts but less inclined to charge as ferociously and, more importantly, prepared to skirmish away if the moment was unfavourable. Some Muslim cavalry horses also wore barding, possibly concealing chain mail. An additional 12,000 unpaid and less well-equipped Kurdish, Bedouin and Turcoman cavalry fighting for loot and slaves seems likely. Finally, there was an unrecorded number of infantry: spear-and-shield- or bow-equipped volunteers from the locality as well as from the further corners of the Turkish Empire like Egypt. But not Saladin's Sudanese infantry who had been crushed after a revolt two years previously and had not yet been re-established.

This Turcoman auxiliary is typical of the numerous non-professional light infantry employed in Saladin's army. He is armed with a heavy axe and shield, but has little in the way of body armour.

Opposite: A French nineteenth-century woodcut depicts a romanticized death for the defeated Crusader knights at Hattin. Even 600 years after the event, the battle was capable of inspiring sentimentality.

This Muslim host moved on the town and adjacent castle at Tiberias. The castle was ignored but the town was pillaged. This was very much an invitation to battle.

THE MARCH

The Crusaders obliged and marched out with the True Cross, the most potent symbol in Christendom, in their midst. They camped at Saffuriya, between Acre and Tiberias, a good site with both water and grazing for the horses. Between there and the Saracen camp 9.6km (6 miles) southwest of Tiberias lay the dry, baking-hot Plain of Toran. Raymond, an old hand, counselled against an advance. His castle at Tiberias, governed by his wife, would hold out; they should draw the Muslims on to

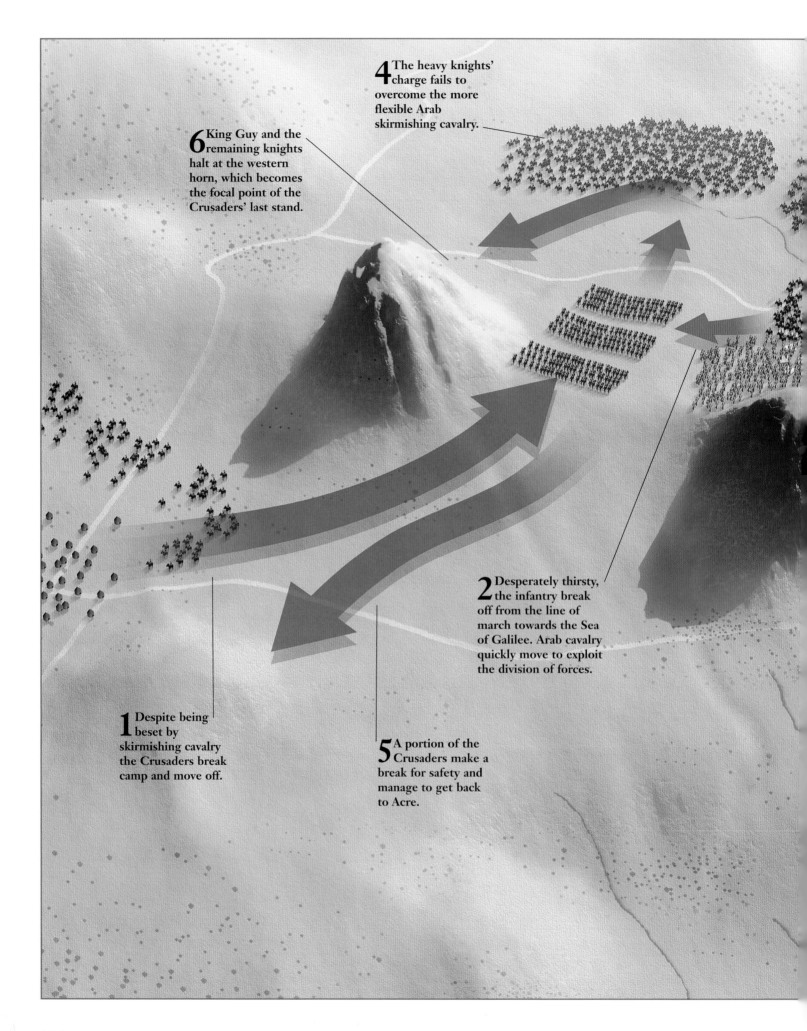

4 The heavy knights' charge fails to overcome the more flexible Arab skirmishing cavalry.

6 King Guy and the remaining knights halt at the western horn, which becomes the focal point of the Crusaders' last stand.

2 Desperately thirsty, the infantry break off from the line of march towards the Sea of Galilee. Arab cavalry quickly move to exploit the division of forces.

1 Despite being beset by skirmishing cavalry the Crusaders break camp and move off.

5 A portion of the Crusaders make a break for safety and manage to get back to Acre.

3 Like so many sheep the Crusader infantry are herded onto the eastern horn. Those that are not cut down are rounded up to be sold into slavery.

TIBERIAS

HATTIN

1187

HATTIN

their position, making them suffer the thirsty approach march. But Reynald de Chatillon and Gerard de Ridefort argued for a bold advance to strike the foe. King Guy vacillated but finally agreed to advance via Wadi Hamman, to the north of the direct route, where the Crusaders expected to find water. Saladin got news of this movement, probably from his scouts, and shifted his position northwards to block this route at the Horns of Hattin.

The Crusaders marched amidst continuous skirmishing from Muslim light cavalry who attacked both the van, under Raymond, and the rearguard of Hospitallers, Templars and Turcopoles. It was a sensible tactic: attack the rear and you will either split the column or make the whole formation slow down or even stop. The Muslims' primary target would have been the Turcopoles, the only ones with a realistic chance of catching the Muslim skirmishing cavalry. Once they were eliminated the Crusaders had little answer to the hit-and-run tactics of the enemy other than to use the plodding infantry as a

shield. Casualties were heavy at both ends of the column and the rearguard was nearly separated from the main column. After just 8km (5 miles) the whole army was forced to halt in the hot early afternoon and the order was given to make camp even though there was no water available. Only Raymond realized they must have water, but the infantry were exhausted and the rearguard was severely battered.

THE BATTLE

The Crusaders got but little respite during the night. The Muslims, however, were re-supplied by camels bringing 400 loads of arrows and 70 loads of water. Early the next morning the Crusaders made one more attempt to reach water at the village of Marescallia but were held back by the Muslims. Anyway the spring was dry. At about nine o'clock the main Muslim force advanced in a crescent formation. Arrows swept before them like rain before a storm. But this was not a charge to contact, merely an intensification of the arrow-storm and a further reduction in the Crusaders' morale.

Louis VII of France, the Emperor Conrad III of Germany and Baldwin III, King of Jerusalem, deliberate on the course of the Holy War, 1148. Baldwin III died without issue so the throne passed through his brother Amalric to Baldwin IV, thence, in 1186, to his brother-in-law Guy of Lusignan, after the short reign of Guy's stepson as Baldwin V.

The Crusaders could charge but all they would meet was another shower of deadly arrows. The Saracens would simply retire before them, keeping within bow range and targeting the Crusaders' horses to dismount the heavily armoured knights.

The tired, disorganized and above all thirsty Crusader infantry could see blue water ahead. They surged past the vanguard to push on to the Sea of Galilee which seemed so tantalizingly close, but they were instead herded onto the easternmost of two hills known as the Horns of Hattin. Halted by despair, frustration and Muslim arrows a mere 12.8km (8 miles) short of their destination, they were a spent force. Even

the king could not persuade them to take any further part in the battle and here those that weren't cut down were rounded up and later sold into slavery by the Saracens.

CAVALRY CLASH

Guy ordered Raymond and the remaining vanguard of about 200 knights to charge. The medieval knight was very much a one-shot weapon. You pointed him at the enemy and let him go. If he collided with the enemy it could be devastating. If not, his horse became blown and he was useless. A good commander might be able to halt the charge, rally the knights and make a second attempt, but it took an awful toll on the

Lower Galilee, Israel – the Horns of Hattin mountains. This photograph gives an excellent impression of the terrain: scrub with patches of rubble and rocky outcrops – sufficient to hinder free movement of the mounted Crusaders but not to impede the arrows of the Muslim horse archers.

horses' strength and exposed the knights to counter-attack from flank or rear when they were unprepared. Nothing saps a horse's strength like thirst. Instead of carefully husbanding his precious but powerful knights, Guy had frittered them away in topping and tailing his more numerous and now dispersed infantry. Richard the Lionheart at Arsuf four years later would use a better strategy.

The Muslims opened their ranks and Raymond's charge passed through, receiving more archery casualties on the way, in a classic response to the charge of Western knights and a tactic from the steppes with a pedigree of more than 1000 years. Raymond, thrice wounded in the charge, knew the day was lost and rode from the field into the steep-sided gorge of Wadi Hamman. The wadi was dry (some say Saladin had the stream diverted) and the Muslims closed behind him. Raymond knew he could not charge back up the slope, so he rode on to Tyre leaving behind at least

one son to be captured by the foe. He had been expected to follow a suicidal plan by people lacking his experience. Perhaps his efforts in securing the original truce persuaded Saladin to let him and his contingent escape.

The remaining knights made two or three more charges, but were still unable to come to grips with their highly mobile foes. Perhaps as many as 300 managed to escape back to Acre. Eventually the survivors were driven back onto the other Horn of Hattin where King Guy's red tent had been erected. The Muslims circled around the hill, cutting the Crusaders down. At some stage Saladin's men even set fire to the tinder-dry brush, sources differing as to exactly when. This was heaping misery upon misery for the parched Crusader soldiers. Finally, the tent was overrun and about 150 remaining knights surrendered. It is a testament to the armour they wore, which made them evidently so hard to kill, and the tenacious determination of the knights that they did not surrender earlier when all reasonable hope had passed. The last few surviving leaders were captured: King Guy, his brother Amalric, Constable of Acre, Reynald de Chatillon and Gerard de Rideford along with so many others that the Muslims did not have enough rope to tie them all.

Muslim soldiers set upon a fallen Crusader cavalryman. Once a horseman had been brought down from his mount, his opponents generally had the advantage. Either he could be taken hostage and ransomed, or, as is most likely in the case of this Crusader at the Battle of Hattin, he would be killed by attacks through vulnerable openings in his armour – at the neck, armpit or groin.

AFTERMATH

The Battle of the Horns of Hattin was the high-water mark of all the seven Crusades to Palestine. Even the briefly combined armies of England and France failed to retake Jerusalem a few years later. Richard the Lionheart of England did learn from the mistakes of his predecessors, however. Four years later on the coast at Arsuf he inflicted a telling defeat on Saladin's warriors.

Saladin had the brutal Reynald de Chatillon executed along with all the surviving Knights Templar and Hospitaller, his most fervent and implacable foes, and the remaining Turcopoles. Raymond's wife, who had faithfully held their castle, was allowed to depart unharmed. The price of Frankish slaves in the Muslim markets tumbled because of the glut. It is recorded that one Frank was sold for a single shoe!

By the end of the year the Muslims had gone on to capture Ascalon and about 30 other Crusader castles; the city of Jerusalem surrendered in October. In addition, as ransom for King Guy and Gerard de Ridefort, Saladin received a further 11 cities. In another 100 years the Crusader presence in mainland Palestine would be eliminated. By then the Muslims were under attack from the east by the Mongols.

A romanticized version of the remaining Crusader leaders surrendering to Saladin after the battle (painting by S. Tahssin). Shortly after this the man who broke the truce, Reynald de Chatillon, and all the surviving Knights Templar and Hospitaller were executed by Saladin.

ARSUF
1191

THE BATTLE OF ARSUF PITTED A CRUSADER ARMY UNDER RICHARD THE LIONHEART AGAINST A SARACEN FORCE UNDER SALADIN. IT WAS A SEVERE TEST OF THE DISCIPLINE THAT RICHARD HOPED TO INSTIL IN THE CRUSADER ARMIES. ULTIMATELY, THE CRUSADER INFANTRY PROVED THEIR WORTH IN THE FACE OF CONSTANT HARASSMENT BY MUSLIM CAVALRY.

WHY DID IT HAPPEN?

WHO A Crusader army under King Richard I of England (1157–99) numbering about 12,000 men was attacked by a Saracen force approximately double in size, commanded by Saladin (1138–93).

WHAT The Crusaders, attempting to march along the Palestine coast, were attacked by the more mobile Saracens but were able to reach and occupy the town of Arsuf.

WHERE The town of Arsuf.

WHEN September 1191.

WHY Having taken Acre, Richard hoped to press on to Jerusalem. Saladin was determined to stop him.

OUTCOME The Crusaders were able to maintain formation and march under fire to Arsuf. A mounted counter-attack then drove off the Saracen force.

The Crusader armies tended to be an ill-assorted mix of troop types and fairly undisciplined. The backbone was provided by mounted men-at-arms and nobles from the Christian kingdoms of Europe. Armoured in chain mail and an open-faced metal helm, the man-at-arms was trained to war all his life. His sidearm was the long sword, but he might also carry an axe or mace as well as his shield and lance. Knights, noblemen and men-at-arms came to the Crusades from all across Europe. The most famous groups were the Knights Templar and the Order of St John (the Hospitallers).

WARRIOR MONKS

The Knights Templar, otherwise known as the Poor Fellows of Christ, were formed after the First Crusade (1096–99) in response to a need for fighting men to defend the conquered lands. Gaining papal approval in 1120, they were an order of warrior monks who took vows of poverty and chastity and lived according to a very strict code. They wore the white surcoat of their order over a plain and unadorned chain mail shirt called a hauberk, along with a mail coif (hood) and leggings. Their helm was plain and open-faced, similar to that worn by Norman knights at the Battle of Hastings. Under the mail hauberk was a padded jerkin to absorb the impact of blows.

The Templars have become the symbol of Christian knights. They were fearsome and unrelenting in combat against their Muslim foes, believing that death in battle against the enemies of Christendom was a direct route to heaven. The Templars had a fierce rivalry with the Hospitallers that did

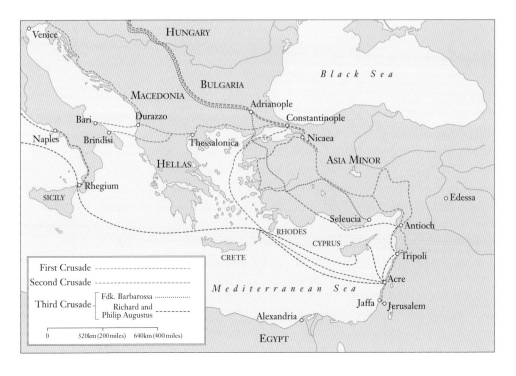

This map shows the routes of the three Crusader armies that gathered for the Third Crusade in 1190. While the forces of Richard I of England and Philip II of France chose to travel by sea, Frederick Barbarossa led the forces of the Holy Roman Empire on a long and arduous overland journey. The emperor was drowned while crossing a fast-flowing river in Turkey.

MAMLUK SOLDIERS (C.1190)

The great wealth of Fatimid Egypt meant that Egyptian commanders could field armies with large numbers of regular troops. The core of the regular troops was made up of Turkish slaves, known as Mamluks (from the Turkish word meaning 'owned'). The Mamluk warrior (left) carries the short cavalry bow favoured in Saladin's armies, which was ideal for skirmishing and harassing Crusader forces. He also carries a sword for close combat, although a single-handed axe was also popular. Askari warriors (right) were members of the emir's personal bodyguard. This Askari is armed with a heavy javelin, which was used for a final shock attack before engaging the enemy at close quarters with sword and shield. Both wear chain mail hauberks.

at times turn violent. Each order had an agreement not to accept men from their rival order.

The Knights of St John began as a charitable order sometime in the 1070s. Their goal was to care for pilgrims to the Holy Land. Booty from the First Crusade, donated to the order, paid for a chain of hospices across the region. Eventually the order took on the duties of protecting the pilgrims and the city of Jerusalem, and became a militant order. Using mercenaries and knights friendly to the order, the Hospitallers garrisoned several fortresses on the route to Jerusalem. After the Crusader army was destroyed at Hattin in 1187, the pope decided to support the various military orders and gave his blessing to the Hospitallers' military role.

THE CAVALRY CHARGE

There is much debate about exactly when the mounted warrior began to charge with the couched lance, i.e. with his weapon held under the arm and braced for a head-on impact. At the time of the Battle of Hastings (1066), some Norman knights were using the lance this way while others thrust downwards with it overarm or rode past and speared enemies out to the side from beyond the reach of their weapons. Some men are known to have hurled their weapons into the mass of their enemies. By

1191 the lance was fairly commonly, though not exclusively, couched.

The impact of a charge of armoured cavalry was a tremendous thing, and many enemy forces broke before contact. This allowed the men-at-arms to ride down their foes with relative impunity, protected from random blows by their armour. Even if the enemy stood and fought, few could withstand the onslaught of the heavily armoured Western knights.

This was one of the problems the Crusaders faced in the Holy Land. There they met a foe who knew how dangerous the knightly charge could be, and was quite prepared to fall back or even run away from it. The result was that many times Crusader knights hurled themselves at the foe and hit only empty air. As their horses tired and their numbers were whittled down by the fire of horse archers, the men-at-arms would become exhausted and often found themselves dangerously far from their supporting forces.

The Crusader armies of the time included considerable numbers of foot-soldiers and crossbowmen. Most foot-soldiers were spearmen with armour of leather or quilted cloth and often a light 'helmet' (i.e. a lesser helm) of leather reinforced with metal bands. Their large shields were their main protection. The crossbowmen were provided with quilted jerkins that offered protection against the relatively weak bows of the Saracen horse archers. Their powerful weapons were slow-firing but outranged the Saracen bows.

LOCATION

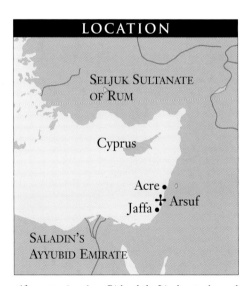

After capturing Acre, Richard the Lionheart advanced along the coast of Palestine in order to strike inland to Jerusalem. However, to achieve this objective, he first had to defeat Saladin in battle.

ARSUF

A woodcut of Richard I. Regal and commanding, he is the epitome of the noble mounted warrior of his age. In Richard's case, his deeds were every bit as impressive as his image.

THE OPPOSED FORCES

CRUSADERS (estimated)
Mounted men-at-arms:	1200
Infantry:	10,000
Total:	**12,200**

SARACENS (estimated)
Cavalry:	10,000
Infantry:	10,000
Total:	**20,000**

Saladin's forces at Arsuf were completely different to those of the Crusaders. The backbone of the force was mounted: a mix of light cavalry equipped with short bows and heavier horsemen able to produce a shock effect with their charge, though not so effectively as the European heavy cavalry. The horse archers of Saladin's force were mainly of Turkish origin. They could attack at close quarters with their light, curved scimitars but these were ineffective against all but the lightest armour.

The horse archers were mainly assigned to harass and skirmish with the enemy, though they would swoop down on isolated or broken enemy units to massacre them. The heavy cavalry were mainly of Arab origin. They were equipped with light mail armour and armed with lances, swords and maces. Usually known as *Mamluks*, these heavy Arab cavalry made up Saladin's personal bodyguard and more of the army besides. Their function was to deliver the fatal blow to an enemy force shaken by endless horse archery. To back up the cavalry, Saladin had pike- and javelin-armed Arab or Sudanese footsoldiers and Nubian archers. Ideally the pikemen could protect the archers from an enemy attack while they shot down their opponents, then complete the victory by charging with their pikes. In practice this was hard to coordinate, but the Muslim armies tended to have good discipline and training, and managed combined-arms cooperation better than many European forces of the time.

THE CAMPAIGN

Arsuf was part of the Third Crusade (1189–92), an attempt by a coalition of Christian forces to capture the holy city of Jerusalem from its Muslim rulers. The city had been lost to the Muslims under Saladin (Salah ad-Din Yusuf) after the disastrous battle of Hattin in 1187. Pope Gregory VIII ordered an immediate Crusade to recapture it. The call was answered by Richard I of England (Richard the Lionheart), King Philip II of France (1165–1223) and the Holy Roman Emperor Frederick I Barbarossa (c.1123–90). The 70-year-old Emperor Frederick was drowned during the march across Europe and most of his army turned for home, leaving Richard and Philip to continue.

Capturing Cyprus as an forward base, the Crusaders landed at Acre and besieged the port, capturing it soon after. King Philip returned home at this point but Richard, now in control of a port through which to supply his army, decided to press on to Jerusalem. With him went much of King Philip's force.

Richard's next objective was the port of Jaffa. Marching down the coast, he imposed strict discipline on his force. The army stayed close to the shore to protect its flank and to benefit from the slightly cooler conditions there. The force was arrayed in three columns plus a rearguard. The knights, suffering terribly from the heat, rode in the column closest to the sea. The two outer columns were of infantry. They suffered from the archery of enemy light cavalry who could ride up, shoot, and escape quickly, but the infantry maintained their discipline and stayed in formation, some men marching with several arrows sticking out of their quilted jerkins. The crossbowmen exacted a steady toll among the horse archers, who could not venture too close to the columns.

Marching under fire in this manner is one of the most difficult of all manoeuvres to carry out. Progress is slow and painstaking, since if the formation breaks up at all the enemy will sweep in and attack. Iron discipline is the key, since the galling fire of the enemy makes individuals want to hurry and opens gaps in the formation for the enemy to exploit. It was particularly impressive that the Crusader army maintained its formation, since discipline in the European armies of the time was very poor. Not only did the knights' warrior instincts tell them to rush out at the enemy but their very way of life had conditioned them to charge at threats regardless rather than plod along hiding behind a screen of common infantry.

For the infantry themselves, the feat is quite remarkable. Often despised by the flower of chivalry they now sheltered, the infantry were forced to bear the brunt of the enemy's fire for hour after baking hour, and all to protect the precious horses of the knights. They, the infantry, were soaking up arrows to protect animals!

There were plenty of reasons for the formation to fall apart – internal divisions, pressure from the enemy, heat and exhaustion should by all the odds have combined to wear down the Christians' resolve. And yet the Crusaders'

A Crusader footsoldier and sergeant. The spearman's thick gambeson of quilted cloth offered excellent protection against arrows but was uncomfortable to wear in the hot Middle Eastern climate. The sergeant's armour is backed by a similar garment worn underneath the mail.

Illustrations of the Third Crusade from a thirteenth-century Venetian manuscript. Note how the noble mounted warrior receives prominence, while the common infantry are relegated to the background.

discipline held. The formation plodded slowly onward, where possible transferring wounded to the ships that followed it down the coast and receiving supplies in return.

On 6 September the Crusader army passed through a wood north of Arsuf, a town north of Jaffa. Had the Saracens fired the wood, it might have become a death-trap, but they did not, perhaps because Saladin had other plans. Thus far the main Saracen force had shadowed Richard's army but made no serious attempt to engage. Now the time was ripe.

DISPOSITIONS

On 7 September the Crusaders had to cover about 10km (6.2 miles) to reach Arsuf, a long day's march in those conditions.

ARSUF

1191

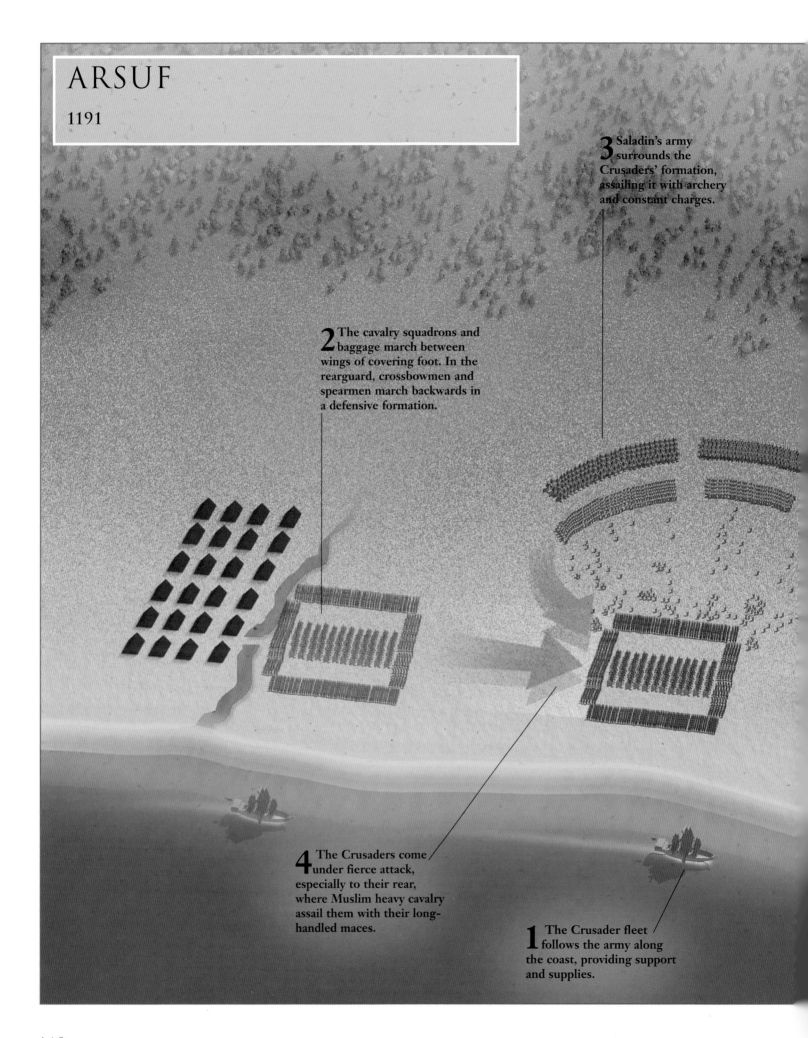

3 Saladin's army surrounds the Crusaders' formation, assailing it with archery and constant charges.

2 The cavalry squadrons and baggage march between wings of covering foot. In the rearguard, crossbowmen and spearmen march backwards in a defensive formation.

4 The Crusaders come under fierce attack, especially to their rear, where Muslim heavy cavalry assail them with their long-handled maces.

1 The Crusader fleet follows the army along the coast, providing support and supplies.

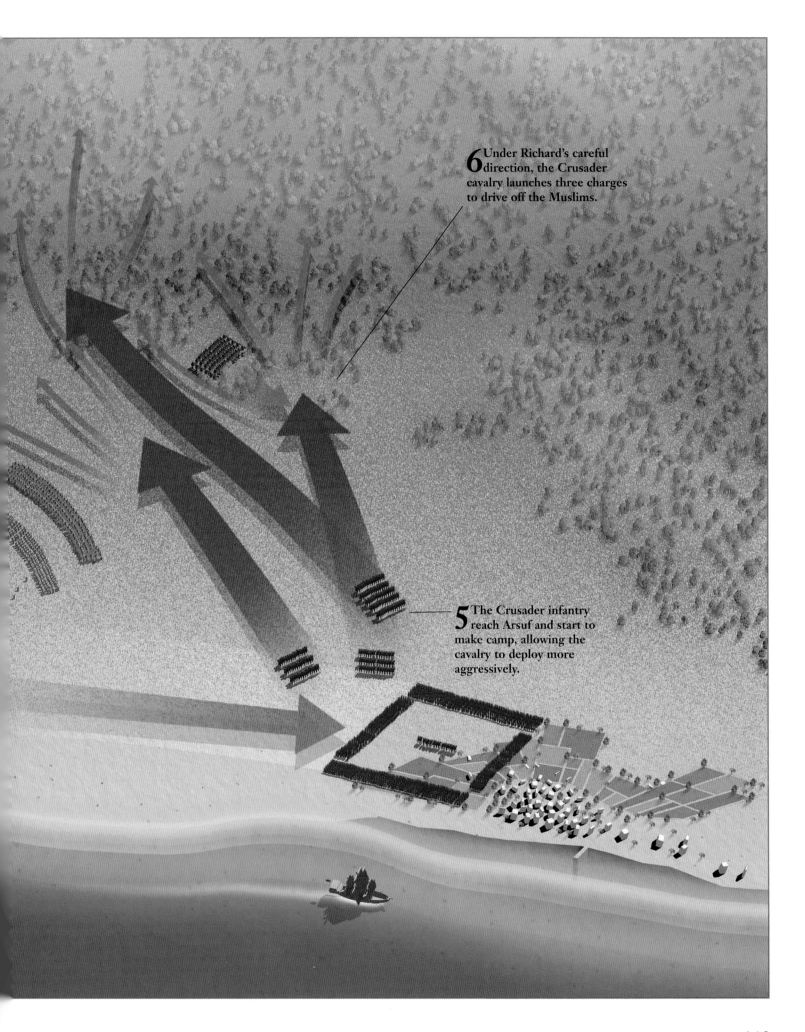

6 Under Richard's careful direction, the Crusader cavalry launches three charges to drive off the Muslims.

5 The Crusader infantry reach Arsuf and start to make camp, allowing the cavalry to deploy more aggressively.

Opposite: Richard the Lionheart leads the great cavalry charge at Arsuf. The impact of heavily armoured men on big horses was awesome and could easily shatter most enemy formations.

Saladin had no intention of letting them reach the town, however. His forces prepared themselves for an attack that would pin the Crusaders against the sea and crush them.

The Saracen formation was typically fluid, with horse archers darting in to shoot in small groups then withdrawing quickly. There was no idea of forming up for battle, just another day of marching and skirmishing. This went on until about 11.00 a.m., at which point the Saracen force attacked in earnest.

The Crusader army was in effect marching in battle formation, organized in a defensive box around its precious supply wagons and the irreplaceable heavy cavalry. In truth the battle had already been going on for days as the defensive formation held off the horse archers and their supporting forces. There had been no serious attack up until that point but now the Saracens were ready to strike.

The forces of Saladin were kept at bay by a fine piece of combined-arms work. Spearmen protected the crossbowmen from direct attack, while the heavy bolts of the crossbowmen exacted a steady toll on the enemy. And in reserve, the threat of the

heavy armoured cavalry prevented the Muslim army from making an all-out assault. For the infantry deployed at the back of the formation, this was in effect a fighting retreat. Most of the time the infantry marched backwards, keeping their shields and weapons facing the enemy. The Crusader army was a 'roving pocket' cut off in enemy territory yet able to continue its march, albeit slowly. The Muslim forces swirled around the human bulwark; ahead, behind and to the left there was nothing but enemies. On the right flank was the sea. The only hope was to march on – and fight on – so the battle became a contest between the pressure exerted by the Muslims and the discipline of the Crusaders.

STEADY PRESSURE

The pressure steadily mounted as the Saracen horse archers came in ever closer and more boldly to shoot. Sometimes the crossbowmen were able to keep the enemy at a distance, but increasingly groups of cavalry were able to race in and attack with lance and sword. Then the spearmen of the Crusader rearguard were forced to engage. Their spears were long enough to be effective against the attacking horsemen and

This Crusader infantry formation of the late twelfth century illustrates how the spearmen braced their spears against the ground while sheltering behind shields to ward off cavalry attacks. The slow-loading crossbowmen then had time to prepare their weapons to drive back any assault. They could even reload in relays, passing the bows forwards to whomever was best placed to shoot.

ARSUF

Bearing a powerful two-headed axe and protected by chain mail, in this illustration Richard I represents the pinnacle of twelfth-century Western military technology. Well-led, Richard's knights were devastatingly effective.

infantry ever lost control of the situation, the knights would have no choice but to engage. They were already itching for a fight; it would not take much more to provoke them into action. Yet somehow, amid the chaos and constant archery, the rearguard held to its task. It is highly unlikely that there was much order to the formation, not with enemy attacks coming in at various points. The scene would be fluid – chaotic even – changing from moment to moment.

Here a band of spearmen is driving a few paces forward, chasing off yet another attack. There a handful of crossbowmen are exchanging fire with horse archers; others load and shoot as fast as they can, covering the retirement of the spearmen back to the column. A gap in the formation is plugged by a handful of infantry just as Muslim cavalry spur at it, hoping to enter the 'box' and cause mayhem. Finally the spearmen regain the main body and struggle to catch their breath. Things are calm for a moment, with only the constant archery taking its toll. But along the line the scene is being repeated as another attack sweeps in …

For the entire morning the rearguard battled on in this manner, holding off attacks at the end of the column while the force as a whole inched forwards. Despite extreme provocation the knights resisted the urge to charge, and the column continued its march towards Arsuf and safety.

As the day wore on, casualties mounted. The whole force was now under fire, and men were falling dead and wounded. Confined within the formation the knights chafed, forced to take casualties and unable to reply in any way. The crossbowmen did their best and the outer column of foot soldiers beat off a series of minor attacks, but the strain was becoming intolerable.

COUNTER-ATTACK

As the army neared Arsuf, the pressure became too much for Richard's knights. The Hospitallers, accompanied by three squadrons of about 100 knights each, burst out of the formation in a reckless charge. Their sudden attack drove back the right wing of the Saracen force, which had been trying to draw such an attack but had ceased to expect it. If Richard did not support the

their shields offered good protection, but they were desperately tired from day after day of marching.

The rearguard could not afford to become embroiled in a mêlée with the attackers. If a group of cavalry broke off and was pursued, even for only a few steps, the spearmen would be quickly surrounded and cut down. So the Crusader infantry was forced to fight a defensive battle. Short rushes to drive off attackers were possible, but it was vital for soldiers to quickly regain the safety of the main force. Dangerous gaps opened up but were sealed by troops who were supposed to be resting inside the defensive formation.

Hoping to draw one of the famously impetuous charges of the Crusader knights, Saladin's forces concentrated mostly on the rear of the column where the Hospitallers and French Royal Guards rode. If the

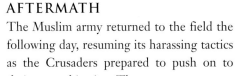

impetuous knights, they would soon be cut off and slaughtered. Yet if he did send more forces after them, he might throw away his whole force. Richard was known for his valour, but he was also a shrewd tactician. His infantry were near to the shelter of the town. Covered by a cavalry charge they could enter and secure the town as a defensive position, protecting the baggage train and giving the army a safe place to retreat to if necessary.

Richard also knew the temperament of his men. They might attack anyway if he did not order it, and without direction their force might be spent for nothing.

Ordering the Templars out, supported by Breton and Angevin knights, Richard launched them at Saladin's left wing. At last given a chance to release their pent-up rage, the knights threw the Saracens back and repulsed a counter-attack by Saladin's personal guard. Now the baggage and its accompanying infantry were entering Arsuf. Richard placed himself at the head of his remaining cavalry, Norman and English knights, and led them at the enemy.

Reeling from heavy blows on both flanks, the Saracen army was shattered by the third charge. Saladin's men scrambled back into the wooded hills above Arsuf leaving behind about 7000 casualties. No less than 32 *amirs* had been killed, almost all of them in the three great charges that broke the army.

SALADIN (1138–93)

Saladin (Salah ad-Din Yusuf Ibn Ayyub) was a courteous and generous individual who was praised even by his Crusader enemies as a man of honour. He was also great warrior and statesman. Representing himself as the champion of Islam, he was able to rally tremendous support which he wielded very effectively. Saladin understood the capabilities and weaknesses of the Crusader armies as well as his own, and shrewdly played to his own forces' strengths. At the Battle of Hattin he was able to draw out the impetuous Crusader knights and isolate them, resulting in a total victory. The same strategy was unsuccessful at Arsuf, but still Saladin was able to keep his force intact and deny the Crusaders their ultimate goal of capturing Jerusalem.

AFTERMATH

The Muslim army returned to the field the following day, resuming its harassing tactics as the Crusaders prepared to push on to their next objective. There was no attempt to launch another full assault, however. Saladin had learned that he could not penetrate the Crusaders' defensive 'box' formation and concluded that he could not draw the impetuous knights out of it either.

Richard the Lionheart did not benefit from his victory at Arsuf. Although he performed a great feat of arms and won a tactical success, his army was not able to take Jerusalem, though a grudging truce was agreed between Saladin and the Crusaders, allowing Christian pilgrims access to the city. Against almost any other Crusader commander, Arsuf would have been another great victory for Saladin. Although defeated in battle he held his army together. Its existence prevented an attack on Jerusalem and brought Saladin an honourable, if less than ideal, outcome to the war.

Tactically, and taken in isolation, Arsuf was a victory for the Crusaders. However, if Arsuf is seen as part of a gradual wearing-down of the European army to make it incapable of capturing Jerusalem, it may be that Saladin came out the strategic victor.

Saladin is depicted here as the wise and kindly father figure who cared for the poor and sick. He was also shrewd and ruthless – an admirable and necessary combination in a leader of his time.

LAKE PEIPUS
1242

THE BATTLE OF LAKE PEIPUS, IN WHICH CHRISTIAN CONFRONTED CHRISTIAN, EXPOSES THE AMBIGUITY OF THE BALTIC CRUSADES. ALTHOUGH A MINOR ENCOUNTER, THE BATTLE EFFECTIVELY ENDED WESTERN CRUSADING AGAINST RUSSIA, AND SECURED PRINCE ALEXANDER NEVSKII OF NOVGOROD'S FAME AS THE HERO WHO HALTED WESTERN AGGRESSION.

WHY DID IT HAPPEN?

WHO A Russian force, largely from Novgorod and led by the city's prince, Alexander Nevskii (1219–1263), defeated a small western army composed of Danish knights, militia from the diocese of Dorpat, Estonian tribal levies and a small number of Teutonic Knights, under the overall command of Bishop Hermann of Dorpat.

WHAT A Novgorodian victory over a mixed Crusader and western colonial army.

WHERE On the shore of Lake Peipus, near the modern Russian–Estonian border.

WHEN 5 April 1242.

WHY Papal desire to force the Orthodox Christians of Russia to acknowledge papal supremacy combined with Scandinavian and German desire to claim Novgorodian resources and trade networks to launch a crusade against Novgorod.

OUTCOME With the Crusader defeat, effective western aggression against Novgorod came to an end. Novgorod's position as the leading Russian state was confirmed, leading in time to the creation of a Russian empire under the Tsars.

The Baltic was the home of Europe's last non-Christian peoples. Twelfth-century Baltic Crusades were largely ineffective, especially because of the difficulty of holding conquered land. Thus a new policy emerged in the thirteenth century. The papacy made a determined effort to create a 'church state' in the Baltic, a state ruled by bishops and papal legates under the supervisory leadership of the popes. Two elements, however, stood in the way of making this dream a reality. First, there was the strong influence of Orthodox Christianity in the region. Second, there were the widely varying motives of the western

This engraving presents the venerable Alexander Nevskii, the subject of later hagiography. In reality, he was only about 22 years old at the time of his victory on Lake Peipus, and died aged 44.

Crusaders, who were willing to accept papal indulgences but did not share in the papacy's goals. The Orthodox Christians of Russia refused to accept papal authority, and to western eyes appeared to be schismatics who were hindering the conversion of the Baltic region. To western merchants and warlords, the Russians, perhaps more importantly, also appeared to be dangerous rivals for the resources of the region. These two factors reached a height by c. 1240, culminating in the Crusaders' defeat at Lake Peipus in 1242.

In the late 1230s, the papal legate William of Modena preached a Crusade and organized a western coalition against Novgorod. Novgorod was the greatest Russian state at the time, a trading centre so impressive by northern European standards that it was often called 'Lord Novgorod the Great'. If any state could contest western control of the Baltic region, it was Novgorod. In the 1230s, however, Russia was reeling under Mongol invasions. Most Russian states had been conquered, and Novgorod, while maintaining technical independence, had accepted Mongol overlordship in 1237. Thus, the time seemed right for a western attack that would defeat Novgorod and finally force its rich and influential townsmen into a reunion of eastern and western Christianity.

William of Modena's efforts to launch a crusade had considerable success, in large part because the kings of Sweden and Denmark were attempting an eastward expansion that they were very happy to label a 'Crusade', thus winning a measure of financial assistance, and of course spiritual rewards, while attracting volunteers from elsewhere in Europe.

Similarly, the Teutonic Knights, members of a military religious order that had begun to carve out a state in the Baltic, were willing to attack their powerful and schismatic neighbour to further their own interests. By 1240, William himself returned to Italy, content that his efforts would lead to a western triumph.

THE CAMPAIGN

The western coalition that William had brought into being had little cohesion, and various elements of the Crusader force set out with no serious thought having been given to a master strategy. The Swedes, led by their king, Eric IX (1222–1250), thrust into Finland in the spring of 1240. The alarmed burghers of Novgorod responded to the threat by recalling their prince, Alexander, who had been driven out of the city shortly before. Alexander assumed leadership in the fight against the Swedes, greatly assisted by the highly trained troops of archers he had taken into exile with him.

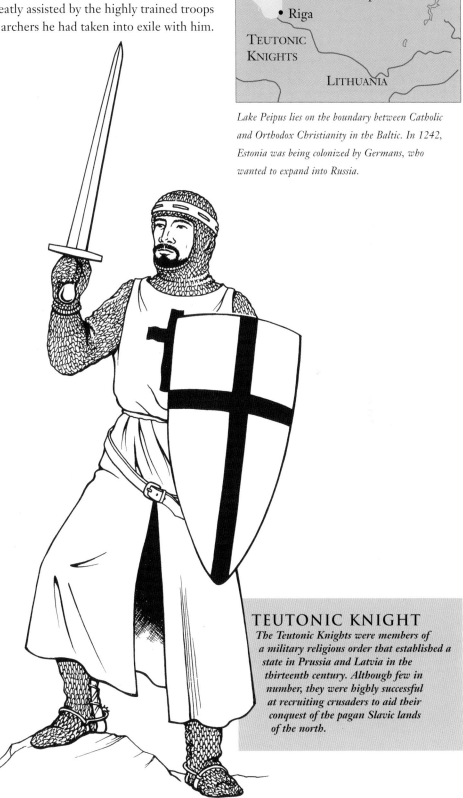

LOCATION

Lake Peipus lies on the boundary between Catholic and Orthodox Christianity in the Baltic. In 1242, Estonia was being colonized by Germans, who wanted to expand into Russia.

TEUTONIC KNIGHT

The Teutonic Knights were members of a military religious order that established a state in Prussia and Latvia in the thirteenth century. Although few in number, they were highly successful at recruiting crusaders to aid their conquest of the pagan Slavic lands of the north.

He defeated the Swedes at a site on the Neva River on 15 July 1240; the delighted Novgorodians commemorated the event by bestowing on Alexander the honorary title 'Nevskii'.

Despite Alexander's great victory over the Swedes, the threat to Novgorod remained. A second western force had already taken the field against them. This second army consisted of former members of the disbanded military Order of Swordbrothers, western knights who had become feudal overlords in Estonia, Danes, the German bishop of Dorpat, a Russian force led by Prince Jaroslav, and a few Teutonic Knights. This second invasion enjoyed considerable success, capturing Isborg in September 1240. The westerners then defeated a relief force sent from the Russian city of Pskov and went on to besiege Pskov itself, which surrendered on terms.

By April 1241, this mixed army occupied lands east of the Neva River, and had constructed a fortress at Kopore. From that base, the westerners launched devastating raids that penetrated to within 32km

(20 miles) of Novgorod. These Crusaders were so certain of victory that they despatched one of the border bishops, Heinrich of Oesel-Wiek, to petition the Pope for authority over the conquered regions.

Although Alexander Nevskii had already abandoned Novgorod again, after another quarrel with the merchant leadership of the city, he was recalled once more. The Novgorodians agreed to his demands, in

Opposite: The Battle on Ice (1942; oil on canvas) by Vladimir Aleksandrovich Serov (1910–68). In Soviet Russia, Alexandre Nevskii was a popular hero, and his victories were exploited to the full in World War II propaganda. This is in part because he came from a pre-Tsarist era, but also because he repelled German invaders from the West.

This Russian druznik *cavalryman is typical of Alexander Nevskii's cavalry at Lake Peipus. More lightly armed than their western counterparts, such troops were especially effective in attacks on disorganized enemies.*

THE OPPOSED FORCES

WESTERN ARMY (estimated)
Teutonic:	
Knights:	20
Order men-at-arms:	c. 200
Danish & Estonian knights	c. 200
Dorpat militia	c. 600
Estonian tribal levies	1000
Total:	**2000**

NOVGOROD ARMY (estimated)
Mixed force, perhaps half cavalry and half infantry

Total:	**c. 6000**

LAKE PEIPUS

1242

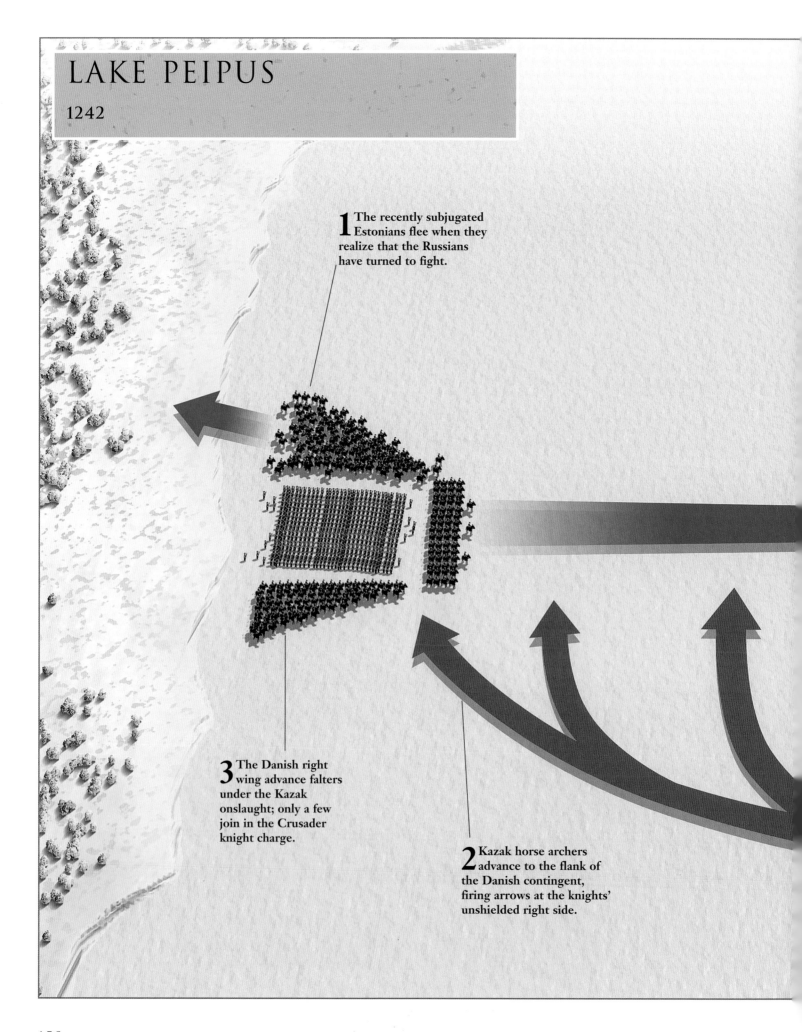

1 The recently subjugated Estonians flee when they realize that the Russians have turned to fight.

3 The Danish right wing advance falters under the Kazak onslaught; only a few join in the Crusader knight charge.

2 Kazak horse archers advance to the flank of the Danish contingent, firing arrows at the knights' unshielded right side.

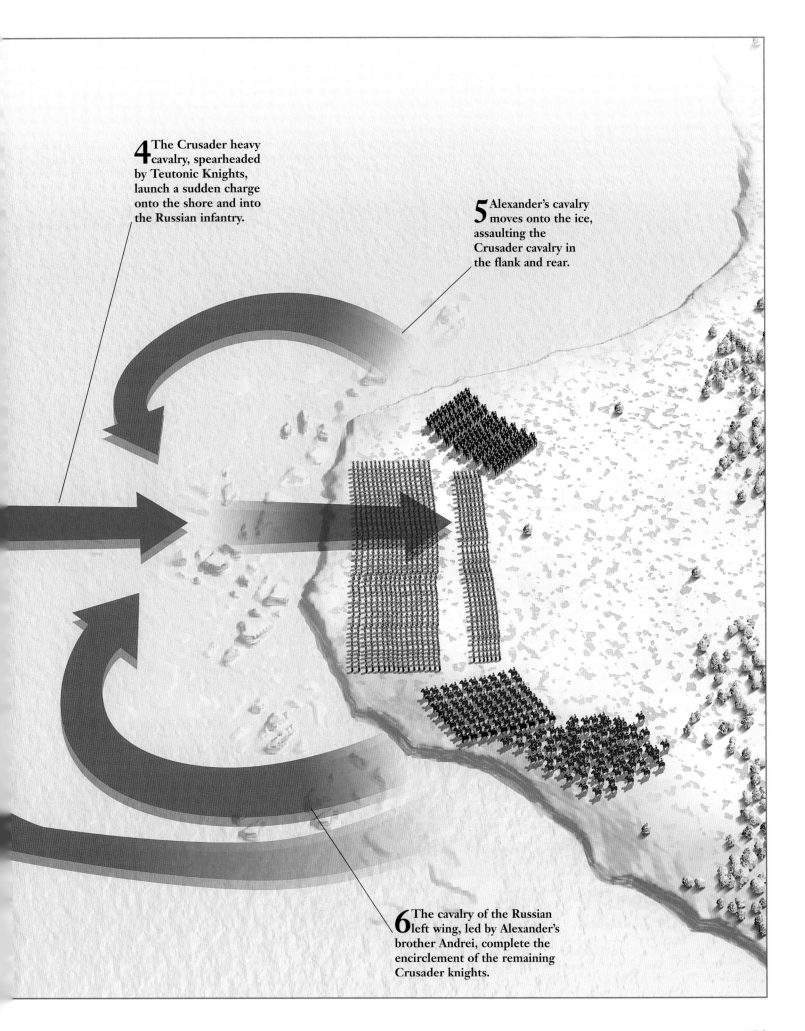

4 The Crusader heavy cavalry, spearheaded by Teutonic Knights, launch a sudden charge onto the shore and into the Russian infantry.

5 Alexander's cavalry moves onto the ice, assaulting the Crusader cavalry in the flank and rear.

6 The cavalry of the Russian left wing, led by Alexander's brother Andrei, complete the encirclement of the remaining Crusader knights.

In this Soviet propaganda image, Alexander Nevskii appears as a staunch defender of Russia against foreign aggression. He was also a practical man who later accepted Mongol overlordship and ruled Novogorod in their name.

return for his agreement to fight the German–Pskov coalition. Alexander proved worthy of their trust.

He regained the territory east of the Neva late in 1241, and in March 1242 re-took the town of Pskov. Alexander and his force then proceeded to raid deep into the German border diocese of Dorpat, apparently hoping to give the westerners a taste of their own medicine. It is clear that his intention was a major raid and he had no serious plan to expand Novgorod's territory. Apparently content with his success, Alexander and his 6000-man army turned for home after his advance force was driven back from a bridge.

THE BATTLE ON THE ICE

It seems likely that Bishop Hermann of Dorpat misunderstood Alexander's move, interpreting the Novgorodian withdrawal as a flight. It is also possible that Alexander had seriously underestimated the number of troops that the Bishop of Dorpat had at his disposal. Whatever the case, Bishop Hermann appears to have been exhilarated, thinking he had caught his formidable enemy at a considerable disadvantage. Most of the Crusader force from the preceding autumn had disbanded, but some were still present in Hermann's diocese, comprising a force that he clearly thought sufficient for the purpose.

Hermann set out in pursuit of Alexander's army with these troops; a force consisting of somewhere between 1000 and 2000 fighting men (the number given in extant sources varies widely), which seems somewhat foolhardy against an enemy 6000 strong. One must, however, take into account that the westerners were much better armed and armoured than most of the Russians – and probably intended merely to harry the retreating force rather than meet them in pitched battle.

Alexander's army retreated across the frozen waters of Lake Peipus; the Crusader army, close behind, also took to the ice, north of where the Russians were crossing. The Russians won the race to the shore and Alexander Nevskii had time to organize his force before the westerners arrived. He drew up the Russian army at a place on the eastern shore called Raven Rock, where the broken ground would cause difficulty for a manoeuvring and mounted attacker. The ground was made even more awkward by the build-up of ice ridges on the shore, caused by Lake Peipus freezing and refreezing during the course of the winter.

The site was well chosen for a defensive battle, especially since the terrain limited the effectiveness of the western heavy cavalry. Alexander placed his infantry, armed with spears, bows and axes, in the centre. It should be noted that, despite Sergei Eisenstein's magnificent portrayal of

the battle of Lake Peipus in his celebrated 1938 film *Alexander Nevsky*, the Russian force consisted largely of professional soldiers – not peasant militia desperately struggling to save Holy Mother Russia, as the highly propagandistic film portrays. Alexander also had some light cavalry, which he placed on his flanks. Some of these cavalrymen were mounted archers, probably Kazaks or Cumans.

The fact that the Russians had drawn up their army and offered battle apparently caused some consternation among the outnumbered Crusaders. This is suggested by the behaviour of their native Estonian levies, who were probably not very willing to fight in the first place; they are reported to have fled immediately when they caught sight of the enemy. Nevertheless, despite the fact that the western force was

This scene from Eisenstein's film Alexander Nevsky *(1938) presents the Russians as a peasant militia defending their homeland. In reality, they were a highly professional force.*

A Novgorod Polk infantryman (c. 1240). Russia was first settled by the Vikings travelling along its rivers. They met the nomadic tribes who roamed the steppes. So Russian arms and armour reflect both Western (Norse) and Eastern influences. This infantryman wears chain mail armour with a sleeveless, waist-length quilted tunic and a round, Turkic-style breastplate. He has a simple, Norse-style conical helmet with a nose guard, and is armed with a long-handled axe.

charge against the Russian position. Clearly, they were hoping to force the Russian centre to flee in disorder, allowing the escaping foot soldiers to be picked off at leisure. The Crusaders thus formed their heavy cavalry in a wedge, with the Teutonic Knights and their men-at-arms – the best troops – at the forefront.

With very little preliminary manoeuvring, this wedge charged deep into the massed infantry that formed the centre of the Russian line. The line, however, did not break. It is probable that the Crusader charge was fatally slowed by a combination of the large number of Novgorodian archers (whose weapons would have been particularly effective against Crusader horses) and the broken terrain they had to cross.

FLANKING ATTACK

The charge might still have won the day if the Russian cavalry, posted on either wing, had not engaged at about the same time. These lighter horsemen hit the flanks of the western army, the horse archers on the Russian left flank causing particularly serious damage to the Danish knights on the Crusader right. The Russians outnumbered the Crusaders by such a large margin that they were able to surround the westerners completely.

Many of the Danish knights turned back and tried to re-cross Lake Peipus, only to be pursued by the Russian cavalry. This is the only point at which fighting is likely to have taken place upon the frozen lake itself. Even if some of the heavier western horses broke through the ice with their riders, it is unlikely that anyone drowned, since the lake is extremely shallow (in areas as little as 30cm [12in] deep). Nonetheless, this manoeuvring on the frozen lake was enough

outnumbered at least three to one, the Crusaders still had a reasonable chance of success. The core of their army was heavy cavalry, both knights and men-at-arms. Wearing heavy mail, reinforced with plate, and being mounted on large warhorses, each knight would literally have far outweighed any opponent he faced. More importantly, the knights were trained in western chivalry's signature close-order cavalry charge, which in the thirteenth century achieved victory in battle after battle, especially when launched against unsupported infantry.

The Crusader leaders (we have no information on who commanded during the actual battle; it may have been Bishop Hermann himself) decided on a sudden to win the battle of Lake Peipus the nickname 'Battle on the Ice'.

About 400 Crusaders were killed, close to half the force that actually engaged the enemy; six Teutonic Knights and 44 others were captured. The casualties might have been higher but Alexander Nevskii permitted the pursuit of the defeated westerners to continue only to the far shore of the lake.

AFTERMATH

Lake Peipus was, in reality, an unimportant battle that was made into a centrepiece of Russian anti-western ideology by later legend, most notably Eisenstein's compelling theatrical spectacle *Alexander Nevsky*, with its blood-stirring soundtrack by Sergei Prokofiev. After winning his victory, Alexander offered favourable peace terms, again confirming that Novgorod intended no westward expansion. The bishop of Dorpat and his allies promptly accepted. Novgorod withdrew from the border territories it had seized and Alexander freed his prisoners, while the westerners released their hostages.

The battle did, however, have an effect on western prestige and may have encouraged several of the conquered Baltic peoples to rebel against their western masters. Shortly after Lake Peipus, the Prussians rebelled against the Teutonic Order that had subjugated them, although such a revolt may have been inevitable anyway. It is certain that the Order was not seriously weakened in the Battle on the Ice. Very few Teutonic Knights participated in the battle, and neither the order's grand master, master for Livonia, or the latter's acting master was even present on the occasion. The next year, the Estonians rebelled against Denmark, a revolt that was also doomed to failure.

This failed Crusade against Novgorod also revealed the weakness of the papacy's grandiose schemes for the region, as the Pope proved unable to channel the divergent interests of the north into a single master plan that might have had some effect. Perhaps the most important impact of the battle, though, was to enhance the prestige of the Russian prince Alexander Nevskii. The legend of the

battle on the Neva and the battle of Lake Peipus grew over time, leading to Alexander's eventual veneration as a saint for his role in protecting Russian orthodoxy. He also emerged as the clear victor in political terms, allowing him to begin the consolidation of power in Russia that would culminate several centuries later in the union of Russia under the Tsars.

This Soviet propaganda poster, likening the Crusader invasion of Russia in 1242 to the German invasion in World War II, helps explain the exaggerated importance given to the Battle of Lake Peipus.

TANNENBERG
1410

IN MILITARY HISTORY THE POLES CELEBRATE THEIR SPECTACULAR VICTORY AT TANNENBERG, OR GRÜNWALD, OVER THE TEUTONIC ORDER WITH SPECIAL REVERENCE. THIS IS BECAUSE THE VICTORY ENSURED THAT THE NEWLY CREATED KINGDOM OF POLAND-LITHUANIA SURVIVED AND COULD PUT A HALT TO THE ADVANCE OF THE GERMAN ORDER.

WHY DID IT HAPPEN?

WHO The Teutonic Knights, led by their Grand Master Ulrich von Jungingen (d. 1410) sought to divide Lithuania from Poland, but were annihilated in a single battle with King Wladislaw II Jagiello's Polish-Lithuanian army.

WHAT Lightly armed but swift-moving Lithuanian cavalry and heavily armed Polish knights outflanked, encircled and destroyed the Teutonic Knights.

WHERE Between the villages of Tannenberg and Grünwald, in the western forests of East Prussia.

WHEN 15 July 1410

WHY The Teutons took the Polish-Lithuanians by surprise, forcing a reluctant King Jagiello to fight on ground chosen by them.

OUTCOME Instead of attacking at once Ulrich remained on the defensive, counter-attacking only when the Polish-Lithuanians retreated, but fell into a trap that saw his army destroyed.

The Teutonic Order had been founded as a Crusader order of knights at Acre in 1190 but transferred its seat of war in the name of Holy Christ to the Baltic, fighting Prussian, Latvian, Livonian and Estonian pagans. The pagan Prusy raided across the frontier into the Polish Duchy of Masovia and in order to put a stop to these attacks Duke Conrad invited the Teutonic Order to counter this menace. The knights arrived in 1230 and had crushed the Prusy within a decade of fierce fighting. But once their mission had been accomplished these increasingly unwelcome alien intruders refused to return to Germany. The Teutonic Order continued to expand and by 1283 controlled both western and eastern

Pruthenia (Prussia) stretching from the Vistula River in the west to the port of Memel in the east.

Later on, by merging with the Order of the Sword, the Teutonic Order gained control over the great trading port of Riga and the lands of Estonia, Livonia, Latvia and Courland. The order now controlled the entire eastern coastline of the Baltic and was a regional great power backed by a superlative army.

Military might made the Teutonic Order unpleasant neighbours for Poland and Lithuania and for the Russian principality of Novgorod. Conquest by the Teutons was followed by colonization by German peasants and in 40 short years

In this romanticized nineteenth-century oil painting by the Polish artist Maksymiljan Piotrowski (1813–75) the Polish-Lithuanians, led by their venerable-looking king, Wladislaw II, prepare for battle on 15 July 1410.

(1310–50) some 1400 German villages were established in Prussia.

The Teutonic Order's inexorable *Drang nach Osten* (March to the East) was greatly facilitated by the state of political chaos and division that reigned in Poland during the 1200s – the country was divided into a series of squabbling duchies and lacked a united front against the German menace to the west and north. In 1320 Poland was united under King Wladislaw I (1260–1333; reigned 1320–33), and then in 1386 Wladislaw Jagiello (c.1350–1434), the Grand Duke of Lithuania, married Queen Jadwiga of Poland. Two sworn enemies had united against the Teutonic Order, and the Lithuanians, by turning to Catholicism, deprived the order of a propaganda weapon – they were no longer fighting 'pagans'. The Poles wanted a corridor to the sea and coveted above all the port city of Danzig but their overriding ambition – in the long term – was no doubt to crush the order once and for all. The order for its part saw its role as continuing the expansion ever southwards and eastwards at the expense of the Poles and Lithuanians. An uneasy period of 'peace' came to an end when the order and Poland-Lithuania clashed over the fate of the province of Samogitia.

Of the two sides, the order was militarily the stronger and more experienced. They had known almost constant success during the previous century and a half against Slav and pagan enemies. The core of their army consisted of the 2–3000-strong Teutonic Knights themselves. They were superbly mounted, armoured, armed and disciplined. In conventional cavalry battles between armoured knights they had few equals. But during the previous decades they had had to supplement their cavalry arm with a numerous German and European mercenary infantry force and specialist troops such as English archers, Genoese crossbowmen and Italian artillery. All in all the order was a formidable war machine compared with its enemies.

The united Royal, or Commonwealth, army under King Jagiello was in fact composed of two entirely different armies

that had almost nothing in common in tactics, strategy, combat experience or equipment. The striking arm of the Polish army was its cavalry, which was composed of proud, aggressive and bold armoured knights on some of the finest mounts in Europe. These knights were, man for man, more than a match for their Teutonic enemy. But as for the infantry, it was as poorly equipped and disciplined as the cavalry were not. The Polish infantry was made up of peasant levies with only the most rudimentary weaponry, armour, training and discipline. They were no match for the Teutonic Knights in open battle except in terms of their customary almost suicidal Polish bravery. The Lithuanian army was more Asiatic than European in training, equipment and tactics since it had spent the last centuries fighting and defeating the formidable Mongols across western Russia. As a consequence they relied upon lightly armed and armoured cavalry that was highly mobile and fought the enemy with lightning raids, skirmishes and ambushes. It also contained a large contingent of 'Tartar' (Mongol) cavalry who served as mercenaries and were armed with bows and lassos and mounted on small,

TEUTONIC KNIGHT

One can see in this illustration that the roots of the Teutonic Order were military-monastic in the simple white garb with its equally simple cross as the only decoration upon shield, uniform and horse. The main strength of the order's military might was its mounted knights, who acted as the foremost offensive arm in any battle. But the use of scale armour, instead of plated armour, was to improve mobility, speed and the striking power of the knight in the face of ever better-equipped, better-disciplined and better-led infantry armies. Tannenberg was a cavalry battle but one in which infantry and support forces played a vital role in the defeat of the hitherto invincible Teutonic Knights.

LOCATION

The Battle of Tannenberg, or Grünwald, was fought north of the Vistula River, in the forested areas of southern East Prussia (Mazuria) ruled by the Teutonic Order. This region is today part of Poland.

T
A
N
N
E
N
B
E
R
G

This painting by Polish military artist Wojciech von Kossak (1824–99) gives a taste of the bloody battle, with the Royal army in close combat with the Teutons – the screams of wounded men, the neighing of horses, the clank of armour; dust, heat, and sudden death.

THE OPPOSED FORCES

POLES-LITHUANIANS (estimated)
Cavalry:	40,000
Infantry:	10–20,000
Total:	**50–60,000**

TEUTONIC KNIGHTS (estimated)
Cavalry:	21,000
Infantry:	6000
Total:	**27,000**

shaggy steppe ponies. Although these Asian warriors and the Lithuanians were superb light cavalry they were of dubious value in a pitched battle against Teutonic Knights.

THE CAMPAIGN

In December 1409 Jagiello and his cousin, Grand Duke Witold, Viceroy of Lithuania, met at Brest-Litovsk to discuss the forthcoming campaign. They agreed their armies would combine at Czerwinsk on the Vistula – it was not only equidistant between them but provided a safe and well-protected point to cross the mighty river. Meanwhile Jagiello secured a diplomatic triumph when he got the *Landmeister* (Master) of the Livonian Knights to agree to a truce. The Lithuanians thus would not face a diversionary attack in the rear from Livonia. The King of Hungary assured Jagiello that his alliance with the order, signed in March 1410, was not worth the paper it was written on: he would not take to the field with a large army. Thus Poland's rear was also secured.

To keep the order guessing as to what their enemy's intention was Witold sent Lithuanian forces against Memel while Jagiello's forces raided the Pomeranian frontier. Jagiello wanted the order to believe that this was where he would attack. But the first ordeal was simply getting his Polish army across the Vistula. A pontoon bridge spanned the 601m (550-yard) wide river at Czerwinsk and it took the Poles three days to get across. By 30 June Jagiello's Poles and Witold's Lithuanians had combined. As they set off on 2 July the Bishop of Plock gave the troops a stirring sermon to fight the enemy to the death. His words would no doubt resound on the battlefield.

Meanwhile the Grand Master of the Teutonic Order, Ulrich von Jungingen, had failed to concentrate his army, as he was still in the dark about the intentions of his enemy. But he was quite sure the Poles and Lithuanians were easy prey – he could not believe the Poles (whom he looked upon as Slav 'barbarians') were technically advanced enough to construct pontoon bridges. As Jagiello's army moved north from Czerwinsk Ulrich was forced to move his army from Pomerania to Kurzetnik on the Drweça River. On 9 July the allied army crossed into Prussia singing *Bogurodzica* (Mother of God) having covered 90km (82 miles) in a mere eight days. The following day the Polish-Lithuanian army camped at Lake Rubkowo, opposite Kurzetnik where the order had erected a strong line of fixed defences. Jagiello was now commander-in-chief of the combined Royal army while Pan Zyndram of Maszkowice (a Cracow nobleman) was appointed commander-in-chief of the Polish army. Witold remained commander of the Lithuanians.

DISPOSITIONS

The Grand Master built a series of bridges across the Drwęca and his army crossed over to the eastern bank where the battle was to be fought. Here in a rough triangle between the villages of Grünwald, Tannenberg and Ludwigsdorf (Lodwigowo) was the battlefield. It was far from ideal, as the visibility was poor due to the wooded and uneven terrain in this shallow depression that measured 3km (1.9 miles) across. Jagiello's Polish-Lithuanian army numbered 40,000 cavalry and 10-20,000 infantry. The order's army, reflecting its origins, numbered a mere 6000 footsoldiers, but was strong in cavalry – some 21,000.

The Royal army's camp was situated near Lake Lubien some 7.2km (4.5 miles) east of Grünwald. Early in the morning of 15 July a Polish knight, by the name of Hanko, rode into camp with news that the enemy was already drawn up for battle. The allies had only begun to get into formation and if Ulrich had attacked immediately he might have won a decisive victory. As it was, the Teutonic army had arrived earlier and dug ditches facing the enemy with two lines ready for battle. Here was open ground with a few woods and isolated copses of trees sloping for 6562m (6000 yards) at a gentle gradient down towards Tannenberg. There was a sharper gradient towards the thicker forests that flanked Lake Lubien. Towards the northern shore of the lake the terrain was highly unsuited to the order's style of warfare.

THE FIRST ATTACK

As stated above, had Ulrich attacked with his ready troops straightaway he might have crushed the disorganized Poles and

Lithuanians but the Grand Master wanted them to attack him first. Not wanting to displease Almighty God, whose support was ardently invoked by both sides, Jagiello had spent all morning in fervent prayer in his own private chapel in the camp. He finally bestirred himself and rode out with his bodyguard to the Weissberg – a small hill that gave a good view of the battlefield. If Ulrich thought the enemy would rush into battle in their usual impetuous manner then he was sadly mistaken. Three hours passed with the scorching sun rising ever higher without a single Pole or Lithuanian stirring. Ulrich called one of his aides, telling him if Jagiello could not be enticed into attacking

This dramatic battle scene shows Grand Duke Jagiello supposedly tearing the standard from a Teutonic Knight, signalling the order's defeat.

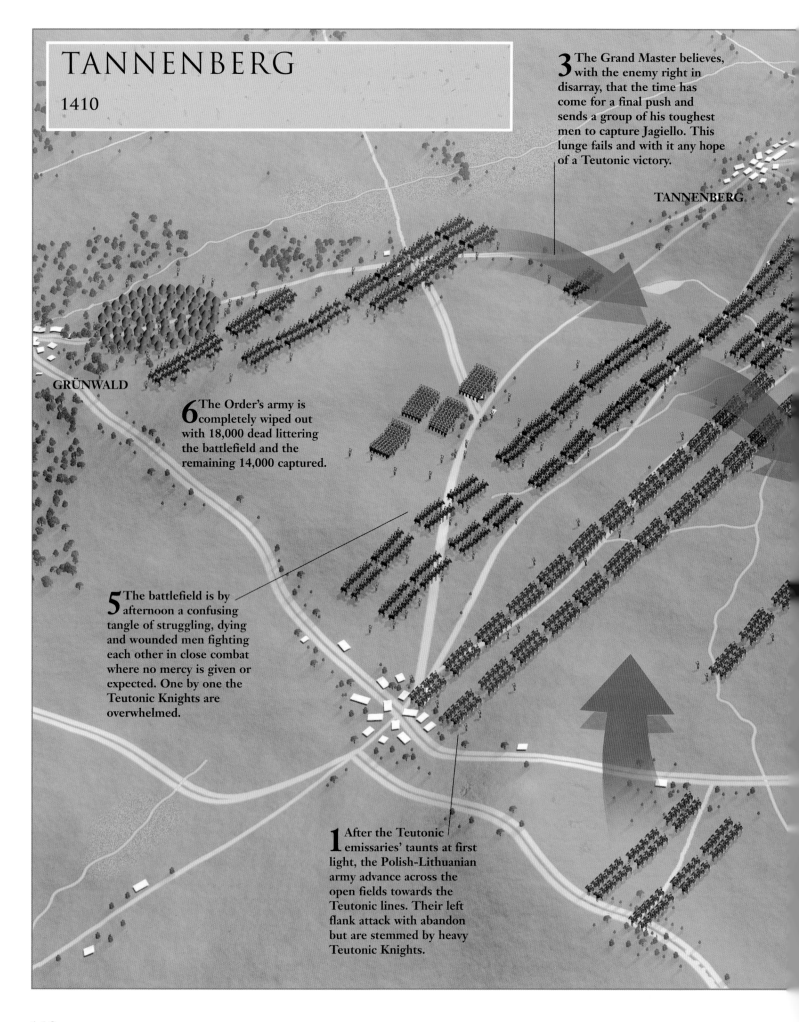

TANNENBERG

1410

3 The Grand Master believes, with the enemy right in disarray, that the time has come for a final push and sends a group of his toughest men to capture Jagiello. This lunge fails and with it any hope of a Teutonic victory.

TANNENBERG

GRÜNWALD

6 The Order's army is completely wiped out with 18,000 dead littering the battlefield and the remaining 14,000 captured.

5 The battlefield is by afternoon a confusing tangle of struggling, dying and wounded men fighting each other in close combat where no mercy is given or expected. One by one the Teutonic Knights are overwhelmed.

1 After the Teutonic emissaries' taunts at first light, the Polish-Lithuanian army advance across the open fields towards the Teutonic lines. Their left flank attack with abandon but are stemmed by heavy Teutonic Knights.

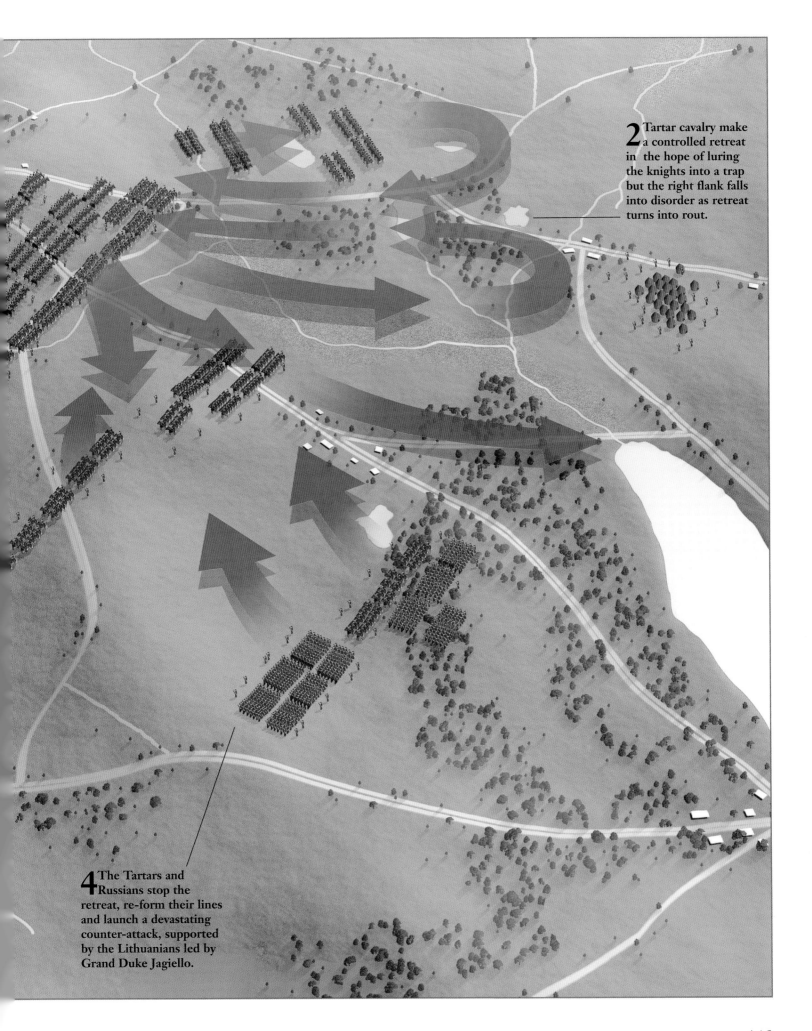

2 Tartar cavalry make a controlled retreat in the hope of luring the knights into a trap but the right flank falls into disorder as retreat turns into rout.

4 The Tartars and Russians stop the retreat, re-form their lines and launch a devastating counter-attack, supported by the Lithuanians led by Grand Duke Jagiello.

TANNENBERG

In this painting by Jan Matejko (1838–93), the Polish-Lithuanian army is at the point of crushing the reeling and bleeding troops of the order, with a triumphant Jagiello in the centre of the action.

then he would have to be goaded by an appropriately insulting gesture.

The Grand Master sent out his two highest-ranking knights to provoke the 'slow-witted' Jagiello into attacking. One was the Imperial German herald, whose shield displayed the Black Eagle (symbol of the emperor) on a gold background, and the other – with a red griffon on a white background – was Duke Kasimir of Stettin. They rode forth across the fields under a white flag of truce and were politely received by Jagiello – who had hoped the Teutons might be willing to negotiate instead of fighting.

Instead the two knights, rudely and arrogantly, rebuked Jagiello and the Polish-Lithuanian army for 'cowardice'. They should come out, said the knights, on the open field and fight like real men. Not surprisingly Jagiello lost his monumental patience, told the Teutonic Knights that they would regret their insolence, told them to return and gave Witold, the actual commander of the army, the signal to commence battle.

The Poles advanced in good order with lances and spears at the ready. On their right the Lithuanians, with their Russian and Tartar auxiliaries, could not be restrained any longer. With an almighty battle cry they crashed into the Teutonic lines, sweeping all before them until the Grand Master committed his knights. These heavily armoured troops fought the Lithuanians to a standstill. The Tartars tried to spring their trap of the controlled retreat to lure the Teutonic Knights into a trap but the plan backfired. Their own troops thought the Tartars were fleeing and began to flee themselves. The knights moved forward methodically, coldly butchering the fleeing Tartars, Lithuanians and Russians. Only three squadrons of Lithuanians and Russians held the line as Witold cut his way through the confusion to beg Jagiello to swing the Poles around and save the right flank from total collapse.

Jagiello could not have made out what was going as the whole battlefield was enveloped in thick dust stirred up by the hooves and feet of thousands of horses and

men. A sudden downpour settled the dust and finally the two sides could make out what was going on and who was fighting whom. Witold called up his last remaining reserves to stem the Teutonic attack that had seemed unstoppable only half an hour before. But the enemy had clear visibility. Jagiello was only protected by a small guard and Grand Master Ulrich ordered an attack upon the Weissberg by some of his best knights. One of these, clad in white, rushed forward but was stopped by the king's secretary, Count Zbigniew of Olesnica, who thrust a broken lance into the German's side. The white knight fell to the ground where he was bludgeoned and stabbed to death by Polish infantrymen.

THE TIDE TURNS

Meanwhile the fleeing Lithuanians, Tartars and Russians had been prevailed upon to halt and now streamed back as fast as they had fled before. They rode at the enemy with their customary courage and élan. A rain of arrows fell on the Teutonic troops as the Tartars, riding at full gallop, shot at them with their bows, while the Lithuanians and Russians used their swords and battle-axes to good effect.

The Poles had in the meantime held more than half of the order's army at bay and had forced them back in close combat. As the Lithuanian army streamed back to the fight the Teutonic army began to give way, some even fled while others died where they stood. As the Teutons began to give way they were surrounded on all sides by the enemy. To their credit the Order did not capitulate or flee in wild disorder – most of them, including the Grand Master himself, fought to the death. Others who had been able to disengage from the advancing enemy continued to fight on the road that led to Grünwald. It was in this village that the Teutonic army made its last stand and fought to the death with the Poles and Lithuanians. By 7.00 p.m. the battle was finally won.

The Teutonic Order had ceased to exist as a proper military force. The number of Teutonic dead was 18,000 and 14,000 had been taken prisoner. The Grand Master, his deputies and most of his district commanders (*komturs*) lay dead on the battlefield. Only two senior knights had survived: Prince Conrad the White of Silesia and Duke Kasimir of Stettin – the same man, presumably, who had taunted Jagiello for his 'cowardice' at the outset of the battle.

AFTERMATH

Instead of marching on the Teutonic Order's capital of Marienburg to the west the Polish-Lithuanian army – utterly exhausted – remained on the battlefield to divide the loot, rest and recuperate. When it was ready to march on Marienburg – held by Count Heinrich von Plauen and 3000 troops – it was too late. This immense fortress complex with stone walls 8.2m (27ft) high and 2.1m (7ft) thick and ample supplies of food and water proved impregnable. Jagiello's victorious army arrived on 25 July but failed to make any headway during the two-month-long siege. The war would continue for years and the Order would recover. For the Prussians this defeat left a permanent, humiliating scar that never healed, and in 1914, General Paul von Hindenburg – a Prussian – named his epic World War I victory over the Imperial Russian army in the same region after the village of Tannenberg.

This manuscript illustration by Stanislaw Durink from 1448 shows the colours and heraldry found on captured Teutonic standards seized at Tannenberg (from Biblioteka Jagiellonska, *Cracow).*

AGINCOURT
1415

THE BATTLE OF AGINCOURT PITTED A TIRED AND DISEASED ENGLISH ARMY AGAINST A FRENCH HOST ALMOST FIVE TIMES ITS SIZE. THE FRENCH WERE DETERMINED TO BREAK THE CHAIN OF ENGLISH VICTORIES AND TO PREVENT KING HENRY V FROM REACHING CALAIS WITH HIS ARMY.

WHY DID IT HAPPEN?

WHO An English army numbering 5700 under King Henry V (1388–1422), opposed by 25,000 French under Charles d'Albret (1369?–1415), Constable of France.

WHAT The main action took place between French men-at-arms (mounted and dismounted) and a combined force of English archers and dismounted men-at-arms.

WHERE East of the village of Agincourt, between Abbeville and Calais.

WHEN 25 October 1415.

WHY Marching to winter in Calais, Henry's tired and sick army was brought to battle by a vastly superior French force.

OUTCOME The French initially intended to fight a defensive action, but instead attacked down a narrow frontage between two woods. The result was a shattering defeat for the French.

The English system of making war was by this time well established. The firepower of longbow-armed archers combined with the staying power of dismounted men-at-arms was a potent force in a defensive battle.

The English longbowman in 1415 was little different than his predecessor who fought at Crécy or Halidon Hill. His main weapon had a combat range of 250m (273 yards) and could shoot perhaps 100m (109 yards) further. The plate armour of the time

King Henry V, a portrait by Benjamin Burnell (1790–1828). One of England's great captains, Henry's real-life deeds at Agincourt and Harfleur would grant him a place in heroic legend, even if he had never been immortalized in Shakespeare's plays.

was difficult to penetrate but the longbow was sufficiently powerful to drive an armour-piercing bodkin arrow through it into the man beneath at up to 50m (55 yards). Conventional broadhead arrows would bring down an unarmoured man or a horse at greater distances. Most archers carried a back-up weapon. In some cases this was a sword; more often a hatchet, dagger or a maul – a huge mace-like weapon that could be deadly in the hands of a strong man. Few archers wore armour of any sort. What there was included quilted or leather jerkins and a very basic helmet made of *cuir boulli* – leather boiled in oil or wax to make it almost as hard as metal. Many of King Henry's troops were suffering from dysentery contracted during the recent siege of Harfleur. Thus when some men went into action stripped to the waist, others chose to remove their hose for convenience instead.

All archers were professionals, recruited and paid for the campaign. They were well supplied with arrows and, more importantly, could shoot fast and accurately. At longer ranges a cloud of arrows could be arched into any target, falling directly downwards to wound the horses' backs and make looking up hazardous despite a visored helm. At close ranges hitting a moving target such as a mounted man was an easy shot for any archer competent enough to be able to hold up his head among his fellows. Most archers were good enough to shoot for the head, resulting in large numbers of men shot through their visors.

ENGLISH MEN-AT-ARMS

The 750 or so English men-at-arms that accompanied King Henry were equipped in a full-body suit of plate armour and armed with the knightly sidearm – a long sword. The sword was merely a back-up in most cases, however. To get through an enemy's armour something more substantial was necessary. Thus a mix of axes and maces was also borne, along with pole-axes and similarly lethal instruments. Henry's men-at-arms were accustomed to fighting on foot alongside the archers, though of course they were also skilled with the lance and in horsed combat.

The English army was wracked with disease, half-starved and tired from its long march. It was not in good shape for a battle even without the immense advantage in numbers of the French. However, the army did have great confidence in King Henry V, who had shown his courage and warrior skills at the recent (victorious) siege of Harfleur.

FRENCH KNIGHTS

On the French side, the main striking force was, as usual, men-at-arms encased from head to foot in steel. Improvements in armour meant that the shield had largely been abandoned, permitting knights to fight with two-handed weapons on foot and to have recourse to the sword only when disarmed. Specialist armour-piercing weapons such as military picks were much in evidence.

Although the French had lost some of their reluctance to fight on foot, the massed charge of lance-armed chivalry was still their ideal of warfare. Despite a string of humiliating defeats at the hands of the English, the French seemed determined to disprove the old adage that 'defeat breeds innovation'. This was, as much as anything, for social reasons.

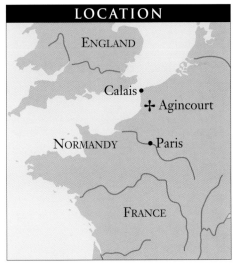

ENGLISH ARCHER AND MAN-AT-ARMS (1415)

The English men-at-arms (a term which embraced knights, squires and some non-noble warriors) were always prepared to dismount to fight alongside the archers, who were their social inferiors. These longbowmen usually deployed on the flanks or in broken ground to give them protection against more heavily armed opponents should it come to hand-to-hand fighting. At Agincourt, King Henry V ordered that every archer should cut himself a stake to provide portable protection against cavalry charges. This worked to great effect in defeating the French. The miserable state of the English army, starving and living on filthy water, is shown in the archer's need to let down his breeches, due to diarrhoea.

LOCATION

ENGLAND

Calais
† Agincourt

NORMANDY •Paris

FRANCE

The village of Agincourt lay on the Calais road 50km (32 miles) south of the port. The battle was fought in a narrow gap between two woods, which still survive to this day.

Henry V (centre, with crowned helm) was a fearsome warrior who personally saved the life of the Duke of Gloucester during the battle. More than great speeches, such deeds inspired his followers to fight on when things looked bleak.

footsoldiers from, and no desire to create one. The idea of arming peasants made French noblemen uneasy, and rightly so. What good was victory over the English if the way of life of the French rulers was swept away in the process?

And so, as always, it was the upper echelons of society who came to the field of Agincourt with banners flying, their numbers filled out by professional men-at-arms who might aspire to winning a knighthood on the field. The rivalry between these noble warriors, whose status in society depended upon what they did on the field of battle, made them impetuous and unreliable. Their charge would be furious, but it was also uncontrolled. One concession to the dominance of the English archer was to provide many of the knights' horses with barding – horse armour – to give them a measure of protection. In earlier battles the charge of the knights had foundered as their mounts were shot down. The French hoped that even if barding slowed their mounts it would enable more of them to reach the enemy line. The French also brought a force of about 3000 crossbowmen and some early cannon to the field, but they played little part in the battle.

THE CAMPAIGN

The Battle of Agincourt was part of the so-called Hundred Years War (actually 1337–1453) between England and France. The war was not continuous, and at times subsided into an uneasy peace of sorts.

In 1415, France was weakened by civil war, and Henry V of England decided that the time was right to resume hostilities. In mid-1415, his army landed in France and laid siege to the fortress of Harfleur. Five weeks later, despite dysentery and all the other hardships of siege, Henry had captured the fortress. He then set off with what remained of his army to march to Calais, intending to winter there.

The French, intimidated by their string of defeats, tended to adopt a very defensive stance when the English attacked. In practice this meant withdrawing into fortresses and surrendering the initiative to the English. However, with a clearly far superior force at hand, the Constable of France, Charles d'Albret, decided to bring

The feudal system in France included a sharp divide between the ruling class, whose right and responsibility was to bear arms, and the peasantry, who were generally ground underfoot and had to be kept disarmed to reduce the chances of a rebellion. The miserable performance of peasant levies whenever they were taken to the battlefield had served to further convince the French nobility of the futility of arming the lower orders. There was therefore no proud yeoman class to recruit

the English to battle. His men placed stakes and broke down the banks at river crossings, making the English march a lengthy and dangerous one.

Henry's army was already short of provisions as it set out for Calais. Struggling to find a usable river crossing wasted more time, but at length the army managed to cross the Somme at St Quentin. Struggling onward, the sick and weary English then found d'Albret's powerful host camped across its line of march. With his men starving and soaked by a downpour during the night, Henry nevertheless resolved to fight his way through to safety.

DISPOSITIONS

Knowing very well that the English were short of food – and wishing to avoid a repeat of previous defeats, where French charges had battered themselves to pieces on a static English line – d'Albret was determined to force the outnumbered English to come to him. By refusing to attack he would force the English into moving forward. His enemy was constrained by his lack of supplies, while d'Albret had all the advantages – numbers, mobility and position. He could wait; Henry could not.

D'Albret's force was drawn up in three battles, as was usual. The front and second

THE OPPOSED FORCES

ENGLISH (estimated)

Men-at-arms:	750
Archers:	4950
Total:	**5700**

FRENCH (estimated)

Men-at-arms (mounted):	7000
Men-at-arms (dismounted):	15,000
Crossbowmen:	3000
Others: Some primitive cannon	
Total:	**25,000**

Charles, Duke of Orléans. One of the French commanders at Agincourt, Duke Charles was captured and spent 25 years imprisoned in the Tower of London. He spent much of his time there writing poetry.

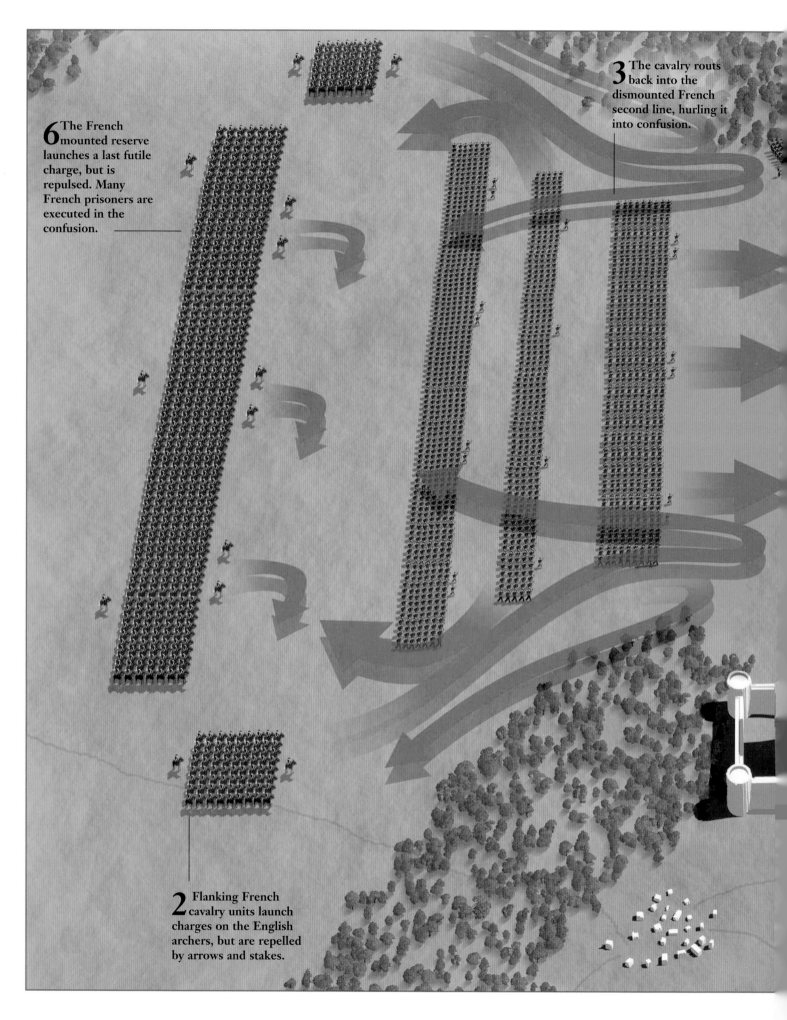

6 The French mounted reserve launches a last futile charge, but is repulsed. Many French prisoners are executed in the confusion.

3 The cavalry routs back into the dismounted French second line, hurling it into confusion.

2 Flanking French cavalry units launch charges on the English archers, but are repelled by arrows and stakes.

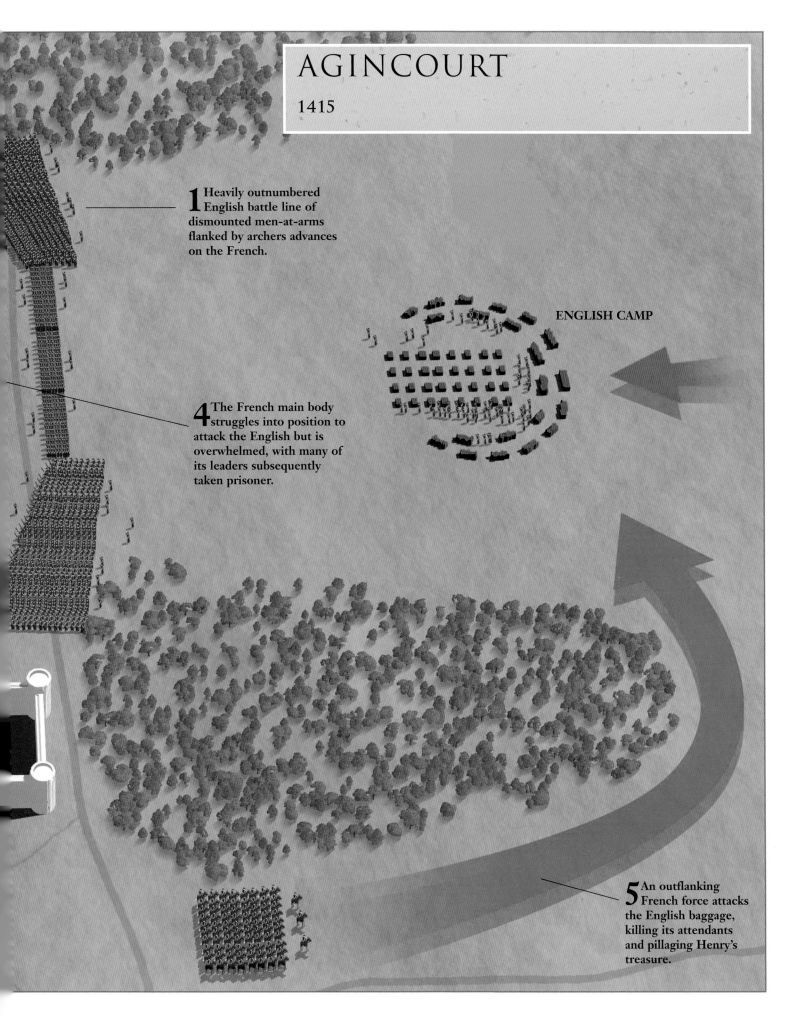

AGINCOURT
1415

1 Heavily outnumbered English battle line of dismounted men-at-arms flanked by archers advances on the French.

ENGLISH CAMP

4 The French main body struggles into position to attack the English but is overwhelmed, with many of its leaders subsequently taken prisoner.

5 An outflanking French force attacks the English baggage, killing its attendants and pillaging Henry's treasure.

At Agincourt King Henry fought on foot, but the horse was a powerful status symbol. Thus in this manuscript illustration showing the seal of the king he is depicted as a mounted warrior bearing a sword, another symbol of power and rank.

lines were mostly dismounted, while the third was composed of mounted men. The 3000 crossbowmen attached to the French force were also in the rear where they could achieve little.

Given what had happened to the Genoese at Crécy, the crossbowmen were probably grateful that at least they would not be ridden down by their own side. D'Albret also positioned two forces of mounted men-at-arms, each numbering about 600 men, on the flanks. He hoped to be able to launch a mounted charge directly at the English archers and either scatter

them or at least distract them from shooting into the main attack. The force assigned to make this assault included many knights mounted on barded horses. He was sure that Henry could be induced to attack, which would in turn lead to the ruin of the English army.

DEPLOYMENT

The English deployed in what had become the conventional manner, with three blocks of men-at-arms flanked by triangular formations of archers. The centre block was commanded by Henry himself, with the right commanded by Edward, Duke of York, and the left by Lord Camoys. Henry knew of the French plan to destroy his archers, and came up with a counter to it. During the march, the archers were commanded to furnish themselves with long stakes, sharpened at both ends. These were rammed into the ground in front of and among the archer formations, pointing forward and offering a measure of protection against an enemy charge. The archers were easily able to step around the stakes and move within their protective hedge, but to a horseman approaching at speed the chances of being impaled were considerable. Some of the men were charged with uprooting the stakes and moving them if the archers were ordered to change position.

Henry's flanks were protected by woods. On the right lay Tramcourt woods and on the left were Agincourt woods. To the rear lay the English baggage camp, virtually undefended. Some accounts claim that Henry placed archers and men-at-arms in the woods, but this is unlikely. The English scarcely had enough men to form a line and could not afford a reserve, let alone a flanking force.

While the English nobles and men-at-arms knew that they might expect some degree of mercy from their enemies, there was no such hope for the common soldiery. So hated were the infamous longbowmen that 300 had been hanged after the fall of Soissons to the French. Indeed, one reason for the provision of stakes to the archers was the rumour that the French intended to 'make a dead-set' against the archers and massacre them at the first opportunity.

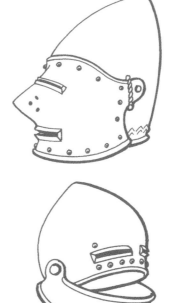

Late medieval cavalry helmets varied in style with the wearer's preference. They generally fitted more tightly to the face and neck. Still, some soldiers and leaders felt that they limited vision and communication too much. Therefore, they chose to raise their visors or fight without them.

Their preparations made, the two armies faced one another across the sodden ground. Each waited for the other to attack. For four hours the stand-off continued.

Eventually, Henry was forced to act. If the French would not attack, he had to advance against them. It seemed that the enemy had learned from their previous headlong attacks. There was little chance for the tiny English army to make a successful assault, but there was no alternative. At the command to advance, the English crossed themselves, the archers pulled up their stakes, and the whole force slowly moved forward. Eventually, having paused more than once to allow the men-at-arms to rest and maintain their formation, the English reached longbow range. The archers re-emplaced their stakes in the wet ground and began to shoot.

THE FRENCH ATTACK

The English halted at bow range and opened a steady fire on the front battle of the French army, which had no means of reply. The only troops able to match the

In this nineteenth-century illustration of Agincourt, it is the mounted knight that takes centre stage. Even today, it is widely (and erroneously) believed that medieval warfare was the exclusive province of the armoured nobleman.

179

AGAINST THE ODDS

Given the disparity in numbers and sheer fighting power of the two armies deployed at Agincourt, it is obvious that the odds were heavily in the French favour. Yet the English won. The main reason was the tactics employed by both sides. Outnumbered by foes with superior mobility, Henry could not afford to be flanked. He thus carefully chose ground where his flanks were covered. Meanwhile the French threw away their main advantages – mobility and numbers – by attacking on a narrow frontage over muddy ground that slowed their assault and gave the English archers more time to barrage the attacking force. The French did employ some basic good practice, such as the flanking forces and dismounting the first line of attackers, but overall they gave the advantage to Henry's tiny army and suffered terribly for it.

Longbowmen depicted in a fifteenth-century manuscript. Their only armour is a helmet of metal or more likely leather. The bowmen are shown with a sheaf of arrows stuck in their belts; at Agincourt many archers stuck arrows in the ground in front of them for convenience.

archers at that range, the French crossbowmen, were far to the rear and unable to contribute to the action. The French were forced to take the offensive after all, or else stand under fire all day. First the cavalry of the flanking forces advanced against the archers on the English flanks. The flanking forces were smaller than they should have been due to command and control issues that resulted in many knights being out of position or deployed in the wrong units.

Despite this, the flanking cavalry make a brave attempt. On the English left flank, the charge was broken up by archery and the majority of the force turned back. Three knights pressed the attack but were soon brought down. On the right, the assault fared a little better. Part of the force managed to come to handstrokes despite the re-emplaced stakes and intense archery. The attack was quickly repulsed, however.

Meanwhile the lead battle, under d'Albret and the Duke of Orléans, began to advance. The going was slow, through ankle-deep mud churned up by the cavalry

Opposite: King Henry V makes a rallying speech to his troops on St Crispin's Day, inspiring his men for the desperate battle ahead. By nightfall the English had won one of the greatest victories of all time.

and weighed down by armour. Even for the mounted men the pace was not fast. This was no headlong charge but a steady advance coming forward at a slow walk, and it offered a perfect target for the English longbowmen. As d'Albret's force pushed laboriously forward, it was disrupted by the routing cavalry and riderless horses of the initial attack.

The formation was also compressed onto a smaller frontage by the woods, which acted as a funnel. The French force was bunched together as it approached the shorter English line. So tightly compressed were the French that some men struggled to find room to wield their weapons. Two-handed swords, then just entering service, were useless in the press.

The lead French battle finally came into contact with the English line and a fierce

mêlée developed. Unable to shoot, the archers took to their hand weapons and assailed the French alongside their armoured companions. Although the French had the advantage of numbers they were exhausted by their laborious advance and, jammed together, could not fight effectively. Many were killed or taken prisoner in the fighting. Offensive weapons were not the only killers in that desperate struggle. A man-at-arms who slipped or fell wounded into the thick mud had little chance of rising easily, even if he was not trampled down by others.

Men died of drowning in the mud or suffocated under the weight of their armour and that of others. This fate befell the Duke of York. Still others were slain by the vengeful longbowmen, who dispatched downed noblemen with a knife through the joints in their armour or beat them to death with mauls.

The second French battle came up to support the first, and the battle intensified.

The Count d'Alencon and a party of knights, sworn to kill King Henry or die trying, cut their way through to the English monarch, who was fighting heroically in the front rank. Henry covered himself with glory once more, coming to the rescue of the Duke of Gloucester who was in serious trouble at d'Alencon's hands.

Although part of the crown that surrounded his helm was cut away, Henry emerged victorious from the combat. Eventually, d'Alencon's assault was beaten off and his band of knights were dispatched. The French assault gradually ebbed and the English eyed the third French battle, as yet uncommitted, across the corpse-strewn and sodden ground.

A LATE REVERSE

King Henry boldly – some might say cheekily – sent a herald to the remaining French battle saying that that it must leave the field immediately or receive no quarter.

Having seen what had happened to the other two-thirds of their army, the men of the third battle began to comply.

Even as the French third battle was retreating, one of its leaders, de Fauquemberg, scraped together a force and made a minor, though determined, attack through the knee-deep mud and the carnage of previous assaults. At much the same time, the local lord, Isembert d'Azincourt, made an attack into the English rear with his own forces.

The English were at this time occupied with the removal of prisoners to the rear and reorganizing their weary army. Then came word that the French had attacked the baggage camp. This meant that a French force of unknown size was in the English rear area and might at any moment fall upon Henry's battered force. Worse, the French third battle

French crossbowmen of the late fifteenth century are depicted in a nineteenth-century engraving based on a medieval manuscript. Here they demonstrate the importance of the large pavise, often carried by an accompanying pavisier, to the slow-loading missilemen.

had returned to the field and begun to slowly advance.

Henry did not have enough men to guard the prisoners, repulse the force in his rear and face the remainder of the French army. The order was given to put the prisoners to the sword, since they posed a severe threat if they obtained weapons. However, although the baggage was pillaged, the threat posed by d'Azincourt's force proved to be fairly minor and it was soon driven off, at which point the remaining prisoners were spared.

The rallied French forces, even though they still outnumbered Henry's entire force, thought better of pressing their attack against the English line. They drew off, leaving the field in English hands and the road to Calais open.

AFTERMATH

King Henry was able to reach Calais with what remained of his army, though he was not in a position to pursue the beaten French and make more of his victory.

Agincourt was the third of a trio of great English victories – after Crécy and Poitiers – won by English archers over heavily armoured French men-at-arms. The battle cost France half of its nobility, including three dukes, 90 other nobles and about 1560 men-at-arms. About 200 more were captured. The English lost about 400 men.

However, the total dominance of the English archer was drawing to an end by 1415, with the emergence of gunpowder and the increasing use of firearms. The pattern of victories of steady English troops over aggressively advancing Frenchmen would continue for many years, however. Four centuries later, during the Napoleonic Wars, the Duke of Wellington observed that the French continued to come on in the old manner, and that the English continued to defeat them in the old manner.

The Battle of Poitiers, fought on 19 September 1356, was the second great battlefield defeat of the French by the English during the Hundred Years War. Using a combination of longbow archers, infantry and dismounted cavalry, the English Black Prince led a force that withstood charges from both French cavalry and infantry to capture the opposing general, France's King John II. This defeat forced the French to agree to the Treaty of Brétigny, which ceded large amounts of land to the English.

CONSTANTINOPLE
1453

THE OTTOMAN TURKISH SIEGE OF CONSTANTINOPLE IN 1453 WAS ONE OF THE GREATEST SIEGES OF ALL TIME. IT SAW THE TURKS USE – FOR THE VERY FIRST TIME – HEAVY SIEGE ARTILLERY TO BREAK THROUGH THE ENORMOUS THEODOSIAN WALLS THAT HAD HELD OFF ATTACKERS FOR MORE THAN A MILLENNIUM.

WHY DID IT HAPPEN?

WHO Ottoman Sultan Mehmed II (1432–81, reigned 1444–46 and 1451–81) besieged the city with 120,000 troops, opposed by some 8–10,000 Christian defenders under Emperor Constantine XI Palaeologus (1405–53, reigned 1449–53).

WHAT The Turks used Urban's massive cannon against the finest fortification works in Europe.

WHERE Siege of the Imperial Byzantine capital of Constantinople (Byzantium) on the Bosporus and Sea of Marmara. The city is better known today by its Turkish name of Istanbul.

WHEN 5 April–29 May 1453

WHY Mehmed II wished to eliminate this tiny Christian stronghold deep behind the Turkish frontier and make it the new capital of his growing empire.

OUTCOME The fall of Byzantine Constantinople to Mehmed's expanding Ottoman Empire.

The fall of the capital of the Byzantine Empire, Constantinople, to the Muslim Turks in May 1453 was a disastrous event for the Christian world, especially for Orthodox Christians, who viewed it as the beginning of the end for their faith. That Constantinople was going to fall to the Ottoman Turks was a foregone conclusion. The beginning of the end for the Byzantine Empire had been the disastrous defeat of their once-victorious army at the hands of the Seljuk Turks at the battle of Manzikert in 1071. During the following centuries the Turks conquered the whole of Anatolia and

A medieval illustrated map from the British Library showing in the centre the formidable walls of Constantinople. Across the waters of the Golden Horn is the fortified suburb of Galata (Pera) held by the neutral Genoese.

were united under the Ottoman dynasty into one single sultanate. The Catholic West, instead of aiding the hard-pressed Byzantines, stabbed them in the back. In 1204 'Crusaders', paid by Venice, sacked Constantinople, and the city itself, like the rest of the empire, began a long, sad decline.

The Western invaders were eventually expelled but the Ottoman Turks, taking advantage of the ravages of the Black Death, crossed into the Balkans in 1356, seizing Byzantine lands there. By 1396 the whole of Bulgaria was in Ottoman hands, and Constantinople itself – practically all that was left of the empire – was surrounded by Turkish-occupied territory and cut off from the West.

The city was a mere shadow of its former self and its disastrous decline was reflected in the city's population – an impressive one million in the twelfth century had been reduced by the 1450s to a mere 100,000. Constantinople, however, continued to trade both with the West and the East, while the Theodosian Walls – built in the fifth century in the reign of Emperor Theodosius II (401–450) – remained intact and protected the city from enemy attack with their 5.7km (3.5-mile) long moats and triple line of walls and fortified towers which stretched from the Sea of Marmara to the Golden Horn.

Constantinople was given a respite when a most unlikely saviour appeared in the East in the shape of the savage but brilliant Mongol warlord Timur Lenk, or Tamerlane (1336–1405), who defeated the Ottomans at the battle of Ankara in 1402. This gave the city a reprieve for half a century mainly due to Ottoman civil wars and the fact that after a failed siege in 1422 Sultan Murád II (1404–51) chose to live in peace with the Byzantines. He argued, sensibly, that Constantinople posed no threat in the hands of the feeble Byzantines and that an Ottoman attack upon the city might unite the divided and decadent Christians against the Muslim menace.

MEHMED II

Unfortunately Murád II – admired and respected by Ottomans and Byzantines alike – died in February 1451 and his place as sultan was taken by a callow, arrogant,

TURKISH JANISSARY (C.1450)

Founded in 1330, these Turkish slave-soldiers, drawn from converted Christian tribute-children and prisoners of war, were essential to the military success of the Ottoman state and went on to become the model for discipline in the Western armies of the sixteenth century. This infantryman is armed with the standard curved scimitar of the period and a short bow. Janissary bowmen first proved their worth at the Battle of Nicopolis (1396), where they were deployed against cavalry to great effect behind stakes in a skirmishing formation. By the time of the siege of Constantinople, they were an essential part of the Ottoman Turkish army.

drunken and aggressive youth of 19, Mehmed II, who was to rule and make war on his neighbours until his death from overindulgence at the age of 49. Mehmed II had many bad qualities but he was determined and was to prove, with time, a good military leader. His one overriding, indeed consuming, passion was to take Constantinople and make it the capital of an Ottoman Empire that would straddle the world. He had the temerity to call himself the 'Shadow of God upon Earth' and with the fall of the Byzantine capital that seemed justified. After all, walls that had stood for a thousand years had been breached and stormed by his Ottoman troops.

In the summer of 1452 Mehmed II had recruited and paid a Hungarian gunmaker, Urban, a huge sum to build him a monstrous gun that would be able to breach the walls of Constantinople. By January 1453 Urban's gun was ready for inspection at Adrianople (the Ottoman capital to the west of Constantinople): its barrel measured 8.1m (26ft 8in) in length, had a calibre of 20.3cm (8in) and required a crew of 700, but could lob a cannonball weighing a tonne (1 ton) over 1.6km (1 mile).

Obviously Mehmed II had the hardware for a successful siege and during the spring he called up men from across his vast empire that stretched from the Balkans in the west to Anatolia in the east. He had a huge army concentrated at Adrianople

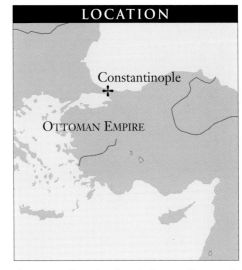

LOCATION

Constantinople stood at the point between Europe and Asia Minor and also between the Mediterranean and the Black Sea. In 1453 it remained the last vestige of ancient Byzantium not yet conquered by the Turks.

CONSTANTINOPLE

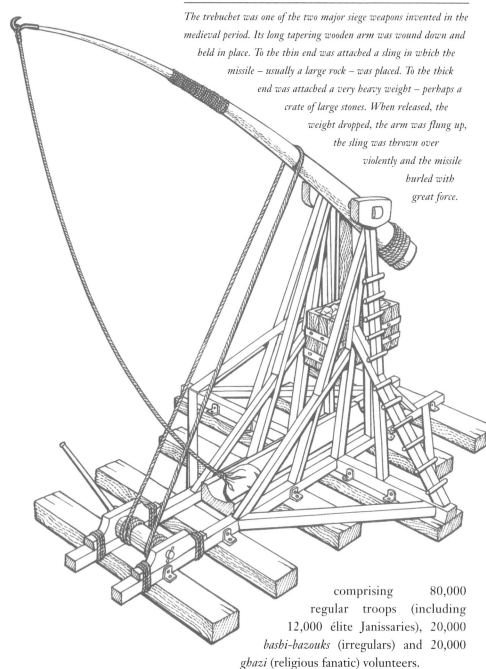

The trebuchet was one of the two major siege weapons invented in the medieval period. Its long tapering wooden arm was wound down and held in place. To the thin end was attached a sling in which the missile – usually a large rock – was placed. To the thick end was attached a very heavy weight – perhaps a crate of large stones. When released, the weight dropped, the arm was flung up, the sling was thrown over violently and the missile hurled with great force.

comprising 80,000 regular troops (including 12,000 élite Janissaries), 20,000 *bashi-bazouks* (irregulars) and 20,000 *ghazi* (religious fanatic) volunteers.

THE SIEGE BEGINS

The first step in Mehmed's relentless assault upon Constantinople began a year before he commenced the formal siege of the city. First and foremost Constantinople's access to grain from the Black Sea had to be cut. Mehmed, no respecter of Christians or the niceties of diplomacy, broke all his father's agreements with the Emperor Constantine XI – who had ascended the throne in 1449 – and sent his army to occupy Byzantine territory along the Bosporous.

The Ottomans, partly using Christian slave labour, began to construct a fortress at the shoreline. In only five months, between 14 April and 31 August 1452, the Turks had

constructed a fort named, in appropriately grisly fashion, Boghaz-Kesen, or the 'Throat Cutter', by Mehmed. The fort soon lived up to its name. In November 1452 a Venetian ship – ignoring the Turkish blockade of Constantinople – was hit with a single shot and sunk. The crew were slaughtered and the captain, Antonio Rizzo, was impaled. His body was left to rot as a warning for others that they ignored the fort's guns at their peril.

None of the Italian states, except for the pope, lifted a finger to aid Constantinople and in the doomed city the population realized that the hapless Venetian captain's gruesome fate was only a foretaste of what the barbaric Turks would do to them. For once all the disparate elements of the city's population – Greeks, Balkan Slavs, Italians and others – united in a desperate resolve to fight to the bitter end. One man had more reason that any other to fear Turkish atrocities. He was in fact an Ottoman Turk and a distant relative of Mehmed: Prince Orhan. He and his men would fight with more desperation and courage than the Byzantines.

Mehmed II spent the following winter making elaborate and meticulous preparations to attack Constantinople by the following spring. An unpleasant surprise in March 1453 was the appearance of the Ottoman fleet under Suleyman Baltoghlu in the Marmara. Thus Constantinople's seaborne lines of communication were cut.

DISPOSITIONS

The first Ottoman detachments arrived beneath the walls of Constantinople on 1 April and were met by Byzantine skirmishers. As more Turks arrived Constantine XI, who took an active part in the defence, ordered the bridges across the outer moat burnt and the gates shut and bolted; meanwhile the walls were manned. It was a valiant effort but he had only 7000 Byzantines and 5000 foreigners (mainly Italians) facing over 100,000 Turks.

On 6 April Mehmed moved his main camp closer to the walls. He faced an unenviable task, despite his enormous numerical preponderance, since the walls were in good repair. Where should he attack? The Marmara Sea Wall was strong

THE OPPOSED FORCES

OTTOMAN TURKS (estimated)
Regular infantry:	68,000
Janissary infantry:	12,000
Bashi-bazouks militia:	20,000
Ghazis (Islamic volunteers):	20,000
Total	**120,000**

CHRISTIAN DEFENDERS (estimated)
Byzantine Greeks:	7000
'Foreigners or Latins' (Italians, Catalans & other European volunteers):	5000
Total	**12,000**

and was protected by a strong current and underwater reefs. The Golden Horn Wall was also strong. So the assault had to be made against the massive Land Wall. A logical place would be to attack the Blachernae district that protruded northwards from the wall. But the Byzantines – brilliant fortifiers – had reinforced its defences. The actual Theodosian Walls consisted of three separate but parallel lines of walls fronted by a 18.2m (60ft) moat that could be flooded in an emergency. The Outer Wall – which lay behind this moat and a low crenellated breastwork – was 7.6m (25ft) high and had a strong square tower every 46–56m (50–60 yards). Facing a powerful enemy with few troops the emperor decided to man the Outer Wall with Byzantines and his Italian allies. Prince Orhan's Turks held the harbour while Don Péré Julia's Catalans held the Hippodrome. The Sea Walls were thinly held as the Byzantines, rightly, expected Mehmed to launch his main attack against the Land Wall. The defenders' artillery was unusable due to the shortage of saltpetre in the besieged city but the troops had good armour, far superior to that of the lightly armoured Turks.

Mehmed placed the Rumelian army under Karadja Pasha from the Golden Horn to the Lycus Valley and from there to the Marmara, Ishak Pasha's Anatolian army. Mehmed pitched his red and gold silk tent about 400m (440 yards) from the Land Wall with his best troops and Urban's monstrous gun around him.

THE ATTACK BEGINS

On 9 April the Ottoman admiral Baltoghlu Pasha made an unsuccessful attempt to break through the boom erected by the defenders across the Golden Horn. That same day the Turks began to attack two forts, Therapia and Studius, to the west of the Land Wall. The castles held out until 11 April when both capitulated. The brave defenders, some 76 men, were impaled on Mehmed's express orders in front of the Land Wall to show what happened to those that resisted his will. A third fort, on the island of Prinkipo, held out and the garrison chose to burn itself to death rather than fall into the hands of the Turks.

On 12 April the Turks began bombarding the Theodosian Walls and the artillery fire would continue without interruption for six weeks. The Ottoman guns were heavy and unwieldy with a tendency to slide off their mud and wood firing platforms. Urban's giant gun only fired seven times a day, so complex and time-consuming was the process of loading and firing it, but it had a deafening roar and did great damage to the wall and the defenders' nerves.

By 18 April the wall across the Lycus Valley – the weakest section of the

An illustrated 'map' from a medieval document that shows in high colour and fascinating detail the camp of the besieging Ottomans east of Constantinople's Theodosian Walls (bottom of picture).

1 Mehmed II establishes his camp outside the Land Wall in early April 1453. The city is cut off and the walls receive a constant battering.

4 On the night of 28/29 May the Turks break in over the wall and through a small postern gate.

5 Constantine XI is killed in the final battles for the city. For three days the city is sacked and looted.

CONSTANTINOPLE

1453

3 Mehmed sends Turkish ships overland round Pera on rollers and into the Golden Horn. Constantinople is now fully blockaded.

2 A small Italian fleet breaks through and is let into the Golden Horn, giving temporary relief.

Theodosian Walls – had been completely destroyed but General Giustiani Longo (the emperor's field commander) had it repaired by Byzantine volunteers. That same day, two hours after sunset, Mehmed launched his first attack against this area, known as the Mesoteichion. The Turks had filled in the moat and rushed the wall but were thrown back by heavily armoured Byzantines and Italians led by Longo. The fighting lasted for four hours with the Turks losing 400 men to no loss for the Christians. Morale among the defenders soared.

NO RELIEF

Two days later came an even greater success when Baltoghlu Pasha tried and failed to defeat a fleet of Italian ships that were sailing to Constantinople with badly needed

This restored section of the Theodosian Walls shows their formidable strength, with three parallel lines of towers and thick crenellated walls. Breaching such defences proved near impossible for many centuries.

supplies of grain. The Turkish galleys were no match for the heavy Italian ships which blasted their way through with cannon and Greek Fire. The enraged Mehmed – who had seen the defeat unfold before his eyes – dismissed the hapless admiral.

Mehmed took charge and managed to move part of his fleet overland to the Golden Horn without the Byzantines being able to stop it. Now Constantinople was threatened from the north and a bravely led night attack, on 28 April, to launch fire

ships against the flotilla failed due to spies in Pera. The Venetians and Genoese, sworn enemies, began to fight amongst themselves prompting Constantine XI to tell them: 'The war outside our gates is enough for us. For the pity of God do not start a war between yourselves.' Thus admonished, the squabbling Italians buried the hatchet – but only temporarily.

On 7 May the Turks made a night attack against the Mesoteichion section of the

The Cannon of Mehmed II (below) was cast in 1464 and used by the Turks to protect the Bosporus strait. The gun was divided into two parts for ease of transportation. It weighed 18.2 tonnes (18 tons) and was 5.25m (17ft) long.

Opposite: The Turks entered Constantinople on 29 May 1453. The Byzantine Emperor, Constantine XI, was killed. The sultan, Mehmed II, gave the city up to his troops to destroy and loot for three days.

saw their massive siege tower opposite the Mesoteichion go up in flames after the Byzantines made a night raid and blew it up with a powder keg. By 23 May further tunnels had been eliminated after the Byzantines captured the Serb mining engineer in the sultan's service. After refined torture he revealed everything he knew and Grant's anti-mining unit set to work. But that very same day a lone Venetian vessel sailed into the harbour with the devastating news that there would be no Western fleet to save Constantinople. Morale began to slide.

On 24 and 25 May morale collapsed. In an age of deep religious fervour and belief in omens or signs, the events of these two days could only have a catastrophic impact. The first day during a procession, the Holy Icon of the Mother of God was dropped and the whole proceedings were interrupted by a thunderstorm that flooded the street. The following day, the city was blanketed in a thick fog that was unusual for the time of year. The populace, remembering the ancient prophesy that Constantinople would fall when the emperor had the same name as the founder, Constantine the Great, was convinced the fog hid God's departure from the Holy City.

What the defenders did not know was that morale among the besiegers was also low. After a seven-month-long siege with an army that now numbered 150,000, only setbacks and humiliations had been experienced. The sultan's ministers – all Murád II's men – and especially the Grand Vizier, Halil Pasha, were unimpressed with the boasts and arrogance of the 21-year-old ruler. Mehmed wanted a grand assault during the night of 28/29 May and agreed to withdraw if that failed.

THE GRAND ASSAULT

Medieval armies besieging a stubborn enemy would offer terms. If these were rejected then the city would, if stormed, be shown no mercy. This was the fate that would now befall Constantinople. By 28 May all the preparations had been completed on both sides. Across the doomed city the Christian populace, knowing that the last battle was upon them, assured each other that they would fight. In

This highly romanticized and propagandistic illustration from 1832 shows Mehmed II Fatih leading his men over the walls of Constantinople while (at the bottom of the picture) the Byzantine Emperor Constantine XI is killed.

Theodosian Walls that ended with the sultan's standard bearer, Amir Bey, being killed by the Byzantine knight Rhangabe. Five days later another night assault ended in defeat. Turkish attempts to build underground tunnels for mining were discovered. The Scottish mercenary knight, John Grant, in Byzantine service, led the defenders in counter-mining and flooding the Turkish tunnels. On 18 May the Turks

the evening, everyone, including the emperor, attended mass where both Orthodox and Catholic prayed to God for deliverance. Catalans, Castilians, Venetians and Genoese as well as the Byzantine Greeks stood shoulder to shoulder and took Holy Communion together from their respective clergy.

At 1.30 a.m. Mehmed signalled for the huge horde of poorly disciplined and lightly armed *bashi-bazouks* to attack in the Lycus Valley. During two hours of fighting the Christian defenders stood their ground, leaving hundreds of enemy dead. But Mehmed was only wearing down the defenders in preparation for further assaults. The Anatolian army attacked – in wave upon wave – but each successive surge of men was halted, cut to pieces and sent reeling back in retreat. Similar attacks against the Sea Walls failed equally miserably and even Mehmed began to lose faith in a Turkish victory. There were now only the Janissaries – some 12,000 of them – left for a final, desperate attack.

At that moment, as the Janissaries, accompanied by the Ottoman musical corps, attacked, two disasters befell the defenders. Firstly the Turks discovered that someone had left a small gate (Kerkaporta) open between the Blachernae and the Theodosian Walls. The attackers wasted no time in rushing the open gate. The Byzantines hurried to defend it but were simply swamped by sheer numbers. At the same time Giustiani Longo was wounded and despite Emperor Constantine XI pleading with him to stay he was taken aboard a Genoese ship which sailed to Chios where he died two days later. The Genoese fled in panic down to the harbour or to Pera. The Venetians claimed betrayal while the Byzantines fought on in sheer desperation; the emperor died fighting. The Turks opened the gates, more of their troops poured in and they penetrated the city. Orhan's Turks fought to the death, knowing they would die slowly at the hands of the bloodthirsty Mehmed, and the Catalans fought to the last man defending the Hippodrome and Old Palace. The Turks ran amok in the city, looting, killing and raping, until even Mehmed had had enough and by evening imposed some order. Some 50,000 Byzantines were enslaved while 4000 were killed in the battle. The greatest siege of all time was over.

AFTERMATH

The fall of Constantinople was a high point in the relentless and ruthless expansion of the Ottoman Empire. Mehmed II became known by his honorific title, *Fatih*, or 'Conqueror'. During the next three centuries, until an equally famous siege and battle beneath the walls of Vienna in 1683, the Turks remained the scourge of Christian Europe.

Crossbowman were more effective in a siege situation, and a number of Aragonese and Genoese crossbowmen mercenaries were employed to defend Constantinople. By this time Western plate armour had become so heavy that knights ceased using a shield, freeing them to use heavy two-handed weapons.

NAGASHINO
28 June 1575

THE BATTLE OF NAGASHINO WAS A CLASH OF OLD AND NEW TECHNOLOGIES. THE TRADITIONAL JAPANESE 'WAY OF THE SWORD' CONFRONTED THE REALITY OF EARLY FIREARMS, WITH DECISIVE RESULTS THAT WERE TO CHANGE THE WAY BATTLES WERE FOUGHT IN JAPAN.

WHY DID IT HAPPEN?

WHO The *daimyo* (feudal lord) Takeda Katsuyori (1546–82) fought the combined forces of Oda Nobunaga (1534–82) and Tokugawa Ieyasu (1543–1616).

WHAT Takeda besieged Nagashino Castle, to which Oda and Tokugawa sent a massive relief army that was heavily armed with arquebus gunners.

WHERE The area around Nagashino Castle, in Totomi Province, central Japan.

WHEN 28 June 1575.

WHY Takeda had wider territorial ambitions for central Japan and was aiming to defeat the Tokugawa armies and advance against Kyoto.

OUTCOME An eight-hour battle saw the almost complete destruction of Takeda's army, with devastating casualties caused by volley fire from enemy arquebusiers.

The Battle of Nagashino was born out of a time of great social turmoil in Japan. The decline of the Ashikaga shogunate (1336–1573), previously a unifying presence within Japan, in the second half of the fifteenth century led to the country's splitting into numerous different fiefdoms, each ruled by *daimyo* leaders and their own personal armies. The *daimyo* fought amongst themselves for the next century, trying to gain control over greater territories and over the still symbolically powerful figure of the shogun, the emperor's military commander-in-chief and effectively ruler of Japan. By the end of the 1560s, one of the big winners in the struggle was Oda Nobunaga. Oda was a great and ruthless samurai general, who from 1568 took the Japanese capital, Kyoto, installed a puppet shogun and controlled a large swathe of territory in central Japan.

Oda's enemies, however, were not far away. One of the greatest threats lay in the eastern provinces controlled by the *daimyo* Takeda Shingen (1521–73), who also had his eyes set on Kyoto. The chief obstacles to Takeda's ambition were the territories of the Tokugawa family (Totomi and Mikawa Provinces), which along the Pacific coast separated Takeda's provinces from those of Oda. In 1572, Takeda went for broke, pushing into Tokugawa territory and besieging the castle of Noda, seat of the Tokugawa leader and general Tokugawa

Okazaki Castle, Tokushima, Shikoku, Japan. It was here that the great Tokugawa Ieyasu was born in 1542. Ieyasu proved himself a brilliant politician and soldier, and became Shogun in 1603.

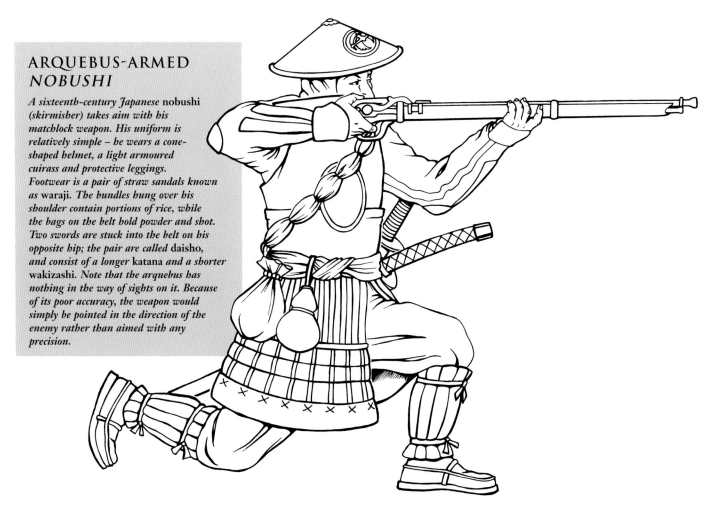

ARQUEBUS-ARMED *NOBUSHI*

A sixteenth-century Japanese nobushi *(skirmisher) takes aim with his matchlock weapon. His uniform is relatively simple – he wears a cone-shaped helmet, a light armoured cuirass and protective leggings. Footwear is a pair of straw sandals known as* waraji. *The bundles hung over his shoulder contain portions of rice, while the bags on the belt hold powder and shot. Two swords are stuck into the belt on his opposite hip; the pair are called* daisho, *and consist of a longer* katana *and a shorter* wakizashi. *Note that the arquebus has nothing in the way of sights on it. Because of its poor accuracy, the weapon would simply be pointed in the direction of the enemy rather than aimed with any precision.*

Ieyasu (1542–1616). There his ambitions were thwarted – Takeda was killed by a sniper's musket ball.

Takeda's son Takeda Katsuyori, however, kept the candle of expansionism burning. In 1575, he invaded Tokugawa territory, but quickly found himself in difficulties. An attempt to take Okazaki Castle in western Mikawa Province was abandoned when Takeda's man on the inside, who was to open the castle gates for the invaders, was unmasked in advance and executed. A subsequent onslaught against Yoshida Castle, further to the south on Mikawa Bay, was stopped militarily, the Tokugawa having brought the garrison up to a strength of 6000 men. Yet Takeda soon found another target – the castle of Nagashino, further north along the Toyokawa River.

SIEGE CONDITIONS

Nagashino Castle sat between the forks created by the Takigawa (west) and Onogawa (east) rivers, where they joined to form the Toyokawa. The banks of the rivers towered up to 50m (164ft) high, hence placing the castle in a strong defensive position. The castle itself consisted of a series of wooden dwellings contained within the stone walls of the *hon-maru* (inner bailey) and protected by two more ranks of outer defences, the *ni-no-maru* (second bailey) and *san-no-maru* (third bailey). Four gates punctuated the outer walls; holding these would be critical to the defence. Though physically well protected, the castle contained a military garrison of only some 500 men against the 15,000 troops that began to surround the fortification in mid-June 1575. Between 17 and 27 June, Takeda threw his army against Nagashino Castle in several major attacks. Remarkably, all were battered off by stubborn defence. Takeda therefore decided to place the castle under siege and starve the defenders out.

Yet by this time Takeda had a larger problem than Nagashino Castle looming. An enemy relief force was on its way. On 24 June, Oda Nobunaga and Tokugawa Ieyasu, both at Okazaki, were informed of the situation at Nagashino and, motivated by reports that the garrison had only three more days of supplies, quickly moved to raise a relief force. A total of 38,000 troops was assembled (Oda 30,000 and Tokugawa 8000) and marched for Nagashino.

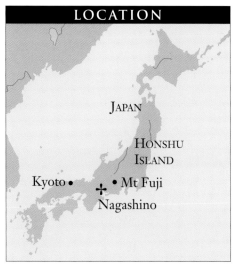

LOCATION

JAPAN

HONSHU ISLAND

Kyoto •

+ • Mt Fuji

Nagashino

The cross here marks the location of Nagashino Castle. The struggle for political power in sixteenth- and seventeeth-century Japan focused upon central Honshu, which contained the capital Kyoto.

A member of a reenactment society displays traditional samurai armour, with bow and horned helmet, at the Nara Festival, Japan. Archers provided more accurate fire than arquebusiers, but required much more training to bring to any level of competence.

THE OPPOSED FORCES

ODA/TOKUGAWA (estimated)

Total:	**38,000**

TAKEDA (estimated)

Total:	**15,000**

ARMIES AND ARQUEBUSES

The Japanese armies of the sixteenth century were basically split into two different orders. Occupying leadership and warrior roles were the samurai, highly trained armoured troops who traditionally fought mounted, although economic conditions in the late 1500s forced many to operate on foot. The classic samurai weapons were the sword, bow and, most tactically important, the *mochi-yari* spear, a stabbing and slashing weapon some 3.5–4m (11.5–13.1ft) long. The samurai cavalry were a true elite, and were used to smash or outmanoeuvre enemy lines in close-quarter combat.

Beneath the samurai – but critical in forming the bulk of an army – were the *ashigaru* footsoldiers. The *ashigaru* were more lightly armoured than the samurai, and as combatants they were principally armed with spears, bows and arquebus firearms, although around 25 per cent of *ashigaru* were non-combat support troops. Dedicated spear units armed with weapons up to 6m (19.7ft) long would make up the largest combatant portion of the *ashigaru*. By contrast, the smallest portion consisted of the archers, their numbers restricted by the skill and time-demanding training required of their profession. The great advantage of the archers was their accuracy over a 400m (437-yard) range and their rate of fire – an arrow could be unleashed every five to six seconds.

The third type of armed *ashigaru* were those equipped with the arquebus. First introduced into Japan by the Portuguese in 1543, the arquebus was a simple muzzle-loaded matchlock firearm, light enough to

Opposite: A gentle depiction of a samurai warrior of the Ashikaga period, seated beside his bow, fanning himself. Composite bows such as this one would have a range of up to 400m (437 yards).

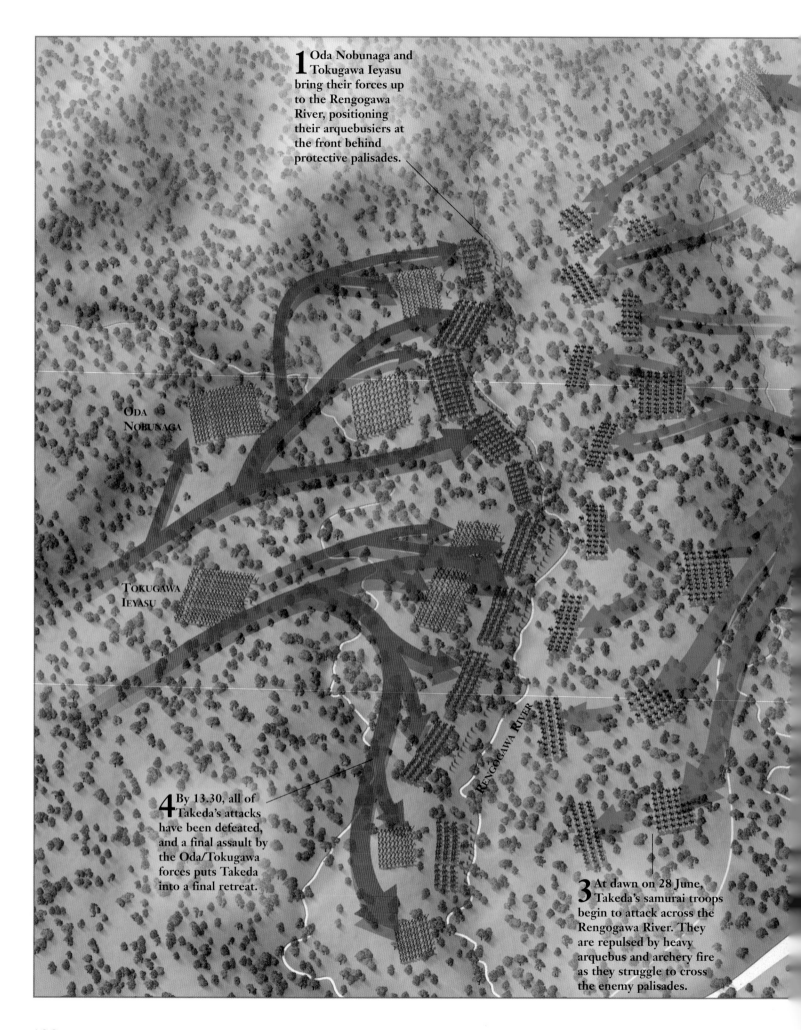

1 Oda Nobunaga and Tokugawa Ieyasu bring their forces up to the Rengogawa River, positioning their arquebusiers at the front behind protective palisades.

ODA
NOBUNAGA

TOKUGAWA
IEYASU

4 By 13.30, all of Takeda's attacks have been defeated, and a final assault by the Oda/Tokugawa forces puts Takeda into a final retreat.

RENGOGAWA RIVER

3 At dawn on 28 June, Takeda's samurai troops begin to attack across the Rengogawa River. They are repulsed by heavy arquebus and archery fire as they struggle to cross the enemy palisades.

NAGASHINO CASTLE

TAKEDA KATSUYORI

2 Leaving behind a 2000-strong siege force at Nagashino Castle, Takeda Katsuyori pulls the bulk of his troops away to face the combined Oda/Tokugawa army.

5 Later, Takeda's siege lines on Tobigasu Hill are breached by a 3000-strong raiding party from Oda's army, bringing the siege to an end.

NAGASHINO
28 JUNE 1575

NAGASHINO

be fired from the shoulder, although heavy versions that required a support were also used. The capabilities of individual arquebuses were extremely limited. Accuracy was very poor; range was limited to just a few hundred metres, although the effective range against armour plate was little more than 50m/55 yards; misfires were common; and a laborious loading procedure meant that the maximum rate of fire was some three rounds per minute, and often much slower if the gun was in inexperienced hands or was fouled. The true advantage of the arquebus, however, emerged when the weapon was used in volley. Oda had learned this lesson himself when fighting against Buddhist Ikko-Ikki rebels around Ishiyama Hongan-ji in 1570 – volleys from some

3000 arquebusiers had a lethal impact upon his army's ranks. Furthermore, handling an arquebus required a fraction of the skill demanded of a bowman; therefore an army could more rapidly increase its firepower.

Both sides in the Battle of Nagashino had enthusiastically embraced firearms, but it was Oda, drawing on his brutal experience, who best understood the tactical applications of such weapons. Oda took 3000 arquebusiers with him to the Nagashino battlefield, and had trained them in the application of disciplined volley tactics. During the lulls in reloading, the archers would take over to maintain a constant rain of direct fire on the enemy. Takeda also had arquebus-armed troops, but at the time of Nagashino he still relied on cavalry dash.

THE BATTLE

By 27 June, the Nagashino relief forces were assembling on the battlefield. This was not the immediate surrounds of the castle; instead the Oda–Tokugawa troops gathered on the plain of Shidarahara, some 5km (3.1 miles) from the castle, behind the banks of the Rengogawa River. The river was actually little more than a shallow stream, but sitting 100m (109 yards) in front of the relief force's lines it provided a soggy obstacle to cavalry. A three-tiered palisade of wooden stakes just high enough to prevent a horse jumping over it was also built a short distance behind the river, which served to further break up Takeda's cavalry. The wooden structure, with gaps to enable counterattack movement, also provided cover for Oda's arquebusiers, who were sited forward. Protecting the Oda–Tokugawa right flank was the Toyokawa, which bent around beneath the army to the west, while on the left flank there was forested and hilly ground.

The relief troops acted as a carrot for Takeda, despite commanders such as Baba Nobuharu (1514–75) urging that the castle be taken first. Baba wisely argued that it would be make better sense to fight Oda from defensive positions within the castle rather than to take heavy casualties from ball and arrow while charging across open ground. Nevertheless Takeda, tempted by prospects of glory, ordered all but 2000

Mounted samurai with banners here make a ferocious charge. These soldiers are obviously wealthier samurai, since by the time of the Nagashino battle many samurai did not have the financial means for horses.

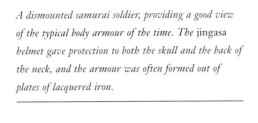

A dismounted samurai soldier, providing a good view of the typical body armour of the time. The jingasa *helmet gave protection to both the skull and the back of the neck, and the armour was often formed out of plates of lacquered iron.*

troops to leave the castle siege and head out for the confrontation. The 12,000 men going into battle would be arranged in four divisions, each consisting of some 3000 troops and together forming right, centre and left wings plus a headquarters reserve. In addition, a further 1000 men were based in wooden forts near the castle, on Tobigasu Hill to the east.

FRONTAL ATTACK

A frontal attack seemed the most judicious plan, since from woodland at the east of the plain to the nearest point of Oda's lines was a distance of little more than 200m (219 yards). Although open to enemy fire, this could theoretically be covered at speed. Takeda also surmised that many of the enemy arquebuses would prove useless because of wet weather. As it happened, the arquebusiers' powder had been kept dry, and the principal effect of the rain was to create soggy ground that was ill-suited to a fast cavalry charge.

The battle began on 28 June at 0600, as Takeda's cavalry emerged onto the plain and began a thunderous, drum-motivated charge towards the enemy lines. The charge was initially uncontested, except by the Rengogawa River, which slowed the cavalry in its crossing. However, as the horsemen emerged up the far bank, a withering fusillade of fire rippled out from the 3000 matchlockmen, arranged behind the palisade in three ranks, each rank firing in turn. Some 9000 rounds were fired in the first three rapid volleys alone, and cavalrymen and horses dropped in horrifying numbers as shot hit home from around 50m (55 yards). Oda had placed some of his best commanders in charge of the arquebusiers; Takeda had done likewise with his cavalry, meaning that with each volley he lost some of his most important leaders, while Oda's finest remained behind the protective wooden shield. Those cavalrymen who survived the gunfire found themselves pressed up against the palisade. Here they were easy prey for *ashigaru*

Katsutaka (below right), besieged in Nagashino castle, broke out and sought help from Tokugawa Ieyasu. He was captured when he tried to return, but in an act of heroism he shouted to the castle garrison that they would soon be relieved. He was immediately killed.

Right: A statue of Tokugawa Ieyasu. As a military commander, Tokugawa was known for his personal bravery, a man who would endure physical injuries to prosecute an attack. He held the position of Shogun from 1603 to 1605.

Below: An extensive set of samurai body armour, as would have clad the more affluent warrior. Such armour could be time-consuming to put on. One method for speeding up the entire process was to hang the set of armour from cords, then stand up into it.

spearmen, who simply drove their long spears up through the defences to pierce horse or rider. Other cavalrymen who found themselves channelled through the gaps in the palisade were attacked by further Oda–Tokugawa *ashigaru* and the dismounted samurai.

Successive waves of attackers were soon throwing themselves against the palisade, with similar results. Meanwhile, the battle was widening. Oda had sent the Tokugawa officer Sakai Tadatsugu (1527–96) with a raiding party of several thousand troops – including 500 matchlockmen – to attack the Takeda siege lines around Nagashino Castle, focusing on the four forts commanded by Takeda Nobuzane (d. 1575). The attack went in at 0800, and such was its success that defenders from Nagashino Castle itself entered the battle. Takeda Nobuzane was killed, along with 200 of his men. The battle was beginning to tip in favour of the Oda–Tokugawa army.

FINISHING THE FIGHT

On the Shidarahara Plain, the efforts of Takeda's army to break the Oda–Tokugawa lines were steadily failing. Throughout the morning, the cavalry and other troops threw themselves in vain against the palisade defences, while taking constant losses from arquebus fire, arrows and spears. Dozens of Takeda's top commanders fell. Flanking attacks over on the left wing of the battlefield had proved to be futile and had more than justified Oda's choice of battleground. Over on the right wing, however, the battle was going somewhat differently, principally because here the Oda–Tokugawa troops under Okubo Tadayo (1531–93) had no protective barrier in front of them. Here the enemy soldiers of Yamagata Masakage (1524–75) made a powerful assault that resulted in bloody hand-to-hand combat, with the samurai of both sides given the opportunity to show their courage in action and their skill with sword and spear. One notable victim of the clash was Yamagata himself. Fighting from horseback, supported by three samurai, he was finally killed by a fusillade of arquebus fire. In traditional samurai style, his head was cut from his body as a battle trophy.

FINAL ASSAULT

While Yamagata was fighting his last battle, Takeda had also launched his forces in a final all-out attack, pulling in his reserves for the fight. Close-quarter combat raged up and down the line for several hours until, at around 1300, Oda gave the signal for disengagement and a withdrawal to fall-back positions. However, this order was quickly reversed into an attack command when it became apparent that Takeda's forces themselves were in retreat. Now the Oda–Tokugawa mounted samurai could have their day. They charged the fleeing enemy, killing hundreds of men and adding to the toll of commanders who were left on the battlefield.

Some eight hours after the fighting had first begun, the battle was over. The Oda–Tokugawa army was victorious, having killed 10,000 of Takeda's 15,000 men, including more than 50 per cent of his samurai commanders. The siege of Nagashino was broken, and Takeda Katsuyori, who survived the battle, retreated back to Kai and Shinano Provinces, where he fought on the defensive for the next seven years. Steadily his allies deserted, and then turned on him, giving the opening, in 1582, for the Oda and Tokugawa to deal the finishing blow. Takeda committed suicide at Toriibata, only 300 soldiers remaining by his side.

Historical studies of the Battle of Nagashino have frequently overplayed the

contribution of the arquebus to its outcome. That the battle lasted eight hours suggests that the bow, sword and spear must also have played their part in the Oda–Tokugawa victory. Nevertheless, it is certain that the arquebus was central to the battle's outcome, its correct application as a volley-firing weapon, combined with an excellent defensive arrangement, causing a high level of casualties and dealing a crushing blow to a force that was employing traditional methods of warfare.

The samurai were meant to embody the essence of martial ferocity. Here, in a picture from the nineteenth-century artist Yoshitoshi, a mounted samurai smashes through a foot soldier, splitting his opponent's sword in half in the process.

ARMADA
1588

LONG-STANDING TENSION BETWEEN PROTESTANT ENGLAND AND CATHOLIC SPAIN TURNED INTO OPEN WAR IN 1585. IN JULY 1588, THE SPANISH FLEET ENTERED THE ENGLISH CHANNEL, INTENDING TO INVADE THE BRITISH ISLES.

WHY DID IT HAPPEN?

WHO A Spanish fleet of 22 galleons and 108 armed merchant vessels under the Duke of Medina Sidonia, opposed by an English fleet comprised of 35 galleons and 163 other vessels and commanded by the Lord High Admiral, Charles Howard.

WHAT The Spanish intended to invade England in conjunction with a Dutch-based army, who were to be transported by the Armada from the Spanish Netherlands.

WHERE A series of running engagements in the English Channel, with a decisive battle off Gravelines near the Belgian coast.

WHEN July and August 1588.

WHY Conflict was ongoing between Protestant England and Catholic Spain, largely due to religious differences.

OUTCOME The Spanish fleet was defeated off Gravelines and was forced to sail north around Britain to return home. Losses to weather were severe during this voyage.

The struggle between Protestants and Roman Catholics in England was part of a wider pattern of religious conflicts. Protestant England supported a revolt in the Dutch provinces against Catholic Spain, while Spain supported the Catholic Scottish queen, Mary I, against the Protestant English queen, Elizabeth I.

Although no formal declaration of war was ever made, an effective state of war existed between Spain and England from 1585 to 1604. This arose from a treaty signed at Nonsuch Palace in Surrey, England. Under the treaty, England sent funds and troops to assist the Dutch United Provinces in their revolt against their Spanish overlords, in return for territorial concessions. Naturally, Spain considered this English interference to be an act of open hostility.

Direct confrontations were rare, though English privateers used the conflict to enrich themselves by attacking Spanish treasure fleets coming back laden with riches from the New World. The unofficial nature of privateering allowed England to attack Spanish revenue sources without provoking direct conflict between the nations, while still inflicting considerable damage on the Spanish war effort.

Largely to curtail English assistance for the Dutch rebels, King Philip II of Spain decided to invade England. The execution of Mary I in 1587 had given Philip a clear claim to the English throne because Mary had named him her successor in her will over the claims of her half-sister, Elizabeth. The invasion had the support of Pope Sixtus V, who took the view that removing a Protestant monarch from England was a

With a relatively short gun deck mounting fewer and smaller cannon, Spanish warships such as the San Martin *were at a disadvantage against faster and more heavily armed English vessels.*

worthy crusade. The Pope agreed to support whomever Philip installed as ruler of England.

An invasion of England was a significant undertaking, requiring extensive preparations. The basic plan was for a large fleet, named the 'Invincible Armada', to sail up the English Channel and rendezvous with a ground force in Flanders. This required communications to be carried out over great distances. In addition, just assembling a fleet of this size was a serious logistical problem.

The Spanish fleet was commanded by Alvaro de Bazan, Marquis of Santa Cruz (1526–88), who began assembling his force early in 1587. Of necessity, the vessels were marshalled in different ports, making preparations hard to keep secret.

Spain was at that time primarily a land power, with a large army that had gained experience fighting in the Low Countries. Its navy, however, was not very experienced or effective. On the other hand, England did not maintain a standing army, relying on militia for home defence and raising forces for overseas service only when required, but it did have an experienced navy. So if the Spanish could get past the English navy and get its forces ashore, they stood a good chance of success, whereas the best chance for English victory lay at sea.

English naval superiority was demonstrated once war broke out in 1585. Francis Drake (1540–96) sailed for the West Indies in September 1585 with 25 ships. In his 'descent on the Indies', his forces caused havoc in the Carribbean, capturing and looting the major cities of Santo Domingo (in modern-day Hispaniola) and Cartagena (in Columbia).

Not long after his return, Drake set out again in early 1587, leading a raid on Cadiz in Spain. The English force possessed such seamanship that it was able to manoeuvre in the confines of the harbour, make its attack and escape more or less unscathed.

Drake's expedition also destroyed several Spanish fortresses and captured a treasure fleet, inflicting delay on Armada preparations and humiliation on the Spanish king and his navy. The Spanish gave chase but ran into heavy storms, eventually returning to port, where Alvaro

de Bazan died of illness. His replacement was the inexperienced Duke of Medina Sidonia, Don Alonso Perez de Guzman el Bueno (1549–1615). Preparations continued, and in 1588 the Armada was finally ready.

OPENING MOVES

The Spanish Armada sailed on 28 May 1588. It contained 130 ships, most of which were armed merchant vessels. This was not unusual: there was little difference at the time between the construction of merchant vessels and warships, though the armament of the galleons warships was heavier.

The galleons of Spain had high 'castles' fore and aft, and it was from these that their large contingent of soldiers fought, while

SPANISH SOLDIER

The move from hand weapons to firearms was not complete by 1588, but the musket-armed infantry formed the backbone of many armies, including that of Spain. This infantryman carries several pre-prepared cartridges in clay pots hanging from his belt, speeding the loading process. His weapon is a caliver, *a lighter version of the* arquebus.

Although firepower was important, hand-to-hand combat was still likely, so the soldier also carried a sword. He was protected by a leather or padded jerkin and a bronze helmet.

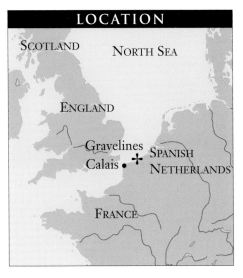

LOCATION

SCOTLAND

NORTH SEA

ENGLAND

Gravelines
Calais ✦ SPANISH
NETHERLANDS

FRANCE

The defeat of the Armada took the form of a week-long running engagement with heavy clashes at times, culminating in the decisive action at Gravelines.

ARMADA

Francis Drake was second-in-command of the English fleet that faced the Spanish Armada. His naval career included a circumnavigation of the globe and many successful attacks on Spanish shipping.

THE OPPOSED FORCES

ENGLISH

Warships:	34
Armed Merchant Ships	163

SPANISH

Warships:	22
Armed Merchant Ships	108

the cannon were used mainly to force enemy ships onto the defensive before closing in to board and fight hand-to-hand. The galleons were unwieldy vessels, prone to rolling and unable to sail very close to the wind. Although such ships had proven effective in previous wars, they were now becoming obsolete.

The Armada was crewed by about 8000 sailors, with 19,000 soldiers aboard. It was to pick up a force of 30,000 more soldiers under the command of Alexander Farnese, Duke of Parma (1540–95) and convey them to England. There was some doubt as to exactly when the Duke of Parma's force would arrive at the rendezvous, so the Armada was instructed to anchor off the Dutch coast and await his arrival. But first it had to get past English warships in the Channel.

As the Spanish laboured against heavy seas, the English tried to sail out to meet them but were themselves driven back by gales. This worked in favour of the English, enabling them to put a fresh and combat-ready force to sea to engage the Spanish, tired from struggling through the difficult weather in the English Channel.

The English force also included many merchant ships in addition to its war vessels, but the latter were superior to those of the Spanish. English naval vessels were designed as true warships rather than seagoing infantry platforms. They were lower because they did not possess high castles. The forecastle was almost completely dispensed with and the sterncastle was cut down considerably.

Perhaps more importantly, the English ships had much finer lines than their Spanish opponents – in other words, they were narrower . A Spanish galleon typically had a length-to-beam ratio of 2.5:1, whereas an English ship was closer to 4:1.

In addition to improving speed, these dimensions also created a longer gun-deck in which to mount cannon. The lower gun-deck of the larger English galleons mounted seven 18-pound cannon known as 'culverins' along each side, with five-pound 'sakers' or nine-pound 'demi-culverins' guns along the main deck. In addition, a number of smaller anti-personnel guns named Robins and Falcons were shipped.

English warships were thus faster and more manoeuvrable than their opponents, enabling them to avoid being grappled and boarded while bringing their guns to bear. They were designed to be mobile artillery platforms rather than the floating siege towers of previous generations. At the time, this new approach to warship construction had not been properly tested in action; the English were staking the defence of their nation on an unproven concept.

In command of the English fleet was the Lord High Admiral, Charles Howard, Earl of Nottingham (1536–1624). Under him were three squadron commanders – Francis Drake, Martin Frobisher (1535–94) and John Hawkins (1532–95). Hawkins, as Treasurer of the Navy, had been instrumental in creating the new style of warship, of which 18 were constructed in the initial production run.

THE FLEETS ENGAGE

Warned by a string of beacons, the English commanders were informed on 19 July that the Spanish were sailing off Cornwall in southwest England. It was not possible to intercept them due to difficult weather conditions, but on 30 July, the English fleet came out of Plymouth harbour and formed up for battle.

The Spanish fleet adopted a battle formation on 31 July, with two wings of about 20 ships and a central force of 36 galleons protecting the main body of merchant vessels. This formation withstood English attacks off Eddystone and Portland, and on 4 August, the Spanish reached the Isle of Wight, off the south coast of England, with their force intact. The intent was for the powerful wings to fall on any vessels trying to attack the vulnerable transports in the central group. However, the superior sailing qualities of the English fleet enabled its vessels to choose the range and nature of any engagement.

The English fleet took advantage, moving to windward of the Spanish and following the Armada up the English Channel. A low-key running battle ensued. The English plan was to remain in this position, known as maintaining the 'weather gage', and to destroy the Armada with their superior gunnery. However, despite a great expenditure of shot and powder, decisive results were not achieved.

The warships of the Armada tried to turn back and engage the English, who stood off out of range while they waited for reinforcements. Unable to get into cannon range, the Spanish warships rejoined the rest of the Armada and moved on, but not without incident. The galleon *Neustra Senora del Rosario*, one of the squadron flagships, was involved in a collision with another vessel. She lost her bowsprit but was able to struggle on until the following morning, when a sudden change in the wind caused her foremast, which lacked the support of stays from the missing bowsprit, to collapse.

Left behind with a small escort by the Armada, *Neustra Senora del Rosario* was captured by Drake's flagship. The galleon *San Salvador*, damaged by an accidental powder explosion, was also taken. Meanwhile, Lord Howard, with just three ships, had become detached from the fleet during the night and at dawn was dangerously within cannon range of the main Spanish force. Good seamanship enabled the outnumbered English vessels to withdraw and rejoin the main body.

INDECISIVE ENGAGEMENTS

Medina Sidonia intended to anchor in sheltered waters off the Isle of Wight, but was successfully prevented by further English attacks. Two of his galleons ran aground, but the rest of the fleet regained open waters and the Armada was able to press on. Finally it reached the Calais region of northern France and anchored off Dunkirk. Both sides had cause to be disappointed thus far. The Spanish had hoped to seize the Isle of Wight to use as a base, and had failed. The English had not made much impression on the Armada despite hard fighting, and powder was in short supply.

The Spanish defensive formation was extremely effective, and their ships, although outdated, were tough. More than once, a vessel, including Medina Sidonia's own flagship *San Martin*, became isolated under difficult sailing conditions. Surrounded by English ships, the vulnerable vessels withstood heavy attack until other Spanish ships came up in support. At that point, the English drew off to stay out of range of the Spaniards' guns.

However, the Spanish tactical position was weak. The Duke of Parma's army was not ready to board the Armada's ships, and in any case the nearby port of Dunkirk was blockaded by Dutch naval forces, who referred to themselves as the 'Sea Beggars'. The threat from the English fleet made it impossible to send Spanish naval units to dislodge them.

As the Armada lay off Dunkirk, unprotected by a harbour, the English launched a fireship attack. Vessels carrying barrels of gunpowder, and loaded with a highly combustible mix of tar and pitch, were sent downwind against the Spanish force. Normally, expendable vessels were used to prepare fireships, but the English fleet was forced to use good-quality

After discovering that long-range bombardment could not inflict serious damage on the Spanish vessels, English warships closed to point-blank range in the later engagements.

ARMADA

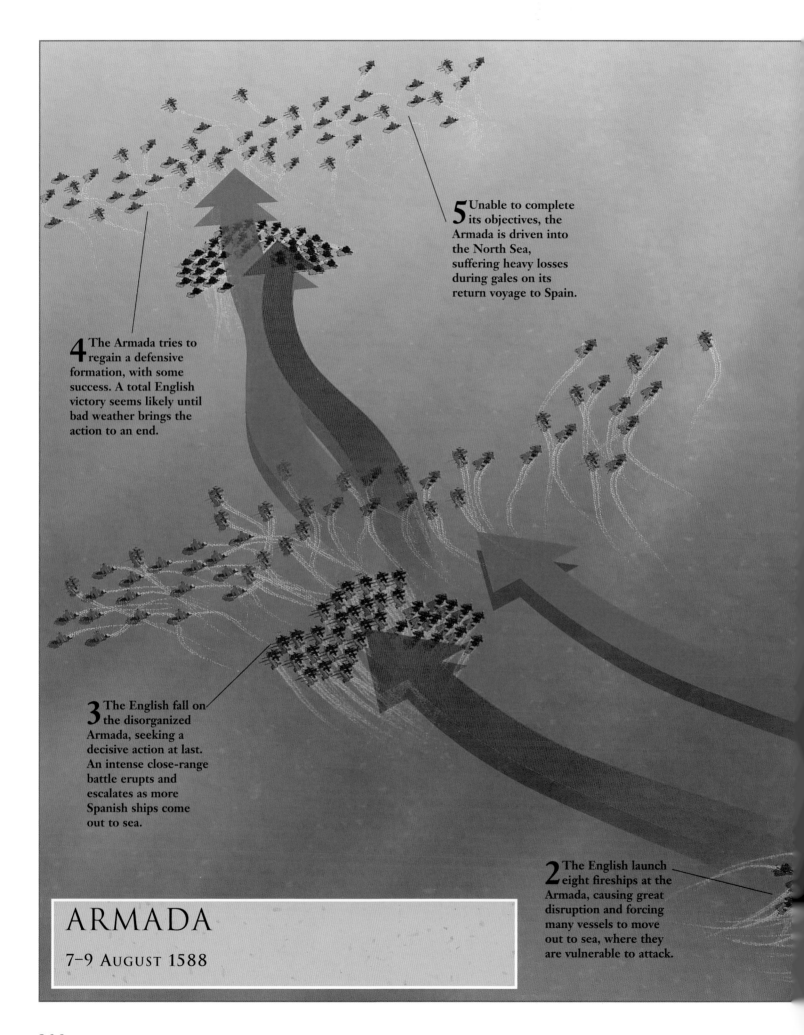

5 Unable to complete its objectives, the Armada is driven into the North Sea, suffering heavy losses during gales on its return voyage to Spain.

4 The Armada tries to regain a defensive formation, with some success. A total English victory seems likely until bad weather brings the action to an end.

3 The English fall on the disorganized Armada, seeking a decisive action at last. An intense close-range battle erupts and escalates as more Spanish ships come out to sea.

2 The English launch eight fireships at the Armada, causing great disruption and forcing many vessels to move out to sea, where they are vulnerable to attack.

ARMADA

7–9 AUGUST 1588

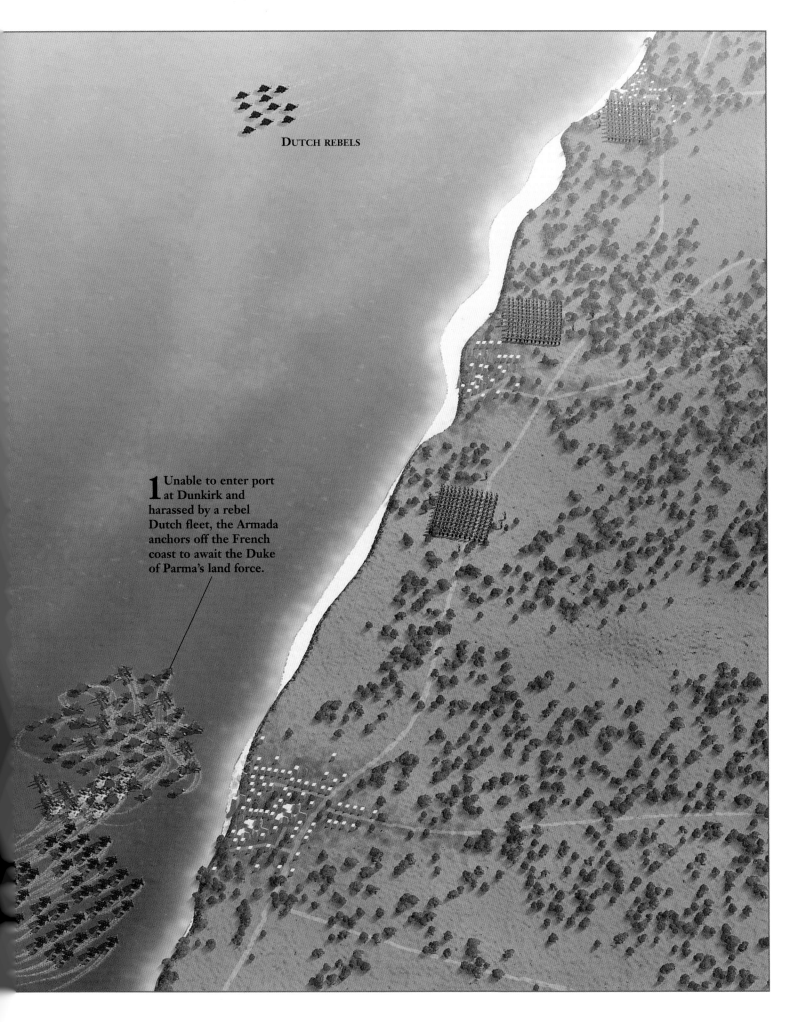

DUTCH REBELS

1 Unable to enter port at Dunkirk and harassed by a rebel Dutch fleet, the Armada anchors off the French coast to await the Duke of Parma's land force.

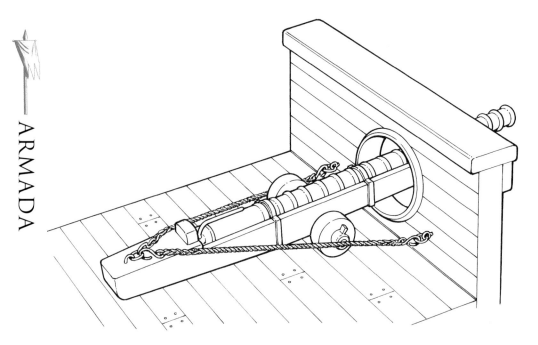

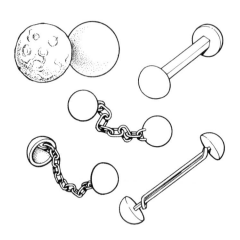

Although the guns themselves were rather primitive, they could fire a range of ammunition for various purposes. Specialist projectiles were available for attacking the hull, crew or rigging of an enemy vessel.

warships instead, lacking the time to prepare other vessels.

Strong nerves and good seamanship were required to defeat a fireship attack. If the fireships could be intercepted in time they could be towed away from the fleet, though this was hazardous given the possibility of an impending explosion. Two of the eight English fireships were intercepted in this manner, but the others got through.

The large size of the English fireships made the Spanish fear that they were 'hellburners', a variant on the standard fireship which carried a large quantity of gunpowder and was prone to destroy itself in a massive explosion. Two such vessels had been used at the Siege of Antwerp, and their fearsome reputation added to the already unsettling effect of a fireship attack.

Although part of the Spanish fleet remained in formation, large numbers of vessels were forced to cut their cables to evade the attack, causing confusion within the fleet. One Spanish vessel was set on fire, but the main effects of the attack were to dent morale and cause confusion. Blazing vessels careering through a fleet at anchor caused considerable consternation, and now the Armada was in difficulty as it was driven from its anchorage back into open waters, where the English had the advantage.

THE SPANISH FLEE

As the Armada struggled to regain its formation, it was driven gradually eastwards by the winds. Off Gravelines, it was forced

to halt; the Dutch coast became extremely hazardous beyond that point. The English now had a chance to fight a decisive action, and just as importantly they now had the measure of their opponents. Previously they had been 'playing at long bowls', standing off and firing from a distance, which had so far proven ineffective.

To have a chance of penetrating the Spanish ships' thick hulls, the English had to fire from within a range of 100m (109yd), but this was risky as the Spanish wanted to draw their enemies in close in order to grapple and board. However, by maintaining an advantageous windward position, and by means of good seamanship, the English were able to close in, pound the Spanish and retire to a safe distance.

Spanish gunnery was largely ineffective, for several reasons. Their guns were made of bronze and fired more slowly than the English iron guns, and their crews were not well trained. Indeed, the Spanish doctrine was to fire once, then rush aloft to join the anticipated boarding battle. Against some foes this was effective, but the English ships were too manoeuvrable to be caught this way. In addition to its tactical disadvantages, the Spaniards' leeward position meant that penetrating hits often occurred in areas that were below the waterline when the vessel was not heeling over due to the wind, and their guns were pointing at the sky much of the time for the same reason.

Estimates of the losses at Gravelines vary, though no more than 11 Spanish ships were lost in the battle. Many more were damaged, and the Armada was driven into the North Sea, where the English, though almost out of ammunition, pursued them as far as the Firth of Forth in Scotland.

At the time, it was not clear in England that the threat had passed. An English army was mustered at Tilbury in case of invasion up the Thames, and the Queen Elizabeth herself visited this army to deliver a famous inspiring speech. In the event, the encouragement was not needed; the threat of invasion had been averted.

AFTERMATH

Short of supplies and drinking water after a long voyage, and worn down by constant skirmishing and defeated in battle, the

Queen Elizabeth I of England pursued a foreign policy that was openly hostile to Spain, supporting rebels and sending privateers to attack Spanish shipping. Added to religious differences, this made war between England and Spain almost inevitable.

Armada could not rejoin battle, so Medina Sidonia took the only course open to him – returning to Spain by sailing around Scotland.

Struggling through unfamiliar waters, with battle-damaged ships short of supplies, the Armada ran into a series of gales that wrecked many vessels. Those ships that had cut their cables in the fireship attack found it impossible to anchor in sheltered waters, and even those that could do so suffered terribly. Eventually, only about 67 vessels and 10,000 men arrived back in Spain, many suffering from disease and malnutrition.

The undeclared war went on until 1604, exhausting the treasuries of both Spain and England. Although politically indecisive, the war was extremely significant in military terms, since it demonstrated the superiority of the manoeuvrable warship-as-gun-platform over the older style of vessel employed by the Spanish. Previously, boarding actions had been the main tool of decision in naval warfare, but from 1588 it was apparent that the cannon was the arbiter of victory.

Spain underwent a naval revolution after the Armada was defeated, and soon became far better able to defend her treasure fleets and overseas holdings. England, on the other hand, had established herself as the pre-eminent naval power, ushering in an era of dominance at sea that would permit the creation of the British Empire.

LUTZEN
6 NOVEMBER 1632

THE THIRTY YEARS' WAR WAS CHARACTERIZED BY A SHIFTING POLITICAL LANDSCAPE THAT MADE DECISIVE VICTORIES HARD TO ACHIEVE. CAMPAIGNS WERE THEREFORE LAUNCHED TO PUT INDIVIDUAL STATES OUT OF THE WAR, OR AT LEAST WEAKEN THEM ECONOMICALLY BY RAVAGING THE LAND. THE BATTLE OF LUTZEN AROSE PRIMARILY OUT OF AN IMPERIAL ATTEMPT TO NEUTRALIZE SAXONY.

WHY DID IT HAPPEN?

WHO A Swedish army, commanded by King Gustavus Adolphus (1594–1632), opposed by an Imperial army under Prince Albrecht von Wallenstein (1583–1634).

WHAT Despite the death of Gustavus Adolphus, the hard-pressed Swedish army was able to win a hard-fought victory.

WHERE Lutzen, near Leipzig in Saxony.

WHEN 6 November 1632.

WHY Saxony, a Swedish ally, was threatened with invasion by Imperial forces.

OUTCOME Saxony was preserved, but the war continued for another 16 years.

The mix of religious conflict and political ambition among the states of Europe at the beginning of the seventeenth century created a complex political situation that could have resulted in war for any number of different reasons. When what became the Thirty Years' War did break out, it began as a religious conflict, with alliances drawn up according to Protestant or Catholic allegiances. However, as time went on, the war took on a more political character. Many of the combatant states had their own agenda and chose a side that would best suit their ambitions.

The result was that many allied states, while fighting a common foe, were not united by ideology, friendship or even, sometimes, a common cause. Bargaining between allies was common, as was mistrust. Even within the Holy Roman Empire, which was comprised of Catholic states, there were disputes over policy and the allocation of power, which at times hamstrung the war effort.

HOW ARMIES WORKED

Although large forces were fielded, logistical arrangements were very primitive. Armies were expected to support themselves on campaign by foraging, much to the detriment of the local population. This was an accepted part of war-making; indeed, ravaging an area to weaken its economy was an important tactical tool.

The military forces of the time were not national armies in the way we understand

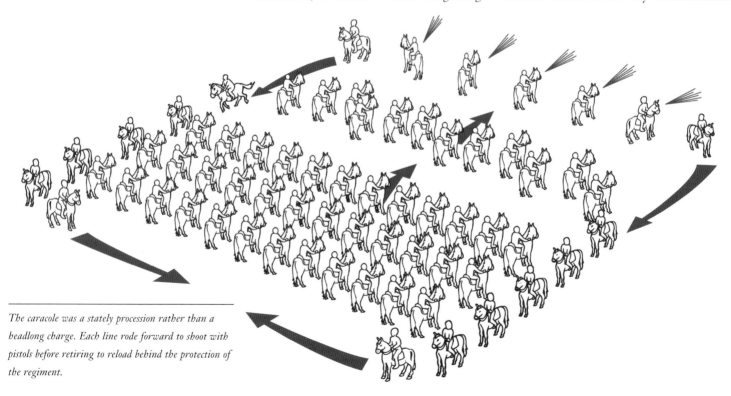

The caracole was a stately procession rather than a headlong charge. Each line rode forward to shoot with pistols before retiring to reload behind the protection of the regiment.

them today. Soldiers did show allegiance to a king or prince, but in general they served for pay rather than out of duty. While it was more convenient to recruit within home territory, most states enrolled large numbers or professional soldiers from any source they could find.

Some of these mercenaries were recruited as individuals, while others were hired as whole companies or regiments. Since non-payment by the hiring state was frequent, it was not uncommon for unpaid troops to desert or even change sides. One answer to this problem was to allow soldiers to loot a city that had been stormed, or to turn a blind eye to plundering that went far beyond simply obtaining food. A town or city might face a demand for a 'contribution' by a nearby army, creating what was essentially a huge protection racket. Armies at the time were very prone to disease and, as a result, the proximity of soldiers to civilian populations triggered several major epidemics. When added to ravaging and the unintentional destruction of farmlands by marching armies, war caused tremendous suffering in the regions where fighting took place or armies camped. The worst of it fell on Germany, which was the main theatre of the war, but the whole of Europe suffered to a greater or lesser extent.

SWEDEN ENTERS THE WAR

Sweden had territorial ambitions in Europe, seeking control of the states of northern Germany along the Baltic. As a Protestant country, Sweden was also willing to help protect European Protestants against Catholic powers. These two aims aligned Sweden against the Holy Roman Empire. Ruled by the Habsburg dynasty, the Holy Roman Empire was a major force in European politics and had been the main combatant on the primarily Catholic side of the conflict since the beginning of the Thirty Years' War.

The Holy Roman Empire was, by 1630, an extremely fragmented collection of fairly large states (some of which paid only lip service to the Empire), plus all manner of free cities (small states that were sometimes nothing more than a single town) and

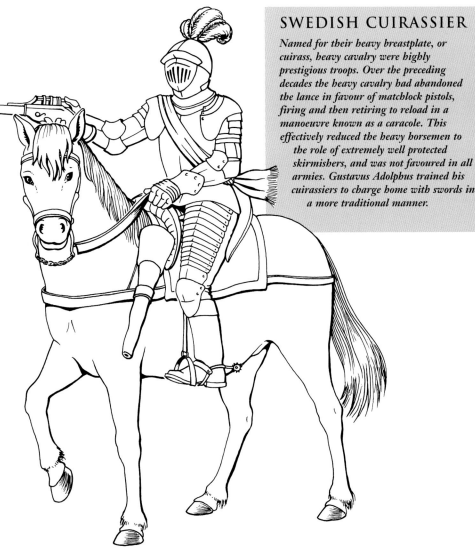

similarly inconsequential political entities. Its core territories, however, were powerful. They included Austria, Hungary, Bohemia and Bavaria. Imperial forces raised from these major states had recently won a string of major victories under the command of Count Albrecht von Wallenstein (1583–1634), who was then dismissed from command for political reasons.

This proved advantageous to the King of Sweden, Gustav II Adolphus, more commonly known as Gustavus Adolphus (1594–1632), because Wallenstein was an extremely effective commander. So too was Gustav, having gained experience as a commander in wars against Poland and Russia. This experience had led him to undertake a number of reforms in his army, which vastly increased its effectiveness.

THE SWEDISH ARMY

The Swedish Army of 1630 was the first modern-style professional standing army in

LOCATION

Sweden's interests along the Baltic coast were protected by advancing far inland to support allied Saxony against Imperial invasion.

213

LUTZEN

Gustavus Adolphus was responsible for reforming and modernizing the Swedish army. His innovations gradually spread to other forces that witnessed or were victims of the Swedes' increased effectiveness.

THE OPPOSED FORCES

SWEDISH ARMY (estimated)

Infantry:	12,800
Cavalry:	6200
	60 guns
Total:	**19,000**

IMPERIAL ARMY (estimated)

Infantry:	10,000
Cavalry:	7000
	24 guns
Total:	**17,000**

Europe. This had many benefits. Troops could be trained for longer and gain experience of soldiering even when there was no major war in which to fight. Unit identities and habits of loyalty were ingrained by regimental tradition and frequent drilling, giving units superior cohesion and esprit de corps. This made formations more likely to stand and fight when things went badly, or to remain together and combat-effective after experiencing a reverse.

The army also received improved equipment. Gustavus Adolphus introduced lighter gun-carriages for the artillery, making his guns far more mobile on the battlefield. The heavy cavalry dropped the practice of attacking with pistols and

retiring to reload in favour of a more traditional headlong charge with swords. The infantry was also reorganized and re-equipped. The practice of the time was to deploy units of musketeers protected by pikemen. Both received lighter equipment in the Swedish army, increasing their mobility. A reduction of the army's baggage train also contributed to an increase in marching speed.

EARLY CAMPAIGNS

Gustavus Adolphus was concerned that Imperial forces might capture Stralsund on the Baltic coast. This would create a threat to Sweden itself, and also endanger Swedish sea trade in the Baltic. In response, the Swedes landed in northern Germany on 6 July 1630 with 13,000 men. This force was augmented by allies, though not always willing ones. Saxony joined forces with Sweden to gain protection from Imperial invasion, while other forces were coerced into joining Gustavus' army by the threat of seeing their homes destroyed by the Swedes.

After the dismissal of Wallenstein, command of the Imperial army fell to Count Tilly (1559–1632), who favoured traditional tactics developed by the Spanish. The 'Spanish' style of warfare had previously shown its effectiveness, but was becoming outdated in the face of new developments, which were demonstrated by the Swedes at the battle of Britenfeld, which arose out of an encounter as the Swedes marched on Leipzig.

Tilly deployed his forces in *tercios*, essentially giant squares of musketeers and pikemen, with around 1500–2000 men in each square. Around 10,000 cavalry were deployed on the flanks. The Swedes used a more flexible formation, with Swedish and Finnish troops, plus large numbers of Scottish mercenaries, in the centre. The right was held by the Saxons, with a mix of Swedes and Germans on the left.

The Imperial cavalry launched an attack on the Swedish flank, which was misinterpreted as a signal for a general advance. The huge Imperial *tercios* rolled forwards, causing the Saxons to panic and flee the field. This robbed Gustavus Adolphus of a third of his force and left him without a right flank. It was now that the superior mobility of the Swedish army showed its worth, allowing Gustavus to rapidly move troops into the gap left by the departing Saxons.

The ponderous Imperial *tercios* could not move fast enough to exploit the situation, and were unable to achieve a decisive advantage. The battle became a hard slogging match, in which the ability of the Swedish artillery to shoot much faster than its Imperial counterparts was of great importance. Eventually the Imperials began to waver, then retired in great disorder. Victory at Britenfeld allowed the Swedes to overrun much of southern Germany in 1631–32, defeating Tilly again at Lech on 16 April 1632.

WALLENSTEIN RESUMES COMMAND

Faced with a threat to Vienna itself and unable to halt the Swedes any other way, the Holy Roman Emperor recalled Wallenstein to command and permitted him to implement his chosen strategy. This strategy was subtle, and involved avoiding battle while trying to goad the Swedes into attacking Wallenstein on ground of his own choosing. The result was a failed Swedish attack on the fortified camp of the Imperial army on 4 September 1632.

After inflicting a defeat – and about 3000 casualties – on the Swedish army, Wallenstein marched into Saxony. There, he decided to go into winter quarters and detached some of his cavalry. This was an error, as the Swedes were still in the field and seeking a decisive battle. One reason for this was the inability of the ravaged countryside to support an army on campaign; Gustavus Adolphus needed a victory before his supplies ran out.

Joining forces with the Saxons to create an allied army, Gustavus marched on the

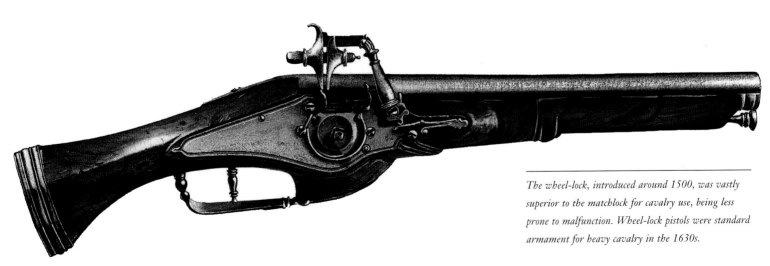

The wheel-lock, introduced around 1500, was vastly superior to the matchlock for cavalry use, being less prone to malfunction. Wheel-lock pistols were standard armament for heavy cavalry in the 1630s.

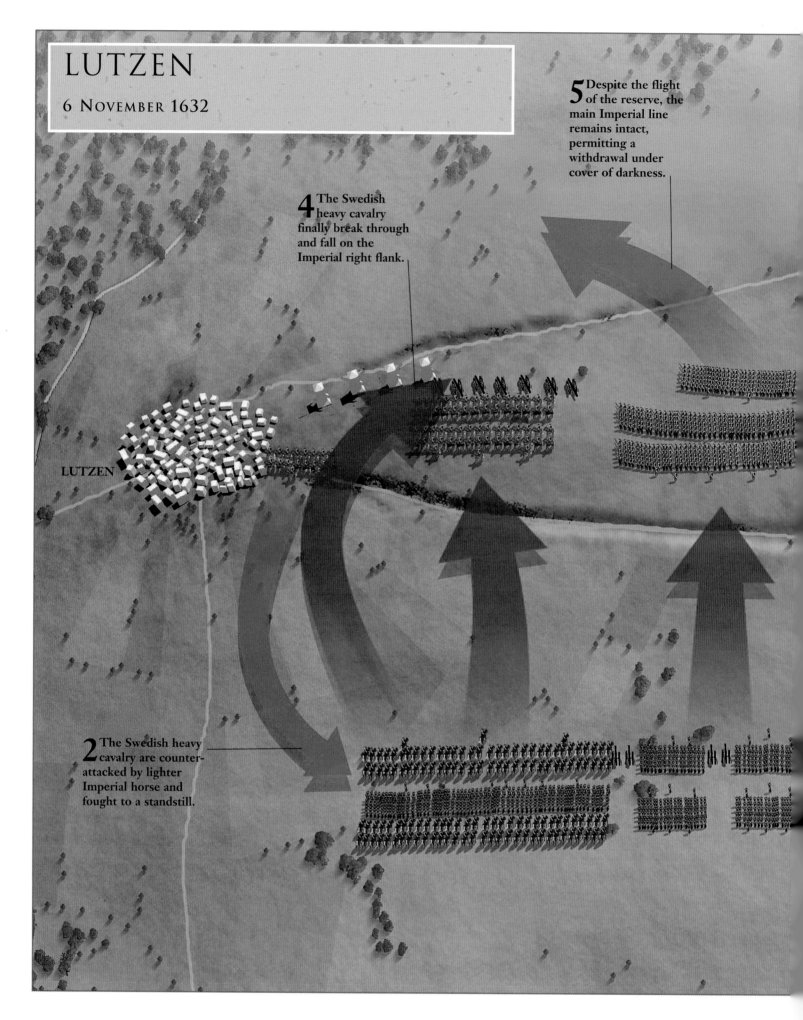

LUTZEN

6 NOVEMBER 1632

5 Despite the flight of the reserve, the main Imperial line remains intact, permitting a withdrawal under cover of darkness.

4 The Swedish heavy cavalry finally break through and fall on the Imperial right flank.

LUTZEN

2 The Swedish heavy cavalry are counter-attacked by lighter Imperial horse and fought to a standstill.

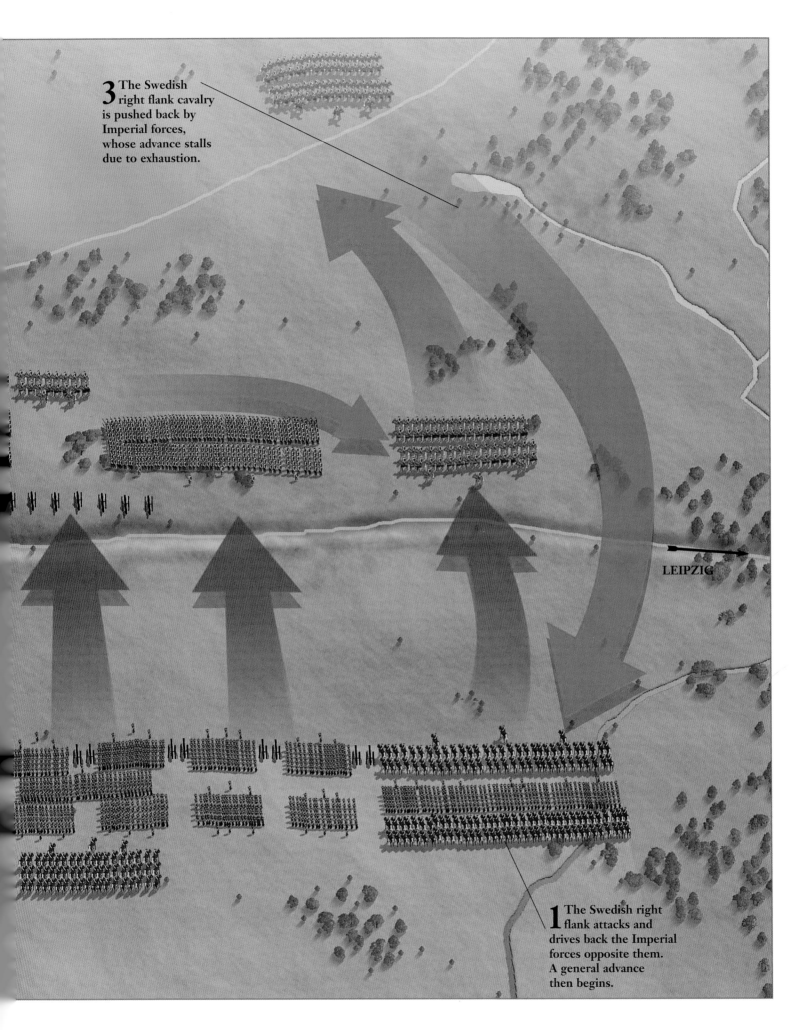

3 The Swedish right flank cavalry is pushed back by Imperial forces, whose advance stalls due to exhaustion.

LEIPZIG

1 The Swedish right flank attacks and drives back the Imperial forces opposite them. A general advance then begins.

Gustavus Adolphus leading a cavalry charge. As well as being a skilled administrator who reformed both army and government, the Swedish king was a personally courageous commander.

Imperial camp but was halted by Imperial cavalry at the Rippach stream. The allied army camped on the night of 5/6 September near Lutzen, on a flat plain with little shelter. The Imperial army was nearby, just 5km (3 miles) away, but was seeking to avoid battle if possible. If he had to fight at all, Wallenstein wanted a defensive action. To this end, his troops spent much of the night fortifying themselves along the line of a ditch that ran approximately parallel to the road to Leipzig.

OPENING MOVES

Wallenstein had implemented some reforms in the Imperial army, in terms of both tactics and organization. His infantry used formations that were flexible and smaller than previously, enabling it to react more quickly to events on the battlefield. Expecting, though not wanting, a battle, Wallenstein deployed his army with the infantry in four *tercios* occupying the centre, and the cavalry on the flanks. The right rested on a rise known as Windmill Hill, while the left relied on cavalry for protection against a flanking attack. Light artillery supported the infantry while the field artillery was deployed in well-protected positions. To conceal his dispositions, Wallenstein ordered Lutzen to be set alight, creating a smokescreen.

The Allied army was forced to postpone its attack until 11:00, due to thick morning fog that did not lift as expected. The attack did not go well, being halted by heavy musket and artillery fire in the centre and on the left. On the right, a primarily Swedish and Finnish force under the personal command of Gustavus Adolphus made more progress, though at a heavy cost in terms casualties. Fog then descended on the battlefield once more, heavily restricting visibility. The result was a close-quarters battle of attrition with heavy casualties on both sides.

CRISIS FOR THE SWEDES

In the midst of the fighting, Wallenstein's detached cavalry returned. Approximately 5000 horsemen under Count Pappenheim (1594–1632) joined the battle, and the Swedish cavalry were almost driven from the field. They were rallied by the Swedes' chief army chaplain and returned to the fight. Meanwhile, Gustavus Adolphus had taken personal command of one of his cavalry units when its commander was wounded. As he led an advance, the fog thickened until it was impossible to see in any direction. This covered the attack of a force of Imperial cuirassiers, who charged into Gustavus' unit.

In the ensuing mêlée, Gustavus Adolphus was shot in the arm and lost his sword as he tried to keep control of his horse. He became separated from his command and was shot again, this time in the back. Despite the efforts of his bodyguard to save him, Gustavus fell from his horse when it was shot and was dragged for some distance with his foot caught in a stirrup. He was still alive when the Imperial cavalry found him, and was finished off with a pistol shot. His clothing and weapons were taken as trophies.

THE SWEDES RALLY

Recognizing the wounded horse that fled through their lines, and hearing that the king was dead, the Swedes began to waver. However, the army second-in-command, Bernhard of Saxe-Weimar (1604–39), was able to rally them and lead an advance. On the way, they found the body of Gustavus Adolphus and became determined to take revenge. A general attack developed that pushed the Imperial flanks back but could not break them. Instead, a bitter close-range firefight developed.

In a final effort to break the murderous deadlock, Bernhard of Saxe-Weimar ordered an attack on the Imperial artillery battery located on Windmill Hill. Supported by intense artillery fire, the allies launched their assault at 15:00, but were initially repulsed. A second assault succeeded, but only after two further hours of close combat. With Windmill Hill in the possession of the allies, the Imperial position was badly compromised. However, although the Imperial reserve force had fled the field, the main line held out until nightfall.

Wallenstein's army was demoralized and exhausted and, although his opponents were in scarcely better condition, it was the Imperial forces that retreated. The allied victory had cost them 3000 casualties, against 4000 Imperial losses. Despite this battlefield victory, the overall strategic victory sought by Gustavus Adolphus had eluded him, and whatever advantage was gained at Lutzen was bought at the price of his own life.

AFTERMATH

The battle of Lutzen was a close-fought victory for the allies, but did little to change the political landscape. The most significant outcome was the loss of Gustavus Adolphus himself, depriving the Protestant cause of a truly great commander.

Wallenstein was murdered the following year, while Bernhard of Saxe-Weimar was defeated at Nordlingen in 1635. The war continued, with frequent variations in terms of participants, until it was finally brought to an end by the peace of Westphalia in 1648.

Attacked by Imperial cuirassiers, Gustavus Adolphus was separated from his troops and shot repeatedly before succumbing to his wounds. His death caused a crisis in the Swedish army.

BLENHEIM
13 AUGUST 1704

KNOWING THAT THE FALL OF VIENNA MIGHT SPELL THE END OF THE GRAND ALLIANCE, THE DUKE OF MARLBOROUGH EMBARKED UPON A DARING MARCH FROM THE LOW COUNTRIES TO THE DANUBE, PUTTING HIS FORCES IN POSITION TO DEFEAT A FRANCO-BAVARIAN ARMY THREATENING THE AUSTRIAN CAPITAL.

WHY DID IT HAPPEN?

WHO An allied force commanded by the Duke of Marlborough (1650–1722) and Prince Eugène of Savoy (1663–1736), opposed by a Franco-Bavarian army under Marshal Count de Tallard (1652–1728).

WHAT The allies exploited their advantages, notably in infantry and artillery, with bold strategic movement and aggressive tactics on the field of battle.

WHERE The village of Blenheim in Bavaria.

WHEN 13 August 1704.

WHY The Grand Alliance sought to limit Franco-Bavarian power by defeating their army in the field.

OUTCOME A decisive victory for the allies protected Vienna and forced Bavaria out of the war.

The War of the Spanish Succession resulted from the death of King Carlos II of Spain on 1 November 1700. Europe had just emerged from the War of the Grand Alliance (1688–97), which had pitted France against Britain, Spain, the Dutch Republic, Savoy, Sweden, Portugal and the Holy Roman Empire. The war ended mainly as a result of financial exhaustion, and none of the states of Europe had recovered sufficiently to pursue new campaigns.

However, given the events that transpired, conflict eventually became inevitable.

FRANCE AND SPAIN

Carlos II of Spain had no natural heir, and left his realm to Duke Philip of Anjou. Duke Philip was part of the French ruling family, which meant that France would also control all the territories of the powerful Spanish empire. This was unacceptable to many European states. The Holy Roman

Although heavy armour had gone out of fashion for the battlefield, it was still considered appropriate for portraits. Thus the Duke of Marlborough is depicted here wearing armour from a previous century.

Empire proposed its own candidate for the Spanish throne. This was Leopold I, the Holy Roman Emperor. The Habsburg dynasty, of which Leopold I was part, had previously ruled Spain and Leopold had a solid claim to the throne, but the French could not accept the Habsburgs returning to rule powerful states that were on the opposite side to France.

In order to protect French interests, King Louis XIV of France took a number of risky actions. He cut off Spanish trade to the Netherlands and Britain, and moved forces into the Spanish Netherlands. Meanwhile, a confused diplomatic situation existed. France negotiated a treaty with the United Provinces and the Holy Roman Empire. Signed in 1701, this treaty recognized Louis XIV's grandson, Duke Philip of Anjou, as king of Spain in accordance with the will of Carlos II. In return, Austria received Spain's territory in Italy as well as the Spanish Netherlands. However, the agreement did not last long.

FRANCE AND BRITAIN

Although Louis XIV had previously accepted William III of England as legitimate ruler, he decided to instead recognize his fellow Catholic James Edward Stuart, son of the deposed James II, as king. Conflict between England and France therefore began, though on a small scale at first. Austrian forces moved to annex the Duchy of Milan, which belonged to Spain, and elements in Spain itself declared a desire to be ruled by the Austrian Habsburgs. England, Austria, the United Provinces and various German states, including Hanover and Prussia, formed an alliance to oppose France. The Austrians were primarily active in Italy while the rest of the allies operated in the Low Countries. The war was also prosecuted at sea and in the New World.

Although William III of England died in March 1702, this did little to change British involvement in the war. William's sister-in-law, Anne, assumed the throne and reigned for more than a decade, 1702–1714. The North American segment of the War of the Spanish Succession is known as Queen Anne's War for this reason. Among Queen Anne's chief ministers was Sir John Churchill, Duke of Marlborough. Known as

'Corporal John' among the troops he commanded, Marlborough was a talented commander who had fully grasped the potential of recent military innovations.

INNOVATIONS IN WARFARE

One of the most important inventions of the time was the socket bayonet. Firearms had gradually replaced hand weapons and bows on the battlefield, but their slow rate of fire, coupled with a relatively short lethal range, made it likely that determined enemy troops could close with a unit of musketeers and engage in hand-to-hand combat. A weapon was needed for such an eventuality. For many years, it was common practice to field mixed units of 'pike and shot', with the musketeers protected by a body of pikemen. However, firepower was considered to be the decisive weapon, and pikemen could not shoot.

The answer was to issue every man in a unit with a musket, greatly increasing firepower, and to give him a hand weapon as well. Weapons like hangers (oversized knives or small swords) were not really satisfactory, nor was using a musket as a club. The answer was the bayonet; fitting a blade to the muzzle of a musket turned it into a spear that could be used

Marlborough's march from the Spanish Netherlands to the Danube was an extremely risky undertaking, though the risk was justified by the certainty of defeat if Vienna were not protected.

FRENCH DRAGOONS

French dragoon (mounted) and officer (standing), 1704. Originally infantrymen mounted on cheap horses for mobility, dragoons were developed to carry out a true cavalry role, though they retained the ability to fight on foot as well. The name 'dragoon' comes from dragon, the French name for the firearm that originally equipped the dragoon units. This weapon was shorter than the standard infantry musket, making it easier to use on horseback. For close combat, dragoons were also armed with a cavalry sabre and, often, a pair of pistols.

221

to fend off cavalry or outreach shorter hand weapons such as swords. The first bayonets were of the 'plug' type, fitting directly into the muzzle of the musket. This made firing impossible, so judging when to fix bayonets was a matter for delicate judgement.

From 1678 onwards, experiments were conducted with socket bayonets, which fixed to a socket on the musket and did not block the barrel. After some early troubles, socket bayonets were proven effective. Pikes were deleted from the English and most German armies from 1697 onwards, replaced by the musket-and-socket bayonet combination. The French army did not receive the socket bayonet until 1703. It was still common for non-commissioned officers to be issued with pikes at this time. One reason was to enable the sergeant to place his weapon lengthways across the backs of a line of men, encouraging them to stand their ground.

Muskets themselves had also become more effective than previously, due to the adoption of the flintlock mechanism. Invented in 1610, the flintlock was superior to the earlier matchlock and wheel-lock systems, and replaced them through the mid-1600s. However, the effective range of even massed muskets was still little more than 100m (110yd) due to accuracy issues

with the smoothbore barrel, and the fact that the large ball lost speed quickly due to wind resistance. However, armed with massed muskets, and capable of making a charge or resisting one with the bayonet, infantry had become far more effective than they had previously been.

THE CAMPAIGN OPENS

France had been generally successful in the war up to 1704, and was allied to Bavaria, which caused new problems for the allies. Indeed, early in 1704 the future of the Grand Alliance was in some doubt. A Bavarian army was threatening Vienna, while Austrian forces were distracted by a revolt in Hungary. The French army in northern Italy could also pose a threat to the capital of the Holy Roman Empire. There was a very real threat that Vienna would be taken and one of the major powers of the alliance put out of the war.

The only source of assistance for Vienna was the allied army in the Low Countries, very far off and engaged in hostilities against a French army. Marlborough therefore decided upon a daring march to the Danube, since the war in the Low Countries was lost anyway if Vienna fell. The Dutch United Provinces were opposed to any move away from their territory

For much of the day, allied and Franco-Bavarian forces engaged in a series of exhausting attacks and counter-attacks that wore down both sides. Poor use of reserves resulted in the French centre finally giving way.

because it left their homelands exposed to attack. Marlborough knew that the Dutch would not agree to his planned movement, and in any case he needed to conceal his intentions from the enemy. So he informed the Dutch that he was going to march his army only as far as the Moselle River, while intending to go much further.

An allied force of about 70,000 men was left to assist the Dutch if the French attacked, and Marlborough's force was joined by reinforcements on the march, bringing it up to a similar number. However, he faced about 60,000 French at Strasbourg and 60,000 more in the Franco-Bavarian army. It was necessary to keep these two forces apart if Marlborough was to have any chance of victory, a task that fell to a force of about 30,000 under Prince Eugène of Savoy. It was extremely important to avoid French intervention because Marlborough's supply lines were very exposed, and he could not afford to lose forces in minor actions en route if he were to stand a chance of defeating the Franco-Bavarian force threatening Vienna.

CROSSING THE DANUBE

While Eugène occupied French attention around Baden, Marlborough made a rapid march to the Danube, reaching the town of Donauworth on 1 July. The town commanded a river crossing that Marlborough intended to use and was held by 14,000 men under Marshal d'Arco. The defenders were making preparations for a defence, constructing a fortification named the *Schellenberg*. A forced river crossing was difficult enough at any time, but against fortified troops it was likely to be extremely expensive in terms of casualties, which Marlborough could not afford.

The answer was to launch a surprise attack. The defenders were aware of Marlborough's army as it took up positions in front of the *Schellenberg* on the afternoon of 2 July, so complete surprise was out of the question. Marlborough ordered his army to pitch tents and make camp, suggesting that he was not intending to attack straight away. However, that is exactly what he did, with artillery preparation beginning at 05:00 and the first

assault going in at 06:15. Although the defenders were caught by surprise as a result of the ruse, three assaults were beaten back.

The attacks fixed the defenders' attention on one sector of the battle, and at 07:15 a renewed assault from a new direction broke into the *Schellenberg*. A furious hand-to-hand fight ensued, leaving Marlborough's force in control of the fortress. The cost was high – some 1400 dead and 3800 wounded – but the Bavarian defenders suffered worse casualties, estimated at around 10,000. More importantly, the allies had forced a crossing of the Danube and were now in a position to operate against the Franco-Bavarian army, which was now commanded by Marshal Count de Tallard.

TALLARD STANDS AT BLENHEIM

Marlborough tried to draw out the Franco-Bavarians by laying waste to the countryside, but Tallard was unwilling to fight on his enemy's terms. On 11 August, Marlborough requested Prince Eugène to bring up his force to join the allied army and began to advance against Tallard's army. Tallard had chosen a good defensive

In the early eighteenth century, infantry were supported by a single rank of pikemen, who would come to the front if the musketeers were threatened by cavalry. This was very disruptive to the formation, and eventually led to the development if the bayonet.

THE OPPOSED FORCES

ALLIES

Infantry and cavalry:	52,000
Guns	66

FRANCO-BAVARIAN

Infantry and cavalry	56,000
Guns	90

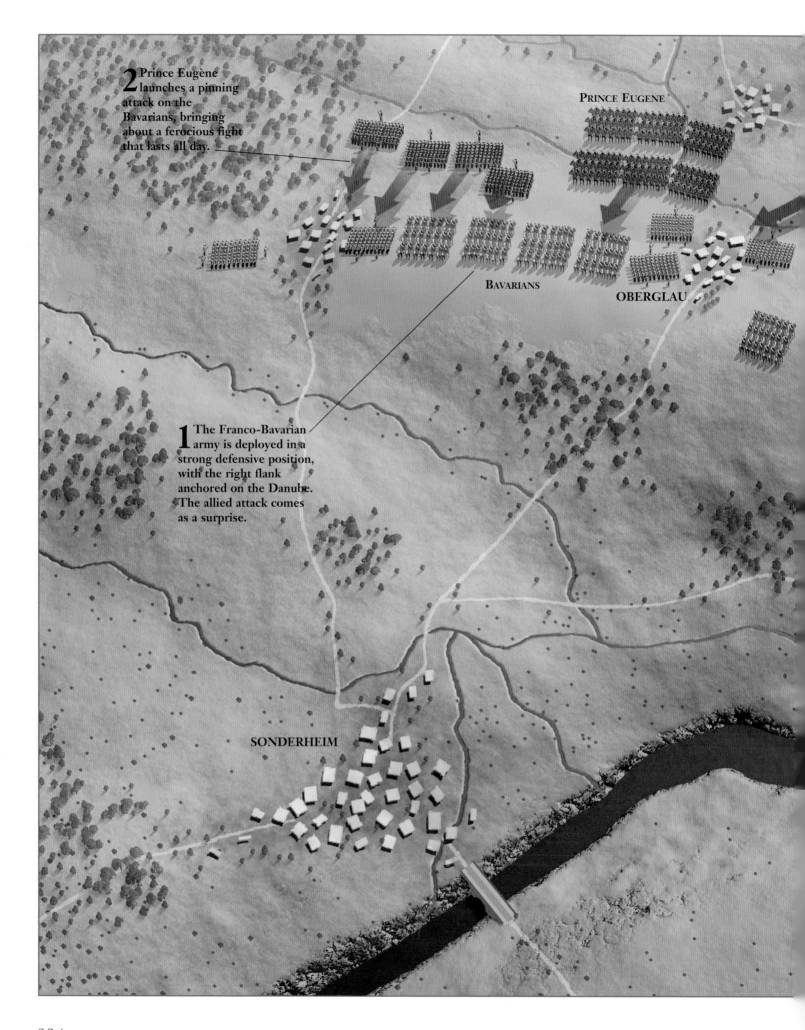

2 Prince Eugène launches a pinning attack on the Bavarians, bringing about a ferocious fight that lasts all day.

PRINCE EUGENE

BAVARIANS

OBERGLAU

1 The Franco-Bavarian army is deployed in a strong defensive position, with the right flank anchored on the Danube. The allied attack comes as a surprise.

SONDERHEIM

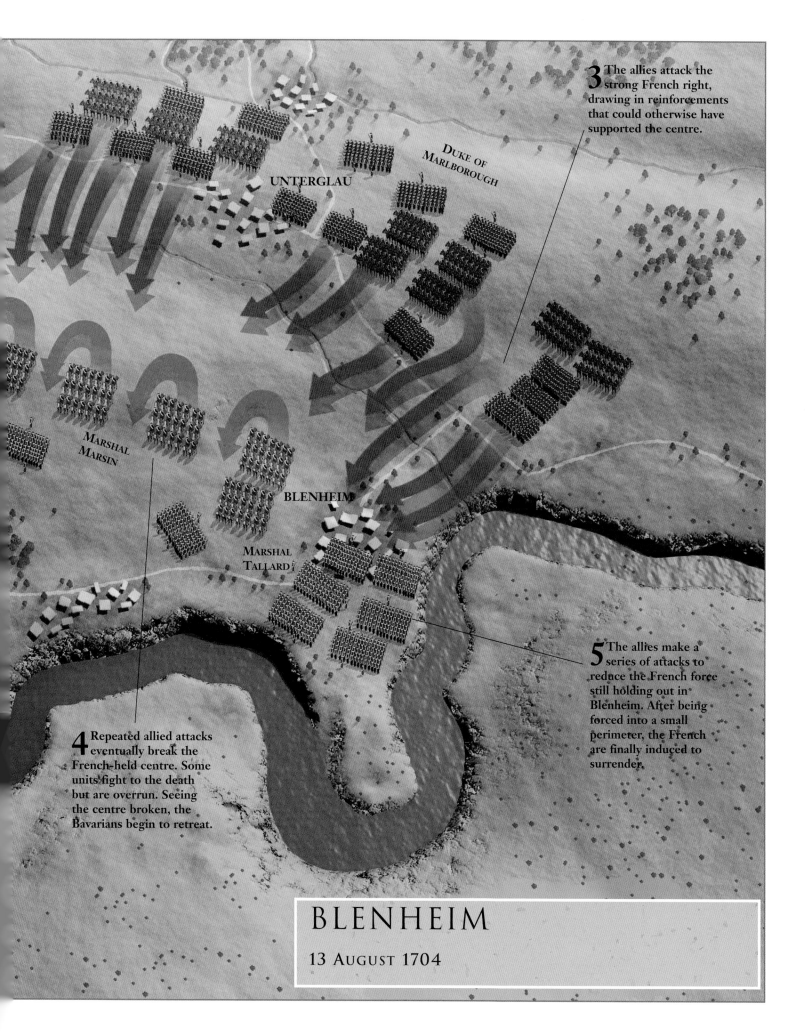

3 The allies attack the strong French right, drawing in reinforcements that could otherwise have supported the centre.

DUKE OF
MARLBOROUGH

UNTERGLAU

MARSHAL
MARSIN

BLENHEIM

MARSHAL
TALLARD

5 The allies make a series of attacks to reduce the French force still holding out in Blenheim. After being forced into a small perimeter, the French are finally induced to surrender.

4 Repeated allied attacks eventually break the French-held centre. Some units fight to the death but are overrun. Seeing the centre broken, the Bavarians begin to retreat.

BLENHEIM

13 AUGUST 1704

225

The Duke of Marlborough signs despatches at the end of the battle of Blenheim. The whole operation was a huge gamble that literally changed the course of the war.

position around Blenheim. His right flank was secured by the Danube and his left by high, forested, ground. The villages of Blenheim, Oberglau and Lutzingen formed strong points in the line, with low-lying and wet areas, as well as the Nebel stream, forming natural obstacles to any enemy advance.

The Franco-Bavarian force felt secure in its positions, and with good reason. However, Marlborough was an aggressive and skilled commander who was not daunted by fortified enemies. On 12 August, he made a personal reconnaissance of the enemy dispositions and decided that he could break them. Again, he decided upon a surprise attack and started his army moving into position at 02:00 on 13 August. By 07:00, Marlborough's army was close to the enemy line, while Tallard's force was unaware that anything was happening. As the morning mist cleared, the over-confident Franco-Bavarians were presented with the prospect of an imminent attack.

Although slightly outnumbered – 56,000 to 60,000 – the allies had achieved surprise and had the advantage of fighting an unprepared enemy who just minutes before had felt safe and secure. The Franco-Bavarians were unable to coordinate their plans effectively, and so were forced to fight as three more or less separate commands. Tallard himself commanded the strongest component of the line, at Blenheim, on the right flank. The centre was commanded by

Marshal de Marsin, with the Bavarian contingent under Maximilian II Emanuel, Elector of Bavaria.

INITIAL ATTACKS

The battle was opened by the artillery of both sides as the allied army advanced. Marlborough was wary of Tallard's dispositions, noting that his personal command on the right flank was the strongest part of the Franco-Bavarian line. It seemed likely to Marlborough that Tallard intended to counterattack with this force if the opportunity presented itself. He therefore decided to occupy this force while he broke the weaker centre.

In order to prevent Bavarian interference, Marlborough ordered Prince Eugène to launch an attack on the Bavarians holding the enemy left. This required a lengthy approach through rough and marshy ground, holding up the allied attack. In the meantime, the artillery pounded away, inflicting casualties on both sides. Once the Bavarians were engaged, the pinning attack on Blenheim could begin. This went in at 12:45, with the attacking troops crossing the Nebel stream at five points using pontoon bridges.

The initial attack penetrated Blenheim at a few points, but the allies were swiftly ejected and were then counterattacked in the flank by cavalry. Fire from an allied infantry brigade drove off the counterattack in turn, allowing a renewed attack to be launched. This drew in French reinforcements, with the result that there were far more men in the village than were necessary to beat off the allied assault. The attack on Blenheim was an expensive failure, in that it did not drive the French from the village, but it served the purpose of pinning large numbers of French troops in a position where they could not influence the critical phase of the battle.

SUCCESS IN THE CENTRE

The point of decision was Oberglau, held by the French under Marsin. As the allied infantry advanced, they were charged by French horsemen, who were beaten off by allied cavalry. These in turn were repulsed by infantry fire and additional French cavalry. More French cavalry attacks were launched, but these became confused and were beaten off. However, the allied infantry were unable to advance in the face of this pressure. Had Tallard's infantry reserves not been drawn into Blenheim, a counterattack in the centre might have borne fruit. The deadlock was broken by additional allied cavalry, including heavy squadrons sent by Prince Eugène to assist his ally. This permitted the advance of allied infantry and artillery, pushing the French centre back into the village of Oberglau. The French cavalry was driven off and the infantry overwhelmed despite a gallant stand. The centre finally disintegrated after many battalions formed square and fought to the last man.

VICTORY FOR THE ALLIES

On the allied right flank, Prince Eugène's force had been hotly engaged all day. Some units were wavering and the issue was still in doubt. Prince Eugène personally led another attack, regimental colour in hand, and finally broke the Bavarian line. With many units in retreat and seeing their French allies breaking, the Bavarians began a retreat that, while disorderly, remained short of rout. The allies were too exhausted to pursue.

With the centre and left broken, only the French right flank force held out in and around Blenheim. Allied reinforcements were fed into the fighting, gradually forcing the French into the centre of the village, where they made a stand in a walled churchyard. There, they beat off repeated attacks with heavy casualties on both sides until the allies offered a parlay. The defenders eventually agreed to surrender, bringing the action to a close.

AFTERMATH

The Franco-Bavarian army was shattered, with 13,600 casualties and 15,000 prisoners. The Bavarian contingent managed to return home, but Bavaria was taken out of the war and placed under Austrian rule. The cost was high – 4500 dead and 7500 wounded – but the threat to Vienna was eliminated. This ensured the survival of the Grand Alliance and meant that France would not come to dominate Europe. In recognition of the importance of his victory, Marlborough was gifted a palace by the crown and elevated to the rank of Duke.

Another tradition of an earlier age was the depiction of cavalry as the decisive arm in battle. Blenheim was, in fact, won by the cooperation of all arms and especially by intense infantry combat.

SIEGE OF QUEBEC
13 SEPTEMBER 1759

ALTHOUGH THE FORCES INVOLVED WERE NOT LARGE, THE SIEGE OF QUEBEC HAD PROFOUND CONSEQUENCES FOR THE COURSE OF THE SEVEN YEARS' WAR IN THE AMERICAS, AND FOR THE SUBSEQUENT EMERGENCE OF THE NATION OF CANADA.

WHY DID IT HAPPEN?

WHO A British army under Major-General James Wolfe (1727–59), numbering 4441 men, opposed by a 4500-strong French army under Major-General Louis-Joseph de Montcalm (1712–59).

WHAT The British sought and eventually found a route onto the Heights of Abraham surrounding Quebec, at which point the French army advanced to confront them.

WHERE Just west of Quebec, Canada.

WHEN 13 September 1759.

WHY Britain and France were on opposite sides in the Seven Years' War.

OUTCOME The French were defeated and Quebec surrendered days later.

The Seven Years' War (1756–63) was a European conflict – it originated there and was fought mainly between European powers. It has, however, been described as a 'world war', since conflict took place in the Americas and India as well as within Europe itself. Indeed, it was in the colonial territories that the conflict made the most lasting changes.

The component of the war fought in North America actually began two years before the European conflict, in 1754, and went on for nine years. Despite this, the colonial segment is still usually referred to as the Seven Years' War since it formed part of that conflict. A further alternative title, the French and Indian War, is sometimes used.

The Seven Years' War arose out of ongoing political conflict among the powers of Europe. The resolution of the War of the Austrian Succession (1740–48) created a situation in which renewed conflict was almost inevitable, as Austria had agreed concessions only to buy time to ready themselves for war. Austria made alliances with France and Russia against Prussia, which threatened British holdings in Hanover and pushed Britain into an alliance with Prussia.

Britain and France were at that time engaged in what amounted to an undeclared war over territory in America, most notably the Ohio region. This conflict had been a small-scale affair fought in the colonies, but once the alliance structure began to form in

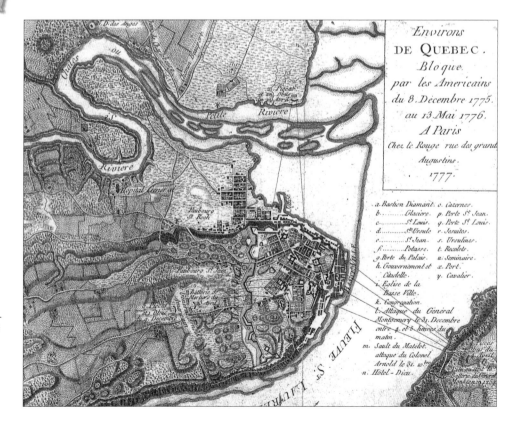

This 1776 map of Quebec shows the American siege of British forces that year. The map illustrates the difficulties facing a besieging force. Protected on two sides by the river, the city was also fortified on the landward side.

GRENADIER INFANTRY

Recognizable by their distinctive 'mitre' caps, grenadiers were originally specialist grenade-throwers and were thus chosen for their size and strength. Over time, they evolved into elite infantry whose stature and physical prowess made them more effective and imposing than other troops. All regiments contained a Grenadier company, which traditionally deployed on the right of the regiment's flank. However, Grenadier companies could also be detached to form elite units. These were often deployed at critical points on the battlefield, or sometimes to 'stiffen' lesser infantry formations by standing behind them with bayonets fixed.

Europe, with France in one camp and Britain in the other, this provided additional impetus towards large-scale war in Europe.

Britain's contribution to the war on land in Europe was largely financial. Britain was a major colonial power, whose military capabilities were primarily naval. Her army was small and unable to make much difference in continentental Europe. Thus the Prussian army of Frederick the Great, backed by British gold, fought on land while the British employed a maritime strategy. This included the blockade of ports as well as operations against overseas holdings. This suited the expansionist ambitions of the British Empire perfectly.

CONFLICT IN THE COLONIES

Seeking to limit British influence in their territory, the French ordered the local Native American tribes to break off trade relations with British settlers, an order that was largely ignored. A punitive expedition was launched to punish the locals for their disobedience, and soon afterwards a larger force, around 2000 in number, moved into the Ohio Valley to enforce French claims to the region.

This force was a mix of French troops and men recruited from the local tribes. They

built forts and garrisoned them, and drove out British trading parties. This displeased the Iroquois Confederacy, who demanded that the British respond to what the Iroquois saw as French encroachment. The British delivered an ultimatum requiring a French withdrawal, sending it via a member of the Virginia Militia: Major George Washington, later General and subsequently the first President of the United States. The French response was a polite refusal, citing a claim on the region predating the British one.

In January 1754, Washington returned with the news that the French had declined to comply with the British ultimatum. By then, a small British force had been sent to build a fort in the disputed region, but was driven off by French, who now built a fort of their own. It was named Fort Duquesne, after the commander who oversaw its construction. Washington was sent back with a larger force to deal with the French, and built a fort of his own. He was forced to surrender it by a French attack, negotiating the withdrawal of his command in return for abandoning the fort.

THE BRITISH RESPONSE

These small colonial hostilities involved only a few men, but it was understood that

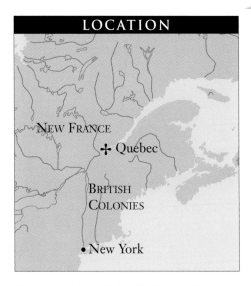

Quebec occupied a critical position between the British colonies along the coast and New France, further inland. The city controlled access to the Great Lakes region.

Louis-Joseph de Montcalm-Gozon, Marquis de Saint-Veran, commanded French forces in the American colonies from 1756 until his death at Quebec in 1759. He was initially successful but was defeated by superior numbers of British troops.

the outcome could affect colonial affairs on a much wider scale. Thus a British expeditionary force was assembled to be sent to the contested region. The French found out what was going to happen and sent their own troops. The Royal Navy tried to blockade the French expeditionary force in port, but was too late; it had already sailed. An attempt to interfere with the deployment resulted in British ships firing on French vessels and capturing some.

The British expeditionary force attempted to capture Fort Duquesne in June 1755, but failed in the face of French resistance. Worse, French troops captured the British plans for their colonial campaign, which included expeditions to fortify key areas. A series of inconclusive, though often bloody, small-scale actions took place during the remainder of 1755. At that time, war had not been declared, and these actions pushed Europe ever closer to a general conflict.

THE SEVEN YEARS' WAR

France and Britain both sent reinforcements to the American theatre in 1756, as the Seven Years' War began. The French were generally more active, pursuing a campaign of raids against the British supply chain and outposts. Although not decisive, this campaign gradually improved the French strategic position. The British, on the other hand, proceeded cautiously and in some confusion. A planned attack on Quebec in 1757 was reassigned to Louisburg, arriving there by sea after considerable delay, only to find a strong French naval force in position. The expedition was called off, having achieved nothing.

The British were both more aggressive and more successful after 1757. An attempt on Fort Ticonderoga failed in July 1758, but a renewed effort drove off the French the following year. Meanwhile, Fort Duquesne was taken near the end of 1758. The capture and destruction of these forts deprived the French of bases that could have been used to threaten British operations against Canada, and particularly Quebec.

With the situation in the colonies deteriorating, French policy switched to preparations for an invasion of Britain, hoping to pull British forces back from the

American theatre by threatening the homeland. This increased concentration on events in Europe was made necessary in part by British naval supremacy. Although both sides were operating at the end of an extremely long supply chain, the Royal Navy was better able to protect its own interests and impede French efforts to keep their forces in the New World combat-worthy. Supply ships did get through, but they were forced to run the gauntlet of British blockades off the French and American coasts, as well as the risk of an interception on the open sea.

THE QUEBEC CAMPAIGN

Although short of supplies and facing desertion by some of their Native American allies, the French still held a strong position in Quebec. The British plan was to advance on Quebec from Louisbourg while other forces moved along Lake Champlain. The offensive was supported by a large force of ships and smaller boats, which made the difficult journey up the Saint Lawrence River and landed British troops on the Île de Orleans on 28 June 1759.

An attempt by the French to dislodge the fleet using fireships floated down the river was defeated by British sailors using their ships' boats to tow the fireships aside. With a secure base established, the British quickly landed on the south bank of the river and established artillery positions to bombard the city.

It was one thing to fire artillery at Quebec, but assaulting it was a different matter. Quebec was protected by the wide Saint Lawrence River, making a direct assault from that direction impossible. It was still essential to establish a force on the north side of the river, albeit away from Quebec itself, and attack the city from the west. However, even approaching Quebec was a difficult undertaking, as the defenders had positioned troops at every likely crossing point on the river.

THE BATTLE OF BEAUPORT

The best point for a landing on the north shore seemed to be the strongly held town of Beauport, east of Quebec. A direct assault was certain to be costly, so the British commander, James Wolfe, planned to

outflank Beauport by landing at a point beyond the mouth of the Montmorency River, where the French defensive line terminated.

Wolfe landed with part of his force on the north shore of the Saint Lawrence River on 10 July and set about building a fortified camp to support his attack. As he prepared for an attack, the Navy succeeded in running several ships upriver, past the defences of Quebec. This created the possibility of a crossing upriver of the city, but Wolfe persisted with his plan for an assault on Beauport.

In order to reach Beauport, it was necessary to cross the Montmorency River, which, although much smaller than the Saint Lawrence, was still a real obstacle. A ford was found but it was garrisoned by the French, who fought off an attempt to force a crossing. Nevertheless, the attack on Beauport went in on 31 July.

The main attack was made across the Saint Lawrence River by forces landing from boats and naval transports, while additional forces crossed the Montmorency River and launched a diversionary attack. However, the plan went wrong from the start. Some troops reached the shore while others were held up by unexpected shallows in the river. Soon after the action opened, heavy rainfall began, making musketry impossible. Wolfe now had no option but to order a retreat.

THE SIEGE CONTINUES

Having failed to establish a force across the Saint Lawrence, the British continued to besiege and bombard the city. Disease broke out in the British camp, making a rapid end to the campaign essential before the army became incapable of offensive operations. Despite becoming ill himself, Wolfe worked on various plans to get across the river and attack Quebec, finally deciding to try for a landing upriver of the city. Wolfe hoped to establish a force across the river, thereby forcing the French to come out to fight in order to protect their supply lines to Montreal.

Meanwhile, the French commander, Montcalm, was well aware that his victory at Beauport was only a setback for the British. He set about strengthening his position by reinforcing Beauport and sending troops to observe the British ships, which had previously run past Quebec and were now anchored upstream. Montcalm rightly considered that these vessels might pose a threat, but failed to predict the landings that took place on 12 September 1759.

SCALING THE HEIGHTS OF ABRAHAM

Wolfe did not decide on the location for his landings until almost the last minute. He had been considering landing sites well upstream of Quebec, some as much as 32km (20 miles)

This contemporary painting indicates the importance of naval power in operations against Quebec. The Saint Lawrence River was the city's main defensive asset; once across it, the British were able to take the city.

THE OPPOSED FORCES

BRITISH

Total: 4441

FRENCH

Total: (approximate) 4500

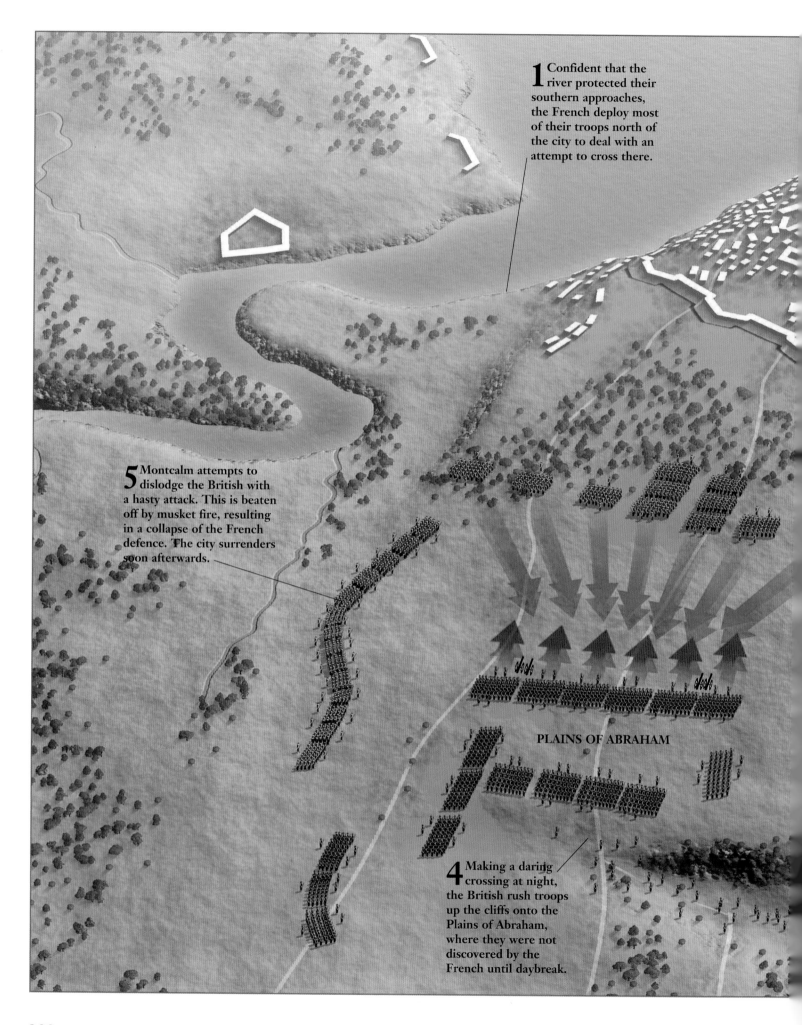

1 Confident that the river protected their southern approaches, the French deploy most of their troops north of the city to deal with an attempt to cross there.

5 Montcalm attempts to dislodge the British with a hasty attack. This is beaten off by musket fire, resulting in a collapse of the French defence. The city surrenders soon afterwards.

PLAINS OF ABRAHAM

4 Making a daring crossing at night, the British rush troops up the cliffs onto the Plains of Abraham, where they were not discovered by the French until daybreak.

2 British artillery on the south bank causes considerable damage in the lower town but cannot achieve a decisive result.

BRITISH BATTERIES

QUEBEC CITY

ST LAWRENCE RIVER

3 Having run vessels upriver past the defences of Quebec, the British are able to make a crossing. After considering many options, a point close to the city is finally selected.

SIEGE OF QUEBEC

13 SEPTEMBER 1759

Wolfe and Montcalm in action on the Plains of Abraham. Montcalm's insistence on commanding from horseback made him a target, probably resulting in his mortal wound during the retreat.

away, but finally settled on a daring plan to land at a cove called L'Anse-au-Foulon, close to the city. The initial landing was to be made by a small advance party, which would quickly scale the cliffs and deal with French troops watching the river. Additional troops would be fed across the river as quickly as possible, establishing themselves on the Plains of Abraham in front of Quebec before the French could react.

The plan was risky, involving a night-time crossing of the river followed by climbing up a 50m (164ft) cliff. This was likely to be followed by an engagement with enemy troops coming out of the city, with no easy line of retreat. Even a small force could stall the advance indefinitely from the top of the cliffs, so the utmost stealth and speed was essential.

In the event, the assault received inadvertent French assistance. The defenders observed boats on the river, but assumed that these were part of their own supply run – they had not been notified that the run had been cancelled. The defenders did challenge the British advance party as it disembarked, but a French speaker among the British force gave an answer credible enough to convince the French soldiers that they were dealing with friendly sailors. Thus the garrison at the top of the cliffs was caught by surprise and overrun, enabling the British to rush a sizable force up the

road leading to the top of the cliffs before sunrise made their presence obvious.

BATTLE ON THE PLAINS OF ABRAHAM

Even when word arrived that the British were on the Plains of Abraham, Montcalm was not convinced. He expected a renewed attack at Beauport, and this assumption was encouraged by a demonstration attack and feigned landings by the British. However, the true situation then became apparent and Montcalm realized that he had to dislodge the British quickly. Although there were over 13,000 men in Quebec who could theoretically be considered combat-capable, many of these were militia or other irregulars who were unwilling or unable to take part in a set-piece battle against British regulars.

Montcalm advanced out of Quebec to find the British deployed with their backs to the cliff. Their only line of retreat was back down the road and across the river, ensuring that a defeat would be catastrophic. This may have been a factor in Montcalm's decision to attack immediately. The British line was nearly 1km (0.6 mile) long, and held by only 3300 men. It seemed that a determined attack would drive the British into the river.

Montcalm's force of regulars and militia were not really suited to European-style tactics, which emphasized close-order drill and massed volleys from smoothbore muskets. Many of the militia were armed with long rifles that fired more slowly than muskets but had a far greater accurate range. Thus Montcalm might have done well to stand off and use long-range skirmishing tactics, but instead he advanced for a set-piece musket-and-bayonet fight.

The British left flank was secured on a small hamlet, which came under attack from a force of militia who fired from cover or rushed in to fight at close quarters with hatchets and tomahawks. Their plan was to gain control of the buildings in the hamlet and thus turn the British flank. This force harassed the British throughout the action and pulled back only when the French centre collapsed.

As the main French force advanced against Wolfe's centre regiments, the British held their fire. Wolfe had ordered his men to double-load their muskets with two balls, creating a very deadly volley but only at close range. The French hesitated and then began firing volleys, but coming from a mix of rifles and muskets in the hands of volunteers and irregulars these were mostly ineffective. At a range of about 30m (98ft), the British centre finally opened fire with their double-shotted muskets, causing severe casualties. As the French stalled, the British advanced a little and fired again.

The French then began to retreat, though firing continued for a time before the retreat became a general flight. However, Wolfe had been mortally wounded in the exchange of fire and died on the field of battle. The loss of their commanding officer caused great confusion in the British force, and as a result the pursuit was not very effective.

The main French force was routed, and the battle now apparently won, but more French troops arrived in the British rear, having marched from their positions on Montcalm's orders. The British hurriedly threw together a defensive line, and the French decided to pull back. This brought the battle to an end.

AFTERMATH

Montcalm was wounded during the retreat. He was carried back into Quebec, where he died the next day. The main French force pulled out of Quebec and the associated defensive deployments, moving west to continue the war elsewhere. Quebec surrendered on 18 September.

Further fighting took place around Quebec, but it was at Quiberon Bay on the French coast that the fate of the American theatre was decided. A massive naval defeat rendered the French incapable of supporting their army in America. As a result, French forces in Montreal surrendered on 8 September 1760, and at the end of the Seven Years' War, the former French possessions in America became British territories.

Wounded in the arm, shoulder and chest, Wolfe lived long enough to receive news that the French were beaten and in flight. His last act was to order his troops to cut off the French retreat.

SIEGE OF YORKTOWN
28 SEPTEMBER–19 OCTOBER 1781

AFTER REALIZING THAT THE ADVANCE INTO VIRGINIA WAS A MISTAKE, THE BRITISH WITHDREW TO THE COAST. HAD THE ROYAL NAVY ENJOYED ITS USUAL SUPREMACY AT SEA, THIS WOULD HAVE BEEN THE RIGHT DECISION. HOWEVER, FRENCH NAVAL FORCES WERE ABLE TO BLOCKADE YORKTOWN, PREVENTING RESUPPLY OR REINFORCEMENT BY SEA.

WHY DID IT HAPPEN?

WHO A British army of 8000 men under Major-General Charles Cornwallis (1738–1805), opposed by a 17,000-strong Franco-American army under Lieutenant-General George Washington (1732–99) and Lieutenant-General Jean-Baptiste de Rochambeau (1725–1807).

WHAT Cornwallis advanced into Virginia without orders, placing his force in a compromising position. He then retreated to Yorktown, where he was besieged.

WHERE Yorktown, on the York River in Virginia.

WHEN 28 September–19 October 1781.

WHY Cornwallis believed that an advance into Virginia would improve the British hold on the southern states.

OUTCOME The British army was forced to surrender, convincing Parliament that the war in the colonies was not winnable.

Charles Cornwallis (1738–1805) was a competent officer who had gained experience in the Seven Years' War (1754–1763). He personally sympathized with the colonists in North America and had voted against the Stamp Act that taxed the colonists so heavily. Nonetheless, when war broke out in 1775 he offered his services to the British government and was posted to America under the command of Lieutenant-General Henry Clinton (1730–95).

Cornwallis participated in several major actions of the war and confronted George Washington (1732–99) in battle more than once. He was notably duped by Washington after the second battle of Trenton in 1777, when Washington disengaged his forces during the night, leaving campfires burning to create the illusion that he remained in position. Cornwallis fell for the ruse, allowing Washington to move off and attack Princeton.

On other occasions, however, Cornwallis was successful. His flanking movement at the battle of Brandywine and his counter-attack while in command of the rearguard during the retreat from Philadelphia to New York were both effective and well-judged actions. He had the confidence of his superiors and, after leave in England during 1778–79, returned to the American war in July 1779.

Cornwallis' return coincided with a shift in emphasis from the northern theatre to the southern. Despite winning battles, the British had failed to achieve victory in the

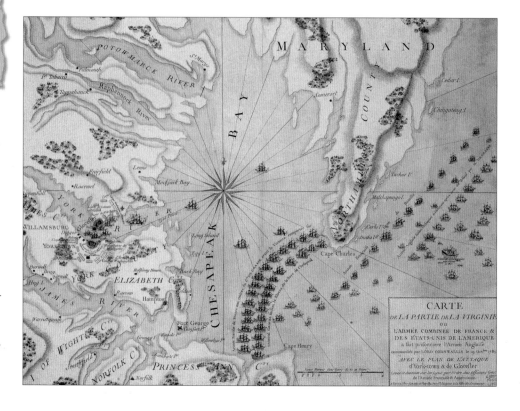

This contemporary map shows the Yorktown region, where Cornwallis was besieged. Had the Royal Navy not lost naval supremacy and thus been able to resupply the British force, the outcome might have been entirely different.

north, and so transferred troops southwards to seek a decisive action there. At first, the campaign went well. In early 1780, Charleston was forced to surrender, taking its defenders out of the war. Clinton left Cornwallis in command of the southern region and returned to New York, where a large British force held the city against any attempt to retake it.

Cornwallis embarked on an aggressive campaign, defeating an American force under Horatio Gates (1727–1810) at the Battle of Camden on 16 August 1780. This secured South Carolina under British control, and Cornwallis pushed into North Carolina. There, he inflicted a marginal defeat on a force of American regulars at Guildford Court House on 15 March 1781.

With the Carolinas cleared of regular enemy forces, Cornwallis made the fateful decision to advance into Virginia. Irregular forces were still conducting guerrilla operations in the Carolinas and it might have been more productive to operate against these, but Cornwallis reasoned that they could be mopped up or would dissipate with the defeat of regular forces and the capture of cities. This was perhaps a flawed assumption; defeats in the northern theatre had not taken the fight out of the American rebels.

THE VIRGINIA CAMPAIGN

Cornwallis moved into Virginia in May 1781 and took command of British troops already operating there, giving him a force of around 7000 effectives. Cornwallis initially tried to bring Franco-American forces under Lafayette (1757–1834) to battle, but the outnumbered Lafayette avoided battle, fighting occasional skirmishes while withdrawing to link up with other rebel forces. Unable to defeat the main enemy force in the area, Cornwallis then primarily busied himself with the destruction of supplies that could be used by the rebel army.

Clinton finally became aware of the situation in Virginia – Cornwallis had not told his superior of his intentions – and ordered Cornwallis to move to the coast, locating and securing an area suitable for ships-of-the-line to anchor. A move back

LIGHT INFANTRY

British light infantry, officer and soldier, 1780. The British Army was very quick to adapt its training and equipment to meet the demands of colonial warfare, as illustrated by these soldiers (based on sketches by De Loutherberg) with caps and shortened coats – although some considered these garments more showy than useful. These men were armed with the 'Brown Bess' flintlock musket.

into the Carolinas might have been a better option, but Clinton faced political pressure to back the move into Virginia. Thus Cornwallis marched to Yorktown and began the work of fortifying his position.

Meanwhile, American attention was also shifting south. An attempt to take New York had been planned, or at least considered, by George Washington. His army had been reinforced by French troops, but the French commander, de Rochambeau, suggested that New York would be too costly to attack and that there was no guarantee of success. A campaign further south had the advantage that it could be supported by French naval forces under Admiral Comte de Grasse (1722–88).

CUT OFF AT YORKTOWN

The British war effort in America depended upon sea links for communication, resupply and the movement of reinforcements, so a position on the coast made strategic sense. The navy needed secure anchorages and the

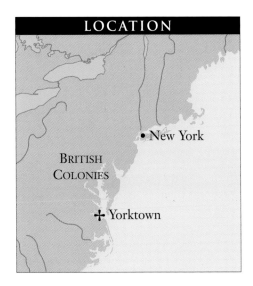

LOCATION

• New York

BRITISH COLONIES

✝ Yorktown

The Virginia Peninsula offered the British the opportunity to develop a secure base with access to the natural harbour of Chesapeake Bay, but instead it turned into a trap when control of the sea lanes was lost.

George Washington had gained experience as a commander of militia forces in the French and Indian War. He had worked with British regulars and was familiar with their doctrine.

Charles Cornwallis had studied at the Turin military academy and was praised for his personal courage while leading troops in the Seven Years' War. Although his career was largely successful, he is remembered mainly for his surrender at Yorktown.

army needed to receive support from naval and transport vessels. Dominance of the seas around North America was taken almost for granted. Certainly there was nothing that the American colonists could do to challenge the Royal Navy. However, the same was not true of the French navy.

A clash between French and British ships took place off Chesapeake Bay in March 1781, resulting in a French defeat. The French were not discouraged, however, and sent a larger force, including 24 ships of the line, to prevent the Royal Navy from supporting Cornwallis in Yorktown. The fleet also carried French infantry, who were landed as soon as the fleet arrived on 29 August to assist in siege operations.

On 5 September, the British fleet, with 19 ships of the line, arrived off Chesapeake Bay. There, they found the French at anchor. A splendid opportunity was on offer to savage the unprepared French fleet, but instead the British fleet adhered to traditional naval tactics and formed line of battle outside the bay. The French cut their cables and sailed out, forming a hurried line. Difficult wind conditions prevented some vessels from closing enough to attack, forcing the lead ships of both lines to take the brunt of the fighting.

After more than two hours of

inconclusive fighting, the fleets separated. The battle was not decisive in any tactical sense, but it prevented the British from resupplying their force ashore, and so aided the Franco-American strategic position. For the next few days, the British and French fleets remained in contact without a resumption of the action. The arrival of French reinforcements, bringing the fleet up to 36 sail of the line, made further British attacks pointless. The reinforcements also brought artillery, which was used in the siege of Yorktown.

THE SIEGE BEGINS

Cornwallis was dismayed when he realized what a huge mistake he had made, and did not defend Yorktown with his usual aggression and vigour. He was also hampered by a shortage of supplies and ammunition, and disease among his troops. Nevertheless, a system of defences and outworks were put in position and manned. Yorktown was defended by seven main redoubts, with artillery batteries covering the river narrows as well. An inner line of earthworks protected the town itself.

On 28 September, the Franco-American army approached Yorktown and began reconnaissance of the defences. British artillery fired on the besiegers as they made preparations during 29 September, but these were made unnecessary by the decision to fall back to the inner earthworks.

Although somewhat thinly held, the outer line of defences was well constructed and should have posed a formidable obstacle to the attackers. Cornwallis had heard from Clinton that reinforcements were on their way, and felt that the shorter inner lines could be more effectively held until assistance arrived.

As a result, the French and Americans were able to move into most of the outer line of defences, setting up their own batteries to fire on the defenders. Artillery sited in the inner ring attempted to

George Washington, depicted here surrounded by officers and regulars of the Continental Army, fired the first gun of the Yorktown bombardment. According to legend, the shot struck a table at which British officers were dining.

discourage them, and British engineers attempted to strengthen the inner line. A French assault on 30 September, against one of the few outposts still held by the British, was beaten off.

SIEGE OPERATIONS

The British were already short of food, and slaughtered a large proportion of their horses to avoid having to feed them. Enough were retained to allow a foraging party of cavalry to be sent out on 3 October, but this force was chased back into the siege lines, which continued to tighten as the besiegers began work on a trench parallel to the defences. This was beyond effective musket range from the defences and included battery positions covering the defences and the river.

From the river batteries, British ships anchored on the York river were bombarded. Some were set alight and others were so badly damaged that they had to be scuttled. Meanwhile, the defenders' artillery positions came under fire from heavier and more numerous guns in the Franco-American siege train. The

barrage covered the digging of a second parallel (a system of trenches), much closer to the defence lines. This was ready by 12 October, though it was not a complete encirclement because two

British-held redoubts blocked the path to the river. These were named Redoubts 9 and 10 by the British.

ASSAULT ON REDOUBTS 9 AND 10

As work continued to construct trenches ever closer to the British lines, Washington planned an assault on the outlying redoubts. These were blasted with artillery for an extended period, but were still formidable when the assault went in. To ensure success, deception and stealth were employed. French troops made a diversionary assault, against another position named the Fusiliers' Redoubt. Troops also formed up as if to attack Yorktown itself, diverting

Americans assaulting the fortifications at Yorktown. Attacks mounted by American and French troops on the British redoubts did not breach the main perimeter but served notice that the position was untenable and so induced Cornwallis to open negotiations for surrender.

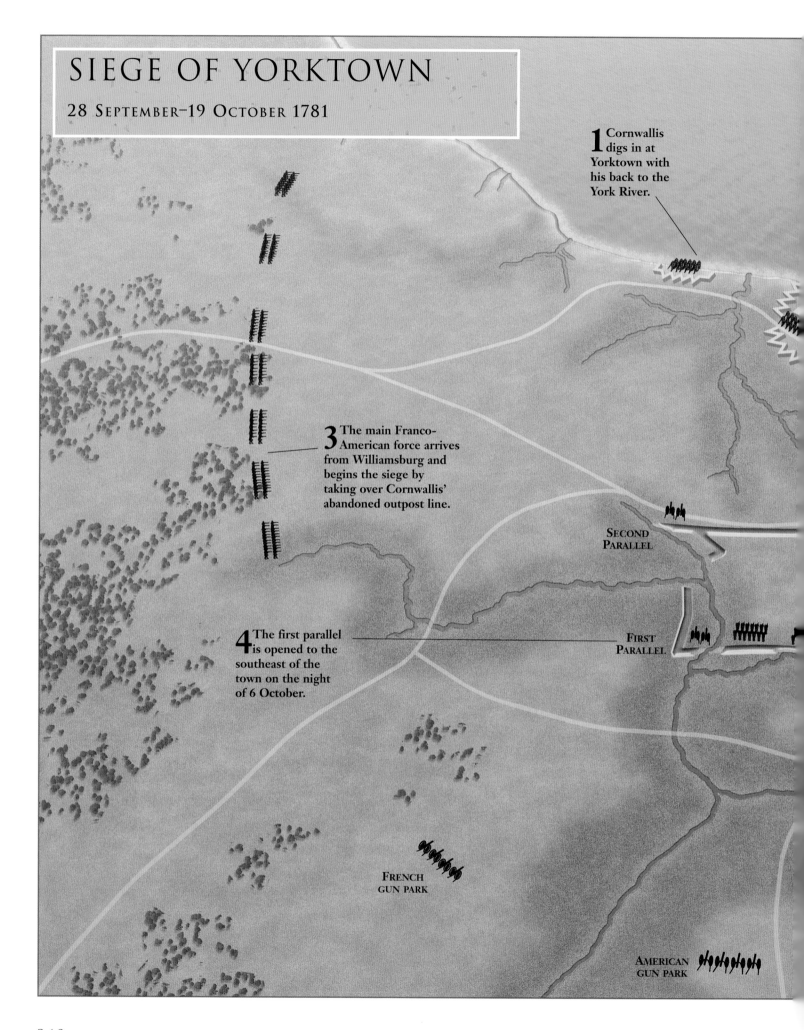

SIEGE OF YORKTOWN

28 SEPTEMBER–19 OCTOBER 1781

1 Cornwallis digs in at Yorktown with his back to the York River.

3 The main Franco-American force arrives from Williamsburg and begins the siege by taking over Cornwallis' abandoned outpost line.

SECOND PARALLEL

4 The first parallel is opened to the southeast of the town on the night of 6 October.

FIRST PARALLEL

FRENCH GUN PARK

AMERICAN GUN PARK

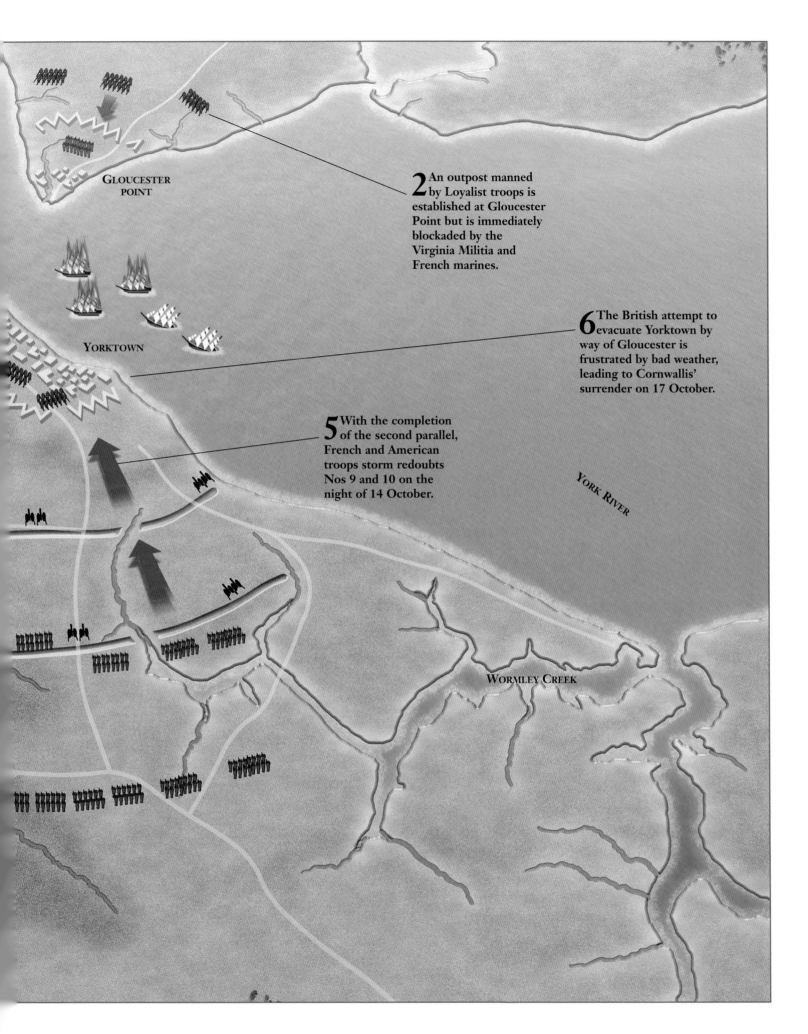

GLOUCESTER POINT

2 An outpost manned by Loyalist troops is established at Gloucester Point but is immediately blockaded by the Virginia Militia and French marines.

YORKTOWN

6 The British attempt to evacuate Yorktown by way of Gloucester is frustrated by bad weather, leading to Cornwallis' surrender on 17 October.

5 With the completion of the second parallel, French and American troops storm redoubts Nos 9 and 10 on the night of 14 October.

YORK RIVER

WORMLEY CREEK

The regular infantry of the Continental Army was lightly equipped and, in the early stages of the conflict, inexperienced. They gained their skills in the course of the war rather than by extensive peace-time training. Although not usually capable of the sort of large-scale evolutions required by a formal European battlefield, the American infantry were adept at fighting fluid, small-scale actions in their home terrain. Over time, the army gained experience and began to evolve into a more formally organized military force.

attention and, more importantly, reinforcements from the redoubts. These demonstrations were made at nightfall, and then, under cover of the moonless night, the attacking troops advanced with unloaded weapons, ensuring that surprise would not be compromised by a premature shot.

The French attack on Redoubt 9 was held up by *abatis*, large obstructions constructed of wood with spikes or blades sticking out. The French were challenged and then fired on as they began their assault, but were able to break through. As the French advanced with the bayonet, the 120 or so defenders wisely surrendered. The American force sent against Redoubt 10 found the *abatis* smashed by artillery fire, but the defenders, approximately 70 strong, kept up heavy fire until the Americans gained entry to the redoubt with a charge. After a bayonet fight, the defenders were overwhelmed and forced to surrender.

ENDGAME

With the redoubts in Franco-American hands, Yorktown came under artillery fire from three directions. It was clear that the defenders could not hold out much longer unless the artillery bombardment was slackened. To this end, the British formed a storming party of about

350 men, and on 15 October advanced under cover of their own artillery barrage. The attack caught the besiegers unaware and was at first successful, with several guns spiked. However, the storming party was driven back to its starting position by a counter-attack and the spiked guns were soon back in commission.

As the British defences crumbled under heavy fire, Cornwallis decided that his only chance to avert disaster was to try to break out. It was impossible to go through the Franco-American positions, but there was an alternative. Boats were collected and began rowing troops across the York River, to Gloucester Point on the far bank. It was hoped that once enough men were in position, a break-out might be possible. However, increasingly bad weather made it impossible to get many troops across the river and the plan had to be abandoned.

With even more artillery being moved into position by the besiegers, the situation in Yorktown was completely hopeless. Surrender terms were requested on 17 October, with negotiations taking place the next day. On 19 October, the British force surrendered, though Cornwallis claimed to be too ill to attend the ceremony and instead sent a deputy, General O'Hara. O'Hara offered

Cornwallis' sword as a symbol of surrender to the French commander, Rochambeau, but the Frenchman refused, indicating that George Washington should instead take the sword, a sign of the courtesy that had existed between the two commanders since the outset of the campaign.

But Washington, too, declined to take Cornwallis' sword. Instead he gave the honour of receiving the British surrender to his second-in-command, General Benjamin Lincoln (1733–1810). Lincoln had been defeated by the British at Charleston, but merely held the weapon for a moment before returning it as his own gesture of respect. Those British troops that had managed to reach the far side of the river were included in the surrender, along with over 200 artillery pieces.

AFTERMATH

The reinforcements promised by Clinton arrived by sea on 24 October, five days after the surrender. There was nothing they could do but remain aboard and sail back to New York, which was still in British hands.

Washington's army moved back northwards to New Windsor, where it remained observing the British force in New York.

Surrender at Yorktown did not end the war, but it did convince the British parliament that military victory was not likely. As a result, there were no more major operations and the war wound down until peace was formalized by the Treaty of Paris in September 1783, which recognized the United States of America as an independent nation. George Washington became its first President, and set the tone for future Presidents with his character and manner.

Cornwallis returned to England in 1782, and while he was criticized for his role in the Yorktown disaster, he retained his high status. His later career included a period as Governor-General in India, where he was instrumental in paving the way for British dominance. After a long career, which included signing the Treaty of Amiens with Napoleon I of France in 1802, Cornwallis returned to India as Governor-General but died soon after his arrival.

The siege of Yorktown, by Louis Couder. The American commander-in-chief and future president George Washington stands in the centre of the group of officers, but this is unambiguously depicted as a French operation conducted by French engineers – note the surveying instruments in right foreground.

TRAFALGAR

21 OCTOBER 1805

THE WAR BETWEEN ENGLAND AND FRANCE WAS A CLASH BETWEEN A GREAT NAVAL POWER VERSUS A GREAT LAND POWER. IN THE SAME YEAR THAT EMPEROR NAPOLEON OF FRANCE WON HIS GREATEST LAND VICTORY AT AUSTERLITZ, HIS CHANCE TO INVADE THE BRITISH ISLES WAS FOREVER LOST OFF THE COAST OF SPAIN.

WHY DID IT HAPPEN?

WHO A Franco-Spanish fleet of 33 ships under Admiral Pierre Villeneuve (1763–1806), opposed by an English fleet of 27 ships under Vice-Admiral Horatio Nelson (1758–1805).

WHAT Rather than a conventional engagement between lines of battle, the English made a risky attack that allowed them to gain local superiority over the enemy.

WHERE Off Cape Trafalgar near the Straits of Gibraltar.

WHEN 21 October 1805.

WHY The English needed to cripple the Franco-Spanish fleet to protect England from invasion.

OUTCOME The Franco-Spanish fleet was decisively defeated.

With the defeat of the Spanish Armada in 1588, Britain emerged as the greatest of the world's maritime powers. This both permitted and was made necessary by vast mercantile interests in all corners of the world. As an island nation, Britain relied on her navy for protection but had relatively small land forces compared to land powers such as France.

Land forces could be raised when required for an overseas campaign, but a large navy was always necessary for defence and so was kept in constant service. However important experience may have been in land warfare, it was even more critical at sea. The

Royal Navy honed its shiphandling and gunnery skills in small engagements, and maintained a high standard of seamanship by constant experience.

Thus at the outbreak war with France, the Royal Navy was operating at a high level of efficiency. The French fleet, on the other hand, was given lower priority than the French land army, and was not as effective as a fighting force. It was further weakened by a purge of its officers that took place during the French Revolution. Many experienced seamen were sent to the guillotine or dismissed from service for their real or assumed aristocratic connections.

The army underwent a similarly traumatic period, but was in a better position to recover from it. The armies of Revolutionary France were forced to fight for the very survival of their nation, forcing them to evolve and adapt to the new circumstances that prevailed, and enabling a new class of leaders to arise from the chaos.

Conversely, the navy spent much of its time languishing in port, especially after the Royal Navy implemented a blockade of French ports. Soldiers can train on any available land, but ships' crews need to put to sea to gain experience. When the French navy did leave port, its inexperienced crews suffered at the hands of the Royal Navy, as well as the usual

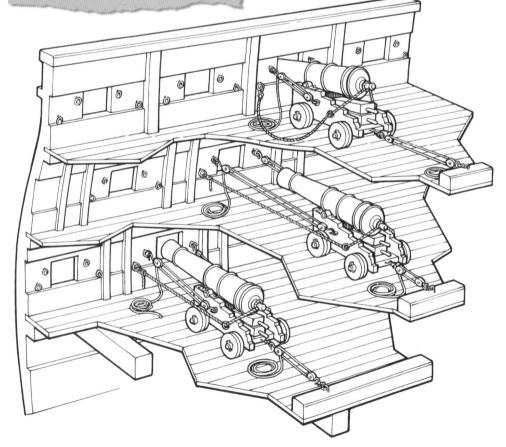

Most line-of-battle warships carried their guns on three decks. Here the guns are depicted run out for firing (top), at full recoil position for reloading (middle), and secured for travel. In bad weather, a loose (unsecured) cannon could smash its way out of the side of a heavily rolling ship.

GUN CREW

Serving a gun like this 32-pounder aboard HMS Victory required a high degree of teamwork if a reasonable rate of fire was to be maintained. Each man had a specific task that had to be carried out in the right order. Swabbing out the barrel before the next charge was inserted prevented an accidental explosion while loading, after which the charge and ball were loaded. The heavy gun then had to be run back out to firing position, at which point the gunner took aim.

hazards of wind and weather. This created a vicious cycle, in which ships were reluctant to come out of port but met disaster if this reluctance was overcome.

PREPARATIONS

To defeat Britain, a land invasion would be necessary, but that was impossible unless the Royal Navy's ability to defend the British Isles was reduced. The end result was that the French fleet was going to have to challenge the Royal Navy. Emperor Napoleon I of France appointed Pierre Villeneuve (1763–1806) to command his fleet, which was at that time scattered among several ports. The main squadrons were at Toulon on the Mediterranean coast and Brest on the Atlantic. Brest was under close blockade by a British fleet, while the British commander, Admiral Nelson, maintained a looser blockade at Toulon. Nelson wanted the French fleet to come out and fight, so that he could destroy it.

Villeneuve was unenthusiastic about fighting the British for several reasons. First, he had been present at the Battle of the Nile in 1798, when Nelson's fleet had shattered the French in Aboukir Bay. He also had a personal dislike of Napoleon

himself and was unimpressed with his battle plan: the French fleet was to concentrate and then link up with allied naval forces from Spain in the West Indies before returning to European waters. The intent was to clear the English Channel of British warships and thus enable a fleet of small boats to land Napoleon's 'Army of England' in Britain.

The early stages of the plan went well enough. Taking advantage of a storm that scattered the British blockading force, Villeneuve led his fleet out of Toulon on 30 March and into the Atlantic Ocean. Nelson, who was expecting a move eastwards towards Egypt, did not become aware of the Villeneuve's position until 12 May, by which time the French were almost at the Caribbean island of Martinique. Nelson set off in pursuit but was not able to prevent a rendezvous between the French and Spanish forces, after which this Combined Fleet sailed eastwards once more. Nelson failed to make contact and followed Villeneuve back across the Atlantic.

ACTION OFF FINISTERRE

While Nelson was out of position, searching the Caribbean for the French and

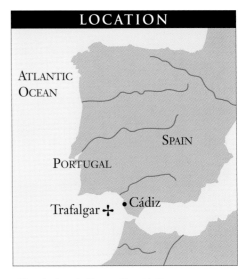

LOCATION

After chasing the Franco-Spanish fleet across the Atlantic Ocean and back, Nelson's fleet brought it to action off Cape Trafalgar and inflicted a decisive defeat.

then making his way back across the Atlantic, Villeneuve set about trying to break the blockade of Brest. With 21 ships of the line and seven frigates under his command, he engaged 15 British ships of the line under the command of Admiral Robert Calder (1745–1845) off Cape Finisterre in Spain. Thick fog hampered the ensuing action, in which Calder's force captured two ships and damaged four others, and prevented a decisive action.

Villeneuve made for Ferrol after the action, but was sent back out by Napoleon almost immediately with orders to try to again break the blockade at Brest and allow the ships located there to join his force. In the hope of deceiving the British about his intentions, Villeneuve first led his Combined Fleet to Cadiz. However, Napoleon was expecting this Fleet to appear in the English Channel. When by 26 August it had still not arrived, Napoleon reassigned his Army of England to a campaign against Russia and Austria, and marched eastwards. The invasion of Britain was postponed

indefinitely, but the naval campaign to make it possible was still in process.

NELSON SAILS

Nelson had meanwhile returned to England, where he received a hero's welcome. When word arrived that the Combined Fleet was in Cadiz, preparations began to send a British fleet to engage it. Nelson's flagship, HMS *Victory*, was not ready until 15 September, but by 29 September he had taken up station off Cadiz in command of a squadron that grew in size as reinforcements from the Brest blockade arrived.

Once again, Nelson implemented a loose blockade, hoping to tempt the enemy out to fight. A force of five frigates and two smaller vessels watched the harbour while the line-of-battle ships remained out to sea. Short of supplies, Nelson sent off part of his force to reprovision; these ships were then reassigned to convoy duty in the Mediterranean. However, other vessels arrived, bringing up the total force to 27 ships of the line.

Nelson's battle plan brought about a confused action, with many ships crowded together and firing at point-blank range. Under such conditions, the advantage lay with the best-trained crews, who could keep up a high rate of fire.

Line versus column. Breaking the enemy line with a column was a risky manoeuvre, but had a high payoff if the ships in column managed to cut the line in two. If more than one ship could break the line at different places, the attacking vessels could fire on an individual enemy ship from both sides simultaneously.

The Combined Fleet was also short of supplies due to the blockade, and its crews were inexperienced and understrength. However, orders from Napoleon arrived, to the effect that the fleet was to put to sea and link up with additional Spanish vessels before sailing to Naples in Italy. The fleet was to seek battle if it encountered a British fleet of lesser size. Thus, on 19 October, the Combined Fleet left port and headed for the Straits of Gibraltar to enter the Mediterranean.

DISPOSITIONS

Villeneuve commanded an impressive fleet in terms of gunpower and number of ships. He had more line-of-battle ships than the British fleet, and some of the most powerful warships in the world under his command. The Spanish contingent included four first-rate warships, of which the largest carried 136 guns as opposed to the 74 of the standard British ship of the line.

Villeneuve also correctly deduced that Nelson would try to bring about a 'pell-mell battle' by charging into his battle-line instead of turning parallel to it for a traditional, formal gun duel. This standard line-versus-line action permitted close control by an admiral and allowed one side or the other to break off if things went badly. This made it difficult to achieve a decisive result, and Villeneuve knew that Nelson wanted a decisive result.

However, although he had guessed his enemy's intentions, Villeneuve did nothing to

counter them. Thus Nelson's force found the Combined Fleet in a long, straggling line on 21 October, headed east for the Straits of Gibraltar. At 08:40, the Combined Fleet reversed course to offer battle, placing the Spanish contingent, which had previously been leading, in the rear.

The Combined Fleet was in some disorder as the British formed up into two columns with the intent of punching through the enemy line at two points and achieving local superiority by 'doubling up' on enemy ships. This manoeuvre was risky because it exposed the lead ships – including HMS *Victory* – to broadside fire that could rake them from end to end. However, Nelson felt that the poorly trained enemy gunners could not inflict much damage, especially since a rising sea made gunnery difficult.

One advantage of breaking though the enemy line was that the ships at the front would take time to turn around and return to the action, keeping them from bringing their weapons to bear while their comrades were being mauled. In the end, Nelson felt, it would come down to morale and training as the ships of both sides battered one another at close range. Victory would go to the side that could shoot the fastest and most accurately, and Nelson believed that it was his side that could do it.

At 11:00, Nelson ordered his signals officer to hoist flags stating that 'England confides that every man will do his duty'. Realising that 'confides' would have to be spelled out, the officer suggested that

THE OPPOSED FORCES

BRITISH

Total: 27 ships of the line

COMBINED FLEET

French: 18 ships of the line
Spanish: 15 ships of the line

Total: 33 ships of the line

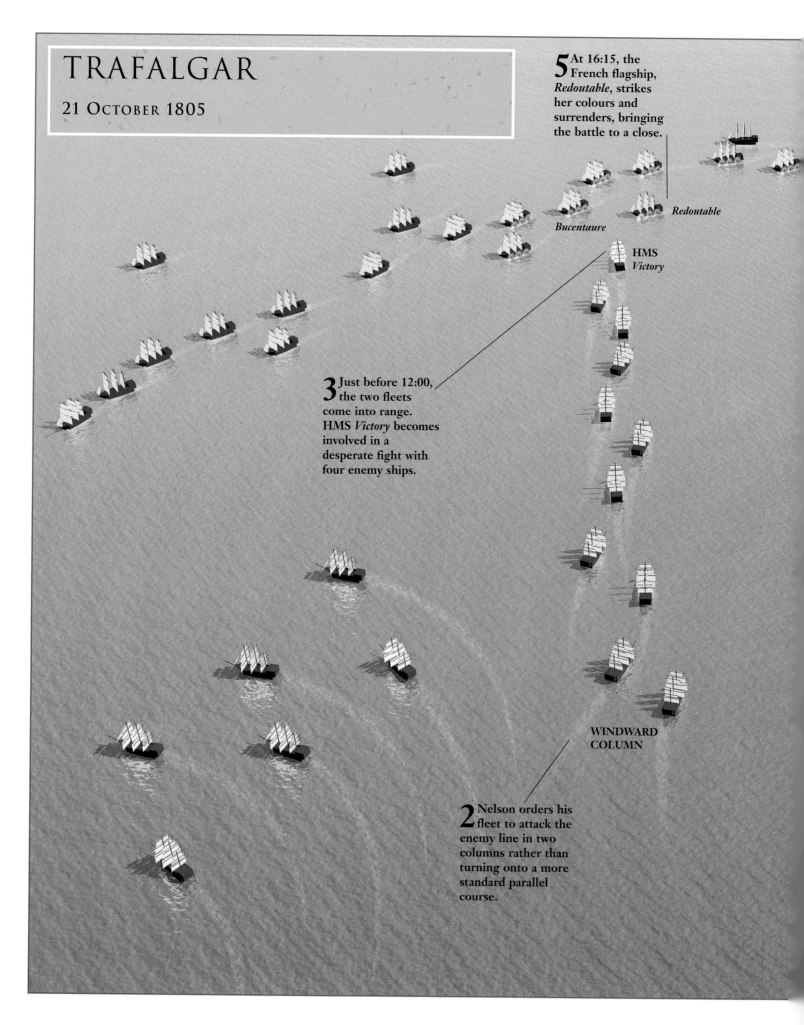

TRAFALGAR

21 OCTOBER 1805

5 At 16:15, the French flagship, *Redoutable*, strikes her colours and surrenders, bringing the battle to a close.

Redoutable

Bucentaure

HMS *Victory*

3 Just before 12:00, the two fleets come into range. HMS *Victory* becomes involved in a desperate fight with four enemy ships.

WINDWARD COLUMN

2 Nelson orders his fleet to attack the enemy line in two columns rather than turning onto a more standard parallel course.

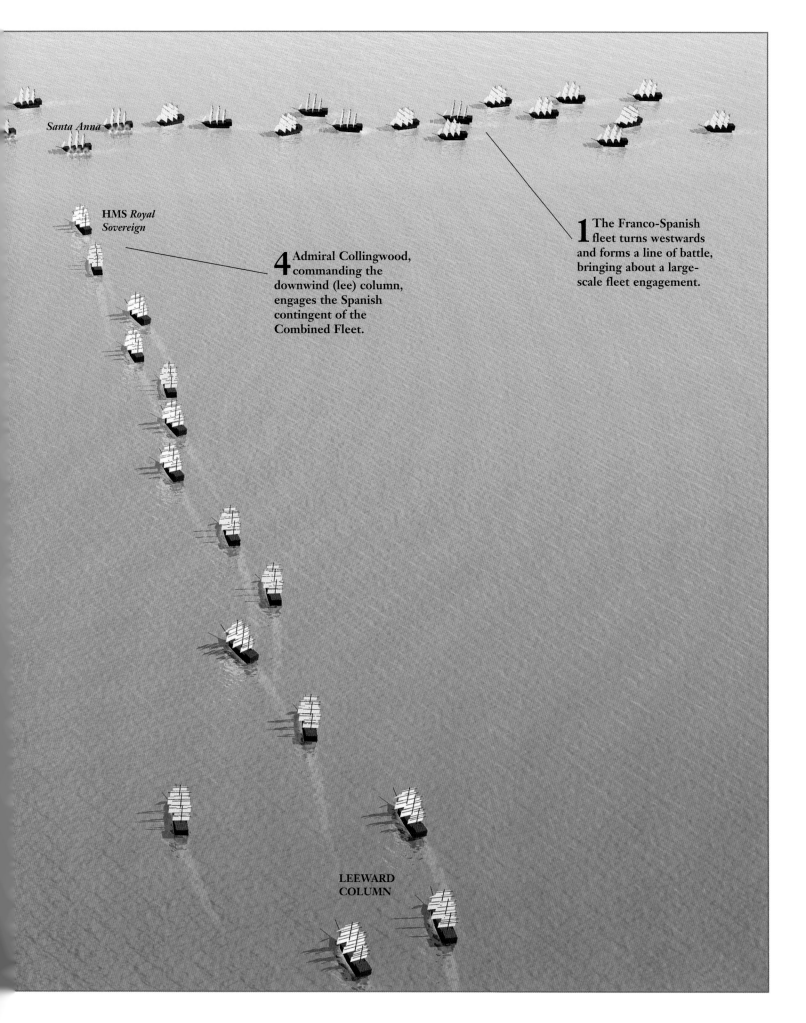

Santa Anna

HMS *Royal Sovereign*

1 The Franco-Spanish fleet turns westwards and forms a line of battle, bringing about a large-scale fleet engagement.

4 Admiral Collingwood, commanding the downwind (lee) column, engages the Spanish contingent of the Combined Fleet.

LEEWARD COLUMN

Surrounded by men manning cannon and sharpshooters trying to clear the enemy rigging of their opposite numbers, Admiral Nelson is hit by a musketball fired from aboard the French warship Redoubtable.

'expects' – which was represented by a single flag – could be substituted. Nelson agreed and the now-famous signal was hoisted.

THE BATTLE BEGINS

At 11:50, HMS *Victory* hoisted the signal 'engage the enemy more closely' as the first shots of the battle were fired. Within minutes, *Victory* was engaged with no less than four enemy vessels. These included the most powerful warship in the world, the Spanish 136-gun first-rate *Santissima Trinidad* along with *Heros*, *Redoubtable* and the French flagship *Bucentaure*. Despite serious damage, *Victory* was able to pass under the stern of *Bucentaure*, allowing her entire broadside to fire down the length of the French flagship.

With damage to her masts and steering, *Victory* was difficult to control and it was almost impossible to tell what was going on as a confused mêlée of ships began to develop – exactly as Nelson had hoped. He had refrained from making detailed plans with his captains, instead making them aware that they could do little wrong if they put their ship alongside one of the enemy and pounded it with guns. A chequered yellow and black recognition pattern on all the British ships helped avoid 'friendly fire' incidents. Anything not bearing the pattern was fair game.

Leaving *Bucentaure* to be dealt with by following vessels, *Victory* engaged the *Redoubtable* and became entangled with her.

Like most French captains, Captain Jean-Jacques Lucas (1764–1819) of the *Redoubtable* was aware of the limitations of his crew, but he had done his best to overcome them. Since gunnery and sailing training were problematic while under blockade, Lucas had drilled his crew in boarding actions and sharpshooting from the rigging.

Morale was high aboard *Redoubtable*, which carried a large force of marines. One of her sharpshooters hit Nelson, the bullet lodging in his spine. Nelson was taken below, where he died three hours later. In the meantime, Lucas and his crew were preparing to board *Victory*. Their attempt was disrupted when the second British ship in the line, the 98-gun *Temeraire*, fired into the crew assembled on *Redoubtable's* deck.

Under fire from *Victory* and *Temeraire*, *Redoubtable* fought on until her crew had sustained almost 90 per cent casualties, most of them fatal. At 13:55, *Redoubtable* finally struck her colours (indicating surrender), permitting *Victory* and *Temeraire* to double up on *Bucentaure*. Other ships fired into the French flagship as they passed, or joined the cannonade. *Santissima Trinidad* suffered the same treatment, refusing to surrender for hours despite not having any guns left to fight with.

The front third of the French fleet, cut off by Nelson's windward column, had come about and made a vague pretence of joining the action before withdrawing. By the time that a shattered *Bucentaure* surrendered to HMS *Conqueror*, it was 16:15 and the battle was ending. The French and Spanish had lost some 22 ships, the British none, though many vessels were severely damaged.

At 16:30, Admiral Nelson died, having lived long enough to know that the battle was won. By this time, the wind was rising. In the ensuing gale, many of the captured Franco-Spanish vessels were sunk or ran aground. Other ships were scuttled by the British and a few were recaptured by their former owners.

AFTERMATH

Nelson, who was already a national hero, was elevated still further in the eyes of the public by his posthumous victory at

Trafalgar. Monuments to him were built all over the country, most notably in what became Trafalgar Square in central London. Villeneuve, uninjured, surrendered aboard his smashed flagship. He was paroled to return to France in 1806, and was found dead from stab wounds in an inn on the road to Paris.

The Franco-Spanish fleet was destroyed as a fighting force. Only 11 vessels of the Combined Fleet reached the safety of Cadiz. Of these, the most seaworthy sallied out two days after the battle and managed to recapture two of the vessels taken by the British. However, British naval superiority had been enhanced still further, and the threat of invasion was completely eliminated.

Defeat at Trafalgar was offset by the brilliant French victory at Austerlitz, which cemented the position of France as the pre-eminent military power in Europe. Although Napoleon ordered an ambitious naval expansion programme, he was never again able to challenge Britain at sea. He did try to damage the British economy by creating the 'Continental System', whereby Britain was not permitted to trade with any European nation. However, Britain could not be defeated by a trade freeze-out, only by direct military action. After Trafalgar, that became impossible.

Above: Surrounded by debris, gunners aboard a damaged warship take aim at their next target. The ability to keep up effective fire despite casualties and damage to the ship required constant training.

Left: Having been wounded repeatedly in the past, Nelson almost certainly knew he was mortally injured. Upon being hit he exclaimed, 'They finally succeeded; I am dead.' He was taken below, where he died three hours later.

AUSTERLITZ
2 DECEMBER 1805

THE BATTLE OF AUSTERLITZ WAS ARGUABLY NAPOLEON BONAPARTE'S FINEST HOUR AS A GENERAL. HE HAD WON PREVIOUS VICTORIES BY RAPID MANOUEVRE, BUT THIS TIME HE CONFRONTED A LARGER ARMY AND DEFEATED IT BY A COMBINATION OF EXCELLENT GENERALSHIP AND HARD FIGHTING.

WHY DID IT HAPPEN?

WHO 73,000 French troops under Emperor Napoleon Bonaparte (1769–1821), opposed by an 85,000-strong Austro-Russian army commanded by Emperor Francis II (1768–1835) and Czar Alexander I (1777–1825)

WHAT The allies were drawn into an attack on the French left. Once committed on the flank, their centre was broken by a French attack.

WHERE Near Austerlitz in Bohemia, 113km (60 miles) north of Vienna.

WHEN 2 December 1805.

WHY The allies feared that Napoleon intended to dominate Europe and moved to oppose him. The French responded with a brilliant campaign culminating in the victory at Austerlitz.

OUTCOME The allies were totally defeated, greatly weakening the Third Coalition that had formed to oppose Napoleon.

The French Revolution (starting in 1789) and the execution of King Louis XVI (1754–93) alarmed heads of state in other European countries, and for a time, Revolutionary France fought for survival against a coalition of foreign states. From this struggle emerged an equally threatening entity – the French Empire. Ruled by Napoleon Bonaparte (1769–1821), a former artillery officer who had clawed his way to power through Revolutionary politics and military genius, the Empire was as much a threat to the established European order as the Revolution.

With the defeat of the Austrian and Russian-led Second Coalition in 1801, France gained considerable territories, creating client states in Italy and the Low Countries, and extending the French sphere of influence up to the Rhine, inside western Germany. The situation was formalized by the Treaty of Amiens in 1802, and for a time there was peace in Europe. However, tensions between Britain and France led to a renewal of hostilities in 1803. Britain faced a real threat of invasion by French forces at this time, though the powerful Royal Navy provided an effective barrier. After French and British navies clashed at the Battle of Trafalgar in 1805, the French threat of invasion was almost removed.

A new coalition against France emerged in 1804, largely as a result of British diplomacy and French actions that suggested a dangerous intent to expand national interests still further. The coalition grew as other states decided it was in their interests to curb French ambitions, and it came to include Britain, Sweden, Portugal, Naples and Sicily, and most significantly, Austria and Russia. Austria had lost territory and influence in Italy to France twice already, and was eager to reverse the situation. It was a powerful coalition but contained geographically separated states whose agendas were divergent from one another.

France, on the other hand, could bring to bear its own resources and those of a

French hussars depicted in the fur busby of elite companies and the universal laced dolman worn by hussars of many nations. Hussars made up the majority of light cavalry in every army.

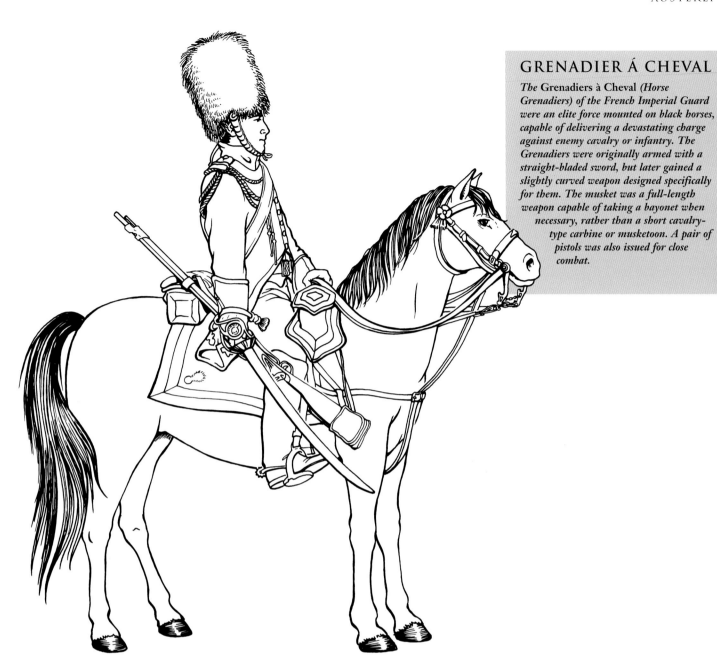

GRENADIER Á CHEVAL

The Grenadiers à Cheval (Horse Grenadiers) of the French Imperial Guard were an elite force mounted on black horses, capable of delivering a devastating charge against enemy cavalry or infantry. The Grenadiers were originally armed with a straight-bladed sword, but later gained a slightly curved weapon designed specifically for them. The musket was a full-length weapon capable of taking a bayonet when necessary, rather than a short cavalry-type carbine or musketoon. A pair of pistols was also issued for close combat.

number of small client states whose military forces were incorporated as part of the French army, rather than operating under independent command. This gave France the advantages of a single set of political goals and a unified command structure under a commander-in-chief who happened to be one of the greatest generals in history.

FORCES AND DISPOSITIONS

It had become obvious to Napoleon that an invasion of Britain was impracticable, but he had gained one advantage from the preparations undertaken. An army of about 200,000 men was assembled around the French port town of Boulogne on the English Channel, and was training for the invasion. This force was titled, in the French style of the time, *L'Armée*

d'Angleterre (the Army of England), referring to its intended area of operations. When invasion plans were abandoned, this army was then used as the basis of a new a force, *La Grande Armée*, which would campaign eastwards against the Continental members of the Coalition.

By 1805, a force of some 350,000 troops had been assembled, to be divided between the main and subsidiary theatres of war. It was possible, though unlikely, that Britain might try to land troops in France, but local reserves were available to deal with this eventuality. At the time, Britain had a small army, relying on sea power and a militia system for defence. Thus *La Grande Armée* could defend France against the Coalition by advancing against the landward foes and defeating them.

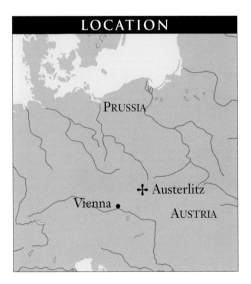

LOCATION

Although the French occupied Vienna, the Austrian army remained intact, and it was not until the decisive clash at Austerlitz that victory was achieved.

La Grande Armée used a flexible organizational structure, within which units could be transferred between formations at need. The basic unit was the corps, into which the army had been divided since 1800. Each corps was a self-contained all-arms force of infantry, artillery and cavalry, capable of dealing with many opponents unsupported and defending itself until assistance arrived if it encountered a superior force. Any given corps could be strengthened by units transferred from others, or could detach a smaller force to secure important objectives.

A cavalry screen preceded any advance, behind which followed the advance corps, while other corps took parallel roads, no more than two days' march away on the right and left flanks. This helped deceive the enemy about the army's actual objective, while good communications allowed the

army to concentrate on supporting any of the corps if opposition emerged.

In addition to the standard corps, a large cavalry reserve was formed, with horse artillery in support. This formation could detach regiments, brigades or whole divisions to carry out required tasks, or be used en masse as a single, powerful attacking force. The Imperial Guard formed an additional corps-equivalent, which acted as a final reserve for the Emperor's personal use.

The Russian and Austrian (allied) armies that opposed Napoleon's main advance were much less flexible in their organization. Training levels were not so high as in the French army, with soldiers commonly punished for fairly minor infractions with beatings. Officers commanded rather than led, and obedience was enforced harshly. This worked well

Napoleon Bonaparte generally wore military uniform even on state occasions, where he appeared as Emperor. This encouraged his troops to think of him as a fellow soldier rather than a politician.

This Russian painting celebrates the capture of the only French standard taken at Austerlitz. Taking a regimental standard was a glorious feat of arms, even amid a defeat.

enough under most conditions, but once the system broke down an army could rapidly disintegrate. In particular, it was very hard to rally a unit that had broken, and an officer trying to do so was liable to be killed by his own men.

Thus, the infantry component of both allied armies that fought at Austerlitz was generally poorer than those of their French opponents. However, the Austrian cavalry, mostly recruited from aristocratic families with long traditions of military service, were very good. The Russian army possessed a highly capable artillery arm, whose gunners were proud of their weapons and were willing to defend their guns in order to avoid the shame of abandoning their guns.

THE CAMPAIGN OPENS

The allies assumed that Napoleon would make Italy his main theatre of operations, as he had done so in two previous campaigns (1796–97 and 1800). In fact, although a subsidiary campaign was launched against Naples, the main force under the Emperor himself advanced into Bavaria. The Austrians, too, had moved into the same area. Beginning on 8 September 1805, a large Austrian force under General Mack von Leiberich (1752–1828) marched on the Bavarian city of Munich. Bavaria's small army could not prevent the occupation of the city, nor of the towns of Ulm and Ingoldstadt. From here, Mack reasoned, he could block a French advance

on southern Germany as it emerged from the Black Forest.

Mack thought his northern flank was secure. Since France already faced a large coalition of powerful enemies, it seemed unlikely that Napoleon would violate Prussian territory and risk fighting Prussia, too. Unfortunately for Mack, he was mistaken in this belief. While one corps moved through the Black Forest and occupied Mack's attention, the remainder of the army made a rapid march and encircled the Austrian force in Ulm. Although Mack ordered a breakout, this was not pressed home with any real determination and the army remained trapped. Caught in an impossible position and unable to achieve anything further, Mack surrendered on 25 October 1805.

According to an Order of the Day issued after the surrender at Ulm, French soldiers lavished praise upon their genius commander, proclaiming that he had invented a new form of warfare, which made use of their legs rather than their arms. It is likely that Napoleon himself was the origin of this accolade, as he was well known for making use of army communications for propaganda. However, the achievement was still impressive; by rapid marching, the French army had made it impossible for the enemy to effectively oppose them, and won a great victory at very little cost.

The Russian vanguard was also almost caught by a rapid French advance at

THE OPPOSED FORCES

FRENCH

| Infantry and cavalry: | 73,000 |
| Guns: | 139 |

AUSTRO-RUSSIAN

| Infantry and cavalry: | 85,000 |
| Guns: | 278 |

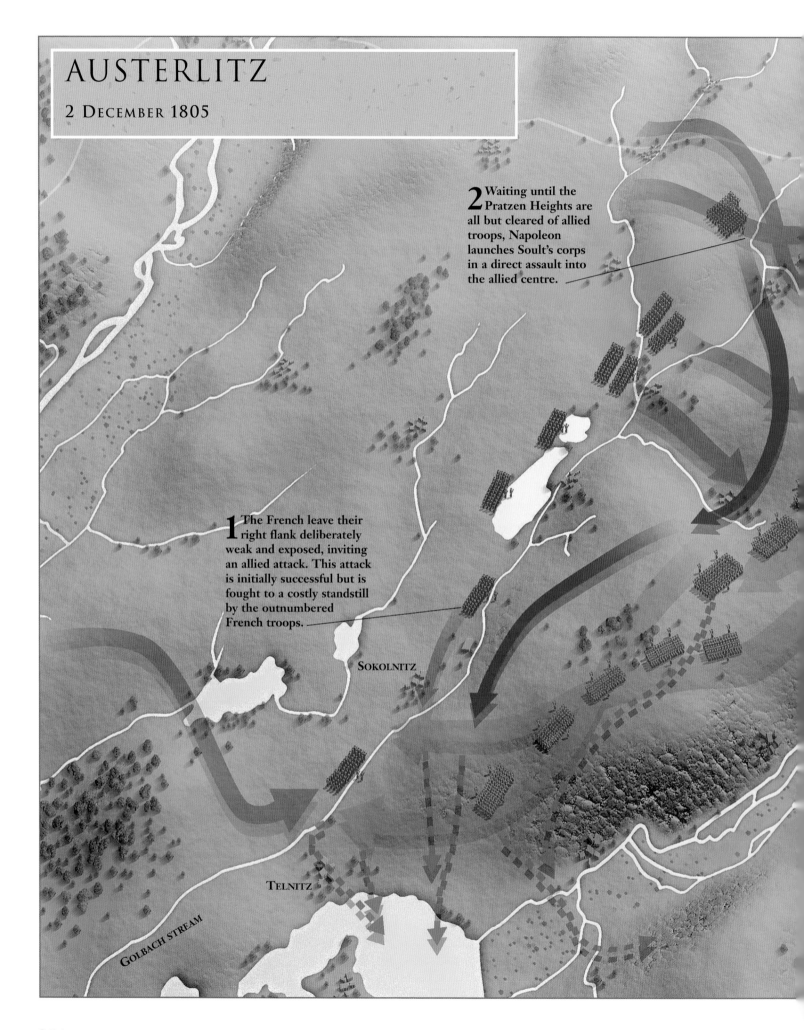

AUSTERLITZ

2 DECEMBER 1805

2 Waiting until the Pratzen Heights are all but cleared of allied troops, Napoleon launches Soult's corps in a direct assault into the allied centre.

1 The French leave their right flank deliberately weak and exposed, inviting an allied attack. This attack is initially successful but is fought to a costly standstill by the outnumbered French troops.

SOKOLNITZ

TELNITZ

GOLBACH STREAM

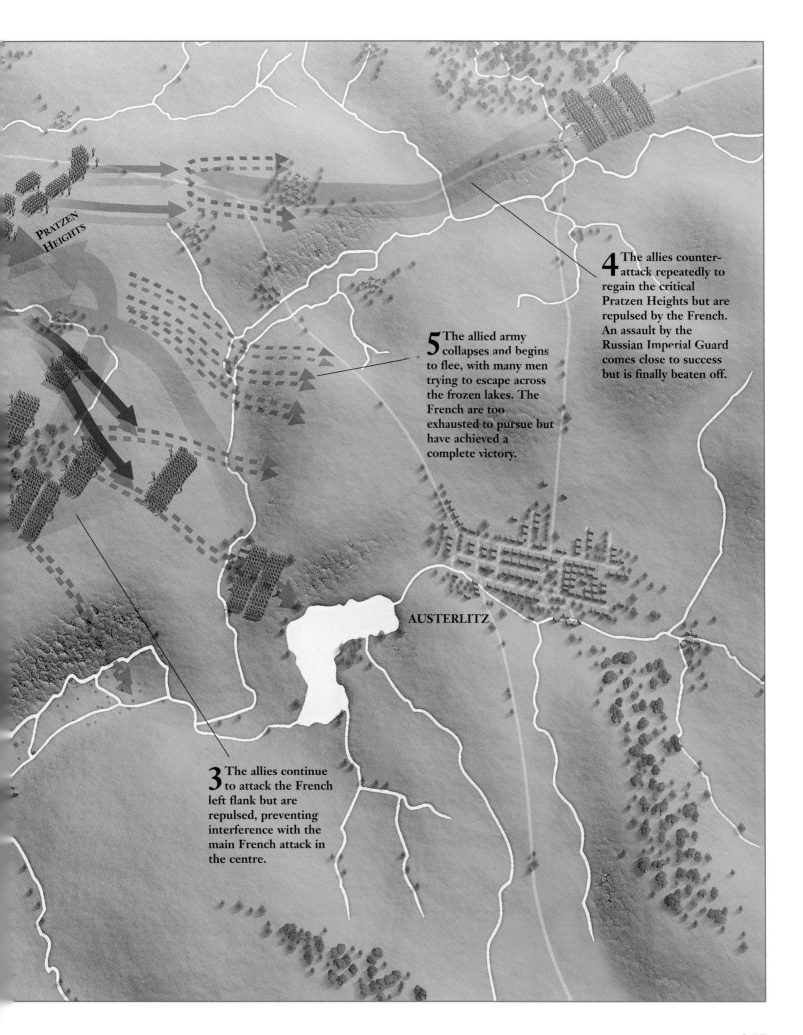

PRATZEN
HEIGHTS

4 The allies counter-attack repeatedly to regain the critical Pratzen Heights but are repulsed by the French. An assault by the Russian Imperial Guard comes close to success but is finally beaten off.

5 The allied army collapses and begins to flee, with many men trying to escape across the frozen lakes. The French are too exhausted to pursue but have achieved a complete victory.

AUSTERLITZ

3 The allies continue to attack the French left flank but are repulsed, preventing interference with the main French attack in the centre.

AUSTERLITZ

The Russian infantry were equipped more or less the same as their Austrian and French counterparts. However, Russian muskets were notoriously badly manufactured and prone to malfunction.

Branau-am-Inn late in November 1805. A combination of caution, a quick retreat and deft handling of the ensuing rearguard action permitted the Russians to escape. However, it was not possible to prevent the French from occupying Vienna on 12 November 1805. The Austrian army chose not to fight and lose in a vain attempt to protect the capital, but instead moved off to concentrate for a better chance of eventual victory.

There was some possibility that Austrian forces from Italy might coordinate with the main army and catch Napoleon's forces in a pincer movement, but the Austrian army was slow-moving and, at that time, intent on a defensive strategy. Thus it was possible for the French to push on and seek a decisive action. This was necessary, for although the French held Vienna, Austria's forces remained in the field and remained a threat.

THE AUSTERLITZ CAMPAIGN

Reaching Brunn (Brno, now in the Czech Republic) on 23 November, Napoleon decided that he wanted to fight the Allies at a nearby location, next to the Pratzen Heights and the village of Austerlitz. He examined the ground and decided it was suitable for a masterstroke. In order to draw out the allies, Napoleon posted forces on the Pratzen Heights and in Austerlitz, then hurriedly withdrew them as the enemy approached. To further consolidate the impression that he was in a bad position and

wanted to avoid a battle, he entered into negotiations, and these were carried out with less of the arrogant self-confidence that characterized his usual manner.

The French abandoned the Pratzen Heights, which dominated the battlefield, on 30 November and were reinforced the next day by additional corps, in a move concealed from the allies. Although still outnumbered, the French had reduced the disparity in forces to a manageable level and had mostly convinced the opposing commanders that the French forces were weak and hesitant. The allies thus decided to strike at the French right flank, which was understrength and in exposed positions. The intent was to break this flank while making a subsidiary attack on the opposite flank, opening the way for a final blow to rout the French army. This was exactly what Napoleon wanted them to try.

THE ALLIES ATTACK

Despite counsel from some allied generals that preparations seemed to be going suspiciously well, and that the planned assault would leave their centre, on the critical Pratzen Heights, exposed to a counterattack, the allies proceeded with their plan and on the morning of 2 December 1805. The attack opened at 06:00 with an advance against the village of Tellnitz on the French right flank. This was held by the Corsican Legion, an elite formation, which stood off the superior allied force for an hour before pulling back.

There was a real danger for the French at this point that a determined allied attack could drive in the flank as planned, but the allied advantage was not pressed home. Perhaps unnerved by the stubborn French defence of Tellnitz, the attacking allied commander, General Doktorov (1756–1816), waited for reinforcements from General Langeron's (1763–1831) corps before advancing. The French had by this time reformed their line and were able to hold up the allied advance despite being outnumbered by five to one.

NAPOLEON'S MASTERSTROKE

Emperor Napoleon waited until the allies were fully committed to the attack on his right flank and had largely vacated the Pratzen Heights before giving the order to attack. At 0845, he asked how long it would take the corps of Marshal Soult (1769–1851) to ascend the Heights and was told it would take 20 minutes. Choosing his moment carefully, the Emperor gave the order and Soult's men advanced in silence, concealed in mist for at least some of the way.

The move was spotted, but not soon enough, and Soult's corps was able to take possession of the Heights. A series of Russian counterattacks failed to dislodge the French, who consolidated their position until they were in firm control, by 1100, of the centre of the battlefield. Czar Alexander ordered his Imperial Guard, the elite of his army, to retake the Heights. Despite heavy resistance, they broke through the first French line and caused thousands of French soldiers to flee in panic.

As the French clung to the Heights, the Horse Grenadiers of the French Imperial Guard charged into action, beginning a cavalry mêlée that drew in large numbers of horsemen from both sides. This engagement was very closely fought but eventually the French, supported by horse artillery and steady infantry, gained the upper hand. Meanwhile, another large cavalry fight had developed on the French left. This went on for some time before the allies were pushed back.

By 14:00, the allies had little left in reserve. Their attacks had failed on the flanks and the surviving units were heavily engaged in close fighting, while the centre was shattered. On the French right, the allies finally broke and began to flee across the frozen lakes. The French artillery caused additional casualties by firing into the lakes to break the ice. However, there was little pursuit; the French, too, were exhausted by the heavy fighting.

AFTERMATH

The French lost 9000 men at Austerlitz as opposed to 27,000 on the Allied side – a full third of their army. The numbers, however, do not tell the whole story. The political consequences of the battle were far more important. The Coalition had been dealt a heavy blow and Austria itself was reduced to military impotence. In addition, the military reputation of the French army and the legend of Napoleonic invincibility was greatly enhanced. Such was the prestige of the Emperor Napoleon that it was said of him that on the battlefield 'the sight of his hat is worth 40,000 men'.

Austria was put out of the war as a result of the battle, making peace at Pressburg (Bratislava, now in Slovakia). She was forced to recognize previous French gains and ceded additional land to French client states. But for all the genius of Napoleon's masterstroke and the crushing defeat that followed, Austerlitz did not end the War of the Third Coalition. It would require two more years of warfare to subdue Prussia, which entered the war in 1806, and bring Russia to terms at Tilsit, in 1807.

François Gérard's painting of Napoleon at Austerlitz, commissioned in 1810. General Rapp presents Napoleon with captured cavalry standards after the battle. Rapp was one of the emperor's aides-de-camp.

BORODINO
7 SEPTEMBER 1812

NAPOLEON HAD NOT INTENDED TO MARCH SO DEEP INTO RUSSIA WHEN HE PLANNED HIS CAMPAIGN, BUT UNABLE TO FORCE A DECISISVE ENGAGEMENT WITH THE RUSSIANS, HE WAS DRAWN ONWARDS. TAKING MOSCOW SEEMED TO OFFER A WAY TO END THE CAMPAIGN IN VICTORY. AS THE OVER-EXTENDED *GRANDE ARMÉE* ADVANCED ON THE RUSSIAN CAPITAL, THE DEFENDERS FINALLY MADE A STAND AT BORODINO.

WHY DID IT HAPPEN?

WHO The French Emperor Napoleon, leading some 130,000 men, opposed by a Russian army totalling around 120,000 men (including militia), commanded by Prince Mikhail Illarionovich Golenishchev-Kutuzov (1745–1813).

WHAT The main French force was advancing on Moscow. After a series of attempts at resistance, the Russians established a defensive position at the village of Borodino.

WHERE The village of Borodino on the Moskwa River.

WHEN 7 September 1812.

WHY The breakdown of the Treaty of Tilsit resulted in renewed war between Imperial Russia and Republican France. Napoleon hoped to force a new treaty on Russia.

OUTCOME A bloody and indecisive action. The French retained the battlefield and thus claimed victory. The advance on Moscow continued.

Having long been an enemy of France, Russia agreed to make peace and even enter into an alliance after the battle of Friedland in 1807. The resulting Treaty of Tilsit was biased towards the French, and gradually the Russians abrogated the clauses they considered most onerous. Tensions between Russia and France were thus increased until Emperor Napoleon I of France (1769–1821) eventually decided that his former ally was once again his enemy.

Napoleon's method of dealing with this sort of diplomatic crisis was straightforward. Launching a military campaign, he threatened an important city, usually the enemy capital, to force a decisive battle. After shattering the enemy's military capability or occupying the capital, he would

Prince Mikhail Kutuzov took command of the Russian army facing Napoleon on 17 August 1812. His cautious approach led to the eventual destruction of the French army despite a marginal defeat at Borodino.

dictate a treaty favourable to his interests. The main problem with this approach was that it imposed a short-term military solution that did little to resolve longer-term diplomatic tensions, which were almost certain to reappear at some point in the future.

It was also an all-or-nothing approach: if the French army could not achieve a decisive result quickly, there was no alternative but to continue the campaign until it was resolved. With the notable exception of Spain, this approach had always worked, but failure there had created the 'Spanish Ulcer', which bled off French military strength. This was one of the two main causes of ultimate French defeat in the Napolenic Wars. The other was the invasion of Russia and the catastrophic march home that followed, depleting the *La Grande Armée* and killing many of its best men.

PREPARATIONS FOR INVASION

In 1812, Napoleon ruled Europe as far east as Poland, and it was there that *La Grande Armée* assembled. The army could not advance as a single unit because of its size, so the campaign was to be prosecuted by a main army under the personal control of the Emperor, while subsidiary forces were deployed to the flanks or to secure important objectives, as well as the line of communication along which supplies and reinforcements had to pass.

Preparations were meticulous, at least in the headquarters of the Emperor. An incredible stream of orders was produced, specifying what would be needed, in what quantity, and where it was to be delivered. However, actually obtaining the necessary stocks of ammunition, food, greatcoats and shoes, along with wagons to carry it all, was much harder. Thus when *La Grande Armée* set off into Russia it was with supplies that were barely sufficient to maintain a short campaign – a state of affairs that was acceptable to the Emperor, who intended to win a decisive battle early on.

The Russians, meanwhile, were making preparations of their own. Their command

structure was undermined by internal squabbles, which hampered efforts to concentrate forces and set up an effective defensive line. As a result, the initial French advance caught the defenders unprepared, and they were forced to pull back to try and find a suitable point to make a stand. The characteristically fast French advance made this impossible and also hampered Russian efforts to send reinforcements to their field forces; it was not possible to say for certain where their army would be at any given time, and it was therefore difficult to direct additional troops to the battle area.

THE FRENCH ADVANCE

The ability of the French army to move rapidly was mostly due to its skill in foraging on the march and thus travelling

LOCATION

SWEDEN FINLAND

RUSSIA

Moscow

Borodino ✝

Kiev

By the time La Grande Armée *reached Borodino, it had advanced much further than intended. Failure to win a decisive victory necessitated a continued advance with disastrous consequences.*

BORODINO

Polish lancers (left) engage with General Duka's 2nd Cuirassier Division in front of the Great Redoubt in this panoramic painting by artist Franz Roubaud (1856–1928). The charge by just 100 or so Polish lancers saved the Great Redoubt from being recaptured by the Russian cavalry at a crucial point in the battle.

THE OPPOSED FORCES

FRENCH

Infantry:	56,000
Cavalry:	28,000
Total:	**84,000**
Guns:	587

RUSSIAN

Infantry:	82,000
Cavalry:	24,500
Total:	**106,500**
Guns:	640

light. This was possible in the fertile countryside of central Europe, but in Russia there was little forage to be had. Thus *La Grande Armée* used up its supplies quickly as logistics struggled to bring up more from the depots. The supply line was also subject to Russian attacks from the very beginning of the campaign, mostly by bands of fast-moving Cossacks.

Czar Alexander I (1777–1825) lost confidence in Count Michael Barclay de Tolly (1761–1818), who commanded the Russian forces facing Napoleon, and replaced him with Prince Mikhail Kutuzov (1745–1813), hoping that he would be able to stand and fight. In fact, Kutuzov was forced to continue the retreat, but this worked in favour of the Russians. Not only was the French supply line lengthening but the French army was gradually weakening due to disease, accidents, harassment by irregular forces and straggling. This 'friction' gradually wore down the French capability to fight, and by the time Kutuzov was able to set up a defensive position near Borodino, the French main army had dwindled from 286,000 to 161,000 men.

PRELUDE AT THE SHEVARDINO REDOUBT

The Russian army took up a defensive stance in a naturally strong position near

Borodino. The Moskwa river protected the Russian right flank, with some forces stationed on the far riverbank across to provide further security. A series of ravines and thick belts of woods covered the Russian front, and these were strengthened by a series of field fortifications. The greatest of the fortifications was the *Raevski*, or 'Great' Redoubt. A set of smaller earthworks known as *flèches* (arrows, named after their arrowhead shape) were dug to protect the obvious avenue for attack between two belts of woods. An outlying fortification called the Shevardino Redoubt covered the expected line of advance to the battlefield.

The Russian position was very strong on the right, but weaker on the left where the flank rested on the village of Utitsa. Despite this, Kutuzov deployed his best troops on the right. His aim was to cross the river and, once strengthened by the arrival of reinforcements, hook into the French left flank. The best troops in the Russian army, other than the elite regiments of the Imperial Guard, were the artillery, and it was hoped that guns would turn the tide of the battle. Thus a powerful reserve containing nearly half the artillery batteries of the entire Russian army was formed, ready to be committed wherever it was most needed. However, the death of its commander, General Kutaisov, disrupted control of the artillery reserve for much of the battle.

Preliminary engagements happened on 5 September, when French cavalry under Marshal Joachim Murat (1767–1815) approached and were engaged by Russian horsemen. A large-scale but indecisive cavalry engagement ensued, and was repeated the next day. However, the Russians pulled back as French reinforcements arrived, leaving the Shevardino Redoubt open to attack. It was assaulted from the front by cavalry and from the rear by infantry. Capturing the Redoubt cost the French about 4000 casualties, although the Russians suffered more heavily. More significantly, the confidence of the Russian army was shaken by the defeat.

FRONTAL ASSAULT

Napoleon was at this time past his peak as a general. Had he been confronted with the situation at Borodino in his prime, he would almost certainly have launched a daring manoeuvre to flank the Russians by wheeling around their southern positions at Utitsa. Indeed, he was advised to do just this by his marshals, but instead decided on a straightforward frontal attack. Napoleon hoped to use the superior fighting power of his army to punch his way through the heavily defended Russian positions.

To support the frontal attack, Napoleon, himself a former artillery officer, deployed a Grand Battery of 102 guns to face the main Russian positions at the *flèches*, which were a crucial French objective. Many of these guns were heavy 12-pounders capable of inflicting serious damage on the defenders, despite the protection of their earthworks. At 0:600 on 7 September, these guns opened fire and soon afterward the infantry began to advance. Despite Russian cannon fire, the infantry forced its way into the *flèches*, gaining control by 07:30.

The *flèches* were retaken in a Russian counterattack, but renewed French assaults secured them once again. However, these earthworks were only the first component of a deep Russian defence, and the French came under heavy fire, from which the open-backed *flèches* offered no protection.

Also, to prevent further penetration of their centre, elements of the Russian Imperial Guard and supporting elite Grenadier formations, with artillery support, were moved up.

French cavalry joined the fight but were repulsed by their Russian counterparts. The way was now open for a Russian counter-attack, but this was destroyed by French artillery, which had moved up to help hold the taken ground. Finally, the Russians fell back in some disorder, but exhaustion and the chaos of the battle prevented the French from exploiting their advantage.

BORODINO AND THE GREAT REDOUBT

In addition to approaching the Great Redoubt from the front, a second French approach was possible by crossing the Kolocha river, a tributary of the Moskwa upon which Borodino stood. The Borodino crossings were protected by a force of Russian *Jaegers* (light infantry) deployed in the village of Borodino itself. These were pushed out of the village by French troops, but these became disorganized as they attempted to cross the river, and were driven back into Borodino by the Russians. A second attempt saw the French established across the river and able to bring up artillery. With this

Recruited from the warlike peoples of the Russian steppe, the Cossack light cavalry were a vital part of the Russian army. They were natural fighters who favoured the lance and sabre, often striking from ambush and then disappearing back into the countryside to wait for another opportunity. Capable of acting as scouts and foragers, Cossacks could also fight effectively on a large-scale battlefield, although they were best in small-scale, highly fluid operations. Cossack cavalry harried La Grande Armée *to destruction during the retreat from Moscow.*

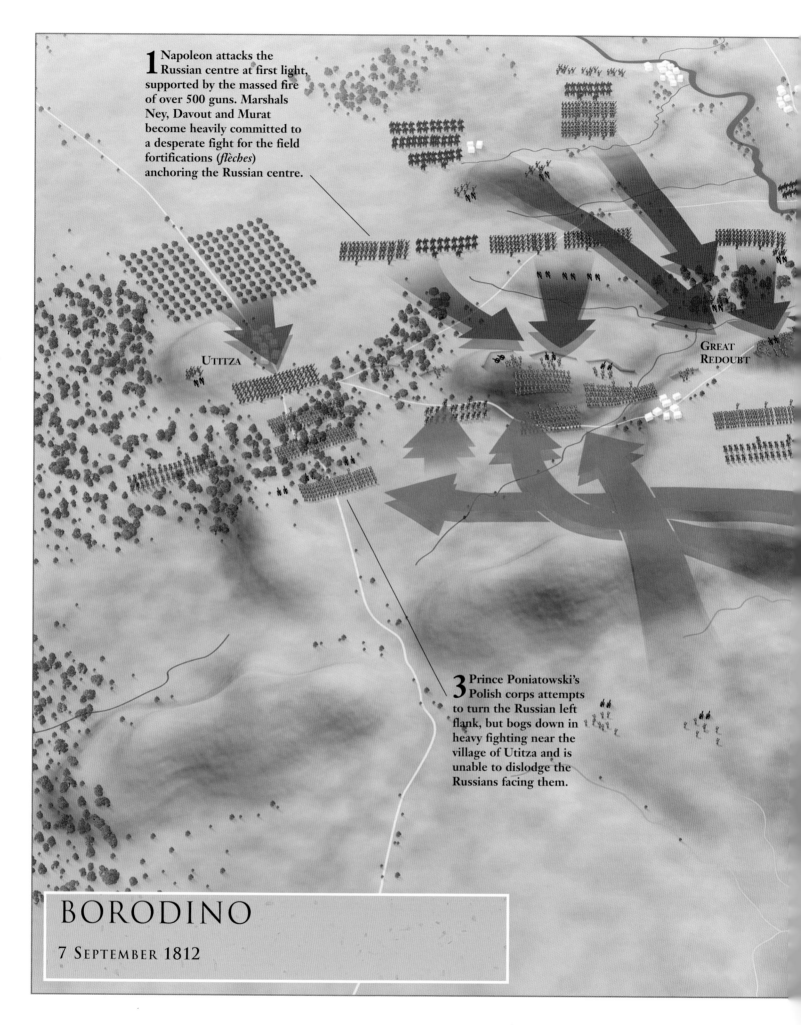

1 Napoleon attacks the Russian centre at first light, supported by the massed fire of over 500 guns. Marshals Ney, Davout and Murat become heavily committed to a desperate fight for the field fortifications (*flèches*) anchoring the Russian centre.

UTITZA

GREAT REDOUBT

3 Prince Poniatowski's Polish corps attempts to turn the Russian left flank, but bogs down in heavy fighting near the village of Utitza and is unable to dislodge the Russians facing them.

BORODINO

7 SEPTEMBER 1812

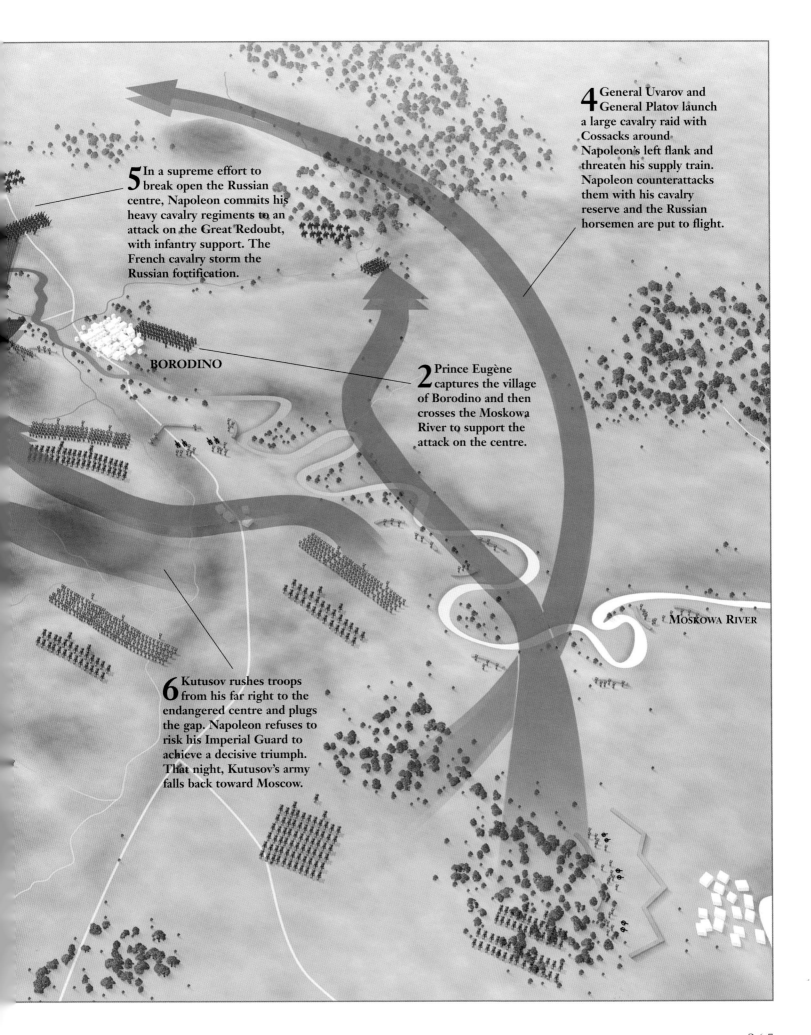

4 General Uvarov and General Platov launch a large cavalry raid with Cossacks around Napoleon's left flank and threaten his supply train. Napoleon counterattacks them with his cavalry reserve and the Russian horsemen are put to flight.

5 In a supreme effort to break open the Russian centre, Napoleon commits his heavy cavalry regiments to an attack on the Great Redoubt, with infantry support. The French cavalry storm the Russian fortification.

BORODINO

2 Prince Eugène captures the village of Borodino and then crosses the Moskowa River to support the attack on the centre.

Moskowa River

6 Kutusov rushes troops from his far right to the endangered centre and plugs the gap. Napoleon refuses to risk his Imperial Guard to achieve a decisive triumph. That night, Kutusov's army falls back toward Moscow.

BORODINO

support, they began to advance on the Great Redoubt.

The Great Redoubt was taken at bayonet point but was then retaken by a Russian counterattack. Both sides fed in troops and played their artillery on enemy units moving up to join the fighting. The French gradually gained the upper hand and around 14:00 put in a concentrated attack. Preparations for this assault were obvious, and the attacking regiments, as they formed up, should have made an excellent target for Russian artillery fire. However, the artillery reserve commander was dead, and proper control had not been reasserted so the great mass of Russian guns were not available.

However, French artillery was available, and in large numbers. As the Russians concentrated their forces to meet the French attack, they came under heavy fire, which caused some units to become badly disorganized. The bombardment by the artillery was also demoralizing, weakening the Russian response further. The French attack was a success, finally forcing the Russians out of the Great Redoubt and consolidating the French hold on it.

However, the attacking force was in great disorder and was desperately tired after its titanic effort; a pause was necessary in order to reorganize and rest.

THE BATTLE WINDS DOWN

The pause drew out into a gradual wind-down of the action, though the artillery of both sides continued to fire and skirmishing took place all across the battlefield for some time. Although the defensive line had been broken and the Russians had been pushed back, they were not defeated in any real sense. To do that would require a final push, and the only troops available to make it were the French Imperial Guard. Napoleon refused to commit the guard, perhaps because it was his only remaining reserve, so the Russians were able to retreat without pursuit. This left the French in possession of the battlefield, which is a traditional measure of victory. However, although it was possible for the French to claim a tactical win, however marginal, they had not in practice achieved any of their strategic aims. Both sides had lost 30,000–40,000 men, but, unlike the Russians who were on home

Russian infantry and artillery at Borodino. The Russian Army was deployed in a series of field fortifications (flèches) and a large earthen fort that came to be known as the Great Redoubt. Cavalry was considered impotent against fortified infantry and guns, yet at Borodino French and Allied cuirassiers would perform the impossible by storming the Great Redoubt.

At Borodino, Napoleon showed little sign of his previous inspired generalship, dispensing with manoeuvre in favour of a head-on attack and the inevitable heavy casualties that accompanied it.

soil, the French could not replace their losses. Strung out at the end of a long supply line, the French needed a decisive victory while the Russians only had to avoid total defeat. The Russians had achieved this and, although bloodied, had hurt the invaders badly, denying Napoleon the short campaign he had envisaged.

AFTERMATH

Kutuzov realized that his army was in no condition to fight another battle, and chose to preserve what remained rather than make a last stand before Moscow. In this he was correct, although by moving off, he allowed Napoleon to capture Moscow. The expected surrender did not occur, and the French were left in control of an empty city, with little to eat and no prospect of resupply. The only option was to retreat, and on 19 October 1812 *La Grande Armée* began its homeward march.

The intent was not to retreat along the same route that the French had used for their advance, as this had been denuded of supplies by foraging and a deliberate scorched earth policy implemented by the retreating Russian forces. A more southerly route was intended, but the preservation of the Russian army after Borodino now paid off handsomely. The French advance guard was confronted at Maloyaroslavets on 24 October by the

Russian army, resulting in a bloody clash. Although the Russians were again narrowly defeated, they were not pushed aside.

Napoleon decided that a breakthrough would be too costly in terms of casualties and instead began to retire along his original route of advance, back towards the Baltic countries. Casualties during what was known as the Moscow Retreat were immense, from hunger, cold and on-going attacks by Russian forces. In particular, the Cossack cavalry showed their worth as skirmishers, continually harassing the French army as it disintegrated on the march. In the end, only about 30,000–40,000 troops of the 630,000 that had entered Russia re-emerged in formed units. About the same number eventually straggled to safety.

The French army never recovered from the appalling losses it suffered in Russia. In addition, Napoleon's reputation for invincibility was destroyed. This in turn caused unrest among both allies and conquered peoples, and encouraged enemies to renew their efforts. Napoleon did manage to assemble a new army for the next year's campaign season but it was of a much lower standard than that of 1812 and could not do more than stave off defeat for a time. It could be argued that the failure to win a decisive victory at Borodino doomed the French Empire to eventual defeat.

WATERLOO
18 JUNE 1815

A SERIES OF DEFEATS FOR NAPOLEON BONAPARTE (1769–1821) LED TO HIS EXILE ON THE ISLAND OF ELBA. HOWEVER, HE ESCAPED BACK TO FRANCE, REASSEMBLED HIS ARMY AND CROSSED THE FRENCH BORDER, INTENDING TO PREVENT AN ALLIED INVASION. ALLIED FORCES RETALIATED, BRINGING ABOUT HIS DECISIVE DEFEAT AT WATERLOO.

WHY DID IT HAPPEN?

WHO Over 60,000 British, German, Belgian and Dutch allies, led by the Duke of Wellington (1769–1852), plus 50,000 Prussian troops under Marshal Blücher (1742–1819), were opposed by Emperor Napoleon's reformed *Grande Armée* of 74,000 men.

WHAT Napoleon resolved to attack the Allied forces before other powers could come to their aid. With 74,000 troops and 250 guns, he faced 23,000 British and 44,000 Allied troops and 160 guns.

WHERE Approximately 5km (3 miles) south of the village of Waterloo, which is approximately 13km (8 miles) south of Brussels.

WHEN 18 June 1815.

WHY In 1814, 25 years of European war ended and the major European powers started restoring their countries to normality. To their alarm, Napoleon returned from Elba and assumed his earlier title of Emperor, clearly intent on regaining his former conquests and raising and equipping a new army. Wellington and Blücher also began building up their forces.

OUTCOME After Napoleon's defeat at Waterloo, a new peace treaty was signed in Paris, on 20 November 1815. On the same day, another document, the Quadruple Alliance, was signed by those who had fought at Waterloo. It was designed to protect the balance of power created by the peace treaty, with the intention that the signatories would consult one another if they were threatened.

In 1812, France invaded Russia. In doing so, Napoleon's *Grande Armée* suffered very serious casualties. A coalition of Austria, Prussia, Russia, Britain and a number of German states finally defeated France, forcing Napolean to abdicate on 11 April 1814. He was then exiled to Elba, where he was granted the right to rule the island and retain the title of Emperor.

The European allies were therefore shocked when Napoleon escaped from Elba in February 1815 and arrived in France, intent on the reconquest of the territories he had previously seized but lost. Seven days later in Vienna, Prince Karl von Schwarzenberg (1771–1820), field marshal of the Austrian army, sent urgent instructions to mobilize his various army corps. A call to arms was issued against the man the Allies declared to be an outlaw and a 'disturber of world repose'. It was made clear that there would be no laying down of

---

Unlike most nations during the period, who deployed their infantry in three ranks, the British routinely made use of a two-rank line. This provided a much larger number of muskets for effective volley fire.

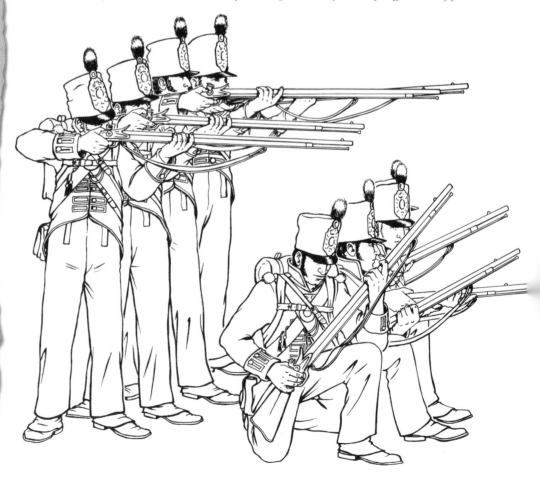

HIGHLAND SOLDIER

Within a year of being raised in 1798, the men of the 92nd Regiment of Foot (Gordon Highlanders) paraded proudly in their distinctive tartan, intent on serving the future Duke of Wellington, notably in some of the fiercest battles at Waterloo against the French. At the charge of the Scots Greys, every rider yelling 'Scotland For Ever!', the regiment, amid thundering hoofs and deafening cheers, fiercely routed attacking infantry, sabring its gunners and laming its horses, but going on to sustain some of the heaviest losses of the entire campaign.

their bid to overthrow Napoleon. The campaign started badly. To his dismay, Wellington, arriving in Brussels from Vienna on 4 April 1815, discovered that his Anglo-Dutch forces consisted of a scant 33,000 men. He proclaimed to a friend: 'I have an infamous army, very weak and ill-equipped, and a very inexperienced staff'. Despite demands for reinforcements, more troops were slow to arrive, not least because the Prussians, under Marshal Gebherd Leberecht von Blücher, were desperately short of money to pay their troops, because of levies Napoleon had previously extracted. But, fuelled by hatred of the French, volunteers gradually emerged and by June, the Prussian army had doubled in size to around 120,000 men.

Wellington was not expecting a French attack, regarding Napoleon's preparations on the other side of the frontier as purely defensive. Napoleon himself deliberately set out to give this impression by operating from Paris and building a network of fortifications to imply that he intended to block any enemy incursion rather than unleash a wholesale advance. However, the opposite was true and on 6 June, the French started to assemble their forces in complete secrecy for an offensive.

At dawn on the 12 June, Napoleon left Paris, reaching an already established headquarters at Beaumont on the Belgian frontier in just two days. His army was itching to march when his Order of the Day to advance came through, which concluded with the flourish: 'The moment has come to conquer or to perish'. The Emperor's forces, thrusting from Beaumont in brilliant sunshine, took the

arms until Napoleon was crushed. Meanwhile, with whirlwind energy, Napoleon equipped his new army. Paris workshops produced over 1200 uniforms a day while 12,000 cartridges were made within two months. By June, 124,000 men were concentrated near the French border, while the Allies gathered near Brussels.

WELLINGTON'S COMMAND

The European allies, under the overall command of the Duke of Wellington (1769–1852) reassembled their armies in

LOCATION

Napoleon sought to deal a knock-out blow to the Anglo-Allied forces in Belgium before the arrival of Blücher's Prussians army.

The assault on the chateau at Hougoumont was a disastrous miscalculation by the French. What should have been a feint to draw away some of Wellington's forces from the main action developed into a day-long struggle which availed nothing. Troops from the Coldstream Guards clashed with the enemy vainly trying to gain the outside of the building. Hougoumont remained in British hands throughout.

THE OPPOSED FORCES

ALLIED FORCES (estimated)

Total: **113,000**

FRENCH FORCES (estimated)

Total: **72,000**

frontier city of Charleroi, which lay at a junction of roads leading to Brussels. Napoleon was greeted by enthusiastic citizens who lined the streets, cheering 'Vive l'Empereur!'

Meanwhile, Wellington and Blücher were in disarray, their troops scattered all over the countryside in billets so many miles away that they were unable to assemble into an effective fighting force. Intelligence between the British and Prussians was also chaotic, with instances of Blücher neglecting to pass on essential knowledge of the enemy's movements.

QUATRE BRAS AND LIGNY

Napoleon's plan was to push on to Brussels with the main part of his army slashing through Wellington and Blücher's forces. Wellington's strength was centred on the crossroads at Quatre Bras, 32km (20 miles) south of Brussels, while Blücher was with his Prussian army at the village of Ligny, 8km (5 miles) to the southeast.

As it turned out, Napoleon was obliged to close with the enemy at both points. At Quatre Bras, *L'Armée du Nord*, under Marshal Ney (1769–1815), was concentrated into a dense formation. Three cannon shots gave the signal for attack, followed by a furious clash of arms, with

shot and shell flying overhead. The situation in Ligny turned out to be scarcely better. Here, Napoleon's strong right wing forced the Prussian Army to retreat, then enforced a withdrawal towards Brussels. The village was set ablaze and destroyed during the furious fighting between the Prussians and French.

While regrouping, Wellington received an assurance from Blücher, bruised by a fall from his horse at Ligny, that he would be able to join him for what was intended to be the conclusive battle. On the afternoon of 17 June, the Duke halted on the ridge that crossed the road to Brussels at the point where it emerged from the woods surrounding the town of Soignies, south of Waterloo.

Through his eye glass, Wellington was able to witness a spectacle in which Napoleon clearly revelled. Amid trumpet calls, drum rolls and martial music, the Emperor rode past his troops, who shouted 'Vive l'Empereur!', while cavalrymen raised their plumed helmets and sabres as if they had already won the battle.

The nature of the terrain over which the battle was to be fought was far removed from any conventional idea of a battlefield. It comprised a network of small roads intersected by hedgerows with a succession of orchards and prosperous farms, and fields of rye carpeting an area of countryside barely 5 square km (3 square miles).

The centre of action Wellington chose lay in the valley situated in front of the right wing of his front line. This was the château of Hougoumont Farm, held by the light companies of the Coldstream and Third Guards. Two other farms in the valley played a crucial role – Germans troops occupied La Haye Sainte and the French appropriated the nearby La Belle Alliance as their headquarters. The French would approach the battle from the south of this farm.

THE BATTLE COMMENCES

Napoleon regarded Hougoumont of secondary importance, perceiving Wellington's grouping of forces in the centre around La Haye Sainte as being of far greater importance. His views brought him into to serious conflict with his brother Prince Jerome, whose division decided to lead a bitter attack on Hougoumont anyway. The Battle of Waterloo was underway.

Obliged to support Jerome, Napoleon undertook a major assault, calling on howitzers to shell the chateau, which caught fire. Soon, the conflagration spread to surrounding buildings. But valuable time had been lost and Napoleon had to return to what he regarded as the main target – the Allied centre.

At around 1330 on 18 June, Marshal Michel Ney (1769–1815), the former French royalist who had changed sides to become one on Napoleon's most trusted aides, brought forward 74 French guns over the ridge opposite La Haye Sainte, followed by 17,000 infantry, to start the attack on Wellington's centre and left.

The effect of the French cannonade was partly lessened by an order from Wellington that his infantry battalions should move behind the ridge and lie down for protection, shielding them from the worst of enemy fire. However, the Belgian-Dutch brigade was unprotected and suffered heavy casualties. For a while, Wellington was able to rely on the King's German Legion, recruited from Hanover and boasting a consistently reliable force. But gradually the legion was worn down, largely due to dwindling ammunition, although the defensive line held.

As the French troops under Ney approached the top of the ridge, they were greeted with a fierce volley and a bayonet charge from the infantry division lead by General Sir Thomas Picton. This charge cost him his life from a bullet through the head. This attack was followed by a charge from the heavy cavalry of the Union and Household Brigades, led by Lord Uxbridge, (1768–1854), the former infantry colonel who had switched to the cavalry and was now the British second in command.

'SCOTLAND FOR EVER'

The day's most heroic action came from the Scots Greys, part of the Heavy Brigade. To the sound of bagpipes, they came thundering down the slope from the ridge on their magnificent grey chargers, yelling 'Scotland For Ever' and slashing at the enemy to the right and left. But in the mêlée, recall orders did not reach them all. Sergeant Ewart had managed to seize the eagle banner of the French 45th Regiment, the 'Invincibles', and in the euphoria the Scots Greys advanced too far. A fierce French counterattack then followed, which had deadly consequences. Wellington lost

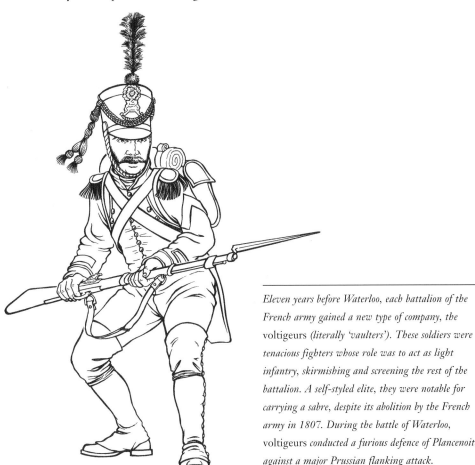

Eleven years before Waterloo, each battalion of the French army gained a new type of company, the voltigeurs (literally 'vaulters'). These soldiers were tenacious fighters whose role was to act as light infantry, skirmishing and screening the rest of the battalion. A self-styled elite, they were notable for carrying a sabre, despite its abolition by the French army in 1807. During the battle of Waterloo, voltigeurs conducted a furious defence of Plancenoit against a major Prussian flanking attack.

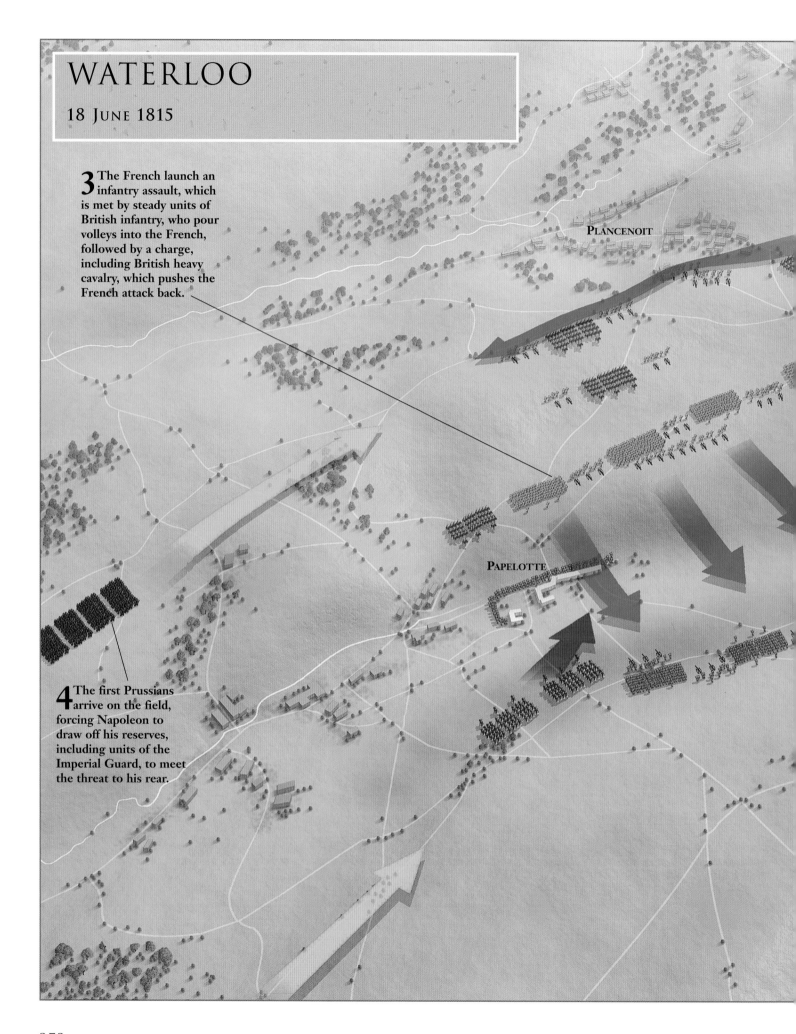

WATERLOO

18 JUNE 1815

3 The French launch an infantry assault, which is met by steady units of British infantry, who pour volleys into the French, followed by a charge, including British heavy cavalry, which pushes the French attack back.

4 The first Prussians arrive on the field, forcing Napoleon to draw off his reserves, including units of the Imperial Guard, to meet the threat to his rear.

PLANCENOIT

PAPELOTTE

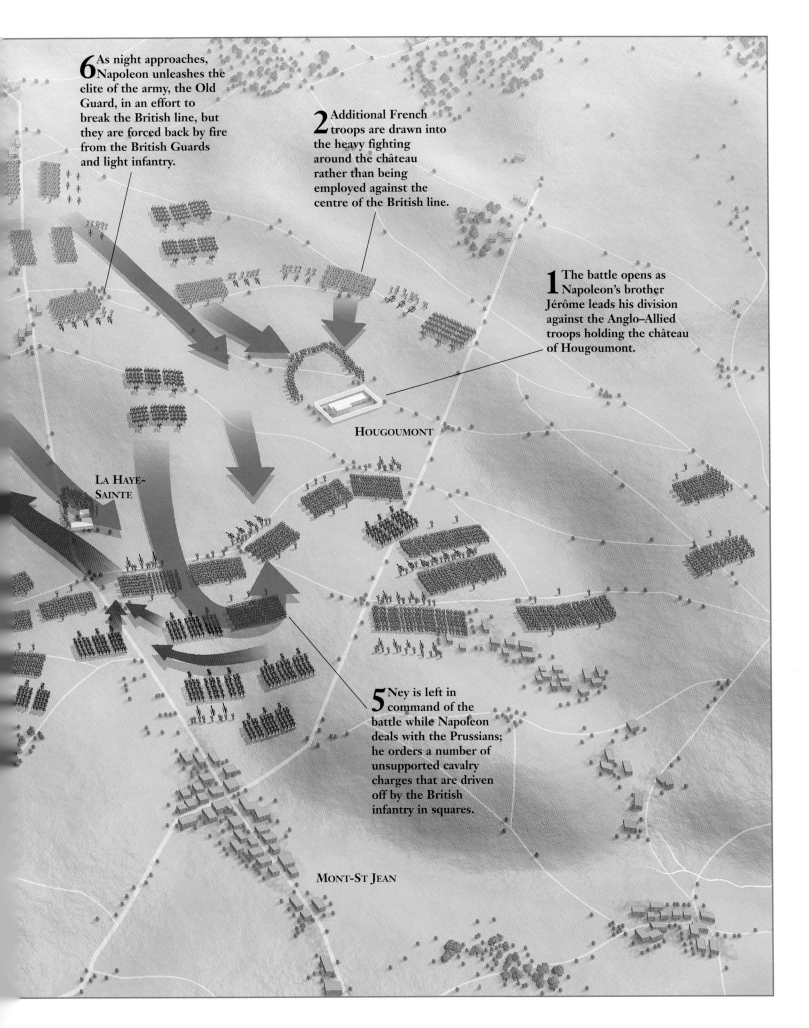

6 As night approaches, Napoleon unleashes the elite of the army, the Old Guard, in an effort to break the British line, but they are forced back by fire from the British Guards and light infantry.

2 Additional French troops are drawn into the heavy fighting around the château rather than being employed against the centre of the British line.

1 The battle opens as Napoleon's brother Jérôme leads his division against the Anglo–Allied troops holding the château of Hougoumont.

HOUGOUMONT

LA HAYE-SAINTE

5 Ney is left in command of the battle while Napoleon deals with the Prussians; he orders a number of unsupported cavalry charges that are driven off by the British infantry in squares.

MONT-ST JEAN

Trooper of the 2nd Royal Scots Greys. The Scots Greys spent most of the Napoleonic Wars in Great Britain, but were deployed to the continent with Wellington's forces for the 1815 campaign. Assigned to Ponsonby's Union Brigade of heavy dragoons, they were deployed with the main Anglo–Allied army at Waterloo.

'The Field of Waterloo' by Robert Alexander Hillingford shows a Highland infantryman helping a wounded British cavalry officer following the charge of the Union Brigade.

approximately 800 of his best men, along with 1000 horses.

This action marked a lull in the battle, except for the continued shelling of Hougoumont. However, it was soon the turn of the French to suffer a major setback. Napoleon ordered Ney to secure La Haye Sainte, which he considered to be a key to Allied strength. Ney called on two battalions, feeling reasonably confident that these were sufficient for the task, particularly as he saw what he took to be signs of Allied withdrawals. His attacking force was made up of Cuirassiers cavalry – men equipped with helmets and breast plates – primed to reach Allied lines. But the Allied army, far from having withdrawn, had formed into squares interlaced with artillery barriers, creating a solid defensive position that the by now exhausted French troops could not overcome.

Allied morale was high, and attention turned to attacking the small hamlet of Plancenoit, the key to Napoleon's rear. Blücher's assurances of full support for the British were threatened by heavy rain, which caused his guns and transport to become bogged down in the network of narrow farm lanes, where wagons loaded with equipment were unable to overtake one another. Bülcher's distance from the battlefield made communication with

Wellington almost impossible and Wellington had no idea whether Blücher would arrive in time to be effective. Blücher's contingents had been expected mid-morning, but were unable to arrive until around 1600.

SHARPSHOOTERS IN POSITION

French sharpshooters were defending the cottages in Plancenoit, but Napoleon was eventually forced to send 4000 of his elite reserve troops, the Young Guard, to stem the Prussian advance. But within two hours, a second Prussian corps entered from the east to support the forces of General Friedrich Wilhelm von Bulow (1755–1816), who commanded the IV Corps of Blücher's army. The French were heavily defeated and were forced to abandon the village.

Napoleon was now faced with the nagging presence of the farm of La Haye Sainte in Wellington's centre. Very vulnerable, it was held by just one battalion of the King's German Legion, and came under constant fire from the French. Allied resistance ultimately proved futile – the farm had to be abandoned to Ney's continued assaults, which drove out the defenders and torched the barns and outbuildings. The Allied practice of creating protective squares for the troops in

WATERLOO

a bid to drive off the French infantry had to be abandoned. In the chaos of the battle, too many troops were left unprotected and fell victim to Ney's cavalry. The force of the attack succeeded in turning the farm into a fortified outpost for the French.

Before releasing his men for what was to prove the final attack on the Allied lines, Napoleon concentrated on keeping Wellington's and Blücher's troops apart. He reasoned that if one of these commanders was forced to retreat it was likely that the other would follow. Ney, on the other hand, was in favour of continuing the push on the Allied centre, pleading with the Emperor for more troops. Napoleon at this point was more interested in deploying the Young Guard to drive the Prussians back from Plancenoit, to be followed by an assault at the main Allied line. Wellington was thus given the opportunity to reorganize his forces and Ney's chances of pressing home a decisive attack had gone. With the Middle and Old Guard brought out from the reserve, Napoleon passed command to Ney, who led five battalions up the Brussels road. However, they were met by a surprise attack

by Allied batteries that had been assembled to meet them.

FOOT GUARDS ADVANCE

At first, men of the Middle Guard threw back the British battalions, only to be assaulted in turn by Allied Belgian and Dutch troops who drove the French back down the hill. Men of the British Brigade of Foot Guards were then urged on by Wellington, who commanded, 'Up Guards, ready'. Needing no further encouragement, the Foot Guards fired a volley and charged with their bayonets, forcing the French Guard back. It took 15 minutes for Wellington to appear on the skyline and wave his hat, giving the signal for the all-out pursuit of the retreating French, and a mêlée of Allied forces quickly attacked. The French retreat became a rout. Three battalions of the Old Guard hung on to enable the Emperor to escape. He made no attempt to stay and rally his soldiers or conduct their retreat but rode for his life. The Battle of Waterloo was over.

As for the casualties, the Allied army lost 15,000 men, or one in four troops engaged.

This famous painting by Philippoteaux shows French cuirassiers attacking a square of British infantry, in this case a battalion of Highlanders. The artillery pieces in the foreground and background would have been manned until the last moment, the gunners seeking protection within the square after firing one last shot at point-blank range.

The Prussians lost 7000 men. The casualties of the French army were estimated at 25,000 dead and wounded, with 8000 prisoners and 220 guns lost.

NAPOLEON'S FINAL ECLIPSE

The Battle of Waterloo saw the end of 26 years of fighting between the European allies and France and the end of Napoleon's 100 days reign. He was permanently exiled to the island of St Helena, where he died in 1821. Officers who had fought for Napoleon received harsh punishment. Most notable was Marshal Ney, who was regarded as a traitor and was executed by a firing squad. Wellington, too, fought his last battle at Waterloo, and became a hero throughout Europe.

CHARGE OF THE LIGHT BRIGADE

25 OCTOBER 1854

THREE NOTABLE FEATS OF ARMS WERE PERFORMED BY BRITISH TROOPS AT THE BATTLE OF BALAKLAVA. THE HEAVY CAVALRY BRIGADE AND THE INFANTRY WERE BOTH HIGHLY SUCCESSFUL IN REPULSING THE RUSSIAN CAVALRY. THESE EVENTS WERE OVERSHADOWED BY THE GALLANT ACTION OF THE LIGHT BRIGADE'S CHARGE INTO THE 'VALLEY OF DEATH'.

WHY DID IT HAPPEN?

WHO The British Light Cavalry Brigade, under the command of Major General the Earl of Cardigan (1797–1868), numbering around 670 effectives, opposed by an unknown but large force of Russian cavalry and artillery.

WHAT The Light Brigade advanced against Russian artillery despite enfilading fire from cannon on both flanks.

WHERE North of Balaklava in the Crimea, Russia.

WHEN 25 October 1854.

WHY Confusion arising from poorly worded orders sent the Light Brigade forward against the wrong objective.

OUTCOME Despite massive losses, the Light Brigade reached the Russian guns and overran them before retiring though heavy fire.

The Ottoman Empire, founded in 1299, reached its zenith in the sixteenth century. It held territories in Europe, Asia and Africa, and was a major naval power in the Mediterranean. However, by the 1800s, it was in decline. It had lost considerable amounts of land and was significantly weaker than in previous centuries, to the point where the Empire needed alliances with European powers to support its ambitions. Conversely, the weakening Ottoman Empire was a region where European diplomats and entrepreneurs could make gains. Businessmen and military adventurers sought opportunities while foreign states became increasingly involved in Ottoman affairs.

Among the issues that arose was control over the Holy Land. Disputes between Orthodox and Catholic Christians and Muslims were further complicated by national allegiances, resulting in a complex question of who should have authority over the holy places. Accusations of mistreatment and discrimination by one group against another were made, some of which were true although some were invented as a pretext for new demands by national or religious leaders.

Catholic France sought to become the supreme authority in the Holy Land, and forced a treaty on the Ottoman Empire to this effect. This was partially a diplomatic offensive but was backed up by the threat of force in the form of a French warship deployed to the Black Sea, in violation of international treaties. Almost immediately, Russia made her own show of force, deploying troops to the Danube, and demanded a reversal of the decision. This was granted, with Russia assuming responsibility for protecting the interests of Christians in the Holy Land, with all the prestige and authority that went with it.

British cavalry officers pictured early in the Crimean campaign. The vast increase in infantry firepower since the beginning of the century rendered cavalry far less effective than in previous wars.

A flurry of diplomacy ensued, backed up by ship and troop deployments. Russian forces moved into Moldavia and Wallachia, under the pretext of protecting Christians there. This was permitted by treaty even though these were Ottoman provinces. French and British diplomats, fearing the expansion of Russian power in Europe, tried to convince the Ottoman Empire to rebuff Russian demands. Both nations sent fleets to the Dardanelles to demonstrate their commitment to supporting any stand taken by the Ottoman Empire. A conference between Britain, France, Austria and Prussia produced a proposal that was acceptable to Russia but not the Ottoman Sultan. Amendments were proposed, but Russia this time was not agreeable.

THE WAR BEGINS

With the diplomatic situation unresolved and Russian troops on Ottoman soil in the Balkans, war was declared by the Ottoman Empire on 23 October 1853. For a time the war was a local affair, fought in the Caucasus and the Danube region of the Balkans. However, a Russian naval attack against Ottoman vessels anchored at Sinop, on 30 November 1853, triggered international intervention. Issuing a joint ultimatum that required Russia to withdraw from Ottoman territory, Britain and France prepared for war.

On 28 March 1854, Britain and France declared war on Russia, which had not complied with the ultimatum. The possibility of Austrian intervention against Russia prompted a withdrawal, but by then Britain and France had made new demands and were prepared to fight to enforce them. The intent was to reduce Russian power and influence, and to this end, the allies landed troops near Sevastopol, the main Russian port on the Black Sea. From here, Russian ships could threaten Ottoman territory and possibly transit the Dardanelles into the Mediterranean.

THE ADVANCE ON SEVASTOPOL

In order to reach Sevastopol, the allies landed troops approximately 53km (33 miles) north of the port and began marching south. This required crossing several rivers, each of which offered the Russian army a good defensive position. The Russians, under General Menshikov (1787–1869), made a stand at the Alma River on 20 September 1854 but were driven back after an intense fight. The allies had a real opportunity to shatter the Russian army, which was shocked and demoralized by its defeat, but there was little attempt to exploit the victory and the Russians were able to retire to Sevastopol.

It was not until 23 September that the allies got moving again after the battle of the Alma. A divided command structure, with poor cooperation between French and British forces and their commanders, hampered the advance and the formulation of strategy. Allied troops were advancing from the north, but the defences in this direction were very strong. Reconnaissance indicated that the southern approaches were less powerfully defended, so it was decided to hook around Sevastopol and come up from the south. This move also made it possible to capture one or more of the smaller ports in the region for use as supply bases.

The main Russian army marched out of Sevastopol as the allies approached, preventing it from being besieged and permitting mobile operations against the allies. Defence of the city fell to around 18,000 personnel, most of whom were drawn from the navy. To strengthen the defences, guns were used from Russian naval ships, which were then scuttled to prevent capture.

LOCATION

RUSSIAN EMPIRE

BATTLE OF BALAKLAVA

BLACK SEA

Constantinople

OTTOMAN EMPIRE

The port of Sevastopol was an important Russian base, critical to the projection of power in the Black Sea and against the failing Ottoman Empire.

BRITISH LANCER

Like many other lancer units, the uniform of the British 17th Lancers was heavily influenced by the dress of the Polish Uhlans (lancers). So this soldier wore a czapka, *a square-topped, four-pointed cap. His primary weapon was a long-hafted lance, giving him a considerable reach advantage in combat. Note the wrist loop, which allowed the lancer to release his grip upon impact but still retain his weapon. If his lance was lost or broken, he also carried a sabre.*

CHARGE OF THE LIGHT BRIGADE

James Thomas Brudenell, Earl of Cardigan, lived aboard his private yacht during the Crimean campaign. He had little time for officers who were not well-connected noblemen.

THE OPPOSED FORCES

BRITISH AND FRENCH

Infantry:	1500
Cavalry:	1750
Total:	**3250**
Guns:	9

RUSSIAN

Infantry:	22,000
Cavalry:	3400
Total:	**25,400**
Guns	78

The city was open to an assault from the south, so work parties toiled to shore up the city's defences.

PREPARATIONS AT BALAKLAVA

Although the allies had an opportunity for rapid action, they proceeded with methodical slowness. First they proceeded to occupy the port of Balaklava for use as a supply base, then began landing equipment for a siege that was not necessary at that time. In fact, the delay in getting the siege train ashore actually meant that it became necessary to use it. In addition, the port was not large enough to support both the British and French armies, and since the allies were not proceeding quickly they would have been better served by securing more ports.

The British assumed responsibility for covering the eastern flank of the operation against Menshikov's still-intact army as the Allies finally moved into position to begin a siege. The presence of Menshikov's army

made it necessary to build redoubts on the Causeway Heights to the north of Balaklava, which were manned by Turks and armed with guns landed from naval ships. British infantry and artillery were also deployed as a second line to protect Balaklava. Control of the port was rightly judged to be critical to the campaign; its loss would cripple allied logistics and probably force the siege to be ended.

The allies finally began the long task of reducing the Russian defences at Sevastopol, but they were in a vulnerable position. Manpower was stretched thin due to the deployments, and the situation was made worse by poor logistics and disease. Cholera took its toll among the troops, weakening the Allied army. The Russians under Menshikov, on the other hand, were receiving reinforcements, with more still to come. However, political pressure forced Menshikov to launch an attack before they arrived.

THE BATTLE OF BALAKLAVA

Rather than strike at the troops of the besieging army around Sevastopol, Menshikov decided to break the siege by capturing Balaklava, defeating the entire allied operation at a stroke. His first move had to be against the redoubts of the Causeway Heights, which covered the approaches with their artillery. Clearing aside the allied pickets with cavalry, the Russian army advanced at dawn on 25 October. As the guns of the redoubts opened fire on the Russians, the allied commanders realized that a major attack was underway. Their response was less than decisive.

The main infantry force covering Balaklava was the 93rd Highlanders under Sir Colin Campbell (1792–1863), who was in overall command of the Balaklava defences. Although too far from the Causeway Heights to assist the defenders, the 93rd were able to prepare themselves to meet an attack if the Russians broke through. In the hope of influencing the battle on the Causeway Heights, the Heavy Brigade was sent forward. This had no effect, so the heavy cavalry pulled back to their deployment positions and waited for orders.

The British horse artillery did manage to contribute usefully, advancing to positions on the heights between the allied redoubts to fire on the Russians. They were forced to retreat after a time by a combination of heavy Russian fire and lack of ammunition. As the horse artillery pulled back, the Russian assault went in. The Turkish defenders of the redoubts, although shaken by artillery bombardment, resisted until 0730, at which point they were driven from one of the redoubts. This caused the defenders of the other positions to fall back, pursued by Cossacks.

FEATS OF ARMS

By 08:00, the Russians were in firm possession of the artillery positions on the Causeway Heights, and began preparing to advance through the South Valley towards Balaklava. The French had sent reinforcements to help protect the port, but they were some distance off as were British infantry, ordered from the siege lines. All that stood between the Russians and Balaklava was the 93rd Highlanders, a horse artillery battery and a scratch force of invalids and rallied Turkish infantry, plus the British cavalry division. This was composed of Heavy and Light Brigades.

The cavalry division was sent an ambiguous order that placed it to the north of the Causeway heights, in the North Valley. A follow-up order sent the Heavy Brigade back into the South Valley, leaving the Light Brigade in place. The heavy cavalry returned to their starting positions in time to sight two to three thousand Russian cavalry assembling on the Causeway Heights. Some of these were detached to attack the Highlanders and their supporting forces, opening the way to Balaklava.

In the path of the Russians stood the Highlanders with bayonets fixed, a 'thin red streak tipped with steel' (according to *The Times* correspondent, William H. Russell, who observed the battle). As the cavalry approached, the Highlanders opened fire, joined by the artillery and the supporting infantry. The Russian charge was halted and the survivors began to retreat. As they did so, the Heavy Brigade wheeled to face the main Russian cavalry force on the heights and, after pausing to dress ranks, charged uphill into the teeth of greatly superior numbers.

The lead squadrons of the Heavy Brigade became surrounded, creating a desperate situation. Additional squadrons hit the Russians' flanks and rear as they enveloped the lead formations. After a fierce close-quarters fight, the Russians fell back, pursued a short way by the Heavy Brigade. They halted after a few hundred metres, allowing the horse artillery to shoot up the

The Heavy Brigade advances against Russian cavalry threatening Balaklava. The Charge of the Heavy Brigade was a short action lasting no more than 10 minutes. The Russians suffered 40–50 killed and over 200 wounded, while the British lost 10 killed and 98 wounded.

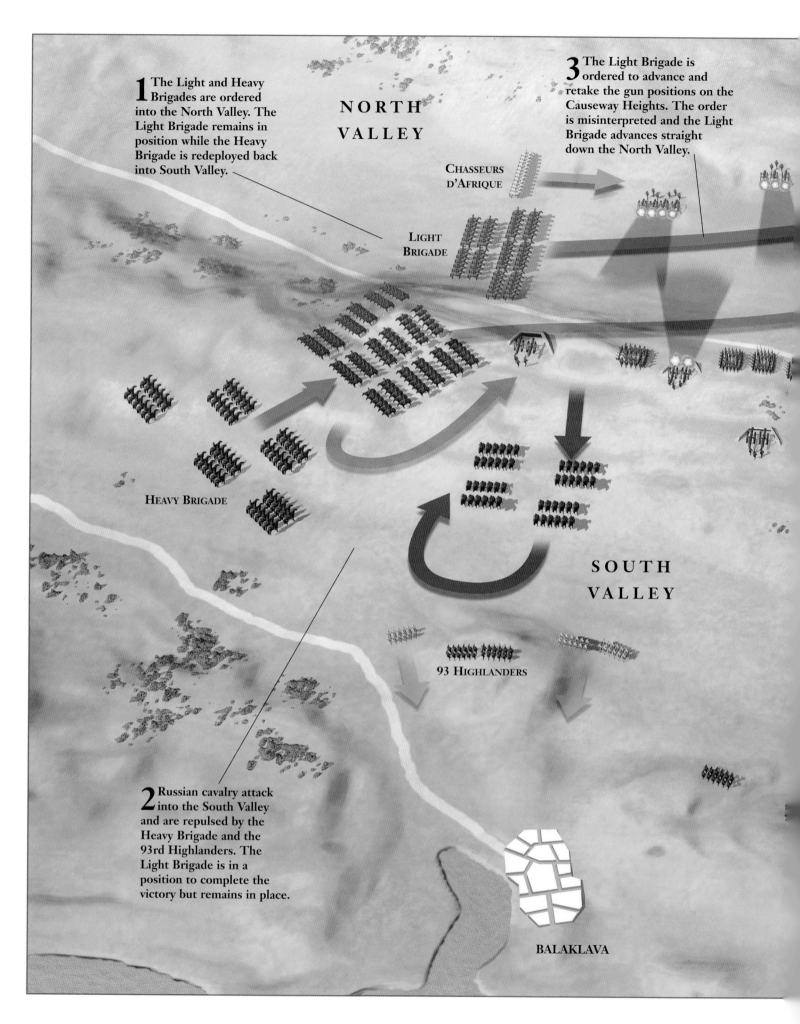

1 The Light and Heavy Brigades are ordered into the North Valley. The Light Brigade remains in position while the Heavy Brigade is redeployed back into South Valley.

3 The Light Brigade is ordered to advance and retake the gun positions on the Causeway Heights. The order is misinterpreted and the Light Brigade advances straight down the North Valley.

NORTH VALLEY

CHASSEURS D'AFRIQUE

LIGHT BRIGADE

HEAVY BRIGADE

SOUTH VALLEY

93 HIGHLANDERS

2 Russian cavalry attack into the South Valley and are repulsed by the Heavy Brigade and the 93rd Highlanders. The Light Brigade is in a position to complete the victory but remains in place.

BALAKLAVA

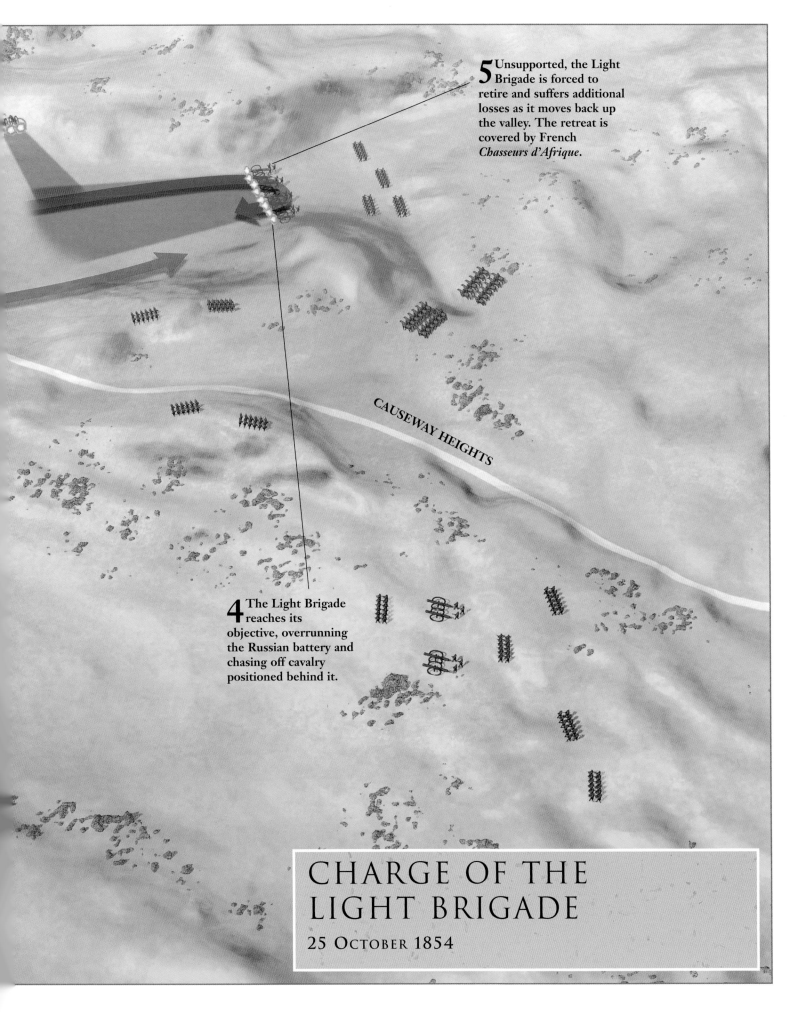

5 Unsupported, the Light Brigade is forced to retire and suffers additional losses as it moves back up the valley. The retreat is covered by French *Chasseurs d'Afrique*.

CAUSEWAY HEIGHTS

4 The Light Brigade reaches its objective, overrunning the Russian battery and chasing off cavalry positioned behind it.

CHARGE OF THE LIGHT BRIGADE
25 OCTOBER 1854

retreating Russians. The Light Brigade was in a perfect position to attack the disorganized Russians as they fell back, but did not do so for reasons that are still unclear.

CONFUSED ORDERS

The fight in South Valley had defeated the Russians' advance on Balaklava but left them in possession of the artillery redoubts on the Causeway Heights. These were lightly held at 09:30, and there was a possibility of dislodging the Russians. However, infantry reinforcements were some way off and could not be in position much before midday, while Russian reinforcements were strengthening their hold on the ridge all the time. Thus at 10:00, the cavalry division was ordered to advance and 'take advantage of any opportunity to recover the Heights'. The order also mentioned that infantry support was on its way.

Lord Lucan (1800–88), commanding the cavalry division, interpreted the order as meaning that he should wait for the infantry and then advance, which was not what Lord Raglan (1788–1855), in overall command of the army, intended. Raglan wanted a show

of force to persuade the Russians to retreat, and became exasperated when Lucan did nothing. His annoyance increased when the Russians began moving British guns out of the redoubts – losing artillery pieces was considered a dishonour.

Raglan sent additional orders demanding that the cavalry act immediately. These were written hurriedly and with little clarity. Fatefully, the fourth and final order stated that the cavalry was to 'advance rapidly to the front' and prevent the enemy carrying away the guns. It was delivered by Captain Lewis Nolan (1818–54), who was given a verbal addition to the orders: 'Tell Lord Lucan that the cavalry is to attack immediately'.

This stream of vague orders confused Lucan, who was not aware of any guns being moved by the Russians. He could see a Russian battery at the far end of the North Valley, which was 'to his front' while the Causeway Heights were more to his right. Lucan asked Captain Nolan for clarification and received a vague gesture in response, with the angry words: 'There are your guns!' Nolan's gesture was down the valley, where Lucan could see the Russian guns.

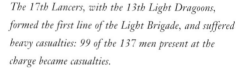

The 17th Lancers, with the 13th Light Dragoons, formed the first line of the Light Brigade, and suffered heavy casualties: 99 of the 137 men present at the charge became casualties.

Lucan had an order to attack immediately, and his target had – he thought – been indicated clearly. The attack was extremely hazardous, with artillery in the flanks and infantry within rifle range, but Lucan now had no choice. He ordered Lord Cardigan (1797–1868), commanding the Light Brigade, to advance, and overruled Cardigan when he raised the same objections that Lucan himself had made.

THE LIGHT BRIGADE CHARGES

At 11:10, Cardigan began to lead the Light Brigade down the North Valley. The Heavy Brigade moved forward in support but was held back by Lucan, who was determined that some of his command at least would not sacrificed. After about 200m (219yd), Captain Nolan apparently realized that the orders had been misunderstood and tried to indicate the correct target. He was killed by a shell almost immediately, and the Light Brigade trotted onwards.

Receiving fire from both flanks, the Light Brigade accelerated to the gallop some 250m (273yd) from the Russian guns. Despite heavy casualties from canister rounds fired by the guns to their front, the cavalry broke into the battery and began sabring the gunners. A large number of Russian cavalry was deployed to the rear of the battery, intending to counter-charge the Light Brigade. Some of the British cavalrymen charged the Russian cavalry, who panicked and fled.

The Light Brigade had somehow managed to achieve its misunderstood aim, and was in possession of the Russian battery. However, as it began reforming what remained of its squadrons, the realization dawned that the heavy cavalry had not followed and the brigade was unsupported. Russian cavalry began to close around the brigade's rear, attempting to prevent their escape. There was no alternative but to fight clear and retire back up the valley, under fire all the way. Despite vastly superior numbers, the Light Brigade did manage to break through and returned to the British-held end of the valley by noon. Their escape was greatly assisted by a charge of the French *Chasseurs d'Afrique*, whose attack helped cover the British retreat.

AFTERMATH

The Light Brigade started the attack with around 670 men, and suffered about 40 per cent casualties – 118 dead and 127 wounded – but it achieved an incredible feat of arms. Advancing under fire from three sides, the Brigade overran a critical position and drove off the supporting cavalry. Had additional forces – the Heavy Brigade, for example – moved up in support, a decisive result might have been achieved. Instead, the battle of Balaklava ended inconclusively.

Avoiding defeat at Balaklava was enough for the Allies to eventually win a strategic victory. The siege of Sevastopol continued and eventually the port fell to the Allies. However, the recriminations went on for much longer than the war, and the charge of the Light Brigade is remembered as an act of futility.

Such was the outrage in Britain about the fiasco that the other great feats of arms at Balaklava – the repulse of the Russian cavalry by the 93rd Highlanders and the charge of the Heavy Brigade – are now virtually unknown, yet the Light Brigade lives on as a shining example of dramatic catastrophe. What is usually forgotten is that despite all the odds stacked against it, the Light Brigade achieved all of its objectives and presented its commanders with an opportunity to win a decisive victory.

Lord Cardigan depicted in combat with Russian cavalry after overrunning the Russian batteries. Cardigan was accused of deserting his troops and fleeing just after the first line reached the guns.

SECOND MANASSAS
28–30 AUGUST 1862

THE SECOND BATTLE OF MANASSAS (ALSO KNOWN AS THE SECOND BATTLE OF BULL RUN) WAS THE HIGH POINT FOR THE CONFEDERACY'S ARMIES. GENERAL ROBERT E LEE TOOK AN INCREDIBLE RISK IN DIVIDING HIS FORCES IN THE FACE OF SUPERIOR NUMBERS, BUT WAS ABLE TO GAIN A DECISIVE ADVANTAGE THAT RESULTED IN A TOTAL VICTORY.

WHY DID IT HAPPEN?

WHO Union Army of Virginia (63,000 men) under Major-General John Pope (1822–92) opposed by the Confederate Army of Northern Virginia (55,000 men) under General Robert E Lee (1807–70).

WHAT Pope attacked Major-General Thomas 'Stonewall' Jackson's (1824–63) corps in a disjointed fashion and was unable to defeat it before Lee arrived with the remainder of the Confederate army.

WHERE Near Manassas, Virginia, 42km (26 miles) southwest of Washington DC.

WHEN 28–30 August 1862.

WHY Lee wished to prevent a junction between Pope's army and the Union Army of the Potomac under Major-General George B McClellan (1826–85). He advanced against Pope's supply line and drew the Army of Virginia into a fight on approximately equal terms.

OUTCOME After some initial successes, Pope's force was soundly defeated. Pope was dismissed from army command. Lee's victory opened the way for an invasion of the North.

The ground around Manassas was not auspicious for the Union forces. It was here, in July 1861, that a Union army had broken on the bulwark of Jackson's brigade and thus earned the Southern general his nickname of 'Stonewall'. More recently, three independent Union forces had been unable to defeat a badly outnumbered Jackson in the Shenandoah Valley.

Nonetheless, victory here was necessary. Washington was just 42km (26 miles) away and had to be protected, while the Confederate capital at Richmond was also within striking distance. To bring about this much-needed victory, the Union forces in the region were combined under the command of Major-General John Pope, who managed to antagonize his own side as well the enemy. Even Robert E Lee, a man

not normally given to animosity even towards his enemies, took a personal dislike to the Union commander.

Pope's newly formed Army of Virginia was a serious threat to Lee, who was already outnumbered by the 90,000 strong Army of the Potomac under Major-General George McClellan. If the two Union forces made a junction, Lee was in real trouble. It would have to be prevented.

Lee knew that McClellan was much given to procrastination and was unlikely to make a decisive move any time soon, so he decided to hit Pope hard before McClellan realized what was going on. He sent Jackson north against Pope with just 12,000 men, then ordered Major-General AP Hill (1825–65) to support Jackson, bringing another 24,000 men under Jackson's hand.

Thomas Jonathan Jackson was a strong-willed and eccentric man with deeply held religious beliefs. Although a staunch Christian who disliked fighting on a Sunday, he was also a fearsome battle commander.

The three Union corps that had been formed into the Army of Virginia were still dispersed, and Jackson decided to defeat them in detail by use of a central position from which to lunge against each one in turn. However, Jackson was so concerned with secrecy that he did not fully brief his commanders (including AP Hill) and disorganized his own force in the process.

Jackson's force ran into the Union corps under Major-General Nathaniel Banks (1816–94) at Cedar Mountain and was driven back by a very aggressive assault until Hill's force arrived on the field. Banks had neglected to request reinforcements and could not cope with the setback; his force was soundly defeated.

However, by now McClellan was moving to reinforce Pope. This was a slow business, but Lee knew that his time was limited. He decided to crush Pope as quickly as possible, using Clark's Mountain to conceal his advance until he could launch a decisive attack on Pope's eastern flank. This was more than a tactical flanking movement; if successful, it would drive a wedge between Pope and McClellan, and also knock Pope off his line of retreat to Washington.

Things did not quite go according to plan. Lee's staff was slow to organize the attack, and then his cavalry commander Major-General JEB 'Jeb' Stuart (1833–64) was almost captured when his headquarters was attacked. His adjutant was taken, and in his possession was a copy of Lee's entire battle plan. Stuart struck back with a raid on Pope's headquarters and came back with dire news: in five days McClellan's forces would be in position to aid Pope, bringing the Union army up to 130,000 against Lee's 55,000 or so. Pope already had 75,000 men but if Lee was going to act, it had to be now, before things got any worse.

UNCONVENTIONAL MOVES

Even though he knew that conventional strategy became the norm because it worked, and that those who ignored the rules invited disaster, Lee threw away convention and caution (and, some said, sanity), and split his forces in the face of a superior foe. It may be that he had no choice – it was either this desperate gamble or certain defeat by superior forces.

PRIVATE, IRON BRIGADE

First known as Rufus King's Brigade and later as 'that damn Black Hat Brigade', the formation that became known as the Iron Brigade was composed mainly of units from Wisconsin, plus one from Indiana and, later, one from Michigan. The unit's nickname came from its ability to stand 'like iron' under intense fire – one reason why the formation suffered very high casualties during the war.

Before the Second Battle of Manassas the Iron Brigade was able to muster 2100 men of all ranks. Afterwards, only 1250 answered the roll call. The brigade was recruited back up to just under 1900 in time for Gettysburg but suffered a staggering 1212 casualties there. Some of the units of the brigade took 75–80 per cent casualties.

Whatever the reasoning, Lee sent Jackson's corps, supported by Stuart's cavalry, off on the morning of 25 August. They marched first to Salem (42km/26 miles) and, after covering a remarkable 58km (36 miles) the following day, fell on the Union depot at Manassas on the night of 26 August, destroying the supplies found there.

POPE'S REACTIONS

Pope now found himself in the central position, with 75,000 men available. He could move against Jackson's 24,000 or Major-General James Longstreet's (1821–1904) corps of 30,000, leaving a small force to cover the other. Pope had already

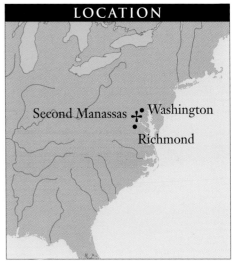

LOCATION

Second Manassas · Washington
Richmond

Lying just 42km (26 miles) from Washington, about midway between the Union and Confederate capitals, Manassas Junction was a critical point that had already seen heavy fighting earlier in the war.

THE OPPOSED FORCES

FEDERAL
Total: 63,000
(troops of all arms)

CONFEDERATE
Total: 55,000
(troops of all arms)

begun redeploying his forces to counter Jackson's move, and now had a real chance to smash the Confederate corps. However, Jackson was a master of what would come to be known as deception operations. Manoeuvring his forces in a manner designed to mislead and confuse Pope as to his intentions, Jackson moved to Sudley Mountain and reformed his corps on Stony Ridge. His forces were in position by midday on 28 August.

Pope was thoroughly confused by Jackson's movements and did not have adequate reconnaissance information to hand. The captured Confederate battle plan did not help at all. Pope's men reached Manassas too late to catch Jackson and wasted more time in confused movements. Pope then heard that there were Confederates in Centreville and jumped to the conclusion that he had found his enemy.

He sent his entire force racing towards Centreville to engage the enemy. He had been so busy trying to intercept and destroy Jackson that he forgot about Longstreet, permitting the two Confederate forces to make a junction.

ACTION AT GROVETON

Late in the day on 28 August, Jackson's forces attacked Union troops moving down the turnpike towards Centreville. Jackson did not want the Federal forces to take up good defensive positions in Centreville, so

Troops from one of the many New York regiments to fight at Second Manassas pose for the camera. The Civil War was the first conflict to be extensively photographed. Posed images like this one were a novelty at the time, as were the newspapers they appeared in soon after being taken.

The opening of the Second Manassas Campaign came on 9 August in the shadow of Cedar Mountain in northern Virginia, where Brigadier-General Nathaniel Banks's corps fought with Major-General Thomas J. 'Stonewall' Jackson's Second Corps. The battle cost the Federal forces 314 killed, 1445 wounded and 662 missing, totalling 2381 of the 8000 troops engaged. The Confederate forces suffered casualties of 241 killed, 1120 wounded and 4 missing for 1365 of the 16,800 troops employed.

he accepted the risk inherent in making his position known to Pope (who was still groping around for him) and fired on elements of Brigadier-General Rufus King's (1814–76) division as they moved down the Warrenton Turnpike.

Six thousand Confederates attacked about 2300 Union troops under Brigadier-General John Gibbon (1827–96). The Union troops were green but Gibbon was an experienced and determined commander who led his men at the advancing Confederate force. Lines shook out and the firing started. For over two hours the opposing lines stood, in places just 100m (110 yards) apart, and blazed away at one another. There was no attempt at flanking or manoeuvre, just raw firepower poured into the enemy in the hope of breaking them. Gibbon's brigade was reinforced during the battle, bringing his strength up to about half that of the Confederates. At nightfall, the battle petered out, leaving about 1300 casualties on each side. The Confederate force withdrew. Pope misconstrued the action as evidence that Jackson was retreating towards the Shenandoah Valley. He ordered his army to concentrate at Groveton, ready to annihilate Jackson.

SECOND MANASSAS OPENS

Pope was wrong about his opponents' intentions, but Jackson's position was not all that good. He had 20,000 men, who were positioned behind an unfinished railroad line, with the cut as a defensive obstacle. Longstreet was on his way but was still some hours out. Despite his mistakes thus far, Pope had a real chance to pulverize Jackson's force. The first attack went in on the morning of 29 August.

Pope's force advanced against Jackson in a disjointed fashion, making repeated attacks that caused heavy casualties but did not drive Jackson back. About an hour into the fighting, Longstreet's corps came up on Jackson's right and began extending the Confederate line to the south.

On the Union side, Major-General Fitz John Porter's (1822–1901) corps did make a probing attack against what seemed to be Jackson's right flank. In fact, Porter's troops, who were moving up from Manassas Junction, had encountered Longstreet, whose flank was, in turn, held by Stuart's cavalry. After a minor skirmish, Porter withdrew and refused an order to attack, presumably thinking he was unlikely to succeed. He led his force to join the main Union body.

Proving that mistakes were not the sole preserve of the Union army, Longstreet did not attack once he was in position. A dangerous gap had opened up in the Union army, and Longstreet was ideally positioned to exploit it. However, his thinking was defensive at the time and although the Confederates did press forward somewhat as their opponents fell back, there was no

John Pope held general rank more or less from the outset of the war and helped raise some of the earliest volunteer units to be recruited. Although successful in the west, he is mainly remembered for his defeat at Second Manassas and for his arrogant address upon assuming his new command in the east.

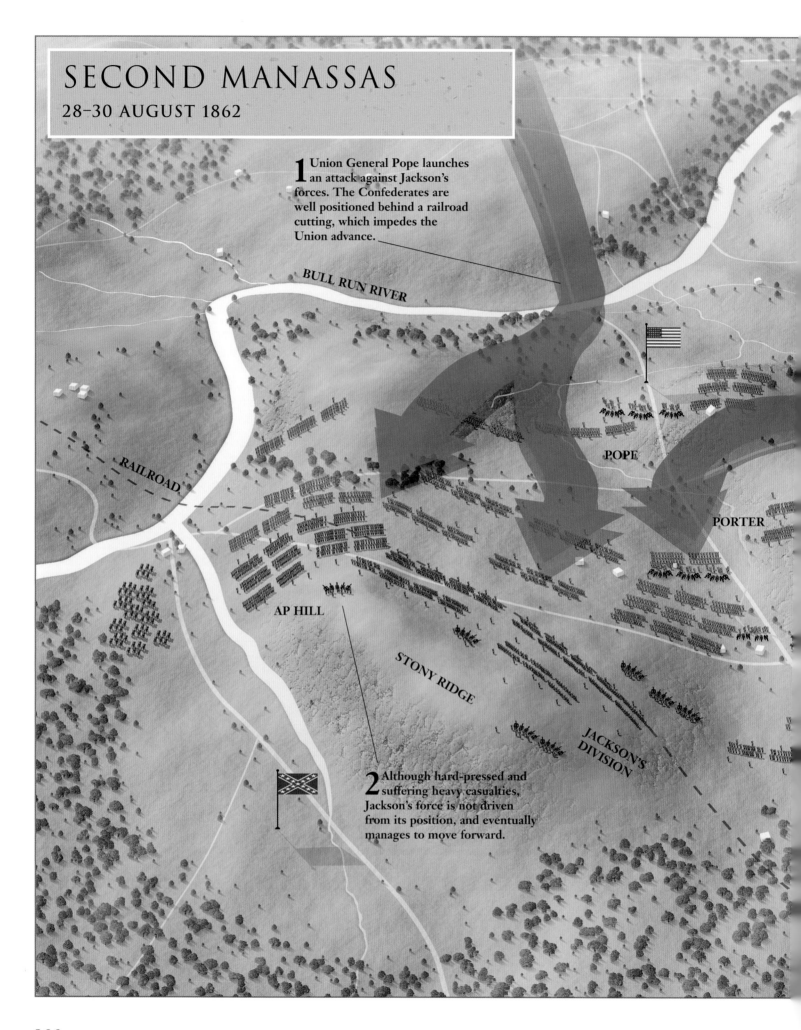

SECOND MANASSAS
28–30 AUGUST 1862

1 Union General Pope launches an attack against Jackson's forces. The Confederates are well positioned behind a railroad cutting, which impedes the Union advance.

BULL RUN RIVER

RAILROAD

POPE

PORTER

AP HILL

STONY RIDGE

JACKSON'S DIVISION

2 Although hard-pressed and suffering heavy casualties, Jackson's force is not driven from its position, and eventually manages to move forward.

288

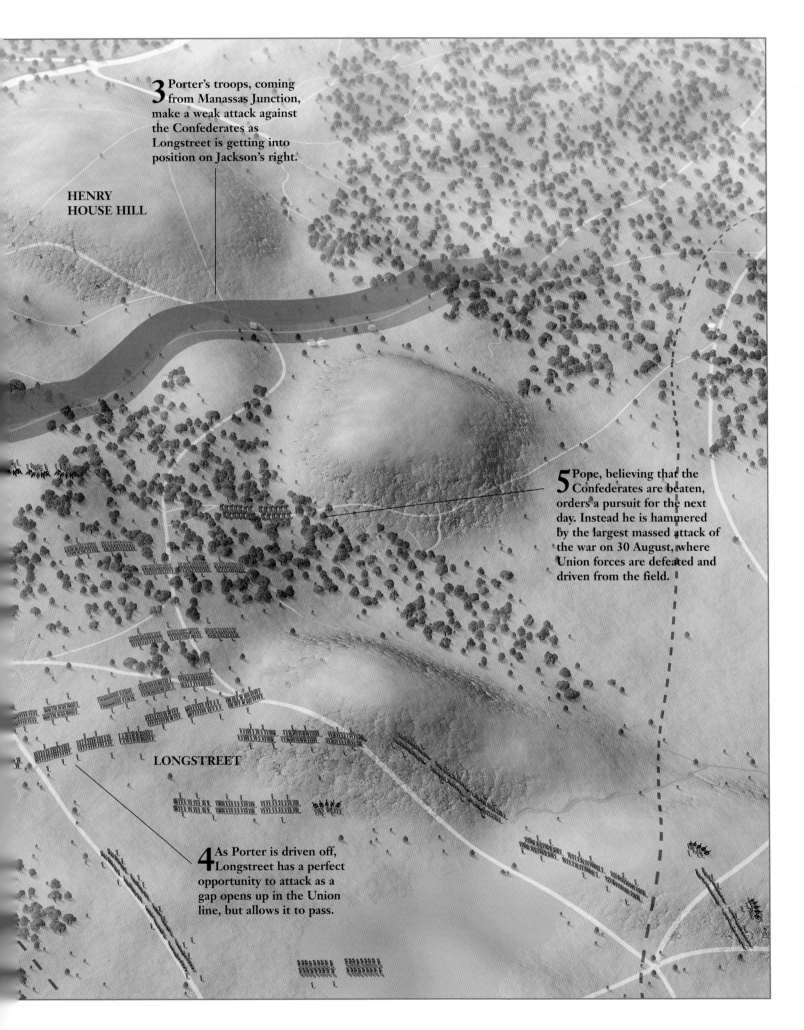

3 Porter's troops, coming from Manassas Junction, make a weak attack against the Confederates as Longstreet is getting into position on Jackson's right.

HENRY
HOUSE HILL

5 Pope, believing that the Confederates are beaten, orders a pursuit for the next day. Instead he is hammered by the largest massed attack of the war on 30 August, where Union forces are defeated and driven from the field.

LONGSTREET

4 As Porter is driven off, Longstreet has a perfect opportunity to attack as a gap opens up in the Union line, but allows it to pass.

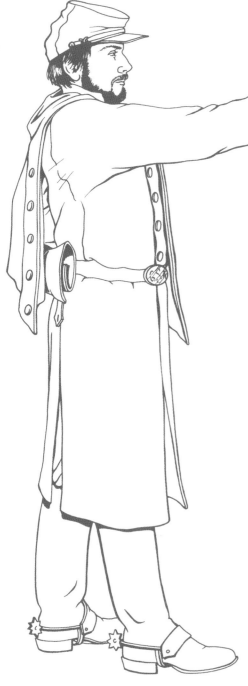

A Confederate Kentucky cavalryman fires his service revolver. Cavalry were mainly effective as scouts, raiders and skirmishers in the Civil War. Infantry firepower was such that a traditional sabre charge was unlikely to be effective. The cavalryman's combination of mobility and firepower made him an important asset all the same.

pursuit or attempt to exploit the repulse of the Union army. Indeed, Jackson ordered his troops to withdraw from the ground they had taken and resume their previous defensive positions. Pope, as usual, misconstrued the move.

This time, Pope decided that the Confederates were in retreat, and ordered a pursuit for the following day. He still did not know that Longstreet was on the field, nor that Lee was coming up as well.

THE SECOND DAY

The second day opened with Jackson's force returning to its former positions and the Union army beginning a new series of attacks. Pope finally became aware of Longstreet's presence but still thought the Confederates were retreating. Skirmishing went on all day, with casualties mounting on both sides.

In the early afternoon, Pope decided to put in a decisive assault. This began at about 3:00 p.m., and was launched with great determination. Successive lines went forward and fierce close-range firefights broke out all along the Confederate line.

Jackson's corps had a good defensive position and confidence born of the previous day's victory. But the men were tired and the enemy far more numerous. Many battles of the Civil War were decided by raw firepower, with victory going to the side that hung on longest. Would the Rebels be broken first by the hammering they were receiving, or would the Federal troops run out of aggression and fall back? The crisis point had arrived.

THE DECISIVE MOMENT

Porter's force put in an attack, which was met with massed Confederate artillery fire and hurled back. Seeing that the moment had arrived, General Robert E Lee, who

had reached the battlefield with his own force, ordered Longstreet forward against the Union left flank.

Longstreet had 28,000 men under his hand, who had thus far played little part in the battle. They were relatively fresh and were opposed by only weak forces. The advance, which was the largest massed assault of the entire war, smashed into the

weak Union line and flung it back. This endangered the flank of the forces assaulting Jackson, and resulted in a general movement towards the rear. For a time, it appeared that Pope's army was going to be chased from the field and devastated.

Despite the extremely aggressive advance of Longstreet's corps, elements of the Union force were able to rally and make a stand on Henry House Hill, the same place where Jackson's brigade had broken the Union assault at the First Battle of Manassas. Although the rearguard was hard-pressed by determined Confederate attacks, it was able to hold out and prevent the total collapse of the Union Army.

As a result of the rearguard action, Pope's army came off the field at Second Manassas defeated and bloodied but generally intact. It remained a viable fighting force, which was an improvement on the situation after First Manassas.

Below: The Confederate 5th Texas Regiment charge the Federal 5th New York Zouaves at the battle of Second Manassas.

SECOND MANASSAS

Left: Confederate commanders and staff at the Second Battle of Manassas. Commanders on both sides relied on mounted messengers to bring information and carry orders to the commanders actually engaged. A 'galloper' who failed to find the recipient of his message could tip a battle one way or the other.

Opposite: James Longstreet resigned a commission in the US Army to serve the Confederacy. Although controversy dogged his career there is no doubt that he performed very well in battle.

PURSUIT (1 SEPTEMBER)

Following on from this success, Lee continued to attack. He made a second large flanking manoeuvre, hoping to cut off the retreating Union army and obliterate it. However, the going was slow even for Jackson's hard-marching 'foot cavalry'. Jackson's force reached Chantilly and there encountered Union forces under Major-General Isaac Stevens (1818–62) and Major-General Philip Kearny (1815–62) on 1 September.

A sharp fight ensued, in which both Union commanders were killed, but Jackson was unable to complete his flanking movement and the Union line of retreat remained open. Pope was shaken by the string of defeats and retired into the defences of Washington, even though reinforcements were available to him.

AFTERMATH

Lee had not quite managed to destroy Pope's army, mainly due to Longstreet's failure to attack on the first day and the determined rearguard action on Henry House Hill. Pope's decision to send troops north to cover his flank, thus precipitating the inconclusive but important fight at

Chantilly, also did much to stop a tactical defeat becoming a strategic disaster. Pope was blamed for the fiasco and relieved of his command. Porter's career was also wrecked by allegations that his refusal to attack Longstreet was calculated to cause Pope's defeat and McClellan's reinstatement as overall commander.

Lee was not able to make an attempt on Washington's defences with the forces he had to hand, and McClellan remained a threat. However, the way was now open for

an advance across the Potomac into the North. Lee had shown that he could gamble when he had to and that, overall, the Southern forces were better led than their Northern counterparts.

Victory at Second Manassas was a turning point for the Confederacy. Not long beforehand, Lee was facing certain defeat; now the Union forces were in disarray and there was a real chance of winning the war.

Up until Second Manassas, the Confederacy had been trying to stave off defeat in Virginia, which would mean the loss of the capital and probably the end of the war. Now a new campaign opened, which would lead to Antietam and another turning point.

Thanks to the stand at Henry House Hill, the Federal army was able to cross the Bull Run and withdraw in good order. Thousands of men were funnelled across this narrow bridge.

ANTIETAM
17 SEPTEMBER 1862

THE YEAR 1862 BEGAN WELL FOR THE UNION. IN THE WEST, UNION ARMIES ACHIEVED A NUMBER OF IMPORTANT VICTORIES, INCLUDING GRANT'S SUCCESS AT SHILOH. LIKEWISE, THE UNION NAVY WON SOME SIGNIFICANT GAINS, INCLUDING THE CAPTURE OF NEW ORLEANS AND THE USS MONITOR'S FORCING THE CONFEDERATE IRONCLAD VIRGINIA (FORMERLY THE UNION FRIGATE USS MERRIMACK) TO YIELD HAMPTON ROADS AND THE MOUTH OF THE JAMES RIVER TO FEDERAL CONTROL.

WHY DID IT HAPPEN?

WHO Major-General George B McClellan's (1826–85) Union Army of the Potomac (87,000) confronted General Robert E Lee's (1807–70) Confederate Army of Northern Virginia (45,000).

WHAT McClellan's army attacked while the Confederates were drawn up along Antietam Creek on the Maryland side of the Potomac River, inflicting some 10,300 casualties while losing 12,400 men.

WHERE Sharpsburg, Maryland, some 80.5km (50 miles) northwest of Washington DC.

WHEN 17 September 1862.

WHY McClellan's natural caution, his belief that he was outnumbered, plus poorly coordinated attacks allowed Lee to repulse Union attacks and withdraw to Virginia.

OUTCOME While the Army of Northern Virginia remained a significant force, Southern hopes of Maryland joining the Confederacy were dashed, as was the possibility of foreign intervention on their behalf. Lincoln also had the victory he needed to issue the Emancipation Proclamation.

Despite these successes on other fronts, the Union was unable to make significant progress in the central theatre of the war, that 161km (100-mile) front between the capitals of Washington DC and Richmond. Here, the main Confederate army of 60,000 men under General Joseph E Johnston (1807–91) faced the Union army of more than 100,000 under the command of Major-General George B McClellan. Under pressure from Lincoln (1809–65), McClellan came up with a plan for a grand flanking manoeuvre that required transporting his army to the Virginia Peninsula for an attack on

Richmond. By late March McClellan had concentrated a large army of nearly 100,000 on the Peninsula, but he was slow to act and so missed an opportunity to strike at Richmond from the Peninsula while he was opposed by a force of only 17,000 men. Johnston and his army moved to block McClellan's advance.

At this point, McClellan, noting that with the withdrawal of Johnston to the Peninsula Washington was no longer in danger, requested the release of a corps that had been left to defend Washington. He was thwarted by the advice of Robert E Lee, who suggested that Major-General Thomas

This is the railroad bridge at Harpers Ferry. The town was an important Union garrison and supply centre. The heights in the background were captured by Confederate troops and it is clear from the photograph how these dominate the town.

'Stonewall' Jackson's (1824–63) troops in the Shenandoah Valley make a feint to tie down Union forces. Jackson executed a masterful campaign, not only pinning, and defeating, large numbers of Union forces in and around the Valley, but also convincing Lincoln not to release the corps McClellan had requested.

Although McClellan would advance to within 8km (5 miles) of Richmond, he would be forced to retreat when Robert E Lee assumed command of the Confederate army there after Johnston had been wounded. During June and July, the two armies fought a number of engagements and, although the battles were indecisive and costly to the Confederacy, Lee's skilful manoeuvring forced the Union army to halt its efforts to seize Richmond.

POPE TO THE FORE

In early August, Lincoln decided to concentrate Union forces in northern Virginia under the command of Major-General John Pope (1822–92) as the Army of Virginia. He also ordered McClellan to begin withdrawing his forces from the Peninsula, intending for the two forces to join together and create a huge army to march on Richmond from the north. Lee reacted quickly, ordering a probing attack by Jackson against Pope and moving the bulk of his own forces north in support. At the Second Battle of Manassas (28–30 August), Pope's army was mauled by Jackson and by Longstreet, whom Lee had sent to support him.

Lee had hoped to annihilate the Army of Virginia, but Pope began an orderly retreat to Centreville, and the exhaustion of the Rebel troops, especially those of Jackson's command, a vigorous defence by the Union rearguard and impending arrival of Union reinforcements, made this impossible.

By the end of the summer, Confederate fortunes on the war's central front were on the rise. Lee had turned back a major Union effort against the Rebel capital, Richmond, and, in conjunction with Jackson, had counterattacked and won a significant victory. At the same time, Union forces in the western theatre had become bogged down and lost the initiative. It was at this point that the Confederacy planned a major

series of coordinated offensives against the Union forces both in the east and the west.

THE CAMPAIGN

The Union Army was in disarray. Pope and his subordinates blamed one another for the debacle at Manassas. President Lincoln was despondent because he was unable to find a commander who seemed capable of winning the decisive victory he so sorely wanted. In the event, he appointed, once again, George McClellan as the commander of the reinforced Army of the Potomac. Many in the Lincoln administration were against the general's reappointment, including Secretary of War Edwin Stanton (1814–69). Although Lincoln perhaps

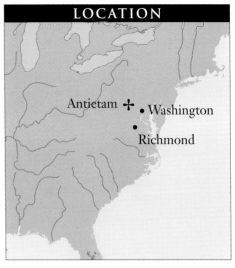

The battle took place in Maryland where Confederate forces could threaten the capital, Washington, as well as the rich farms and towns of Pennsylvania. It was further hoped that a Confederate army in Maryland would bring that state over to the Confederate cause.

1ST SOUTH CAROLINA REGIMENT OF RIFLES

Also known as Orr's Rifles, the regiment was formed in July 1861 and was engaged in many of the important battles of the war. At Antietam, it was part of Brigadier-General Maxcy Gregg's (1814–62) brigade of AP Hill's (1825–65) Light Division along with four other units of South Carolinians. The unit was involved in Hill's counterattack against Major-General Ambrose Burnside (1824–81). Hill notes that Gregg's brigade was composed of veterans and while engaging in a firefight, poured in 'destructive volleys' against the advancing Union troops. Three Confederate brigades, including Gregg and his South Carolina regiments, numbering only 2000 men, were able to drive off Burnside's corps.

This illustration shows the difficulty that faced the troops of Burnside's corps as it tried to push across the Rohrbach Bridge. Only one unit at a time could cross the bridge and so the Union forces were forced to launch piecemeal attacks rather than coordinated ones.

realized that McClellan's cautious nature made him less than ideal as an aggressive battlefield commander, McClellan had, nonetheless, demonstrated his skills as an excellent military administrator. After the defeat at Second Manassas, it was these skills that were needed to reforge the demoralized Union army.

While the Union forces were regrouping, the Confederacy was planning its coordinated offensives for the autumn of 1862. There were to be three separate campaigns launched. Two western armies under General Braxton Bragg (1817–76) and Major-General Earl Van Dorn (1820–63) were to invade Kentucky and Tennessee respectively. In the meantime, Lee and the Army of Northern Virginia were to move north through Maryland, pushing on to Harrisburg, the capital of Pennsylvania. If successful, the Confederacy would see a number of positive strategic

effects. First, it was hoped that the arrival of a Confederate army in Maryland, which was home to a number of Southern sympathizers, would bring that state within the Confederacy, providing both manpower and resources.

Secondly, Lee's army had suffered from the constant and arduous campaigning earlier in the year and his troops were in desperate need of all manner of supplies. Many of these could be procured in Pennsylvania. Lastly, Harrisburg was an important centre of communications that sat astride road and railroad lines that would allow Lee and his army to threaten a number of important Northern cities, such as Philadelphia, Baltimore and Washington, with either direct attack or by cutting their supply lines.

On 5 September, Lee led his Army of Northern Virginia across the Potomac River into Maryland. Unfortunately, it quickly became apparent to him that, despite the sympathetic leanings of many Marylanders, the state and its population were not actively going to support him or his army. One reason for this may have been the appearance of the Army of Northern Virginia. Although the troops were flushed

with victory and very confident, they hardly looked like a triumphant army. Few units had a uniform appearance and many of the troops' clothing was threadbare and their equipment was worn out.

HARPERS FERRY

Lee continued to move north towards Frederick, which he occupied. While there he learned that the Union forces in and around Harpers Ferry, about 13,000 men, had not retreated even though they were now cut off by his invasion force. Lee decided to have Jackson cross the Potomac with 15,000 men while two other divisions supported Jackson by occupying the heights on the Maryland side of the river. He would take the remainder of the army and move towards Hagerstown.

On 9 September, Lee had orders drawn up, Special Orders 191, outlining his plan, with copies sent to the pertinent commanders. This did not seem to be a particularly risky manoeuvre given McClellan's propensity for caution and his tentative movements. Lee believed that the army would be reunited before it faced a major engagement. Having received its marching orders, the Army of Northern

Virginia divided into four columns and departed the next day.

Unfortunately for Lee, McClellan moved more quickly than usual, perhaps spurred on by the panic that Lee's invasion had caused. On 7 September, the Army of the Potomac left Washington in pursuit of Lee's forces. The army's morale had not improved much since the defeat at Second Manassas a little more than a week before. But as the Union troops marched though western Maryland, a profound change occurred. Unlike Lee, the Union troops were met with great enthusiasm by the local population, who came out in large numbers to cheer them on and provide them with food and drink. For the first time, the Army of the Potomac was on the defensive, fighting on its own soil, and with the outpouring of support morale soared.

On 12–13 September, Confederate troops occupied the heights east of Harpers Ferry, facing only minor resistance, and,

after a brief bombardment, the town and its garrison, less 1500 cavalry who managed to break out, surrendered to Jackson the following day. But while Jackson was enjoying success at Harpers Ferry, fate struck a serious blow to the Army of Northern Virginia.

On 13 September, McClellan's army entered Frederick and received an enthusiastic greeting from the inhabitants. One Union regiment, the 27th Indiana, halted that morning at a farm just outside town. As troops fell out to rest, a corporal in the unit found an envelope containing three cigars wrapped in a sheet of paper. The soldier unwrapped the paper and discovered that it was a copy of Special Orders 191, detailing Lee's campaign plan. The captured document was quickly passed up the chain of command until it reached General McClellan's headquarters. But McClellan was indecisive; although he had the enemy's plans, he believed, as he all too

THE OPPOSED FORCES

FEDERAL
Army of the Potomac,
consisting of 7 army corps   **87,000**

CONFEDERATE
Army of Northern Virginia,
consisting of 2 army corps   **45,000**

Major-General Ambrose Burnside, seated in the centre with his legs crossed, commanded the Union Army's Ninth Corps. He is shown with his staff. Photographs of commanders and their staffs taken either before or after a battle were very popular.

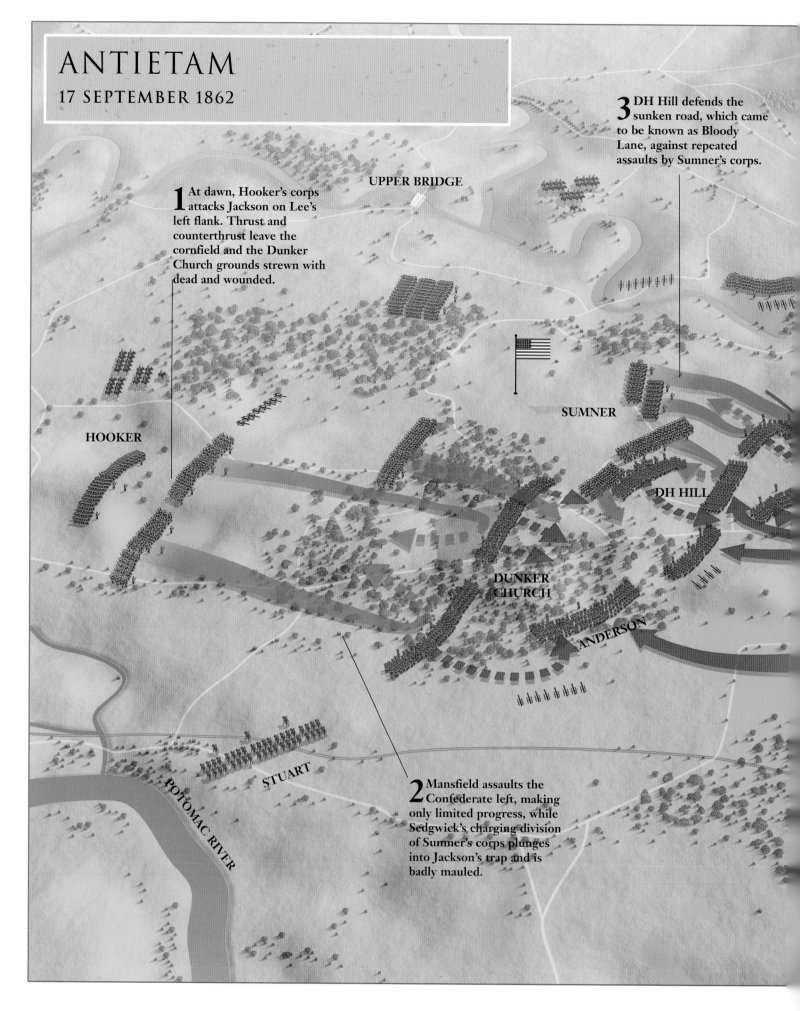

ANTIETAM
17 SEPTEMBER 1862

3 DH Hill defends the sunken road, which came to be known as Bloody Lane, against repeated assaults by Sumner's corps.

UPPER BRIDGE

1 At dawn, Hooker's corps attacks Jackson on Lee's left flank. Thrust and counterthrust leave the cornfield and the Dunker Church grounds strewn with dead and wounded.

SUMNER

HOOKER

DH HILL

DUNKER CHURCH

ANDERSON

STUART

POTOMAC RIVER

2 Mansfield assaults the Confederate left, making only limited progress, while Sedgwick's charging division of Sumner's corps plunges into Jackson's trap and is badly mauled.

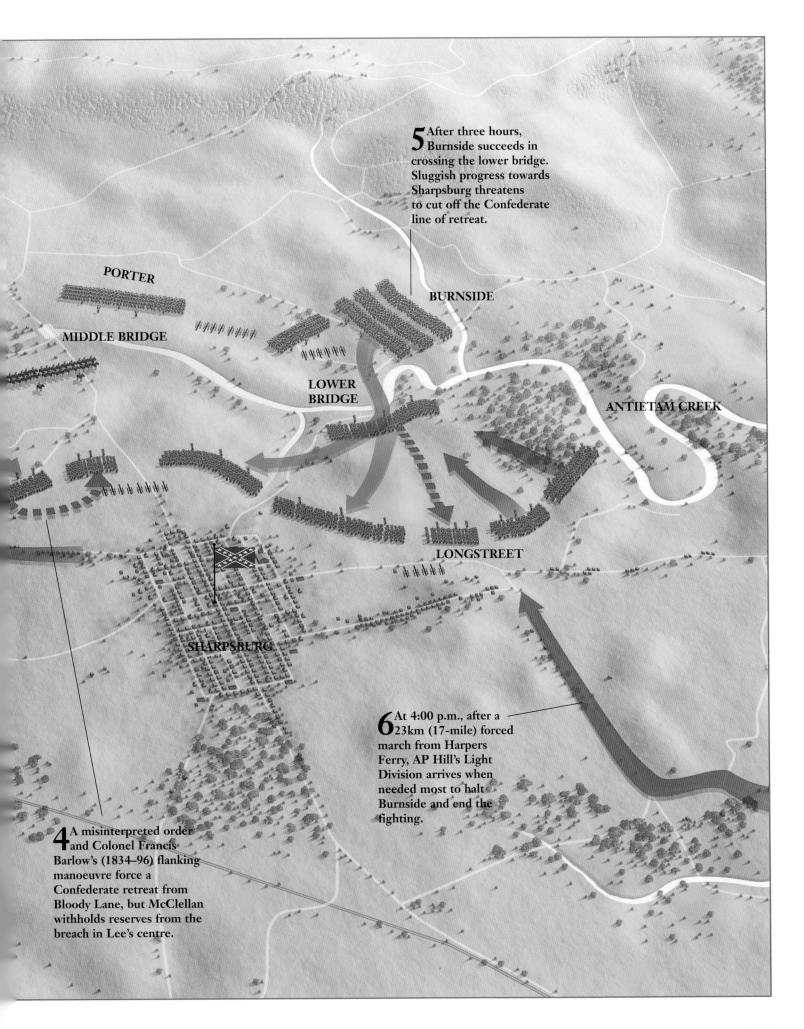

PORTER

MIDDLE BRIDGE

5 After three hours, Burnside succeeds in crossing the lower bridge. Sluggish progress towards Sharpsburg threatens to cut off the Confederate line of retreat.

BURNSIDE

LOWER BRIDGE

ANTIETAM CREEK

LONGSTREET

SHARPSBURG

6 At 4:00 p.m., after a 23km (17-mile) forced march from Harpers Ferry, AP Hill's Light Division arrives when needed most to halt Burnside and end the fighting.

4 A misinterpreted order and Colonel Francis Barlow's (1834–96) flanking manoeuvre force a Confederate retreat from Bloody Lane, but McClellan withholds reserves from the breach in Lee's centre.

Above: A soldier of a Zouave unit which formed part of Major-General Ambrose Burnside's Ninth Corps. His regiment had the distinction of being the Union unit which advanced farthest during the battle, attacking the outskirts of Sharpsburg in the afternoon.

often did, that Lee's force was much larger than it actually was. As a result, it took hours for orders to be drafted and the Union forces did not begin moving until the next morning.

Lee, however, received intelligence regarding the impending movement of the Union army. Colonel JEB 'Jeb' Stuart's (1833–64) cavalry scouts had noted the unusual activity among the Union units and a message was received from a Southern sympathizer that McClellan had obtained a copy of his orders. Had McClellan moved quickly on 13 September, he might have taken and held the passes in the South Mountain range. Lee, however, moved more quickly and blocked the three key passes with his available forces, perhaps 16,000 men. On 14 September, these forces were attacked by more than twice their number of Union soldiers. Although the fighting was fierce, the Southern troops were forced to yield the passes to the enemy.

Things looked bleak for Lee on the night of 14 September and he was planning to abandon the campaign and retreat back to Virginia when he received word that Harpers Ferry was about to surrender to Jackson. This strengthened his resolve and so Lee determined to make his stand where

he had received the message – Sharpsburg. This was a strong position, protected by a series of hills and Antietam Creek. At noon on 15 September, Lee received confirmation that Harpers Ferry had in fact surrendered and sent orders to all of his units to converge on Sharpsburg for what could be, if they were victorious, a decisive battle.

DISPOSITIONS

On 15 September, Lee had managed to gather some 18,000 troops at Sharpsburg, but they had not had the time to fully deploy. McClellan's forces began arriving that afternoon as well but, cautious as ever, he did not cross the unguarded Antietam Creek; indeed, he did not even make an effort to reconnoitre the far bank by sending out a cavalry screen. The next day, troops arrived on both sides. Lee's force increased to perhaps 25,000 men while McClellan had some 55,000 men deployed with another 14,000 or so men only a few

Hooker's First Corps launched a sustained attack along the Hagerstown Turnpike on the morning of 17 September and there was heavy fighting stretching the length of the road. The bodies are those of Confederate soldiers killed in the fighting.

kilometres away. But rather than attacking on 16 September, McClellan spent the entire day planning rather than moving. Once again, he assumed that Lee's forces were far stronger than they actually were and so he delayed attacking. This was a missed opportunity for the Union to defeat the Army of Northern Virginia while it was divided. By the time the battle began on the morning of 17 September Lee had gathered most of his available forces at Sharpsburg. Only Major-General AP Hill's division was not present, as it was on the march and expected to arrive later that day.

Lee had deployed his forces to the north and east of Sharpsburg along a ridgeline with both wings protected by water; the left rested on a bend in the Potomac River, while the right was anchored on Antietam Creek. Stuart's cavalry held the extreme left of Lee's line. The main body of the

Confederate left was composed of Jackson's corps, while Longstreet's corps held the Confederate right flank.

McClellan had finally sent troops across the Antietam on the evening of 16 September. He sent Major-General Joseph Hooker (1814–79) and his First Corps, later followed by Major-General Joseph K Mansfield's (1803–62) 12th Corps, as the right wing of his army. On the eastern bank of the Antietam, the remainder of his army was placed, beginning with Major-General William B Franklin (1823–1903) and his Sixth Corps, closely followed by Major-General Edwin Sumner's (1797–1863) Second Corps. Then came the Fifth Corps under Major-General Fitz John Porter (1822–1901) supported by Brigadier-General Alfred Pleasonton's (1824–97) cavalry division and, finally, Major-General Ambrose Burnside's Ninth Corps, which

This painting shows Union troops advancing at the double. Although tactics of the time, such as Hardee's Rifle and Light Infantry Tactics, emphasized firepower, moving forward at the double in order to come to grips with cold steel was seen as a possible counter to the infantry firefight.

In an era without radios and on battlefields that were quickly covered with billowing smoke, signal towers like the one shown provided both a vantage point as well as a way of communicating across the battlefield through the use of semaphores and heliographs.

formed the army's left flank. The plan called for 'Fighting Joe' Hooker supported by Mansfield and Sumner to sweep down the Hagerstown Turnpike and engage the Confederate left flank. Once this had been done and Lee's attention was fixed on his left, Burnside would force his way over the Antietam by the Rohrbach Bridge. The remaining two corps and Pleasonton's cavalry were to be kept in reserve.

THE BATTLE

The battle began at dawn with Hooker's First Corps quickly moving to the attack along the Hagerstown Pike. As the Union troops entered the cornfield that lay to the east of the Pike between two large woods, they became heavily engaged with Jackson's troops. The fighting was intense, with both sides suffering heavy losses. Particularly devastating was the artillery fire. Both sides engaged in stiff counterbattery fire and the Union artillery fired at point-blank range into the cornfield, inflicting massive casualties. For nearly two hours both sides fed divisions into the fray without gaining the advantage. It was not until 7:00 a.m. that troops from the next Union corps, Mansfield's 12th, joined the action. Sadly, this was to be typical for the battle –

McClellan's inability to coordinate attacks that would have allowed him to take advantage of his superiority in numbers. By the time Mansfield engaged the enemy, Hooker's division had been rendered nearly combat ineffective. Moreover, Lee used the time to move additional troops to support his left flank.

Once again, the Union troops of the 12th Corps attacked, but without much support and thus with limited success – when the troops did make a breakthrough they were unsupported. The only support came from one division of Sumner's corps, which, having crossed the cornfield and entered the West Woods without reconnoitring first, was ambushed and badly mauled.

Sumner's remaining two divisions advanced around 9:00 a.m., moving south to engage the centre of Lee's line. Here, the Confederates occupied an 800m (880-yard) stretch of road that had been eroded by years of use and provided a natural trench line for the Confederates holding it. For nearly four hours the Union troops launched attacks against the enemy in 'Bloody Lane' until, finally, they managed to take and hold it.

Once again, a lack of coordination, in this case not committing the troops held in reserve from the corps of Major-Generals Porter and Franklin, allowed an opportunity to be lost. It is clear that McClellan assumed that he needed to keep these troops in reserve to counter Lee's reserve forces – which did not exist.

While the Union army was hotly engaged in the cornfield, the West Woods, and then at Bloody Lane, Burnside, who was to have engaged in early assault, remained inactive. This allowed Lee to move units facing Burnside to other parts of the battlefield at critical moments. At 10:00 a.m., however, Burnside received direct orders to attack and he now faced a considerably reduced Confederate force. Although he outnumbered the enemy by more than three to one, Burnside was unable to force a crossing of the Antietam for several hours.

His actions at Rohrbach, soon to be evermore known as Burnside's Bridge, were both unimaginative and lethargic. He suffered heavy casualties by sending units to attack across the bridge. It was not until the early afternoon that some of his troops turned the Confederates' position by fording the creek downstream; and it was not until nearly 3:00 p.m. that he was prepared for a more general advance against the Confederate right and began forcing them back towards Sharpsburg, cutting off their line of retreat across the Potomac. But Burnside's lack of initiative proved costly since at 4:00 p.m. AP Hill arrived from Harpers Ferry with badly needed reinforcements and attacked Burnside's left flank, collapsing it.

Although Burnside's left flank was in serious trouble, his right continued to press the Confederates, driving them towards Sharpsburg, but McClellan refused to send in his reserves, assuming himself still to be outnumbered.

As night fell, both sides were exhausted and had suffered horrific casualties. On the morning of 18 September Lee could muster perhaps 30,000 effectives and had no hope of fresh troops. McClellan, meanwhile, had received some 13,000 reinforcements who, together with his uncommitted reserves, gave him more fresh troops than Lee had fit for duty in his entire army. But his belief that Lee had hidden reserves kept him from engaging on 18 September, and so the Army of Northern Virginia was able to slip away unmolested that night.

Although McClellan had missed an opportunity to destroy Lee's army and likely end the war, the strategic effects of the Battle of Antietam were nonetheless significant. The Union had turned back a major Confederate offensive on to their soil and, in so doing, had kept Maryland out of the Confederacy. This also ended any hope of foreign intervention on behalf of the South. Finally, President Lincoln, who did not wish to appear desperate when he issued the Emancipation Proclamation, could now do so in the wake of a major strategic victory.

This photograph shows President Lincoln (centre) with Allan Pinkerton (1819–84, left), head of the Secret Service, and Major-General John McClernand (1812–1900, right). The victory at Antietam was important to Lincoln since it provided him with a much-needed success before announcing the Emancipation Proclamation.

GETTYSBURG
1–3 JULY 1863

GETTYSBURG IS OFTEN THOUGHT OF AS THE TURNING POINT OF THE CIVIL WAR, BUT IT WAS NOT IMMEDIATELY DECISIVE. HOWEVER, THE SOUTH NEEDED A MAJOR VICTORY MORE THAN THE NORTH, AND FAILURE TO WIN ONE TIPPED THE BALANCE IN FAVOUR OF THE UNION. IT WAS IN SOME WAYS A BATTLE DECIDED BY MISTAKES, AND, IN THE END, THE UNION ARMY MADE FEWER OF THEM THAN ITS OPPONENTS.

WHY DID IT HAPPEN?

WHO The Union Army of the Potomac under the command of Major-General George G Meade (1815–72) numbering about 95,000, opposed by General Robert E Lee's (1807–70) Confederate Army of Northern Virginia, about 75,000 strong.

WHAT A 'meeting engagement' gradually drew in both armies, developing into a major battle in which the Confederate army generally attacked and the Union force fought from defensive positions atop Cemetery Ridge.

WHERE Gettysburg, Pennsylvania.

WHEN 1–3 July 1863.

WHY The Confederate army was operating in Union territory during Lee's Second Invasion of the North and was foraging for supplies. The location was a matter of chance, though it was inevitable that a clash would occur.

OUTCOME Lee's army was unable to defeat the Union force opposing it, and took casualties that it could not afford. Although the battle was indecisive in immediate military terms it was important politically and strategically.

In the summer of 1863, both sides were facing their own crises. In the North, with presidential elections looming, there was a real danger that a pro-peace president might be elected, who would be willing to let the secession states go in return for an end to the war. In the South, it was becoming increasingly difficult to find supplies, weapons and manpower to maintain the war effort. With Vicksburg under siege, there was a real possibility that the Confederacy might lose the use of the vital Mississippi waterway.

General Robert E Lee's advance into the North was critical for both sides. He might even take Washington and dictate the terms of peace in Napoleonic style, but his mere presence on Union soil was an affront to the prestige of President Lincoln (1809–65), who needed public confidence if he was to win the coming election. Just by having an army 'in being' in enemy territory, Lee was a threat to the Union. But he was also exposing his irreplaceable Army of Northern Virginia to defeat.

The Union Army of the Potomac was shadowing Lee's force, trying to prevent it from moving against Washington. It, too, could not risk defeat or the capital would be open to attack. During this tense period, Lee's army was sending out units to forage across the countryside in search of vital

Arriving during the battle, Meade positioned his headquarters in this farmhouse, sufficiently close to the action that stray artillery rounds narrowly missed the general and his staff during the battle.

114TH PENNSYLVANIA ZOUAVES

At the time of the Civil War there was a fashion for all things French in America, and several regiments were raised and equipped in the fashion of the Zouaves who fought for the French government. They were among the best light infantry in the world, and were widely copied. The original Zouaves were North African mercenaries but were gradually replaced by Frenchmen, while the distinctive clothing of the original soldiers was retained in its style but altered to French national colours.

The 114th Pennsylvania was raised in late 1862. It was renowned for its excellent drill and fighting ability. The regiment served with the Army of the Potomac at Gettysburg and through the remainder of the war, being appointed to the position of headquarters guard for General Meade in 1864.

supplies, including food and shoes. This further confused the issue as reports of these detached units made it difficult to be sure exactly where Lee was.

Unfortunately, Lee was robbed at this time of his own best reconnaissance asset, the cavalry of Major-General JEB 'Jeb' Stuart (1833–64). Stuart was somewhat in eclipse and wanted to renew his fortunes with attention-grabbing operations. He had taken his command off on a raid, which turned into an attempt to repeat his previous exploit of riding right around the Union army. He caused a certain amount of disruption to the enemy but would have been more use to Lee if he had been available to provide reconnaissance and screening.

The general confusion was increased by the resignation of Union army commander Major-General 'Fighting Joe' Hooker (1814–79) after a dispute with Major-General Henry Halleck (1815–72). His replacement, Major-General George G Meade, would need time to familiarize himself with the situation and his new command, but time was not to be had; events precipitated a major battle whether or not anyone was ready for it.

COLLISION AT GETTYSBURG

The town of Gettysburg, Pennsylvania, was an important road junction and was said to contain a warehouse with large supplies of shoes, something the Confederate army badly needed. A brigade under Brigadier-General James Pettigrew (1828–63) was sent into the town to forage, and was encountered there by a Union cavalry force under Brigadier-General John Buford (1826–63). Buford's cavalry were trained as mobile infantry, fighting in a dismounted skirmish line.

Buford's force was something of an experiment, and among the ideas on trial was the use of repeating rifles. So, when

Pettigrew's brigade began to advance against them, Buford's outnumbered men were able to hold their ground on McPherson Ridge for a time, though they were hard-pressed. The arrival of elements of the Union First Corps turned the tide, and now the Confederate force was pushed back. Other units were coming up as quickly as possible, and the fight began to spread out as units fell in on the flanks of those already engaged.

The situation was chaotic, with units arriving unexpectedly and rushing straight into action. Sometimes, this led to dramatic success and sometimes to disaster. Occasionally, both occurred in rapid succession, as when Brigadier-General James Archer's (1817–64) Confederate brigade made a dramatic attack on McPherson's Woods and captured the area, only to be outflanked by the Union Iron Brigade and captured – almost to a man.

LOCATION

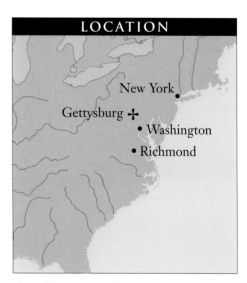

General Lee's Invasion of the North was intended to threaten Washington and other strategic locations, and resulted in a period of countermanoeuvres that culminated in the clash at Gettysburg.

It was during the fight for McPherson's Woods that Major-General John Fulton Reynolds (1820–63), at that point the senior Union officer on the field, was killed. It was also the point at which the true situation began to become clear. Seeing the black hats of the Iron Brigade advancing, a voice in the Confederate ranks was heard to call out: 'Hell, that ain't no milishy, that's the Army of the Potomac!'

The advantage swung one way, then the other. At one point the Rebels outnumbered the Federal troops on the field but were forced to attack across a railroad cut and took heavy casualties. The cut was bitterly contested for hours, and gradually two semi-coherent battle lines began to emerge from the chaos.

The Confederates were getting the better of it, and the Federal troops were gradually pushed back into, and through, Gettysburg. Thousands were taken prisoner and whole units were broken, with the survivors rallying on or behind Cemetery Ridge. They were covered by a determined rearguard action fought by the Union First Corps, which reached the ridge battered but in fairly good order.

Meanwhile, a succession of increasingly senior Union officers were reaching the field and assuming command, as each had a right to do. This created more confusion but gradually order asserted itself, with units being sent to defensive positions on the ridge.

This was the best chance Lee had of winning the battle, with the Union army shaken and disorganized. Lee gave orders to the effect that the Confederate army was to advance and push the enemy off the heights, but the attack was delayed too long and the moment passed.

By nightfall on the first day, the Union army was formed in a 'fish-hook' shape along Cemetery Ridge, with the Confederate army in a similar shape along Seminary Ridge and curving around the top of the fish-hook to the north. This gave the Union force the advantage of a shorter line, allowing reinforcements to be moved quickly from one point to another. Lee did have control of the Chambersburg and Hagerstown roads, however, and thus good communications to his rear.

THE SECOND DAY DAWNS

Both the Union and the Confederate armies spent the morning of the second day improving their position and their situation, slotting newly arrived units into their corps and divisional positions, and sorting out the chaos of the previous day's hurried deployments. Skirmishers exchanged fire but there was little major activity.

However, it was obvious that a battle was going to be fought here. Meade knew he had a strong position and was determined to defend it. Lee had the initiative and was equally determined to attack. Lee moved his forces into position and, as noon approached, began to mass troops opposite the southern end of the Union line. Lee had

John Fulton Reynolds was a career soldier from a military family, who had served with great distinction in the Mexican War. He was one of the best Federal corps commanders and a severe loss to the Union cause.

in fact ordered an attack to be launched at daybreak, but it was delayed, a problem that beset the Confederate army.

Detecting the movement opposite his command, Union Major-General Daniel Sickles (1819–1914) moved his Third Corps forward into a better position to meet the coming attack, occupying a peach orchard and the surrounding terrain. He had already asked for (and not been given) permission to do so, and now acted on his own initiative, leaving a dangerous gap in the Union line.

LEE ATTACKS ON THE LEFT

Lee was becoming increasingly impatient with Lieutenant-General James Longstreet (1821–1904), who was still stalling instead of attacking as ordered. Longstreet was short of one of his divisions, commanded by Major-General George Pickett (1825–75), which was still on the road. He did not want

to 'fight with one boot off', but was finally pushed into action by Lee.

The attack opened with a massive artillery bombardment of the Union troops occupying the Peach Orchard. Then Longstreet's assault finally went in. As a result of his earlier stalling, Longstreet's attack was disjointed but, despite hard resistance from Sickles' Third Corps, the Union forces were pushed back.

During the next four hours, the Union left flank was in severe danger. Six times the Confederates captured the Wheat Field but were driven off, and skirmishers hunted one another through the tumbled rocks of the Devil's Den. First one side, then the other, gained the advantage, but eventually Sickles' corps was pushed back. One Rebel brigade, under Brigadier-General Ambrose R Wright (1826–72), gained Cemetery Ridge but was pushed off again.

The confusion that reigned during the first day of the Battle of Gettysburg prevented either side from realizing the importance of the hill of Little Round Top. The subsequent defence of the hill was one of the decisive moments of the Civil War.

THE OPPOSED FORCES

FEDERAL
Army of the Potomac

95,000

CONFEDERATE
Army of Northern Virginia

75,000

A Confederate infantryman of the 1st Texas Brigade lunges forward with his bayonet-tipped musket. Troops of the 1st Texas were heavily engaged in the capture of Devil's Den on 2 July 1863, at Gettysburg.

FIGHT FOR ROUND TOPS

Meade reacted decisively and quickly to the news that Sickles was in trouble, committing most of his army reserve, and weakening his right flank, to send reinforcements to the embattled left. This was a courageous move: the Union centre

As the Union line was broken, crisis loomed. On the Union right were two hills: Round Top and Little Round Top. The former was too steep and rocky to be much use. Little Round Top, however, could be used as a position for artillery to enfilade the Union line along Cemetery Ridge, and it was entirely undefended other than by a signals detachment.

and right were also under attack, but Meade correctly decided that the most serious threat was to his left.

However, they could not have reached the Round Tops in time to prevent them being occupied in strength. Meade needed time, and that time was bought for him on the personal initiative of the Chief Engineer of the Union Army, Brigadier-General Gouverneur K Warren (1830–82).

Realizing the importance of Little Round Top, Warren rushed to the nearest troops – Brigadier-General James Barnes's (1801–69) division of Fifth Corps – and borrowed a brigade under the command of Colonel Strong Vincent (1837–63). These troops reached the crest of Little Round Top just as Confederate troops – elements of Major-General John Bell Hood's (1831–79) division, which had already taken Round Top – were coming up the other side.

For a while the fate of Little Round Top was undecided but, despite being badly outnumbered, Vincent's brigade was able to cling on and then even counterattacked downhill at bayonet point. Although there was still heavy fighting going on, the successful defence of Little Round Top meant that the crisis had passed for the Union army. Reinforcements arrived and the situation was gradually restored.

LEE ATTACKS ON THE RIGHT

Meanwhile, another Confederate attack was going in against the northern end of the fish-hook, with the aim of dislodging the Union army from Culp's Hill and turning its right flank. After an artillery preparation that was met by overwhelming counterfire

from Cemetery Hill, Lieutenant-General Richard S Ewell's (1817–72) corps finally moved forward with Major-General Edward 'Allegheny' Johnson's (1816–73) division in the lead.

Exploiting the weakened Union position (caused by sending brigades south to assist Sickles), Johnson's division was able to take the southern slopes of Culp's Hill and to advance almost as far as the Baltimore Pike. It was chiefly opposed by a single brigade under Brigadier-General George S Greene, (1801–99) which held out long enough to receive reinforcements. Meanwhile, Brigadier-General Jubal Early's (1816–94) command made an attempt on Cemetery Hill but the expected support did not materialize and the attack was beaten off.

As night fell, the Confederates were in possession of important terrain at the right of the Union line, and were within a few hundred metres of the Union supply wagons. However, darkness concealed the situation and the fighting died down.

THE THIRD DAY OPENS

The Union army was still in danger as the third day began. Although there had been no big successes on the Confederate part, they held part of Culp's Hill and some territory around the bases of the Round Tops. They had exerted serious pressure and, arguably, had only failed to win a victory due to lack of coordination.

On the Union side, more reinforcements had arrived in the form of Major-General John Sedgwick's (1813–64) 15,000-strong corps, but the Confederate army had also been reinforced by late arrivals, including that of Stuart's cavalry. On balance, however, it would appear that Lee had missed his chance. He did not have an objective viewpoint, and things probably looked more favourable from where he stood. He still believed that he could win.

Having attacked heavily on the right and left, and only weakly in the centre, Lee reasoned that the Union centre must have been weakened to meet his thrusts on the second day. Meade correctly predicted this move and reinforced his centre with infantry plus an artillery redeployment to allow massed fire down the hill.

Equally importantly, Meade bolstered the centre psychologically by informing Brigadier-General John Gibbon (1827–96) of Lee's intentions and his preparations to meet them, saying that Gibbon's command would be where the blow was to fall – and be repulsed. Seeing their commander proven correct must have been good for morale among the defending troops.

One other thing was necessary to remedy the Union position: Culp's Hill must be retaken. Twelfth Corps was given the task,

and reinforced accordingly. Some of the troops involved in the assault had an affront to avenge – they had been sent off to reinforce Sickles and had returned to find their positions in enemy hands. This deprived them of food and, they told themselves, a more comfortable night than the one they had just spent in the open.

Johnson's Confederate division wished to widen the penetration it had made into the Union line, and the Federal force wanted to see it off. Johnson's men came out to attack and fighting rapidly spread until about 10:00 a.m., when the Federals finally dislodged Johnson's division from its captured positions. Forced to retreat to the main Confederate line, Johnson's division was shot up badly by Union artillery on the way.

LEE PLANS A DECISIVE BLOW

Although his scouts (and General Longstreet) informed him that it would be possible to manoeuvre around Meade's

This was the terrain so bitterly fought over; hilly and liberally sprinkled with obstacles to break up an infantry advance. The same obstructions provided cover for sharpshooters on both sides.

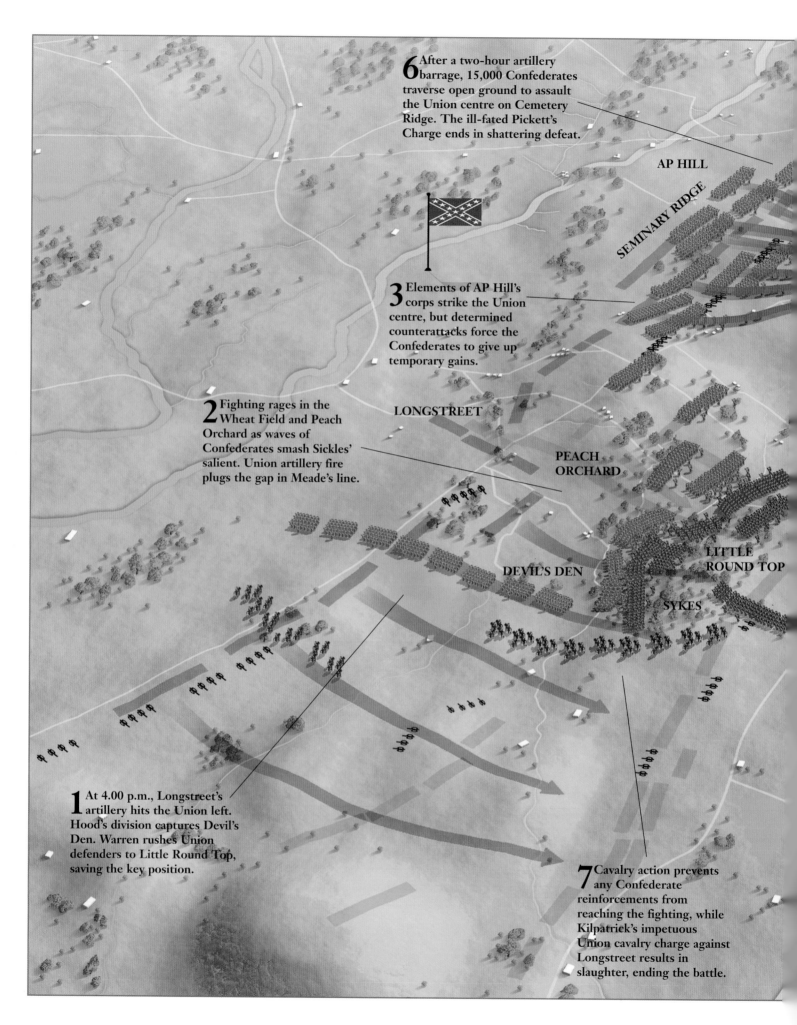

6 After a two-hour artillery barrage, 15,000 Confederates traverse open ground to assault the Union centre on Cemetery Ridge. The ill-fated Pickett's Charge ends in shattering defeat.

AP HILL

SEMINARY RIDGE

3 Elements of AP Hill's corps strike the Union centre, but determined counterattacks force the Confederates to give up temporary gains.

2 Fighting rages in the Wheat Field and Peach Orchard as waves of Confederates smash Sickles' salient. Union artillery fire plugs the gap in Meade's line.

LONGSTREET

PEACH ORCHARD

DEVIL'S DEN

LITTLE ROUND TOP

SYKES

1 At 4.00 p.m., Longstreet's artillery hits the Union left. Hood's division captures Devil's Den. Warren rushes Union defenders to Little Round Top, saving the key position.

7 Cavalry action prevents any Confederate reinforcements from reaching the fighting, while Kilpatrick's impetuous Union cavalry charge against Longstreet results in slaughter, ending the battle.

4 In gathering darkness, Ewell fails to capture Culp's Hill, while Early gains the summit of Cemetery Hill but, without reinforcements, is compelled to abandon the effort.

GETTYSBURG

JOHNSON

HOWARD

CEMETERY HILL

CULP'S HILL

5 Ewell vainly renews the assault at Culp's Hill and Spangler's Spring, and Union counterattacks end the threat to the heights on Meade's right.

NEWTON

ROCK CREEK

GETTYSBURG
1–3 JULY 1863

army and perhaps force it to attack on ground of his choosing, Lee was determined to end this matter here and now. Pointing to Cemetery Ridge, he stated that 'the enemy is there and I am going to strike him'.

Lee's strike would take the form of 15,000 men advancing en masse to break through the Union centre. Many of his troops had been only peripherally involved the previous day and Lee believed that they were fresh enough and sufficiently determined to carry Cemetery Ridge. Longstreet disagreed, suggesting that 'no fifteen thousand men ever arrayed for battle can take that position'. But Lee was in command, not Longstreet, and the only concession to the latter was some compromise over details of the plan.

PICKETT'S CHARGE

Preparations were made, troops were shifted and the hour approached. Longstreet's misgivings grew, but at about

1:00 p.m., the artillery preparation began. This was not as effective as Lee had hoped for, partly due to lack of ammunition, and partly because the guns were firing upwards and tended to shoot over the ridge rather into the forces arrayed along its crest. A tremendous storm of fire came from the massed Federal artillery in reply.

Finally, Pickett, who had been detailed to lead the assault, asked Longstreet if he should advance. Longstreet was unable to give him an answer but nodded, and Pickett's Charge began. This was one of the great military undertakings of the period – a full 15,000 men advancing with their colours, almost as if on parade. There was a brief lull in the firing, during which the Rebel lines crossed about half the distance to the base of the ridge. Then, the Federal artillery began firing.

The massed Union guns fired ceaselessly as the Confederate infantry struggled forward and began to ascend the hill. Gunners changed from roundshot to shell and finally canister as Pickett's Charge came towards them, but the Rebels just closed ranks and kept coming. More artillery (including some guns positioned, ironically enough, on Little Round Top) enfiladed the lines, and as the range dropped, rifle fire broke out along the crest line.

Gaps were opening up between Confederate units, but the advance continued. However, Union Major-General Winfield Scott Hancock (1824–86) pushed a brigade into the gap and began firing into the flank of the advancing enemy units. They broke up two brigades on the Confederate right and sent the survivors back towards their own lines.

By now the leading elements of the Confederate force were approaching the main Union line. Pickett positioned himself, an inviting target on his black horse, to direct units coming up and remained there within range of enemy

A cavalryman from Rush's Lancers, 6th Pennsylvania Cavalry. The lance was going out of fashion in the 1860s, though some units still carried it. The Union cavalry made better use of their firearms than hand weapons. Note that the revolver is worn in 'reverse cavalry' position.

A section of the Gettysburg Cyclorama, painted in 1883 by French artist Paul Phillippoteaux (1845–1923), depicting Pickett's Charge on the final day of the battle. In many ways this was the last hurrah for the Confederacy. Afterwards, the tide had fully turned in favour of the North.

sharpshooters. He fed in units as they arrived, trying to maintain some kind of organization to the assault.

On the left, Pettigrew's division came under murderous flanking fire and broke up. With both flanks stalled and falling back, the only chance for success lay with Pickett's central units. They came forward, pausing only to shoot, and were within 100 metres (110 yards) of the stone wall behind which Gibbon's men waited with loaded weapons. Just as Meade had predicted, the main thrust was coming straight at Gibbon.

Gibbon gave the command to fire, and within five minutes the determined assault was shot to pieces. A scant 150 Confederate soldiers reached the stone wall and clambered over it, led by Brigadier-General Lewis Armistead (1817–63). A Union brigade under Brigadier-General AS Webb (1835–1911) broke and ran, and nearby gunners were chased off or shot down.

This was the high watermark, the point where Pickett's Charge crested and began to ebb. Rallied Union troops, assisted by artillery firing point-blank, blasted the intrepid general and his tiny force off the hill. The assault began to thin out and break up as the Union defenders returned to their positions and continued firing. Soon, Confederate regiments began to break and scatter back down the ridge. The charge was over, and Lee's chance of winning the battle was gone with it. Estimates of Southern dead and wounded in the assault range from 7000 to more than 10,000.

ENDGAME

Longstreet did what he could to rally the shattered survivors and form some kind of battle line in case of a counterattack. It did not come, however. The reason might have been that Meade was thinking defensively and was unable to switch to aggressive operations. It might have been that the Union army was exhausted, and there is also the possibility that Meade did not know that the Confederates were beaten. He may have been expecting another assault from his highly determined enemies.

Lee knew he was beaten, though. Despondently telling Pickett that he and his men had done all that could possibly be asked of them, he accepted the blame for the failure with the simple words: 'This was all my fault.'

The Rebel army was perhaps less despondent. Once out of immediate danger most of the survivors of the charge returned to their units at a walk rather than fleeing into the distance. They knew they had been dealt a beating, but defeat was a new experience for them and, rather than breaking their spirit, it provoked a desire for

revenge. It is perhaps as well for the Army of the Potomac that Meade did not choose to counterattack, given the mood in the Confederate lines at that point.

CAVALRY SKIRMISHES

As Pickett's Charge was going in, a cavalry fight broke out at the southern end of the battlefield. This was an inconclusive but violent business, and went on for some time. Meanwhile, to the north, a rather more serious cavalry action took place. Four Confederate brigades under the legendary 'Jeb' Stuart fought it out with three Union brigades. The prize was control of the roads in the Union army's rear. Lee had hoped that the sudden appearance of Stuart's cavalry in the Union rear would be a factor in breaking the Army of the Potomac, coinciding with Pickett's Charge. In the event the fight, though hard, did not materially affect the result of the battle.

The cavalry fight involved dismounted men fighting as skirmishers and several

batteries of artillery as well as the more traditional running fight. In general, the Union cavalry was inferior to that of the Confederacy in terms of horsemanship and dash. As a result, the Rebels liked to get stuck in with sabres and revolvers, while the Union cavalry tended to come off worse in such engagements. However, one brigade on the Union side was only too willing to meet the Confederate *beau sabreurs* on their own terms – headlong at the point of the sword. This brigade was commanded by a man who had been a captain on the staff a few days earlier and had been promoted, with two others, to general rank for lunatic bravery. His name was George Armstrong Custer (1839–76).

Custer's brigade clashed with the advancing Rebels in a violent mutual charge that became a classic cavalry mêlée of charge and countercharge, while a firefight around Rummell House drew in ever-larger numbers of dismounted men. The fight went on for some time before winding

Entitled 'Come on you wolverines!', this modern painting depicts General George Armstrong Custer leading the Michigan Brigade in a charge at the Battle of Gettysburg, 3 July 1863.

Photographer Timothy O'Sullivan (c1840–82) recorded this grisly scene of Union dead in a meadow near the Peach Orchard. These soldiers were probably killed on 2 July 1863, defending the advanced positions of the Union Third Corps.

down somewhat inconclusively. The Confederate cavalry withdrew into the gathering darkness.

One other cavalry action took place that day. While Confederate General James Longstreet was trying to rebuild the battle line, the Union cavalry commander Major-General Hugh Judson Kilpatrick (1836–81) decided to make a cavalry attack. It is possible that he believed that Meade might be about to counterattack and was trying to assist. Whatever the reason, he ordered one of his regiments forward.

Led by the newly promoted Brigadier-General John F Farnsworth (1820–97), 300 Union cavalrymen charged. They punched through the Confederate line and into the rear, then broke through and came back without their commander, who was killed.

LEE RETREATS

As darkness fell on the third day of Gettysburg, there was a real possibility that the fighting would be resumed on 4 July. However, after waiting for a Union attack

and choosing not to launch one of his own, Lee began a withdrawal.

It seems that Meade was not entirely sure that Lee was withdrawing until 5 July, at which point he sent orders to some of his detached troops to impede and harass the retreat. The most effective action against the retreating Confederates was a cavalry attack made at night, which caused a fair amount of damage.

Union cavalry intermittently harassed the withdrawing Army of Northern Virginia and were driven off at times by walking

wounded who had retained their rifles. However, there was no serious attempt at a close pursuit. Heavy rains, which had flooded the Potomac, hampered the retreat and made the going difficult.

However, Meade was reluctant to press the pursuit and, once the river had subsided, Lee was able to get his army across and out of danger.

AFTERMATH

Gettysburg was, in truth, an inconclusive affair, but the Union could afford to fight a struggle of attrition and the Confederacy simply could not. There was a point when Lee might have broken the Army of the Potomac and perhaps even taken the Federal capital of Washington, but that moment had now passed. The odds against the Confederacy were growing ever longer, especially with a victory to shore up Lincoln's bid for re-election.

Gettysburg was, therefore, the point at which the Confederacy lost its best chance to win to war, and from then onwards it was on the road to defeat.

In one of the few photographs taken during the dedication of the Gettysburg National Cemetery on 19 November 1863, President Abraham Lincoln is barely visible seated at the left on the crowded speakers' platform. Lincoln's Gettysburg Address, consisting of slightly more than 200 words, remains one of the principal documents of American freedom.

SEDAN
1 SEPTEMBER 1870

CHANCELLOR OF THE NORTH GERMAN CONFEDERATION, COUNT OTTO VON BISMARCK USED THE SPANISH SUCCESSION CRISIS IN EARLY 1870 TO PROVOKE A WAR AGAINST FRANCE RULED BY NAPOLEON III, WHO WAS FORCED AGAINST HIS BETTER JUDGMENT TO DECLARE WAR ON PRUSSIA ON 15 JULY 1870.

WHY DID IT HAPPEN?

WHO French Army of Châlons under Napoleon III (1803–73) and Marshal Patrice MacMahon (1808–93) versus Prussian Third Army and Army of the Meuse under General Helmuth von Moltke (1800–91).

WHAT The superior Prusso-German armies brilliantly led by master strategist Moltke manoeuvred to trap, encircle and annihilate MacMahon's army. Superior Prussian artillery played a key role in securing a Prusso-German victory.

WHERE Sedan, France, near the Franco-Belgian border.

WHEN 1 September 1870.

WHY Bismarck sought to crush France, which was suspicious of a united Germany under Prussian control; victory at Sedan helped realize this political ambition.

OUTCOME Sedan led to the collapse of the Second Napoleonic Empire of France (1850–70). The war continued until early 1871 and ended with a draconian peace that left France a vanquished, but vengeful, enemy.

The Franco-Prussian War of 1870–71 is something of a forgotten war. Yet the conflict, which saw the French defeated under humiliating circumstances, would leave deep scars and contribute to the outbreak of the Great War in August 1914. Ultimately the war, engineered by Bismarck (1815–98), was about power and the chancellor's ruthless ambition that Germany should be united under Prussian control. Only by defeating France and eliminating that country's obvious opposition to a unified Germany could Bismarck realize his dream.

Bismarck therefore pushed a cousin of King William I (1797–1888) of Prussia to seek the Spanish throne, and France, unable either to accept a Hohenzollern as king of Spain or to persuade Berlin to retract the candidacy, declared war on Prussia on 15 July 1870.

Officially France was branded the aggressor; in reality, it was the other way around – in the infamous Ems Dispatch, Bismarck manipulated the Prussian reply to France's request for a withdrawal of the candidacy in a way certain to provoke the proud and prickly French into fury.

As matters now stood, in late July, the politically divided and weak France, ruled by an ailing emperor and lacking allies or even friends, faced a stronger, better-equipped German enemy, champing at the bit to fight and with a ruthless political and

A Hessian infantry regiment stands firm to prevent the breakthrough of the French Chasseurs d'Afrique cavalry, battle of Sedan. This painting is based on an original by Professor Georg Koch.

military leadership. The omens for France and for Europe were dire.

WAR PREPARATIONS

Caught unawares with its best troops in Algeria, the vaunted Imperial French Army was in no fit state to fight the Prussians. The French had rested upon their laurels since the Crimean War (1853–56) and made too much of their Napoleonic legacy; they had grown complacent while their hereditary enemies to the east sharpened their swords. The army had no reserves to speak of, and the supply, support and engineering services were in a poor state. Furthermore, it was armed with obsolete artillery and muskets, and relied upon outdated notions of élan and frontal attack. A mere 220,000 French frontline troops were strung out along the Rhine and German frontier in an almost slapdash manner and lacking direction. The question of whether to remain on the defensive or attack remained unresolved, and the French generals did not even have good maps of the frontier region.

If chaos and indecision reigned in France, the same was not true on the other side of the border. In 1866, the Austrians had almost defeated the Prussians at Sadowa with their modern artillery. Four years later, the French were still equipped with light smooth-bore muzzle-loaded artillery, while the Prussians had equipped themselves with the finest artillery in the world. The Krupp-manufactured 6-pounders, for field service, and 24-pounders were superior in all meaningful ways to the French 4- and 12-pounders. With their better rifling, breech-loading mechanism and percussion-detonated shells, the Krupp guns were three times as accurate, had twice the rate of fire, a third longer range and many times the destructiveness of the French guns.

In addition, troops in the Prussian Army were issued with breech-loading rifles; their commanders were professional and dedicated to their 'art'; their NCOs were numerous; and the men themselves, besides being well armed and supplied, were battle-hardened and experienced. Morale – after the victories over Denmark and Austria in 1864 and 1866 respectively – was at a peak. France was the hereditary enemy and the Germans itched to give the French a bloody nose. The 380,000 German troops (mainly Prussians but also Saxons and Bavarians) were divided into three armies – the First Army (60,000) at Mosel, the Second Army (190,000) around Mainz and the Third Army (130,000) on the Rhine.

MOLTKE'S MOUSETRAP

The fighting got under way at the beginning of August with minor early actions at Saarbrücken and Weissenburg before the Germans defeated the French at Wörth on 6 August, the battle costing the French 11,000 dead and 9000 men taken prisoner. The cost for the Germans was 10,000 – an expensive victory. What shocked the French most was the accuracy and rate of fire of the German artillery. French attacks were literally torn to shreds by the breech-loading guns, not to mention accurate rifle fire. News of this unexpected defeat left Paris in a state of denial.

Napoleon III divided his frontline armies into two – the Army of Châlons under Marshal Patrice MacMahon and the Army of the Rhine under Marshal François Achille Bazaine (1811–88). It was to no avail. Moltke defeated Bazaine at Gravelotte and sealed his army of 180,000 men inside a

LOCATION

Sedan lies in the strategically crucial northeastern French region of the Ardennes close to both the Belgian and German borders.

PRUSSIAN FIELD GUN C64 (8CM)

Prussia had already begun manufacturing steel-barrelled rifled breech-loaders in the 1850s and the Prussians were fully equipped with these artillery pieces model C64s from 1867. In 1870, her allies were similarly equipped. The strong new barrels allowed for a longer range and stronger charges to be used by the field artillery. In general use was the 4 pounder C64 with a 77 (3.03in) or 80mm (3.15in) calibre, and in 1867 a new breech-block was introduced, given the designation C64/67. The gun was very effective within 900m (981 yards) and had shells with reliable percussion fuses. Shrapnel was also being used with range of 2.2km (1.36 miles) with deadly effect.

This colour chromolithography from the late nineteenth century shows French cavalry attacking German infantry (formed up on the right) at the battle of Sedan, 1 September 1870. French cavalry did launch some desperate attacks during the battle, and suffered heavy casualties as a result.

pocket, or cauldron (*Kessel* in German), around Metz.

Paris – or rather, Empress Eugénie (1826–1920) – responded by ordering MacMahon to relieve Bazaine. What he should have done was to retreat westwards, trading space for time and weakening the advancing Germans while gaining numerical strength. This 'offensive' towards Metz was soon mired in mud, with rain and grumbling, plundering troops. Hoping to gain time to re-form his army, MacMahon moved to the small frontier town of Sedan, 145km (90 miles) from Metz.

MacMahon could not have chosen a worse spot for a battle from a French point

of view. Sedan was in a sunken valley where the Meuse made a loop before turning north; the area to the north was wooded, rough terrain, and to the east lay the brook of Givonne, with a series of hamlets, orchards and fields blocking the field of fire. It was the perfect spot for the French Army to be trapped against the rapidly manoeuvring and advancing Germans and the nearby Belgian frontier.

When told the news by a courier, Moltke could not believe his luck. Without much effort on his part, the French marched right into the cauldron, where he would simply wipe them out. He told his staff, 'We have them in a mousetrap! We attack at dawn!'

THE BATTLE BEGINS

A thick white mist shrouded the valley around Sedan at 0400 on 1 September as General Ludwig von der Tann's (1815–81) Bavarians advanced across the Meuse bridges. This sector was held by the French XII Corps under General Barthélémy Lebrun (1809–89), who had been up all night waiting for the inevitable German assault. There were no French pickets, so the Bavarians captured a few houses and the main street of the village of Bazeilles without a single disturbance. Even so, they were headed for the toughest soldiers on the French side – the *Infanterie de Marine*, or Marine Infantry. These elite troops had erected barricades and taken up positions in the village's remaining houses, intending to fight for each street and building. The Marines' gallant defence of Bazeilles rescued France's military reputation from being completely tarnished that day.

Two hours later, the mist had lifted and the Bavarian artillery opened fire from the far side of the Meuse in support of the three brigades and the XII Saxon Corps, which now began a bloody fight for Bazeilles. Lebrun was, like his men, astonished at the range, rate of fire and accuracy of the German breech-loading artillery. The fighting for the village raged around the church, marketplace and Montvilliers Park for hours with unabated ferocity, forcing von der Tann to call up reserves. By contrast, the village of La Moncelle fell to the XII Saxon Corps after it had been strewn with artillery shot from the Saxon batteries. Lebrun came to call this

The loser of Sedan: Field Marshal Patrice MacMahon (1808–1893) went on to become President of the Third Republic of France between 1875 and 1879.

THE OPPOSED FORCES

PRUSSO-GERMAN ARMY

Troops	250,000
Artillery pieces	500

IMPERIAL FRENCH ARMY

Troops	100–120,000
Artillery pieces	420

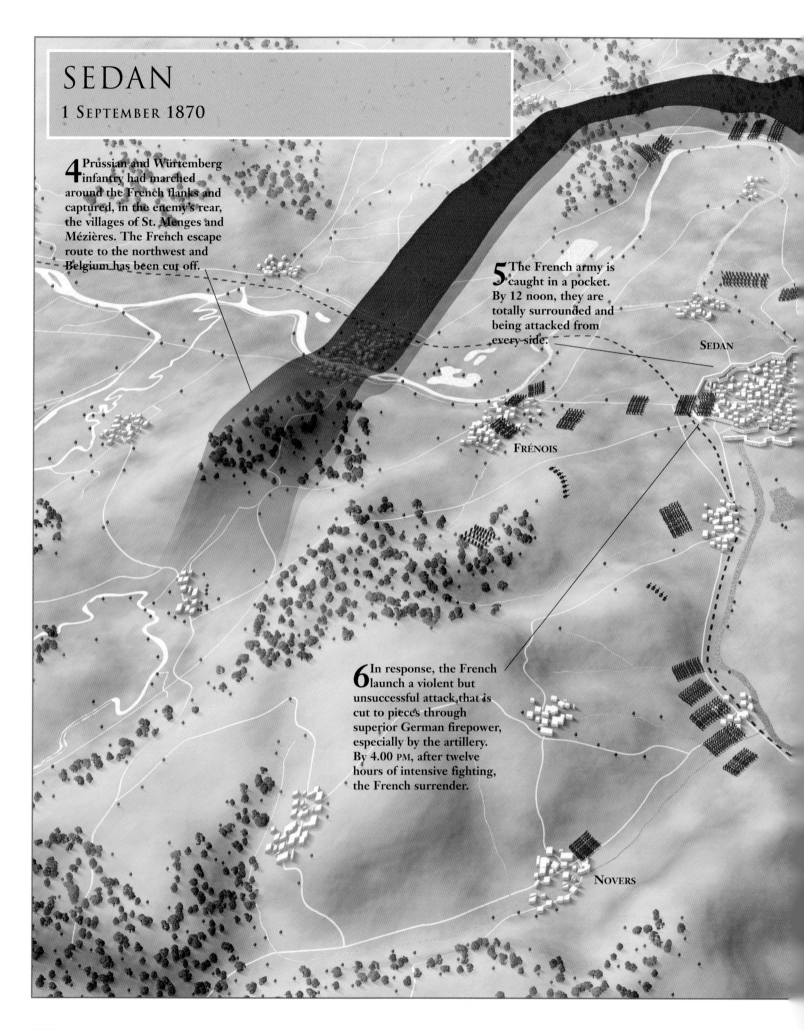

SEDAN

1 SEPTEMBER 1870

4 Prussian and Würtemberg infantry had marched around the French flanks and captured, in the enemy's rear, the villages of St. Menges and Mézières. The French escape route to the northwest and Belgium has been cut off.

5 The French army is caught in a pocket. By 12 noon, they are totally surrounded and being attacked from every side.

SEDAN

FRÉNOIS

6 In response, the French launch a violent but unsuccessful attack that is cut to pieces through superior German firepower, especially by the artillery. By 4.00 PM, after twelve hours of intensive fighting, the French surrender.

NOVERS

3 At 09.00 AM, the French counterattack along the Givonne River led by North African Zouaves. The French attack is cut to pieces by the German artillery with the C64 guns.

ST. MENGES

GIVONNE

VILLERS CERNAY

BAZEILLES

2 As the fog lifts, the Bavarian artillery open fire as their German allies, the XII Saxon Corps, attacks Bazeilles.

1 The Bavarians engage the elite *Infanterie de Marine* in the village of Bazeilles on the Meuse at the crack of dawn.

RIVER MEUSE

DOUZY

The French infantryman's uniform of baggy trousers, knee-length coat and characteristic kepi remained unchanged, with the exception of the rifle, until 1914.

unremitting German bombardment '*avalanche de fer*' (avalanche of iron), and it almost killed him and his entire staff.

Lebrun was fortunate. Not so MacMahon, who was hit at around 05.00 by a German shell fragment. This forced him to relinquish his command to General Auguste-Alexandre Ducrot (1817–82), commanding I Corps, who now gave the order to retreat. Had this order been issued earlier in the morning, MacMahon's army might have been saved, but now there was

no choice but to fight to the bitter end. General Emmanuel Félix de Wimpffen (1811–84), who had been given secret orders to take over if MacMahon was incapacitated, now did so – and immediately countermanded Ducrot's order to retreat. These changes of order inevitably enfeebled the French defence of the Givonne Line, leaving it vulnerable to a full-scale German attack.

THE BATTLE SPREADS

By 0900, the fighting had spread up the Givonne as the Royal Prussian Guards began to advance just as the French decided to do so as well. Ducrot's I Corps and Lebrun's XII Corps launched an attack with all the dash and élan that only the French seemed able to muster. The offensive was soon pushing back the hard-pressed Saxons, who buckled and reeled under the onslaught. But with the Saxons reinforced by the Prussians and Bavarians, especially the deadly *avalanche de fer*, French resolve collapsed under the withering fire. One unit of Zouaves fled into Belgium. The combination of 96 German guns and Bavarian and Saxon infantry broke the French.

Soldiers from the 3rd Westphalian Infantry Regiment advance in line, armed with their distinctive 1857 'needle carbines'. The pioneering breech-loading bolt action system of the needle carbine offered a much faster rate of fire than the old muzzle-loading muskets, giving the Prussian infantry a distinct advantage over their enemies.

At Bazeilles, the Marine Infantry not only held but also gained ground. But when the Saxons cut their way through Montvilliers Park with billhooks, and fresh Bavarian troops attacked, this proved too much even for the Marines. Their stronghold, a villa in the northern part of the village, was broken into by the Bavarians, driving them out. Meanwhile, the Prussian Guards had pushed the French out of their remaining villages along the Givonne, forcing them to set up a new line west of the small river. At 09.00, there were six Prussian Guards batteries firing at the French; just two hours later, no fewer than 14 batteries were firing away – with deadly effect.

FLANK ATTACK

While the main German army set out to tie up the French along the Givonne, with Wimpffen swallowing the bait whole, Moltke had sent Crown Prince Frederick (1831–88) with the Württemberg Division and two Prussian corps to intercept the French and prevent their escape west via Mézières. At 07.30, this force crossed the Meuse while the battle for Givonne was

raging to the northeast. At this point, they received orders from Moltke for V and XI Corps to march on St Menges and thereby trap the French completely. French scouts failed yet again to notice the advancing enemy, who took St Menges by surprise. The French cavalry launched a dashing but doomed attack that was cut to pieces by a renewed *avalanche de fer* from 24 German batteries (some 114 guns). Having toppled the German skirmishers, French horses and men fell in a bloody heap well before they reached the German main line.

THE TRAP IS CLOSED

By midday, the Germans had effectively won the battle. They held both banks of the Givonne plus the villages of Balan, Bazeilles and Illy, while Sedan was cut off. The French were now caught inside Moltke's 'mousetrap'. Facing a total of 71 artillery batteries, they had no hope of escape. The German guns opened up, silencing the French artillery despite their best efforts to answer the enemy's deadly and accurate fire.

Cornered, the French lashed out. General Jean-Auguste Margueritte (1823–1870) launched a cavalry attack so

This contemporary illustration showing French troops surrounded by Prussian forces represents in figurative terms how the French army became trapped and slowly annihilated by the Prussian rifle and artillery fire at the battle of Sedan.

SEDAN

In this painting by Paul Louis Narcisse Grolleron (1848–1901), French Zouave infantry defend a damaged farm house under pressure from Prussian troops. They are armed with the distinctive Chassepot rifle.

By 16.00, the French attack had spent itself, and German corps were converging from all directions on Sedan. Napoleon III now in turn overrode Wimpffen – it was obvious that the bloody and increasingly pointless slaughter had to end. A white flag was hoisted.

There were parleys, and the returning German staff officers told Moltke, Bismarck and King William that among the French was Emperor Napoleon III himself. They were thunderstruck. The following morning, 2 September, Bismarck and Napoleon III met alone along the road to

ferocious and desperate that it carried all before it – the Chasseurs d'Afrique light horse rode down the Prussian infantry and almost captured a battery, but after half an hour they, including their commander, lay scattered on the battlefield, dead and dying. By 14.00, the cavalry had retired – less than half of it survived – and Napoleon III, who was with his army at Sedan, ordered the white flag raised. Wimpffen, as was his prerogative, overrode his emperor's command. With the Germans advancing from all sides, the French fought on with the determination of the damned, especially in the east.

Wimpffen belatedly adopted Ducrot's idea. He massed what remained of his army for an assault against Balan and an attempt at a breakout towards Carignan and the west. The French attacked with such fury that the Germans were stunned and almost overwhelmed, but their discipline, their steady rifle fire in massed columns and, above all, their artillery stemmed the tide of men and horses.

the German field HQ. The French surrendered 104,000 troops, 6000 horses and 419 artillery pieces.

AFTERMATH

Napoleon III chose to share his army's captivity in Germany. On 4 September, the Third Republic was proclaimed in France, and continued the struggle against Prussia and its allies despite dwindling hopes of victory. The Germans advanced, laying siege to Paris, and under the Treaty of Frankfurt of May 1871 forced a humiliated France to cede Alsace–Lorraine and to pay the new German Empire (declared at Versailles on 18 January) five billion francs in indemnity. It is little wonder that this 'peace', imposed on France despite Bismarck's objections, was a contributory factor to the outbreak of World War I (1914–18) two generations later.

The mobility of the Prussian artillery arm and the superior accuracy and rate of fire of the breech-loading guns proved decisive in the victory at Sedan, and was to announce the dominance of artillery in the wars of the early and middle parts of the twentieth century.

In this chalk lithograph by W. Loeillot depicting the events of 2nd September 1870, Napoleon III (left) is shown handing over his rapier to German Emperor William I (centre) as a sign of capitulation. Otto von Bismarck is third from right.

TSUSHIMA
27–29 MAY 1905

THE ANNIHILATION OF THE RUSSIAN FLEET AT THE BATTLE OF TSUSHIMA REALIZED JAPAN'S ASPIRATIONS TO BE BOTH THE DOMINANT POWER IN THE KOREAN-MANCHURIAN AREA AND ONE OF THE TWO KEY NAVAL POWERS IN THE PACIFIC OCEAN.

WHY DID IT HAPPEN?

WHO The Imperial Japanese Navy's Combined Fleet, under Vice Admiral Heihachiro Togo (1848–1934), engaged the Imperial Russian Navy's Second and Third Pacific Squadrons, commanded by Admiral Zinovy Rozhestvensky (1848–1909).

WHAT The largest and most intense naval fleet engagement since the Battle of Trafalgar (1805), and which was not eclipsed until the Battle of Jutland (1916).

WHERE The battle took place in the narrow passage of the Straits of Tsushima, located between the southern Korean coast and the northwestern coast of Japan.

WHEN 27–29 May 1905.

WHY Russia had sent a fleet from the Baltic Sea to shore up its position in Korea and Manchuria during its conflict with Japan – termed the Russo-Japanese War – which was waged to secure dominance in this part of southeast Asia.

OUTCOME A stunning victory for the Imperial Japanese Navy that saw the obliteration of the Russian Fleet and led directly to a negotiated peace that ceded Russian influence in the region to Japan.

The origins of the 1904–05 Russo-Japanese War lay in the rivalry that emerged over the preceding decade, as both nations attempted to expand their influence over the Korean peninsula and Manchuria at the expense of a weak and internally volatile China. Japan eventually decided that further Russian expansionism into Korea was intolerable and so, on 8 February 1904, the Imperial Japanese Navy launched a surprise attack on Port Harbour, Dalny and Chemulpo, the three naval bases in Korea leased by Russia from China. The Japanese needed to remove the threat posed by the Russian Navy's Pacific Fleet, based at Vladivostok, as well as the three bases in Korea, so that a Japanese amphibious landing on Korea could take place. Having secured Korea, Japanese ground forces were to then expel Russian forces from Manchuria.

Vice Admiral Heihachiro Togo (1848–1934) commanded The Imperial Japanese Navy's Combined Fleet at the Battle of Tsushima. He was an effective and ruthless leader, and this battle was the crowning glory of his long naval career.

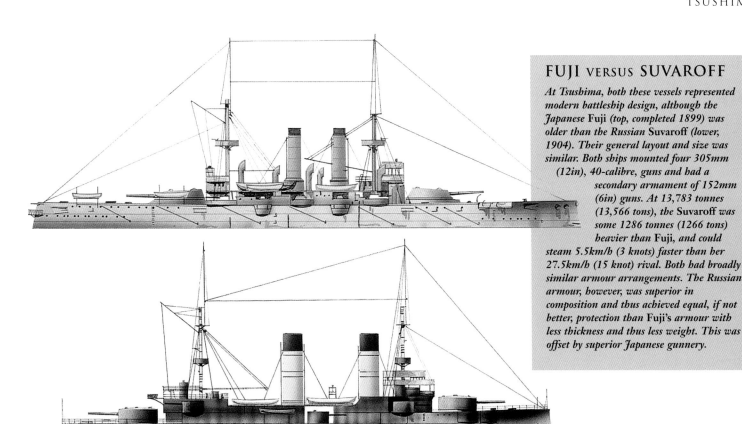

FUJI VERSUS SUVAROFF

At Tsushima, both these vessels represented modern battleship design, although the Japanese Fuji (top, completed 1899) was older than the Russian Suvaroff (lower, 1904). Their general layout and size was similar. Both ships mounted four 305mm (12in), 40-calibre, guns and had a secondary armament of 152mm (6in) guns. At 13,783 tonnes (13,566 tons), the Suvaroff was some 1286 tonnes (1266 tons) heavier than Fuji, and could steam 5.5km/h (3 knots) faster than her 27.5km/h (15 knot) rival. Both had broadly similar armour arrangements. The Russian armour, however, was superior in composition and thus achieved equal, if not better, protection than Fuji's armour with less thickness and thus less weight. This was offset by superior Japanese gunnery.

While the naval attacks sunk fewer Russian warships than had been hoped, it did create some room for Japanese ground forces to land on Korean soil. Over the next eight months, bitter naval and ground campaigns ensued between Japanese and Russian forces, which left the latter forced back towards Mukden in Manchuria and into the isolated enclave of Port Arthur.

LONG VOYAGE TO BATTLE

During early autumn 1904, the Russian Czar, Nicholas II, ordered much of his navy's Baltic Sea Fleet to undertake the staggering 28,800km (18,000 mile) journey round the world to Port Arthur. The Russian plan was to break the blockade of Port Arthur and wrest back control of the seas in the theatre, thus buying time for Russian ground troop reinforcements to arrive via the Trans-Siberian Railway. The naval force dispatched – now known as the Second Pacific Squadron – was led by Admiral Rozhestvensky (1848–1909), a 56-year-old career sailor well-known for his taciturn leadership. The 33 vessels of the Second Pacific Squadron, organized into five divisions, left Russian waters on 15 October 1904. These five divisions included two of capital ships and one each of cruisers, auxiliaries and destroyers.

The first division comprised the four modern battleships, *Kniaz Suvaroff*, *Imperator Aleksandr III*, *Borodino*, and *Orel* (all completed during 1904). The second (capital-ship) division comprised three battleships – the modern *Oslyabya* (1901), as well as the old and technologically backward *Sissoi Veliki* (1897) and *Navarin* (1895) – together with the even older armoured cruiser *Nakhimov* (1888). In the third (cruiser) division came the three cruisers *Oleg*, *Aurora*, and *Svietlana*, and the three light cruisers *Zemchug*, *Izumrud*, and *Almaz*. The remaining two divisions were made up of seven auxiliary vessels, nine destroyers and two hospital ships.

To his credit, Rozhestvensky had persuaded the Russian Naval High Command not to dispatch the Baltic Fleet's Second Division (subsequently termed the Third Pacific Squadron), which comprised six old and slow semi-obsolescent vessels: the old 9144 tonne (9000 ton) battleship *Imperator Nikolai I* (1890), the ancient 6096 tonne (6000 ton) armoured cruisers *Vladimir Monomakh* (1885) and *Dimitri Donskoï* (1883), and the three coastal defence ships *General Admiral Graf Apraxin* (1900), *Admiral Seniavin* (1896), and *Admiral Ushavov* (1896).

For the Russian fleet, simply getting to the Korean theatre was an enormous

LOCATION

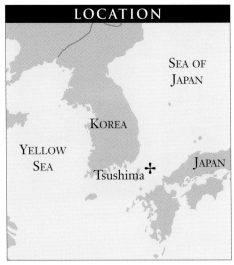

The narrow waters of the Straights of Tsushima separated the southern coast of Korea from the northwestern coast of Japan, and was divided into a 'western' and 'eastern' channel by the small island of Tsushima.

Night battle: this contemporary print depicts the intense battle that raged throughout most of the night 27/28 May, when Japanese destroyers and torpedo boats engaged at close range the battered remnants of the Russian fleet.

undertaking. The long, tedious, journey found several vessels beset with engine problems, while most of the ships, dangerously over-laden, struggled in heavy seas and could manage only 22km/h (12 knots) at best. The journey also involved multiple recoalings at sea from a fleet of 70 chartered colliers, as well as a minor 'engagement' with British trawlers in the North Sea, which the nervous Russians mistook for Japanese attack craft.

After the fleet had reached Madagascar in January 1905, it heard the demoralizing news that the Russian Fleet at Port Arthur had been destroyed and the port captured, leaving a solitary Russian armoured cruiser intact at Vladivostok. The fleet's mission now became to take on and destroy the Japanese Fleet without assistance from other Russian squadrons. At this time, Rozhestvensky also learned that the obsolescent ships of Rear Admiral Nebogatoff's Third Pacific Squadron, which he had previously rejected, were now on their way to join his fleet.

RUSSIANS REACH FULL STRENGTH

On 16 March, the fleet left Madagascar, before the Third Pacific Squadron had linked up with it but after reaching French Indo-China, the two Russian squadrons joined up and the combined fleet of 38 vessels proceeded into the South China Sea. Here they headed for the narrow passage between Korea and Japan called the Straits of Tsushima – a choice of route that made a climactic encounter with the Japanese Fleet inevitable.

On the night of 26/27 May, the Russian fleet entered the Straits, expecting that they would encounter the Japanese Fleet the next day. Before dawn, the Japanese auxiliary cruiser *Shinano Maru* spotted the Russian Fleet through the mist and alerted the Japanese Fleet. At 0505 the Japanese Fleet left the ports of Masampo, on the southeastern Korean coast, and Takeshii on Tsushima Island. That morning, some of the 16 available Japanese cruisers shadowed the Russian Fleet as it headed east-northeast at 15km/h (8 knots) through the 'eastern channel', the passage between Tsushima Island and the Japanese coast. The Russians had abandoned a single line formation in favour of line abreast, but the manoeuvre had not been completed successfully and the fleet was now in two, uneven, parallel columns.

THE FLEETS ENGAGE

At 1339 on 27 May, the main Japanese Fleet heading southwest at 26km/h (14 knots) spotted the Russian fleet, then heading northeast at 16.5km/h (9 knots), 11km (7 miles) to the south-southwest. The main Japanese Fleet comprised 12 ships – four battleships and eight armoured cruisers in single line abreast, supported by 16 cruisers, and 21 destroyers; the heavy seas kept the 44 Japanese torpedo boats back near the Korean coast.

The Japanese capital ships were all modern and remarkably homogenous in their design and technology. At the van came Togo's Flagship, the 15,443 tonne (15,200 ton) battleship *Mikasa* (completed

THE OPPOSED FORCES

IMPERIAL JAPANESE NAVY'S COMBINED FLEET

Battleships	4
Armoured Cruisers	8
Cruisers and Light Cruisers	16
Destroyers	21
Torpedo Boats	44
Auxiliary Vessels	10
Total:	**103**

IMPERIAL RUSSIAN NAVY'S SECOND AND THIRD PACIFIC SQUADRONS

Battleships	8
Coastal Defence Ships	3
Armoured Cruisers	3
Cruisers and Light Cruisers	6
Destroyers	9
Auxiliary Vessels	7
Hospital Ships	2
Total:	**38**

1902), followed by the three battleships *Shikishima* (1900), *Fuji* (1899) and *Asahi* (1901), then the eight armoured cruisers *Kasuga*, *Nisshin*, *Idzumo*, *Azuma*, *Tokiwa*, *Yakumo*, *Asama* and *Iwate*, all of which were completed between 1900 and 1904. At 13:55, echoing Admiral Nelson's famous signal at Trafalgar, Togo sent to his fleet the following message: 'The Empire's fate depends on the result of this battle, let every man do his utmost duty.'

By 14:15, the Japanese main fleet, having executed complex manoeuvres, was sailing northeast on a course now parallel with the Russian fleet, which was still in a partially disorganized two-column formation. Both sides had by now opened fire, with the Japanese concentrating their fire against the *Suvaroff* and *Oslyabya*. Over the next 45 minutes, both sides scored successes. The *Asama* pulled out of the line with disabled steering gear; meanwhile, at 14:43, the *Suvaroff* lurched out of control from the Russian line while the *Oslyabya*, virtually stationery and burning fiercely, finally sank at 1505, taking 515 Russian sailors with her. By 16:00, after successfully out-manoeuvring the Russian fleet's attempts to pass across their rear, the Japanese fleet continued to pour fire into the enemy, which was disintegrating into isolated groups of vessels. By 17:30, both fleets were heading northwards, and with Rozhestvensky now incapacitated, having been wounded for a third time, Rear Admiral Nebogatoff assumed command. He received what were Rozhestvensky's final orders before losing consciousness; that the fleet should endeavour to flee to the Russian port of Vladivostok, some 1040km (650 miles) to the north.

ADVANTAGE JAPAN

The two fleets now lost contact but at around 18:00, the Japanese Fleet, amid mist and smoke, again made contact with what remained of the Russian line. Within the hour, withering Japanese fire had sunk the already damaged *Aleksandr III* and *Borodino*; one shell from *Fuji* detonated the latter's magazines, causing her to capsize and sink. Just five men from these two ships' combined complement of 1660 crew survived these cataclysms. Shortly afterwards, Japanese torpedo boats sank the

Destruction of the fleet: this contemporary colour print evocatively depicts the carnage inflicted on the crew of a Russian capital ship during the battle. The Russian fleet suffered appalling casualties – no fewer than 4380 sailors were killed.

TSUSHIMA

27–29 MAY 1905

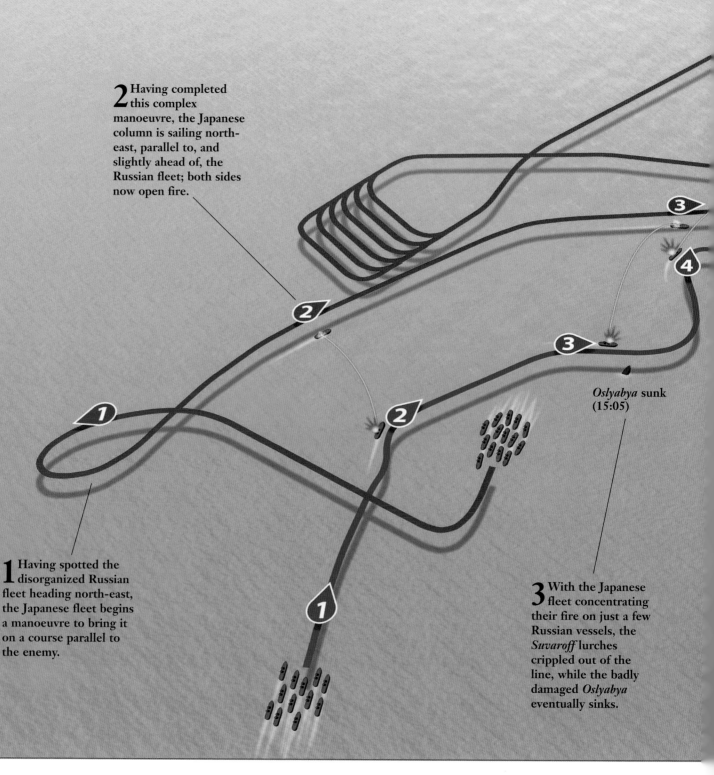

2 Having completed this complex manoeuvre, the Japanese column is sailing north-east, parallel to, and slightly ahead of, the Russian fleet; both sides now open fire.

Oslyabya sunk (15:05)

1 Having spotted the disorganized Russian fleet heading north-east, the Japanese fleet begins a manoeuvre to bring it on a course parallel to the enemy.

3 With the Japanese fleet concentrating their fire on just a few Russian vessels, the *Suvaroff* lurches crippled out of the line, while the badly damaged *Oslyabya* eventually sinks.

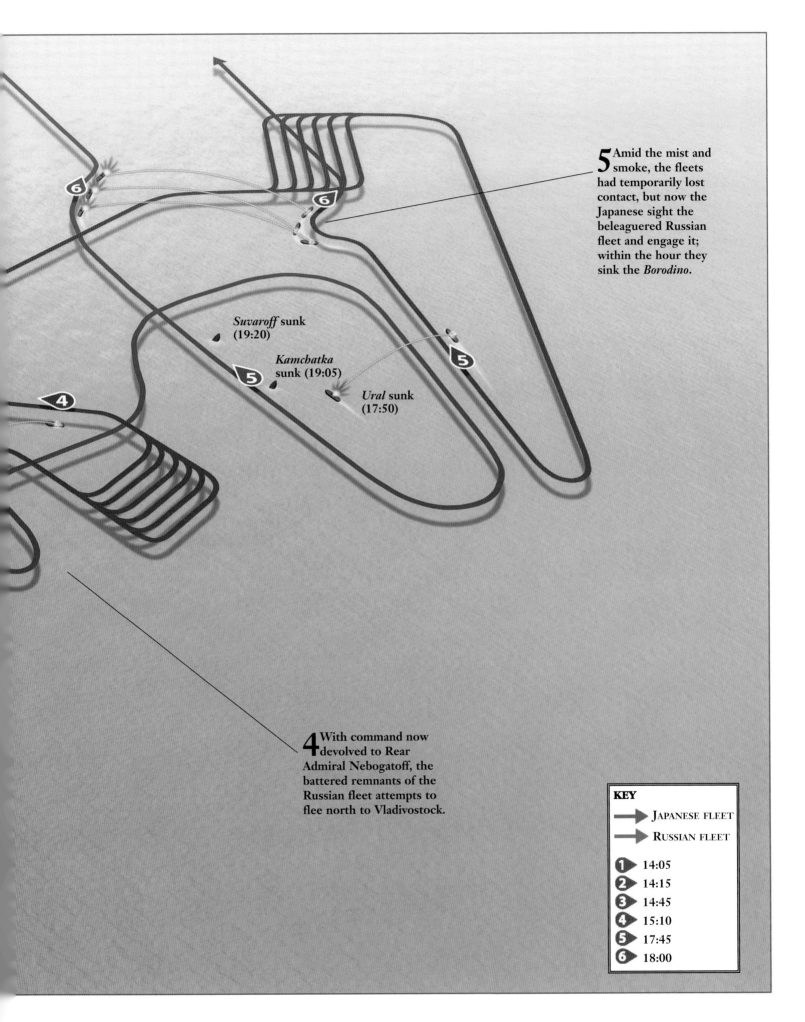

5 Amid the mist and smoke, the fleets had temporarily lost contact, but now the Japanese sight the beleaguered Russian fleet and engage it; within the hour they sink the *Borodino*.

Suvaroff sunk (19:20)

Kamchatka sunk (19:05)

Ural sunk (17:50)

4 With command now devolved to Rear Admiral Nebogatoff, the battered remnants of the Russian fleet attempts to flee north to Vladivostock.

KEY

→ JAPANESE FLEET

→ RUSSIAN FLEET

1 ▶ 14:05
2 ▶ 14:15
3 ▶ 14:45
4 ▶ 15:10
5 ▶ 17:45
6 ▶ 18:00

Russian cruiser Oleg *shown here after the battle, having interned herself in the neutral port of Manila in the Philippines. Some of the damage the vessel incurred during the battle is clearly visible in this photograph.*

crippled *Suvaroff*. As daylight faded, the day's battle had been a stunning Japanese success; for the cost of 144 successful Russian hits, 514 personnel casualties and no ships lost (although several were seriously damaged), Togo's vessels had sunk four of the five modern Russian battleships, and seriously damaged three other capital ships.

During that evening and night, 21 Japanese destroyers and 37 torpedo boats repeatedly attacked the ragged remnants of the Russian fleet as it headed north towards Vladivostok at 22km/h (12 knots), the maximum speed it could now obtain. These attacks, which achieved seven torpedo hits from a total of 100 delivered, sunk the old battleship *Navarin*, as well as crippling the outdated battleship *Sissoi Veliky* and the ancient armoured cruisers *Nakhimoff* and *Vladimir Monomakh*. The crippled ships all succumbed the next morning: *Sissoi Veliky* eventually foundered, while *Nakhimoff* and *Vladimir Monomakh* both scuttled themselves when the Japanese attempted to board them. Meanwhile, the squadron comprising the cruisers *Oleg*, *Aurora* and *Zemchug* had lost contact with the rest of the fleet and eventually headed to Shanghai; subsequently, they made for Manilla in the Philippines and there interned themselves.

THE END FOR THE RUSSIANS

At 09:30 on 28 May the Japanese Fleet, supported by three cruiser squadrons, made contact with the largest grouping of what remained of Nebogatoff's fleet. This comprised the badly damaged *Orel* (the sole remaining modern battleship), the old battleship *Nikolai I*, the ancient coastal defence ships *Apraxin* and *Seniavin*, plus the fast and modern light cruiser, *Izumrud*. The Japanese vessels surrounded and engaged this squadron, but at 10:34, Nebogatoff, realizing that further resistance was futile, surrendered four of his ships to Togo's forces. He ordered, however, the swift and relatively undamaged *Izumrud* to make a break for it. The light cruiser successfully threw off her pursuers and almost made it back to Vladivostok before running aground to become a complete wreck. That afternoon, the coastal defence ship *Ushavov*, which had been languishing behind the main Russian grouping, was set upon by the armoured cruisers *Iwate* and *Yakumo*. Around 1800, *Ushavov* sank, thus dispatching the sole remaining operational asset from the original Russian capital ship line of 12 vessels.

Elsewhere that day, Japanese cruisers, supported by destroyers, hunted down other Russian warships that had become detached from the main fleet. The badly damaged auxiliary cruiser *Irtysh* beached herself on Minoshima Island and off-loaded her crew into captivity, while at 1102 Japanese fire sunk the cruiser *Svietlana*. At 16:40, the destroyer carrying the still unconscious Rozhestvensky surrendered. That evening and night, moreover, the ancient armoured cruiser *Dimitrï Donskoï* heroically resisted the fire poured into her by six Japanese cruisers, plus repeated torpedo boat attacks, before being scuttled the next morning. Some vessels, however, escaped the relentless Japanese pursuit of the remnants of the Russian fleet enacted during 28/29 May. The cruiser *Almaz*, together with the destroyer *Bravy*, managed to evade the enemy hunt by hugging the coast, and eventually reached the sanctuary of Vladivostok, where they were joined by the destroyer *Grozny*. A British steamer also towed the almost immobile destroyer *Brody* into Shanghai, where she was interned. Subsequently the auxiliaries *Svir* and *Korea* were also interned at this port. Finally, the auxiliary transport *Anadyr* successfully made it to Madagascar, before subsequently making its way back to the Russian Baltic Sea port of Kronstadt.

The Battle of Tsushima, therefore, had been a stunning success for the Imperial Japanese Navy. For the loss of just three torpedo boats sunk, and 117 personnel killed and 583 wounded, the Imperial Japanese Navy had devastated the Russian Second and Third Pacific Squadron's. Russian personnel losses amounted to 4380 dead, 5917 captured and 1862 interned in neutral countries, together with an unknown number of wounded, which must have reached many thousands. In terms of Russian vessel losses, 20 ships (out of a total of 38) were lost; this included seven (out of eight) battleships, all three armoured cruisers, one (of three) coastal defence ships, two (of six) cruisers, and five (of seven) destroyers. In addition, the Japanese captured seven vessels, (including the battleship *Orel*) and a further six warships (including three cruisers) were interned in neutral ports. Just three vessels made it back to the sanctuary of the Russian port of Vladivostok – the light cruiser *Almaz* and two destroyers – while the auxiliary transport *Anadyr* managed to steam all the way back to the Baltic Sea.

JAPAN DOMINATES THE PACIFIC

The annihilation of the Russian Fleet at Tsushima gave the Japanese Fleet control of the seas in the Korean theatre of war. The loss of naval control was also the end of attempts by Russian ground forces to resist the Japanese advance into Manchuria; the former had already been decisively defeated at the Battle of Mukden during February–March 1905. Indeed, the scale of the debacle at Tsushima so stunned the Russian Czar and his ministers that they began peace negotiations. The Treaty of Portsmouth was signed on 5 September 1905. Russia ceded to Japan the southern half of Sakhalin Island, the ports of Port Arthur and Dairen, as well as railway rights in Manchuria; it also formally recognized Japan's predominant interest in Korea.

The Battle of Tsushima was one of the most decisive and one-sided naval encounters of the modern age. Japanese success owed much to superior leadership, the use of subordinate initiative, superior crew training and tactics, as well effective higher-tempo gunnery. It also represented the triumph of accurate long-range main armament fire concentrated by a number of vessels on one target; this led to the birth of a new type of super-battleship – the Dreadnought – with four or five main armament turrets instead of the two typical of pre-1905 battleships. The Japanese success established them as the dominant naval power in the Pacific, alongside the United States of America. The ensuing rivalry would ultimately lead to the spread of World War II to the Pacific.

Japanese vessels tow surrendered Russian warships: by the end of the battle, the Japanese had captured no fewer than four Russian capital ships, including the battleships Orel *and* Nikolai I, *as well as two coast defence vessels.*

VERDUN
21 FEBRUARY–18 DECEMBER 1916

THE TEN-MONTH GERMAN OFFENSIVE AGAINST THE HEAVILY DEFENDED FRENCH SALIENT AT VERDUN REPRESENTS, ALONG WITH THE BATTLE OF THE SOMME, ONE OF THE BLOODIEST AND MOST FUTILE OPERATIONS OF THE GREAT WAR.

WHY DID IT HAPPEN?

WHO The German Fifth Army engaged the French Second and Third Armies.

WHAT The Germans attempted to capture the strategically vital French city of Verdun, aiming to leave the defending French forces 'bled white', in the words of the Chief of the German General Staff.

WHERE Along the French-controlled salient that extended around the city of Verdun in the province of Lorraine in eastern France.

WHEN 21 Feb–18 Dec 1916.

WHY The Germans, by attacking towards the strategically vital city of Verdun, hoped to force the French to wage a protracted defensive battle during which the employment of massed German artillery power would lead to the defenders being 'bled white'; whether the Germans actually aimed to capture the city or not remains unclear.

OUTCOME A French defensive victory. After 10 months of intense conflict, the Germans had held onto only a proportion of their limited territorial gains made during the earlier phases of the offensive; had not captured Verdun; and had been decimated by their attack almost as much as the French had been by their defence.

The Battle of Verdun, waged between the German and French Armies for just under ten months during 1916, was one of the horrifying nadirs of the World War I. General Erich von Falkenhayn (1861–1922), Chief of the German General Staff, was the architect behind the German offensive. He planned to attack the French front line around the city of Verdun-sur-Meuse in northeastern France, a location of huge symbolic importance to the French. Falkenhayn expected the French to defend the Verdun salient fanatically, enabling the German forces to inflict a terrible, costly defeat on the defenders using massed artillery firepower. Falkenhayn subsequently claimed that he never intended to capture the city, simply to compel the French to wage a prolonged defensive battle in which the latter would be 'bled white' in the remorseless maul of industrial-scale attritional warfare. It is doubtful, however, that this was his real intent at the start of the offensive; this explanation is probably simply Falkenhayn's subsequent rationalization of what transpired during the battle. Certainly at the time, his subordinates, including Fifth Army Commander Crown Prince Wilhelm of Hohenzollern, believed that the offensive's objective was indeed to capture the city.

In early 1916, the French front line in northwestern Lorraine bulged towards the north and northeast into the German lines along the Verdun sector, creating a large salient that extended about 11km (7 mile) around the city. Consequently, Verdun was surrounded on three sides by the German front line, and this reduced the supply routes into the city from the rest of France to just a solitary main road (later known as *La Voie Sacrée*, the Sacred Way) and a single semi-operational railway line. Furthermore,

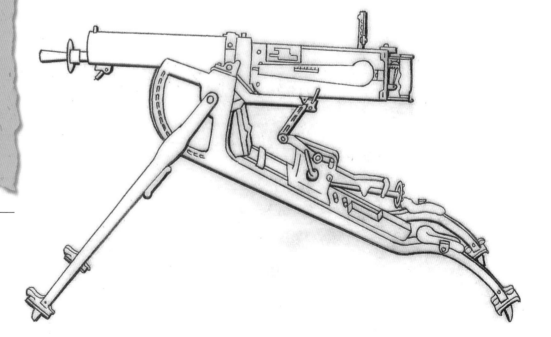

The German Maxim 08 machine-gun fired a devastating 600–700 rounds a minute, cutting a swathe through enemy infantry. Although heavy to manoeuvre, German infantry would drag the gun forwards with them when attacking because of the firepower it offered.

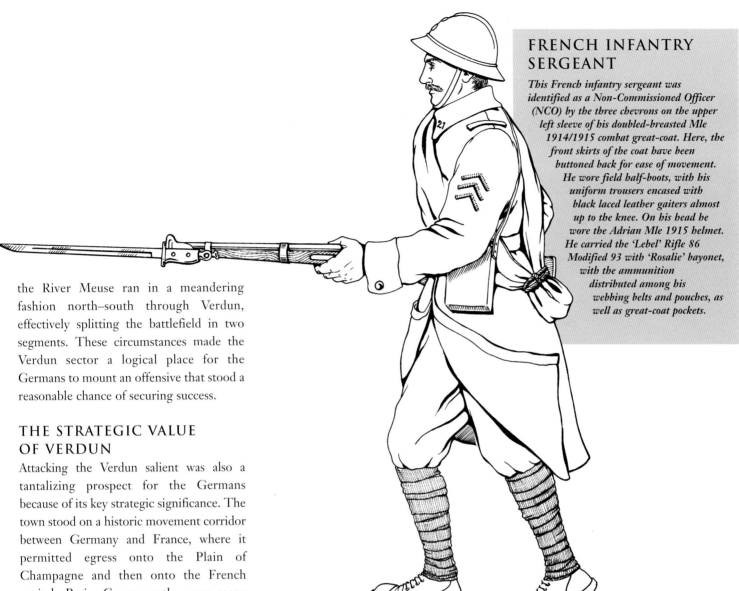

FRENCH INFANTRY SERGEANT

This French infantry sergeant was identified as a Non-Commissioned Officer (NCO) by the three chevrons on the upper left sleeve of his doubled-breasted Mle 1914/1915 combat great-coat. Here, the front skirts of the coat have been buttoned back for ease of movement. He wore field half-boots, with his uniform trousers encased with black laced leather gaiters almost up to the knee. On his head he wore the Adrian Mle 1915 helmet. He carried the 'Lebel' Rifle 86 Modified 93 with 'Rosalie' bayonet, with the ammunition distributed among his webbing belts and pouches, as well as great-coat pockets.

the River Meuse ran in a meandering fashion north–south through Verdun, effectively splitting the battlefield in two segments. These circumstances made the Verdun sector a logical place for the Germans to mount an offensive that stood a reasonable chance of securing success.

THE STRATEGIC VALUE OF VERDUN

Attacking the Verdun salient was also a tantalizing prospect for the Germans because of its key strategic significance. The town stood on a historic movement corridor between Germany and France, where it permitted egress onto the Plain of Champagne and then onto the French capital, Paris. Consequently, over many centuries, a wide variety of fortifications had been established around Verdun. By 1916, the French had established an outer ring of 18 powerful fortresses – sited on ground that dominated the area – to protect this key town, as well as a supporting ring of artillery batteries. The most famous of these fortresses were Fort Douaumont, Fort Souville and Fort Vaux, all of which covered the northeastern approaches to the city. Given the strategic importance, it was not surprising that the German High Command decided, on 24 December 1915, to launch an attack on the Verdun salient – codenamed Operation Judgement. The new offensive was slated to begin on 12 February 1916.

In the weeks prior to the start of the offensive, the Germans – with as much secrecy as possible – brought forward several dozen additional infantry battalions, as well as hundreds of supporting artillery pieces. While the local French commanders

detected this build-up, senior French commanders were slow in redeploying reinforcements to the sector because they did not think it rated highly in the enemy's offensive calculations. By 11 February, the German forces were ready to initiate the offensive. Bad weather, however, forced the Germans to postpone the attack for 10 days until 21 February. This delay would subsequently prove crucial; senior French commanders had belatedly concluded a German attack was imminent and the pause allowed the French enough time to redeploy two additional divisions to the Verdun sector. Nevertheless, at the start of the offensive, the Germans still significantly outnumbered the defenders. The German Fifth Army had assembled 72 battalions and 1300 artillery pieces, including some 860 heavy guns, designed to smash French fortifications.

LOCATION

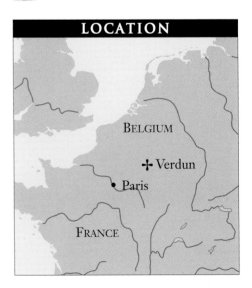

Verdun-sur-Meuse, in the northwestern part of the province of Lorraine, in northeastern France, blocked the classic German movement corridor from Germany to the Moselle Valley, then into the Champagne region and onto Paris.

French troops from the garrison of Fort Vaux relax during a quiet period of the battle. During June a bitter battle raged throughout the fort's underground corridors before what remained of the garrison surrendered.

THE OPPOSED FORCES

FRENCH ARMY (estimated)

Total:	180,000

IMPERIAL GERMAN ARMY
  (estimated)

Total:	220,000

However, just 34 battalions from the French Third Army, supported by only 300 guns, opposed them.

The German plan was to pulverize the defenders through the protracted use of massed artillery fire, which included 42cm (16.5in) guns, the heaviest pieces then in the German arsenal. The aim, therefore, was to pit a vast concentration of explosives against the willpower of the defending French troops. The defenders enjoyed only one key advantage – their extensive system of fortifications, although these were not as effective as they should have been. The forts were in a poor state of repair, had seen most of their heavy guns removed to other parts of the front, and their defending garrisons were seriously undermanned.

This lamentable state of affairs had arisen for two reasons. Firstly, the French Army was doctrinally wedded to the concept that the power of the offensive outweighed that of the defensive. Secondly, the Germans had, through the employment of their heaviest artillery pieces, easily overwhelmed the powerful Belgian forts back at the start of the Great war in August 1914, and so the French Army now placed little faith in such fortifications.

THE BATTLE STARTS

At 07:15 on 21 February, the German offensive commenced. Some 1300 guns delivered over one million shells during a nine-hour bombardment of the French positions along the Brabant-Ornes sector, located north of Verdun; at the time, this was the largest fire-plan ever enacted in the history of warfare. Late that afternoon, German infantry assaults commenced along much of this 16km (10 mile) sector of the front. While many of the defenders had been killed, wounded or stupefied by the devastating ordeal of the bombardment, enough remained capable of firing their weapons to make the Germans have to fight to move forwards.

The Verdun sector as a whole, however, still remained undermanned and this shortage of infantry reserves hampered the continuing French defence. Consequently, over the first 48 hours, the Germans made good progress, capturing the southern half of the Bois de Caures and the nearby village of Haumont. Over the ensuing three days, the German advance continued to progress south, so that by 25 February, the Germans had, in places, advanced as much as 8km (5 miles) from their start lines.

That day, moreover, the Germans achieved the spectacular success of easily capturing the key position of Fort Douaumont. This was a modern artillery fortress, protected by reinforced concrete that was up to 12m (39ft) thick. However, with many of its guns removed and garrisoned by just 30 men, it turned out to be a much less formidable objective than

VERDUN

the Germans had envisaged. Indeed, in a testimony to French incompetence, German forces managed to infiltrate the fortress and capture it without a single shot being fired. With this cornerstone of the French defensive system taken, Crown Prince Wilhelm now looked forward to a rapid German advance into Verdun itself.

After 25 February, however, the French High Command poured reinforcements – in the form of General Philippe Pétain's (1856–1951) Second Army – into the Verdun sector; Pétain's command then assumed control of the salient in place of the Third Army. The immediate local counterattacks undertaken by these forces slowed the German advance to a crawl and inflicted heavy casualties. For example, it took the Germans eight days to advance less than 1km (½ mile) from Fort Douaumont to the adjacent village of the same name. Pétain immediately decided to strongly garrison the perimeter fortresses as the principal bulwarks of the French defence. The general also initiated a system of round-the-clock traffic along *La Voie Sacrée* into Verdun, the sole route left for bringing supplies into the city.

These French efforts to exploit fully the few supply routes into Verdun played a key part in sustaining the combat power of the French forces defending the salient during the dark days of late February. The German Fifth Army attempted to batter its way through this reinvigorated French resistance, but the offensive soon ground to a halt. An increasing problem was that the German assaults now lacked adequate artillery support; many German guns simply found it impossible to move forward across sodden, cratered ground to get into a position where they were in range of the German spearheads.

With stalemate emerging across the front, Falkenhayn decided to kick-start his offensive by assaulting a different sector of the salient. So, from 6 March, German forces launched an offensive to the west of the River Meuse in the Forges-Haucourt sector, located northwest of Verdun. The preliminary artillery strike delivered a staggering four million shells onto the defenders; so many rounds fell on Point 304

that afterwards the hill was 4m (13ft) lower than it had been previously. The ensuing German assaults gradually advanced south until they had secured the line from Hill 304, east through Dead Man's Hill and onto the village of Champ.

By then, General Robert Nivelle (1856–1924) had replaced Pétain as commander of the Verdun sector, the later being promoted to command the Central Army Group, which controlled the entire front in northeastern France. Nivelle believed that the defence of the salient required an offensive element. Therefore, on 22 May, to the northeast of Verdun, the French mounted a counterattack to recapture Fort Douaumont. After a massive bombardment, three divisions attacked on a

General Robert Nivelle (1856–1924) assumed command of the Second Army in the Verdun sector on 1 May 1916, replacing General Philippe Pétain. Subsequently promoted to become Commander-in-Chief, Nivelle's reputation dwindled during 1917 after the failure of the 'Nivelle Offensive'.

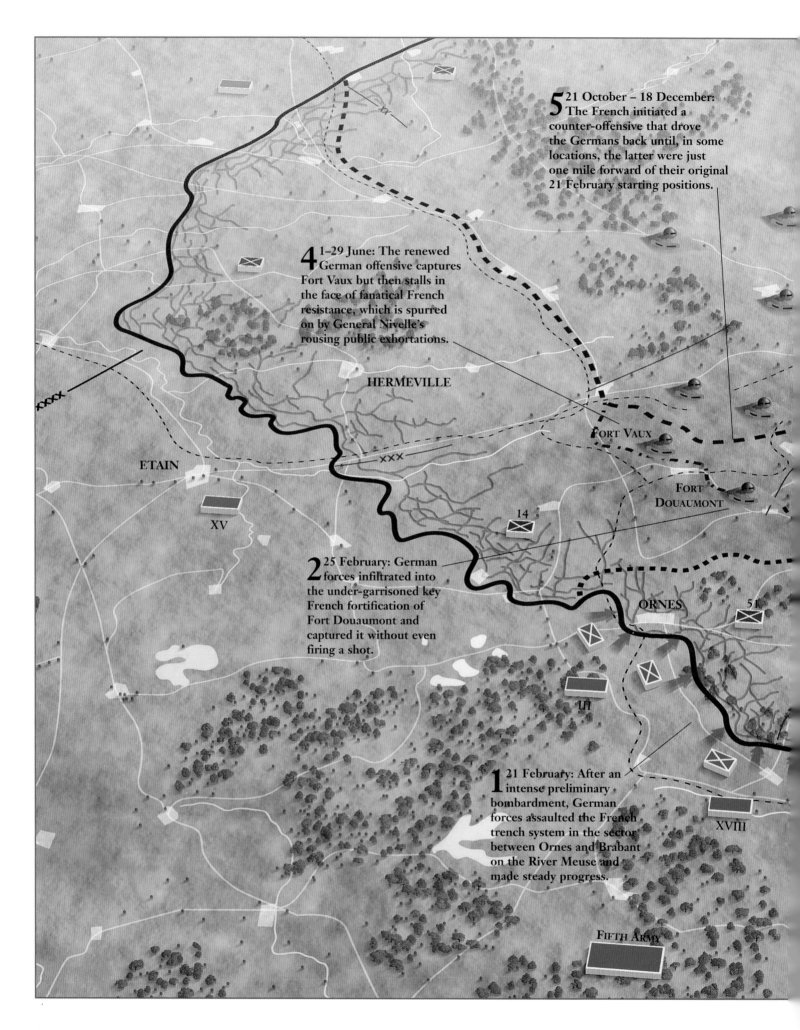

5 21 October – 18 December: The French initiated a counter-offensive that drove the Germans back until, in some locations, the latter were just one mile forward of their original 21 February starting positions.

4 1–29 June: The renewed German offensive captures Fort Vaux but then stalls in the face of fanatical French resistance, which is spurred on by General Nivelle's rousing public exhortations.

HERMEVILLE

FORT VAUX

ETAIN

FORT DOUAUMONT

XV

14

2 25 February: German forces infiltrated into the under-garrisoned key French fortification of Fort Douaumont and captured it without even firing a shot.

ORNES

51

III

1 21 February: After an intense preliminary bombardment, German forces assaulted the French trench system in the sector between Ornes and Brabant on the River Meuse and made steady progress.

XVIII

FIFTH ARMY

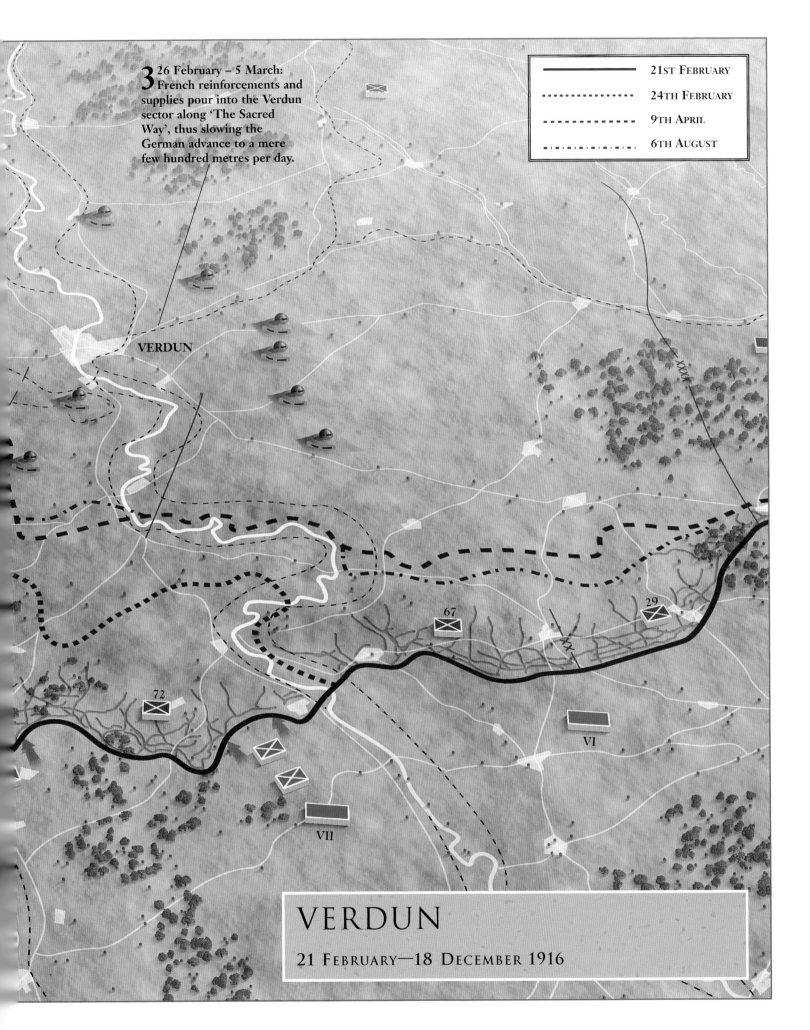

3 26 February – 5 March: French reinforcements and supplies pour into the Verdun sector along 'The Sacred Way', thus slowing the German advance to a mere few hundred metres per day.

————————————	21ST FEBRUARY
····················	24TH FEBRUARY
– – – – – – – –	9TH APRIL
·–·–·–·–·–·–·	6TH AUGUST

VERDUN

72

67

29

VI

VII

VERDUN

21 FEBRUARY—18 DECEMBER 1916

narrow frontage. For three days, the battle raged in and around the fortress before the French were compelled to withdraw and abandon the operation. With both sides exhausted, a short tactical pause emerged on this sector of the front.

ATTACK AND COUNTERATTACK

However, the lull was short-lived. On 1 June, the Germans resumed their offensive, striking southeast from Fort Douaumont to try to capture the strategic fortress of Fort Vaux. The Germans had attempted to capture this objective back in early March, but had been repulsed by fanatical French resistance. In this second attack, approximately 10,000 German assault troops engaged in six days of bitter fighting within the fortresses' underground

corridors before what remained of the French defending forces capitulated, having run out of water. The assaulting German forces then gradually fought their way southwest from Fort Vaux through the village of Fleury toward Fort Souville, positioned on dominant ground overlooking Verdun to the southwest. The Battle of Verdun had now reached a critical turning point – a fact conveyed by Nivelle on 23 June, when he exhorted his troops to even greater defensive tenacity by declaring that the Germans 'shall not pass'.

Intense German bombardments then rained 300,000 artillery shells, plus 60,000 phosgene gas rounds, onto Fort Souville, but the defenders nevertheless tenaciously defended the ruined structure. After days of bitter combat – and after temporarily securing the roof – the Germans failed to capture the fort and withdrew. With the Germans withdrawing a number of infantry battalions and many artillery pieces to support their defensive actions during the Battle of the Somme, which was raging to the northwest, the Verdun sector degenerated into stalemate. The Germans had also changed their command structure and Falkenhayn had been replaced as Chief of the General Staff by Field Marshal Paul von Hindenburg (1847–1934), ably assisted by his de facto deputy, Erich Ludendorff.

THE GERMANS ARE DRIVEN BACK

During October 1916, the French forces defending Verdun again resumed a counter-offensive across the 6.5km (4 mile) wide sector between the village of Bras and Fort Vaux, to the northeast of Verdun. These attacks were facilitated by innovative artillery support; in addition to the usual preliminary bombardment, French artillery laid down creeping barrages, which aimed to suppress enemy resistance while the attacking infantry closed to make contact with the enemy. By 24 October, the French assaults had recaptured Fort Douaumont, and by 2 November the Germans were compelled to abandon what remained of Fort Vaux. Within days, the German High Command had relieved Crown Prince Wilhelm of Hohenzollern (1882–1951) of

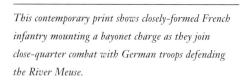

This contemporary print shows closely-formed French infantry mounting a bayonet charge as they join close-quarter combat with German troops defending the River Meuse.

his command of the Fifth Army and replaced him with General Max von Gallwitz (1852–1937).

Despite this change, continuing French attacks over the next six weeks slowly drove the Germans back north until, by 18 December, the French in places had closed to within 1.5km (1 mile) of the original February 1916 front line. However, with the French troops now exhausted, their supplies dwindling and winter fast approaching, the French counter-offensive petered out. The Battle of Verdun was over.

THE RESULT

During the course of this 10-month bloody attritional battle, around 260,000 military personnel died and a further 500,000 were wounded. It is estimated that the two sides expended a staggering total of 40 million artillery rounds during the battle. At the height of their success, the Germans had secured an advance south of no more than 11km (7 miles); subsequently, some of these gains were lost in the French counter-offensive mounted from October.

Indeed, in reality, the German offensive against Verdun had largely been a failure. The French Army had indeed been 'bled white', but then the same was true of the German Fifth Army – the German losses were about 85 percent of their enemy's. Crucially, the German offensive, despite pushing French resolve to breaking point, did not succeed in destroying French morale. Indeed, if the Battle of Verdun proved anything it was that the limits of human endurance could be stretched to a unbelievable degree without breaking. To many others, however, the Battle of Verdun simply epitomises the futility of modern industrialized warfare – where each square kilometre of territory permanently gained by the Germans had been bought at the truly terrible price of tens of thousands of combatant's lives.

During the first day of the offensive, assaulting French infantry seemingly shelter behind a shallow ridge in the terrain as enemy mortar round explodes close-by, showering the troops with earth and debris.

THE SOMME
1 JULY–18 NOVEMBER 1916

THE ALLIED SOMME OFFENSIVE REPRESENTS TO MANY THE FUTILITY OF ATTRITONAL INDUSTRIAL-SCALE WARFARE, WITH 615,000 CASUALTIES INCURRED FOR AN ADVANCE OF JUST 13KM (8 MILES). TO OTHERS, IT WAS A HARSH LESSON, NECESSARY FOR THE TACTICAL IMPROVEMENTS THAT LED TO ALLIED VICTORY IN 1918.

WHY DID IT HAPPEN?

WHO The British Fourth and Reserve/Fifth Armies, under Lieutenant-Generals Rawlinson (1864–1925) and Gough (1870–1963), together with the French Sixth Army under General Fayolle (1858–1928), engaged the German First and Second Armies commanded by General Fritz von Below (1853–1918) and General Max von Gallwitz (1852–1937).

WHAT A protracted Anglo-French offensive that raged for nearly five months in its attempt to break through German positions in the Somme sector.

WHERE The valley of the River Somme in northern France.

WHEN 1 July–18 December 1916.

WHY The Somme represented one element within a coherent Allied strategy for 1916, which aimed to mount offensives against the Central Powers simultaneously on three fronts; it also served to draw German forces away from their ongoing offensive against Verdun.

OUTCOME After 142 days of combat, the Allies had managed to advance no more than 13km (8 miles) deep into the German lines across a 35km (22 mile) frontage, but failed to achieve a decisive breakthrough, despite incurring 632,000 casualties and inflicting just 230,000 on the enemy. This was possibly a marginal and pyrrhic Allied victory, bought at intolerable cost; more likely is that it was a German defensive triumph.

The Battle of the Somme – the climactic five month-long Anglo-French offensive on the Western Front in 1916 – remains the most controversial battle of the Great War, and perhaps of any conflict in history. Daily gains, measured merely in metres, were bought by the sacrifice of many thousands of lives. Indeed, the calamitous British casualties incurred on the offensive's opening day, 1 July, have seared themselves into the British national psyche. To others, the offensive was a triumph of the ordinary British soldier's endurance and perseverance, during which vital offensive tactical skills were honed – a 'learning curve' that made the eventual Allied victory in 1918 possible.

While popular perception of the Battle of the Somme focuses on the events of 1 July, the offensive was actually a protracted, multi-national, campaign that witnessed 12 distinctive British subsidiary battles alone.

A STRATEGY EMERGES

During December 1915, the Allies agreed their overarching strategy for the forthcoming 1916 campaign. Britain and France agreed to mount a combined offensive that summer on the Western Front, timed to coincide with further attacks against the Central Powers on the Italian and Eastern Fronts. At this time, General Douglas Haig (1861–1928) became Commander-in-Chief of the British Expeditionary Force on the Western Front.

British heavy artillery pieces, such as this gun, proved devastating against even deep and well-fortified German bunkers; unfortunately most British guns were of the lighter field piece type.

In February 1916, the French and British decided to mount their joint offensive in the Somme valley in Northern France, along which the dividing line between their respective armies ran. Allied planning for this Somme offensive had scarcely began when the Germans initiated their own offensive against Verdun on 21 February. The increasing French commitment to defending the Verdun salient, however, led to the British assuming a larger proportion of the burden of executing the Somme offensive. The ongoing struggle at Verdun also led the strategic purpose behind the future Somme offensive to evolve from one of inflicting a decisive defeat on the Germans to one of drawing enemy forces away from Verdun.

Haig, however, continued to believe that the offensive could achieve a decisive breakthrough of the German lines. His conception of what was feasible remained at odds with that of Lieutenant-General Henry Rawlinson, Commander of Fourth Army, who was responsible for executing the Somme offensive. Rawlinson preferred a 'bite and hold' approach, where a sequenced series of short mini-offensives would each secure modest territorial gains while withstanding the inevitable local German counterattacks; an aggregation of these modest victories would eventually deliver a decisive penetration of the enemy trench system.

The battlefield of this future offensive was located in the valley of the River Somme, between the towns of Albert and Bray in the west, and Bapaume and Peronne in the east. The River Somme flowed in from the southeast, heading due north to Peronne, then northwest to Clery; the river then wound its way west through Bray. The front line ran broadly north–south to the east of Bray and Albert, with the Allied positions to the west. At the start of the offensive, the boundary between the British and French forces ran from the frontline at Mancourt down to Bray on the River Somme, before following the river west into the rear areas. The Germans, positioned to the north and east, tended to hold the high ground, providing them with good observation of the Allied lines. The Germans had held this sector with little

disturbance since late 1914, and therefore their defences had been transformed into an elaborate trench system that stretched deep into their own lines. The first German trench system, to the immediate east of no-man's land, contained many deep-dug bunkers that proved resistant to even intense bombardment. Behind this,

BRITISH 'TOMMY'

The ordinary British rifleman, or 'Tommy', went 'over the top' on 1 July 1916 carrying a mass of kit and equipment. Over his shoulder he has slung a 7.69mm (.303in) Lee Enfield rifle with bayonet. He carried 100 rounds of ammunition in his webbing belts and pouches, while strung round his neck was a bag containing his gas mask and cape. On his back he carried a small day-sack, which contained a canteen of water, two days' rations, shaving kit, clean socks, and any small personal items such as photographs of his loved-ones.

LOCATION

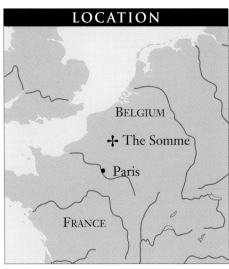

The Somme valley in northern France was a sensible location for the proposed combined Anglo-French offensive of 1916, because the boundary between these countries' respective army contingents on the Western Front ran through the valley.

THE SOMME

British infantry en route to the frontline along the Somme sector take a much needed rest along the edge of a tree-lined French road. While the men relax the officers busy themselves in communicating with the troops.

THE OPPOSED FORCES

ALLIED (estimated)

British and Commonwealth troops;	500,000
French troops:	250,000
Total:	**750,000**

CENTRAL POWERS (estimated)

Total:	**400,000**

0.8–5km (1–3 miles) further back, the Germans had constructed a second defensive line that ran east of Serre to Pozières, then east of Montauban down to the Somme. A third line was also under construction, positioned 3km (2 miles) behind the second one, and covered the villages of Warlencourt, Pys and Flers.

THE BOMBARDMENT STARTS

The preliminaries to the Battle of the Somme commenced on 24 June 1916. That day, the 1437 British artillery pieces assembled for the offensive opened fire on the German positions, while to the south, the French bombardment also commenced. For seven days, the preliminary bombardment continued, raining 1.5 million shells down on the enemy along a 29km (18 mile) sector, in what was the largest British fire-plan then delivered in the history of warfare. While this bombardment unfolded, British tunnelling companies dug 17 mines under the principal German bunkers, while in the skies above Allied aircraft – enjoying temporary air superiority – provided

spotting missions for the guns. The British expected that this overwhelming artillery bombardment would have killed most of the defending German troops, destroyed much of their equipment and obliterated their barbed-wire obstacles; the assaulting British infantry would therefore face only light enemy resistance as they advanced swiftly through the entire enemy trench system.

Events on 1 July proved how wrong these expectations had been. Unfortunately, despite the impressive total number of rounds delivered, the British bombardment was relatively ineffective. Some 960 of the British guns were field pieces that had fired relatively light shrapnel rounds. These could be devastating against enemy troops caught in open trenches, but inflicted little damage on troops sheltering in the deep, well-fortified dugouts that the Germans had constructed within their trench system. Another key problem was that fuses in the British shells had been manufactured hastily by inexperienced workers; it is estimated that as many as a third of the rounds delivered by the British bombardment failed to explode.

TROOPS GO OVER THE TOP

The offensive was due to commence on 29 June but, due to bad weather, was postponed until 1 July. This first phase of the offensive, the Battle of Albert, lasted until 13 July, but popular perception of this phase is dominated by events on 1 July. That day, the 11 divisions of Rawlinson's Fourth Army, plus two divisions of the Third Army led by Lieutenant-General Edmund Allenby's (1861–1936), which was located on the northern flank, went 'over the top'. Further south, 11 divisions from General Marie Fayolle's French Sixth Army joined the assault. At 0728, the Allies detonated most of the underground mines, devastating the key enemy strong points. Then, at 0730, as the artillery shifted to engaging targets deeper within the German lines, thousands of British assault infantry climbed out of their trenches. In order to maintain command and control, the assaulting troops advanced, as they had been trained to, in close order. The advancing soldiers were stalled by still-standing barbed-wire obstacles and were met by a hail of devastating enemy small-arms, machine-gun, and artillery fire, which cut them down in droves.

North of the Albert–Baupaume road, the British attack was a dismal failure with the assault troops suffering horrendous casualties and managing to get a foothold in the initial enemy trenches in just a few places. In the abortive attack on Beaumont Hamel, for example, the 1st Newfoundland Regiment suffered 90 per cent casualties. The only British notable successes that day were the capture of Mametz and Montauban along the southern flank. Further south, the French – facing a weaker defensive position and with a more effective preliminary artillery bombardment – secured greater success. For the cost of 7000 casualties, they advanced 1.6km (1 mile) deep into enemy lines, capturing all their first day objectives. The day for the British, however, had been disastrous: they suffered no fewer than 57,470 casualties, including 19,240 killed. Some 32 battalions – including 20 'Pals' battalions – lost over 500 casualties on this first, bloody, day of the Somme offensive. ('Pals' battalions were men allowed to enlist together, on the understanding that they would serve alongside their friends, neighbours and work colleagues – or 'pals'.)

In the following 48 hours, the British reorganized while Lieutenant-General Hubert Gough's Reserve Army took over the northern part of the British sector. Over the

A German infantry section man their Maxim MG08 water-cooled machine gun, which has been established in an open field position amid scrub-like undergrowth. This weapon inflicted many of the casualties incurred by the Allies during the offensive.

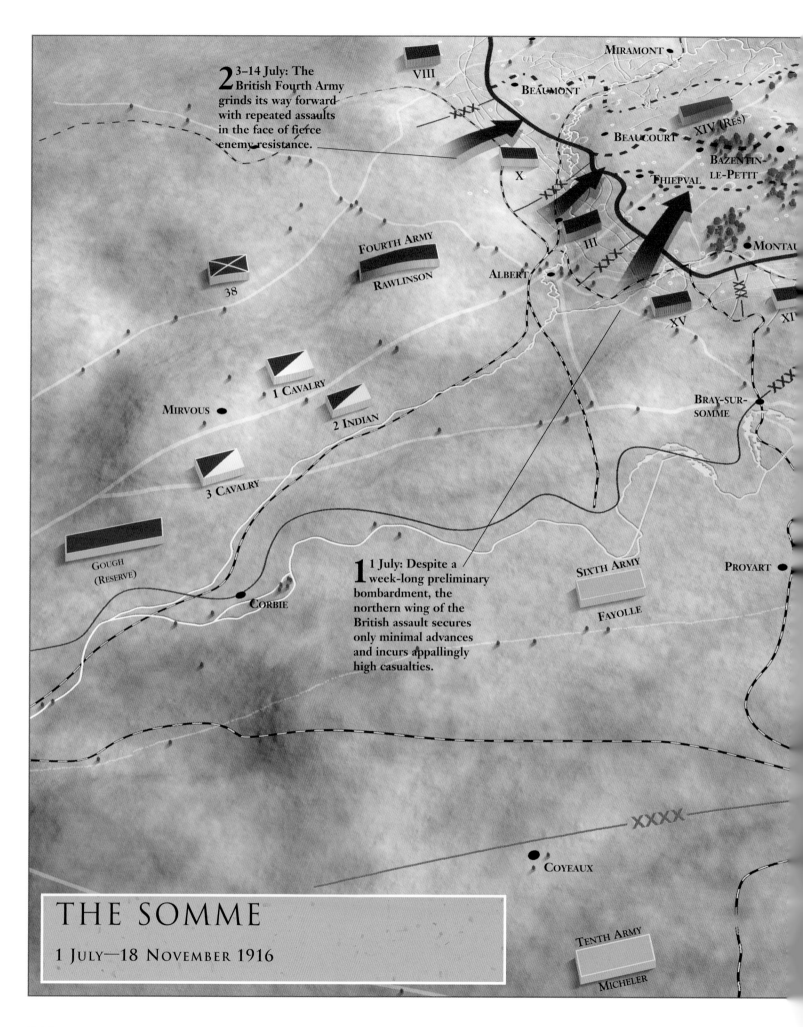

2 3–14 July: The British Fourth Army grinds its way forward with repeated assaults in the face of fierce enemy resistance.

VIII

MIRAMONT

BEAUMONT

BEAUCOURT

XIV (RES)

BAZENTIN-LE-PETIT

THIEPVAL

X

FOURTH ARMY
Rawlinson

III

ALBERT

MONTAU

38

XV

XI

1 CAVALRY

MIRVOUS

2 INDIAN

BRAY-SUR-SOMME

3 CAVALRY

GOUGH
(RESERVE)

CORBIE

1 1 July: Despite a week-long preliminary bombardment, the northern wing of the British assault secures only minimal advances and incurs appallingly high casualties.

SIXTH ARMY
FAYOLLE

PROYART

COYEAUX

THE SOMME

1 JULY—18 NOVEMBER 1916

TENTH ARMY

MICHELER

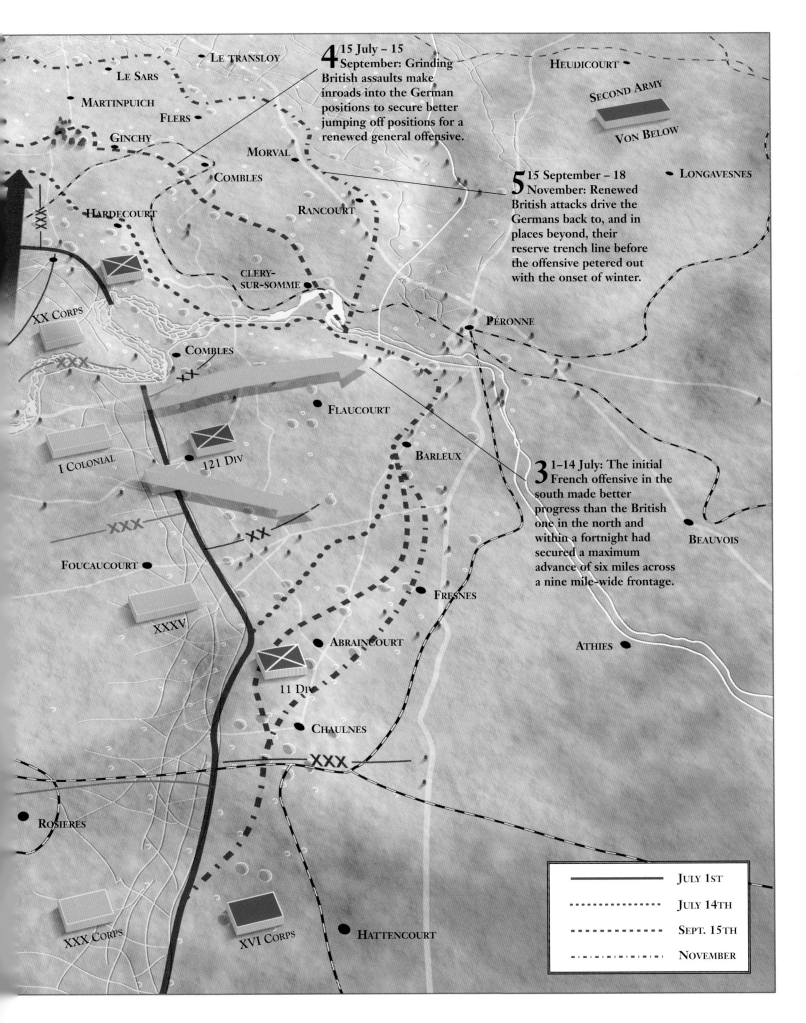

4 15 July – 15 September: Grinding British assaults make inroads into the German positions to secure better jumping off positions for a renewed general offensive.

5 15 September – 18 November: Renewed British attacks drive the Germans back to, and in places beyond, their reserve trench line before the offensive petered out with the onset of winter.

3 1–14 July: The initial French offensive in the south made better progress than the British one in the north and within a fortnight had secured a maximum advance of six miles across a nine mile-wide frontage.

SECOND ARMY

VON BELOW

HEUDICOURT

LONGAVESNES

LE TRANSLOY

LE SARS

MARTINPUICH

FLERS

GINCHY

HARDECOURT

MORVAL

COMBLES

RANCOURT

CLERY-SUR-SOMME

PÉRONNE

XX CORPS

COMBLES

FLAUCOURT

I COLONIAL

121 DIV

BARLEUX

BEAUVOIS

FOUCAUCOURT

FRESNES

XXXV

ABRAINCOURT

ATHIES

11 DIV

CHAULNES

ROSIÈRES

XXX CORPS

XVI CORPS

HATTENCOURT

———————	JULY 1ST
··················	JULY 14TH
- - - - - - -	SEPT. 15TH
-·-·-·-·-·-	NOVEMBER

THE SOMME

ensuing 10 days, the Fourth Army undertook 46 assaults, driving forwards painfully slowly against fierce enemy resistance, to capture Mametz Wood. By 13 July, the British forces had advanced up to 4km (2.5 miles) across a 14.5km (9 mile) frontage. The French to the south, meanwhile, continued to make good progress, securing a maximum advance of 9.5km (6 miles) into the enemy positions across a 16km (10 mile) frontage. The combined Allied offensive had inflicted severe casualties on the defending Germans, and it was only the rapid arrival of seven fresh divisions that kept the German line from breaking.

SECOND PHASE BEGINS

Next, before dawn on 14 July, the second phase of the Allied offensive began, the Battle for Bazentin Ridge. After a brief five-minute bombardment fired by 950 guns, four British divisions attacked the second German line between Pozières and Ginchy. The attack proved successful and left the British with footholds in Delville Wood and, temporarily, in High Wood, which had been taken in the face of intense enemy fire by two cavalry regiments. The ensuing struggle to actually secure Delville Wood and High Wood would rage until September. On 19 July, meanwhile, the Germans reorganized their command structure: General von Below took over the newly arrived First Army, while General

Max von Gallwitz assumed command of Second Army.

British offensive attention now switched to the vital Pozières Ridge, from where the British hoped to attack, intending to 'roll-up' the German second line from the south. Troops from I ANZAC Corps, part of Gough's Reserve Army, assaulted Pozières village on the night 22/23 July. During the ensuing seven weeks, in an attempt to outflank the potent German positions at Thiepval, the ANZACs fought a bitter series of actions enabling them to advance to the fringes of the German strongpoint of Mouquet Farm; these actions cost the Corps 23,000 casualties. Eventually, troops from I Canadian Corps captured the farm on 27 September. Further south, during August and early September, Rawlinson's Fourth Army continued to batter its way against the German positions in and around Guillemont and Ginchy, locations which did not fall until early September. The capture of these hamlets finally left the British forces deployed in a coherent 11km (7 mile) line from Mouquet Farm down to Combles, where the French sector began.

These successes now meant that British had finally achieved the essential pre-conditions for a larger-scale offensive that would yet again seek to secure decisive success. This coherent line, however, had been reached only through a terrible expenditure of soldier's lives; for gains of

This photograph, taken from an Allied aircraft, shows French infantry advancing across a heavily-cratered landscape behind a smokescreen during the Somme offensive.

THE SOMME

less than 1.5km (1 mile), the British forces had suffered 82,000 casualties.

FIGHTING CONTINUES

Subsequently, nine divisions from the Fourth Army and two Canadian divisions from the Reserve Army initiated the Battle of Flers–Courcelette on 15 September. This operation is best known for the appearance of the tank in warfare; 29 vehicles lumbered across the battlefield, breaking down barbed wire obstacles and providing mobile direct fire support for the infantry. The operation secured some success with advances of up to 3km (2 miles) deep into enemy positions across an 8km (5 mile) front, which captured parts of the German reserve trench line. The German positions around the Quadrilateral redoubt, east of Ginchy, and at Guedecourt near Thiepval held firm, however, and it was not until 25 September that British assaults were finally able to capture these locations.

Next, on 26 September, Gough's Reserve Army – now renamed Fifth Army – launched a major attack against the remaining part of the formidable German enclave at Thiepval. British troops captured the hamlet as well as the nearby Mouquet Farm. Throughout October and into early November, Gough's forces fought numerous bitter actions to secure the important terrain of the Ancre Heights, including Regina Trench, most of which was captured on 11 November.

Meanwhile, Haig still hoped that a decisive breakthrough could be achieved, and on 1 October the Fourth Army launched attacks against the German Transloy trench line, which was located between Le Transloy and Le Sars on the Albert–Baupaume main road. Despite appalling weather conditions that turned the ground to a quagmire, the Fourth Army's units pressed their attacks vigorously, eventually capturing Le Sars on 7 November; in the aftermath of an abortive attack on Butte de Warlencourt on 5 November, however, Fourth Army operations eventually petered out.

During 13–18 November, the last subsidiary operation of the Somme offensive, The Battle of the Ancre, was played out. During this, the 51st (Highland)

Division captured the village of Beaumont Hamel – one of the original objectives of 1 July – while the 4th Canadian Division secured the remainder of Regina Trench. With winter fast approaching, and his forces exhausted, Haig suspended operations.

LOSSES AND GAINS

By the end of the offensive on 18 November 1916, the British had secured an advance of 3–13km (2–8 miles) across a frontage of 17.5km (11 miles), making a total gain of approximately 166 sq km (64 sq miles). The French had advanced 1.5–9.5km (1–6 miles) deep into the German lines across the same frontage. The human price of this 'victory' was appalling, with 432,000 British and Commonwealth and 200,000 French combat casualties alone; the Germans, by contrast, are estimated to have suffered 230,000 combat losses. Irrespective of the controversy that still follows such slaughter, the Somme offensive stands out as a testimony to the sheer endurance of ordinary front-line British and Commonwealth, French and German soldiers, who, despite the cold, wet, hunger, and terror of ever-present mortal danger, did their duty and fought through one of the darkest periods in the history of warfare.

British infantry marshal a group of German prisoners-of-war, one of whom is wounded, through a trench in the aftermath of the bitter battle waged around the village of Thiepval.

CAMBRAI
NOVEMBER–DECEMBER 1917

ON 20 NOVEMBER 1917, AT THE BATTLE OF CAMBRAI, THE TANK CAME OF AGE. AS A WEAPON SYSTEM, ALONG WITH AIR POWER, IT WOULD FUNDAMENTALLY CHANGE THE NATURE OF LAND WARFARE AND DOMINATE THE CONVENTIONAL HIGH-INTENSITY BATTLEFIELD FOR THE REST OF THE TWENTIETH CENTURY.

WHY DID IT HAPPEN?

WHO The British Third Army commanded by Lieutenant-General Sir Julian Byng (1862-1935) and the Tank Corps under Brigadier-General Hugh Elles (1880-1945) against the German Second Army led by General Georg von der Marwitz.

WHAT The Tank Corps deployed its tanks *en masse* over suitable terrain. The tanks were supported by infantry trained in co-operation with armour and supported by artillery using new 'Silent Ranging' techniques. On the first day, the British made unprecedented advances at minimal cost.

WHERE The Hindenburg Line, west of Cambrai in Northern France.

WHEN 20 Nov – 3 Dec 1917.

WHY To maintain pressure on the Germans after the tremendous efforts of the Third Ypres offensive and, perhaps, to salvage something from the campaigns of 1917, General Sir Douglas Haig authorized the attack.

OUTCOME Although the British achieved spectacular success on 20 November, the gains were lost to a German counterattack. However, the tank-infantry-artillery tactics used presaged the combined-arms approach that would break the German line in 1918.

At Cambrai, tanks were concentrated on a large scale for the first time on suitable terrain, using specially developed tactics. The result was an 8km (5-mile) penetration through German lines at minimal cost in comparison to the lengthy and extremely costly offensives that had preceded the battle. Although the gains were short-lived, the Battle of Cambrai demonstrated the immense potential of the tank, which would be instrumental in breaking the deadlock of trench warfare and

then, 20 or so years later, revolutionize warfare itself.

Despite the technological advances of the late nineteenth and early twentieth centuries, such as rapid-firing artillery, the magazine-loading rifle, the machine-gun and barbed wire, all armies entered World War I in August 1914 expecting a war of movement. Therefore, cavalry still made up a substantial proportion of the forces deployed, even though a century, perhaps a century and a half, of experience pointed to

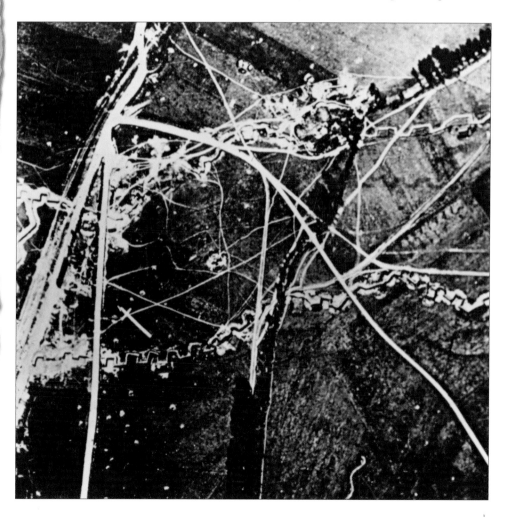

An aerial reconnaissance photograph showing the deep trenches, mine craters and shell strikes on an important sector of the Hindenburg Line. The relatively unscathed terrain at Cambrai made it more suitable for the employment of tanks.

CAMBRAI

the vulnerability of mounted men in combat. In the opening weeks of the war, whenever cavalry met well-formed infantry, they were shot from their horses in droves. Within six weeks, the horse was banished from the Western European battlefield.

Although cavalry were maintained in order to exploit the hoped-for breakthrough, and remained useful in the East and subsidiary theatres such as the Middle East, a key element of tactical and strategic mobility had been driven forever from the battlefield.

Even less expected was the fact that the firepower which shattered the cavalry proceeded to do the same to the bayonet charges of the infantry. At a terrible cost to themselves, the outnumbered British, French and Belgium armies managed to fight to a standstill the invading Germans. The shovel became the essential weapon as the exhausted armies dug in and the war settled into a stalemate.

BREAKING THE STALEMATE

The problem of breaking that stalemate was to exercise the generals for the next three years. Initially, a heavy reliance was placed on artillery, but unfortunately there were usually enough of the well dug-in defenders left, or enough men in reserve, to repulse the infantry following the barrage or recapture any lost ground. Yet, the High Commands persevered through Vosges, Lorraine and Neuve Chappele in 1915; Lozono, Verdun and the Somme in 1916; and Arras, Chemin des Dames and Ypres in 1917, at the cost of hundreds and thousands of their men's lives. There were some attempts at innovation, such as the introduction of poison gas or large-scale mining operations, but none proved decisive. The Battle of the Somme provides a suitable example of the difficulties and costliness of attacking on the battlefields of World War I. Despite a seven-day bombardment that preceded the battle, the attacking British sustained some 60,000 casualties on the first day. Over the following four months of the Somme offensive, at a cost of 400,000 men, British troops advanced no further than 16km (10 miles). Modern technology had reduced mobility to almost nothing.

In the midst of the slaughter of the Somme, however, the British introduced a new weapon, the tank. Development of a tracked armoured fighting vehicle capable of crossing trenches and overcoming barbed wire began in early 1915. A prototype tracked armoured vehicle, 'Little Willie', was ready by December, and 'Mother', an actual vehicle intended for combat and based on the famous rhomboid shape, was trialled in late January 1916.

Its performance was impressive enough for the vehicle to be put into production: 100 were ordered, half of them 'males' armed with 6-pounder (57mm) guns in sponsons on the sides; and half of them 'females' armed with machine-guns. The vehicles were referred to as 'Water Tanks' for security reasons, and the name stuck. An entirely new weapon system had been conceived, designed, built and put into production in less than 12 months. The driving force behind the programme, Colonel Ernest Swinton, had specific ideas about how the new weapon should be used:

Not only…does it seem that tanks will confer the power to force successive comparatively unbattered defensive lines, but…the more speedy and uninterrupted their advance the greater the chance of their surviving sufficiently long to do this. It is possible, therefore, that an effort to break right through the enemy's defensive zone in one day may be contemplated as a feasible operation.

Swinton was determined that the tank 'should not be used in driblets…but in one great combined operation'. Unfortunately, a mere 36 crossed the start-line and were deployed to prop up the Somme Offensive at Flers-Courcelette on 15 September 1916. There was no big breakthrough that day. Yet, despite the fact that the tanks achieved very little – most broke down, became stuck in the appalling terrain or were quickly knocked out – the British

Cambrai lies to the south of the battlefields of the 3rd Ypres offensive. It was a important railhead and a key part of the German communications network in northern France.

TANK OFFICER

This Lieutenant of the Tank Corps has a tank qualification badge on his right sleeve. His equipment includes a 1914 leather pattern belt and a holstered .455 revolver. He carries a box respirator slung to his left and wears a standard British helmet and an anti-splash mask to protect against fragments of the interior of a tank knocked lose by bullet strikes.

A colourized photo of Mark IV 'male' tanks in action. These made up the bulk of Tank Corps forces at Cambrai. The 'male' Mark IV was armed with two 57mm (6 pounder) guns, one in each sponson, and had armour ranging in thickness from 6mm (0.24in) to 12mm (0.47in). The tank was manned by a crew of eight.

THE OPPOSED FORCES

ALLIED ARMY

2 Infantry Corps

Tanks:	476
Tanks knocked out	**179**
Total casualties:	**42,000**

GERMAN ARMY

1 Infantry Corps

Total casualties:	**45,000**

commander in France, General Sir Douglas Haig, decided to order 1000 more.

THIRD BATTLE OF YPRES

The next major commitment of tanks was at Arras in April 1917. Sixty Mark I and II tanks were employed in conditions similar to the Somme, in terrible weather, across ground churned up by preliminary bombardment, and with similar results. There were some local successes: six tanks operating in support of 37th Division captured a very heavily fortified village at very little cost. As the Corps Commander Lieutenant General Aylmar Haldane remarked: 'I certainly never again want to be without tanks, when so well commanded and led.' Although it had achieved little thus far, the tank had been accepted, at least temporarily, as a useful weapon system and was deployed by the British across the front and other theatres.

The Tank Corps, as the new arm became in July, was committed to the major British offensive of 1917: the Third Battle of Ypres,

often known as Passchendaele, which lasted from 31 July to 6 November. Again, the conditions for tank operations were not ideal and they added little to the conduct of operations. At great cost, the British broke into German defences, but were unable to convert these occasional tactical successes into a strategic breakthrough. Yet, as the Third Battle of Ypres petered out, plans were being made that might provide some hope for the future.

There had been a couple of small tank actions in the midst of the slaughter of Ypres that had proved the weapon had some potential, and after an attack on German pillboxes in St Julien area on 19 August, the General Staff approved a plan for larger tank operation on Cambrai. The Chief of Staff of the Tank Corps, Colonel JFC Fuller, proposed a large-scale tank raid, with the reasonably limited aim of getting the tanks onto the German gun-line. His ideas were seized upon and expanded into a major offensive by the commander of the Third Army, General Sir Julian Byng (1862-

1935). Fuller and the commander of the Tank Corps, Brigadier-General Hugh Elles (1880-1945), had their doubts about this, given the commitments made at Ypres, but, knowing the Corps desperately needed a success, they concurred.

In Operation GY, as the offensive was codenamed, the Third Army intended to break the German line with tanks and then push cavalry across the St Quentin Canal to seize Bourlon Wood and the town of Cambrai. Haig, however, made it clear to Byng that, should results prove disappointing, he would close the offensive down quickly.

A LEARNING EXPERIENCE

It had taken some time and bitter experience to learn the lesson that tanks needed to be used on suitable ground. The rolling, firm chalk downland in the Cambrai sector, relatively untouched by artillery fire, had drawn Fuller to the area in the first place. Despite this, the tanks still faced a considerable task in terms of breaking through the German defences. The approach to the first line of trenches was through linked outposts and strong points. The forward trench itself, full of dugouts and machine-gun posts, had been widened to more than 4m (12ft) across, making it tank proof in German eyes. Beyond that, at a distance of 274m (900ft), were the similarly constructed support trenches. To counter this, the Tank Corps developed new tactics. It equipped its tanks with large brushwood fascines strapped to their roofs.

The tanks would advance in sections of three in an arrowhead formation, with the infantry following in file 23m (75ft) behind them. The tanks were responsible for crushing the wire in front of the trenches for the infantry. The leading tank, when it reached the forward trench, would turn left and fire into it with its starboard guns. The second tank would drop its fascine into the trench, cross it, turn left and fire on both the forward and support trenches. The third tank would drop its fascine into the support trench, turn left and fire on the defenders from their rear. Then, the first tank would come forwards with the infantry, while the tanks and infantry would regroup on the objective and resume the advance.

Co-operation between tanks and infantry was vital because, if machine-guns held up the infantry, the tanks would deal with them; and if artillery stopped the tanks, it was up to the infantry to suppress the gunners. The tanks and infantry trained extensively together prior to the opening of the offensive.

COMMITMENT TO BATTLE

The entire Tank Corps was committed to the battle, divided between the two British corps that would take part: III Corps (four infantry divisions, including the reserve) on the right flank, and IV Corps (two divisions) on the left, at a rate of 64–72 tanks per division. This was a total of 476 tanks. The bulk of these were 378 Mark IVs, the main combat type of the time. The Mark IV still resembled the original Mark I, but was up-armoured, had an external fuel tank in effort

General Julian Byng commanded the British Third Army and was responsible for the attack at Cambrai. He was an effective leader and had commanded with some success at Gallipoli and Vimy Ridge.

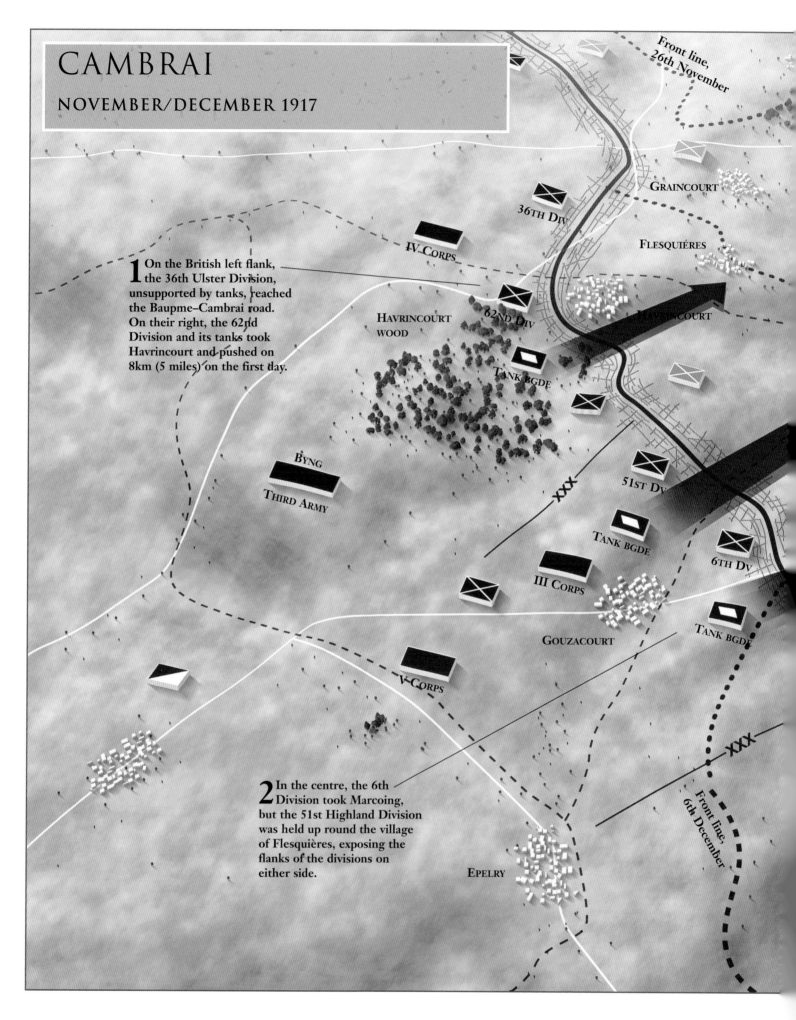

CAMBRAI

NOVEMBER/DECEMBER 1917

1 On the British left flank, the 36th Ulster Division, unsupported by tanks, reached the Baupme–Cambrai road. On their right, the 62nd Division and its tanks took Havrincourt and pushed on 8km (5 miles) on the first day.

2 In the centre, the 6th Division took Marcoing, but the 51st Highland Division was held up round the village of Flesquières, exposing the flanks of the divisions on either side.

Front line, 26th November

GRAINCOURT

FLESQUIÉRES

36TH DIV

IV CORPS

62ND DIV

HAVRINCOURT WOOD

HAVRINCOURT

TANK BGDE

BYNG

THIRD ARMY

51ST DV

TANK BGDE

6TH DV

III CORPS

TANK BGDE

GOUZACOURT

V CORPS

Front line, 6th December

EPELRY

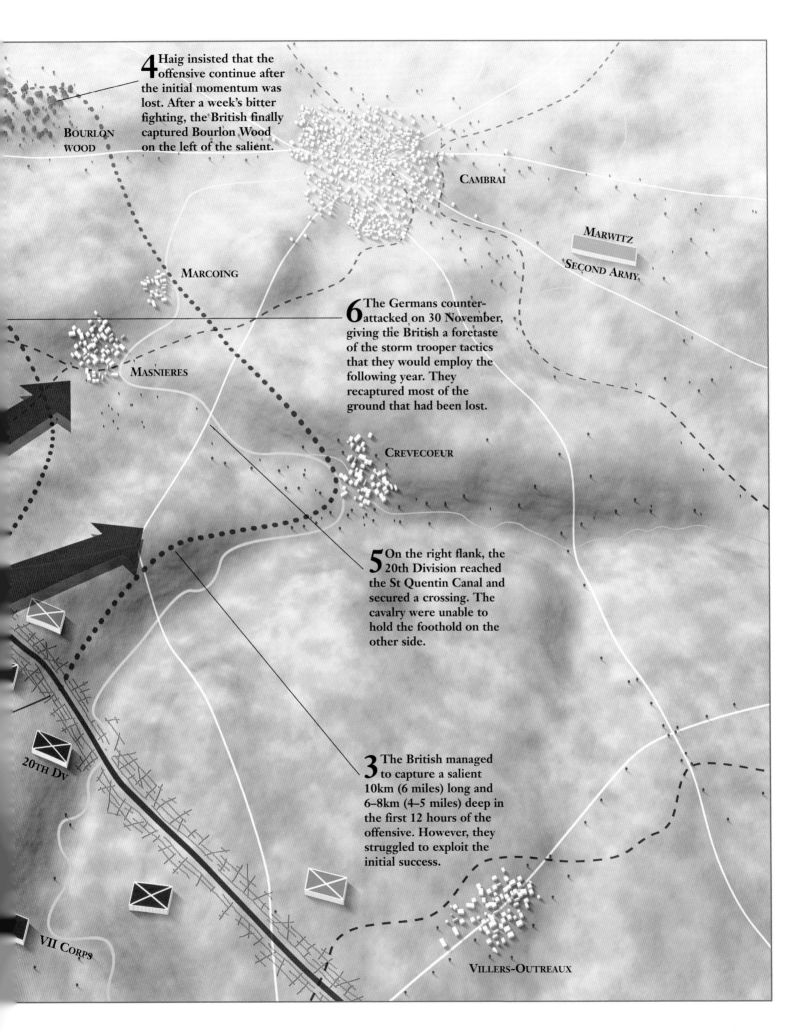

4 Haig insisted that the offensive continue after the initial momentum was lost. After a week's bitter fighting, the British finally captured Bourlon Wood on the left of the salient.

BOURLON WOOD

CAMBRAI

MARWITZ

SECOND ARMY

MARCOING

6 The Germans counter-attacked on 30 November, giving the British a foretaste of the storm trooper tactics that they would employ the following year. They recaptured most of the ground that had been lost.

MASNIERES

CREVECOEUR

5 On the right flank, the 20th Division reached the St Quentin Canal and secured a crossing. The cavalry were unable to hold the foothold on the other side.

3 The British managed to capture a salient 10km (6 miles) long and 6–8km (4–5 miles) deep in the first 12 hours of the offensive. However, they struggled to exploit the initial success.

20TH DV

VII CORPS

VILLERS-OUTREAUX

to improve crew safety, and a new engine and transmission, which proved surprisingly quiet. The remainder were more lightly protected Mark Is and IIs, which had been converted to act as specialist support tanks for supply, communication and laying bridges. Many carried grapnels for pulling wire out of the way of the cavalry. Nine were equipped with radios. After dark, on the evening of 19 November, the tanks were moved up to the start line, their noise masked by overflying aircraft and sustained machine-gun fire. Quite apart from the innovative use of tanks, Cambrai would also reintroduce the concept of surprise to the Western Front.

Cambrai is rightly remembered for the achievement of the tank arm used *en masse* for the first time, yet much of the initial success was down to the innovative use of British artillery. There would be no long 'Somme-style' bombardment. Indeed, there were no preliminary ranging shots, as the guns were ranged 'silently', based on intelligence, air reconnaissance and ballistic data, a method pioneered by Brigadier-General Henry Tudor, the commander

Royal Artillery in 9th Division. The purpose of the short, sharp opening barrage was to keep the enemy's head down and neutralize his artillery, and then shift to a 'creeping barrage' 274m (900ft) in front of the advancing troops and tanks. A large number of smoke shells were to be fired to mask the attackers. The British had mustered about 1000 guns, and these opened up at 0620 on 20 November 1917. At the same time, the tanks and infantry began to move forwards.

Reeling from the opening bombardment, the German outpost line put up little resistance to the tanks and infantry looming out of the early morning mist. The British were soon into the forward trenches, crushing paths in barbed wire, dropping their fascines into the trenches, and crossing and swinging left as the infantry followed. Many Germans were captured and some desperate counterattacks broken up as the Germans moved across open ground.

On the extreme right of the British assault, the 12th (Eastern) Division captured Bonavis and Lateau Wood, dug in on the flank and allowed the cavalry to pass

German troops pose beside a captured British tank. The British lost 65 tanks to enemy action on the first day of Cambrai.

Commonwealth troops clear Germans from their position on Passchendaele Ridge. The attack at Cambrai initially made similar gains but at far less cost.

Below: The German response to the deadlock was to improve their infantry tactics. Elite storm trooper units made an appearance when the Germans counter-attacked at Cambrai.

through as intended. Next to them, the 20th (Light) Division advanced as far as the St Quentin Canal and managed to secure a bridge at Masniéres, which promptly collapsed under the weight of a crossing tank. Some cavalry managed to cross the canal but were driven back. The 6th Division captured Marcoing, but the 5th Cavalry Division that passed through them did not get much further. In the centre, the 51st (Highland) Division faired less well. The Division took its first objectives to schedule, but was slowed by the stiff German defence of the village of Flesquières, where there were a couple of German anti-tank batteries still intact. Its commander, Major-General George Harper, has been blamed for introducing tank-infantry tactics of his own, particularly for holding his infantry further back than was the norm.

It seems that there was poor co-operation between his infantry and tanks. That said, the 51st was assaulting the strongest point of the German line and the defenders might well have halted any division. Whatever the case, the 51st did not take the village on the first day. The 62nd (2nd West Riding) Division fought its way through Havrincourt and pushed on 8km (5 miles) by nightfall. This was a remarkable achievement. On the left flank, the 36th (Ulster) Division reached the Baupme–Cambrai Road.

BREAKTHROUGH

It had been an extraordinary day's fighting. The British had carved out a salient 9.6km (6 miles) long and 6–8km (4–5 miles) deep in a mere 12 hours, taking 7500 prisoners and 150 guns. This had been achieved at the cost of 4000 casualties. Sixty-five tanks were lost to enemy action, 71 broke down and 43 were ditched or abandoned. To put this into perspective, similar territorial gains of the Third Battle of Ypres had taken three months and cost 250,000 casualties. Little surprise, then, that bells were rung in England for the first time in the war. The celebration proved premature, however, as the Germans rapidly recovered. Their defences stiffened the following day and, despite the loss of momentum, Haig ordered the offensive to continue. The Germans counterattacked on 30 November, recapturing most of what they had lost.

The importance of Cambrai lay not so much with the outcome, but rather in demonstrating that the tank, supported by new artillery tactics and in close co-operation with the infantry, could achieve the long-sought breakthrough on the Western Front. The modern combined-arms battle was not far away.

BATTLE OF BRITAIN

10 July–15 September 1940

THE BATTLE OF BRITAIN WAS A SUCCESSION OF AIR COMBATS BETWEEN THE ROYAL AIR FORCE (RAF) AND NAZI GERMANY'S *LUFTWAFFE*. THE GERMANS FIRST ATTACKED BRITISH COASTAL DEFENCES, RADAR STATIONS AND SHIPPING, LATER SWITCHING INLAND FOR AIR-TO-AIR COMBAT AND ATTACKS ON CITIES.

WHY DID IT HAPPEN?

WHO Operations were led by two World War I flying veterans: Air Marshal Sir Hugh Dowding (1882–1970), Chief of Fighter Command and *Reichsmarschal* Hermann Göring (1893–1946), Commander-in-Chief of the *Luftwaffe*.

WHAT The Germans had succeeded in overrunning Belgium, the Netherlands and northern France in May 1940, using *Blitzkrieg* ('Lightning War') methods. Then they attempted to win air superiority by destroying the Royal Air Force (RAF) and the British aircraft industry.

WHERE The Battle of Britain was waged mainly over southern England and the English Channel. At the start, German aircraft assembled in France near Calais to take on Spitfire and Hurricane fighters ordered up from Manston, Kent, together with Hurricanes from Croydon, south of London. Raids later extended to other centres throughout the country.

WHEN 10 July–15 September 1940.

WHY Victory over the RAF was seen by the Germans as essential if they were to mount a successful invasion of the British Isles.

OUTCOME Though heavily outnumbered, the RAF put up a spirited defence, aided considerably by its use of radar. The battle was the first significant failure of the Germans in World War II, forcing Hitler to abandon plans for invasion.

With the outbreak of World War II, Britain faced the very real risk of a vast air assault by Germany's *Luftwaffe*. But throughout the autumn and winter of 1939 and the spring and summer of 1940 the British Isles experienced an uneasy peace, broken dramatically by the Germans entering the smouldering ruins of Dunkirk in France. Within 48 hours, on the night of 5/6 June, 30 German bombers crossed the east coast of England, homing in on airfields. Contrasted with later armadas, it was a light incursion, followed by a further misleading lull as the *Luftwaffe* changed priorities, supporting German armies advancing into France.

Once the French sought an armistice, the situation changed. On 18 June 1940, the British Prime Minister Winston Churchill (1874–1965) pronounced: 'The Battle of France is over. I expect that the Battle of Britain is about to begin … The whole fury and might of the enemy must very soon be turned on us'. By way of preface to a full daylight air offensive in August, the Germans repeatedly despatched bombers against a wide variety of targets in England.

At first, the RAF was faced with a superior *Luftwaffe*, many of whose pilots had gained valuable combat experience from campaigns in Spain, Poland and France. In the sky, the Messerschmitt Bf 109 became the pacesetter for all new fighters, being a slender 550km/h (342mph) single-seat monoplane with two machine guns and two cannon. It was a rival to the Hurricane and the Spitfire. During August 1940, Sir Hugh Dowding's RAF Fighter Command could

Dogfights, often taking place in British skies during the Battle of Britain, consisted of aerial combat between fighter aircraft, the most common participants being the British Spitfire and the German Bf 109.

call on 749 Hurricanes and Spitfires to take on the *Luftwaffe's* 702 Me 109s, which were backed-up by long-range Me 110s.

The day of Tuesday 13 August had been designated by Göring as *Adlertag* (Eagle Day), the start of *Adlerangriff* (Eagle Attack) – a series of *Luftwaffe* attacks against the Royal Air Force (RAF) as part of preparations for a seaborne invasion of Britain. His main objectives were the forward airfields near the Kent coast, chains of radar stations as well as docks and shipping. Göring was also faced with changeable weather and *Adlertag* dawned over southeast England in thick cloud. Amid considerable confusion – some pilots had already taken off while others received no instructions at all – a postponement was ordered until the afternoon. British airfields then experienced the full fury of the German attack.

Thursday 15 August saw some of the fiercest fighting conducted over a wide area, ranging from Tyneside in northeast England, down the east coast and along the south coast to Devon. German resources were heavily stretched and losses were high – 75 *Luftwaffe* aircraft destroyed compared to 34 British fighters. The next day, the *Luftwaffe* lost another 45 aircraft during further attacks on airfields. However, not all ripostes by the RAF were successes. Air Vice-Marshal Trafford Leigh-Mallory, commander of No 12 Group in the Midlands, pitched a squadron of Spitfires against 50 unescorted Junkers Ju 88 bombers incoming from Denmark. Seven bombers were shot down, but the rest, although unescorted, went on to bomb a Yorkshire aerodrome. In the south, bombers, heavily escorted by by Me 109s, attacked airfields and aircraft factories.

From 8 August to 18 August, the RAF destroyed 363 *Luftwaffe* aircraft. But during the same 10 days, the RAF lost 211 Spitfires and Hurricanes, along with 154 experienced fighter pilots. In such circumstances, it was possible that Göring could gain the upper hand, a grim truth of which Dowding was well aware. Pilots as young as 18, their training times slashed, were thrust into combat with just 10 hours experience of flying single-seat fighters. Dowding's role was that of a juggler, shifting men from one squadron to another while desperately scouring for new talent. But both sides shared a shortage of aircraft, creeping exhaustion and low morale.

TALES OF HEROES

However, Fighter Command numbers were boosted by an input of Polish, Czech, French and a few American air crew, flying alongside Commonwealth, Fleet Air Arm and bomber pilots. And there emerged fighter pilots who became legends as Allied aces, often fuelled by a deep hatred of the Nazis. Outstanding among these was the South African Adolph Gysbert Malan (nicknamed 'Sailor' because he had originally trained for the merchant navy). He never attempted to conceal his

RAF FIGHTER PILOT
A pilot from a front-line squadron dressed in full flight gear. His day could begin as early as 03:00, carrying on until a stand-down at 20:00. It was impressed on each pilot that the need for fast scramble was vital. Each 30-second delay in getting airborne meant 305m (1000ft) less altitude available when it came to to meeting the enemy. A Spitfire caught in a climb was an easy target for a Messerschmitt attacking in a dive.

LOCATION

The proximity to Britain of German-occupied France and Belgium made the United Kingdom particularly vulnerable to air attack. Nazi triumphs in France and Norway led UK Joint Intelligence Chiefs in early July 1940 to warn that they believed invasion would be the enemy's next move.

intentions and believed that it was better to send a German aircraft home crippled rather than shoot it down, graphically saying: '... with a dead rear gunner, a dead navigator, and the pilot coughing up his lungs as he lands ... I think if you do that it has a better effect on their morale'. He was given command of 74 (Tiger) Squadron, with the rank of Acting Squadron Leader, on 8 August. By this time, he was already the holder of the Distinguished Flying Cross. Three days later, starting at 07:20, he was tasked to intercept a hostile raid rapidly approaching Dover, which called for four separate air battles. By the time the weary Squadron finally returned to base, it had downed 38 enemy aircraft. Malan's subsequent comment was characteristic understatement: 'Thus ended a very successful morning of combat'.

By the end of 1941, Malan was the unrivalled top scorer with 32 kills, plus two unconfirmed, a record he held for three years. He drew up 'Ten Of My Rules For Air Fighting', and had them pinned up in many crew rooms. They included: 'Never fly straight and level for more than 30 seconds in the combat area; When diving to attack, always leave a proportion of your formation above to act as a top guard; Go in quickly, punch hard, get out!'

Instances of individual heroism served as vital propaganda for the relentless battle against the *Luftwaffe*. But they could not conceal the unpalatable truth that for scores of combatants there was to be appalling physical suffering as a result of enemy fire. Pilot Office Geoffrey Page of 56 Squadron underwent 15 major surgical operations for horrific burns to face and hands, as well as gunshot wounds to both legs after parachuting from his Hurricane, following an attack by German Dornier Do 17s. While laying in a hospital bed unable to move or speak but determined to fight his way back to operational flying, he made a vow to take one German life for each of the operations.

OPERATION SEA LION

For all the achievements of the legendary RAF fighter pilots, there remained the threat of seaborne invasion via the English Channel. Although Hitler feared that the cost to his naval fleet would be considerable, the bucaneering Göring, oozing self-confidence, assured the *Führer* that such an invasion, to be codenamed Operation Sea Lion, would be possible in mid- to late September, given favourable tides.

By way of preparation, Göring ordered his bombers to step up their attacks around Britain, but here caution also ruled. London was the one forbidden target because it was thought likely that any major raids there would lead to retaliation against German cities on a similar or greater scale. As it happened, London was attacked – by accident. On the night of 24/25 August, during the course of night operations, a

Fighter Command pilots scrambling for take off to intercept hostile aircraft. Many of these men, some as young as 18, had minimal flying training and scant experience of air combat. Fighter Command depended heavily on reservists and part-timers to man the fighters, in contrast to many of Göring's elite Luftwaffe pilots, who had gained battle experience in Spain, Poland and France.

flight of Heinkels He 111s lost their way to their intended targets and in the confusion dropped their bombs over the city. The need to retaliate quickly fast was clear. The next night, 81 British bombers flew to Berlin and carried out four successful raids on the capital. The effect on morale throughout Germany was devastating, particularly among ordinary citizens who had considered their capital inviolate. In response, Hitler threatened that if British attacks went on 'we will raze their cities to the ground'. By early September, the situation had escalated and the Blitz on London raged, first against the industrial and port areas of the East End, then spreading to other areas of the capital and finally to towns and cities beyond.

On Saturday 7 September, Göring stood on the cliffs at Cap Blanc Nez, southwest of Calais, watching the German formations sweeping overhead and announced over the radio: 'I myself have taken command of the *Luftwaffe's* battle of Britain'. With him stood a staunch collegue, Field Marshal

Albert Kesselring, commander of *Luftflotten 2* (Air Fleet 2) and one of the most charismatic senior *Luftwaffe* figures, warmly nicknamed 'Smiling Albert' by his crews. Kesselring was a supporter of the move to shift bombing from airfields to cities. Although it was of little consolation to the civilian victims of such bombing, the shift away from targeting airfields was actually a strong contributor to British success because it meant that its aircraft were able to enjoy a greater freedom of the skies.

And relishing that freedom in particular was Leigh-Mallory, despatching five squadrons – part of a so-called 'big wing' – to take on two of Kesselring's attacks on London. In command was Squadron Leader Douglas Bader, who had lost both legs in an air crash in 1931 while doing low-level acrobatics and had been retired as a consequence. Possessed of a giant ego and a determination that recognized no obstacles, Bader had achieved entry to Bomber Command and 242 Squadron of Leigh-Mallory's No 12 group. Fights over

The iconic fighter of the RAF, the Spitfire (above, lower), became best known for its role during the Battle of Britain. Twenty-four versions were eventually produced during World War II. The Supermarine model 1A, with its eight 7.69mm (.303in) Browning machine guns, could reach a maximum speed of 583km/h (362mph) at 5793m (19,000ft), and had a range of 636km (395 miles). The Spitfire was particularly effective against the Messerschmitt Bf 109 (top), the principal German fighter of the era.

THE OPPOSED FORCES

RAF (estimated)

1963 aircraft

LUFTWAFFE (estimated)

4074 aircraft

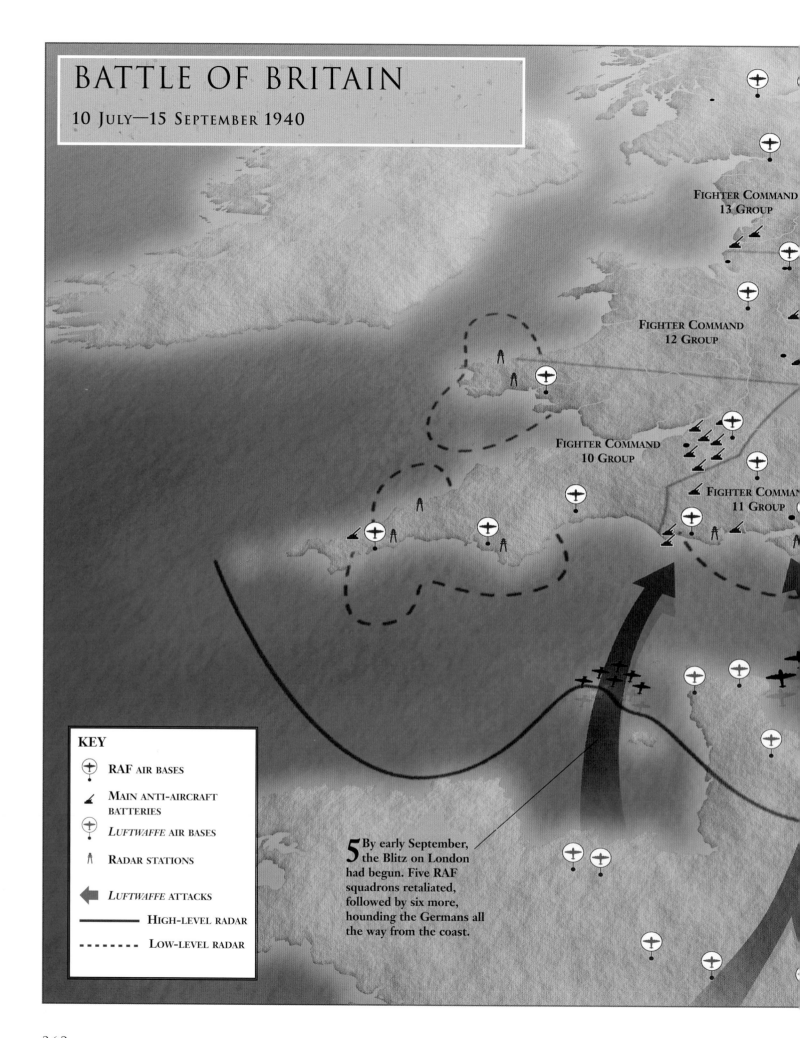

BATTLE OF BRITAIN

10 July—15 September 1940

FIGHTER COMMAND 13 GROUP

FIGHTER COMMAND 12 GROUP

FIGHTER COMMAND 10 GROUP

FIGHTER COMMAND 11 GROUP

KEY

- ⊕ RAF AIR BASES
- ◣ MAIN ANTI-AIRCRAFT BATTERIES
- ⊕ *LUFTWAFFE* AIR BASES
- ⋔ RADAR STATIONS
- ◀ *LUFTWAFFE* ATTACKS
- ——— HIGH-LEVEL RADAR
- - - - - LOW-LEVEL RADAR

5 By early September, the Blitz on London had begun. Five RAF squadrons retaliated, followed by six more, hounding the Germans all the way from the coast.

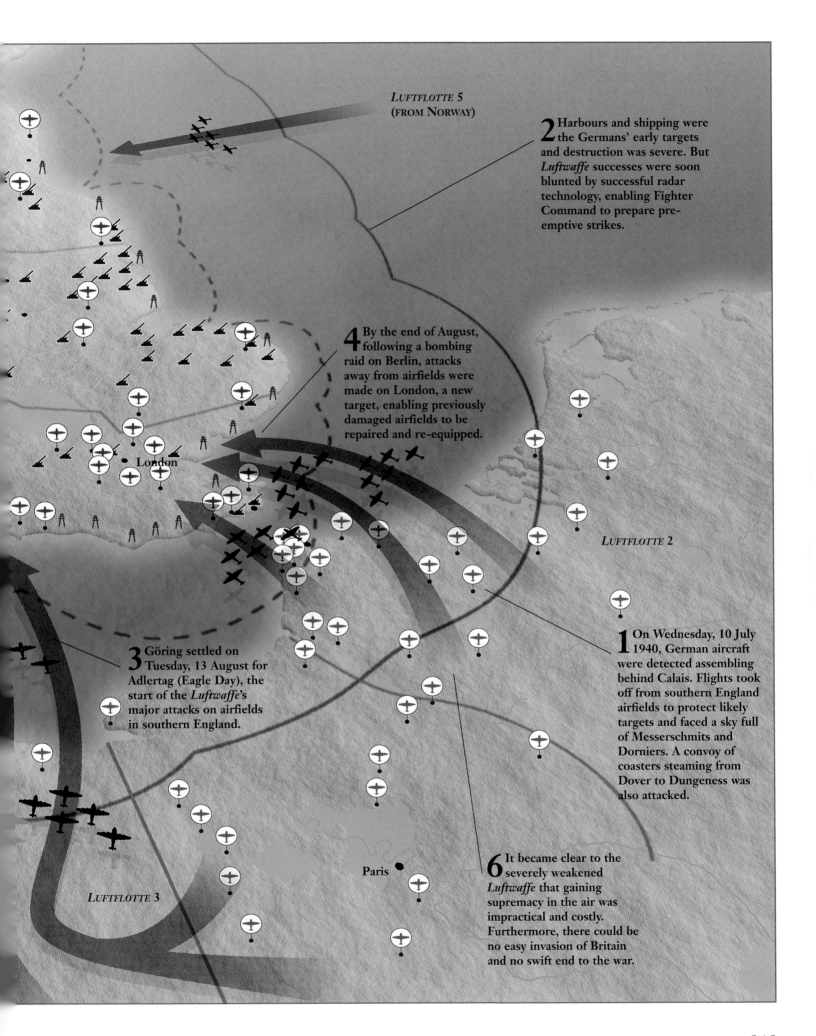

LUFTFLOTTE 5
(FROM NORWAY)

2 Harbours and shipping were the Germans' early targets and destruction was severe. But *Luftwaffe* successes were soon blunted by successful radar technology, enabling Fighter Command to prepare pre-emptive strikes.

4 By the end of August, following a bombing raid on Berlin, attacks away from airfields were made on London, a new target, enabling previously damaged airfields to be repaired and re-equipped.

London

LUFTFLOTTE 2

1 On Wednesday, 10 July 1940, German aircraft were detected assembling behind Calais. Flights took off from southern England airfields to protect likely targets and faced a sky full of Messerschmits and Dorniers. A convoy of coasters steaming from Dover to Dungeness was also attacked.

3 Göring settled on Tuesday, 13 August for Adlertag (Eagle Day), the start of the *Luftwaffe*'s major attacks on airfields in southern England.

6 It became clear to the severely weakened *Luftwaffe* that gaining supremacy in the air was impractical and costly. Furthermore, there could be no easy invasion of Britain and no swift end to the war.

Paris

LUFTFLOTTE 3

363

BATTLE OF BRITAIN

Early in September 1940, the Luftwaffe *turned its attacks from RAF stations to London and southern English towns. Its forces killed or wounded nearly 2000 people in the capital on 7 September alone. In subsequent raids, countless homes were destroyed as the London Docks, near the River Thames, became an inferno.*

London, though, were costly affairs. In the first weeks of September, Fighter Command lost 185 aircraft and the *Luftwaffe* 225.

THE BLITZ INTENSIFIES

On the afternoon of 7 September, controllers at Bentley Priory, headquarters of Air Vice Marshal Keith Park and his No 11 Group Squadron, reported a surge of approaching formations. All 21 fighter squadrons around London were primed. They encountered a formation of *Luftwaffe* aircraft an astounding 2.5km (1½ miles) high, covering 2072 sq km (800 sq miles) of sky. The approach was clearly towards London and no area of the capital escaped the devastation, which spread right along

the Thames, from the working class East End to the wealthy areas of the West End.

The following morning, another 300 bombers attacked in waves, torching the entire 14.5km (9 miles) of the River Thames waterfront, and 448 Londoners were killed. In its efforts to counter these daylight formations, 31 fighters were lost in combat. Six Hurricanes alone were lost from 249 Squadron in one action without destroying a single German aircraft. By the end of 8 September, Germans had lost 39 aircraft.

Further heavy night raids confirmed the change in strategy – the *Luftwaffe* were targeting British cites, rather than trying to reduce the RAF's capability to defend the island. A particularly heavy daylight raid on London on 12 September claimed 412 victims, including 50 people in a single block of flats. During the night, the German assault continued. In the business area of the City of London, a further 370 civilians were killed. Three days later, Kesselring mustered all his resources to make two attacks on London, while assaults were also made by another powerful air fleet, *Luftflotte 3* (Air Fleet 3) under *Generalfeldmarschall*

Hugo Sperrle, which attacked Portland and Eastleigh near Southampton on the south coast. Forces marshalled against Kesselring included those of Park with his No 11 Group Squadron and, commanded by Bader, a 'big wing' of five squadrons from Leigh-Mallory.

The fighting raged so intensely along the coast, that Park sent up six more squadrons. But Kesselring gave no quarter. When his attack resumed in the afternoon, he sent in fighters ahead of the Heinkel and Dornier bombers with the aim of destroying the RAF interceptors. In the meantime, the German bombers were hitting the East End of London. A plea was made to Leigh-Mallory for the use of three squadrons of No 12 Group, bolstered by about 60 Hurricanes and Spitfires from Bader's 'big wing' to try to fight them off.

Göring received reports from his pilots that they were encountering weakening opposition. On Sunday 15 September, the *Luftwaffe* tried to press home their likely advantage, summoning two waves of fighters and bombers over the Pas de Calais. But these were soon detected by British radar and harassed all the way to their targets by Park, aided by a wing of No 12 Group. In the face of such strong defence, the Germans scattered their bomb loads, mainly over south and east London, and were forced to withdraw. Gradually, figures began to look better for the British: by 30 September, Fighter Command's loss was 242 aircraft against the *Luftwaffe's* 433. In addition, output of aircraft from the factories, previously a source of anxiety to Dowding, had speeded up considerably.

Despite his weakening position, Göring persisted in his belief that the *Luftwaffe* could still crush Fighter Command in preparation for an invasion. But Hitler had become increasingly reluctant to endure further losses, which included RAF counter-raids raids on his assembled invasion barges. On 17 September, Grand Admiral Erich Raeder of the *Kreigsmarine* recorded: 'The enemy airforce is by no means defeated. On the contrary, it shows increasing activity. The *Führer* therefore decides to postpone [Operation] Sea Lion indefinitely.' In effect, the invasion was abandoned. Increasingly, Hitler was focusing on long cherished plans for the invasion of the Soviet Union.

AFTERMATH

Still raging, however, was the bombing of London and other British cities. A notable victim was Coventry, a manufacturing centre for armaments and engine parts. On the night of 14 November 1940, it came under a heavy *Luftwaffe* attack, codenamed *Mondlichtsonate* (Moonlight Sonata). Along with its cathedral, which was devastated and whose destruction became a symbol of German brutality, there were 568 civilian deaths and 1256 injuries. Over 4000 homes were destroyed and three-quarters of its factories damaged.

Both Nazi Germany and Britain failed to gain air superiority and both were destined to endure ongoing bombing raids for the next four years. The threat of sea invasion receded from late September 1940, but with the end of the air war came the recognition that there would be no quick end to the conflict. The British triumph in the Battle of Britain was won at a heavy cost. Total British civilian losses from July to December 1940 were 23,002 dead and 32,138 wounded.

By mid-September, the Heinkel He111 with its 1646kg (4410lb) maximum bomb load and 397km/h (247mph) speed had been superseded by faster bombers and switched from daylight to night bombing.

PEARL HARBOR
7 DECEMBER 1941

THE JAPANESE ATTACK ON PEARL HARBOR DEMONSTRATED SPECTACULARLY THE POSSIBILITY OF CARRIER-BORNE AIRPOWER. AIRCRAFT OF THE JAPANESE IMPERIAL NAVY'S STRIKE FORCE SUNK SIX US BATTLESHIPS AND NUMEROUS SMALLER WARSHIPS. DESTROYED 164 AIRCRAFT AND KILLED 2403 US PERSONNEL. THE ATTACK CONFIRMED THE AIRCRAFT CARRIER AND NAVAL AVIATION AS THE DOMINANT WEAPON SYSTEM IN MARITIME WARFARE.

WHY DID IT HAPPEN?

WHO The Japanese Combined Fleet's Air Fleet 1, aboard a task force commanded by Vice-Admiral Chuichi Nagumo (1887–1944), against the US Pacific Fleet and various land installations commanded by Admiral Husband Kimmel (1882–1968) and Army and USAAF units in Hawaii under Major-General Walter Scott.

WHAT The Japanese Combined Fleet assembled six fleet carriers to launch an audacious attack on the US Pacific Fleet base of Pearl Harbor, 5472km (3400 miles) away.

WHERE Pearl Harbor, on Oahu, one of the Hawaiian Islands in the middle of the Pacific Ocean, west-southwest of the United States mainland.

WHEN 7 December 1941.

WHY In the face of both US and British sanctions, Japan needed to neutralize US naval power in Pacific, at least temporarily, in order to seize British and Dutch resources in the region, particularly oil.

OUTCOME Tactically, Japan caused considerable damage at little cost to itself, but, in the words of Vice-Admiral Nagumo, it managed only 'to awaken a sleeping giant and fill her with a terrible resolve'.

Despite the brilliant execution of the Japanese plan in attacking Pearl Harbor on 7 December 1941, it had landed a stunning, not a knockout, blow. Japan was subsequently drawn into a struggle of attrition in the Pacific, against an adversary it could not hope to defeat.

Almost as soon as the Wright Brothers made the first controlled flight by an aeroplane in 1903, sailors could see the possibilities that aircraft had for maritime warfare. The US Navy was the first to fly a plane off a naval vessel in 1910. By the outbreak of World War I, specialized aircraft, usually seaplanes, and seaplane carriers were in service, primarily for fleet reconnaissance. Nonetheless, a year later, in August 1915, Flight Commander CHK Edmonds made history by sinking a Turkish transport ship with an airborne torpedo launched from his Shorts seaplane.

Subsequently, a number of merchant ships and cruisers were converted to carry aircraft. Ship-launched Sopwith Pup fighters had some success against German Zeppelins over the North Sea. However,

Taken on 18 January 1941 in Honolulu, Hawaii, this photograph shows Rear Admiral Husband E. Kimmel in a good mood on hearing that he was to be appointed Navy commander of the US Fleet at Pearl Harbor. Kimmel would be relieved of duty after the Japanese attack on 7 December.

after take-off, these aircraft had to be ditched or landed ashore. It was not until 2 August 1917 that Squadron Commander EH Dunning landed his Sopwith Pup on HMS *Furious*, making the first deck landing on a ship at sea. More ambitious operations followed.

On 19 July 1918, Sopwith Camels, operating off *Furious*, attacked the airship base at Tondern, destroying two German Zeppelins. The Admiralty, however, shelved plans for a concerted carrier-borne air offensive against German naval bases. In September 1918, HMS *Argus*, the first carrier with an unobstructed flight deck or flush deck, was commissioned, setting the pattern for modern aircraft carrier design.

THE WASHINGTON TREATY

Britain, the United States and Japan continued to experiment with naval aviation after the war, with Japan launching its first carrier, the *Hosho*, in 1921. The Washington Naval Treaty of 1922 limited Japan's carrier tonnage to 82,300 tonnes (81,000 tons), in comparison to Britain and the United States with 137,000 tonnes (135,000 tons). Each carrier was restricted to 27,500 tonnes (27,000 tons), but Japan and the United States were permitted to convert two battle cruisers each to carriers of up to 33,500 tonnes (33,000 tons). Increasingly powerful aircraft made larger carriers more appealing, so the Treaty was allowed to lapse in 1936.

However, reasonably scrupulous observance of its terms meant that the three carrier-operating fleets went into World War II with relatively few of these vital weapons, and Japan faced something of a deficit, if it was to face the European powers and the United States in the Pacific. Thus freed of constraints, the Japanese Navy launched an ambitious naval construction programme the following year.

By 1939, the Commander-in-Chief of the Japanese Combined Fleet, Admiral Isoroku Yamamoto (1884–1943), was faced with this problem. He was a keen proponent of naval aviation, had worked in the Naval Air Corps and captained carriers earlier in his career. He was determined to move his navy's emphasis away from the battleship and towards a modern force with airpower

JAPANESE PILOT

This Japanese Lieutenant is wearing a lightweight gabardine flight-suit. This would have been complemented at Pearl Harbor by water-proofed fur-lined overalls, a flying helmet and a thick Kapok life jacket, which also provided some protection against flack. It was not unknown for naval aviators to take their swords with them on missions. The Japanese Naval Air Crew of this period were superbly trained and equipped and many had gained vital combat experience over China.

as its key component. He ordered new 30,400-tonne (30,000-ton) carriers capable of taking 80 aircraft. He was instrumental in the design and development of the Mitsubishi A6M Zero, a carrier-borne fighter far superior in performance to British and US equivalents. Japan also had its first carrier-borne monoplane attack aircraft in the shape of the Nakajima 97 Kate. Priority was given to the training of combat fliers. Though Yamamoto reorganized the Combined Fleet, he was well aware that challenging the United States was a dangerous game. He told Japan's Prime Minister Prince Konoe: 'We can run wild for six months or a year, but after that I have utterly no confidence, I hope you will try to avoid war with America.'

AN INEVITABLE CONFLICT

Yet Yamamoto was well aware that the aggressive policies of his government made such a challenge quite likely. The Japanese Army had been engaged in an intractable war in China since 1937. There had also been clashes with the Soviet Union on the Mongolian border in 1938 and 1939. After the Fall of France in 1940, Japan joined Germany and Italy in the Tripartite Pact and used the weakness of France and Britain to close down supply routes to Nationalist Chinese forces.

Yet the defeat of the democracies in Europe led the United States to look to its own defence. Accordingly, Congress passed the Two-Ocean Expansion Act in June

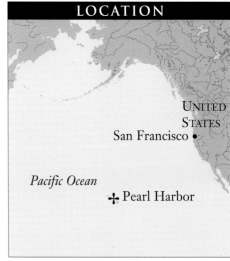

LOCATION

UNITED STATES

San Francisco

Pacific Ocean

Pearl Harbor

Pearl Harbor was the forward base and home of the Pacific Fleet since May 1940. Basing the fleet there placed US naval power deep in the Pacific, and it became the logistical hub of subsequent US operations in this theatre.

A portrait of Vice Admiral Chuichi Nagumo of the Imperial Japanese Navy, who commanded the carrier group that bombed Pearl Harbor.

THE OPPOSED FORCES

IMPERIAL JAPANESE NAVY

Carriers	6
Battleships	2
Cruisers	3
Destroyers	9
Aircraft	183

US NAVY

Warships	
(including 8 battleships)	70

1940, a massive naval building programme that would eventually dwarf Japanese sea power. Relations with the United States deteriorated further as Japan occupied French Indo-China and the United States and Britain imposed sanctions. An increasingly desperate Japanese leadership accepted that it would have to go to war with the United States if it was to secure the resources of the British and Dutch Eastern Empires. As early as the winter of 1939, Yamamoto, although he doubted the wisdom of such a course, began thinking about just such an eventuality.

PREEMPTIVE STRIKE

The only hope was first to reduce the superiority of the US battle fleet. Yamamoto reckoned that he needed a plan to destroy the US Pacific Fleet in one devastating strike, and he drew on a number of inspirations. Ironically, in 1938, the United States had staged a mock attack on the Pacific Fleet's base in the Hawaiian Islands, at Pearl Harbor. A total of 150 aircraft from the attack wings of the aircraft carriers *Lexington* and *Saratoga* managed to make a completely undetected and unopposed pass over the anchorage and thereby, in theory, destroy the fleet.

The US Navy may have been unimpressed, but Yamamoto had taken note. If a similar stroke could be pulled off by the Japanese Navy to cripple US military power, Japan should gain enough time to seize the Dutch and British possessions that were its main objectives. Of course, the British and Dutch forces in the region had to be dealt with too, but the United States was the real long-term threat to Japanese plans. The hope was that by the time the United States had recovered, Japan would

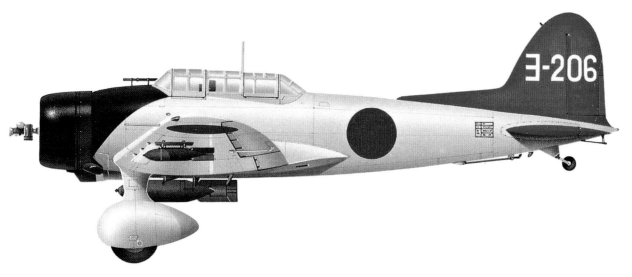

have secured its gains, forcing a weakened US Navy to come forwards and fight in Japanese-dominated seas. Alternatively, the United States might be dragged into the European war and possibly seek some sort of compromise with Japan.

The Naval General Staff did not universally accept Yamamoto's proposal. However, his case was immeasurably strengthened by the British attack on the Italian Fleet at Taranto in November 1940. British carrier-based aircraft succeeded in sinking three battleships, half the Italian capital strength. Surely, the larger and more modern Japanese Naval Air Arm was equally capable of such a coup? Indeed, Yamamoto's naval building programme,

initiated in the late 1930s, was beginning to pay dividends. The Naval Air Arm had grown to six large and three smaller carriers, equipped with the most advanced carrier-borne aircraft in the world.

By May 1941, a plan had been drawn up, and one that Yamamoto believed would guarantee success, as long as he could use six carriers and absolute secrecy was maintained. Although final authority had not been granted, rehearsals were undertaken at Kagoshima Bay on the southern island of Kyushu, which bore a striking similarity to Pear Harbor.

Torpedoes were modified to operate in the shallow waters of the US base. The Japanese Navy had plenty of information on

The Aichi D3A 'Val' bomber was a carrier-borne, single-engine dive bomber. Single-engine bombers made up nearly a third of the attacking aircraft at Pearl Harbor. It is credited with sinking more Allied shipping than any other Axis dive bomber in World War II.

Mitsubishi A6M5 Zero fighters prepare to take off from an aircraft carrier (reportedly Shokaku*) to attack Pearl Harbor during the morning of 7 December 1941.*

PEARL HARBOR

7 DECEMBER 1941

3 At 07.55, Kate torpedo bombers target ships to the northwest of Ford Island. This was where the missing carriers were normally berthed.

6 The USS *Nevada* attempted to make for the safety of open water, but was attacked by wave after wave of torpedo and dive bombers.

MIDDLE LOCH

FORD ISLAND NAVAL AIR STATION

USS *CALIFORNIA*

US NAVY YARD

5 Attacked by both the first and second waves, Hickam Field suffers the heaviest damage of Oahu's airbases.

SOUTHEAST LOCH

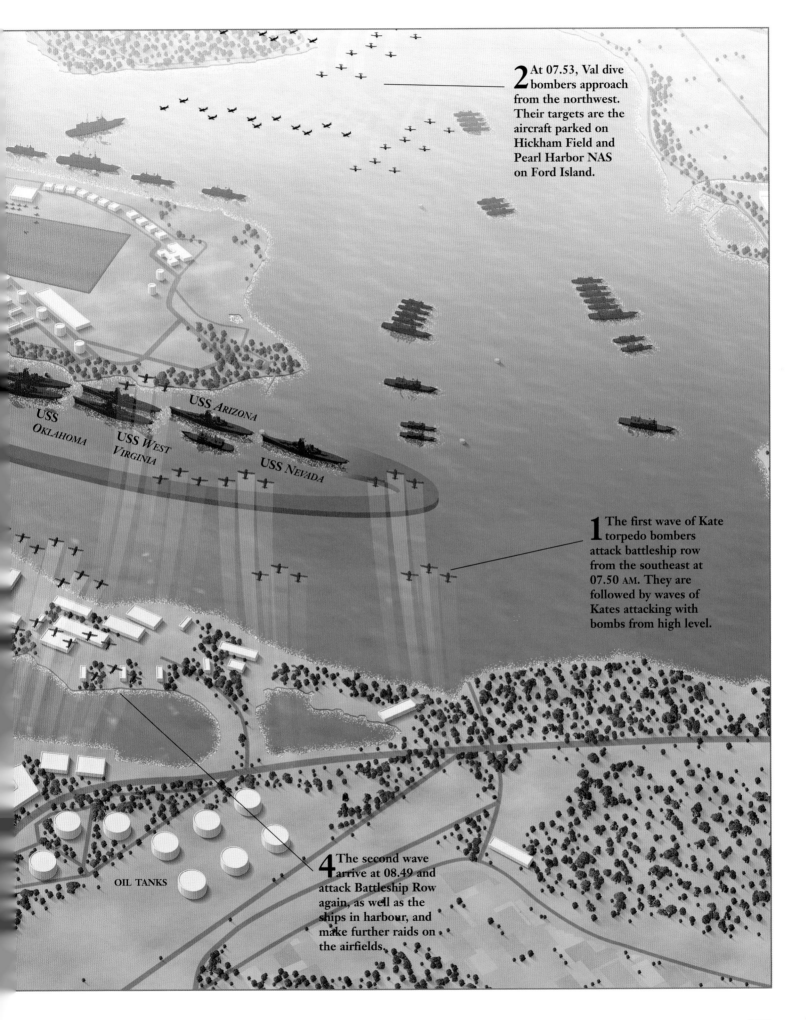

2 At 07.53, Val dive bombers approach from the northwest. Their targets are the aircraft parked on Hickham Field and Pearl Harbor NAS on Ford Island.

USS OKLAHOMA

USS WEST VIRGINIA

USS ARIZONA

USS NEVADA

1 The first wave of Kate torpedo bombers attack battleship row from the southeast at 07.50 AM. They are followed by waves of Kates attacking with bombs from high level.

4 The second wave arrive at 08.49 and attack Battleship Row again, as well as the ships in harbour, and make further raids on the airfields.

OIL TANKS

371

US personnel man air defences at Pearl Harbor. These men are armed with 7.62mm (0.3in) Browning medium machine guns. The Browning was a multipurpose machine gun used by all US forces during World War II, and could be seen mounted on tanks, aircraft and infantry trucks.

The 20,574 tonne (20,250 ton) aircraft carrier Hiryu took part in the Pearl Harbor attack. Slightly small for a fleet carrier, she could carry 70 aircraft. The Hiryu was sunk at the Battle of Midway on 5 June 1942.

Pearl Harbor, as it was in plain view of the city and aerial sightseeing trips across it were permitted.

THE HAWAII OPERATION

The Naval General Staff finally accepted Yamamoto's plan, known as the Hawaii Operation, on 3 November 1941. A week later, the first minor units of the fast carrier striking force under Vice-Admiral Chuichi Nagumo sailed for a secret rendezvous at Tankan Bay in the Kurile Islands. At the same time, a force of 16 submarines, five of which carried a number of midget submarines, left harbour to co-ordinate their attack with the main carrier force. On 26 November 1941, Nagumo, aboard the

flagship *Akagi*, led out the fleet carriers *Kaga*, *Shokaku*, *Zuikaku*, *Hiryu* and *Soryu*. These six carriers made up the largest concentration of naval airpower ever assembled. They boarded a total of 423 Zero fighters, Kate torpedo-bombers and older Aichi D3A Val dive-bombers.

Their supporting force consisted of two battleships, two heavy cruisers, a light cruiser, nine destroyers and eight replenishment tanks and supply ships. Negotiations with the United States were continuing, though neither side seems to have expected a successful outcome.

On 27 November 1941, all US Army and Navy commanders received a final war warning. Despite the heightened tensions, life at the US base continued much as normal. The Commander-in-Chief of the Pacific Fleet, Admiral HE Kimmel, was more concerned with the nearest Japanese possession, the Marshall Islands to the southwest, the likeliest launching point for any Japanese assault. Not that the United States anticipated an air attack, its main concern being sabotage or, perhaps, submarines.

Indeed, the fact that a large number of P40 fighters had just been transferred to Wake and Midway Island confirmed the extent to which the United States did not consider it a serious threat. Anti-aircraft positions around the harbour had no ready ammunition and the USAAF fighters lay undispersed on their airfields. Because of the shallowness of the harbour, torpedo nets were considered unnecessary. Worrying intelligence gleaned from Japanese diplomatic ciphers, which indicated a Japanese interest in the islands, was not even passed on to Hawaii.

'CLIMB MOUNT FUJI'

Nagumo's force sailed for five days under cover of a weather front moving at a similar pace to the fleet. The route took them well

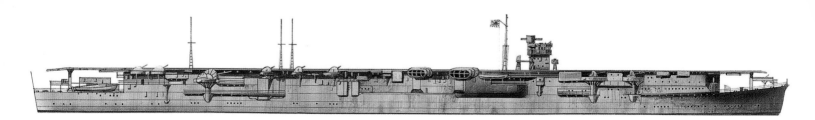

PEARL HARBOR

clear of shipping routes. The task force successfully refuelled on 28 November. On 2 December, Nagumo received a fleet signal from Yamamoto, 'Climb Mount Fuji', meaning that the attack was to go ahead as planned. On 4 December, the weather improved, and by 6 December the seas were clear at last. By the time the task force had reached the attack point, 443km (275 miles) north of Pearl Harbor, the conditions were perfect. This seemed so miraculous that both Nagumo and the first strike wave's leader, Air Commander Mitsuo Fuchida (1902–1976), believed that it signified divine intervention.

On 7 December, Nagumo received the disappointing news that the US carriers were absent, but Yamamoto, well aware of the implications, allowed the attack to go ahead. Fuschida briefed his pilots one final time. The torpedo-bombers were to go in first, followed by the dive-bombers. The

fighters would concentrate primarily on the two USAAF bases, Hickam and Wheeler Field, strafe the ships and deal with any US planes that managed to get into the air. If they failed to gain the surprise, Fuschida would fire two flares, indicating that the dive-bombers should go in first to cause maximum confusion. He and his aircrews boarded their planes at 0600. Fuschido's force of 183 aircraft took off, assembled in formation, climbed to 3048m (10,000ft) and headed southwards towards Pearl Harbor.

The United States' first indication of an enemy presence was a contact made with a submarine at 0342. That or another was depth-charged at 0645 at the entrance of the harbour. Yet it was only at 0725 that Admiral Kimmel was informed. American radar had also picked up an earlier Japanese float plane reconnaissance mission, but for some reason no action was taken. Even when the main assault wave was detected,

The carnage at the Ford Island Naval Air Station following the Japanese raid. Smoke from the USS Arizona billows behind the Catalina and Kingfisher aircraft in the foreground.

A rescue launch plucks a man from the water, as the USS West Virginia *burns in the background. The USS* Tennessee *lies behind her.*

no report was made because a flight of B17s was expected from the same direction. In harbour that Sunday morning were some 70 warships, including eight battleships.

The Japanese formation flew over Oahu Bay at 0749, having achieved complete surprise. Due to a mix-up, Fuschida fired two flares, which meant the Val dive-bombers and Kate torpedo-bombers made their attack at the same time, though it seems to have made very little difference to the effectiveness of their attack. Five battleships were torpedoed, as well as two cruisers. Armour-piercing bombs hit two more. The fighters strafed the Army and Marine air bases. By 0825, the first wave had withdrawn. Fuschido remained, waiting for the second wave, which arrived

24 minutes later. Some 170 planes led by Lieutenant-Commander Shegekazu Shimazaki now attacked Battleship Row, as well as the ships moored in docks, and then made further runs on the airfields. Despite the fact that smoke obscured the target, they were able to cause serious damage, and the fleet flagship USS *Pennsylvania* was hit, as were several destroyers.

By 0945, the attack was over and the Japanese planes were on their way back to the carriers. Nagumo, pleased by the reports of the action, refused to launch a third strike. This decision ignored the advice of Fuschido and it proved to be a serious mistake; in particular, he missed the opportunity to attack the port repair facilities and fuel installations. The task

Right: The shattered remains of aircraft at Wheeler Field in the aftermath of the attack. Amongst the wreckage are the remains of a Curtiss P-40 Warhawk fighter and an amphibian.

force steered away for a replenishment rendezvous and then back to Japan.

NEW ERA OF NAVAL WARFARE

In less than two hours, Japan had sunk six battleships and damaged two others, sunk three destroyers and three light cruisers; four other vessels had also been sunk. The battle squadron of the Pacific Fleet had ceased to exist.

On the airfields, 164 planes had been destroyed and 128 damaged. Altogether, 2403 Americans had been killed and a further 1176 wounded. The cost to Japan was just 29 aircraft and 54 pilots and aircrew. It had been a carefully planned and superbly executed raid.

Yet, there were a number of flaws in what appeared to be a perfect operation. The base facilities of the base remained intact, as did the vast oil-storage tanks full of fuel. Therefore, the US Pacific Fleet could remain at, and operate out of, Pearl Harbor

rather than having to retreat to San Diego. Furthermore, amongst all the ships sunk and damaged, there were no carriers. Longer term, six of the battleships would be repaired and returned to service.

Japan had ushered in a new era of naval warfare, but it had also brought upon itself war with a nation that would eventually ensure it suffered a comprehensive defeat of terrible proportions.

Below: Japanese torpedo bombers attack Battleship Row at about 0800 on 7 December, seen from a Japanese aircraft. The ships are, from lower left to right: USS Nevada; USS Arizona with Vestal outboard; Tennessee with West Virginia outboard; Maryland with Oklahoma outboard; Neosho and California. White smoke in the distance is from Hickam Field.

STALINGRAD
23 AUGUST 1942—2 FEBRUARY 1943

THE BATTLE FOR STALINGRAD WAS A TURNING POINT IN WORLD WAR II. THE RED ARMY INFLICTED A TELLING DEFEAT ON THE PREVIOUSLY VICTORIOUS GERMANS, DEMONSTRATING A REAL GRASP OF SUCCESSFUL STRATEGIC AND OPERATIONAL WARFARE – WHICH WOULD GO ON TO SERVE THEM WELL IN SUBSEQUENT CAMPAIGNS.

WHY DID IT HAPPEN?

WHO The German Sixth and Fourth Panzer Armies under Colonel Generals Von Paulus (1890–1957) and Hoth (1885–1971) against the Soviet Sixty-Second Army under General V. Chuikov.

WHAT Bogged down in urban fighting where their superior mobile tactics were useless, the Germans were unable to completely capture the city before the onset of winter, and were subsequently trapped by a Soviet counter-offensive.

WHERE The city of Stalingrad, located on the western bank of the River Volga, 900km (560 miles) southeast of Moscow.

WHEN 23 August 1942–2 February 1943.

WHY As part of Operation Blue, the German drive on the Caucasus, the Sixth Army was tasked with clearing the western bank of the Volga river. Stalingrad was a major city controlling crossing points across the Volga. Capturing the city also had significant political symbolism, since it bore Stalin's name.

OUTCOME After months of fighting, the Germans and Axis troops had captured most of the city with the Red Army hanging on to only a few toeholds on the western bank of the Volga. But on 19 November, the Soviets launched Operation Uranus, which encircled over 200,000 German troops centred on Stalingrad. The eventual Soviet victory marked a major turning point in the war on the Eastern Front.

Operation Barbarossa, the German invasion of the Soviet Union, was the largest land invasion in history, pitting 3.6 million German and other Axis troops against 3 million Soviet troops, in the western Soviet Union. Hitler's war against the Soviet Union opened on 22 June 1941 with a massive air strike by the *Luftwaffe*. The Germans advanced on three main axes – towards Leningrad in the north, Moscow in the centre and into the Ukraine in the south. The Germans smashed through a Soviet military that was ravaged by the purges of the 1937 and 1938, poorly trained and organized, only moderately equipped, and constrained by its political leadership, particularly Joseph

German senior NCOs take cover in a bomb crater while calling forward other troops to support them. Both men are armed with MP38 submachine-guns – ideal weapons for close quarters and urban fighting.

Stalin, who insisted on a strategy of forward defence.

THE GERMAN ADVANCE

The Soviet dispositions and the rolling, open terrain of the steppes of western Russia and the Ukraine proved ideal for the mobile, fast-moving blitzkrieg warfare at which the Germans excelled. The result was that approximately 3 million Soviet troops were captured in the opening months of the offensive. Towards the end of 1941, German spearheads had reached the outskirts of both Moscow and Leningrad. Hitler had predicted, 'We have only to kick in the door and the whole rotten structure will come crashing down'. Yet despite taking almost unimaginable losses in terms of manpower, equipment and land, the Soviets continued to fight. Unclear strategic goals, logistical overstretch, unexpectedly tough Soviet resistance and the terrible Russian winter meant that the Germans failed to defeat their enemy decisively. Indeed the Red Army was still capable of surprises and its counter-offensive at Moscow on 5/6 December knocked the over-extended, exhausted Germans back more than 160km (100 miles) in places before their line stabilized.

Barbarossa had resulted in massive German losses, too – they had suffered almost 1.1 million casualties and almost all of the army's divisions were below strength. So in the spring of 1942, as the *Wehrmacht* contemplated going back onto the offensive, there could be no question of resuming the offensive across the whole front. The Germans had the resources for a single thrust only. Rather than resume the attack on Moscow as anticipated by Stalin and the Soviet High Command, Hitler instead decided to move towards the south and attack the Soviet oilfields in the Transcaucasus. This was the source of 90 per cent of Soviet fuel, and their capture would have the dual effect of not only depriving the Red Army of its oil but, in the long-term, solving Germany's own oil supply problems. This had become particularly pressing with the entry of the United States into the war in December 1941. With the prospect of the opening of a possible second front (in the west of Europe) and a drawn out attritional war on two fronts, Germany

needed extra energy resources. Hitler outlined this strategy in *Führer* Directive No 41 on 5 April 1942: 'All available forces will be concentrated on the main operations in the Southern sector, with the aim of destroying the enemy before the Don [river], in order to secure the Caucasian oil fields and the passes through the Caucasian mountains themselves.'

GETTING READY FOR BATTLE

Operation Blue, as the plan was codenamed, was undertaken by Army Group South, consisting of 1 million German and 300,000 Romanian, Hungarian and Italian troops,

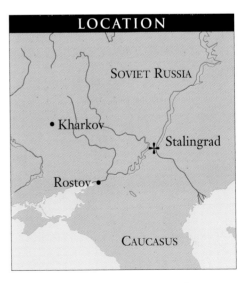

LOCATION

SOVIET RUSSIA

Kharkov

Stalingrad

Rostov

CAUCASUS

Stalingrad sat on a key river crossing on the west bank of the Volga about 900 miles south of Moscow. If it remained in Soviet hands it threatened the left flank of the German advance into the Caucasus.

STALINGRAD

A German officer marshals his platoon in preparation for a local assault in central Stalingrad, October 1942. They are in the goods yard of one the city's railway stations. The men are stripped down to their basic kit of entrenching tool, water bottle, side arm, ammunition and ground sheet – enough to survive on the battlefield for a few days.

THE OPPOSED FORCES

SOVIET (estimated)

Total: 90,000

GERMAN AND AXIS (estimated)

Total: 170,000

supported by *Luftflotte* 4 with 1500 aircraft. There were two main axes of advance – Army Group A would drive for the Caucasus, while Army Group B would secure the northeastern flank of the advance by clearing the western side of the Don and Volga Rivers. Blue opened on 28 June 1942. For the first and only time in the war, Stalin had given permission to the Red Army to trade space for time and so the Germans made excellent progress.

Army Group A reached the oil fields at Maikop on 9 August, but the advance slowed thereafter as resources were switched to Army Group B, which was spearheaded by the Sixth Army, commanded by Colonel-General Friedrich Von Paulus. The Sixth Army was pushing towards the city of Stalingrad, although it faced some hard fighting in front of the Don river.

Hitler ordered that Stalingrad be taken on 23 July. Militarily there were some sound reasons for capturing the city, because it would secure the flank of Army Group South, which was sitting on a major crossing point on the Volga River, blocking an obvious position for a Soviet counterattack. However, the main motivations behind the order were political and psychological. The capture of the city that bore Stalin's name would be of huge value to the morale of both Germany and its allies.

Stalin understood the importance of his city as much as Hitler. It was here he had seen service in the Civil War. On 12 July, he established the Stalingrad Front, made up of Sixty-Second, Sixty-Third and Sixty-Fourth Armies. A week later, the city itself was put on an immediate war footing, but there was to be no mass evacuation of the population because Stalin believed that the troops would fight better for a 'living city'.

On 23 July, he issued Order No 227 that the Red Army would take 'not a step back'. There would be nowhere to retreat if the Germans crossed the Volga. Nonetheless the Germans were able to batter their way through the Sixty-Fourth Army and cross the Don on 23 August. The same day, *Luftflotte* 4, launched a massive air raid on Stalingrad causing 30,000 casualties and a temporary breakdown in civil government.

At the same time, the first German spearheads reached the Volga at Rynok and entered Stalingrad's northern suburbs. However, the main advance on the city slowed in the face of difficult terrain, desperate Soviet resistance and German exhaustion.

Thus, the bulk of Paulus' army had reached only the outskirts of central Stalingrad in early September. Hoth's Fourth Panzer Army suffered similar difficulties in reaching the southern suburbs, yet still the Germans believed that the city was within their grasp.

THE COMMANDERS LINE UP

The Soviets estimated that approximately 170,000 men, 500 tanks and 3000 artillery pieces of the Sixth Army and Fourth Panzer Army faced them on the 64km (40 mile) area of operations round Stalingrad and its environs. The three armies – Sixty-Second, Sixty-Third and Sixty-Fourth – of the South Eastern Front (subsequently the Stalingrad Front) could muster about 90,000 troops, 120 tanks and 2000 guns.

A similar imbalance was present on the narrower front of the city itself, with the defending Sixty-Second Army fielding 54,000 men against about 100,000 Germans. Although the actual numbers fluctuated during the course of the battle, the force ratios of approximately 2:1 remained reasonably constant throughout.

Stalin appointed Georgi Zhukov (1896–1974) as Deputy Supreme Commander and sent him south to organize a counterattack at Stalingrad. However, the Soviet defence rested in the hands of the Front commander General Andrei Yeremenko (1892–1970) and more specifically Vasily Chuikov (1900–1982), who commanded the Sixty-Second Army that held the city itself.

Tough, scruffy and uncompromising, the 42-year-old Chuikov was to prove an inspired choice, holding his nerve through the darkest moments of the battle. He was something of a contrast to his German opposite number General Von Paulus. The tall, neat Von Paulus was an excellent staff officer and had done reasonably well commanding the Sixth Army at Rostov in May and during the drive on Stalingrad. However, he was probably less well suited to the desperate, confused urban battle that confronted him than Chuikov.

The Soviets had chosen their ground well. In the campaigns that proceeded Stalingrad, the Germans had proved masters of the fast-moving warfare that typified the fighting in the wide open spaces of the steppes. Key to their success had been the coordination of their infantry and armour and, particularly, close air support. Indeed Chuikov identified this as a key German strength, noting that: 'The enemy had firm mastery in the air. This dispirited our troops more than anything, and we feverishly thought about how to take this trump card out the enemy's hand'.

Fighting in the close confines of a city would make coordination of the *Luftwaffe's* air attacks much more difficult, particularly if the Soviet troops kept as close to the German lines as possible. Indeed, the urban environment would negate the previous German tactical advantage in mobile operations because there would now be very little room to manoeuvre. Conversely, the

A painting of the crossing of the Volga, in the socialist realist style popular amongst Soviet artists. This captures some of the danger, difficulty chaos that the effort to keep the Sixty-Second Army supplied across the river involved.

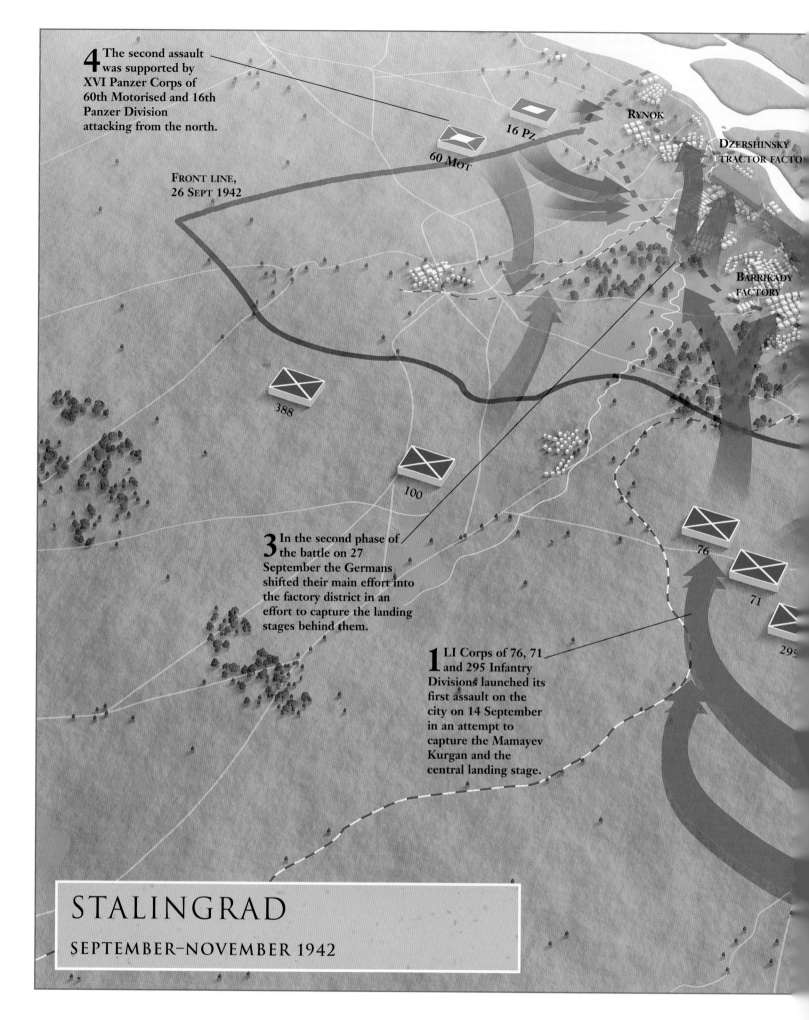

4 The second assault was supported by XVI Panzer Corps of 60th Motorised and 16th Panzer Division attacking from the north.

16 PZ

60 MOT

RYNOK

DZERSHINSKY TRACTOR FACTO

FRONT LINE, 26 SEPT 1942

BARRIKADY FACTORY

388

100

76

71

29s

3 In the second phase of the battle on 27 September the Germans shifted their main effort into the factory district in an effort to capture the landing stages behind them.

1 LI Corps of 76, 71 and 295 Infantry Divisions launched its first assault on the city on 14 September in an attempt to capture the Mamayev Kurgan and the central landing stage.

STALINGRAD

SEPTEMBER–NOVEMBER 1942

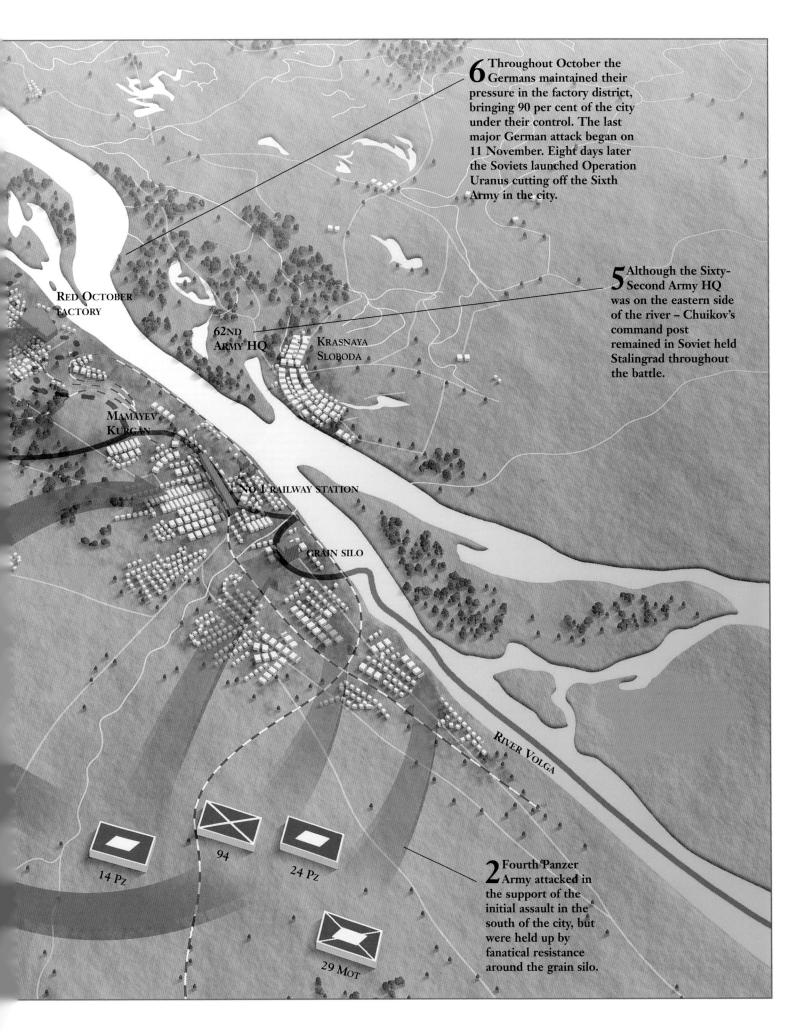

6 Throughout October the Germans maintained their pressure in the factory district, bringing 90 per cent of the city under their control. The last major German attack began on 11 November. Eight days later the Soviets launched Operation Uranus cutting off the Sixth Army in the city.

5 Although the Sixty-Second Army HQ was on the eastern side of the river – Chuikov's command post remained in Soviet held Stalingrad throughout the battle.

RED OCTOBER FACTORY

62ND ARMY HQ

KRASNAYA SLOBODA

MAMAYEV KURGAN

NO 1 RAILWAY STATION

GRAIN SILO

RIVER VOLGA

14 Pz

94

24 Pz

29 MOT

2 Fourth Panzer Army attacked in the support of the initial assault in the south of the city, but were held up by fanatical resistance around the grain silo.

cityscape would play to many Soviet advantages, such as the Red Army's proven defensive tenacity, skill in hand to hand fighting and willingness to engage in a battle of attrition.

THE BATTLE RAGES

The Germans' first assault on the city started on 14 September with a two-pronged assault by 51st Corps on the centre and south, supported by a push from the extreme southern suburbs by Fourth Panzer Army. The aim was to seize the dominating heights of Mamayev Kurgan, where Chuikov had his headquarters, and to capture the central landing stage, splitting the Sixty-Second Army in two and isolating it from resupply. An artillery strike knocked out Chuikov's HQ and the Germans pushed up over the Mamayev Kurgan towards Stalingrad No 1 railway station and the landing stage. Chuikov committed his last tactical reserves and pleaded to his front commander, Yeremenko, to send him Major-General Rodmitstev's elite 13th Guards Division. The division had to fight its way from the landing stage to the station and on to the southeastern slopes of Mamayev Kurgan. The station changed hands 15 times, the German 71st Division finally securing it on 19 September. By then, the 13th Guards, who had entered the battle 10,000 strong, could muster just 2700 men. In the south of city, the Fourth Panzer Army met intense resistance, culminating in the battle around the grain silo, where only 50 naval infantry and guardsmen held up three

German divisions for several days. However, by 26 September, the Fourth Panzer Army had reached the Volga and split Sixty-Fouth Army from Chuikov's Sixty-Second. The Sixth Army held the crest of Mamyev Kurgan and made substantial gains in the centre. Paulus could declare that 'the battle flag of the Reich flies over the Stalingrad Party building', but the fight was far from over.

Although the battle continued around Mamyev Kurgan, the main German effort shifted into the factory district on 27 September. Their attacks against Soviet positions at the vast industrial complexes of the Red October, Barrikady and Tractor factories were intended to capture the landing stages behind them. Controlling the Volga was the key to the battle, as it was the Sixty-Second Army's vital lifeline. Despite the tactical dominance of the *Luftwaffe* and the best efforts of the German artillery, they never managed to stop the flow of supplies and men across the river. After a week of bitter fighting, the Sixth Army managed to cut off the Tractor Factory. There was a lull in fighting and then the Germans redoubled their efforts in the factory district, finally capturing Barrikady and most of Red October.

By the end of October, they held 90 per cent of the city and had all the Soviet controlled areas under fire. This had been achieved at a massive cost. The Sixth Army was battered and exhausted, but it had still not done enough. The Red Army had taken the best the *Wehrmacht* could throw at it, yet it still clung to the banks of the

The T34/76 was, by early 1943, the mainstay of Soviet armoured forces and, when first encountered by the Germans in 1941 easily the best tank in world, belying the myth of Soviet technical inferiority. It remained a formidable tank and was central the success of Operation Uranus. The tank was very reliable in adverse weather conditions, well-armed with the 76mm (3in) cannon and had wide tracks that did not get easily bogged down on the muddy Russian roads.

STALINGRAD

Volga. On 11 November, Paulus launched his last major assault, again in the factory district. It met with some success as German troops managed to reach the west bank of the river.

GERMANS ARE SURROUNDED

To maintain momentum over the seven weeks of bitter house-to-house fighting, the German command narrowed the Sixth Army and Fourth Panzer Army's front, leaving the flanks covered by Italian and Romanian forces. Stalin had given Zhukov the task of organizing a counterattack to cut off the Sixth Army in Stalingrad. He built up one million men and 900 tanks in the hinterland behind the Volga, undetected by the Germans. Zhukov launched his assault, Operation Uranus, on 19 November.

Three Armies of General Vatutin's South-West Front smashed through the Third Romanian Army, and a day later Yeremenko's Stalingrad Front brushed aside the Fourth Romanian Army in the south. The two Fronts met at Kalach on 23 November, completing a perfect encirclement that trapped roughly 250,000 German and Axis troops in the Stalingrad pocket. Paulus requested permission to break out, but Hitler refused. The head of the *Luftwaffe*, Herman Göring, pledged to supply the Sixth Army by air and Hitler ordered Field Marshal Von Manstein to prepare a counterattack to relieve Paulus' trapped troops. Operation Winter Storm, which opened on 12 December, needed to cover about 96km (60 miles). It was stopped 56km (35 miles) south of Stalingrad.

Meanwhile, Zhukov launched Operation Little Saturn, which threatened the entire German position in the south. Winter Storm was the Sixth Army's last hope. The *Luftwaffe* barely managed to land a third of the supplies required, and from 10 January the German position was increasingly constricted by Operation Ring, General Rokossovsky's Don Front's attempt to close the pocket entirely. Despite the futility of the struggle, the Soviets were impressed by the resilience of the German defenders. Nevertheless, the Soviets had taken about half the pocket just a week later and after the last airfield fell, Paulus asked Hitler for

permission to surrender. Hitler refused. By 29 January, the Germans had been reduced to two pockets in the city, one around the Unimag Department Store in the centre, the other in the factory district. On 31 January, Hitler promoted Paulus to Field Marshal. The implications were obvious; no German officer of that rank had ever been captured alive. Paulus surrendered that day although the northern pocket held out to 2 February. German casualties at Stalingrad were about 200,000, with 110,000 of the Sixth Army going into Soviet captivity. Only 5000 ever made it home (the rest died in captivity).

AFTERMATH

Stalingrad was a pivotal turning point in the war against Nazi Germany. The Red Army had inflicted a major operational, arguably strategic, defeat on a broadly numerically similar but tactically more skilled opponent. It had done this by fighting the *Wehrmacht* in an environment that nullified the Germans' advantages. The desperate fighting in Stalingrad had merely served to fix the Germans in place for the devastating counter-stroke of Operation Uranus, a complex, highly mobile double-envelopment that sealed the fate of the Sixth Army. This new Soviet skill and confidence was used from Stalingrad onwards and was the turning point on the Eastern Front.

A soldier from the Sixty-Second Army waves a red flag to celebrate the Soviet victory, Fallen Fighters Square, Stalingrad, February 1943. In the background is the Univermag department store, where Paulus located his headquarters.

NORMANDY LANDINGS

6 JUNE 1944

OPERATION OVERLORD, THE ALLIED INVASION OF EUROPE, WAS LAUNCHED AGAINST NAZI-OCCUPIED FRANCE WITH SOME 5000 SHIPS AND 175,000 MEN. IT WAS THE GREATEST AMBHIBIOUS OPERATION EVER CONCEIVED AND EXECUTED.

WHY DID IT HAPPEN?

WHO General Dwight D Eisenhower (1890–1969), Supreme Allied Commander; Sir Arthur Tedder (1890–1967), Air Chief Marshal; Lt General Omar Bradley (1893–1981), US First Army; General Sir Bernard Montgomery (1887–1967), Allied Land Force Commander; Lt General Miles Dempsey (1896–1969), British Second Army.

WHAT The largest amphibious invasion of all time, codename Operation Overlord, with 175,000 troops and 195,000 Allied naval and merchant navy personnel sailing in over 5000 ships.

WHERE Along an 80km (50 mile) stretch of the Normandy coast, divided into five sectors: Utah, Omaha, Gold, Juno and Sword. US forces assaulted Utah and Omaha beaches, while British and Canadian forces assaulted Gold, Juno and Sword.

WHEN 6 June 1944.

WHY A formidable array of blockhouses and gun emplacements dotted the coastline of occupied Europe, with strong defences stretching from the German border to the Loire river. It was vital that these were rendered impotent if landings were to be effective.

OUTCOME By the time darkness fell on 6 June, the Allies had achieved many of their objectives, crucially securing all five of the planned landing beaches. The Germans had been caught completely by surprise. In addition, bombing and sabotage by the French Resistance had wrought havoc with their communications.

At Spithead, off the Isle of Wight, on 5 June 1944, ships' hailers blasted out jaunty tunes and soldiers cheered enthusiastically as they boarded a vast armada bound for the Normandy beaches. These were Allied troops on the eve of heading for Europe, previously under Nazi occupation but now facing the real prospect of liberation. This frenzied activity had its origins almost a year earlier. In August 1943, the British Prime Minister Winston Churchill (1874–1965), US President Franklin Roosevelt (1182–1945) and the Combined Chiefs of Staff had decided that Normandy would be the location for the landings on 'D-Day', officially codenamed Operation Overlord. It was also decided that the Germans should be deliberately deceived into thinking that the area of Pas de Calais, the shortest route across the Channel, had in fact been chosen. To foster this illusion, the shoreline at Dover (opposite Calais) had sprouted fake jetties, oil storage tanks, pipelines and anti-aircraft guns, news of which reached the Germans.

FIVE SECTOR BEACHES

The real landings were to take place along a 80km (50 mile) stretch of the Normandy coast. The coast was divided into five sector beaches codenamed Utah, Omaha, Gold, Juno and Sword. The assault would be in two phases. The first phase would be American, British, Canadian and Free French airborne troops, followed by an amphibious landing of Allied infantry and armoured divisions. Sword and Gold beaches would be assaulted first, followed by Juno, then Omaha and Utah.

DD-tanks (Duplex Drive, nicknamed Donald Duck) were a type of amphibious swimming assault vehicle developed by the British. A Duplex Drive variant of the medium M4 Sherman, pictured here, was used by the Allies during and after the Normandy landings. DD-tanks worked by erecting a flotation screen around the tank, enabling it to float. The Duplex Drive referred to twin propellers that worked off the main engine. The Sherman was particularly suitable for use with the screen because it could move in water with its gun forward, ready to fire as soon as it reached land.

Forces of Operation Neptune, the seaborne part of the invasion, had a vital defensive role, ensuring that army forces could land without disruption by the German naval forces. The task was given to the Royal Navy's Home Fleet, which was mindful of the risk posed by German U-boats switched from the Atlantic. Three escort carriers and Royal Air Force Coastal Command maintained a cordon west of Land's End. Another area of defence were the Straits of Dover, which was surrounded by a solid band of minefields, accompanied by naval and air patrols, and radar and bombing raids on enemy ports. Co-ordination was also underway with various factions of the French Resistance, whose agents were tasked with disrupting German defences by attacking railway lines, ambushing roads and destroying communications.

MULBERRY HARBOURS

From the beginning, the Allies were aware of the difficulties of landing a huge number of military and earthmoving vehicles on the beaches, which would be in danger of becoming hopelessly overcrowded. A scheme was therefore mooted to use artificial harbours to land and support the invasion.

The harbours, code-named Mulberry, built throughout the United Kingdom by a 40,000-strong workforce, consisted of prefabricated concrete blocks the height of five-storey buildings. These were towed across the Channel and, once assembled, they became the ports, breakwaters and pontoons where vessels could tie up and unload their cargoes. In the early hours of D-Day, 6 June, an invasion fleet of over 1000 ships carrying 156,000 men and sections of the Mulberrries headed towards the Normandy coast. Prior to the overall movement, Eisenhower had transmitted his message to all members of the Allied Expeditionary Force: 'You are about to embark upon the great crusade, toward which we have striven these many months'.

D-Day was slated to begin on 5 June. All plans for invasion depended on favourable weather, which was by no means certain. Although most of May had been fine, there was deterioration in conditions, although a brief improvement was forecast for the 6 June. Eisenhower

seized the chance with just three words: 'Okay, let's go'.

As it turned out, the weather on 'D-Day-plus-one' was atrocious with gusts of wind, heavy clouds and bouts of heavy rain. At first, this proved something of an advantage to the Allies. In the circumstances, the Germans did not expect much enemy activity in the Normandy area, for the most part believing that the invasion would be from Pas de Calais. There were also widespread problems within German intelligence. The *Luftwaffe*, which would once have been able to spot enemy activity, was by now shattered and much of the German's radar and early warning technology had

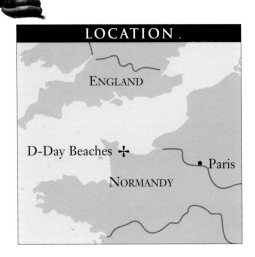

LOCATION

ENGLAND

D-Day Beaches ✠

• Paris

NORMANDY

Successfully landing an army on the Normandy beaches caught the Germans totally off guard, since they had expected that the Allied forces would be launched from the shoreline at Dover, opposite Calais.

Inspired by the successes of British Army Commando units, US Rangers were largely deployed as special infantry in beach landings and in actions against artillery emplacements, machinegun nests and fortified bunkers.

THE OPPOSED FORCES

ALLIES (estimated)

Total:	**150,000**

GERMANS (estimated)

Total:	**60,000**

been rendered impotent by Allied air raids. On 5 June, many senior German commanders were so unaware of the impending invasion that they attended war games at Rennes, Brittany. Field Marshal Erwin Rommel (1891–1944), who was responsible for the defence of the northwest coast, even went to Germany the next day to attend his wife's birthday.

With the exception of Hitler, who had long suspected that the Allied invasion would come at Normandy, senior echelons of the Nazi High Command had thought that the Pas de Calais was the target area for potential invasion. Panzer reserves remained stationed near Paris till around 16:00, when orders were finally given to move to the coast.

PEGASUS BRIDGE CAPTURED

At 0016 on 6 June 1944, the invasion began. At the eastern end of Sword Beach, the British 3rd Infantry Division commenced their assault at 07:15. Comprising a combination of infantry, commando and armoured units, the British forces fought their way off the beach and captured the strongpoint of La Bréche.

Airborne landings took place largely some distance behind the beaches, designed to clear paths for the amphibious forces, aiding a swift progress inland. Pre-dawn glider landings brought in anti-tank guns and support troops for each division. Forces of British 6th Airborne Division had been earmarked for a particular role centred near Sword beach. The area was straddled by bridges that the Germans were certain to cross in their bid to attack the eastern flank of the invasion force. It became essential to take the bridges intact and hold them until relieved. A force of 181 men, led by Major John Howard, took off in six Horsa gliders to capture Benouville Bridge (later renamed Pegasus Bridge) and Horsa Bridge, lying a few hundred metres to the east on the Orne River. The attackers poured out of their battered gliders, taking the German defenders by surprise, snatching the bridges within 10 minutes and losing just two men in the process.

Major Howard had been assured support from one of the most colourful of the British Commando troops, landing on nearby Sword Beach. This was Simon Christopher Joseph Fraser Lovat – Lieutenant Colonel, the Lord Lovat. He could claim worthy ancestors, notably General Fraser of Lovat who had raised the 78th Fraser Highlanders and in 1759 had commanded in the capture of Quebec, when his troops had scaled the Heights of Abraham, their shields proudly emblazoning the *fraises*, an heraldic pun on the cherished 'Fraser'. Lovat's role had been to land at Sword beach, clear a way through the town of Ouistreham and join troops of 6th Airborne at Pegasus Bridge.

The main invasion force at Sword Beach had to capture the village of Ouistreham in the push towards Caen. The assaulting troops faced a solid line of sea front villas, from which the Germans were firing, as well as a casino that had been turned into a fortress. After a massive preliminary bombardment by Allied warships came a launch of tanks, followed by infantry, clearing the shore line and storming the houses one by one. Short work was made of the fortified casino and Ouisterham was cleared, followed by fast progress towards the bridges and the Orne canal.

The ultimate objective had been to capture the area of Caen, just 11km (7 miles) away, but Sword beach came under fire from a German panzer division. There was no swift advance, only a hard battle; Caen was to remain in German hands for some weeks.

US FORCES AT OMAHA

On Omaha Beach, the assault of the 1st and 29th US Infantry Divisions began at 06:30. The US forces making for the beach – forever after to be known as 'Bloody Omaha' – were crammed into landing craft. Packed shoulder-to-shoulder and grey with seasickness, they endured the sound of exploding bombs, the rattle of fighter cannon fire and homing in Allied aircraft. There was co-ordination with craft off neighboring Utah beach, where the first wave of Major General J. Lawton Collins' VII Corps linked up with other airborne contingents inland. Omaha turned out to be the most heavily defended of the beaches. Of the 16 tanks that landed on its shores, only two survived. Defences seemed so overwhelming that the commanders, including General Omar Bradley, even considered abandoning the beachhead. Within a few hours on D-Day, American casualties numbered around 5000 out of 50,000 men.

About 20m (60ft) from the beach, the ramps on the landing craft had been lowered with the American GIs dumped waist-high into the water. Dale L. Shrop, a member of the US Demolition Squad of 1st Engineer Combat Battalion, was one of those who had faced heavy enemy fire. 'A lot of the guys were hit below the waist and lost the use of their arms and legs and the tide came in and got them before the medics got them.'

Ahead of the men loomed a rocky, 33m (100ft) cliff called Pointe de Hoc, which jutted into the Seine Bay in the 29km (18 mile) gap between Utah and Omaha. On the clifftop was a battery bristling with the super-powerful 155 French-made guns with a range of 22,860m (25,000yd). The guns dominated Omaha's western half and its sea approaches and were sufficiently deadly to ensure that no big Allied ships could come in close. This meant that the landing craft had to be manned a full 24km (15 miles) out to sea.

The US Rangers, first onto the beach, had received clear instructions: the heavy guns had to be destroyed. This meant scaling the cliff, and the US troops used rocket-fired rope ladders anchored to the top of the cliffs with grappling hooks. Inevitably, not all the ropes held – the climbers who did not crash to their deaths picked themselves up and began the whole process again.

But those who did reach the top found only ruined gun emplacements; no guns had been installed. It was only later that a patrol found that the guns had been cleverly camouflaged in a nearby apple orchard. Even so, they could still have done serious damage to the forces at both Utah and Omaha. The patrol swiftly immobilized them, saving many lives below.

A desperate plea to the US 1st Division down at Omaha Beach for sorely needed reinforcements and ammunition came to nothing: none were available. The only means of salvation was the firepower of naval destroyers lying off shore. One of them, the USS *Satterlee*, responded, hitting every target the Rangers designated. The need for defence forces remained desperate, but the original purpose of the mission had been implemented and the force that had found and destroyed the missing guns was able to advance.

US troops approaching Omaha Beach met tough resistance from formidable defences. Preliminary bombardments had left enemy positions virtually intact. The Germans trained large calibre guns and machineguns on the beaches, while an additional hazard was heaving seas, which delayed the landing of more men, equipment and supplies.

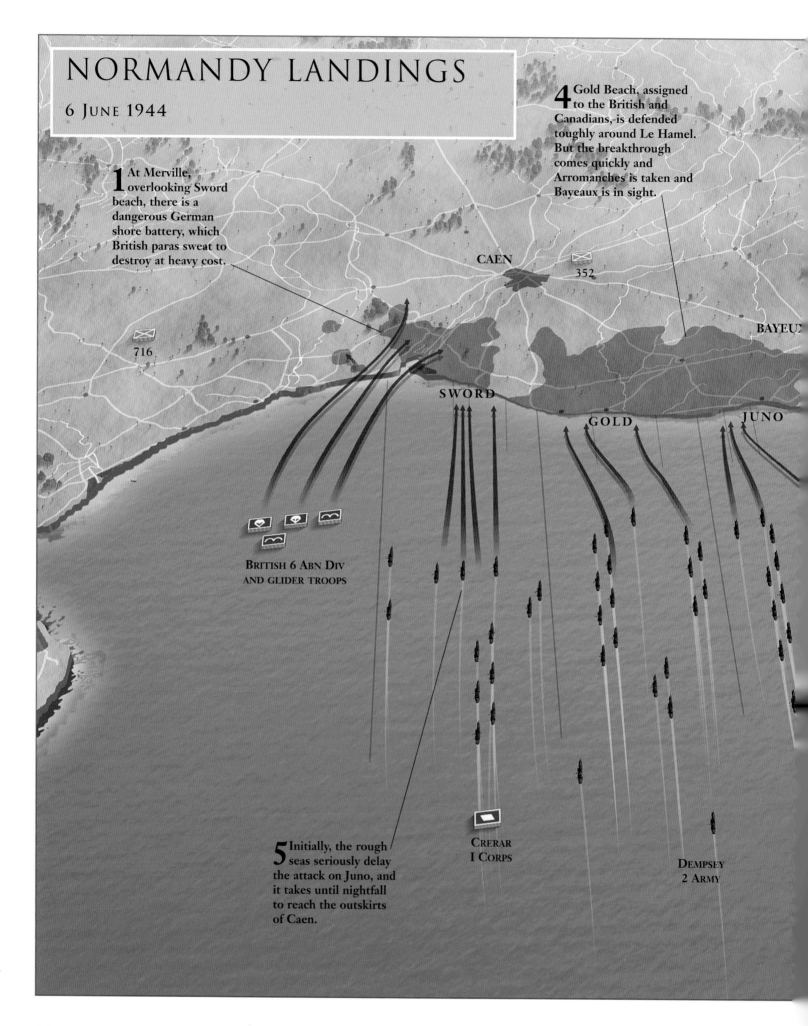

NORMANDY LANDINGS

6 JUNE 1944

1 At Merville, overlooking Sword beach, there is a dangerous German shore battery, which British paras sweat to destroy at heavy cost.

4 Gold Beach, assigned to the British and Canadians, is defended toughly around Le Hamel. But the breakthrough comes quickly and Arromanches is taken and Bayeaux is in sight.

CAEN

352

716

BAYEU

SWORD

GOLD

JUNO

BRITISH 6 ABN DIV
AND GLIDER TROOPS

5 Initially, the rough seas seriously delay the attack on Juno, and it takes until nightfall to reach the outskirts of Caen.

CRERAR
I CORPS

DEMPSEY
2 ARMY

388

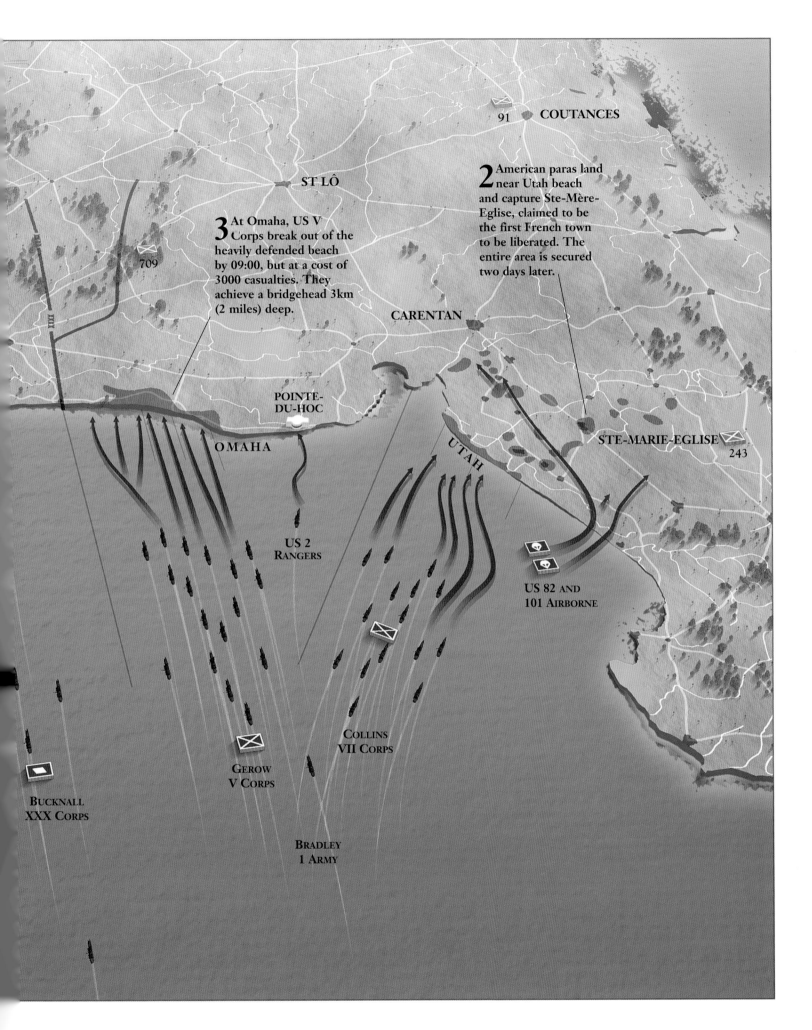

COUTANCES

91

2 American paras land near Utah beach and capture Ste-Mère-Eglise, claimed to be the first French town to be liberated. The entire area is secured two days later.

ST LÔ

3 At Omaha, US V Corps break out of the heavily defended beach by 09:00, but at a cost of 3000 casualties. They achieve a bridgehead 3km (2 miles) deep.

709

CARENTAN

POINTE-DU-HOC

OMAHA

UTAH

STE-MARIE-EGLISE

243

US 2 RANGERS

US 82 AND 101 AIRBORNE

COLLINS VII CORPS

GEROW V CORPS

BUCKNALL XXX CORPS

BRADLEY 1 ARMY

By the day's end, footholds were established on both beaches, but at a high cost on men and matériel.

EVENTS AT OTHER BEACHES

In the Anglo-Canadian sector, at 04:45, two midget submarines helped guide in the invasion fleet using radar and sonar, heralding the start of the naval bombardment. A key hold for the Allies was Juno Beach, stormed by assault troops of the 3rd Canadian Infantry Division, who then linked up with British troops on Gold Beach. Despite facing a tough network of German strongholds and mined beach obstacles, the Canadian tanks secured an advance inland, some of them so speedily that they outran their infantry support and had to temporarily pull back. By the end of the day, the Canadians were able to penetrate further, despite counterattacks by

elements of the German 21st and 12 SS Panzer Division *Hitler Jugend* (Hitler Youth). The increased presence of SS *Hitler Jugend*, which was comprised of fanatical teenagers, was essential for the Germans as they were desperately needed for the defence of Caen.

Further west, Gold Beach was assaulted by the British 50th (Northumbrian) Infantry Division, the assault commencing at 07:30. A preliminary bombardment by Allied ships suppressed much of the German defences, and a beachhead was quickly established with light resistance.

'HOBO'S FUNNIES'

The use of tanks by the Allies throughout was consistent, thanks to the inspiration of Major General Sir Percy Cleghorn Stanley Hobart, or 'Hobo' to his colleagues. Some 10 years before Normandy, he had raised

British troops landing at Juno Beach. Troops on Juno faced an array of machine gun nests, pill boxes and concrete fortifications. But much Allied armour was able to land ahead of infantry, helping to clear the path inland.

and commanded the 1st Tank Brigade, evolving novel methods based on mobility and speed. As part of his innovative approach, Hobart came up with what became known irreverently as 'Hobo's Funnies', which were a variety of devices usually mounted on Sherman and Churchill tanks. These included The Crab, a giant rotating drum with lengths of chain attached to it, which was attached to the front of a tank and used to 'flay' away mines. The Churchill Crocodile had an effective flame gun attached to the front and towed a trailer filled with 1818 litres (400 gallons) of fuel.

The ARK (Armoured Ramp Carrier) had a removable turret and trackway fitted over the top and each end, enabling it to be driven into a ditch to form a causeway over which battle tanks could cross. Other variations included Petards (armed with heavy mortars for destroying fixed emplacements), bulldozers and flails (for clearing mine fields).

As it turned out, the use of tanks on the beaches had varying success. Good results were achieved on Sword beach, where the sea was reasonably calm, and assaults were also effective on Gold. The D-D tanks had been designed to withstand waves up to 30cm (1ft) high, but waves on Omaha were up to 1.8m (6ft) and many tanks were swamped with water.

THE OUTCOME

By the end of the invasion day, the Allies could claim to have secured all five landing beaches and had landed more than 150,000 troops. The establishment of the beach heads meant that finally the Allies had the 'Second Front' they had been seeking. But breakout meant traversing a network of tangled hedgerows and narrow lanes with the ever-present threat of ambush by enemy armour. If Caen had been taken on D-Day, Montgomery could have pushed south and east out of the beachhead area, but German reinforcements had proved too strong and the battle for the town raged on until early August. A breakthrough was not enough; the battle for Normandy was only just beginning.

One of the main reasons for the high casualties at Omaha Beach was that light infantry lacked sufficient armoured support, leaving many of the invaders severely vulnerable. Additionally, tanks had been launched too far out from the beach, many being attacked and sunk.

Scores of solid concrete bunkers in Normandy, built by the Germans with slave labour, were immobilized and were found to consist of a network of corridors, radio and store rooms, accommodation blocks and mounts for heavy guns.

BERLIN
16 APRIL—2 MAY 1945

THE SOVIET OFFENSIVE THAT ENCIRCLED AND CAPTURED BERLIN DURING APRIL/MAY 1945 REPRESENTED THE CULMINATION OF THE BRUTAL WAR WAGED ON THE EASTERN FRONT. THE SOVIET SUCCESS, WHICH LED TO HITLER'S SUICIDE, HASTENED GERMANY'S UNCONDITIONAL SURRENDER ON 8 MAY 1945.

WHY DID IT HAPPEN?

WHO The Soviet Second Belorussian, First Belorussian, and First Ukrainian Fronts, commanded respectively by Marshals Rokossovsky (1896–1968), Zhukov (1896–1974), and Konev (1897–1973), engaged the German Army Groups Vistula and Centre, commanded by Col-Generals Heinrici (1886–1971) and Schörner (1892–1973).

WHAT The Soviet First Belorussian and First Ukrainian Fronts, attacking from the Oder Front, carried out a successful encirclement of Berlin, which led to its capture, while Second Belorussian Front carried out a flank protection offensive further north.

WHERE The Soviets launched the offensive from the Oder Front and, having encircled and captured Berlin, advanced to the Wismar-Schwerin-Wittenberge line in western Mecklenburg and then along the east bank of the River Elbe down to Meissen.

WHEN 16 April–2 May 1945.

WHY Soviets forces had to engage and destroy the powerful German forces deployed along the Oder, whose mission was to protect Berlin. Then the Soviets could drive west to link-up with the Western Allies along the River Elbe, thus completing the defeat of Germany.

OUTCOME Soviet forces encircled Berlin and, after capturing much of the city, forced the remnants of the German defensive garrison to surrender. In the midst of this triumph, the Nazi *Führer*, Adolf Hitler, committed suicide on the afternoon of 30 April.

The Battle of Berlin in spring 1945 represented the climax of the war on the Eastern Front. During January/February 1945, the Red Army advanced through Poland and closed up to the Rivers Oder and Neisse. With key Soviet bridgeheads established over the Oder just 75km (47 miles) from Berlin, a renewed Soviet push to the capital was inevitable. During March and the first half of April 1945, the Soviets poured resources into the Oder front to strengthen the forces deployed by Marshal Rokossovsky's Second Belorussian Front, Marshal Zhukov's First Belorussian Front, and Marshal Konev's First Ukrainian Front. Between them, these three commands fielded 2.4 million troops, 6250 tanks and 41,000 artillery pieces. The German Army Group Vistula and the northern flank of Army Group Centre opposed these Soviet forces, deploying between them 765,000 troops, 1500 AFVs, and 9300 artillery pieces.

The German Army Group Vistula front line stretched south along the Oder's western bank from near Stettin, down to Küstrin, where a Soviet bridgehead west of the river had been established. The front then jutted east of the river around Frankfurt before cutting back west in another Soviet bridgehead. From there it continued south along the western bank of the Rivers Oder and Neisse down into the Army Group Centre sector. The Soviet plan was to execute a double-envelopment

---

A column of IS-2 heavy tanks, on the outskirts of Berlin, March 1945. This Soviet heavy tank, introduced in 1944 and sporting a potent 122mm (4.8in) gun, served in independent regiments that spearheaded the drive on Berlin.

of Berlin. By delineating only the initial boundary between Zhukov and Konev's fronts, Stalin created intense rivalry between the two commanders for the honour of being the first to capture the *Reichstag* in Berlin – the German parliament building.

SOVIET ATTACK BEGINS

On 16 April, the Soviet offensive began after devastatingly powerful artillery bombardments. During 16/17 April, three of Zhukov's armies smashed their way through the initial German positions west of Küstrin, and over the next 48 hours these spearheads gradually fought their way onto the Seelöwe Heights in the face of fanatical German resistance. To overcome this, Zhukov had to commit his key mobile reserves, the 1st and 2nd Guard Tank Armies. Further south that day, six of Konev's armies smashed through the initial German defensive line established along the Neisse's western bank between Forst and Gorlitz. During 17/18 April, Konev's forces surged west towards the River Spree in the beginnings of a huge left-wheel designed to envelop Berlin from the south.

As if these twin offensives were not enough for the Germans to deal with, the neighbouring Second Belorussian Front launched a subsidiary attack on the Oder line south of Stettin on 18 April. Its aim was to drive Army Group Vistula's northern flank – manned by Third Panzer Army – back toward the River Havel, thus protecting the flank of the planned Soviet northern envelopment of Berlin.

From 19 April to 22 April, the Soviet offensives to the northeast and southeast of Berlin continued to advance westwards, permitting the planned encirclement to take form. Zhukov's forces burst through the Seelöwe Heights, enabling the 47th Army to thrust west-southwest to the north of Berlin. Its objective was to reach the eastward course of the River Spree in the Brandenburg-Ketzin area, west of Berlin, where the link-up with Konev's north-westerly advance would take place. Meanwhile, Zhukov's two northern armies advanced northwest to secure an east-west defensive position along the Hohenzollern and Ruppiner Canals to protect the

northern Soviet pincer from any German counterattacks. Simultaneously, four Soviet armies continued to drive the Ninth Army back west from the Seelöwe Heights towards the eastern fringes of Berlin.

BERLIN IS SURROUNDED

Further south, meanwhile, Konev's spearhead armies surged northwest before turning north to approach the Brandenburg–Berlin area from the south; only a 32km (20 mile) gap now separated these forces from the spearheads of Zhukov's Forty-Seventh Army then located northwest of Berlin. In so doing, Konev's forces outflanked much of General Busse's Ninth Army, then still defending

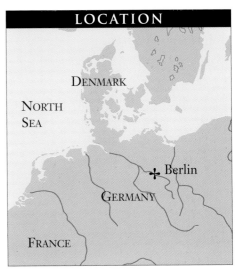
The capital of Germany, Berlin, was located between the River Elbe to the west and the river Oder to the East, in the German province of Brandenburg. To the north, beyond the Ruppiner and Hohenzollern Canals, was the province of Mecklenburg-Vorpommern, while to the south, the River Spree wound its course down to and beyond Bautzen.

BERLIN

Soviet field artillery pieces provided the massive firepower required to soften up the sometimes fanatical German resistance encountered within the hundreds of devastated buildings located in Germany's capital city.

THE OPPOSED FORCES

SOVIET FORCES

SECOND BELORUSSIAN FRONT
(Marshal Konstantin Rokossovsky)

1 x tank army and 5 x armies:
570,000 troops

FIRST BELORUSSIAN FRONT
(Marshal Georgi K. Zhukov)

2 x tank armies and 9 x armies:
980,000 troops

FIRST UKRAINIAN FRONT
(Marshal Ivan Konev)

2 x tank armies and 7 x armies:
850,000 troops

GERMAN FORCES

ARMY GROUP VISTULA
(Col Gen Gotthard Heinrici)

Third Panzer Army
(Pz Gen Hasso von Manteuffel)

Ninth Army (Gen Theodor Busse)

Army Detachment Steiner
(SS Lt Gen Felix Steiner)

Twenty-First Army
(Gen Tippelskirch) (from 27 April)

395,000 troops

ARMY GROUP CENTRE
(Field Marshal Ferdinand Schörner)

Fourth Panzer Army
(Pz Gen Fritz-Herbert Gräser)

Twelfth Army
(Pz Gen Walter Wenck)

370,000 troops

determinedly the Beeskow-Lübben area, southeast of Berlin. Konev's Twenty-Eighth Army, deployed on the inner flank of this envelopment, now wheeled back northeast to link up on 23 April with Zhukov's Sixty-Ninth Army in the area southeast of Berlin. This link-up surrounded much of Ninth Army, plus elements of Fourth Panzer Army, in a pocket located southeast of Berlin. Critically, on 25 April, Konev's spearheads pushed north to link up near Ketzin with Zhukov's Forty-Seventh Army. The Soviets had encircled Berlin.

During this period, Konev's other spearheads had continued to drive west and northwest. By 25 April, they had reached a line that ran from Ketzin, located east of Berlin, southwest via Brandenburg, and thence south via Belzig to Wittenberg on the River Elbe. Konev's front then ran south-southeast along the Elbe's eastern bank, passing close to Torgau and onto Meissen. Konev's southern flank held a line that ran west–east opposing the remainder of Fourth Panzer Army, a part of Col-Gen Schörner's Army Group Centre. That same day, the Western Allies notched up a key milestone. Over the previous fortnight, the US First Army had advanced rapidly east to reach the Rivers Elbe and Mulde between Magdeburg and Halle, where they halted. The Allies now decided to focus on the northern and southern axis of advance, rather than the direct central push onto Berlin.

On 25 April, however, an American patrol pushed further east beyond the Mulde to link up near Torgau with Red Army spearheads that had pushed west beyond the Elbe. Between them, the Allies had split the Reich in two, further hastening the end of the Nazis.

GERMANS COUNTERATTACK

During 21–25 April, as the looming Soviet encirclement of Berlin took shape, Hitler, together with the German Armed Forces and Army High Commands, focused almost exclusively on preventing the Soviet encirclement of Berlin, to the exclusion of everything else going on in the wider war. Their hopes now lay in a series of proposed German counterattacks.

On 22 April, Hitler had ordered the newly formed Army Detachment Steiner to counterattack southwest towards Berlin from the Eberswalde area, thus shattering the northern Soviet pincer. But Steiner's forces possessed more substance in Hitler's mind than in reality, and the counterattack failed to materialize. That afternoon, after a fit of rage at what seemed to Hitler to be Wenck's treasonous failure, the *Führer* suffered a virtual mental collapse: after announcing that the war was lost, he declared his intention both to remain in Berlin to the bitter end and to take his own life should it become necessary to avoid him falling into enemy hands.

BERLIN

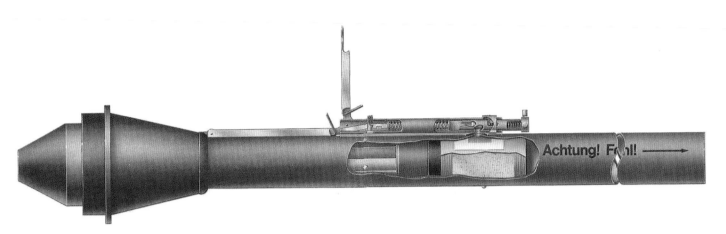

However, that evening, Hitler recovered his poise and now pinned all his hopes on four separate relief efforts that had by then been ordered to begin. First, Steiner's forces, together with elements from the Third Panzer Army, were to attack south and southwest towards Berlin. Second, General Wenck's newly raised divisions were to disengage themselves from the Elbe front around Magdeburg, where they faced the Americans, and counterattack towards Berlin from the southwest, to link up with Ninth Army. Third, the Ninth Army was to smash its way west out of its encirclement around Halbe to link up with Wenck's forces; both commands were then to drive north to relieve Berlin. Finally, Fourth Panzer Army was to thrust north into the southern flank of Konev's advance in the Bautzen area, thus drawing Soviet forces away from Berlin. Hitler placed huge expectations on the prospect that these relief missions would break the Soviet siege around Berlin. In reality, these forces were already fighting for their own survival in a rapidly deteriorating strategic situation and stood little chance of realizing Hitler's grandiose ambitions.

On 25 April, when the Soviets completed their encirclement of Berlin, the defending German garrison, led by General Helmuth Weidling (1891–1955) deployed around 85,000 troops. These forces held a pocket that stretched 6.5km (4 miles) north–south and 9.5km (6 miles) west–east. The defenders comprised one SS and four *Wehrmacht* divisions, together with improvised battle groups formed from Hitler Youth, Home Guard and flak detachments. Some 390,000 Soviet troops, organized into seven armies, now encircled the city.

BERLIN FALLS

Early on 26 April, the final Soviet onslaught, deep into the ruins of Berlin, began. While Soviet artillery, mortars and aircraft unrelentingly poured supporting fire into the ruined buildings, Soviet assault units fought their way forwards building by building, in the face of fanatical German resistance. Conditions inside the German enclave rapidly deteriorated into a humanitarian disaster; thousands of wounded crowded in cellars and bunkers, waiting hours for attention from hopelessly overwhelmed medical staff; corpses lay

B7 1945, the Panzerfaust *was the German infantryman's principal anti-tank weapon. The disposable launcher tube fired a High-Explosive Anti-Tank (HEAT) warhead to a range of 40–100m (130–328ft), depending on the model employed.*

The ISU-152 was a heavy assault gun introduced during late 1943. It mounted a 152mm (6in) gun in a heavily armoured superstructure, built on the chassis of the IS-2 heavy tank. The vehicle was used primarily as an infantry-support weapon, with its main armament proving effective against enemy fortifications as well as troops in trenches. During the war, the Soviets produced 1885 such vehicles, and production continued until well into 1947.

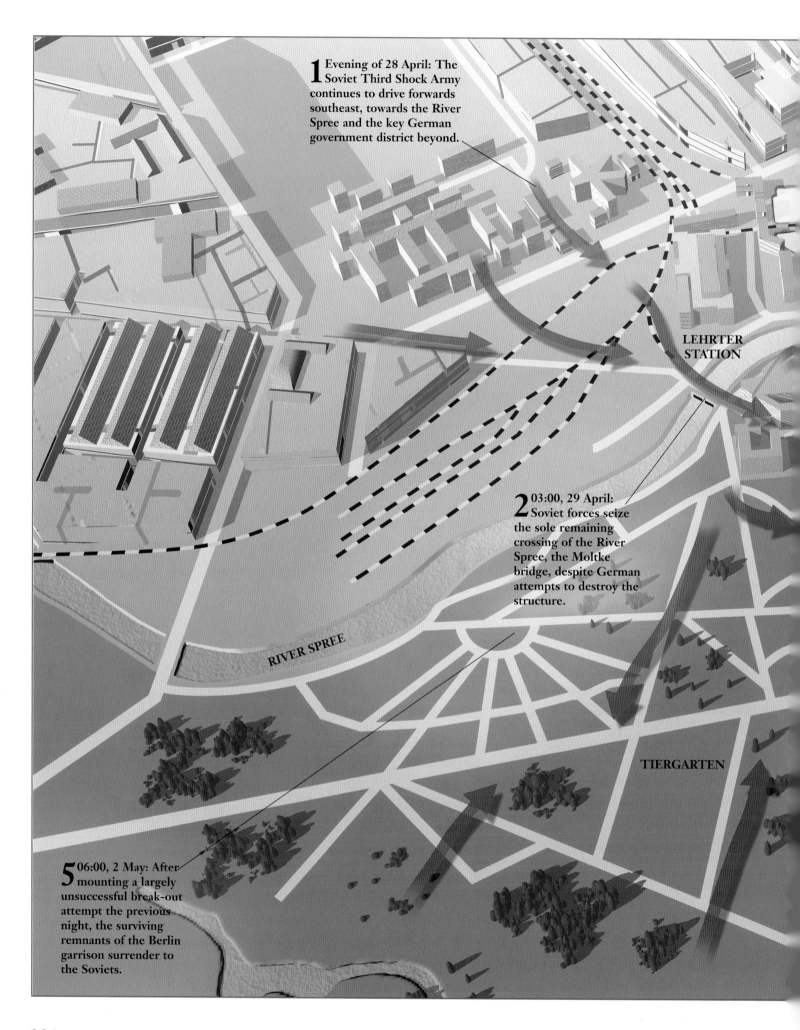

1 Evening of 28 April: The Soviet Third Shock Army continues to drive forwards southeast, towards the River Spree and the key German government district beyond.

LEHRTER STATION

2 03:00, 29 April: Soviet forces seize the sole remaining crossing of the River Spree, the Moltke bridge, despite German attempts to destroy the structure.

RIVER SPREE

TIERGARTEN

5 06:00, 2 May: After mounting a largely unsuccessful break-out attempt the previous night, the surviving remnants of the Berlin garrison surrender to the Soviets.

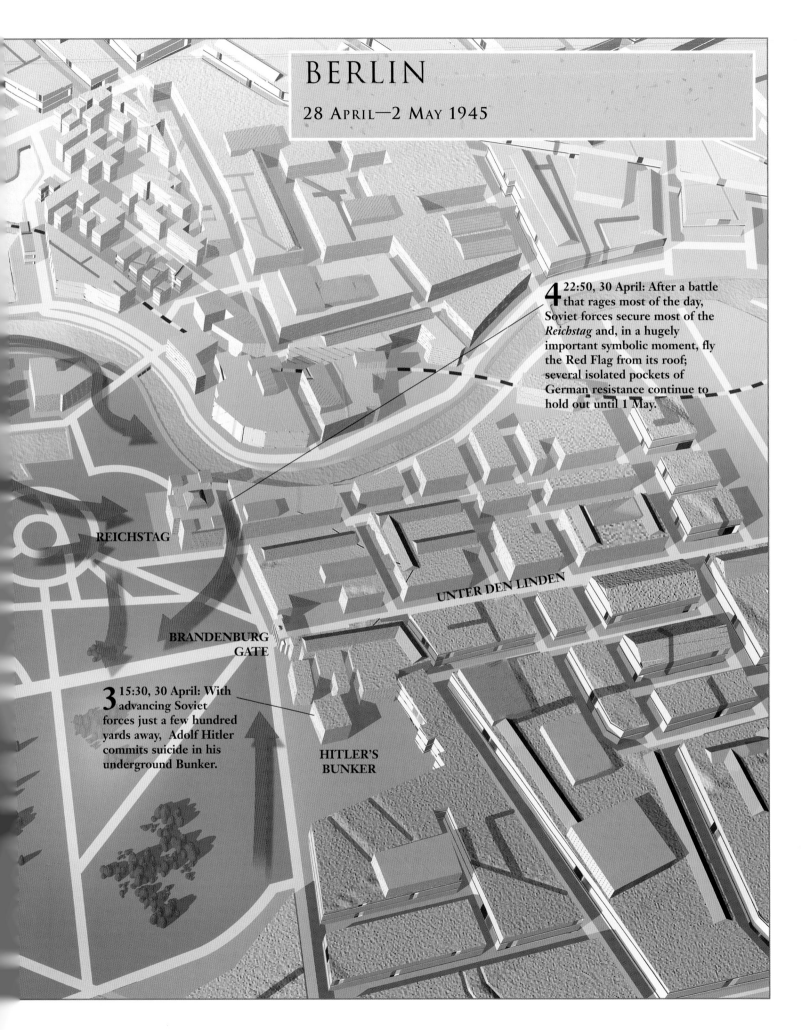

BERLIN

28 APRIL—2 MAY 1945

4 22:50, 30 April: After a battle that rages most of the day, Soviet forces secure most of the *Reichstag* and, in a hugely important symbolic moment, fly the Red Flag from its roof; several isolated pockets of German resistance continue to hold out until 1 May.

REICHSTAG

UNTER DEN LINDEN

BRANDENBURG GATE

3 15:30, 30 April: With advancing Soviet forces just a few hundred yards away, Adolf Hitler commits suicide in his underground Bunker.

HITLER'S BUNKER

festering where they fell; SS teams prowled the ruins, executing any alleged shirker they encountered; starving, dehydrated civilians were compelled to brave the horrors above ground in search of some sustenance; and finally, as the Soviets gradually took control of the city, drunken second-echelon Red Army troops ran amok, looting and raping in an orgy of violence.

During 26–28 April, along the southeastern sector of the German perimeter, three Soviet armies fought their way northwest past Tempelhof airport towards the Reich Chancellery and Hitler's underground bunker. Further west, two further armies fought their way north, pushing back the defenders along the southern German sector to the Kurfürstendamm. Meanwhile, along the northern sector, the Soviet Second Guards and Third Shock Armies gradually drove the Germans back south over the River Spree towards the Zoo Flak Towers and the *Reichstag*. Critically, during the early hours of 29 April, Soviet spearheads captured intact the Moltke

Bridge over the Spree, just 700m (800yd) from the Reich Chancellery. The German commanders, moreover, now assessed that their available ammunition would expire within 24 hours. These twin hammer-blows convinced Hitler that defeat was inevitable; he subsequently married his long-time mistress Eva Braun and then dictated his Political Testament.

Throughout 30 April, the savage battle for the centre of Berlin continued, with the remaining 10,000 defending troops being pressed back into an ever shrinking enclave. Soviet troops fought to secure the ruined *Reichstag* throughout the day, with the building eventually falling that evening, although some German soldiers held out in various rooms for the next 48 hours. That evening, Red Army troops flew the Soviet flag from the building in an act of immense symbolic significance. An even more significant event transpired at around 15:30. With Soviet troops just 360m (400yd) away, Hitler committed suicide. That evening, with the defenders running short of ammunition, the Germans opened

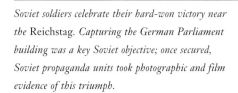

Soviet soldiers celebrate their hard-won victory near the Reichstag. *Capturing the German Parliament building was a key Soviet objective; once secured, Soviet propaganda units took photographic and film evidence of this triumph.*

A Soviet SU-76M assault gun fighting through the rubble of Berlin. The SU-76 was a simple, reliable and highly mobile light-weight Soviet assault gun that was mass-produced from 1942 onwards. It was deployed mainly in an infantry-support role and suffered from one principal defect: its light armour rendered it vulnerable to enemy fire.

surrender negotiations with the Soviets. While these negotiations dragged on, the savage struggle for Berlin continued. Finally, in the early hours of 2 May, General Weidling announced his acceptance of the Soviet demand for unconditional surrender. By then, anyway, the roughly 7000 surviving defenders had launched one last, desperate effort to smash their way out of the Berlin; only a few dozen solders reached Wenck's frontline. At 06:00, the remnants of the Berlin garrison surrendered. Berlin, the capital of the German *Reich*, had fallen.

THE GERMAN SURRENDER

As the final twists in the saga of Berlin's defence unfolded, the battle beyond the city continued to rage. During 28/29 April, Wenck's advance northeast towards Berlin made sufficient progress to raise the hopes of those trapped in the *Führer* Bunker. In the early hours of 30 April, however, news reached Hitler that not only had these relief efforts stalled but that they were also facing powerful enemy counterattacks, which had begun to drive them back west. This report proved devastating, crushing the last hopes in the bunker that rescue was feasible. Within hours, Hitler began preparing to take his own life rather than face Soviet captivity.

Meanwhile, to the south of Berlin, during 24–30 April, the surviving remnants of the Ninth Army had desperately attempted to punch west through the Soviet encirclement. By 1 May, sizable battered groupings had managed to smash through

to Wenck's front line in the Belzig area. By 4 May, the Soviet advance had penned the survivors of Twelfth and Ninth Armies into an area east of the Elbe around Burg. During 6/7 May, these forces surrendered to the Americans holding the western bank of the Elbe.

During this period further south, Soviet attacks pushed the northern flank of Army Group Centre back on Dresden. In the north of the Oder front, moreover, the Second Belorussian Front continued its offensive against the battered remnants of Army Group Vistula, the Third Panzer Army and the newly mobilized Twenty-First Army, which had been formed from cadres that had escaped by sea from East Prussia. By 1 May, the surviving remnants of Third Panzer Army had collapsed into a disorganized flight westwards as the advancing Soviet forces pushed west to meet up with the eastward advance of the British 21st Army Group. During the evening of 2 May, British and Soviet forces linked up at Wismar on the Baltic Coast, and over the ensuing days the remnants of Third Panzer Army surrendered piecemeal to the British forces.

The Soviet encirclement and capture of Berlin and the consequent suicide of Adolf Hitler precipitated the end of an already-crumbling Third Reich; at midnight on 8 May, the German armed forces surrendered unconditionally to all the Allied powers. The Allies had finally won World War II in Europe.

DIEN BIEN PHU
13 MARCH–7 MAY 1954

EVENTS AT DIEN BIEN PHU WERE A MAJOR CAUSE OF THE END OF FRENCH RULE IN INDO-CHINA. THE FRENCH COMMANDER, GENERAL HENRI NAVARRE (1898–1983) CHALLENGED THE COMMUNIST VIET MINH TO ATTACK THE BASE HE HAD ESTABLISHED DEEP IN ENEMY HELD TERRITORY. BUT THE FRENCH UNDERESTIMATED THE FLEXIBILITY AND DETERMINATION OF GENERAL VO NGUYEN GIAP (1911–) AND HIS TROOPS AND, DESPITE A BRAVE STAND, SUFFERED A HUMILIATING DEFEAT.

WHY DID IT HAPPEN?

WHO Operational Group Northwest of the French Expeditionary Force was engaged by four infantry and an artillery division of the Vietnamese People's Army.

WHAT A determined assault by the Viet Minh to crush the French ground air base at Dien Bien Phu.

WHERE The Valley of Dien Bien Phu in northwest Vietnam, 320km (200 miles) west of Hanoi.

WHEN 13 March–7 May 1954.

WHY The French, hoping to provoke a Viet Minh assault, established a base deep in enemy territory that threatened communist operations against northern Laos. Hoping to gain political benefits from defeating a large French force, General Giap accepted the challenge.

OUTCOME After 56 days of combat, Dien Bien Phu finally fell to Viet Minh at the cost of some 25,000 casualties. Despite these losses, it was a major military and political victory for the communists, which would pay dividends at the peace negotiations at the Geneva Conference, starting 8 May.

The shattering defeat of French colonial forces by the Viet Minh had real political and strategic significance. It had a profound effect on the Geneva Conference, which began on 8 May the same year and resulted in a peace treaty and the establishment of North Vietnam. It also demonstrated the dangers of Western over-confidence and reliance on technology and firepower in the face of a determined and innovative opponent. Indeed, it was the first time that a liberation movement had managed to evolve from a guerrilla force into an army that could defeat a European colonial power in a conventional battle.

In May 1953, General Henri Navarre arrived in French Indo-China to take command of the French Expeditionary Corps, which was struggling in a war against the communist Viet Minh, under the political leadership of Ho Chi Minh (1890–1969).

His mission was simple: to strengthen the French negotiating position by achieving enough military success to enable the French government to find an

Col. Christian De Castries, the man who resolved 'We'll fight in Indochina as long as it is necessary', works over some maps of the Dien Bien Phu Area, where he is in command of the defenders.

honourable and favourable way out of the war, which had been running since 1946.

ESTABLISHING A BASE

Believing 'that war can only be won by attacking', Navarre, a cavalryman, was determined to take the war to the Viet Minh. He was faced with a number of strategic imperatives, particularly the need to disrupt the communist offensive against Laos. Therefore, he decided to establish a major *aéroterrestre* (ground-air base) to threaten Viet Minh movement and supply lines, and also prevent them shifting forces southwards against the Mekong Delta. He chose the area around the village of Dien Bien Phu (a name that literally means 'Administrative Centre Near the Border'), nestling deep in a valley 320km (200 miles) west of Hanoi, the centre of French power in northern Vietnam. This was also the site of an old Japanese airbase.

Navarre's plan had supporting precedent. In late 1952, the French had established a base at Na San and, relying on air supply, had been able to inflict a painful defeat on Viet Minh assaulting forces. Navarre's plan, Operation Castor, was fairly straightforward. He would place a major force deep into enemy-held territory and, from there, operate against the Viet Minh communications. This would force the enemy to move against the position, and when it did, French superiority in terms and artillery and firepower would bring victory.

OPERATION CASTOR

On 20 November 1953, Operation Castor began. An initial force of 1800 paratroopers was dropped, reaching a total of 2650 men by night fall. The drop zone proved to be occupied by enemy troops and 15 French soldiers were killed. The Viet Minh suffered 115 casualties. A perimeter was established and a base established. The old Japanese airfield was returned to service using engineers and bulldozers that had been dropped in. A supporting position, complete with its own airstrip, was also set up 7km (4.5 miles) to the south, codenamed Isabelle. (All the positions were given French female names.)

The garrison grew to about 15,000 men, supported by 10 M-24 Chaffee tanks, a

large number of artillery pieces, six F8F Bearcat fighters, a helicopter and a number of light observation aircraft. These were supported by the rest of the French air force in northern Vietnam, which broadly stood at 40 Bearcats based at Hanoi-Bach Ma and two B-26 bomber squadrons of about 35–40 aircraft. The Naval air arm operated a squadron each of fighter-bombers and dive-bombers off the carrier Arromaches in the Gulf of Tonkin.

Serviceability, a shortage of pilots and changeable weather conditions meant the availability of air support varied hugely

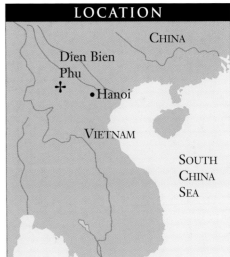

LOCATION

Dein Bein Phu was located 320 km west of Hanoi. It was deep in Viet Minh territory and the French presence threatened Viet Minh operations against northern Laos.

DIEN BIEN PHU

Wounded being airlifted away by helicopter. The Viet Minh routinely ignored Red Cross markings and fired on medical evacuations. The last evacuation helicopter landed at Dien Bien Phu on 23 March 1954.

THE OPPOSED FORCES

FRENCH COLONIAL (estimated)

Total:	15,000

VIET MINH (estimated)

Total:	50,000

during the battle. The ground-air base concept also rested on the provision of heavy artillery support. The artillery commander, Colonel Charles Piroth (1906–1954), had 24 105mm (4.1in) and four 155mm (6.1in) guns, divided between the main base and Isabelle. He was confident his guns would dominate the artillery battle and silence any guns the Viet Minh brought into action.

THE VIET MINH POSITION

The Viet Minh's leadership recognized that a major victory over the Expeditionary Force might hasten a French departure from Vietnam. At the very least, it would give the Viet Minh real political advantage in any subsequent negotiations. But Giap's army, tough and experienced as it was, had never captured a fortified position held by more than two companies. Dien Bien Phu and Isabelle were garrisoned by 12 battalions, meaning that victory would require large numbers of troops. Giap eventually mustered about 50,000 men from four infantry divisions and, crucially, the 351 Heavy Artillery Division, which included numerous 75mm (2.95in) pieces and mortars, as well as 24 105mm (4.1in) howitzers – about which the French knew nothing.

If he had followed convention, Giap would have placed his guns on the reverse slopes of the hills surrounding Dien Bien Phu. However, this would have exposed

them to French air power and might have made counter-battery fire more effective. Rather, he dug his guns into casements on the forward slopes, enabling them to fire directly onto the base. This took an extraordinary effort, given that it was undertaken at night and all work had to be camouflaged by dawn. The guns and the assembling army were protected by about 100 12.7mm (.5mm) and 20mm (.79in) pieces and at least 36 37mm (1.45in) anti-aircraft guns.

THE BATTLE BEGINS

Viet Minh preparations took time, but before dinner on the evening of 12 March 1954, after a wait of almost four months, the garrison commander, Colonel Christian de Castries briefed his senior officers: 'Gentleman, it's tomorrow, at 5 p.m.'. The French held two hills to the north, Gabrielle and Beatrice, which, if in enemy hands, would provide a complete view over the camp. These hills came under 105mm (4.1in) artillery fire just after 1700 (as scheduled) on 13 March. Shells soon began to rain down on the airstrip in the central position too.

Six battalions of Viet Minh leapt from their trenches and swarmed up the slopes towards the 500 defending Foreign Legionnaires, hitting the perimeter at about 1830. After desperate hand-to-hand fighting, organized resistance on Beatrice had ceased by 1315 the following morning. Gabrielle fell two days later.

By this time, a despairing Colonel Piroth had committed suicide. Recognizing the importance of the two lost positions, a couple of companies of Legionnaires and a battalion of Thai infantry, supported by six tanks, made an abortive counterattack on Gabrielle. Holding the two hills allowed the Viet Minh to place anti-aircraft guns much closer to the Dien Bien Phu airfield, further undermining the viability of the airstrip. Elsewhere, Anne-Marie to the west was deemed untenable by the French due to its comparative isolation and was evacuated on 17 March.

The French Bearcat aircraft left Dien Bien Phu once the shelling began on 13 March. Although the occasional Beaver observation aircraft made an extremely dangerous landing and take off, the only aircraft making regular landings were Dakota C-47s delivering medical supplies and evacuating causalities. Other supplies were dropped by parachute or just pushed straight out of the back of cargo aircraft coming in low over the camp. After the fall of Anne-Marie, there followed a lull in the fighting, which allowed the French to replenish their stocks of ammunition. However, on 27 March, French aircraft were ordered to carry out their supply drops from above 2000m (6560ft) due to Viet Minh anti-aircraft fire, which limited the accuracy of the drops.

The assault on the two forward positions, Gabrielle and Beatrice, had been particularly costly for the Viet Minh. Estimates vary, but there were approximately 5000 casualties, necessitating a regrouping of attacking forces. While this went on, Giap completed the encirclement of Dien Bien Phu, cutting it off from Isabelle, although the road connecting the two was reopened by a strong French counterattack on 21/22 March. There were also some changes in command structure for the French defenders, with paratrooper Lieutenant-Colonel Pierre Langlais (1909–88) becoming Castries' chief of operations, responsible for the defence of the central position. This was probably less a coup against Castries, a cavarlyman, than a recognition of Langlais' infantry expertise in the midst of what was a positional defensive battle. Although he had found it hard to cope in the early days of the battle, Castries recovered and continued to shoulder the responsibility for the day-to-day survival of the camp.

THE BATTLE INTENSIFIES

There did appear to be a sense of renewed purpose from the defenders and on 28 March two paratroop battalions and a troop of tanks under Major 'Bruno' Bigeard launched a raid on anti-aircraft positions to the west of Dien Bien Phu, destroying five anti-aircraft guns, numerous heavy machine guns and weapons and inflicting heavy casualties on the Viet Minh. Yet such success could not hide the fact that on the same day the last casualty evacuation C-47 landed and was unable to take off – the runway was effectively closed. The

following day, the road between the main camp and Isabelle was finally cut. In addition, Giap was now ready to resume the offensive.

The multiple Dominique and Eliane strong points were a line of five hills to the east of the Nam Youm River, which bisected the camp on a north–south line. Attacking these was a more daunting proposition than Gabrielle and Beatrice, as each could not be captured in isolation – failure to capture them all would leave the attackers exposed to fire from the other peaks.

But success would bring the rest of Dien Bien Phu into close range of the Viet Minh's lighter support weapons, such as mortars and recoilless rifles. Giap hoped to take the hills all in one night. He was to be disappointed. Although Dominique 1 and 2 fell on the night of 30 March, the Viet Minh regiment that swept across Dominique 2 and threatened to unlock the whole French position were stopped in their tracks by 4th Battery 4th Colonial Artillery Regiment commanded by Lieutenant Paul Brunbrouck (1926–54). His West African gunners fired 1800 shells at point blank range into their attackers, supported by some artillery men acting as infantry and a quad 12.7mm (.5in) anti-aircraft gun mounted by the airfield. Their amazing action saved Dien Bien Phu that night. Eliane 1 was lost, but Major Bigeard's Colonial Paratroopers held on to the most southern hill, Eliane 2. The French counterattacked and regained their lost positions the following morning, but had no-one to reinforce them. The Paratroopers were reluctantly ordered to withdraw. The Viet Minh resumed their offensive that night but still failed to take Eliane 2.

In light of this, Giap shifted his emphasis to the north, chipping away at Huguette 6 and 7. Huguette 7, somewhat isolated to the northwest, was abandoned by the French on 2 April. In fact, across Dien Bien Phu, the defenders were being steadily worn down. Many of the paratroop battalions were down to half strength and the reinforcements being dropped in were not making up the deficit.

This Viet Minh soldier wears black fatigues, typically worn by communist irregular troops during the Indochina/Vietnam wars. He wears a brush hat probably taken from his colonial adversaries and is armed with a French MAT-49 submachine gun.

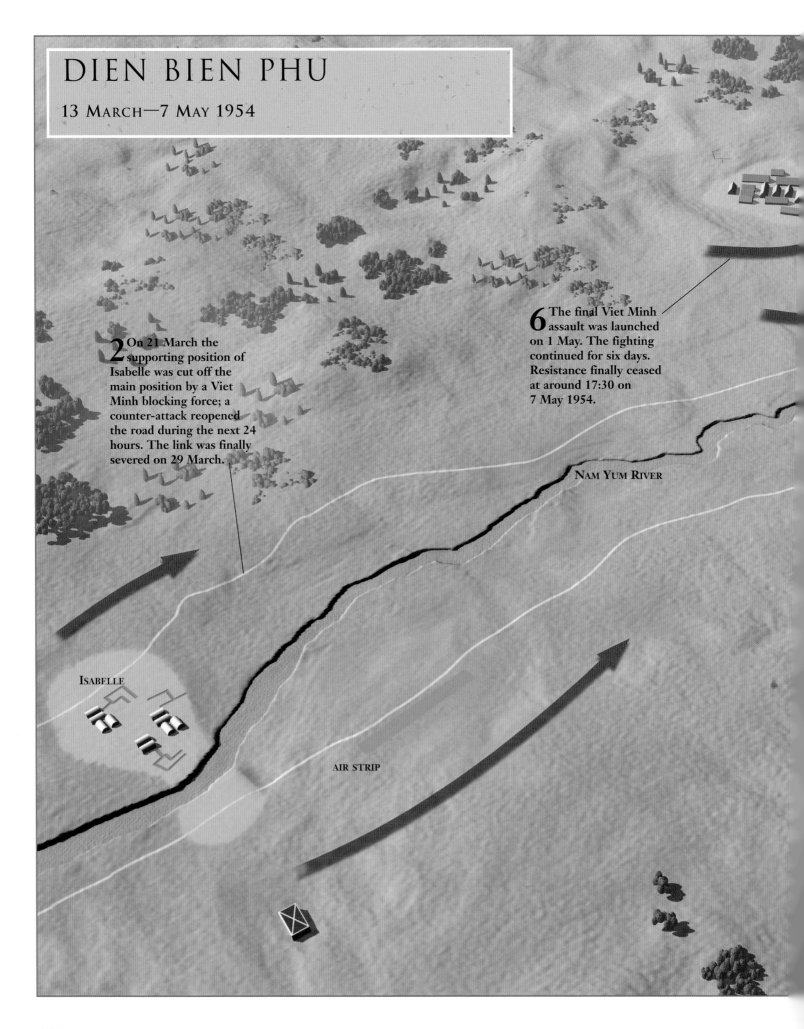

DIEN BIEN PHU

13 MARCH—7 MAY 1954

2 On 21 March the supporting position of Isabelle was cut off the main position by a Viet Minh blocking force; a counter-attack reopened the road during the next 24 hours. The link was finally severed on 29 March.

6 The final Viet Minh assault was launched on 1 May. The fighting continued for six days. Resistance finally ceased at around 17:30 on 7 May 1954.

NAM YUM RIVER

ISABELLE

AIR STRIP

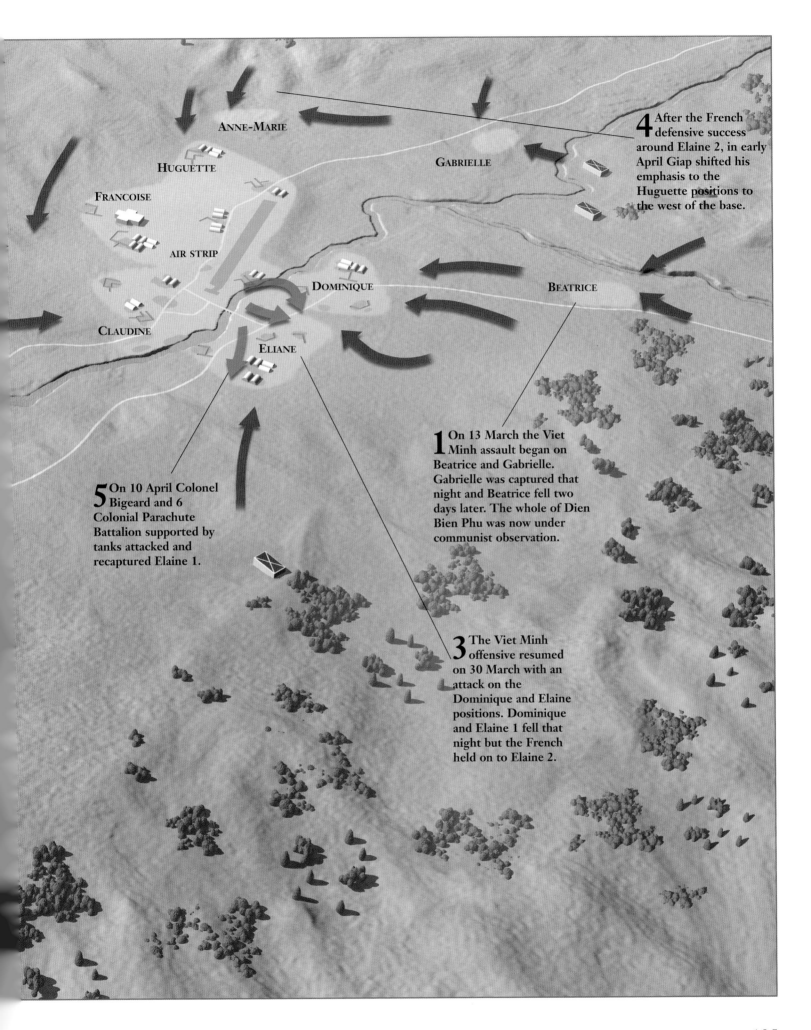

ANNE-MARIE

HUGUETTE

GABRIELLE

FRANCOISE

AIR STRIP

DOMINIQUE

BEATRICE

CLAUDINE

ELIANE

4 After the French defensive success around Elaine 2, in early April Giap shifted his emphasis to the Huguette positions to the west of the base.

1 On 13 March the Viet Minh assault began on Beatrice and Gabrielle. Gabrielle was captured that night and Beatrice fell two days later. The whole of Dien Bien Phu was now under communist observation.

5 On 10 April Colonel Bigeard and 6 Colonial Parachute Battalion supported by tanks attacked and recaptured Elaine 1.

3 The Viet Minh offensive resumed on 30 March with an attack on the Dominique and Elaine positions. Dominique and Elaine 1 fell that night but the French held on to Elaine 2.

The fighting for the eastern hills petered out on 5 April. Giap again paused to consider his next move given the French defensive success around Eliane 2, dismissing a number of commanders who had failed there. He later described the subsequent week or so of operations as 'nibbling away', through entrenching and mining. Bigeard, however, had decided that Elaine 1 could not remain in Viet Minh hands and on 10 April it was recaptured by 6 Colonial Parachute Battalion, supported by tanks. The French held on in spite of continuing counterattacks.

THE VIET MINH EDGE AHEAD

Yet the network of Viet Minh trenches increasingly strangled Dien Bien Phu, despite French raids and occasional successes, such at Eliane 1. The increasingly isolated Huguette 6 at the northern end of the runway was abandoned on 17 April, provoking serious fighting across the airfield, which had been cut off by Viet Minh trenches. A force was sent in to enable

A French soldier takes cover. He appears to be looking out across the airfield towards the wrecked C-47 transport. There was desperate fighting across the runway in middle April.

its French defenders to pull out. Huguette 1 fell on 23 April after the Viet Minh managed to tunnel their way into the position. Their commanders noted with satisfaction the success of their new siege warfare techniques. The 6 Foreign Legion Paratroop Battalion's counterattack failed, taking serious casualties. It was the last major counterattack launched by the defenders. By the end of April, about 4900 French infantry guarded about 2100 wounded and 4000 non-infantry combatants and service troops living in appalling conditions with no hope of relief. Yet morale held.

For the Viet Minh, the issue was less clear cut. Giap's infantry had suffered 50 per cent casualties in six weeks and many of his units were at the end of their reserves of strength. So Giap paused once again before launching the third wave of assaults. He had assembled 50,000 men and intended to take the Elianes and western Huguettes between 1 and 5 May. He would then pause to bring up supporting weaponry before launching the final assault on the central positions on 10 May. The attack opened in the late afternoon of 1 May with a massive bombardment.

The infantry assault against the Elianes and Dominique 3 on the east of perimeter began as darkness fell. There were also

attacks on the Huguettes and the isolated Isabelle to the south. Eliane 1, which had changed hands so many times, fell for the last time that night, but the successful Viet Minh regiment could not maintain its forward moment and was fought to a standstill on the forward slops of Eliane 4 by its defenders, the 5 Vietnamese Parachute Battalion. Dominique 3 was captured after six hours of hand-to-hand fighting that began once the company of 6 Colonial Paratroop Battalion's ammunition ran out. There were some defensive successes on the western side, but Huguette 5 was captured by a Viet Minh regiment, which took 90 minutes to overwhelm its platoon of defenders. Lilli 3 fell on 4 May. Castries, now promoted to brigadier-general, and Langlais toured the positions, trying to maintain moral. Piecemeal reinforcements and supplies were parachuted in, and the garrisons' meagre resources were shuffled as the defenders waited for the final assault.

THE FINAL ASSAULT

During the late afternoon of 6 May, Viet Minh artillery fire intensified to cover the assembly of their infantry for their final assault. Katushka rocket launchers were deployed for the first time. Eliane 2 was the first position attacked that night and, during

assembly of their infantry for their final assault. Katushka rocket launchers were deployed for the first time. Eliane 2 was the first position attacked that night and, during the fighting, the Viet Minh exploded a mine underneath the position, but failed to end the resistance of the Colonial Paratroopers defending the hill.

The fighting continued until sometime between 05:30 and 06:00, when the handful of survivors, ammunition exhausted, were captured round the command post. Eliane 4, held by a mix of French, Legion and Vietnamese paratroopers, fought on into the next morning. Claudine 5 on the western perimeter fell sometime around 22:00.

Meanwhile, Langlais tried to raise a counterattacking force to retake Eliane 2, but this was stopped as the Viet Minh renewed their assault on the morning of 7 May. A thin line of scratch defenders were all that remained on the eastern side of the river, and the attackers were now less than 500m

(547yd) from Castries' command post. He and his commanders discussed and rejected the possibility of a break-out – their remaining men were too exhausted. As this discussion was taking place, the Viet Minh were clearing up the eastern bank of the river. They had enough momentum to dispense with a planned pause since the defenders were on the brink of collapse. Indeed, between 14:00 and 17:30 the fighting petered out and a ceasefire came into effect at 17:30. After 56 days, Dien Bien Phu's agony was over and at 17:40 a red Viet Minh flag was raised above Castries' headquarters. Later that evening, the defenders of Isabelle attempted a largely abortive break-out, although about 70 men were able to reach friendly territory.

THE AFTERMATH

Accurate casualty figures are impossible to come by, but of the slightly more than 15,000 French and colonial troops that

French POWs being marched away. About 10,000 men fell into Viet Minh hands. Only about half of them survived captivity.

fought in battle about 1500 were killed, a similar number were missing and 4500 were wounded. An estimated 10,000 men fell into Viet-Minh hands, about 5500 unwounded. Although they remained in captivity for only four months, only half would return home, so the ceasefire did not immediately end the defenders' suffering. Viet Minh loses are estimated to be approximately 25,000 dead.

The fall of Dien Bien Phu was more than a battlefield setback – it signalled the end of French rule in Indo-China. The Geneva Conference opened on 8 May, the day after the French humiliation. The result was a French withdrawal from Indo-China, the division of Vietnam into two states, the north under Ho Chi Minh's communists and the

TET OFFENSIVE
29 January—8 April 1968

NAMED AFTER THE VIETNAMESE HOLIDAY ON WHICH IT WAS LAUNCHED, THE TET OFFENSIVE WAS A LARGE-SCALE OPERATION THAT WAS INTENDED TO TRIGGER A POPULAR UPRISING IN FAVOUR OF THE COMMUNIST NORTH. ALTHOUGH THE OFFENSIVE WAS A MILITARY FAILURE, THE SUBSEQUENT SHIFT IN PUBLIC OPINION IN THE UNITED STATES TURNED IT INTO A VICTORY FOR THE COMMUNISTS.

WHY DID IT HAPPEN?

WHO Large numbers of North Vietnamese regulars (NVA) and Viet Cong (VC) irregulars opposed by the Army of the Republic of Vietnam (ARVN) and US forces.

WHAT A widespread offensive against military and urban targets in South Vietnam.

WHERE Operations were launched in all regions of South Vietnam, with particularly fierce fighting taking place in the city of Hue.

WHEN 29 January–8 April 1968.

WHY The communists hoped to trigger a popular uprising by overrunning military bases and capturing major urban centres.

OUTCOME The offensive eventually failed after achieving some local victories, which were eventually reversed. However, the offensive created the impression that the war was escalating, with serious political consequences for US involvement.

Communist forces in the Vietnam War belonged to two groups. The North Vietnamese Army (NVA) was a regular, if relatively lightly armed, force capable of undertaking large-scale conventional operations. Its equipment came largely from the Soviet Union. The Viet Cong (VC) were a communist guerrilla force recruited largely in South Vietnam.

These two forces operated in conjunction. In general, the NVA fought a fairly conventional war in the north while the VC were active throughout the whole of the country. VC activities included guerrilla warfare but also political operations, such as

the intimidation of village leaders and the elimination of informants. The VC were responsible for most US casualties despite being relatively poorly equipped. Their ability to use the jungle effectively as well as to hide among sympathetic members of the general population enabled them to ambush US troops with great efficiency while mostly remaining undetected.

The Viet Cong received some supplies from sympathizers in the south, and extorted some from less friendly locals. However, most of its supplies and ammunition were delivered overland via what became known as the Ho Chi Minh

Although the attacks on Saigon achieved little lasting success, they caused significant disruption. Here, fire trucks rush to attend one of the many deliberate fires set by the attacking communists.

Trail. Named after the president of North Vietnam, the Trail ran mostly through neighbouring Laos and was comprised of several small land and water routes that could be used by trucks and boats but were mainly operated by personnel on foot or bicycles. Large quantities of supplies were delivered this way, enabling the Viet Cong to remain combat-capable while operating far from friendly bases.

The strategy of US forces in assisting the Army of the Republic of Vietnam (ARVN) was attrition, gradually wearing down the morale and manpower of the VC and NVA through casualties. VC bases and supporters were rooted out to deny the guerrillas supplies and opportunities to rest, and also to draw them out into combat with superior forces, which would lead to a high 'body count' among the communist forces. In 1967, this strategy was proving effective, causing the VC and NVA leadership to reconsider their options.

The communist leaders were faced with the likelihood that their personnel would be ground down to the point where they could no longer carry out operations in South Vietnam, and understood that what support they had among the population there was being eroded as the US Army and ARVN increasingly took control of the situation. Faced with a gradual defeat, they decided to gamble, staking their success on a large-scale conventional offensive coupled with guerrilla actions.

However, this was not intended to be just a military operation; it had a political objective at its heart. The communists hoped that by attacking and capturing urban centres and inflicting defeats on US and ARVN forces they could trigger a general uprising. This tactic had worked in other conflicts and there was reason to believe that it would succeed in Vietnam. The date chosen for the offensive was the Lunar New Year, an important holiday for which both sides had declared a ceasefire.

PREPARATIONS AND DISTRACTIONS

Although large numbers of VC guerrillas were already operating in South Vietnam, additional personnel were infiltrated into the south along the Ho Chi Minh Trail. In

VC IRREGULAR

The Viet Cong (VC) were irregular forces, lightly equipped compared to the US, ARVN or even NVA forces involved in the Tet Offensive. Well suited to rapid movement through the jungle and guerrilla warfare in dense terrain, VC fighters received support from the local population – not always voluntarily – who supplied them with food and other necessities. The VC expended most of its strength in the Tet Offensive and never really recovered, while the expected surge of popular support in South Vietnam for the communist cause never materialized.

fact, over 80,000 personnel and vast quantities of supplies were laboriously moved along the jungle roads and rivers into position for the offensive. In addition, an element of strategic deception was incorporated into the plan. The aim was to draw US forces away from the main urban areas, which were politically the most important target.

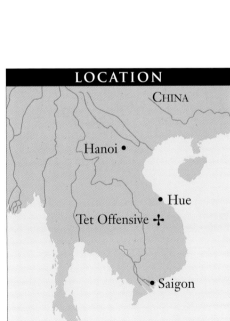

LOCATION

CHINA

Hanoi •

• Hue

Tet Offensive ✚

• Saigon

Important as both a supply base and a politically symbolic city, Hue was the scene of protracted and bitter fighting during the Tet Offensive.

TET OFFENSIVE

A US tank advances along a street wrecked in the fighting for Saigon. Although vulnerable in close urban terrain, armoured vehicles proved effective against lightly equipped VC fighters.

THE OPPOSED FORCES

US AND SOUTH VIETNAM

No reliable estimate

NORTH VIETNAM

Inside South Vietnam	84,000
Additional forces from North Vietnam	

The most significant of these deception operations resulted in a series of 'border battles' along the North–South Vietnamese frontier. A series of protracted battles took place, which seemed to US analysts to have no purpose other than the general one of inflicting US casualties. They did, however, succeed in drawing attention towards the border region and away from the interior, as typified by the siege of the US Marines' base at Khe Sanh.

Located close to the North–South Vietnamese border, Khe Sanh was under constant threat. From October 1967, the base and its outlying posts came under frequent and sustained attack. This included inaccurate but vigorous shelling as well as ground offensives that differed from the more usual pattern of hit-and-run raids by North Vietnamese forces. A major offensive was launched against the base in late January 1968 as final preparations for the main Tet Offensive were underway.

As the enemy forces around Khe Sanh increased, the base was cut off on the ground, although not before reinforcements had arrived. Some of the outlying posts and bases were lost, and at times the Khe Sanh perimeter was penetrated by the NVA, forcing the US Marines to fight hand-to-hand to retain control of the bas. The NVA

also deployed artillery and even armour in the Khe Sanh region, along with specially trained and heavily equipped assault parties, but despite heavy shelling and sustained pressure over many weeks, the Marines held out.

Air transport was used to resupply Khe Sanh, along with intense aerial attack on the surrounding area to disrupt the NVA forces besieging the base. The possibility of using chemical or even tactical nuclear weapons was raised, though the discussion did not get far. Gradually the pressure eased, largely through the success of airborne reinforcement and supply efforts, though the base was not relieved overland until 8 April.

THE TET OFFENSIVE OPENS

With US attention diverted to the border, the Tet Offensive came as a surprise, despite some communist operations starting a day early, so hinting at what was to come. These early operations seemed like isolated incidents until 31 January, when the full scale and co-ordination of the Offensive began to become apparent. South Vietnam had 44 provincial capitals, of which 36 came under attack, along with many other cities and 23 US bases.

The usual pattern was an artillery or mortar attack followed by an infantry assault by VC guerrillas, NVA regulars, or both. Forces up to a division in size were involved in individual battles.

A force of some 35 battalions attacked the capital, Saigon. Some attacks were beaten off by the US Army and ARVN or simply failed, but others succeeded, at least temporarily. A small group managed to seize the National Radio Station in Saigon and was able to make propaganda broadcasts until the transmitter was hastily disconnected. Attacks against the Presidential palace and Navy headquarters did not need to succeed militarily in order to be a major propaganda coup; by taking place at all, such operations shook South Vietnamese confidence and were a rallying cry for pro-communist uprisings.

During the fighting in Saigon, a party of VC guerrillas managed to blast their way through a wall and gain access to the US embassy. They were eventually killed by the embassy guards, but not without a six-hour firefight that was broadcast on television. This, too, was a propaganda coup for the communists. However, military success was short-lived. By 4 February, some ten divisions of ARVN and US troops had been assembled to retake Saigon, a process that took six days.

TET FAILS

Elsewhere, too, the effectiveness of the Offensive was mixed and successes did not last. Although caught by surprise and stunned by the scale of the assault, which came in the middle of a holiday ceasefire declared by both sides, US and ARVN forces managed to avoid defeat in the first critical hours of the Offensive, which bought them time to regroup and start hitting back. In some areas, ARVN forces fought to the death rather than surrender, fearing atrocities by the VC and NVA. This resistance robbed the communists of some victories that they might otherwise have won.

More importantly, the anticipated political outcome did not materialize. The uprising expected from the general population as part of an outpouring of communist sympathy did not happen. Counteroffensives dislodged VC and NVA troops from the captured areas and rapidly restored government control. In some cases, this was done in a matter of hours; in other areas, fighting went on for days.

However, by the time Saigon was secured, most other regions were back under control and the attackers were in retreat. The Offensive had absorbed massive VC and NVA manpower, had taken months of planning, and had resulted in huge casualties for no real military gain. The only real success of the whole campaign was in the city of Hue, and even there, the communists were eventually defeated.

ATTACK ON HUE

The city of Hue, 80km (50 miles) south of the Demilitarized Zone (DMZ) that separated North and South Vietnam, was important to the US and South Vietnamese forces as a supply base, which therefore made it a prime target for the communists.

A US Marine fires his M60 general purpose machinegun (GPMG) during urban fighting. Equipped with automatic weapons, US forces were able to bring overwhelming firepower to bear.

1 Initial communist assaults at Hue are successful, though the citadel and airfield hold out under heavy attack. The airfield is abandoned and ARVN forces concentrate on holding the citadel.

AIRFIELD

OLD CITY

IMPERIAL PALACE

PERFUME RIVER

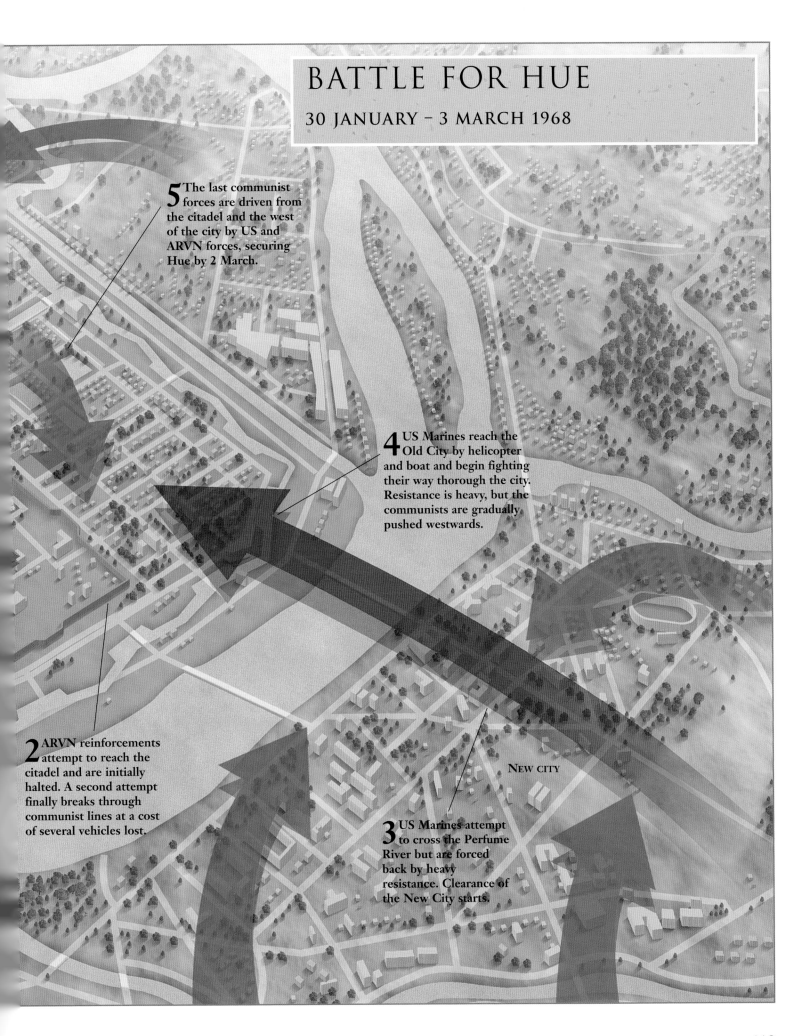

BATTLE FOR HUE

30 JANUARY – 3 MARCH 1968

5 The last communist forces are driven from the citadel and the west of the city by US and ARVN forces, securing Hue by 2 March.

4 US Marines reach the Old City by helicopter and boat and begin fighting their way thorough the city. Resistance is heavy, but the communists are gradually pushed westwards.

2 ARVN reinforcements attempt to reach the citadel and are initially halted. A second attempt finally breaks through communist lines at a cost of several vehicles lost.

NEW CITY

3 US Marines attempt to cross the Perfume River but are forced back by heavy resistance. Clearance of the New City starts.

It was also a symbolic city, as it had been the capital of the Nguyen Dynasty that had ruled Vietnam until 1945. Lying on the Perfume River, Hue was divided into the New City to the south and the Old City, including the citadel, to the north. The latter was built in 1802 and had an outer wall approximately 20ft (6m) thick.

The force tasked with taking Hue was approximately a division in size, backed up with artillery support. The attack overran most of the city very quickly, giving the communists the freedom to carry out executions of anyone they felt sympathized with the enemy or failed to support the communist cause fervently enough. The executions continued throughout the communist occupation of the city, resulting in hundreds of deaths.

However, the communists did not have total success. Tay Loc airfield, outside the city, was successfully defended by ARVN troops for a time, and the attack on the citadel was defeated by a scratch force comprised of clerks and staff from divisional headquarters. Eventually, the airfield had to be abandoned and all forces diverted to holding the citadel. A call for reinforcements brought ARVN troops from a nearby base, but their initial advance was fought to a standstill just 500m (⅓ mile) from the citadel. A second push broke through communist

lines, so some reinforcements reached the defenders, but other ARVN forces were encircled and could not be relieved despite the use of tanks.

Meanwhile, US Marines based at Phu Bai airbase, 16km (10 miles) away, successfully defended themselves against an NVA attack and began making local counterattacks. These had to be abandoned because of the situation in Hue, which necessitated an operation to assist of the city's defenders. Not appreciating the size of the communist force they would encounter, the Marines attempted to enter the city from the south, but were forced to fight from village to village along the way, delaying their arrival considerably. Once in the city, the Marines attempted to advance across the Perfume River into the Old City, but were beaten back by overwhelming communist firepower. US troops were then airlifted into the citadel by helicopter and tried to reach the cut-off defenders, with mixed success.

RETAKING THE CITY

Having failed to oust the communists from the city using local US forces, US and ARVN commanders began planning a more deliberate counteroffensive. On 1 February, a heavily armed convoy using trucks mounting heavy machine-guns, and Ontos

Lightweight and capable of fully automatic fire, the M16 rifle used by US troops was better suited to urban combat than jungle operations, where it was prone to malfunction due to the filthy conditions.

armoured vehicles mounting six 106mm (4.17in) recoilless rifles, smashed its way through to link up with troops cut off in the city. ARVN forces within the citadel were able to go on the offensive as well, gradually driving the communists out.

At first the intention was to avoid shelling Hue or make much use of air support, in the hope of sparing the civilian inhabitants and historic features of the city. However, the stubborn occupation by the communists made a reversal of this policy necessary, and heavy support (air and artillery) became available. Despite this support, the street fighting was bitter, made worse by the inexperience of both the US and ARVN forces in this kind of warfare. Lessons learned in the urban battlegrounds of World War II had been forgotten and had to be relearned at the price of casualties. Nevertheless, a combination of firepower and good, determined infantry work resulted in most of the main points of the New City being secured by 6 February. US and ARVN forces were in full control south of the Perfume River by 10 February.

Crossing into the Old City, US and ARVN forces gradually drove the communists out, retaking the Tay Loc airfield and the Imperial Palace. The communists still held the western fringes of the city and the Gia Hoi district, where they continued to execute anyone accused of being an opponent of their political agenda, and it was not until 2 March that the city was fully secured. The conflict cost the lives of 119 US and 363 ARVN troops, around 6000 civilians and possibly as many as 8000 VC and NVA communist personnel.

THE AFTERMATH

The retaking of Hue spelled the end of the Tet Offensive, though fighting around Khe Sanh went on for several more weeks. Tet was a failure for the communists, resulting in massive numbers of casualties for no lasting gain. The Viet Cong never recovered from the mauling it had taken, and largely ceased to be a factor in the war. Most importantly, there was no communist uprising. However, the Western media portrayed Tet as a disaster for the United States, and took the view that the war was escalating, drawing in an unacceptable number of troops to fight in

a war that was not popular with Americans. A policy of 'Vietnamization' was implemented, whereby the United States began to transfer main responsibility for the war to ARVN forces. Eventually, US troops departed entirely, with US military aid to South Vietnam curtailed entirely after 15 April 1973. Economic aid continued until the end of the conflict.

Two years after US military involvement ended, in April 1975, Saigon fell to the communists, bringing the conflict to a close. The seeds of their victory were sown in the failure of the Tet Offensive, or rather the way it was portrayed in the media. The risk of 'defeat by television' has been a very real factor in all conflicts since.

US Marines move along a road in Hue after the fighting has ended. It was not possible to spare the city's historic landmarks during the bitter fighting that took place during and after the Tet Offensive.

SINAI
6–25 OCTOBER 1973

THE YOM KIPPUR WAR OF OCTOBER 1973 USHERED IN A NEW ERA OF WARFARE. THE DEVASTATING EFFECTS OF GUIDED ANTI-TANK MISSILES RAISED A QUESTION MARK OVER THE FUTURE OF MAIN BATTLE TANKS AS THE PRINCIPAL SPEARHEAD OF ARMIES.

WHY DID IT HAPPEN?

WHO The combined armies of Egypt and Syria, with some minor allies, against the Israeli Defense Forces (IDF).

WHAT Egypt and Syria launched an assault on Israeli-held territories in Sinai and the Golan Heights, aiming to overwhelm the Israeli defence through a two-front strategy.

WHERE Egypt attacked across the Suez Canal into Sinai, while Syria fought in the Golan Heights to the north of Israel.

WHEN 6–25 October 1973.

WHY Egypt hoped that the offensive would force Israel to the international negotiating table, where it would be forced to concede territories captured in the 1967 Six Day War.

OUTCOME After suffering heavy losses on both fronts, Israel rallied and reversed all the gains made by Egypt and Syria, inflicting massive casualties on the Arab armies before a UN ceasefire was imposed.

The seeds of the Yom Kippur War were sown six years earlier in the Six Day War of June 1967. In that conflict, Israel had stunned the world with its military brilliance, particularly in its handling of air power and armour, and had vastly expanded its territory to control the whole of Sinai, the West Bank of the River Jordan and the Golan Heights. The conquests fulfilled their intended purpose – to give the State of Israel a protective 'buffer zone' in a sea of Arab enemies – but did not bring peace. The Arab world demanded the withdrawal of Israel from its conquered territories, something Israel would contemplate only if the Arabs acknowledged Israel's sovereignty and right to exist. Neither side's requirements would be satisfied, so Israel established a string of fortified positions along the east bank of the Suez Canal. This

was known as the Bar-Lev Line, after Lieutenant-General Chaim Bar-Lev (1924–94), chief of the general staff of the Israel Defense Forces from 1968 to 1971. Not always adequately manned or protected, the Bar-Lev Line became the victim of regular Egyptian artillery bombardment from 8 March 1969, the start of what became known as the 'War of Attrition'. This war would steadily escalate into another full-scale showdown between the Arabs and Israel.

REARMAMENT

During the Six Day War and until his death in 1970, Egypt was under the leadership of President Gamel Abdel Nasser (1918–70). Nasser, smarting at the humiliating defeat of 1967, began the job of revitalizing his forces. Central to this effort was the

An Egyptian soldier holds up a portrait of President Sadat. Sadat was a skillful politician, and the Yom Kippur War did much to raise Arab morale, as it broke the myth of Israeli invincibility. Sadat was assassinated, however, in 1981.

expertise and technology of the Soviet Union, Egypt's principal Cold War backer. In particular, Egypt needed solutions to two problems – the Israeli Air Force (IAF) and Israel's armoured formations. To tackle the former problem, Egypt invested heavily in Soviet SA-2, SA-3, SA-6, SA-7 and SA-9 surface-to-air missile (SAM) systems, as well as the formidable four-barrelled ZSU-23-4 radar-controlled self-propelled anti-aircraft cannon. By forging these systems into a tight interlocking network, the Egyptians aimed to created a SAM 'umbrella' that would provide ground forces with relative freedom from IAF ground-attack missions. The different operational altitudes of the various SAM systems meant that an Israeli aircraft's efforts to avoid one type of SAM usually put it within the effective range of another.

The problem of Israeli armour was partly answered by re-equipping Arab tank forces – in total, the Soviet Union supplied over 4000 tanks to Egypt and Syria in the years between 1967 and 1973, mostly T55s and T64s. The other side to Egypt's anti-armour restructuring was to acquire huge supplies of infantry anti-tank weapons. These were the AT-3 Sagger and the now infamous RPG-7. Each had its own capabilities (see box, right).

The rearmament programme of the Arab armies seemed to put them on a secure footing for a coming war. By October 1973, Israel had 275,000 soldiers (one-third were regulars, the rest were reserves), 1700 tanks and 432 aircraft. Egypt had 285,000 men, 2000 tanks and 600 aircraft, but its ally Syria added another 100,000 men, 1200 tanks and 210 aircraft to the Arab arsenal.

CROSSING THE CANAL

Nasser died in September 1970 and was succeeded as president by Anwar Sadat (1918–81). Sadat made great efforts on the international stage to secure a diplomatic solution to the Arab–Israeli problem, but by 1971 he felt that war was his only option. Here lay a problem. Sadat knew that his forces could not match Israeli military professionalism (and that the United States would come to Israel's material aid). His plan, therefore, was to open a multi-front war that was not aimed at crushing Israel but at forcing it and the international community to the negotiating table. The plan was as follows: Egypt would launch an assault across the Suez Canal, penetrate a short distance into Sinai, then hold the ground while Israeli forces battered themselves against the SAM, anti-tank and infantry defences. A simultaneous attack by Syrian forces in the Golan Heights would stretch the Israeli response thin, preventing it from applying the focused *Blitzkrieg*-style warfare it had employed in the Six Day War.

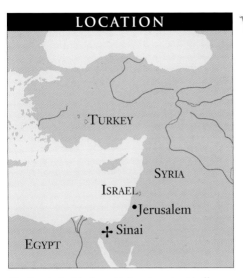

LOCATION

For Israel, the Sinai provided an important buffer zone between its home territories and its Egyptian enemy. Israel was, however, surrounded by potential and real enemies on all other borders.

INFANTRY ANTITANK WEAPONS

The Sagger (see below left) fired a missile 860mm (33.9in) in length, either from a suitcase launcher or from rails mounted on an armoured fighting vehicle (AFV) or a helicopter. It had a range of up to 3000m (3281 yards) and guidance was by the Manual Command to Line of Sight (MCLOS) system. This system relied on the operator guiding the missile to the target via a joystick, a tricky job, especially under combat conditions. A 3000m (3281-yard) flight would take up to 30 seconds, during which time enemy gunners could fire at the tell-tale dust cloud generated by the missile's launch and hopefully knock the shooter off aim. Impact rate for the Sagger could be as low as 30 per cent, even in the hands of a skilled operator. Nevertheless, in quantity and with an armour penetration of over 400mm (15.7in), it remained a very dangerous weapon.

The RPG-7 was a different animal from the Sagger. This shoulder-launched weapon fired an unguided rocket fitted with a High Explosive Anti-Tank (HEAT) warhead, which had an armour penetration of around 260mm (10.2in) at close range. Being unguided, the RPG-7's PG-7V missile gave the weapon an effective range of up to 500m (547 yards), but in practical combat 100–200m (109–219 yards) was more realistic. The great virtue of the RPG-7 was, and remains, its ease of use. Every infantryman trained in the weapon could destroy any of the tanks in the Israeli inventory.

The Arab attack would be codenamed Operation *Badr*. The primary focus of our study here is the Sinai theatre of operations, although this in no way relegates the Golan Heights action to a secondary position.

Under the cloak of a highly effective deception operation, Egypt assembled five infantry, three mechanized and two armoured divisions, plus several other independent brigades, along the Suez Canal in early October 1973. (The timing of the operation was made to coincide with the most favourable tides and weather over the Suez Canal.) The deception operation was designed to make the Israeli high command, headed by Prime Minister Golda Meir (1898–1978) and her minister of defence, Lieutenant-General Moshe Dayan

(1915–81), believe that the force gathering was mere posturing. Such was the skill of its execution that only 18 of the 32 strongpoints on the Bar-Lev Line were occupied, and by fewer than 500 troops. This relaxed attitude was adopted in spite of the IDF's then chief of the general staff, Lieutenant-General David Elazar (1925–76), having stated his belief that the Arab mobilization was a definite prelude to a major offensive.

ATTACK BEGINS

On 6 October at 1400, Egyptian artillery went into action along the Suez Canal, unleashing up to 10,500 shells in the first 60 seconds alone as the Israeli positions came under fire. Meanwhile, the Egyptian

Israeli Centurions mass for the attack in the Sinai. One of Israel's greatest mistakes in the Yom Kippur War was its tendency to commit armour without infantry support, resulting in many losses to Egyptian anti-armour teams.

Air Force embarked on heavy ground-attack missions against Israeli air defence and command-and-control centres, although it quickly lost 40 aircraft to Israeli fighters and anti-aircraft fire. Then, at 1420, the first Egyptian infantry began to swarm across the canal in assault boats. Their way was paved by remarkable combat engineering, the principal challenge of which was cutting through the huge sand berms constructed by the Israelis on their side of the canal. This was accomplished by using the same high-pressure water hoses employed in the construction of the Aswan Dam; the jets of water cut through the berms, and steel matting was laid in the gap to enable armoured vehicles to pass. Huge motorized rafts ferried tanks across the water, and over the next two days 10 massive prefabricated bridges were thrown over the canal to expedite troop and vehicle transfer.

Once the force was across, the Egyptians advanced into Sinai and prepared to face the inevitable Israeli counterattack. Only 208 Egyptian troops were killed during the crossings, and by 7 October 90,000 troops and 850 tanks were on the eastern side.

ISRAELI COUNTERATTACK

Between 6 and 8 October, as fighting raged around the Bar-Lev strongpoints, the Israelis began to mount their response in earnest. Here they made their first mistakes. Self-belief within the Israeli Armor Corps was extremely high, with powerful characters such as Major-General Avraham Mandler (commander 252nd Armoured Division), Major-General Avraham Adan (b. 1926 – 162nd Reserve Armoured Division), Major-General Ariel Sharon (b. 1928 – 143rd Reserve Armoured Division) and Brigadier-General Kalman Magen

Soviet-built Egyptian SA2 anti-aircraft missiles captured by the Israelis on the western bank of the Suez Canal. SA2s provided a high-altitude anti-aircraft 'umbrella' under which Egyptian land forces could operate.

THE OPPOSED FORCES

ISRAEL (estimated)

Total:	275,000

EGYPT (estimated)

Total:	285,000

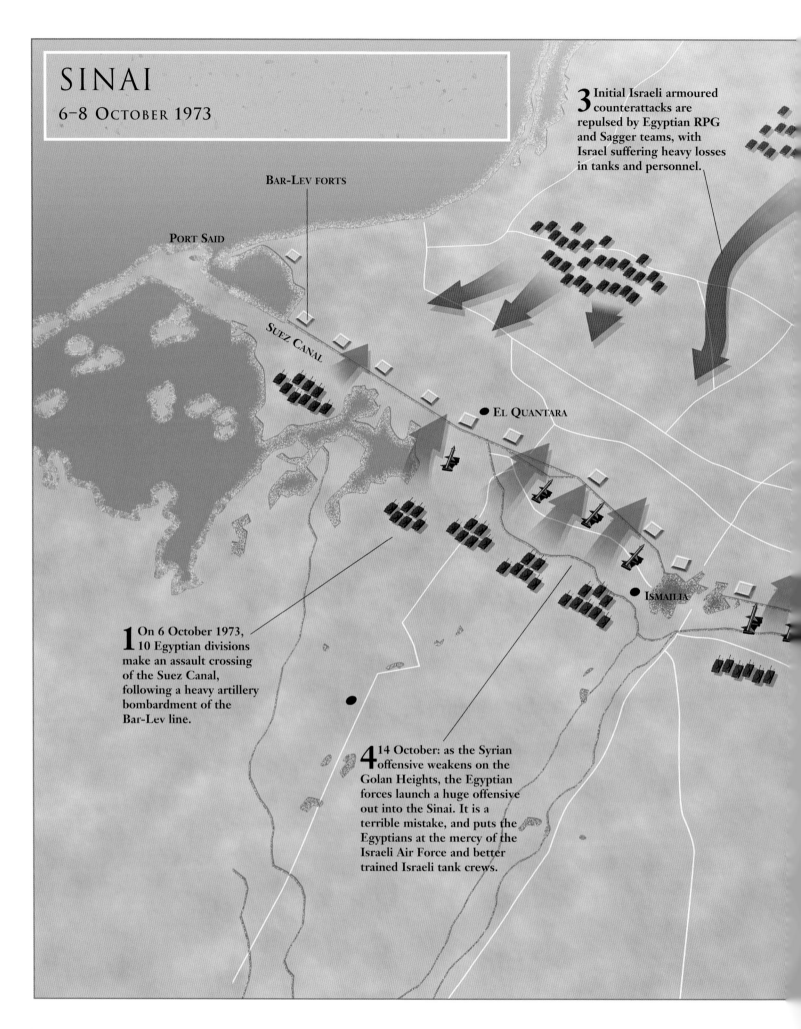

SINAI

6–8 OCTOBER 1973

3 Initial Israeli armoured counterattacks are repulsed by Egyptian RPG and Sagger teams, with Israel suffering heavy losses in tanks and personnel.

BAR-LEV FORTS

PORT SAID

SUEZ CANAL

EL QUANTARA

ISMAILIA

1 On 6 October 1973, 10 Egyptian divisions make an assault crossing of the Suez Canal, following a heavy artillery bombardment of the Bar-Lev line.

4 14 October: as the Syrian offensive weakens on the Golan Heights, the Egyptian forces launch a huge offensive out into the Sinai. It is a terrible mistake, and puts the Egyptians at the mercy of the Israeli Air Force and better trained Israeli tank crews.

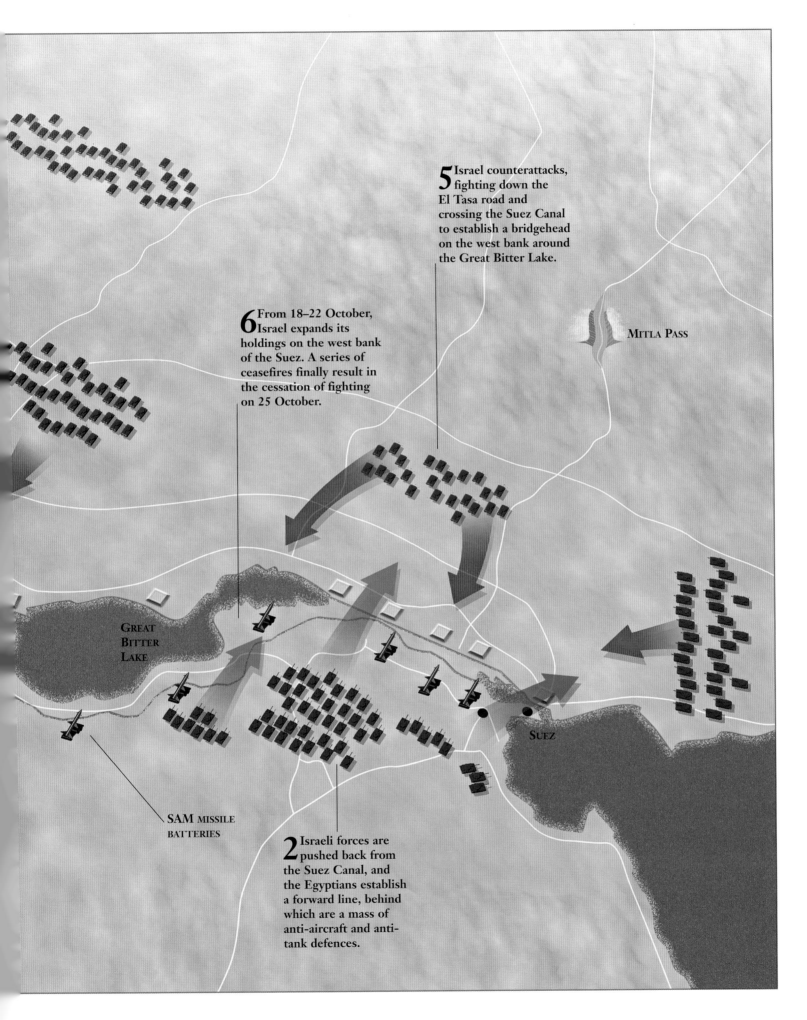

5 Israel counterattacks, fighting down the El Tasa road and crossing the Suez Canal to establish a bridgehead on the west bank around the Great Bitter Lake.

6 From 18–22 October, Israel expands its holdings on the west bank of the Suez. A series of ceasefires finally result in the cessation of fighting on 25 October.

MITLA PASS

GREAT BITTER LAKE

SUEZ

SAM MISSILE BATTERIES

2 Israeli forces are pushed back from the Suez Canal, and the Egyptians establish a forward line, behind which are a mass of anti-aircraft and anti-tank defences.

(146th Reserve Armoured Division) pushing for rapid offensive action. However, the SAM umbrella was already inflicting serious losses on the IAF, and troop mobilization was taking time, so the armoured forces would largely go into action without the cover of air superiority or large troop movements. Artillery support was also slow in materializing.

HEAVY ARMOURED LOSSES

The result was that the Israeli armour threw itself against the Egyptian defences, mostly in battalion-sized packets, making 23 individual counterattacks between 6 and 8 October. Almost all were bloodily repulsed when they encountered Egypt's

anti-tank screen. The experience of Adan's division was typical.

Adan attacked with his three brigades against the Egyptian Second Army south of El Qantara, with Sharon's division ordered either to make a follow-up attack against the more southerly Third Army or to move up as a reserve support to Adan if he found himself in trouble. The overall Israeli plan was to sweep along the eastern side of the Suez Canal, breaking up the Egyptian defences in preparation for taking back the territorial losses.

Adan's manoeuvre seemed to be going smoothly, when Egyptian infantry armed with RPG-7s and Saggers suddenly broke their cover from dug-in positions and

Israeli up-armoured Shermans head to the frontline. Israeli tank commanders often fought stood up with their heads out of the turret hatch. Although this provided better tactical awareness, it resulted in terrible losses amongst the commanders.

SINAI

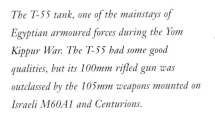

The T-55 tank, one of the mainstays of Egyptian armoured forces during the Yom Kippur War. The T-55 had some good qualities, but its 100mm rifled gun was outclassed by the 105mm weapons mounted on Israeli M60A1 and Centurions.

unleashed dozens of missiles at the Israeli tanks. Twelve tanks were destroyed in quick succession, and more soon followed. One brigade was engaged by the anti-tank units about 1000m (1094 yards) from the canal, and 18 of its tanks were lost. By 1400, Adan's entire counterattack had been smashed, and similar stories were repeated up and down the front.

Israeli armoured counterattacks in the Sinai between 6–9 October were disastrous, with the Israelis losing more than 400 tanks destroyed or damaged in this period. Combined with the air losses to the SAM screen, and the stress of the additional fighting on the Golan Heights, a deep depression started to sink over the Israeli forces and the high command.

CLAWING BACK VICTORY

By the end of 8 October, events seemed to be going in Sadat's favour. Yet the Arab forces would eventually go on to lose the Yom Kippur War, through a combination of foolish strategic changes and the dogged resilience of the Israeli troops, who had the added motivation in the Golan of fighting to protect their homeland. The battle for the Golan Heights, which began with a Syrian assault on 6 October, turned into one of the greatest armour-versus-armour battles in history.

The Syrians unleashed some 1200 tanks against, initially, only two brigades of Israeli armour numbering around 180 tanks, obliterating them by 8 October. Nevertheless, the heroism of the Israeli defenders, plus the steady influx of other Israeli tank and infantry units, began to

inflict unsustainable losses on the Syrians and their allies. In three days of fighting on a battlefield only 16km (10 miles) deep, the Arab forces lost 1400 tanks, several other Arab countries, particularly Iraq, having also deployed tank forces in the sector. In one action alone, an Israeli unit of 50 tanks wiped out 200 Syrian tanks near Yehudia. Although fighting in the Golan would rumble on for several more weeks, the Syrians were effectively defeated by 9 October.

Alarmed by such events, Sadat made a fatal decision. It was decided that Egypt would go on the offensive, abandoning its original plans to fight a defensive battle. The decision was a critical mistake on several levels. First, it would force Egyptian units to fight the fast-moving manoeuvre engagements at which the Israelis excelled, and for which the laborious, centralized Egyptian command and control was poorly suited. Second, an advance would push the Egyptians out from under their SAM umbrella, where they would suffer the depredations of the IAF. Third, the Israelis were beginning to cope with the anti-tank threat. By pouring machine-gun and mortar fire on enemy anti-tank troops, the Israelis could either destroy the anti-tank units or disrupt their aim. Similarly, the IAF

IDF TANK CREWMAN

The personnel of the Israeli Armoured Corps (IAC) were critical to the eventual defeat of the Arab armies during the Yom Kippur War, but they paid for victory with hundreds of lives – some 400 Israeli tanks were destroyed in the Sinai. This first lieutenant (his rank is displayed on the collar straps) gives a typical image of an IAC crewman. He wears a fibre helmet, drilled through with ventilation holes, a simple lightweight fatigue uniform and a communications headset (the junction box is suspended over his chest). Israeli forces have long been known for their informality in dress, the emphasis in training being placed on combat effectiveness rather than what some might feel are minor points of military etiquette.

SINAI

Above: An Egyptian infantryman showing the simplicity of his uniform. Most Egyptian equipment was of Soviet origin, hence this soldier has a Soviet-type Russian helmet and an AKM assault rifle.

began operating in larger formations, overwhelming SAM defences and utilizing US-supplied Walleye guided bombs to destroy launchers and radar systems.

The Egyptian offensive was launched on 14 October, with disastrous results. In only two hours, the attack was crushed. Four hundred Egyptian tanks were committed to battle, but 260 were destroyed by Israeli tanks and units firing US TOW anti-tank missiles. Worse still, the failed effort gave an opening for the Israelis to return to the offensive, this time with improved tactics and against a weakened enemy. On the 15th, IDF armoured formations crossed the canal around Deversoir and consolidated a bridgehead, while more units moved across the Great Bitter Lake to the south, using assault boats and pontoon bridges.

By the 17th, the canal was effectively in Israeli hands, so much so that on the 18th, the IDF launched Operation *Gazelle*, an offensive into the Egyptian interior. Accompanied by extensive air strikes that destroyed 50 Egyptian SAM batteries over four days, three Israeli brigades pushed outwards from the western bridgehead, advancing 56km (35 miles) by the end of 19 October. Many units of the Egyptian Third Army escaped encirclement only by

Israeli troops try out a captured Egyptian Carl Gustav anti-tank weapon. The Israeli solution to Egyptian tank hunters was to saturate their positions with small arms and artillery fire, thereby disrupting their ability to aim and manoeuvre.

directly disobeying Sadat's orders and pulling out. Nevertheless, the going remained hard for the Israelis, and some of their objectives, such as Suez City, remained in the hands of the defenders.

By now, the international community was pushing hard for a ceasefire, especially when Saudi Arabia stopped oil exports to the United States, who had launched Operation *Nickel Grass*, a massive resupply operation to Israel during the early stages of the war. A ceasefire was agreed on 22 October, but it took several more UN Security Council resolutions to bring the fighting to a close on the 25th.

AFTERMATH

The Yom Kippur War inflicted heavy losses on both sides. In total, Israel suffered 2687 dead and 7251 wounded, while the Egyptian losses alone on the Arab side were in the region of 12,000 dead and 35,000 wounded. Ironically, both sides declared the action a victory, although the fact that Israel held onto all of its previously acquired territory, and indeed made some additional conquests, does make their claim appear the more plausible. Nevertheless, the 1973 war shook the IDF to the core, and it came in for heavy criticism both in terms of its prewar intelligence and its tactical choices. What was apparent was that both armour and air force had to refresh their tactics in the light of new battlefield technology.

Some 107 IAF aircraft and 400 IDF tanks were lost in Sinai, and even though these losses were in some way offset by the 277 aircraft and 1000 tanks lost by Egypt, they were still an appalling cost for what was a small armed force.

The Israelis had been totally unprepared for the Egyptian's mass deployment of antitank weapons, such as the Sagger and RPG-7, and these had proved extremely effective against one of the best-equipped professional armies in the world. The Yom Kippur War showed that motivated infantry armed with effective antitank weapons could take on modern AFVs and win.

Arguably, Israel would never again have the total military confidence enjoyed after its 1967 victory, although the war spurred the IDF to become one of the most technologically-advanced forces in the world.

Moshe Dayan (right) was the Israeli Minister of Defence during the time of the Yom Kippur War. While his brilliance in the earlier Six-Day War in 1967 brought him fame, the tactical and intelligence failures of the 1973 conflict eventually led to his resignation in 1974.

THE GULF WAR
JANUARY–FEBRUARY 1991

THE 1991 GULF WAR SAW AN OUT-OF-DATE SOVIET-STYLE IRAQI MILITARY FACE THE FULL POWER OF WESTERN WARMAKING TECHNOLOGY, INCLUDING THE CAPABILITIES OF FORMIDABLE SYSTEMS SUCH AS THE F-117 'STEALTH' FIGHTER.

WHY DID IT HAPPEN?

WHO Iraq versus a US-led Coalition. Both sides had about the same troop numbers, but the Western forces enjoyed technological superiority.

WHAT During Operation *Desert Shield*, the Coalition built up assets for Operation *Desert Storm*, the military campaign to eject Iraqi forces from Kuwait. The F-117 'Stealth' Fighter proved invaluable in knocking out air defences and other key Iraqi assets.

WHERE Kuwait and southern Iraq.

WHEN *Desert Shield* ran from 7 August 1990 to 17 January 1991, when *Desert Storm* began. Kuwait was declared liberated on 27 February 1991.

WHY The Iraqi invasion of Kuwait threatened the security of global oil supplies and raised the possibility that Saudi Arabia would also be invaded.

OUTCOME For less than 400 casualties, the Coalition drove Iraqi forces from Kuwait and inflicted some 150,000 casualties on Saddam Hussein's (1937–2006) military.

At the end of the 1980s, relations between Iraq and its southern neighbour Kuwait were strained. When Kuwait requested the repayment of loans made to Iraq to finance the latter's debilitating eight-year war with Iran (1980–88), Iraq countered by accusing Kuwait of conducting a campaign of economic warfare. Besides Kuwait's pressure over repayments, Iraqi grievances included charges that Kuwait was exceeding its oil production quota, thereby affecting the overall international oil revenues that were so important to Iraq, and stealing oil by cross-border drilling into Iraqi reserves. Outside the realm of economics, the Iraqis also claimed that Kuwait was historically part of Iraq. As Iraqi president Saddam

Hussein massed his forces on the Kuwaiti frontier, talks between the two countries aimed at resolving their differences broke down on 1 August 1990. On the 2nd, the Iraqi Army crossed the border into Kuwait. By the end of the day, this small but oil-rich country was under effective occupation.

The international response to the Iraqi invasion was surprisingly swift and nearly unanimous. The United Nations Security Council immediately passed Resolution 660, calling for Iraq's immediate withdrawal from Kuwait, and Iraq was quickly hit with economic sanctions. By August 1990, Saddam was already well on his way to becoming an international pariah. Nevertheless, he remained a respected power player in the Middle East, with a very

A British Challenger tank makes a stop on the Iraq-Kuwait border during Desert Storm. *Coalition tanks were totally superior in terms of armour, gunnery and crew training when compared to the ageing T-72s, T-62s and T-55s used by the Iraqi forces.*

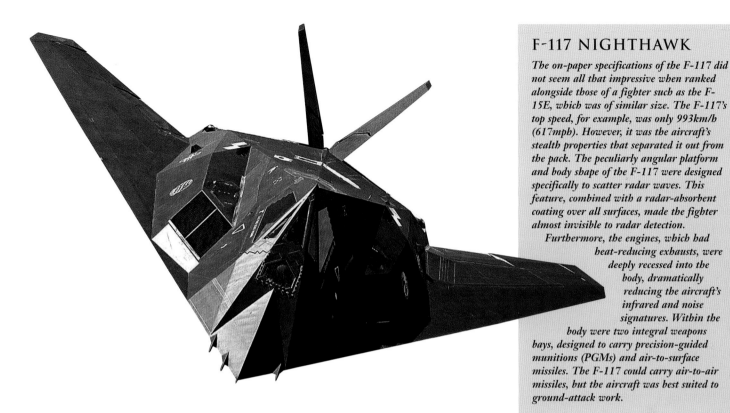

F-117 NIGHTHAWK

The on-paper specifications of the F-117 did not seem all that impressive when ranked alongside those of a fighter such as the F-15E, which was of similar size. The F-117's top speed, for example, was only 993km/h (617mph). However, it was the aircraft's stealth properties that separated it out from the pack. The peculiarly angular platform and body shape of the F-117 were designed specifically to scatter radar waves. This feature, combined with a radar-absorbent coating over all surfaces, made the fighter almost invisible to radar detection.

Furthermore, the engines, which had heat-reducing exhausts, were deeply recessed into the body, dramatically reducing the aircraft's infrared and noise signatures. Within the body were two integral weapons bays, designed to carry precision-guided munitions (PGMs) and air-to-surface missiles. The F-117 could carry air-to-air missiles, but the aircraft was best suited to ground-attack work.

large land army that had quickly engulfed any Kuwaiti resistance. There also remained the possibility that Kuwait could serve as a stepping-stone to an invasion of long-time US ally Saudi Arabia. With the entire balance of Middle Eastern power in jeopardy, and global oil interests threatened, it was time for the West to draw a 'line in the sand', known as Operation *Desert Shield*.

DESERT SHIELD

Almost immediately, a US-led Coalition, with contributions from 34 countries, began a huge military build-up in the region. Between August 1990 and January 1991, more than 500,000 troops – 74 per cent of them US soldiers – were deployed to Saudi Arabia, while major naval assets, including two US carrier battle groups, were sent to the proximate waters.

In addition to the massive build-up in land and naval forces, the Coalition also brought together an impressive volume and quality of air assets. By the beginning of 1991, there were more than 2400 fixed-wing military aircraft deployed as part of Operation *Desert Shield*. As in the case of the land forces, the United States provided the bulk of these air assets, although there were important air contributions from many more Coalition states. All were sewn

together by an enormous electronic network created by intelligence-gathering aircraft, and capably supported by the fleets of transport aircraft that were also critical to the land build-up. Most of the aircraft were based in Saudi Arabia, although some flew from Turkey while long-range B-52s operated from bases as far away as England, Spain and Diego Garcia.

Although the size of Saddam Hussein's army was causing some disquiet in the West, there was no doubting the technological superiority of the Coalition. Perhaps most emblematic of this superiority was a fighter that would occupy the vanguard of future air combat operations – the F-117A Nighthawk 'stealth' fighter.

The F-117's typical payload was two 909kg (2000lb) GBU-27 bombs fitted with the Paveway III laser guidance kit. The aircraft's primary mission was the penetration of enemy air defences to make low-level precision attacks against critical targets. To ensure accurate targeting and terrain-hugging flight at night, the F-117 had an inertial navigational system (INS) and two forward-looking infrared (FLIR) sensors; one sensor gave the pilot images of the terrain around him (beamed onto a multi-function display – MFD – in the cockpit), while the other supplied target

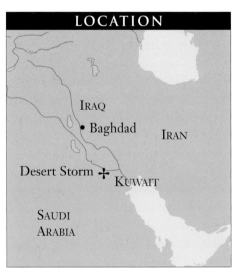

LOCATION

The terrain in which Operation Desert Storm *was fought was perfect for the Allied forces. The flat desert and scrub in Kuwait and southern Iraq gave the ideal conditions for rapid target acquisition.*

THE GULF WAR

pictures and was coupled to a laser designator to provide guidance for the PGMs. The F-117 stood as the most advanced fighter in history, each aircraft costing over $50 million.

The Coalition's purpose was not only to protect Saudi Arabia from possible invasion but also to create the means for future offensive action in the event that Saddam Hussein were to resist all diplomatic efforts over Kuwait. That resistance looked increasingly certain as time went by. Not only did Saddam ignore the demands of leaders such as US President George Bush (b. 1924) to withdraw from Kuwait, he also seemed to be reconfiguring his forces in preparation for a showdown. On 29 November 1990, the UN Security Council passed Resolution 678, which effectively provided the Coalition with the authorization to use military means to enforce their demands if Iraqi troops had not withdrawn from Kuwait by 15 January 1991. Instead of backing down, Saddam

allowed the deadline to expire and promised the 'Mother of all Battles'.

DESERT STORM

The responsibility for taking back Kuwait lay principally in the hands of General H. Norman Schwarzkopf (b. 1934), head of US Central Command (CENTCOM), and his subordinate commanders. On the basis of four months of preparatory intelligence, a two-phase operation was planned. The first phase would be a massive and prolonged air campaign. Under the command of Lieutenant-General Charles A. Horner USAF (b. 1936), this was designed to destroy Iraqi armour, troop concentrations, supply lines, key buildings and, most importantly, the Iraqi command-and-

---

F-117 Stealth aircraft of the 37th Tactical Fighter Wing at their base in Saudi Arabia after operations into Iraqi. A indication of the F-117's heavy use is seen in the bomb-delivery motifs beneath the cockpit.

THE OPPOSED FORCES

COALITION FORCES (estimated)

Total: **880,000**

IRAQI FORCES (estimated)

Total: **500–800,000**

control network. The last-mentioned was especially critical, since once they were 'blinded' (in other words, once without their communications and radar networks) the Iraqi forces would not be able to coordinate air defences, thereby giving the Coalition air superiority over the battlefield. Furthermore, once the land units were without centralized instructions, they were likely to display all the poor tactical decision-making typical of armies with a dictatorial command structure that crushed individual initiative.

Once the air campaign had done its preparatory work, a large Coalition land army would strike into Kuwait and also Iraq from the west, this left wing of the attack cutting off the Iraqi forces in Kuwait from reinforcements and also trapping large numbers of troops within Kuwait itself. In both phases of what would be known as Operation *Desert Storm*, aerial surveillance would be critical.

E-2 Hawkeye and E-3 Sentry airborne warning and control system (AWACS) aircraft would monitor the skies for hostile air threats, while E-8C Joint STARS would track ground targets, transferring their

The Iraqi Republican Guard were Saddam Hussein's elite troops. Their origins were as a bodyguard force to Saddam, but by 1991 they had grown to a strength of some 80–100,000 and formed the main military concern to Coalition leaders in the Gulf War. The Republican Guard uniform was much the same as that of the rest of the Iraqi army, although they often wore red boots and red berets to distinguish themselves. They also had better access to specialist items of clothing and weaponry.

coordinates to land units or, more commonly, vectoring ground-attack air sorties. RC-135 River Joint aircraft would monitor Iraqi communications traffic. In short, the Iraqis would have nowhere to hide.

The air campaign was launched on 17 January 1991 at 0238 (Baghdad time), with a strike by eight AH-64 Apache attack helicopters on Iraqi radar sites on the Iraqi–Saudi Arabian border. Within minutes, Tomahawk cruise missiles were slamming into targets in Baghdad, and F-117s were also making attacks on the city. The air campaign was, apart from some Special Forces actions and localized border clashes,

A GBU 909kg (2000lb) penetration bomb is prepared for an aerial attack mission over Iraq. Even the most basic of such weapons could penetrate up to 1.8m (5.9ft) of reinforced concrete.

the principal method of prosecuting the war until the land campaign began on 24 February. Space here does not allow a detailed insight into one of the greatest air campaigns in history, in which more than 1000 combat sorties were flown every single day, but the contribution of the F-117 is more than representative.

STEALTH KILLER

From the outset of the air campaign, the F-117's role was critical. Although the 42 F-117As used in the war constituted just 2.5 per cent of all combat aircraft deployed to the Gulf, they actually took on 31 per cent of the key strategic targets during the first day of the conflict. The stealth fighters were contained within two squadrons (415th and 417th) of the 37th Tactical

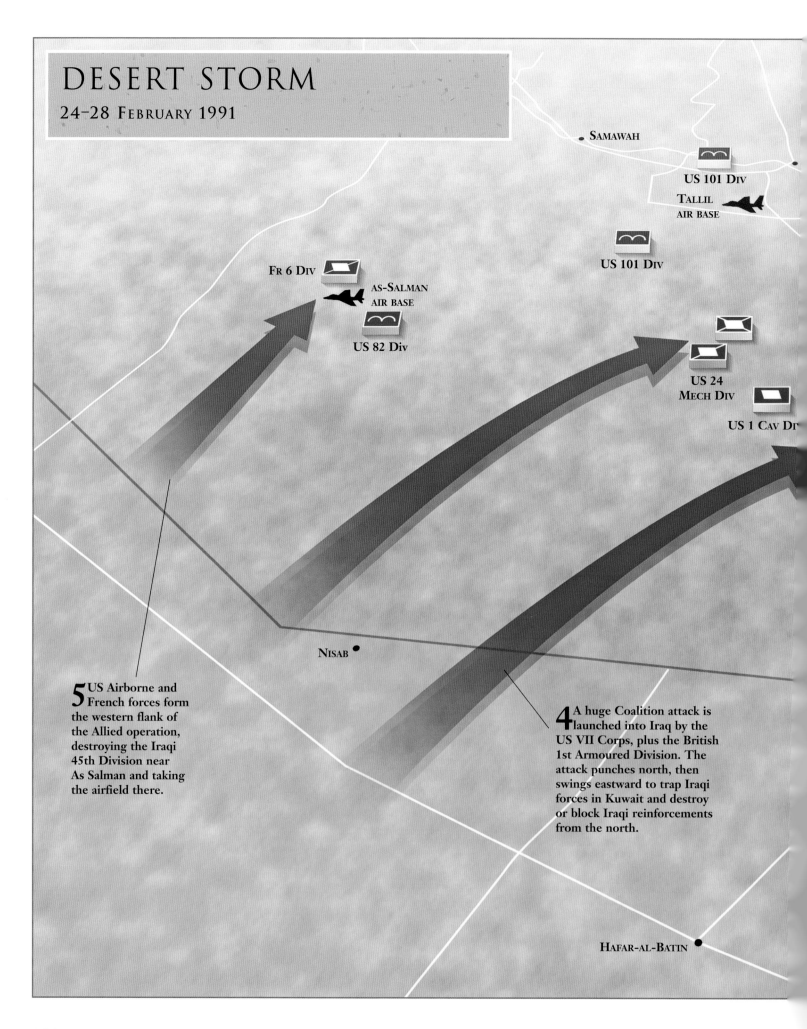

DESERT STORM
24–28 FEBRUARY 1991

SAMAWAH

US 101 DIV

TALLIL
AIR BASE

US 101 DIV

FR 6 DIV

AS-SALMAN
AIR BASE

US 82 DIV

US 24
MECH DIV

US 1 CAV DIV

NISAB

5 US Airborne and French forces form the western flank of the Allied operation, destroying the Iraqi 45th Division near As Salman and taking the airfield there.

4 A huge Coalition attack is launched into Iraq by the US VII Corps, plus the British 1st Armoured Division. The attack punches north, then swings eastward to trap Iraqi forces in Kuwait and destroy or block Iraqi reinforcements from the north.

HAFAR-AL-BATIN

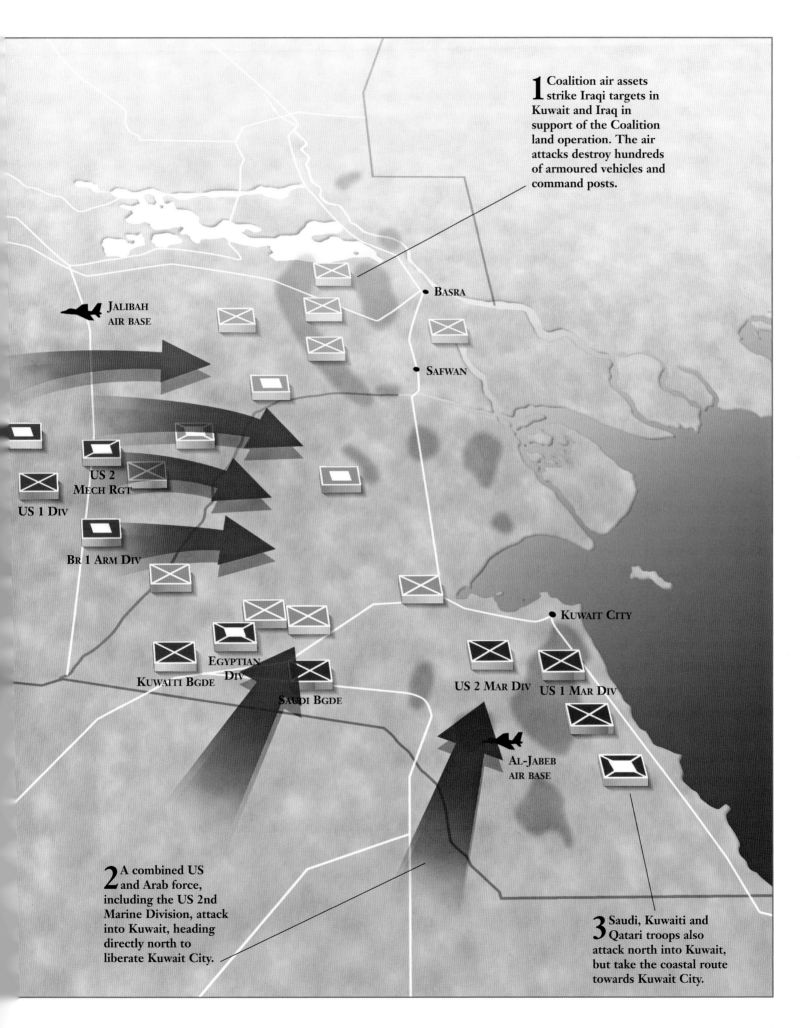

1 Coalition air assets strike Iraqi targets in Kuwait and Iraq in support of the Coalition land operation. The air attacks destroy hundreds of armoured vehicles and command posts.

JALIBAH
AIR BASE

• BASRA

• SAFWAN

US 2
MECH RGT

US 1 DIV

BR 1 ARM DIV

• KUWAIT CITY

EGYPTIAN
DIV

KUWAITI BGDE

SAUDI BGDE

US 2 MAR DIV   US 1 MAR DIV

AL-JABEB
AIR BASE

2 A combined US and Arab force, including the US 2nd Marine Division, attack into Kuwait, heading directly north to liberate Kuwait City.

3 Saudi, Kuwaiti and Qatari troops also attack north into Kuwait, but take the coastal route towards Kuwait City.

THE GULF WAR

Fighter Wing and were based at Khamis Mushait in southern Saudi Arabia. During the course of the war, the F-117s were given a broad range of targets – command centres; communications and radar sites; nuclear, biological and chemical (NBC) facilities; powerplants; bridges; and hardened aircraft shelters. Many of their targets, however, were concentrated in the Iraqi capital, Baghdad, which by January 1991 had an air defence network of 60 surface-to-air (SAM) sites and some 3000 anti-aircraft guns.

Many details of the F-117s' combat sorties remain classified, as the capabilities and tactics of the aircraft are closely guarded secrets. Some operations did become public, however. The first bomb to be dropped on Iraq during the war was delivered by F-117 pilot Major Gregory A. Feest, who flew with nine other F-117s towards Baghdad in the very first hours of the war. Feest's first target was a camouflaged and hardened Iraqi Air Force interceptor operations centre in a town

called Nukhayb. The INS helped guide Feest to the objective, although he changed course often to hamper enemy tracking efforts. Finally he was over the target, and the MFD threw up a grainy picture of the location. He locked the aiming crosshairs onto the bunker, designated the target and released a 909kg (2000lb) bomb. It flew completely true, punching through the roof of the bunker and detonating inside (Feest saw the doors of the bunker blow outwards). Heavy anti-aircraft fire opened up in response, but as would often happen through the night it quickly ceased or was wildly inaccurate, indicating that the Iraqis were unable to track the assaults. Nonetheless, it was a disturbing barrage to fly through.

The flight of F-117s began to swarm over other targets across Iraq. Another key attack – one whose MFD picture was broadcast on public television – was on Baghdad's principal telecommunications centre. As in the case of the bunker attack,

The terrible power of Coalition land assets is illustrated by this bombed-out Iraqi column. Elevated roads such as these presented targets in shooting-range clarity for helicopter gunships and strike aircraft.

An Iraqi T-55 burns in the desert. Iraqi use of armour was tactically inept. Armour relies on its mobility for survival, but all too often Iraqi forces set their tanks in static positions, there to be picked off at leisure by Coalition aircraft and armour.

the target was shattered by a 909kg (2000lb) bomb. During the war, stealth fighters dropped a total of 1814 tonnes (1778 tons) of bombs in nearly 1300 combat sorties. On average, an F-117 pilot conducted 21 combat missions, each lasting about 5 hours 30 minutes, and with about 24 hours' rest in between. In terms of both mission duration and the number of missions flown, the figures for F-117 pilots were lower than those of many other combat pilots during the conflict. However, the highly technical nature of F-117 operations, and the fact that they were always conducted at night against heavily protected targets and at low level, meant that such actions required great skill and concentration.

Of course, although it was important, the F-117's role was just a part of a massive air campaign. Day and night, Coalition aircraft swarmed over Iraq and Kuwait, delivering destruction. Iraq had no effective answer to Coalition air supremacy. Thirty-eight MiGs were shot down in the first week and up to 150 Iraqi jets were flown to Iran by pilots who recognized the futility of resistance. Almost all command-and-control structures were wiped out, and several thousand Iraqi armoured vehicles were destroyed by A-10s, Apache helicopters, F-15Es and other ground-attack aircraft.

Possibly tens of thousands of Iraqi troops were killed when their positions were carpet-bombed by B-52s. By the end of February, conditions were right for the land campaign to begin.

ENDING THE OCCUPATION

Although the air campaign had been a resounding success, there remained an air of uncertainty over the land campaign. Iraq's army was large – with more than 600,000 troops (possibly over one million if all reserves were counted), 11,000 armoured vehicles (including 5800 tanks) and nearly 4000 artillery pieces – and many of its soldiers were combat-proven. Despite this, there were reasons for the Coalition to be confident.

The first reason was the sheer damage done by the air campaign, not only to Iraqi assets but also to Iraqi morale. Moreover, the land campaign would enjoy the cover of complete air superiority. Second, Coalition land warfare equipment – particularly

A British Special Air Service (SAS) soldier in desert camouflage holds an SLR rifle. Special forces played a crucial role in the success of the bombing campaign, provided on-the-ground markers for many of the Allies' lazer-guided bombs.

THE GULF WAR

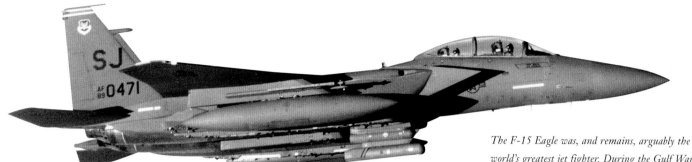

The F-15 Eagle was, and remains, arguably the world's greatest jet fighter. During the Gulf War, F-15s were mostly employed in ground-attack roles, the Iraqi air force being quickly destroyed or fleeing to safety in neighbouring countries.

armoured vehicles and battle command-and-communications systems – was generally superior to that of the Iraqis. GPS systems allowed Coalition units to manoeuvre with precision without getting lost, even in areas of featureless terrain. Finally, the airborne surveillance assets meant that the Iraqis could not move without being spotted (in good weather,

The Abrams M1 was at the vanguard of Coalition armoured forces during Desert Storm. *Its fire-control system enabled crews to engage Iraqi armour at distances in excess of 3000m (9842ft).*

they couldn't really stay stationary either), and their positions could be instantly relayed to fire bases or attack aircraft.

Small reconnaissance and Special Forces operations began in late January, with some larger cross-border actions around 20 February. Yet after further UN demands for an Iraqi withdrawal from Kuwait were ignored, the full force of the Coalition land army surged into Kuwait and Iraq. In effect, the land campaign consisted of three huge sweeps. To the far west, the US XVIII Airborne Corps – with flank protection from the French 6th Light Armoured Division (left) and British 1st Armoured

Division (right) – would attack into southern Iraq, sweeping upwards towards the Euphrates River and then turning eastwards towards Basra. The US VII Corps would make a similar but shorter 'hook punch' into Iraq along the Kuwait–Iraq borderlands before advancing *en masse* into Kuwait itself. US Marine and combined Arab forces would simply cross the border directly into Kuwait from the south. In effect, the Iraqi occupation forces would be crushed against the Gulf coastline.

Within hours of the Coalition invasion, it became apparent that the Iraqis were a shadow force. Poorly handled Iraqi armour could not stop the surge of US M1 Abrams or British Challenger tanks – the British 1st Armoured Division, for example, destroyed 200 Iraqi tanks, while the US 1st Armored Division took out 630. Iraq's Republican Guard units were quickly smashed; they had endured relentless bombing, which had shattered their ranks and their nerves. Mass surrenders gave the Coalition a huge logistical challenge. In addition, convoys of requisitioned and military vehicles fleeing out of Kuwait City to Iraq were shot to pieces in relentless air attacks.

By 28 February, after only 100 hours of fighting, the US president – not wanting to encourage what many would see as a purposeless slaughter – ordered the shooting to stop. The mission of expelling Iraq from Kuwait had been completed and the Iraqis were defeated, although many would rue the fact that the ceasefire allowed a couple of thousand armoured fighting vehicles and thousands of Republican Guard troops to escape. The incongruity between Coalition and Iraqi casualties was striking. Some 358 Coalition troops died from combat and non-combat causes.

By contrast, there were an estimated 150,000 Iraqi casualties, with as many as 50,000 dead. One central reason for the discrepancy is that the Coalition air power, including assets such as the F-117s, not only rendered the Iraqi forces unable to communicate effectively but reduced them to sitting ducks under the sun.

The Gulf War demonstrated the heights to which precision air attacks had ascended. This photograph shows a bridge over the Euphrates river, neatly split in two by a laser-guided bomb.

IRAQI FREEDOM
20 MARCH—1 MAY 2003

HAVING BEEN DEFEATED IN THE GULF WAR (1990–91), IRAQI LEADER SADDAM HUSSEIN (1937–2006) RETURNED TO HIS PREVIOUS POLICY OF BRINKMANSHIP IN INTERNATIONAL POLITICS, WHILE BRUTALIZING HIS OWN PEOPLE. A US-LED COALITION RAPIDLY OVERRAN SADDAM'S ARMY AND REMOVED HIM FROM POWER.

WHY DID IT HAPPEN?

WHO A US-led coalition of forces from Australia, Poland and the United Kingdom plus Kurdish Iraqis, opposed by the regular army of Iraq, the Republican Guard and irregular Iraqi forces.

WHAT The coalition launched an invasion of Iraq, with the intention of removing Saddam Hussein and his supporters from power.

WHERE Between the Kuwaiti border and the Iraqi capital, Baghdad.

WHEN 20 March–1 May 2003

WHY In the wake of the terrorist attacks on 11 September 2001, the United States and other nations sought to curb possible support for terrorist organizations, and to punish non-compliance with United Nations resolutions regarding Iraq's Weapons of Mass Destruction (WMD) programmes.

OUTCOME Rapid military victory and the removal of the Saddam Hussein regime. Ongoing and bloody insurgency after the end of combat operations.

Saddam's regime was a brutal one. The Ba'ath party that he eventually came to lead had assumed power in a coup in 1958 and was well-versed in the use of terror and violence in internal politics. Hussein's own early career included a number of political murders and strong-arm tactics as he rose to power, culminating in his assumption of the presidency of Iraq in 1979. He was a great admirer of the Soviet leader Joseph Stalin, and used similar methods to Stalin in dealing with internal opposition.

During the Iran-Iraq War (1980–88), the Iraqi military used chemical weapons against Iranian forces, and later used them against Kurdish dissidents. This was ignored by the West for political reasons at the time, mostly because an Iranian victory in the Iran-Iraq War was seen as detrimental to Western interests. However, the war cost Iraq a vast amount of money and left the nation in debt to others, notably Kuwait. An invasion of Kuwait offered two possibilities: access to additional oil reserves with which to rebuild the economy, and the

elimination of Iraq's largest creditor. However, the invasion provoked a massive international response, which culminated in the Gulf War.

The remit for the Gulf War was the removal of Iraqi occupying forces from Kuwait. This was achieved by a rapid land campaign (Operation Desert Storm), which followed a long air bombardment that had reduced Iraqi military capabilities. Although there were those in the international community who pushed for the complete removal of Saddam, marching on Baghdad was beyond the scope of the United Nations resolution for the war. Thus, although crushingly defeated on the battlefield, Saddam was able to remain in power, savagely putting down post-war uprisings against him in the cities of Iraq. His rule continued much as before.

Concerns about Iraq's stores of weapons of mass destruction (WMDs), and Saddam's proven willingness to use them, resulted in UN demands for Iraq to allow inspectors to determine that no stocks of weapons or means of delivery existed. Saddam and his government agreed to cooperate but did not do so, resulting in several rounds of negotiation, partial access, renewed UN pressure but ultimately little compliance. However, Saddam complied just enough to cloud the issue and the situation stalled.

Meanwhile, political murders and the harsh repression of opponents was ongoing, especially against the Kurds of northern Iraq. However, the political climate changed considerably after the terrorist attacks of 11 September 2001 (9/11). Tiring of the support by certain nations, such as Syria and Afghanistan, for terrorism, the

General Tommy Franks began his military career as an enlisted man, gaining a commission through Officer Candidate School. He commanded US forces during Operation Iraqi Freedom.

M1A1 ABRAMS

In action in Iraq, the M1A1 Abrams MBT demonstrated its vast superiority over the armoured vehicles opposing it. The Abrams' armour proved impervious to the weapons of enemy tanks, while its 120mm (4.7in) smoothbore main gun could destroy any enemy target. Hits with the main gun were possible from several hundred metres outside the maximum range of its opponents' weapons. Coupled with high mobility and excellent electronic systems, the M1A1 justified its considerable cost with extreme effectiveness.

United States and other nations began to demand that either the terrorist training camps be eliminated by local forces, or that the United States and supporting nations be given permission to do so by the government in whose territory the camps were located.

In the wake of 9/11, Western nations became much more willing to act against nations they perceived as a threat, while maintaining a polite fiction of being unable to deal with the problem. Patience with the endless stalling and obfuscation of the Iraqi government regarding compliance with UN resolutions had also run out. On 17 March 2003, the US President George W Bush (1946–) demanded that Saddam Hussein and his supporters step down from power, and threatened direct military action if they did not.

Unsurprisingly, Saddam did not comply and a US-led coalition invaded Iraq to remove him from power. The military campaign was over quickly and without the enormous loss of life predicted by some observers. A bloody anti-coalition insurgency followed, dividing public opinion about the wisdom of the invasion, but Operation Iraqi Freedom was itself a complete military success.

OPENING MOVES

The key to success was speed and momentum. Coalition planners could not be certain of the Iraqi troop numbers they faced, but estimated there to be around 400,000 personnel, including paramilitary groups, plus several hundred thousand reserves. The Iraqi army was equipped with outdated tanks, but had them in large numbers. The coalition could not afford to become bogged down in urban warfare, in which large numbers of ill-equipped but determined fighters could stall the offensive. Instead, the coalition had to play to its own strengths.

Thus the plan was for an very rapid advance, brushing aside or bypassing resistance in order to strike a knockout blow at the Iraqi government. This was in keeping with the coalition military mission; its forces were there to fight Saddam, not the Iraqi people. The coalition did not desire to, and could not afford to, take on the Iraqi nation. In this regard, the systematic brutalization of his own people worked against Saddam. Often Iraqi people watched the coalition tanks roll by and then simply went back to what they were doing; rallying calls from the government inspired only those who had an interest in supporting the current regime.

Originally, it was planned that the invasion would be launched from Turkey in the north and Kuwait in the south. However, Turkey declined to allow land forces to stage out of its territory, though use of its air bases was permitted. Thus the invasion had to be launched along the narrow and predictable axis of the Kuwait/Iraq border.

LOCATION

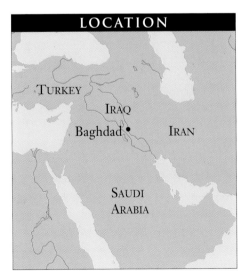

Political considerations required that the advance into Iraq be staged through Kuwait, necessitating a long advance from the Persian Gulf to Baghdad.

IRAQI FREEDOM

Air support for the ground operations was provided by naval as well as Air Force assets. These F/A-18 Hornets are launching from the carrier USS Constellation *in the Persian Gulf.*

From there, the intent was for a primarily British force to secure the flank of the advance by taking the port of Umm Qasr, then advance north to Basra to secure the southern part of the country. Meanwhile, US forces, better suited to long-range operations, would drive northwestwards on two parallel axes, separated by the River Euphrates. These axes were to converge on Baghdad from two directions in a classic pincer movement. Once the capital was secure, resistance in other areas would be mopped up.

The path across the border with Kuwait, from where the invasion was launched, was cleared by a combination of artillery and helicopter gunships, while a missile and air attack was launched at key targets in Baghdad in the hope of 'decapitating' the Iraqi government. The latter did not achieve much, but the preparatory border attacks were extremely successful and allowed the armoured forces of the coalition to advance rapidly.

One reason the Iraqis were caught off guard was the expectation of a lengthy air campaign to precede the land invasion. Instead, the coalition surprised their Iraqi opponents and were able to make rapid gains. On 20 March, a force of US and British Marines captured the port of Umm Qasr, though resistance continued in some areas for the next two days. British armoured forces reached Basra on 21 March but halted outside the city to allow the civilian population time to flee.

Meanwhile the US 1st Marine Division secured the Rumaila oilfields, located on the

Iraq/Kuwait border to prevent a repeat of the destruction wrought in 1991, when retreating Iraqi forces set fire to the oil wells. With this objective secure, the Marines advanced north on the town of An Nasiriyah. This was a key objective because its bridges over the River Euphrates were essential to the continued advance of the left arm of the coalition pincer. Thus far, the advance was progressing well. Resistance was determined in some areas, but it was scattered and thus easily contained or overrun. In many cases, the Iraqi army, suffering from low morale and lack of confidence in their leaders, put up little more than token resistance before surrendering. Many soldiers quietly changed into civilian clothing and went home rather than fight the coalition.

THE ADVANCE

By 23 March, the rapidly advancing coalition was operating at the end of a lengthening supply line, and that supply line ran through areas that were not wholly under coalition control. As a result, US logistics troops were ambushed by pro-Saddam irregulars, loosely called *fedayeen* (martyrs), in An Nasiriyah, and some US troops were captured. The rescue attempt became a bloody street battle, and although passage through the city was cleared for supply movement, fighting went on for a week before the city was brought under control.

One reason for the hard fighting at An Nasiriyah was the arrival of large numbers of these irregular forces, who arrived by whatever private transport they could obtain over 22/23 March. Although they were outsiders and did not know the city well enough to make the best use of its streets and buildings for defence, they were devoutly religious fighters whose irregular nature and defensive positions in urban terrain made them difficult to oust.

The *fedayeen* came from many sources. Some were members of the 'Popular Army' created in the 1970s by Saddam Hussein himself as a political tool. Others were members of the Ba'ath party and others came in from other Muslim states to carry out what they saw as a holy war against the Western invaders. Thus, although the regular army division defending An

THE OPPOSED FORCES

COALITION

US:	248,000
UK:	45,000
Other Coalition Members:	4500
Kurdish/others:	70,000
Total: 367,500	

IRAQ

Tanks:	2000
APCs:	2000
Artillery Piece:	2000
Total:	**200,000 men**

Nasiriyah melted away, US forces faced a difficult urban battle for an objective that was irrelevant except for the fact that it lay on their route.

The advance was further slowed by sandstorms and stiffening resistance as regular Iraqi forces overcame their initial shock and began fighting with greater determination. Overall strategy and military direction was still lacking, however; there was little sign of an attempt to counter-attack or to put a coherent defensive strategy into action. Instead, Iraqi forces held out as best they could when attacked, with little hope of assistance.

For example, at An Najaf, coalition forces became involved in heavy fighting, slowing the advance on Baghdad from that direction. The city was encircled by 26 March and bombarded with artillery as well as air attacks. It was eventually taken by US troops, but only after a hard fight, which demonstrated that some Iraqi soldiers would not give up easily. Some regulars also joined the assortment of irregular forces in harassing coalition supply lines, while others simply held on to the location where they had been posted. Many such areas were bypassed by coalitions forces, but others had to be fought for.

The Republican Guard, the elite of the Iraqi army, put up a determined fight and proved a tough opponent. Its morale was higher than that of the regular army, more because it was a political elite than due to better training or leadership. The Republican Guard owed its status to Saddam and had more to lose in defeat than the typical Iraqi soldier, who rarely had anything to gain by Saddam's continued presidency. The Republican Guard was also better equipped than the regulars, with tanks and other armoured vehicles.

THE BRITISH IN BASRA

After pausing to allow the civilian population to escape, the British contingent advanced into Basra, engaging in conventional operations around the city and street fighting within. During the pause, special forces teams had entered the city and conducted reconnaissance, reporting back on conditions within the city.

Basra was commanded by one of the Iraqi governments' top officials, Ali Hassan al-Majid, better known as 'Chemical Ali' to the media. His personnel had tried to keep the civilian population within the city, hoping to drag the British into the type of street battles that would cause large numbers of civilian casualties and which the Iraqis could then use as propaganda. However, he had little support from the people of Basra themselves because he had savagely punished them for their part in the 1991 rising against Saddam. His regular forces, who were conscripts rather than long-service volunteers, had for the most part rapidly melted away. The remainder were terrorized in order to stiffen their resolve, driving yet more to desert as soon as they could.

Air and missile strikes were launched on Baghdad in the hope of 'decapitating' the Iraqi government by killing Saddam Hussein and his close advisors.

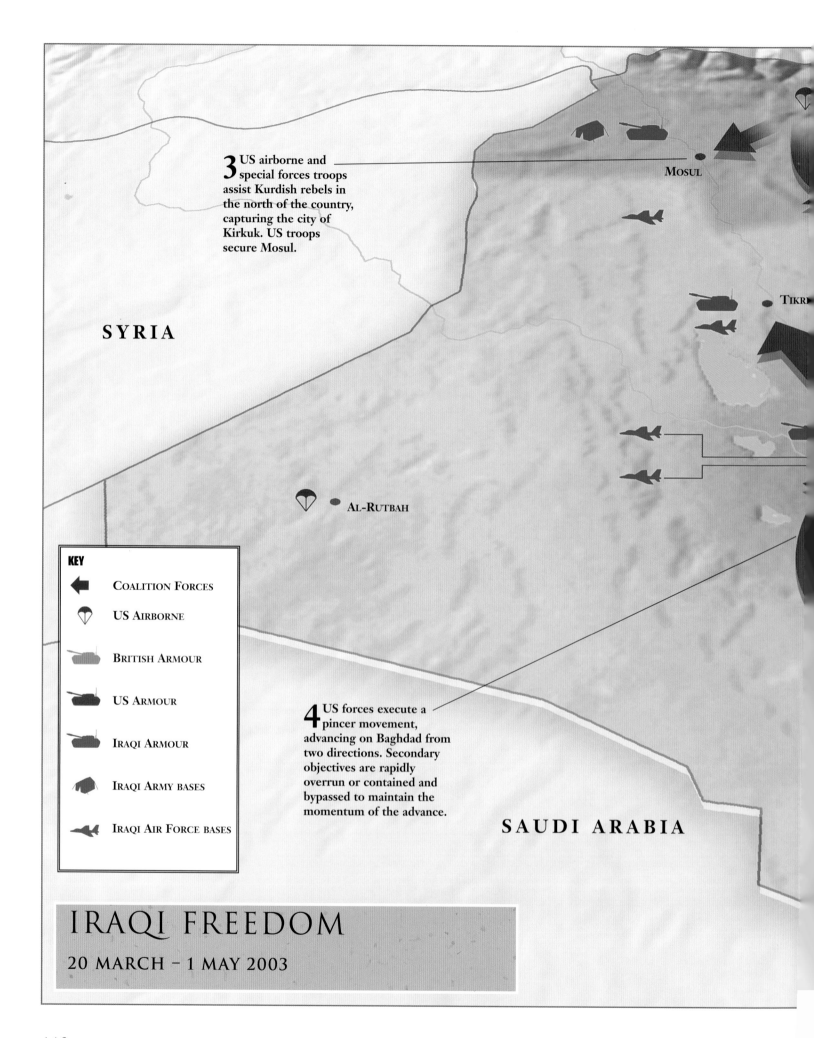

3 US airborne and special forces troops assist Kurdish rebels in the north of the country, capturing the city of Kirkuk. US troops secure Mosul.

MOSUL

TIKR

SYRIA

AL-RUTBAH

KEY

COALITION FORCES

US AIRBORNE

BRITISH ARMOUR

US ARMOUR

IRAQI ARMOUR

IRAQI ARMY BASES

IRAQI AIR FORCE BASES

4 US forces execute a pincer movement, advancing on Baghdad from two directions. Secondary objectives are rapidly overrun or contained and bypassed to maintain the momentum of the advance.

SAUDI ARABIA

IRAQI FREEDOM

20 MARCH – 1 MAY 2003

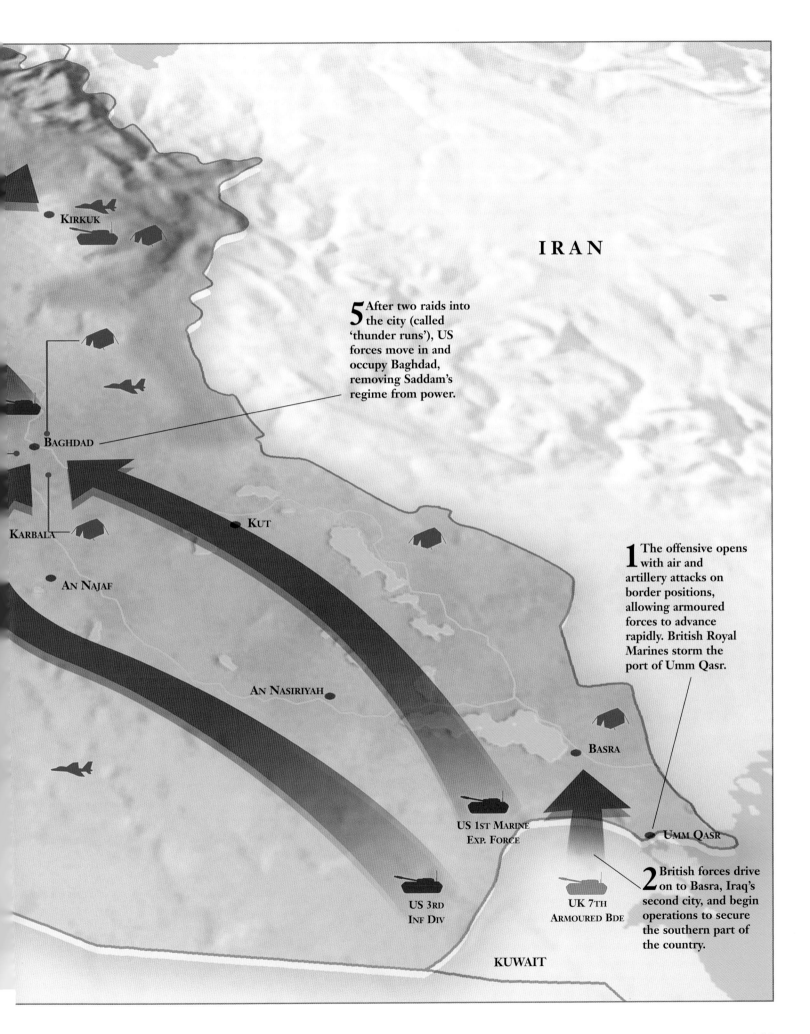

KIRKUK

IRAN

5 After two raids into the city (called 'thunder runs'), US forces move in and occupy Baghdad, removing Saddam's regime from power.

BAGHDAD

KUT

KARBALA

AN NAJAF

1 The offensive opens with air and artillery attacks on border positions, allowing armoured forces to advance rapidly. British Royal Marines storm the port of Umm Qasr.

AN NASIRIYAH

BASRA

US 1ST MARINE EXP. FORCE

UMM QASR

2 British forces drive on to Basra, Iraq's second city, and begin operations to secure the southern part of the country.

US 3RD INF DIV

UK 7TH ARMOURED BDE

KUWAIT

US troops search surrendering Iraqi personnel. The involvement of irregular fighters who dressed and acted like civilians greatly complicated the task of the ground forces.

Thus the defence of Basra was mainly in the hands of Ba'ath Party loyalists, who were deeply resented by the local population, and by *fedayeen* who had reached the city from elsewhere. These forces tried to draw in the British during the period 23–30 March, without success. Handfuls of Iraqi tanks and armoured vehicles made probing attacks on the British positions, which also came under mortar fire. These efforts failed to provoke a response, although a column of 15 Iraqi tanks that ventured too far out of the city was destroyed for no loss by British armour.

During this time, British snipers infiltrated into the city took a steady toll on the Ba'ath Party leadership. By careful observation and the occasional tip-off from locals, it was possible to identify leaders and eliminate them. This weakened enemy command and reduced morale among the defenders.

From 31 March onwards, British strategy became more aggressive. Groups of Warrior Infantry Fighting Vehicles (IFVs) were used to make fast raids into the city, striking known areas of resistance or command posts before withdrawing. The Warrior's 30mm (1.18in) cannon was more than sufficient to deal with lightly armed infantry, though its light protection (relative to a tank) made it vulnerable to anti-armour weapons. Accurate artillery fire was also used to eliminate enemy strong points, based on observation by British troops in the city.

On 6 April, British forces finally made their assault. The original plan was to make

what amounted to a series of raids in force, withdrawing for the night to avoid counter-attack. However, the defence had been so successfully 'crumbled' that the raids achieved more than expected. The British forces involved were quickly organized into ad hoc battle groups comprising a small number of tanks and one or two companies of infantry with their Warrior combat vehicles.

The heaviest resistance was encountered in the vicinity of the College of Literature, which was held by about 300 *fedayeen*. To avoid civilian casualties, the British made little use of heavy weapons but drew out the opposition using traditional infantry urban warfare techniques. Soon afterwards, resistance collapsed and the city was firmly in British hands. The armoured vehicles withdrew and the infantry switched from an assault role to a peacekeeping one, beginning the work of rebuilding security and public confidence.

US FORCES AT BAGHDAD

US forces paused at the end of March, to resupply and prepare for the assault on Baghdad. Despite setbacks and resistance along the route, they had advanced at an incredible rate and were now in a position to make the final thurst. The main worry was that the Republican Guard divisions deployed at Baghdad might retreat into the city and force the US to fight a costly urban campaign. To avoid this, as the ground forces advanced, air units bombarded the rear of the Republican Guard divisions as a broad hint that trying to fall back would be worse than standing to fight.

US forces also approached the city from more than one direction, creating confusion among the defenders as to where the main blow would fall. The keys to the US advance were the Karbala Gap, between Lake Razzazzah and the Euphrates, and Baghdad's airport, Saddam International. The latter was both symbolic and significant in terms of logistics. The first task was to secure the Hadithah Dam to prevent Iraqi engineers from destroying it and flooding the land below. This would make it impassable to armoured forces. US Army Rangers took the dam and successfully held off counterattacks, opening the way for the armoured advance.

Despite heavy opposition, US infantry and armoured forces secured their approach to Baghdad, gaining control of crossings over the Euphrates and advancing on Kabala. By 2 April, some US forces had managed to cross the Euphrates, exploiting the failure of Iraqi engineers to blow changes they had set. From there, the airport was quickly reached.

Once at the airport, US forces deployed to meet the inevitable counterattack. The regular army had effectively disintegrated by this point, and the Republican Guard was occupied elsewhere, so it fell to the lightly equipped *fedayeen* to assault US positions. Several hundred were killed in a series of rushes that were determined but poorly organized and almost completely unsupported. Support did appear from 4 April onwards, when Iraqi tanks joined the fighting. It is not clear who was manning them – possibly a mix of regular army remnants, Republican Guard and *fedayeen*.

These renewed attacks ran onto the 120mm (4.7in) guns of the Abrams Main Battle Tanks (MBTs) and the 25mm (.98in) chain guns of Bradley IFVs. The latter proved effective against even the T-72 tanks of the Republican Guard, disabling at least five. After advancing to locate and eliminate the rest of the Iraqi armour in the area, the US force pushed onwards and secured the rest of the airport. A renewed attempt to dislodge the Americans from the airport, this time made by organized forces of the Republican Guard or regular army (or perhaps both), was also defeated by American armour.

The final objective was the interior of the city itself. This was achieved by a combination of firepower, aggression and speed. Although significant forces remained operational within Baghdad, these were disorganized and in many cases unprepared for attack. The 'thunder runs', as the American attacks into central Baghdad were called, overran several unprepared positions but did encounter heavy resistance. This came mostly from irregulars armed with small arms and RPG-7 anti-armour weapons. Although many vehicles were hit and some disabled, the US forces suffered no fatalities whilst the defenders took casualties numbering in the hundreds.

On 5 April, a breakout by Iraqi forces towards Saddam's home town of Tikrit, supported by Republican Guard armour, had been contained by US forces and thrown back. Now the final remnants of the Saddam regime were cornered and making a last stand. Hordes of *fedayeen* irregulars engaged US forces in a furious battle that at times became desperate as the advance US units clung to their positions and reinforcements battled through to join them.

Fighting went on for several hours before resistance broke and the final advance could begin, and on the night of 7/8 April, the central 'Regime District' of Baghdad was brought under US control. There was little organized resistance after this; a large group of *fedayeen* made a stand at the university on 9 April and small groups continued to fight all over the city, but the operation to take Baghdad was over.

US M1A1 Abrams tanks throw up clouds of dust while moving in the desert. Military vehicles have to be adapted if they are to function for any length of time in such conditions.

On 1 May 2003, the end of the war was declared. It would take some months to hunt down Saddam Hussein and his close supporters, and the country was still the scene of a major insurgency, but the mission of removing Saddam Hussein from power was complete.

AFTERMATH

The symbolic toppling of Saddam's statue on 9 April marked the end of his regime, though it was some time before the dictator himself and his close associates were apprehended. The military operation was a stunning success despite setbacks of a sort that are inevitable in warfare. Even in the face of heavy resistance in some areas, fewer than 160 Coalition personnel were killed during the operation. This was a testimony to good planning and decisive action coupled with excellent equipment and training.

The peace in Iraq has proven more costly than the war, with insurgents fighting coalition forces, the new Iraqi government, and each other. The war has drawn in *jihadists* from other nations seeking to strike at the West, as well as home-grown dissidents, forcing coalition forces to remain in position to fight a wholly different kind of war.

INDEX

Figures in **bold** refer to illustration captions.